Model of personality structure

Three interacting components (id, ego, superego) operating at three levels of consciousness

Conscious
Preconscious
Ego
Superego
Unconscious
Id

Collections of response tendencies tied to specific stimulus situations

Operant response tendencies

Stimulus situation

R_1
R_2
R_3
R_4

Self-concept, which may or may not mesh well with actual experience

Self-concept   Actual experience

Congruence

Incongruence

Hierarchy of traits, with specific traits derived from more fundamental, general traits

Extraversion

Lively   Active   Assertive

View of personality development

Emphasis on fixation or progress through psychosexual stages; experiences in early childhood (such as toilet training) can leave lasting mark on adult personality

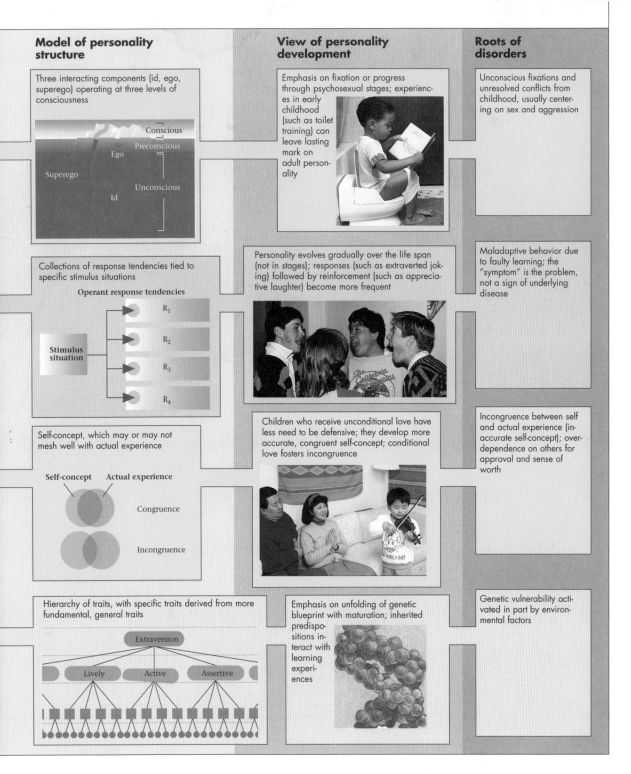

Personality evolves gradually over the life span (not in stages); responses (such as extraverted joking) followed by reinforcement (such as appreciative laughter) become more frequent

Children who receive unconditional love have less need to be defensive; they develop more accurate, congruent self-concept; conditional love fosters incongruence

Emphasis on unfolding of genetic blueprint with maturation; inherited predispositions interact with learning experiences

Roots of disorders

Unconscious fixations and unresolved conflicts from childhood, usually centering on sex and aggression

Maladaptive behavior due to faulty learning; the "symptom" *is* the problem, not a sign of underlying disease

Incongruence between self and actual experience (inaccurate self-concept); overdependence on others for approval and sense of worth

Genetic vulnerability activated in part by environmental factors

7
EDITION

Theories of Personality

Duane P. Schultz
University of South Florida

Sydney Ellen Schultz

Wadsworth
Thomson Learning™

Australia • Canada • Mexico • Singapore • United Kingdom • United States

Psychology Editor: *Marianne Taflinger*
Assistant Editor: *Jennifer Wilkinson*
Editorial Assistant: *Suzanne Wood*
Marketing Manager: *Jenna Opp*
Project Editor: *Trudy Brown*
Print Buyer: *Karen Hunt*
Permissions Editor: *Joohee Lee*

Production Service: *Graphic World Publishing Services*
Text Designer: *Laurie Albrecht*
Cover Designer: *Jennifer Dunn*
Cover Image: © *David Katzenstein/CORBIS*
Cover Printer: *R.R. Donnelley, Crawfordsville*
Compositor: *Graphic World, Inc.*
Printer: *R.R. Donnelley, Crawfordsville*

Printed in the United States of America

4 5 6 7 04 03 02

For permission to use material from this text, contact us by
Web: http://www.thomsonrights.com
Fax: 1-800-730-2215
Phone: 1-800-730-2214

Wadsworth/Thomson Learning
10 Davis Drive
Belmont, CA 94002-3098
USA

For more information about our products, contact us:
Thomson Learning Academic Resource Center
1-800-423-0563
http://www.wadsworth.com

International Headquarters
Thomson Learning
International Division
290 Harbor Drive, 2nd Floor
Stamford, CT 06902-7477
USA

UK/Europe/Middle East/South Africa
Thomson Learning
Berkshire House
168-173 High Holborn
London WC1V 7AA
United Kingdom

Asia
Thomson Learning
60 Albert Street, #15-01
Albert Complex
Singapore 189969

Canada
Nelson Thomson Learning
1120 Birchmount Road
Toronto, Ontario M1K 5G4
Canada

Library of Congress Cataloging-in-Publication Data

Schultz, Duane P.
    Theories of personality / Duane Schultz, Sydney Ellen Schultz—7th ed.
      p.   cm.
    Includes bibliographical references and index.
    ISBN 0-534-55107-6
    1. Personality. I. Schultz, Sydney Ellen. II. Title.
BF698.S36   2000
155.2—dc21
                                    00-039854

To Dad

PHOTO CREDITS

CONTENTS

PART   3   *The Neopsychoanalytic Approach*   *89*

CHAPTER   *Carl Jung*   *91*
   THREE

CHAPTER   *Alfred Adler*   *120*
   FOUR

PART 6   *The Humanistic Approach*   297

CHAPTER
ELEVEN   *Abraham Maslow*   299

CHAPTER
TWELVE   *Carl Rogers*   323

Preface to the Seventh Edition

Each edition of a textbook must be as vital, dynamic, and responsive to change as the field it covers. To remain an effective teaching instrument, it must reflect the development of the field and continue to challenge its readers. We have seen the focus of personality study shift from global theories, beginning with Sigmund Freud's 19th-century psychoanalytic theory of neuroses, to 21st-century explorations of more limited personality dimensions. And we have seen the basis of personality exploration change from case studies of emotionally disturbed persons to more scientifically based research with diverse populations. Contemporary work in the field reflects differences in gender, age, sexual orientation, and ethnic, racial, religious, and cultural heritage (see the "Note on Diversity" section below).

New and Expanded Coverage

Major changes for this edition include new biographical material for the theorists to suggest, where war-ranted, how the development of their theory may have been influenced by events in their personal and professional lives. This approach shows students that the development of science through theory and research is not always totally objective. It may also derive from intuition and personal experience later refined and extended by more rational, analytical processes. Cultural influences on the theorists' beliefs about human nature are described (such as Adler's concept of social interest and Horney's concept of feminine identity).

The sections on personality research have been updated to maintain the emphasis on current problems. Considerable material has been added on gender and ethnic issues in personality development. We present the results of cross-cultural research and a diversity of subject samples.

For Freudian theory, we have added the work of Margaret Mahler and noted additional research on ego development, catharsis, and repressed memories. For Jung, we cover the midlife crisis in women. For Erikson, gender stereotypes in children's play behavior and the use of toys are discussed, as are gender differences in aging. As an outgrowth of Erikson's concept of identity crisis, material has been added on ethnic identity, gender preference identity, and the effect of the Internet on adolescent identity development.

For Allport we include cross-cultural differences in expressive behavior. For the Big Five factor model we report research on cross-cultural stability of personality traits and expand coverage of behavioral correlates and higher-order factors. For Maslow we note gender differences in self-esteem. And for the social-learning theorists there is new material on self-efficacy and on locus of control.

Organization of the Text

The 7th edition of *Theories of Personality* retains its orientation toward undergraduate students who have had little previous exposure to personality theories. Our purpose is to reach out to beginning students and ease their task of learning about the study of personality. We have chosen theorists who represent psychoanalytic, neopsychoanalytic, life-span, trait, humanistic, cognitive, behavioral, and social-learning approaches, as well as clinical and experimental work. The chapter on limited domain theories deals with conceptions that explore a single personality dimension rather than the total personality.

Chapter 18 reviews the seven major perspectives from which to view personality development and suggests ways to help students draw conclusions and achieve closure from their studies. We also introduce the so-called "happy" personality, based on components of subjective well being. This growing field, based on positive subjective experiences, deals with issues such as happiness, self-efficacy, competence, optimism, creativity, and spirituality. It is the subject of the January 2000 special issue of the *American Psychologist*.

Each theory in the text is discussed as a unit. Although we recognize the value of an issues or problems approach that compares theories on specific points, we believe that the issues-oriented book is more appropriate for higher-level students. The theories-oriented text makes it easier for beginning students to grasp a theory's essential concepts and overall flavor. We try to present each theory clearly, to convey its most important ideas, assumptions, definitions, and methods. We discuss each theorist's methods of assessment, and empirical research, and offer our evaluations and reflections. The "Questions About Human Nature" section for each theorist deals with six fundamental issues: free will versus determinism, nature versus nurture, childhood experiences, uniqueness versus universality, goals, and optimism versus pessimism. These are presented in a bar graph format to simplify comparisons among the theories.

Except for placing Freud first in recognition of his chronological priority, we have not arranged the theories in order of perceived importance. They are presented in nine parts, placing each theory in the perspective of competing viewpoints.

A Note on Diversity—We've Come a Long Way!

The first person to propose a comprehensive theory of the human personality was Sigmund Freud, a clinical neurologist who formulated his ideas while treating patients in Vienna, Austria, in the 19th century. His work, known as "psychoanalysis," was based largely on sessions with wealthy white European females who came to him complaining of emotional distress and disturbing thoughts and behaviors. From his observations of their progress, or lack of it, he offered a theory to explain the personalities of *everybody*.

Freud's system was important for the concepts he proposed—many of which are now part of popular culture—as well as for the opposition he provoked, inspiring other theorists to examine and promote their own ideas to explain personality.

Today, in the 21st century, personality theorists and researchers recognize that an explanation based on a small, homogeneous segment of the population cannot be applied to the many diverse groups of people sharing living space in our world. The situation is similar in medicine. Doctors and researchers are recognizing that some medications and treatments appropriate for young adults are not suitable for children or elderly people. Some diseases prevalent in certain ethnic groups are rare in others, requiring differences in medical screening and testing for diverse populations.

Contemporary personality theory and research strives to be inclusive, studying the influences of age, gender, race, ethnic origin, religious beliefs, and sexual orientation. We see examples of this diversity in most of the chapters of this text.

• Chapter 1 considers cross-cultural psychology and the influences of gender, race, and ethnic origin on personality development and assessment. It includes a table of the responses of people from 20 countries to the Adjective Check List, a self-report measure of personality.

• Chapter 2 (Freud) notes racial differences in reported childhood sexual abuse.

• Chapter 3 (Jung) considers personality development at middle age and the midlife crisis in women.

• Chapter 4 (Adler) emphasizes differences in personality development stemming from family context, based on order of birth. Social interest, or social adjustment, is assessed in Latino subjects.

• Chapter 5 (Horney) proposes a feminine psychology to counteract the accepted explanation for gender differences then based on the ancient Chinese doctrine of Yin and Yang, wherein Yin is considered feminine/passive and Yang is masculine/active.

• Chapter 6 (Fromm) studies the evolution of personality in a Mexican subculture, examining socioeconomic structure, health, attitudes, and dreams.

• Chapter 8 (Erikson) discusses ethnic identity as a significant component of the ego. Extensions of Erikson's theory of ego development and the identity crisis in adolescents are proposed for people of African, Hispanic, Asian, and Arab origin. Sexual orientation is explored as an influence on the ego development of gay men and women.

• Chapter 9 (Allport) shows how emotions associated with certain personality traits are found in facial expressions of infants in different cultures.

• Chapter 10 (other trait theories) shows consistencies and differences among major personality dimensions in more than 30 nations.

• Chapter 11 (Maslow) describes gender differences in the development of self-esteem, a basic human need.

• Chapter 15 (Bandura) provides age and gender differences in the development of self-efficacy, the feeling of competence in coping with life. Cultural differences in self-efficacy are found in communist versus capitalist societies.

• Chapter 16 (Rotter) describes the personality component of control (whether we have control over our life or whether it is determined by other people or by fate). Age, gender, and socioeconomic class influence this belief. It has been studied in Native American, African, Hispanic, and Asian populations, showing differences between Eastern and Western cultures and between wartime and peacetime conditions.

• Chapter 17 (limited domain theories) discusses ways in which achievement motivation varies by culture and historical time period and how expectations of success differ by race. The personality variable of optimism/pessimism varies among ethnic groups and is also related to religious beliefs and to sexual orientation.

Features

For the student we offer chapter outlines, summaries, review questions, annotated reading lists, margin glossary terms, a cumulative glossary, tables and figures, and a reference list.

For instructors, the instructor's manual is available both in print and computerized formats. Instructors can also create, deliver, and customize tests and study guides (both print and online) in minutes with ExamView®, an easy-to-use assessment and tutorial system. ExamView offers both a Quick Test Wizard and an Online Test Wizard that guide users step-by-step through the process of creating tests, while its unique WYSIWYG capability previews the test on the screen exactly as it will print or display online. Instructors can build tests of up to 250 questions using up to 12 question types. With ExamView's complete word-processing capabilities, instructors can also enter an unlimited number of new questions or edit existing questions.

InfoTrac® College Edition

Available exclusively from Wadsworth/Thomson learning, *InfoTrac College Edition* is a fully searchable online university library that includes the full text of articles from hundreds of scholarly and popular publications. Hot linked, expertly indexed, and ready to use, the data base is updated daily with articles going back as far as four years. The *InfoTrac College Edition* symbol in the margin suggests search terms students can use to access additional information about a particular topic.

Acknowledgments

We would like to thank the many colleagues and students who have written to us about the book and have offered suggestions for this edition. We are especially grateful to the following reviewers:

William Bailey, Eastern Illinois University
Benjamin Bandiola, University of Tennessee at
  Chattanooga

Francene Bellamy, Chicago State
  University
Evelyn Chisholm, Spelman College
George Domino, University of Arizona–
  Tucson
Kenneth Greenberg, University of
  Maryland
Michael Jones, College of the Ozarks
Betty Miller, University of Wisconsin–
  La Crosse
Pamela Mulder, Marshall University
Lynn Pardie, University of Illinois at
  Springfield
Randall Salekin, Florida International
  University
Edward Samuelewicz, Rosemont College
Mark Smircina, Blackburn College
Vetta Thompson, University of Missouri–
  St. Louis

Duane Schultz
Sydney Ellen Schultz

A Note to Our Readers

You are about to begin a fascinating journey over the last 100 years. This book describes various ideas that psychologists and other scientists have advanced to explain the human personality—your personality. It also tells the story of the great theorists' lives and how their own experiences may have influenced the explanations they proposed.

You already know how important personality is. Everything you have achieved so far, your expectations for the future, and even your general health are influenced by your personality and the personalities of the people with whom you interact.

We have organized the theories by their outlook on human nature, beginning with Sigmund Freud. We consider extensions of his theory of psychoanalysis and discuss the men and women who revised his ideas or rebelled against his system. These chapters are followed by a life-span approach, tracking personality development from birth to old age. We then discuss theories that focus on individual personality traits, on psychological health, on predetermined be-

havior patterns, and on cognitive learning from social situations. The book's final chapter offers conclusions from our exploration of personality and introduces an idea for the 21st century, the happy personality type.

We also recognize that theorists from the last century rarely considered the importance of diversity. You can readily see that it is not appropriate to generalize to all people from, for example, ideas that one theorist based on clinical observations of neurotic European women or that another theorist based on tests given to American college men. Therefore, when we discuss research conducted on these theories, and describe their use for real-world problems of diagnosis and therapy, we show the influence of age, gender, race, ethnic and national origin, religious beliefs, and sexual orientation.

To make your study easier, we include chapter outlines, summaries, review questions, and reading lists. Important words are defined in the margin, and these definitions are also listed in the back of the book. Those of you who have *Infotrac College Edition* will find search terms in the margin. These words link you to an online database containing hundreds of articles that provide additional information about various related topics.

Also, you may want to check out some of the Web sites listed below. They contain a wealth of information on personality.

http://fas.psych.nwu.edu/personality
Personality theories, research, individual differences, training programs, recommended readings, and links to other Web pages and organizations

http://www.learner.org/exhibits/personality
Program notes from the video series on the human brain

http://www.ship.edu/~cgboeree/perscontents.html
A personality e-text with chapters to download

http://wynja.com/personality/theorists
Information on theorists' lives, links to current researchers, and an online bookstore

http://www.med.virginia.edu/personality-studies
Case studies on reincarnation, near-death experiences, and out-of-body experiences

http://www.freud.org.uk
The Sigmund Freud Museum in London, England

http://www1.netaxs.com:8080/people/aca3/1pm.htm
A virtual museum about psychology

http://www.apa.org/science/test.html
Information from the American Psychological Association on FAQ about psychological tests

http://www.davideck.com
Online tests for personality, intelligence, health, and career interests, including tests to take just for fun

http://www.2h.com/tests/personality
Tests for specific personality factors such as self-esteem, Type A, coping with stress, and assertiveness

For information on specific theorists, try the following.

http://plaza.interport.net/nypsan/freudarc.html
For Sigmund Freud

http://www.cgjung.com/webjung.html
For Carl Jung

http://www.behavior.net/orgs/adler/index.html
For Alfred Adler

http://lilt.ilstu.edu/erdesou/horney.html
For Karen Horney

http://www.erichfromm.de/english/index.html
For Erich Fromm

http://www.psych.westminster.edu/psy311/murray/ppframe.htm
For Henry Murray

You get the idea. Happy surfing!

Introduction

Personality theories are maps of the mind.

—Harvey Mindess

O N E

The Study of Personality: Assessment, Research, and Theory

The Study of Personality

Everybody Has One

Everybody has one, and yours will help determine the limits of success, happiness, and fulfillment in your life. We're talking about *personality*, and it is no exaggeration to state that your personality is one of your most important assets. It has already helped shape much of your life and will continue to do so in the future.

All you have achieved thus far, all you expect to achieve in your career, whether you will be a good spouse or parent, and even your general state of health can be influenced by your personality and the personalities of the people with whom you interact.

How often have you described someone as having a *terrific* personality? By that you typically mean the person is affable, pleasant, nice to be around, and easy to get along with—the kind of person you might select for a friend, roommate, or colleague at work. If you are a manager, you might choose to hire this person. If you are prepared to make a commitment to a personal relationship, you might want to marry this person, basing your decision on your perception of his or her personality.

You have also known people you would describe as having a *terrible* personality. Such persons may be aloof, hostile, aggressive, unfriendly, unpleasant, or difficult to get along with. You would not hire them or want to associate with them, and they may be similarly shunned, rejected, and isolated by others.

Your personality can limit or expand your options and choices in life. It can prevent you from sharing certain experiences with other people or enable you to make the most of them. It can restrict and constrain some people and open the world of experience to others.

While you are making judgments about the personalities of other people, they are making similar judgments about you. These mutual decisions that shape the lives of both the judged and the judges are made countless times throughout our lives, every time we encounter a social situation that requires us to interact with new people. Of course, the number and variety of social situations you willingly participate in are also determined by your personality—for example, your relative sociability or shyness. You know where you rate on that factor, just as you no doubt have a reasonably clear picture of your overall personality.

Describing Your Personality

It is glib and facile to attempt to sum up the total constellation of someone's personality characteristics by using such fuzzy terms as *terrific* and *terrible*. The subject of personality is too complex for such a simplified description, because humans are too complex and changeable in different situations and with different people. We need to be more precise in our language to adequately define and describe personality. For that reason, psychologists have devoted considerable effort to developing tests to evaluate, or assess, personality.

You may believe you don't need any psychological test to tell you what your personality is like, and, in general, you may be correct. After all, you probably know yourself better than anyone else. If you were asked to list the words that

TABLE 1.1
Adjective check list. Make a check mark
next to the words you believe apply to your personality.

_____ affectionate	_____ ambitious	_____ assertive
_____ boastful	_____ cheerful	_____ cynical
_____ demanding	_____ dominant	_____ fearful
_____ forceful	_____ generous	_____ highstrung
_____ impatient	_____ insightful	_____ meek
_____ moody	_____ optimistic	_____ opinionated
_____ persistent	_____ prudish	_____ relaxed
_____ sarcastic	_____ sensitive	_____ sociable
_____ submissive	_____ tolerant	_____ trusting
_____ uninhibited	_____ vindictive	_____ withdrawn

best describe your personality, no doubt you could do it without too much thought.

OK. Let's do it. Take a piece of paper and write down as many adjectives as you can to describe what you are *really* like—not how you would like to be, or how you want your teachers or parents or friends to describe you—but the real you. Try not to use the word *terrific*, even if it does apply in your case.

How many words did you select? Six? Ten? A few more? A widely used personality test, the Adjective Check List, offers an astonishing 300 adjectives to describe personality. People taking the test choose the ones that best describe themselves (Gough & Heilbrun, 1983).

No, we're not going to ask you to review all 300 adjectives, only the 30 listed in Table 1.1. Place a check mark next to the ones you believe apply to you.

Now you have a description of your personality in greater detail, but remember that in the actual test, you would have an additional 270 items to pick from.

How Does Personality Develop?

Our focus here is not what *your* personality is like. You don't need a psychology course to learn that. What we will be studying are the forces and factors that shape personality. Later in this chapter we consider some basic questions about the nature of personality—for example, whether we are born with a certain type of personality or learn it from our parents; whether personality is influenced by unconscious forces; or whether personality can change after our childhood years.

In this book we describe a variety of theories that have been proposed to help answer these and related questions about human nature. After we have discussed them—what they are, how they developed, and what their current status is—we will evaluate their usefulness in answering our questions and contributing to our understanding of how personality develops.

We may think of these theorists as all contributing pieces to a grand puzzle, which is why we study their ideas, even though some of their concepts are decades old. Psychologists continue to try to fit these pieces together to bring forth a clearer image, a more complete picture of what makes us the way we are.

The Place of Personality in the History of Psychology

Because the study of personality is so central to an understanding of human nature, you might assume it has always occupied a prominent position in psychology. For more than half of psychology's history as a science, however, psychologists paid relatively little attention to personality.

Psychology emerged as an independent and primarily experimental science from an amalgam of ideas borrowed from philosophy and physiology. The birth of psychology took place in the late 19th century in Germany and was largely the work of Wilhelm Wundt, who established psychology's first laboratory in 1879 at the University of Leipzig.

The Study of Consciousness

The new science of psychology focused on the analysis of conscious experience into its elemental parts. The methods of psychology were modeled on the approach used in the natural sciences. Physics and chemistry appeared to be unlocking the secrets of the physical universe by reducing all matter to its basic elements and analyzing them. If the physical world could be understood by breaking it down into elements, why couldn't the mind or the mental world be studied in the same way?

Wundt and other psychologists of his day who were concerned with studying human nature were greatly influenced by the natural science approach, and they proceeded to apply it to the study of the mind. Because these researchers limited themselves to the experimental method, they studied only those mental processes that might be affected by some external stimulus that could be manipulated and controlled by the experimenter. There was no room in this experimental psychology approach for such a complex, multidimensional topic as personality. It was not compatible with either the subject matter or the methods of the new psychology.

The Study of Behavior

behaviorism The school of psychology, founded by John B. Watson, that focused on psychology as the study of overt behavior rather than of mental processes.

In the early decades of the 20th century, the American psychologist John B. Watson, at Johns Hopkins University in Baltimore, Maryland, sparked a revolution against the work of Wilhelm Wundt. Watson's movement, called **behaviorism**, opposed Wundt's focus on conscious experience. More devoted than Wundt to a natural science approach, Watson argued that if psychology was to be a science, it had to focus only on the tangible aspects of human nature—that which could be seen, heard, recorded, and measured. Only overt behavior—not consciousness—could be the legitimate topic of psychology.

Consciousness, Watson said, cannot be seen or experimented upon. Therefore, like the philosophers' concept of the soul, consciousness is meaningless for science. Psychologists must deal only with what they can see, manipulate, and measure—that is, external stimuli and the subject's behavioral responses to them. According to Watson, whatever happens inside the person after the stimulus is presented and before the response is made cannot be seen. Because we can only speculate about it, it is of no interest or value to science.

Behaviorism presents a mechanistic picture of human beings as well-ordered machines that respond automatically to external stimuli. It has been said that behaviorists see people as a kind of vending machine. Stimuli are put in, and appropriate responses, learned from past experience, spill out. In this view, personality is nothing more than the accumulation of learned responses or habit systems, a definition later offered by B. F. Skinner (see Chapter 14). Thus, behaviorists reduced personality to what could be seen and observed objectively and there was no place in their conception for consciousness or for unconscious forces. However, the more recent social-learning theorists (Chapters 15 and 16), who offer explanations derived from Watson's and Skinner's versions of behaviorism, have restored to personality some measure of consciousness.

If Watson and the early behavioral psychologists dismissed all those notions, feelings, and complexities that come to mind when we use the word *personality*, then where were they? What happened to the consciousness you know you experience every moment you are awake? Where were those unconscious forces that sometimes seem to compel us to act in ways over which we feel we have no control?

The Study of the Unconscious

Those aspects of human nature were dealt with by a third line of inquiry, one that arose independently of Wundt and Watson. They were investigated by Sigmund Freud, beginning in the 1890s. Freud, a physician in Vienna, Austria, called his system **psychoanalysis**. Psychoanalysis and psychology are not synonymous or interchangeable terms. Freud was not by training a psychologist but was a physician in private practice, working with persons who suffered from emotional disturbances.

psychoanalysis Sigmund Freud's theory of personality and system of therapy for treating mental disorders.

Although trained as a scientist, Freud did not use the experimental method. Rather, he developed his theory of personality based on clinical observation of his patients. Through a lengthy series of psychoanalytic sessions, Freud applied his creative interpretation to what patients told him about their feelings and past experiences, both actual and fantasized. His approach was thus quite different from the rigorous experimental laboratory investigation of the elements of conscious experience or of behavior.

Inspired by Freud's psychoanalytic approach, a group of personality theorists developed unique conceptions of human nature outside the mainstream of experimental psychology. These theorists, the neopsychoanalysts (Chapters 3 through 7), focused on the whole person as he or she functions in the real world, not on elements of behavior or stimulus-response units as studied in the psychology laboratory. The neopsychoanalysts accepted the existence of conscious and unconscious forces, whereas the behaviorists accepted the existence only of that which they could see. As a result, the early personality theorists were speculative in their work, relying more on inferences based on observations of their patients' behavior than on the quantitative analysis of laboratory data.

The Scientific Study of Personality

We see, then, that experimental psychology and the formal study of personality began in two separate traditions, using different methods and pursuing different aims.

We should note that experimental psychology in its formative years did not totally ignore personality—some limited aspects of personality were studied—but there did not exist within psychology a distinct specialty area known as *personality* as there was child psychology or social psychology.

It was not until the late 1930s that the study of personality became formalized and systematized in American psychology, primarily through the work of Henry Murray and Gordon Allport at Harvard University (see Chapters 7 and 9). Following their initial efforts, professional books appeared, journals were founded, universities offered courses, and research was undertaken. These activities signaled a growing recognition that some areas of concern to the psychoanalysts and neopsychoanalysts could be incorporated into psychology. Academic psychologists came to believe that it was possible to develop a scientific study of personality.

Today, experimental psychologists are making increasing use of concepts from Freudian theory and its derivatives, and followers of the psychoanalytic tradition are seeing the benefits of the experimental approach. However, a complete merging of the two camps has not occurred. They began separately and so, for the most part, they remain. Each offers advantages and disadvantages, and we shall see examples of both in the chapters to follow.

Definitions of Personality

We frequently use the word *personality* when describing others, and ourselves, and we all believe we know what it means. Perhaps we do. One psychologist suggested that we can get a good idea of its meaning if we examine what we intend when we use the word *I* (Adams, 1954). When you say *I*, you are, in effect, summing up everything about yourself—your likes and dislikes, fears and virtues, strengths and weaknesses. The word *I* is what defines you as an individual, as a person separate from all others.

As Others See Us

In our effort to define the word more precisely, we can look to its source. *Personality* derives from the Latin word *persona*, which refers to a mask used by actors in a play. It is easy to see how persona came to refer to outward appearance, the public face we display to the people around us.

Based on its derivation, then, we might conclude that personality refers to our external and visible characteristics, those aspects of us that other people can see. Our personality would then be defined in terms of the impression we make on others— that is, what we appear to be. One definition of personality in a standard dictionary agrees with this reasoning. It states that personality is the visible aspect of one's character, as it impresses others.

But is that all we mean when we use the word *personality*? Are we talking only about what we can see or how another person appears to us? Does personality refer solely to the mask we wear and the role we play? Surely, when we speak of personality, we refer to more than that. We mean to include many attributes of an individ-

Our personality may be the mask we wear when we face the outside world.

ual, a totality or collection of various characteristics that goes beyond superficial physical qualities. The word encompasses a host of subjective social and emotional qualities as well, ones that we may not be able to see directly, that a person may try to hide from us, or that we may try to hide from others.

Enduring Characteristics

We may also, in our use of the word *personality*, refer to enduring characteristics. We assume that personality is relatively stable and predictable. Although we recognize, for example, that a friend may be calm much of the time, we know that he or she can become excitable, nervous, or panicky at other times. Personality is not rigid and unchanging but can vary with the situation.

In the 1960s, promoted by the psychologist Walter Mischel, a debate erupted within psychology about the relative impact on behavior of such enduring personal variables as traits and needs, as well as variables relating to the situation (Mischel, 1968, 1973). The controversy continued in the professional literature for 20 years and ended in the late 1980s. Most personality psychologists resolved the issue by accepting an interactionist approach, agreeing that enduring personal traits, changing aspects of the situation, and the interaction between them must all be considered in order to provide a full explanation for human nature (Carson, 1989; Magnusson, 1990; McAdams, 1997).

Unique Characteristics

personality The unique, relatively enduring internal and external aspects of a person's character that influence behavior in different situations.

Our definition of personality may also include the idea of human uniqueness. We see similarities among people, yet we sense that each of us possesses special properties that distinguish us from all others. Thus, we may suggest that **personality** is an enduring and unique cluster of characteristics that may change in response to different situations.

Even this, however, is not a definition with which all psychologists agree. To achieve more precision, we must examine what each personality theorist means by the term. Each offers a unique version, a personal vision, of the nature of personality, and that viewpoint has become his or her definition. And that is what this book is all about: reaching an understanding of the different versions of the concept of personality and examining the various ways of defining the word *I*.

Psychologists interested in personality have done more than formulate theories in their attempts to define its nature. They have also devoted considerable time and effort to measuring or assessing personality and to conducting research on its various aspects. Although the primary focus of this book is theories, we will describe for each theory the relevant assessment techniques and research findings.

Gender and Ethnic Issues in Personality

ⓖ **ethnicity**

ⓖ **gender identity**

The personality theorists we discuss in this book offer diverse views of the nature of the human personality. Despite their disagreements and divergences, however, they share certain defining characteristics: All are White, of European or American heritage and almost all are men.

Of course, there was nothing unusual about this situation, given the period during which most of these researchers and theorists were developing their ideas. At the time, nearly all of the great advances in the arts, philosophy, literature, and the sciences, including the development of the scientific method, were propounded and promoted by White men of European or American background. In many fields, educational and professional opportunities for women and for people of ethnic minority groups were limited.

In addition, in the field of personality theory, virtually all of the patients, clients, and laboratory subjects on whom the theories are based were also White. Even the laboratory rats were white. Further, the majority of the patients and subjects were men. Yet the personality theorists confidently offered theories that, by implication, are supposed to be valid for *all* people, regardless of gender, race, or ethnic origin.

None of the theorists stated explicitly that his or her views applied only to males or to Whites or to U.S. citizens, or that their ideas might not be useful for explaining personality in people of other backgrounds. Although the theorists accepted, to some degree, the importance of social and environmental forces in

ⓖ   This logo indicates the occurrence of a search term to be used with the online library, InfoTrac College Edition. The first search word is *ethnicity*.

shaping personality, they tended to ignore or minimize the influence of gender and ethnic background.

An Asian-American psychologist summed up the present-day situation: "In America the overwhelming subject of research is white Americans. The U.S. constitutes less than 5 percent of the world's population, yet from that population we develop theories and principles assumed to be universal" (Sue, quoted in McGuire, 1999, p. 26).

Our own experiences tell us that our brothers and sisters were exposed to different childhood influences than we were and that they grew up to have different personalities. We also know from research in social psychology and sociology that children from different environments—such as a predominantly White Midwestern town, an Asian immigrant community, a Los Angeles barrio, an Appalachian mountain village, a Native American reservation, or an affluent Black suburb—are exposed to vastly different social and cultural influences. If the world in which people live and the factors that affect their upbringing are so different, then surely their personalities can be expected to differ.

They do, as demonstrated by a rapidly growing body of research. For example, consider a study comparing the personalities of Chinese college students in Hong Kong with Chinese students in Canada. Those living in Hong Kong, an Eastern culture, were more introverted than those living in Canada, a Western culture, a finding that supports earlier research showing that Eastern societies, in general, are more introverted than Western societies.

In the same study, recent Chinese immigrants to Canada demonstrated a similarly low level of introversion as the Hong Kong Chinese. However, Chinese immigrants who had lived in Canada at least 10 years, and thus had greater exposure to Western culture, scored significantly higher in extraversion than did more recent immigrants or the Hong Kong subjects. In this instance, cultural forces had exerted an impact on this basic personality characteristic (McCrae, Yik, Trapnell, Bond, & Paulhus, 1998).

A study of approximately 2,000 men and women college students from 20 countries, including the United States, found gender differences in the personality characteristics the students considered the most important. The subjects were asked to indicate which of the 300 adjectives in the Adjective Check List they thought were important. Some of the results are shown in Table 1.2 (Williams, Satterwhite, & Saiz, 1998). The researchers concluded that the important traits chosen by women are seen as more favorable by U.S. cultural standards whereas the traits selected by men are viewed as less desirable.

Cross-Cultural Psychology

The influence of cultural forces on personality is now widely recognized in psychology. A specialty area called cross-cultural psychology developed in the late 1960s, as reflected in new publications such as the *Cross-Cultural Psychology Bulletin* and the *Directory of Cross-Cultural Psychological Research*. In 1970, the *Journal of Cross-Cultural Psychology* began, and in 1980, the *Handbook of Cross-Cultural Psychology* first appeared, revised in 1997.

TABLE 1.2   *Importance of adjectives selected to describe personality*

More important to women	More important to men
clever	sexy
loyal	quick
poised	effeminate
helpful	argumentative
dependable	slipshod
friendly	tense
mannerly	unassuming
patient	rebellious
charming	severe
appreciative	unconventional
optimistic	hurried
warm	complicated

SOURCE: Adapted from J. E. Williams, R. C. Satterwhite, & J. L. Saiz, *The importance of psychological traits: A cross-cultural study.* Plenum Press, 1998, p. 63.

All this attention sounds impressive and represents a major advance after years of neglect. However, the importance of cross-cultural issues has been slow to infiltrate the mainstream personality journals. During the 1990s, some 15 percent of the articles published in the *Journal of Cross-Cultural Psychology* dealt with personality. In contrast, leading personality journals, such as the *Journal of Personality and Social Psychology*, devoted less than 2.5 percent of their articles to the effects of culture on personality (Lee, McCauley, & Draguns, 1999).

In addition, research on cross-cultural psychology has yet to cross many of the world's cultures. Little research has been conducted on personality in African, South American, and Asian nations. Consider, for example, India and mainland China. Although they account for more than 45 percent of the world's population, relatively few studies dealing with personality in those cultures have been published in English-language sources.

Another problem limiting the applicability of cross-cultural personality research is that most studies use college students as subjects. It is questionable whether we can generalize the results of such research to the population as a whole (a criticism made of much psychological research based on college students).

Ethnic and Racial Influences in American Psychology

The situation is more optimistic with regard to the study of ethnic and racial influences on personality. Over the last 20 years there has been an increasing recognition in American personality research of the importance of racial and ethnic differences. In 1986, the Society for the Psychological Study of Racial and Ethnic Minority Issues was established as Division 45 of the American Psychological Association (APA).

In the years between 1988 and 1995, the APA published bibliographies on African Americans, Hispanic Americans, Asian Americans, and Native Americans. This strong interest in ethnic and racial issues is reflected in an increase in relevant research. In the 16 years between 1974 and 1990, APA journals published 2,445 articles citing racial and ethnic differences, an average of 153 articles per year. In the following seven years (1990 to 1997), the average grew to 431 per year (Loo, 1998).

At the same time, the amount of research conducted on the effects of gender on personality increased substantially. It has been suggested that the rapid growth in the number of women Ph.D.s and the lessening of academic barriers to their promotion and tenure has increased the attention paid to male-female differences in personality.

Thus, overall, it is fair to state that personality researchers have become more aware of and sensitive to the substantial impact of gender and ethnic identity. Psychologists expect that this greater recognition will lead to the inclusion of people of different backgrounds in subject pools for psychological research, thus improving and extending the applicability of the research findings.

We discuss throughout this book research results that deal with gender and ethnic issues and note what they portend for personality theory. It is important to keep in mind that these factors can be potent influences on personality, in ways that are only beginning to be understood.

Assessment in the Study of Personality

To assess something means to evaluate it. The assessment of personality is a major area of application of psychology to real-world concerns. Consider a few everyday examples.

Clinical psychologists try to understand the symptoms of their patients or clients by attempting to assess their personalities, by differentiating between normal and abnormal behaviors and feelings. Only by evaluating personality in this way can clinicians diagnose disorders and determine the best course of therapy.

School psychologists evaluate the personalities of the students referred to them for treatment in an attempt to uncover the causes of adjustment or learning problems. Industrial/organizational psychologists assess personality to select the best candidate for a particular job. Counseling psychologists measure personality to find the best job for a particular applicant, matching the requirements of the position with the person's interests and needs. Research psychologists assess the personalities of their laboratory subjects in an attempt to account for their behavior in an experiment or to correlate their personality traits with other measurements. Thus, no matter what you do in life, it is difficult to avoid having your personality assessed in some way.

Standardization, Reliability, and Validity

Assessment techniques differ in their degree of objectivity or subjectivity; some techniques are wholly subjective and therefore open to bias. The results obtained by subjective techniques may be distorted by the personality characteristics of the person making the assessment. The best techniques of personality assessment follow three principles: standardization, reliability, and validity.

standardization The consistency or uniformity of conditions and procedures for administering an assessment device.

Standardization.   **Standardization** involves the consistency or uniformity of conditions and procedures for administering a test. If we want to compare the performance of different people on the same test, then they must all take that test under identical conditions. Everyone taking the test must be exposed to the same instructions, be allowed the same amount of time in which to respond, and be situated in an identical or highly similar environment.

Any variation in the established testing procedure can affect the test-takers' performance, and lead to an inaccurate assessment. Suppose, for example, that the air-conditioning system in the university's counseling center failed on an unusually hot day. The people taking tests that day would be operating under a disadvantage. In their desire to escape the heat, they might answer the questions less carefully than might the people who took the test the day before, when the room temperature was more comfortable.

If an inexperienced tester failed to read aloud the complete test instructions to a group of people, those test-takers would not be taking the test under the same conditions as people tested by a more conscientious test administrator, one who did read the complete instructions. The psychologists who develop a test can design appropriate standardized testing procedures into it, but if those procedures are not followed precisely, an otherwise excellent test can be rendered useless.

reliability The consistency of response to a psychological assessment device. Reliability can be determined by the test-retest, equivalent-forms, and split-halves methods.

Reliability.   **Reliability** involves the consistency of response to an assessment device. If you took the same test on two different days and received two widely different scores, the test could not be considered reliable because its results were so inconsistent. No one could depend on that test for an adequate assessment of your personality. It is common to find some slight variation in scores when a test is retaken, but if the variation is large, then it is likely that something is wrong with the test or with the method of scoring it. Research has shown that test-takers' personal characteristics, such as age and degree of normality of the personality, can affect the reliability of personality tests.

Several procedures are available to determine the reliability of a test before it is used for assessment or research.

- The **test-retest method** involves giving the test twice to the same people and statistically comparing the two sets of scores by calculating the correlation coefficient. The closer the two sets of scores are to each other (the higher the correlation coefficient), the greater the test's reliability.
- In the **equivalent-forms method**, instead of taking the test a second time, the subjects take two equivalent forms of the test. The higher the correlation between the two sets of scores, the greater the test's reliability. This approach is more expensive and time-consuming than the test-retest method because it requires that psychologists develop two equal forms of the test.
- In the **split-halves method** the test is administered once, and the scores on half the test items are compared with the scores of the other half. This is the fastest approach because the test is given only one time. Also, there is no opportunity for learning or memory to influence performance.

validity The extent to which an assessment device measures what it is intended to measure. Types of validity include predictive, content, and construct.

Validity.   **Validity** refers to whether an assessment device measures what it is intended to measure. Does an intelligence test truly measure intelligence? Does a test of anxiety actually evaluate anxiety? If a test does not measure what it claims to, then it is not valid and its results cannot be used to predict behavior. For example, your score on an invalid intelligence test, no matter how high, will be useless for predicting how well you will do in college or in any other situation that requires a high level of intelligence. A personality test that is not valid may provide a misleading portrait of your emotional strengths and weaknesses.

As with reliability, validity must be determined precisely before a test is applied. Psychologists use several kinds of validity, including predictive validity, content validity, and construct validity.

From a practical standpoint, the most important kind of validity is **predictive validity**—how well a test score predicts future behavior. Suppose you apply for flight training to become an astronaut. As part of the selection process, you are given a lengthy paper-and-pencil test to complete. If the majority of the applicants over the last several years who scored above 80 percent on the test became successful astronauts, and the majority of those who scored below 80 percent failed as astronauts, then the test can be considered a valid predictor of performance in that situation. In establishing predictive validity, we must determine the correlation between a test score and some objective measure of behavior, such as job performance. The higher the correspondence between the two, the greater the test's predictive validity.

Content validity refers to the test's individual items or questions. To determine content validity, psychologists evaluate each item to see if it relates to what the test is supposed to measure. For example, the Sensation-Seeking Scale (see Chapter 17) is a test designed to measure the need for stimulation and excitement. One of the test items is the statement "I would like to try parachute jumping." A content analysis would ascertain how well this statement (and all other statements) distinguishes between people high in sensation-seeking behavior and people low in sensation-seeking behavior.

Construct validity relates to a test's ability to measure a construct—a hypothetical or theoretical component of behavior, such as a trait or motive. Anxiety is one example of a construct. How can we tell if a new test that promises to measure anxiety really does so? A standard way to determine this is to correlate the scores on the new test with other established and validated measures of anxiety, such as other psychological tests or some behavioral measure. If the correlation is high, then we can assume that the new test truly measures anxiety.

Methods of assessment.   The personality theorists discussed in this book devised unique methods for assessing personality, ways that suited their theories. By applying these methods, they derived the data on which they based their formulations. The techniques vary in objectivity, reliability, and validity, and they range from dream interpretation and childhood recollections to paper-and-pencil tests. In psychology today, the major approaches to personality assessment are:

- self-report or objective inventories
- projective techniques

- clinical interviews
- behavioral assessment procedures
- thought-sampling assessment procedures

It is important to note that assessment for diagnostic and therapeutic purposes should not be based solely on a single approach. Ideally, multiple assessment measures are used to provide a range of information about a person.

Self-Report Inventories

self-report inventory A personality assessment technique in which subjects answer questions about their behaviors and feelings.

The **self-report inventory** approach involves asking people to report on themselves by answering questions about their behavior and feelings in various situations. These paper-and-pencil tests include items dealing with symptoms, attitudes, interests, fears, and values. Test-takers indicate how closely each statement describes their characteristics or how much they agree with each item. Two widely used self-report inventories are the Minnesota Multiphasic Personality Inventory (MMPI) and the California Psychological Inventory (CPI).

MMPI

Minnesota Multiphasic Personality Inventory (MMPI).   The MMPI has been translated into 140 languages and may be the world's most widely used psychological test (Butcher & Rouse, 1996; Snoxell, 1994). First published in 1943, the MMPI was revised in 1989 to make the language more contemporary and nonsexist (Buchanan, 1994). Items were also rewritten to eliminate words that over the years had acquired alternative meanings or interpretations (Ben-Porath & Butcher, 1989). The 1989 revision, the MMPI-2, is a true-false test that consists of 567 statements. These items cover physical and psychological health; political and social attitudes; educational, occupational, family, and marital factors; and neurotic and psychotic behavior tendencies. The test's clinical scales measure such personality characteristics as gender role, defensiveness, depression, hysteria, paranoia, hypochondriasis, and schizophrenia. Some items can be scored to determine if the test-taker was faking, was careless, or misunderstood the instructions. Examples of the types of statements in the MMPI can be found in Table 1.3.

The MMPI-2 is used with adults in research on personality, as a diagnostic tool for assessing personality problems, and for vocational and personal counseling. In 1992 the MMPI-A was developed for use with adolescents. The number of questions was decreased from 567 to 478, to reduce the time and effort needed to administer it (Butcher, et al., 1992).

Both forms of the test have their shortcomings, however, one of which is length. It takes considerable time to respond diligently to the large number of items. Some people lose interest and motivation long before they finish. Also, some of the items on this and other self-report personality tests deal with highly personal characteristics, and some people consider the questions an invasion of privacy, particularly when someone is required to take the test to get a job. Nevertheless, despite the length and privacy issues, the MMPI-2 is a valid test that discriminates between neurotics and psychotics and between emotionally healthy and emotionally disturbed persons. Thus, it remains a highly valuable diagnostic tool.

T A B L E 1 . 3

Simulated items from the Minnesota Multiphasic Personality Inventory (MMPI). Answer "true" or "false."

At times I get strong cramps in my intestines.
I am often very tense on the job.
Sometimes there is a feeling like something is pressing in on my head.
I wish I could do over some of the things I have done.
I used to like to do the dances in gym class.
It distresses me that people have the wrong ideas about me.
The things that run through my head sometimes are horrible.
There are those out there who want to get me.
Sometimes I think so fast I can't keep up.
I give up too easily when discussing things with others.

California Psychological Inventory (CPI).   Developed in 1957 and revised in 1987 (Gough, 1987), this test is designed for use with normal people age 13 and older. It consists of 462 items that call for a "true" or "false" response. The CPI has three scales to measure test-taking attitudes and provides scores on 17 personality dimensions, including sociability, dominance, self-control, self-acceptance, and responsibility. The CPI has been successful in profiling potential delinquents and high school dropouts and in predicting success in various occupations, such as medicine, dentistry, nursing, and teaching.

Other self-report inventories measure personality traits or focus on larger dimensions, such as sociability, introversion-extraversion, and emotional maturity. Some personality theorists have devised tests to assess the characteristics relevant to their theories, and some theories have inspired other psychologists to develop additional tests.

Although there are self-report inventories to assess many facets of personality, the tests are not always appropriate for children or elderly people, for people whose level of intelligence registers below normal, or for people with limited reading skills (Wolfe, 1993).

Research has shown that even minor changes in the wording of the questions or the response alternatives on self-report measures can lead to major changes in the results. For example, when adults were asked what they thought was the most important thing for children to learn, 61.5 percent chose the alternative "to think for themselves." But when adult subjects were asked to supply the answer—when no list of alternatives was provided—only 4.6 percent made that or a similar response (Schwarz, 1999).

Despite such problems, self-report inventories remain the most objective approach to personality assessment. Their greatest advantage is that they are designed to be scored objectively. Virtually anyone with the proper answer key can score these tests accurately. The test results do not depend on the scorer's personal or theoretical biases. This objectivity in scoring, combined with the widespread use of computers, has led to automated personality assessment programs for the MMPI-2, the CPI, and dozens of other tests. Computerized scoring provides a complete diagnostic profile of the test-taker's responses.

Projective Techniques

projective test A personality assessment device in which subjects are presumed to project personal needs, fears, and values onto their interpretation or description of an ambiguous stimulus.

☞ **projective techniques**

Clinical psychologists developed **projective tests** of personality for their work with emotionally disturbed persons. Inspired by Sigmund Freud's emphasis on the importance of the unconscious, projective tests attempt to probe that invisible portion of our personality. The theory underlying projective techniques is that when we are presented with an ambiguous stimulus, such as an inkblot or a picture that can be understood or interpreted in more than one way, we will project our needs, fears, and values onto the stimulus when asked to describe it.

There are two kinds or levels of interpretation problems with projective techniques, both of which contribute to their subjectivity. The first problem is interpreting the responses to the individual test items, which make up the final score. The second problem is interpreting the final score to provide a personality profile of the test-taker.

Because the interpretation of the results of projective tests is so subjective, these tests are not high in reliability or validity. It is not unusual for different test administrators to form different impressions of the same person, based on the results of a projective test; in such a case, the inter-scorer reliability of the test is considered to be low. Nevertheless, such tests are widely used for assessment and diagnostic purposes. Two popular projective tests are the Rorschach Inkblot Technique and the Thematic Apperception Test (TAT).

☞ **Rorschach**

Rorschach Inkblot Technique.   The Rorschach was developed in 1921 by the Swiss psychiatrist Hermann Rorschach (1884–1922), who had been fascinated by inkblots since childhood. As a youngster he had played a popular game called *klecksographie*, or *blotto*, in which children gave their interpretations of various inkblot designs. Rorschach was known to be so intensely interested in inkblots that as a teenager, he acquired the nickname *Klecks*, which means, in German, blot of ink. Later, when Rorschach was serving a hospital residency in psychiatry after receiving his M.D., he and a friend played *blotto* with patients to pass the time. Rorschach noticed consistent differences between the responses of patients and the responses offered by school children to the same inkblots (Ben-Porath & Butcher, 1991; Ellenberger, 1993; Popplestone & McPherson, 1994).

In developing his inkblot test, Rorschach created the inkblots by dropping blobs of ink on blank paper and folding the paper in half (see Figure 1.1). After trying numerous patterns, he settled on ten blots because he could not afford to have more than ten printed. He wrote about his work with inkblots, but the publication was a failure. Few copies were sold, and the few reviews it received were negative. Although the test eventually became immensely popular, Rorschach became depressed and died nine months after his work was published.

The inkblot cards (some black, others using color) are shown one at a time, and test-takers are asked to describe what they see. Then the cards are shown a second time, and the psychologist asks specific questions about the earlier answers. The examiner also observes behavior during the testing session, noting test-takers' gestures, reactions to particular inkblots, and general attitude.

Responses can be interpreted in several ways, depending on whether the subject or patient reports seeing movement, human or animal figures, animate or inanimate

F I G U R E   1 . 1   *An inkblot similar to a Rorschach inkblot.*

objects, and partial or whole figures. Attempts have been made to standardize the administration, scoring, and interpretation of the Rorschach. The most successful of these, the Comprehensive System, claims, on the basis of considerable research, to lead to improved reliability and validity (Exner, 1993). Since the 1980s there has been renewed interest in the Rorschach, primarily because of the usefulness of the Comprehensive System (Lerner, 1994). Indeed, the Rorschach is now the second most frequently used assessment technique in personality research and clinical practice; only the MMPI is more popular (Butcher & Rouse, 1996).

It is important to note, however, the great difference in validity between these two approaches to personality assessment. This was reinforced by a meta-analysis of more than 160 studies that confirmed the MMPI to be far more valid than the Rorschach (Garb, Florio, & Grove, 1998).

Holtzman Inkblot Technique.   The Holtzman Inkblot Technique, developed by psychologist Wayne Holtzman and originally published in 1961, consists of 45 inkblots. It has a standardized scoring system that yields high reliability for well-trained scorers. The test procedures are simpler than those for the Rorschach, so it can be given to a large number of subjects at the same time. It is widely used in research on assessing personality characteristics (Holtzman, 1988).

Thematic Apperception Test (TAT).   Henry Murray and Christiana Morgan developed the TAT (Morgan & Murray, 1935). The test consists of 19 ambiguous pictures, showing one or more persons, and 1 blank card. The pictures are vague about the events depicted and can be interpreted in several ways. A sample TAT picture and a possible interpretation are shown on page 203. Persons taking the test are asked to construct a story about the people and objects in the picture, describing what led up to the situation shown, what the people are thinking and feeling, and what the outcome is likely to be.

In clinical work, psychologists consider several factors in interpreting these stories, including the kinds of personal relationships involved, the motivations of the characters, and the degree of contact with reality shown by the characters.

There are no objective scoring systems for the TAT, and its reliability and validity are low when used for diagnostic purposes. However, the TAT has proven highly valid for research; for that purpose, scoring systems have been devised to measure specific aspects of personality, such as the needs for achievement, affiliation, and power.

The TAT is frequently used in clinical practice and for employee selection. According to a survey of 50 doctoral programs, however, less than one-fourth of the clinical psychology Ph.D. programs in the United States require coursework on the test. When test interpretation of the TAT is taught, it is typically unstructured and superficial (Rossini & Moretti, 1997).

Word association and sentence completion are additional projective techniques that psychologists use to assess personality. In the word-association test, a list of words is read to the subject, and he or she is asked to respond with the first word that comes to mind. Response words are analyzed for their commonplace or unusual nature, for their possible indication of emotional tension, and for their relationship to sexual conflicts. Speed of response is considered important. The sentence-completion test also requires verbal responses. Subjects are asked to finish such sentences as "My ambition is . . ." or "What worries me . . ." Interpretation of the responses with both of these approaches can be highly subjective. However, some sentence-completion tests, such as the Rotter Incomplete Sentence Blank, provide for more objective scoring.

Clinical Interviews

In addition to the specific psychological tests used to measure an individual's personality, the assessment procedure often includes clinical interviews. After all, it is reasonable to assume that valuable information can be obtained by talking to the person being evaluated and asking relevant questions about past and present life experiences, social and family relationships, and the problems that led the person to seek psychological help. A wide range of behaviors, feelings, and thoughts can be investigated in the interview, including general appearance, demeanor, and attitude; facial expressions, posture, and gestures; preoccupations; degree of self-insight; and level of contact with reality.

Armed with the results of the psychological tests, which are usually administered before or during a series of interview sessions, the psychologist can focus on

TABLE 1.4   *Sample items from the Buss and Plomin EASI Temperament Survey*

Child tends to cry easily.
Child has a quick temper.
Child cannot sit still long.
Child makes friends easily.
Child tends to be shy.
Child goes from toy to toy quickly.

problems indicated by the test results and explore those areas in detail. Interpretation of interview material is subjective and can be affected by the interviewer's theoretical orientation and personality. Nevertheless, clinical interviews remain a widely used technique for personality assessment and a useful tool when supplemented by more objective procedures.

Behavioral Assessment

In the behavioral assessment approach, an observer evaluates a person's behavior in a given situation. The better the observers know the person being assessed, the more accurate their evaluations are likely to be. Psychologists Arnold Buss and Robert Plomin (Chapter 10) developed a questionnaire to assess the degree of various temperaments present in twins of the same sex (Buss & Plomin, 1984). The mothers of the twins were asked, on the basis of their observations of their children, to check those items on the questionnaire that best described specific and easily discernible instances of their children's behavior. Sample items from the questionnaire are listed in Table 1.4.

In a psychiatric ward for adults, hospital staff members were trained to observe their patients' behavior and were asked to watch the patients systematically for two seconds of every hour (Mariotto & Paul, 1974). In this way, the staff developed daily records of patient activities so those behavioral trends could be identified. Some of the specific behaviors observed and recorded included mumbling, pacing, and talking to oneself.

As we noted in the section on clinical interviews, counselors routinely observe their clients' behavior—considering, for example, facial expressions, nervous gestures, and general appearance—and use that information in formulating their diagnoses. Such observations are less systematic than formal behavioral assessment procedures, but the results can provide valuable insights.

Thought Sampling

In the behavioral approach to personality assessment described in the preceding paragraphs, specific behavioral actions are monitored by trained observers. In the thought-sampling approach to assessment, a person's thoughts are recorded systematically to provide a sample over a period of time. Because thoughts are private experiences and cannot be seen, the only person who can make this type of observation is the individual whose thoughts are being studied. In this procedure, then, the observer and the person being observed are the same.

In one study, over several weeks, adolescent subjects were given electronic beepers that sounded whenever it was time for them to record their thoughts, moods, and fantasies. In this way, the psychologists were able to evaluate how various activities, situations, and life events affected the subjects.

In another application of the thought-sampling technique, 88 men and women college students recorded their most positive and negative experiences at intervals every day for two weeks. The students, along with two trained judges, then grouped the experiences around common themes. These themes were compared with the results of objective and projective tests administered to the same subjects. The validity of the thought-sampling procedure was found to be as high or higher than the other assessment techniques and to uncover material that was difficult (or impossible) to obtain by other methods (Hanson, 1992).

The thought-sampling assessment procedure is typically used with groups, but it has also been applied to individuals to aid in diagnosis and treatment. A client can be asked to write or tape-record thoughts and moods for later analysis by the psychologist.

A variation of thought sampling is the experience sampling method. This is conducted similarly to thought sampling but the participants are asked also to describe the social and environmental context in which the experience being sampled occurs. For example, subjects might be asked to note whether they were alone or with other people when the electronic beeper sounded, alerting them to record their experiences. Or they might be asked precisely what they were doing or where they were. The goal of this method is to determine how one's thoughts or moods may be influenced by the context in which they occur (Hurlburt, 1997).

Gender and Ethnic Issues in Assessment

Gender.   The assessment of personality can be influenced by a person's gender. For example, women tend to score lower than do men on tests measuring assertiveness, a difference that may result from cultural sex-role training that traditionally teaches girls not to assert themselves. Whatever the cause, however, personality test data do show differences between men and women on a number of characteristics.

In addition, considerable data from personality tests, clinical interviews, and other assessment measures indicate differential rates of diagnosis based on gender for various emotional disorders. Women are more often diagnosed with and treated for depression, anxiety, and related disorders than are men. Several explanations have been offered. There actually may be a higher incidence of these disorders among women, or the differential rate may be related to gender bias or gender stereotyping in interpreting the assessment results. Also, the therapists who recommend treatment options based on the assessment results may exhibit a bias against women. The average course of therapy for women tends to be longer than that for men, and doses of psychoactive medications prescribed for women tend to be higher than those for men (Pilkington & Lenaghan, 1998).

ethnic attitudes   *Asians.*   Researchers have found that people of Asian heritage tend to hold strong beliefs about the common good of society as a whole. To them, individual competitiveness and assertiveness are undesirable and are contrary to Asian cultural standards (Markus & Kitayama, 1991). American culture is usually depicted as the opposite. An Asian American job applicant who is a recent immigrant to the United States and not yet acculturated to American values and beliefs is likely to score low on a personality test measuring factors such as competitiveness, assertiveness, and self-promotion. This person would probably be judged as deficient—as not measuring up to American standards—and thus would be unlikely to be offered a job.

Research on the personality factors of self-effacement and self-enhancement supported such ethnic differences. Self-enhancement was defined as the tendency to promote oneself aggressively and make oneself conspicuous. Self-effacement, the opposite of self-enhancement, was suggested to be more in agreement with the cultural values of Asian societies. A study of MMPI-2 results from North American and Hong Kong Chinese college-age students upheld this theory. The Chinese students scored considerably lower on self-enhancement variables than did the American students (Yik, Bond, & Paulhus, 1998).

In some Southeast Asian cultures, a belief in supernatural spirits and in communicating with deceased family members is widely accepted. Expressing such beliefs in these cultures is considered normal. Admitting these beliefs on an American personality test, however, could lead to a diagnosis that the person is delusional (Uba, 1994).

Studies of MMPI scores of Hong Kong Chinese college students showed consistently higher rates of depression than for American college students. However, the researchers concluded that these scores reflected cultural differences in social norms and values rather than true differences in psychopathology (Cheung & Ho, 1997). Interpretation of the individual item responses relating to social interaction, activity level, modesty, sex, and admitting to personal problems varied for the different subject samples. Lack of awareness of cultural norms could easily lead to the erroneous belief that the Asian students actually were more depressed. The practice of using American values, beliefs, and norms as the standard by which everyone is judged may help explain much research that shows that Asian Americans tend to receive different psychiatric diagnoses than American patients of European heritage.

Blacks.   On some scales of the MMPI personality test, Blacks frequently score higher than Whites. In a study of Black men and White men (average age 30) in a court-appointed counseling program for domestic violence, the assessment test used was the Millon Clinical Multiaxial Inventory. Black men scored significantly higher than White men on scales assessing mistrust, alienation, vigilance, impulsivity, and cynicism. The researchers pointed out that

> a "blind" interpretation of such results, without consideration of cultural context, could lead to interpretations that view Blacks as exhibiting greater psychopathology than Whites, including sociopathic, paranoid, and even delusional disturbances. . . . such characteristics may actually reflect a realistic adaptation to living in an oppressive and prejudicial society. (Hamberger & Hastings, 1992, p. 94)

A study that involved administering the MMPI to clients at a community mental health center showed that Black men scored higher than White men on the lie scale.

The researchers suggested that the Black men were attempting to give a good impression of themselves, to make themselves appear in a more favorable light. The scores for Black women showed higher energy, higher self-esteem, and more elated moods than did the scores for White women (McNulty, Graham, Ben-Porath, & Stein, 1997).

Blacks respond differently on projective tests of personality. A review of research using the Rorschach found that Blacks offer many fewer responses than Whites to the standard inkblots. This lower rate of self-disclosure may reflect a tendency of Blacks to limit the personal information they reveal to strangers such as clinicians or test administrators, particularly when those strangers are White. In turn, this reticence could influence the clinicians' interpretations and diagnoses (Frank, 1992).

Black children ages five to eight tended to give fewer responses to the TAT. When the people depicted on the TAT cards were changed from White to Black (in terms of facial features, hair texture, and style of dress), the Black children still made fewer responses, although they did express more positive attitudes toward the cards with the Black figures. With college student subjects, White test administrators tended to elicit longer stories from both Black and White college students than did Black test administrators, a finding that held for both Black and White TAT cards (Cramer, 1996).

Hispanics.   Little research has been conducted on personality assessment of Hispanic subjects, and the results of even this limited work have been inconsistent. Some studies show significant differences between Hispanics and persons of European background on some of the MMPI scales; other studies reveal no such differences (Whitworth & McBlaine, 1993).

One study used a paper-and-pencil personality test called the Psychological Screening Inventory, which was administered to 212 Texas college students, approximately half of whom were of Mexican descent. The Mexican American students scored higher on the characteristics of alienation and defensiveness, perhaps reflecting their minority status within the university community and American society at large. However, those Mexican American students who also scored high on an acculturation rating scale—meaning they held more of the values and attitudes of the majority U.S. culture—did not differ significantly from the other students on the alienation and defensiveness scales. These findings demonstrate the interaction between personality and sociocultural beliefs (Negy & Woods, 1993).

When a Spanish-language version of the MMPI was administered to university students in Mexico, where students of Mexican heritage are obviously not a minority group, their scores were found to be similar to those of university students in the United States. This finding reinforces the idea that personality test scores can be influenced by minority-group or majority-group status (Reyes-Lagunes, Reyes-Lagunes, & Scott, 1994).

Cross-cultural issues.   Some personality tests have been translated for use in other cultures, but there are potential problems with their cross-cultural application. This is particularly crucial when a test designed for the population of a Western culture is administered to people in a non-Western culture, such as China or the Philippines (Guanzon-Lapeña, Church, Carlota, & Katigbak, 1998). For example, among traditional Chinese people, important personality characteristics include being gracious, having a family orientation, emphasizing harmony with others, and showing frugality in everyday behavior. None of these factors is typical of those measured by American personality inventories (Cheung & Leung, 1998).

When the MMPI-2 was translated into Arabic, the issue arose of how to treat questions about one's sex life. In Arab countries, any open discussion of sex is considered inappropriate, even offensive. The researchers decided to retain the sex questions in the test but to specify in the instructions that the subjects' responses to these items were optional.

Translators of American personality tests for use in other cultures also face the problem of American slang and colloquial expressions. Phrases such as "I often get the blues," or "I like to keep up with the Joneses" might have little meaning or relevance when translated into another language. Some test questions will also be meaningless because they lack reference to everyday experience. The phrase "I like to ski fast" would have no personal meaning to people who have always lived in the desert or the tropics and therefore would reveal little about their personality.

Even the manner in which people in the United States answer test questions may differ from other cultures. Responding to items in a true-false format or multiple-choice format seems natural to American college students, who have been taking these types of tests since childhood. To others, it may be an awkward and alien way of answering questions.

There have been, as we noted, many successful versions of American personality tests prepared for use with other cultural groups. The MMPI-2 is available in at least 22 languages. But the reworking of personality tests to ensure that they accurately reflect and measure relevant personality variables is difficult and requires knowledge of and sensitivity to cultural differences (Butcher, Lim, & Nezamo, 1998; Paunonen & Ashton, 1998).

Research in the Study of Personality

One criterion for a useful personality theory is that it must stimulate research. In other words, a theory must be testable. Psychologists must be able to conduct research on its propositions to determine which to accept and which to reject. Ideally, a theory will be shaped, modified, and elaborated on—or discarded—on the basis of the research it generates.

Psychologists study personality in different ways. The method used depends on the aspect of personality under investigation. Some psychologists are interested only in overt behavior—what we do and say in response to certain stimuli. Other psychologists are concerned with feelings and conscious experiences as measured by tests and questionnaires. Such self-report inventories are among the most frequently used research techniques. Still other investigators try to understand the unconscious forces that may motivate us. A method useful for examining one aspect of personality may be inappropriate for another aspect. As we discuss the various theories throughout this book, you will see examples of all these expressions of personality—behavior, conscious processes, and unconscious processes—and the techniques used to study them.

The number of subjects used and the ways in which they are studied may also categorize personality research. For example, the **idiographic research** approach involves the intensive study of a small number of subjects—in some cases, only a single subject. Typically, the goal in the idiographic approach is therapeutic, in which the knowledge gained about a subject is used to aid in treatment. An additional goal is gaining general insights into the human personality.

The **nomothetic research** approach involves comparing and analyzing statistical differences among large samples of subjects. The goal in the nomothetic approach is to obtain data that can be generalized to a broad range of people. We will describe examples of both approaches throughout this book.

The three major methods used in personality research are

1. the clinical method
2. the experimental method
3. the correlational method

Although different in their specifics, these methods rely on objective observation, which is the fundamental defining characteristic of scientific research in any discipline.

The Clinical Method

The primary clinical method is the **case study** or case history, in which psychologists search their patients' past and present for clues that might point to the source of the patients' emotional problems. Undertaking a case study is similar to writing a mini-biography of a person's emotional life from the early years to the present day, including feelings, fears, and experiences.

Sigmund Freud used case studies extensively in developing his theory of psychoanalysis. He probed into his patients' childhood years, seeking those events and conflicts that may have caused their present neuroses. One such patient was Katharina, an 18-year-old woman suffering from anxiety attacks and shortness of breath. In reconstructing what he considered to be the relevant experiences in her childhood, Freud traced Katharina's symptoms to several early sexual experiences she reported, including a seduction attempt by her father when she was 14. With another patient, Lucy, Freud linked her reported hallucinations to events in her past that related to her love for her employer, a love that had been rebuffed.

It was through a number of such case studies that Freud developed his theory of personality, with its focus on sexual conflicts or traumas as causal factors in neurotic behavior. Freud and later theorists who used the case study method searched for consistencies in their patients' lives. On the basis of what they perceived as similarities among the reports of large numbers of patients, these theorists generalized their findings to everyone.

To investigate personality, psychologists use a variety of clinical methods in addition to case studies. These methods include tests, interviews, and dream analysis—

idiographic research
The intensive study of a relatively small number of subjects using a variety of assessment techniques.

nomothetic research
The study of the statistical differences among large groups of subjects.

case study A detailed history of an individual that contains data from a variety of sources.

all of which can also be used for assessment. We may distinguish between assessment and research based on whether the data are used to treat a patient (assessment) or to test a theory (research). Some theorists may use the same methods for both purposes.

Although the clinical method attempts to be scientific, it does not offer the precision and control of the experimental and correlational methods. The data obtained by the clinical method are more subjective, relating to mental and largely unconscious events and early life experiences. Such data are open to an interpretation that may reflect the therapist's personal biases, more so than data obtained by other methods. Further, memories of childhood events may be distorted by time, and their accuracy cannot easily be verified. However, the clinical method provides a window through which to view the depths of the personality, and we shall see many examples of its use, especially by the psychoanalytic and neopsychoanalytic theorists.

The Experimental Method

As stated earlier, the fundamental defining characteristic of research in any scientific discipline is objective observation. The clinical method does not meet that requirement very well. Two other requirements of scientific research are even more difficult to fulfill by using the clinical method but are satisfied by the experimental method.

One of these requirements is that observations be well controlled and systematic. Such control is not possible when dealing with a person's past life events or unconscious phenomena. The other requirement involves duplication and verification. With careful control of experimental conditions, a researcher working at another time and in another place can duplicate precisely the conditions under which the earlier research was conducted. Events in a person's life cannot be repeated or duplicated so exactly.

An experiment is a technique for determining the effect of one or more variables or events on behavior. We are constantly exposed to stimuli in our everyday world, such as lights, sounds, sights, odors, instructions, demands, and trivial conversations. If a psychologist wants to determine the effect of just one stimulus variable, he or she can arrange an experimental situation in which only that variable is allowed to operate. All other variables must be eliminated or held constant during the experiment. Then, if the subjects' behavior changes while only the stimulus variable is in operation, we can be certain that it alone is responsible for any change in behavior. The change could not have been caused by another variable because no other variable was allowed to influence the subjects during the experiment.

Scientists distinguish two kinds of variables in an experiment. One is the **independent or stimulus variable**, which is manipulated by the experimenter. The other is the **dependent variable**, which is the subjects' behavior or response to that manipulation. To be sure no variable other than the independent variable can affect the results, researchers must study two groups of subjects: the experimental group and the control group. Both groups are chosen at random from the same population of subjects.

The **experimental group** includes those subjects to whom the experimental treatment is given. This is the group exposed to the stimulus or independent variable.

independent variable In an experiment, the stimulus variable or condition the experimenter manipulates to learn its effect on the dependent variable.

dependent variable In an experiment, the variable the experimenter desires to measure, typically the subjects' behavior or response to manipulation of the independent variable.

experimental group In an experiment, the group that is exposed to the experimental treatment.

control group In an
experiment, the group that
does not receive the
experimental treatment.

The **control group** is not exposed to the independent variable. Measures of the behavior being studied are taken from both groups before and after the experiment. In
this way, researchers can determine if any additional variables have influenced the
subjects' behavior. If some other variable was operating, then both groups would
show the same changes in behavior. But if no other variable was in operation—if the
independent variable alone influenced the subjects—then only the behavior of the
experimental group would change. The behavior of the control group would remain
the same.

Applying the experimental method.   Let us follow the experimental method in action, using data from psychologist Albert Bandura's social-learning theory of personality. Bandura (see Chapter 15) wanted to determine whether children would imitate the aggressive behavior they observed in adults. What was the best way to study
this problem? Bandura could have observed children on neighborhood streets or at a
playground, hoping to catch their reactions if they happened to witness a violent incident. He could then have waited to see whether the children would imitate the aggressive behavior they had seen.

This approach is unsystematic and uncontrolled, and it does not allow for duplication and verifiability; it is unlikely that the same conditions would recur. Also,
observing children who happened to be present on a street corner would not necessarily provide an appropriate sample of subjects. Some of these children might already possess the tendency to behave aggressively, regardless of the adult behavior
they observed. Therefore, it would be impossible to decide whether their behavior
resulted from witnessing a violent act or from some factor that had long been part of
their personality.

Further, observing children at random would not allow the researcher to control
the type of aggressive act to which the subjects might be exposed. Children see many
kinds of violence—television actors in a gun battle, teenagers in a fistfight, drive-by
shootings, parental brawling, action figures in computer games. Each form of aggression would have to be studied individually before its effects on behavior could be determined reliably. For Bandura to study the phenomenon, then, it was necessary that all
the children he observed be exposed to the same instance of aggressive behavior.

Bandura approached the problem systematically by designing an experiment in
which children whose pre-experiment levels of aggression had been measured were
exposed to the same display of adult aggression. Children in the control group witnessed nonaggressive adults in the same setting. Both groups of children were
watched by trained observers to see how they would behave.

Children who watched the aggressive adult behaved aggressively; children in
the control group exhibited no change in aggressiveness. Bandura concluded that aggressiveness can be learned by imitating the aggressive behavior of others.

Limitations of the experimental method.   The experimental method has the potential for being the most precise method of psychological research, but it has several limitations. There are situations to which it cannot be applied; some aspects of
behavior and personality cannot be studied under rigorously controlled laboratory
conditions because of safety and ethical considerations. For example, psychologists

might be better able to treat emotional disturbances if they had data from controlled experiments on child-rearing techniques, to determine what kinds of early experiences might lead to problems in adulthood. Obviously, however, we cannot take groups of children from their parents at birth and expose them to various child-rearing manipulations to see what happens.

Another difficulty with the experimental method is that the subjects' behavior may change not because of the experimental treatment (the manipulation of the independent variable), but because the subjects are aware that they are being observed. They might behave differently if they thought no one was watching. When people know they are participating in an experiment, they sometimes try to guess the purpose and behave accordingly, either to please or to frustrate the experimenter. This kind of response defeats the purpose of the experiment because the resulting behavior (the dependent variable) has been influenced by the subjects' attitudes rather than by the experimental treatment. This is quite a different response from what the researcher intended to study.

Experimental research has its limitations, but when it is well controlled and systematic, it provides excellent data. We will see examples throughout the book of how the experimental method applies to understanding aspects of personality.

The Correlational Method

correlational method A statistical technique that measures the degree of the relationship between two variables, expressed by the correlation coefficient.

In the **correlational method**, researchers investigate the relationships that exist among variables. Rather than manipulating an independent variable, the experimenters deal with the variable's existing attributes. For example, instead of experimentally creating stress in subjects in the psychology laboratory and observing the effects, researchers can study people who already function in stressful situations—such as police officers, race-car drivers, or college students suffering from test anxiety.

Another way the correlational method differs from the experimental method is that in the correlational approach subjects are not assigned to experimental and control groups. Instead, subjects who differ on an independent variable—such as age, gender, order of birth, level of aggressiveness, or degree of neuroticism—are compared with their performance on some dependent variable, such as personality test responses or job performance measures.

Applying the correlational method. Researchers applying the correlational method are interested in the relationship between the variables—in how behavior on one variable changes or differs as a function of the other variable. For example, is birth order related to aggressiveness? Do people who score high on an IQ test make better computer programmers than people who score low? The answers to such questions are useful not only in research but also in applied situations where predictions must be made about a person's chances of success. The college entrance examinations you took are based on correlational studies that show the relationship between the variables of standardized test scores and classroom success.

A great deal of correlational research has been conducted on various facets of the human personality. Consider the need for achievement, a concept formulated by

Henry Murray (see Chapter 7) and subsequently studied by David McClelland (see Chapter 17). Much of the research on that topic compared the measured level of the achievement need with performance on a number of other variables.

For example, researchers wanted to determine whether people high in the need for achievement earned higher grades in college than people low in the need for achievement did. The psychologists could have chosen to use the experimental method and designed an experiment in which children would be reared by adults who had been trained in techniques known to increase the achievement need. Years later, when the children attended college, the grades of those high in the achievement need could be compared with the grades of those low in the achievement need. You can see, of course, that such an experiment is ridiculous to contemplate.

Using the correlational method, the researchers measured the achievement-need levels of a group of college students and compared them with the students' grades. The independent variable (the different levels of the need for achievement, from high to low) was not manipulated or changed. The researchers worked with the existing data and found that students high in the need for achievement earned higher grades than students low in the need for achievement (Atkinson, Lens, & O'Malley, 1976).

We will see many examples of the correlational method in personality research throughout the book, especially in discussions of the development and application of assessment techniques. The reliability and validity of assessment devices are typically determined through the correlational method. In addition, many facets of personality have been studied by correlating them with other variables.

The correlation coefficient. The primary statistical measure of correlation is the correlation coefficient, which provides precise information about the direction and strength of the relationship between two variables. The direction of the relationship can be positive or negative. If high scores on one variable accompany high scores on the other variable, the direction is positive. If high scores on one variable accompany low scores on the other variable, the direction is negative. (See Figure 1.2.)

Correlation coefficients range from $+1.00$ (a perfect positive correlation) to -1.00 (a perfect negative correlation). The closer the correlation coefficient is to $+1.00$ or -1.00, the stronger the relationship and the more confidently we can make predictions about one variable from the other.

Cause and effect. The primary limitation of the correlational method relates to cause and effect. Just because two variables show a high correlation, it does not necessarily follow that one has caused the other. There may indeed be such a relationship, but researchers cannot automatically conclude that one exists, as they can with a well-controlled, systematic experiment.

Suppose a psychologist applied the correlational method and found a strong negative relationship between the two personality variables of shyness and self-esteem: The higher the level of shyness, the lower the level of self-esteem. Conversely, the lower the level of shyness, the higher the level of self-esteem. The relationship is clear: People who are shy tend to score low on measures of self-esteem. We cannot conclude with certainty, however, that being shy causes people to have

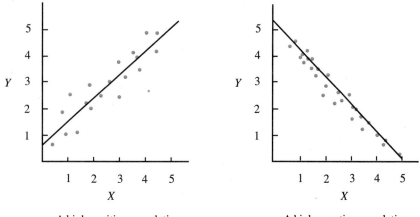

A high positive correlation   A high negative correlation

FIGURE 1.2   *Correlation*

low self-esteem. It could be the other way around—that low self-esteem causes people to be shy. Or some other variable, such as physical appearance or parental rejection, could cause both shyness and low self-esteem.

This restriction on drawing conclusions from correlational research presents difficulties for researchers, whose goal is to identify specific causes. However, for practitioners, whose goal is to predict behavior in the real world, the correlational method is more satisfactory. To be able to predict success in college on the basis of the need for achievement, for example, we need only establish that the two variables have a high correlation. If a college applicant scores high on a test of the need for achievement, we can predict that he or she will earn good grades in college. In this case, we are not concerned with determining whether the level of the achievement need causes good academic performance, only with whether the two variables are related and whether one can be predicted from the other.

Theory in the Study of Personality

Although most scientists use them, theories are sometimes referred to in derogatory terms. "After all," they say, "it's only a theory!" Many people think that a theory is vague, abstract, and speculative—really no more than a hunch or a guess and quite the opposite of a fact.

It is true that a theory without research evidence to support it is speculation. However, a mass of research data can be meaningless unless it is organized in some sort of explanatory framework or context. A theory provides the framework for simplifying and describing empirical data in a meaningful way. A theory can be considered a kind of map that represents the data in their interrelationships. It attempts to bring order to the data, to fit them into a pattern.

Theories are sets of principles used to explain a particular class of phenomena (in our case, the behaviors and experiences relating to personality). If personality theories are to be useful, they must be testable, capable of stimulating research on their various propositions. Researchers must be able to conduct experiments to determine whether aspects of the theory should be accepted or rejected. Personality theories must be able to clarify and explain the data of personality by organizing those data into a coherent framework. Theories should also help us understand and predict behavior. Those theories that can be tested and can explain, understand, and predict behavior may then be applied to help people change their behaviors, feelings, and emotions from harmful to helpful, from undesirable to desirable.

Formal Theories and Personal Theories

Scientists are not the only people who use theories; nor are all theories formal proposals containing numerous postulates and corollaries. We all use implicit personal theories in our everyday interactions with other people. We have some idea of the concept of personality, and we make suppositions about the personalities of those with whom we interact. Many of us speculate about human nature in general. For example, we may believe that all people are basically good or that people care only about themselves.

These suppositions are theories. They are frameworks within which we place the data of our observations of others. We usually base our personal theories on data that we collect from our perceptions of the behavior of those around us. In that respect—that our theories derive from our observations—personal theories are similar to formal theories.

However, formal theories in psychology, as well as in other sciences, have certain characteristics that set them apart from our personal theories. Formal theories are based on data from observations of large numbers of people of diverse natures, whereas personal theories are derived from our observations of a limited number of persons—usually our small circle of relatives, friends, and acquaintances, as well as ourselves. Because a broader range of data supports formal theories, they are more comprehensive. We can generalize more effectively from formal theories to explain and predict the behavior of more kinds of people.

A second characteristic is that formal theories are likely to be more objective because scientists' observations are, ideally, unbiased by their needs, fears, desires, and values. In contrast, our personal theories are based as much on observations of ourselves as of others. We tend to interpret the actions of other people in terms of our thoughts and feelings, evaluating their reactions to a situation on the basis of what we would do or how we would feel. We view others in personal and subjective terms, whereas scientists try to observe more objectively and dispassionately.

Another characteristic is that formal theories are tested repeatedly against reality, often by a scientist other than the one who proposed the theory. A formal theory may be put to many objective experimental tests and, as a consequence, be supported, modified, or rejected in light of the results. Personal theories are not so tested by us or by a neutral party. Once we develop a personal theory about people in general or about one person in particular, we tend to cling to it, perceiving only those behaviors that confirm our theory and failing to attend to those that contradict it.

In principle, scientists can recognize and evaluate data that do not support their theories. Unfortunately, in reality, this is not always true. Many examples exist in both the history of science and the history of psychology of scientists who were so prejudiced by their theory, so emotionally committed to it, that their objectivity was compromised. However, the ideal of objectivity remains the goal toward which scientists strive.

Subjectivity in Personality Theories

The intent of formal theories is greater objectivity; personal theories tend to be more subjective. We might assume that personality theories, because they belong to a discipline that calls itself a science, are exclusively of the formal and objective variety, but that conclusion would be wrong. Psychologists recognize that some personality theories have a subjective component and may reflect events in a theorist's life as a sort of disguised autobiography. The theorist may draw on these events as a source of data to describe and support his or her theory. No matter how hard scientists try to be impartial and objective, their personal viewpoint is likely to influence their perception to some degree. This should not surprise us. Personality theorists are human beings and, like most of us, may find it difficult to accept ideas that diverge from their own experience.

Thus, the distinction between formal and personal theories may not be so notable in the area of personality as in other branches of psychology. This does not mean that all personality theories are personal theories. Personality theories have the characteristics of formal theories. Some are based on the observation of a large number and variety of persons. Some are tested against reality either by the theorist who proposed it or by others. These scientists attempt to be objective in making their observations and in analyzing their data, which may or may not support the theory. Ultimately, the theories are as objective as their subject matter—the complex human personality—permits, but their propositions may owe much to the personalities and life experiences of their originators.

The first stage in constructing a theory may be based primarily on intuition, but in later stages these intuitively based ideas may be modified and refined by the theorist's rational and empirical knowledge. Thus, through the application of reason and data analysis, what began as a personal theory assumes the characteristics of a formal theory. Whatever level of objectivity is found in personality theories (and some are more objective than others), there is no denying that they are also partly subjective, reflecting the experiences and needs of the theorist.

If we want to understand a theory fully, we should learn about the person who proposed it. It is important to consider how the development of a theory may have been influenced by specific events in a theorist's life. Where sufficient biographical information is available, we suggest how a theory reflects those events. At least initially, the theorist may have been describing himself or herself. Later, the theorist may have sought appropriate data from other sources to support the generalization of that personal view to others.

The significance of personal events in a theorist's life has long been recognized, as we noted. William James (1842–1910), considered by many scholars to have been the greatest American psychologist, believed that biography was a crucial subject for anyone who attempts to study human nature. He argued that it was even more important to understand eminent persons' lives than to know their theories or systems so as to learn about the different ways people approach human experience (Simon, 1998).

One historian noted:

> More than any other professional discipline, psychologists have sought to publish biographical and autobiographical sketches of those in their calling. . . . At some level, at least, they seem to have acknowledged that their lives and values are the key to their "scientific knowledge." (Friedman, 1996, p. 221)

We shall see throughout this book several examples of the autobiographical nature of personality theory, but we must also introduce a note of caution into this intriguing relationship between theory and real life. Perhaps it is not the life experiences that influence the development of the theory. Instead, maybe the theory influences what the theorists recall and choose to tell us about their lives (Pervin, 1984). Much of our information about a theorist's life comes from autobiographical recollections. These accounts are usually written late in life, after the person has proposed and defended the theory. The time spent developing the theory and affirming a commitment to it may distort the theorist's memories of earlier years. Does the person recall only those events that support the theory? Are contradictory or troublesome events conveniently forgotten? Are experiences invented to enhance a theory's credibility? Although we cannot always answer these questions, we should keep them in mind while we explore the notion that personality theory may be partly autobiographical.

Questions About Human Nature

An important aspect of any personality theory is the image of human nature formulated by the theorist. Each theorist has a conception of human nature that addresses a number of fundamental questions, issues that focus on the core of what it means to be human (see Table 1.5). For centuries, poets, philosophers, and artists have phrased and rephrased these questions, and we see their attempts to answer them in our great books and paintings. Personality theorists, too, have addressed these troubling questions and have reached no greater consensus than have artists or writers.

The various images of human nature offered by the theorists allow for a meaningful comparison of their views. These conceptions are not unlike personal theories; they are frameworks within which the theorists perceive themselves and other people and within which they construct their theories. The issues that define a theorist's image of human nature are described below. As we discuss each theory, we will consider how the theorist deals with these questions.

Free Will or Determinism?

free will

determinism

A basic question about human nature concerns the age-old controversy between free will and determinism. Theorists on both sides of the issue ask, do we consciously

TABLE 1.5   *Questions about human nature*

1. Free Will/Determinism	Do we consciously direct our own actions, or are they governed by other forces?
2. Nature/Nurture	Are we influenced more by heredity (nature) or by our environment (nurture)?
3. Past/Present	Is our personality fixed by early events in our lives, or can it be affected by experiences in adulthood?
4. Uniqueness/Universality	Is the personality of each human being unique, or are there broad personality patterns that fit large numbers of persons?
5. Equilibrium/Growth	Are we motivated simply to maintain a physiological balance or state of equilibrium, or does the urge to grow and develop shape our behavior?
6. Optimism/Pessimism	Are we basically good or evil?

direct the course of our actions? Can we spontaneously choose the direction of our thoughts and behavior, rationally selecting among alternatives? Do we have a conscious awareness and a measure of self-control? Are we masters of our fate or are we victims of past experience, biological factors, unconscious forces, or external stimuli—forces over which we have no conscious control? Have external events so shaped our personality that we are incapable of changing our behavior?

Some personality theorists take extreme positions on this issue. Others express more moderate views, arguing that some behaviors are determined by past events and some can be spontaneous and under our control.

Nature or Nurture?

nature

nurture

A second issue has to do with the nature-nurture controversy. Which is the more important influence on behavior: inherited traits and attributes (our nature or genetic endowment) or features of our environment (the nurturing influences of our upbringing, education, and training)? Do the abilities, temperaments, and predispositions we inherit determine our personality, or are we shaped more strongly by the conditions under which we live? Personality is not the only topic affected by this issue. Controversy also exists about the question of intelligence: Is intelligence affected more by genetic endowment (nature) or by the stimulation provided by home and school settings (nurture)?

As with the free will–determinism issue, the alternatives are not limited to extreme positions. Many theorists assume that personality is shaped by both sets of forces. To some, inheritance is the predominant influence and environment of minor importance; others hold the opposite view.

Past or Present?

A third issue involves the relative importance of past events, such as our early childhood experiences, compared with events that occur later in life. Which is the more powerful shaper of personality? If we assume, as some theorists do, that what happens to us in infancy and childhood is critical to personality formation, we must consequently believe that our later development is little more than an elaboration of the basic themes laid down in the early years of life. This view is known as **historical determinism**. Our personality (so this line of thought goes) is mostly fixed by the age of five or so and is subject to little change over the rest of our life. The adult personality is determined by the nature of these early experiences.

historical determinism
The view that personality is basically fixed in the early years of life and subject to little change thereafter.

The opposite position considers personality to be more independent of the past, capable of being influenced by events and experiences in the present as well as by our aspirations and goals for the future. An intermediate position has also been proposed. We might assume that early experiences shape personality but not rigidly or permanently. Later experiences may act to reinforce or modify early personality patterns.

Uniqueness or Universality?

Is human nature unique or universal? This is another issue that divides personality theorists. We may think of personality as so individual that each person's action, each utterance, has no counterpart or equivalent in any other person. This obviously makes the comparison of one person with another meaningless. Other positions allow for uniqueness but interpret this within overall patterns of behavior accepted as universal, at least within a given culture.

Equilibrium or Growth?

A fifth issue involves what we might call our ultimate and necessary life goals. Theorists differ on what constitutes our major motivation in life. Do we function like machines, like some sort of self-regulating mechanism, content as long as some internal equilibrium or balance is maintained? Do we act solely to satisfy physical needs, to obtain pleasure and avoid pain? Is our happiness totally dependent on keeping stress to a minimum?

Some theorists believe that people are tension-reducing, pleasure-seeking animals. Others consider us to be motivated primarily by the need to grow, to realize our full potential, and to reach for ever-higher levels of self-actualization and development.

Optimism or Pessimism?

optimism

pessimism

One additional issue reflects a theorist's outlook on life. We may call it optimism versus pessimism. Are human beings basically good or evil, kind or cruel, compassionate or merciless? Here we are dealing with a question of morality, a value judgment, which supposedly has no place in the objective and dispassionate world of science. However, several theorists have dealt with the question, at least implicitly. Some theorists' views of the human personality are positive and hopeful, depicting us as humanitarian, altruistic, and socially conscious. Other theorists find few of these qualities in human beings, either individually or collectively.

Cultural Influences on Human Nature

We noted earlier that cultural differences affect personality development and assessment. It should come as no surprise, then, to learn that cultural factors influence our image of human nature and the questions we may ask about it. Consider the concept of *karma*, which for centuries has shaped the outlook of the peoples of India and other countries that accept Hinduism or Buddhism. It may be seen as a fatalistic and deterministic view of human nature. The consequences of our present and past actions are believed to determine our destiny or fate, our happiness or unhappiness in the future. In other words, "Things do not happen because *we* make them happen. Things happen because they were *destined* to happen" (Laungani, 1999, p. 204).

Thus, in this view, our fortune or misfortune, health or sickness, are preordained by our own actions. This belief may lead to a passive, resigned personality type, accepting of whatever comes one's way and not motivated to take action to change. Contrast this with a view more typical of U.S. culture that emphasizes free choice and action, and the role of personal effort and initiative in engendering personal success or failure.

Or consider the impact of the emphasis on individualism in the United States and on collectivism in Asian countries such as China and Japan. In an individualistic society, the focus is on personal freedom, choice, and action. In a collectivist society, the focus is on group norms and values, group role expectations, and other cultural constraints on behavior. These contrasting views have been shown to promote different approaches to our questions about human nature (Chiu, Hong, & Dweck, 1997).

What we should remember about these issues, then, is that there are diverse ways of understanding personality development and growth. Perhaps one or more of the theories we describe in this book will be congenial to you, or perhaps they will clash with your views and your image of human nature. Few of us can approach this topic without preconceptions because it is, after all, the study of ourselves.

Chapter Summary

Wilhelm Wundt, who used the methods of the natural sciences to analyze conscious experience, formally founded psychology in 1879. Early in the 20th century, John B. Watson developed the behavioral approach to psychology to protest against Wundt's focus on conscious experience. Watson argued that psychologists must study only overt behavior. Psychoanalysis, developed by Sigmund Freud, used clinical observation to probe the unconscious. The study of personality began in American psychology in the 1930s. Personality can be defined as an enduring, unique cluster of characteristics that may change in different situations. Differences in gender, ethnicity, and cultural background can influence personality development. Interest in cross-cultural psychology dates from the 1960s.

Techniques for assessing or measuring personality must meet three requirements: standardization (consistency of conditions and procedures for administering a test), reliability (consistency of responses on a test), and validity (the degree to which the test measures what it is intended to measure). The resulting assessment of personality can be influenced by the subject's gender and ethnic identity and by the test administrator's attitudes and beliefs.

Self-report inventories, in which people report on their own behavior and feelings in various situations, are objective in that scores are not influenced by personal or theoretical biases. Projective techniques attempt to probe the unconscious by having people project their needs, fears, and values into their interpretation of ambiguous figures or situations. Projective techniques are subjective, low in reliability and validity, and usually poorly standardized.

Clinical interviews are used to assess personality, but the interpretation of interview results is subjective. In the behavioral assessment approach, an observer evaluates a subject's responses in specific situations. In thought sampling, people record their thoughts over a period of time.

Psychological research methods include the clinical, experimental, and correlational approaches. Such research requires objective observation, controlled and systematic conditions, and duplication and verifiability. Idiographic research involves the intensive study of one or a few subjects; nomothetic research involves statistical analysis of data obtained from a large sample of subjects. The clinical method relies on case studies, in which psychologists reconstruct patients' backgrounds and lives to find clues to their present emotional problems. The clinical approach does not satisfy the requirements of psychological research as well as the experimental and correlational methods do.

The experimental method is the most precise method of psychological research. Using this method, psychologists can determine the effect of a single variable or stimulus event on the subjects' behavior. The variable being studied (that is, the stimulus to which the subjects are exposed) is the independent variable; the subjects' responses or behavior is the dependent variable.

In the correlational method, psychologists study the relationship between two variables to determine how behavior on one variable changes as a function of the other. The correlation coefficient, the primary statistical measure of correlation, indicates the direction and intensity of the relationship.

A theory provides a framework for simplifying and describing data in a meaningful way. Personality theories must be testable, must clarify and explain the data of personality, and must be useful in understanding and predicting behavior. Formal theories are based on data from observation of large numbers and diverse kinds of people. These theories are objective and are repeatedly tested against reality. Some personality theories may be partially autobiographical, reflecting a theorist's life experiences. The first stage in theory construction may be intuitive; ideas based on intuition may later be modified by rational and empirical knowledge (the results of research and scientific study).

Personality theorists differ on basic questions about human nature: free will versus determinism, nature versus nurture, the importance of the past versus the present, uniqueness versus universality, equilibrium versus growth, and optimism versus pessimism.

Review Questions

1. In your opinion, how does our personality influence our eventual success in interpersonal relations, in our career, and in our general level of health and happiness?

2. Discuss various ways of defining personality.

3. What was the fundamental point of difference between the approaches of Wilhelm Wundt and John B. Watson?

4. When and where did the scientific study of personality begin? What role did Sigmund Freud play in the investigation of personality?

5. In what ways may gender and ethnic factors affect the study and assessment of personality? Describe cross-cultural psychology and its impact on the study of personality.

6. Give examples of everyday situations that involve the assessment of personality. Recount your own experience of having your personality evaluated.

7. How do researchers determine the reliability of a psychological test?

8. Describe the difference between predictive validity and content validity.

9. Distinguish between self-report techniques and projective techniques for assessing personality. What are the advantages and disadvantages of each approach?

10. Describe the behavioral and the thought-sampling procedures for assessing personality.

11. Give examples of ways in which the personality assessment process can be influenced by the subject's gender or race.

12. What are the advantages and disadvantages of the case study approach?

13. What three requirements of scientific research are met by the experimental method?

14. Give an example of personality research that uses the correlational method.

15. Describe the relationship between data and theory.

16. Describe the differences between formal theories and personal theories.

17. How might cultural factors affect our image of human nature?

18. Six questions are asked in our discussion of human nature (Table 1.5, page 35). Write down your thoughts on these issues now. At the end of the book you will be asked to reconsider these questions to see how your views might have changed.

Suggested Readings

Buss, D. M. (1991). Evolutionary personality psychology. *Annual Review of Psychology, 42,* 459–491. Describes a field of study that seeks to identify behaviors and psychological mechanisms that have evolved to help us adapt to our environment.

Butcher, J. N., & Rouse, S. V. (1996). Personality: Individual differences and clinical assessment. *Annual Review of Psychology, 47,* 87–111. Reviews the use of popular assessment instruments such as the MMPI, MMPI-2, Rorschach, and TAT.

Elms, A. C. (1994). *Uncovering lives: The uneasy alliance of biography and psychology.* New York: Oxford University Press. Contains insightful psychological portraits of writers, political leaders, and personality theorists, including Freud, Jung, Murray, Allport, and Skinner.

Enns, C. Z. (1989). Toward teaching inclusive personality theories. *Teaching of Psychology, 16*(3), 111–117. Reviews biases in current personality theory, and recommends inclusion of viewpoints that recognize cultural and gender diversity.

Lee, Y.-T., McCauley, C. R., & Draguns, J. G., Eds. (1999). *Personality and person perception across cultures.* Mahwah, NJ: Lawrence Erlbaum. Reviews issues in studying personality in different cultures and social groups, including the accuracy of stereotypes. Contributors represent diverse cultures and ethnic identities.

Ross, M. (1989). Relation of implicit theories to the construction of personal histories. *Psychological Review, 96,* 341–357. Suggests that people develop personal theories to provide a framework for understanding their own personality and use these theories as a basis for selecting and organizing their memories of past events. They may recall incidents that are consistent with the theory and sometimes invent material to fill in gaps.

Schwarz, N. (1999). Self-reports: How the questions shape the answers. *American Psychologist, 54,* 93–105. Questions the cognitive and communication processes that underlie self-reports of behaviors and attitudes, including how people actually comprehend the task requirements.

Segall, M. H., Lonner, W. J., & Berry, J. W. (1998). Cross-cultural psychology as a scholarly discipline. *American Psychologist, 53,* 1101–1110. Reviews the growing recognition of cross-cultural influences on human behavior focusing on issues such as values, gender differences, intergroup relations, and psychological acculturation.

The Psychoanalytic Approach

The earliest approach to the formal study of personality was psychoanalysis, the creation of Sigmund Freud, who began his work in the closing years of the 19th century. So important and far-reaching were Freud's formulations that many of his ideas and his unique approach to psychotherapy remain influential more than a century later. In addition, nearly every personality theory developed in the years since Freud's work owes a debt to his position—either building on it or opposing it.

Psychoanalysis as Freud conceived it emphasized unconscious forces, biologically based drives of sex and aggression, and unavoidable conflicts in early childhood. These were considered the rulers and shapers of our personality.

Freud's views had an impact not only on psychology but also on the general culture. He succeeded in redefining the human personality and revolutionizing our ways of thinking about human nature.

> Turn your eyes inward, look into your own depths, learn to first know yourself.
>
> —Sigmund Freud

T W O

Sigmund Freud

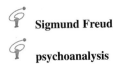

Sigmund Freud

psychoanalysis

psychoanalysis Sigmund Freud's theory of personality and system of therapy for treating mental disorders.

Personality theory has been influenced more by Sigmund Freud than by any other individual. His system of **psychoanalysis** was the first formal theory of personality and is still the best known. Freud's influence has been so profound that more than a century after his theory was proposed it remains the framework for the study of personality, despite its controversial nature. A survey of personality textbooks conducted nearly 60 years after Freud's death found him to be the most frequently cited personality psychologist (Mayer & Carlsmith, 1997). Not only did Freud's work affect thinking about personality in psychology and psychiatry, but it also made a tremendous impact on our view of human nature. Few ideas in the history of civilization have had such a broad and profound influence.

Many of the personality theories proposed after Freud are derivatives of or elaborations on his basic work. Others owe their impetus and direction in part to their opposition to Freud's psychoanalysis. It would be difficult to comprehend and assess the development of the field of personality without first understanding Freud's system.

The Life of Freud (1856–1939)

The Early Years

Freud was born on May 6, 1856, in Freiberg, Moravia (now Pribor, Czech Republic); in 1990 the town changed the name of its Stalin Square to Freud Square. Freud's father was a relatively unsuccessful wool merchant. When his business failed in Moravia, the family moved to Leipzig, Germany, and later, when Freud was 4 years old, to Vienna, Austria. Freud remained in Vienna for nearly 80 years.

When Freud was born, his father was 40 years old and his mother (the elder Freud's third wife) only 20. The father was strict and authoritarian. As an adult, Freud recalled his childhood hostility, hatred, and rage toward his father. He wrote that he felt superior to his father as early as the age of 2.

Freud's mother was slender and attractive. Her behavior toward her first-born son was protective and loving. Freud felt a passionate, sexual attachment to her, a situation that set the stage for his later concept of the Oedipus complex. As we shall see, much of Freud's theory reflects his childhood experiences and can therefore be considered autobiographical in nature.

Freud's mother took pride in young Sigmund, convinced that he would become a great man. Among Freud's lifelong personality characteristics were a high degree of self-confidence, an intense ambition to succeed, and dreams of glory and fame. Reflecting the impact of his mother's continuing attention and support, Freud wrote: "A man who has been the indisputable favorite of his mother keeps for life the feeling of a conqueror, that confidence of success that often induces real success" (quoted in Jones, 1953, p. 5). There were eight children in the Freud family, two of them Freud's adult half-brothers with children of their own. Freud resented them all and expressed anger and jealousy when competitors for his mother's affection were born.

From an early age, Freud exhibited a high level of intelligence, which his parents helped to foster. For example, his sisters were not allowed to practice the piano lest the noise disturb Freud's studies. He was given a room of his own, where he spent most of his time; he even took his meals there so as not to lose time from his studies. The room was the only one in the apartment to contain a prized oil lamp while the rest of the family used candles.

Freud entered high school a year earlier than was usual and was frequently at the head of his class. Fluent in German and Hebrew, he mastered Latin, Greek, French, and English in school and taught himself Italian and Spanish. From the age of 8, he enjoyed reading Shakespeare in English.

Freud had many interests, including military history, but when it came time to choose a career from among the few professions open to a Jew in Vienna, he settled on medicine. It was not that he wished to be a physician, but rather that he believed that medical studies would lead to a career in scientific research, which might bring the fame he fervently desired. While completing work for his medical degree at the University of Vienna, Freud conducted physiological research on the spinal cord of fish and the testes of the eel, making respectable contributions to the field.

The Cocaine Episode

While in medical school, Freud also began to experiment with cocaine. (At that time, cocaine was not an illegal drug. Further, it was not yet known that cocaine could have an addictive effect on some, but not all, users.) He used the drug himself and insisted that his fiancée, sisters, and friends try it. He became highly enthusiastic about the substance, calling it a miracle drug and a magical substance that would cure many ills and be the means of securing the recognition he craved.

In 1884 he published an article about cocaine's beneficial effects. This article was later judged to be a contributor to the epidemic of cocaine use in Europe and the United States, which lasted into the 1920s. Freud was strongly criticized for his part in unleashing the cocaine plague. The matter brought him infamy rather than fame, and for the rest of his life he tried to eradicate his earlier endorsement of the drug, deleting all references to the substance from his own bibliography. However, according to letters published long after his death, he continued to use cocaine well into middle age (Freud, 1985).

The Sexual Basis of Neurosis

A professor discouraged Freud from pursuing his intended career in scientific research, pointing out that it would be many years before Freud could obtain a professorship and support himself financially in the university system of the day. Because Freud lacked an independent income, he believed he had no choice but to enter private practice. A further impetus toward private practice was his engagement to Martha Bernays, which lasted four years before they could afford to marry. Freud established practice as a clinical neurologist in 1881 and began to explore the personalities of those suffering from emotional disturbances.

He studied for several months in Paris with the psychiatrist Jean Martin Charcot, a pioneer in the use of hypnosis. Charcot also alerted Freud to the possible sexual basis of neurosis. Freud overheard Charcot comment that a particular patient's problem was sexual in origin. "In this sort of case," Charcot said, "it's always a question of the genitals—always, always, always" (Charcot quoted in Freud, 1914, p. 14).

When Freud returned to Vienna, he was again reminded of the possible sexual origin of emotional problems. A colleague described a woman patient's anxiety, which the therapist believed stemmed from her husband's impotence. The husband had never had sexual relations with his wife in 18 years of marriage. "The sole prescription for such a malady," Freud's colleague said, "is familiar enough to us, but we cannot order it. It runs: *Penis normalis dosim repetatur!*" (quoted in Freud, 1914, p. 14). As a result of these incidents, and his own sexual conflicts, it can be suggested that Freud was certainly open to the possibility of a sexual basis for emotional disturbance.

Childhood Sexual Abuse or Fantasy?

By 1896, after several years in clinical practice, Freud was convinced that sexual conflicts were the primary cause of all neuroses. He claimed that the majority of his women patients reported traumatic sexual experiences from childhood. These events resembled seduction, with the seducer usually being an older male relative, typically the father. Today we call such experiences child abuse, and they often involve rape or incest. Freud believed that it was these early sexual traumas that caused neurotic behavior in adulthood.

About a year after he published this theory, Freud changed his mind. He decided that in most cases the childhood sexual abuse his patients mentioned had never really occurred. They had been telling him fantasies, Freud claimed. At first this was a stunning blow, for it seemed that the foundation of his theory of neurosis had been undermined. How could childhood sexual traumas be the cause of neurotic behavior if they had never happened?

On reflection, Freud concluded that the fantasies his patients described were indeed quite real to them. They believed that the shocking sexual events had actually happened. And because the fantasies did focus on sex, sex remained the cause of adult neuroses.

In 1984, nearly a century later, a psychoanalyst who briefly headed the Freud Archives charged that Freud lied and that his patients had truly been victims of childhood sexual abuse. Jeffrey Masson claimed that Freud called these experiences fantasies to make his ideas more palatable and acceptable to the public. Otherwise, who would believe that so many fathers and uncles were sexually abusing little girls? In other words, Masson said, Freud covered up the truth to make his theory of neurosis more acceptable (Masson, 1984).

The charges received much international publicity and were denounced by most Freud scholars on the grounds that Masson offered little persuasive evidence (see Gay, 1988; Krüll, 1986; Malcolm, 1984). It is important to note that Freud never claimed that all the childhood sexual abuses his patients reported were fantasies;

what he did deny was that his patients' reports were *always* true. It was, Freud wrote, "hardly credible that perverted acts against children were so general" (Freud, 1954, pp. 215–216).

Today we know that childhood sexual abuse is far more common than once thought, which leads contemporary scholars to suggest that Freud's original interpretation of the seduction experiences may have been correct. We do not know whether Freud deliberately suppressed the truth, as Masson claims, or whether he genuinely believed that his patients were describing fantasies. It may well be that "more of Freud's patients were telling the truth about their childhood experiences than [Freud] was ultimately prepared to believe" (Crewsdon, 1988, p. 41).

A similar conclusion was reached by one of Freud's disciples in the 1930s, and Freud tried to suppress the publication of his ideas. It has also been suggested that Freud changed his position on the seduction theory because he realized that if sexual abuse was so widespread, then many fathers (including perhaps his own) would be considered suspect of perverse acts against their children (Krüll, 1986).

Freud's Sex Life

It is a paradox that Freud, who emphasized the importance of sex in emotional life, experienced personal sexual conflicts. His attitude toward sex was negative. He wrote about the dangers of sex, even for those who were not neurotic, and urged people to rise above what he called the common animal need for sex. The sex act was degrading, he wrote, because it contaminated mind and body. He apparently abandoned his own sex life at the age of 41, writing to a friend: "sexual excitation is of no more use to a person like me" (Freud, 1954, p. 227). He occasionally had been impotent during his marriage and had sometimes chosen to abstain from sex because he disliked condoms and coitus interruptus, the standard birth control methods of the day.

Freud blamed his wife, Martha, for the termination of his sex life, and for many years he had dreams involving his resentment toward her for forcing him to abandon sex. "He felt resentful because she became pregnant so easily, because she often became ill during her pregnancies, and because she refused to engage in any kind of sexual activity beyond [procreative acts]" (Elms, 1994, p. 45). Thus, Freud's periods of impotence may also have been related to his fear that Martha would become pregnant again.

Freud's personal frustrations and conflicts about sex surfaced in the form of neuroses, in the same way he believed sexual difficulties affected his patients. In his forties he experienced a severe neurotic episode, which he described as involving "odd states of mind not intelligible to consciousness—cloudy thoughts and veiled doubts, with barely here and there a ray of light. . . . I still do not know what has been happening to me" (Freud, 1954, pp. 210–212). He was troubled by a variety of physical symptoms, including migraine headaches, urinary problems, and a spastic colon. He worried about dying, feared for his heart, and became anxious about travel and open spaces.

Freud diagnosed his condition as anxiety neurosis and neurasthenia (a neurotic condition characterized by weakness, worry, and disturbances of digestion and circulation), and traced both disturbances to an accumulation of sexual tension. In his writings he had proposed that neurasthenia in men resulted from masturbation, and anxiety neurosis arose from abnormal sexual practices such as coitus interruptus and abstinence. By so labeling his symptoms, "his personal life was thus deeply involved in this particular theory, since with its help he was trying to interpret and solve his own problems. . . . Freud's theory of actual neurosis is thus a theory of his own neurotic symptoms" (Krüll, 1986, pp. 14, 20).

Despite Freud's personal conflicts about sex (or perhaps because of them), he was fascinated by beautiful women. A friend noted that "among [Freud's] students there were so many attractive women that it began to look like more than a matter of chance" (Roazen, 1993, p. 138).

For three years Freud psychoanalyzed himself through the study of his dreams. It was during this period that he performed his most creative work in developing his theory of personality. Through the exploration of his dreams he realized, for the first time, how much hostility he felt toward his father. He recalled his childhood sexual longings for his mother and dreamed of a sex wish toward his eldest daughter. Thus he formulated much of his theory around his own neurotic conflicts and childhood experiences, as filtered through his interpretations of his dreams. As he perceptively observed, "The most important patient for me was my own person" (Freud quoted in Gay, 1988, p. 96).

The Pinnacle of Success

Freud's theory, then, was formulated initially on an intuitive basis, drawn from his experiences and memories. He constructed it along more rational and empirical lines through his work with patients, examining their childhood experiences and memories through case studies and dream analysis. From this material he fashioned a coherent picture of the development of the individual personality and its processes and functions.

As his work became known through published articles and books as well as papers presented at scientific meetings, Freud attracted a group of disciples who met with him weekly to learn about his new system. The topic of their first meeting was the psychology of cigar making. One writer referred to the group as a second-rate "collection of marginal neurotics" (Gardner, 1993, p. 51). Freud's daughter Anna described the early disciples a bit more charitably as

> the unconventional ones, the doubters, those who were dissatisfied with the limitations imposed on knowledge; also among them were the odd ones, the dreamers, and those who knew neurotic suffering from their own experience. (quoted in Coles, 1998, p. 144)

The disciples included Carl Jung and Alfred Adler, who later broke with Freud to develop their own theories. Freud considered them traitors to the cause, and he never forgave them for disputing his approach to psychoanalysis. At a family dinner he complained about his followers' disloyalty. "The trouble with you, Sigi," said his aunt, "is that you just don't understand people" (quoted in Hilgard, 1987, p. 641).

In 1909 Freud received formal recognition from the American psychological community. He was invited to give a series of lectures at Clark University in Worcester,

Massachusetts, and to receive an honorary doctoral degree. Although grateful for the honor, Freud did not like the United States, complaining of its informality, bad cooking, and scarcity of bathrooms.

Freud's system of psychoanalysis was warmly welcomed. Two years after his visit, American followers founded the American Psychoanalytic Association and the New York Psychoanalytic Society. Over the next few years, psychoanalytic societies were established in Boston, Chicago, and Washington, D.C. His ideas, popularized in magazines and books, were tremendously appealing to the American public (Kurzweil, 1998).

During the 1920s and 1930s, Freud reached the pinnacle of his success, but at the same time his health began to decline. From 1923 until his death 16 years later, he underwent 33 operations for cancer of the mouth (he smoked 20 cigars daily). Portions of his palate and upper jaw were removed, and he experienced almost constant pain, for which he refused medication. He also received X-ray and radium treatments and had a vasectomy, which some physicians thought would halt the growth of the cancer.

When the Nazis came to power in Germany in 1933, they expressed their feelings about Freud by publicly burning his books, along with those of other so-called enemies of the state, such as the physicist Albert Einstein and the writer Ernest Hemingway. "What progress we are making. In the Middle Ages they would have burnt me; nowadays they are content with burning my books" (Freud quoted in Jones, 1957, p. 182).

In 1938 the Nazis occupied Austria, but despite the urgings of his friends, Freud refused to leave Vienna. Several times gangs of Nazis invaded his home. After his daughter Anna was arrested, Freud agreed to leave for London. Four of his sisters died in Nazi concentration camps.

Freud's health deteriorated dramatically, but he remained mentally alert and continued to work almost to the last day of his life. By late September 1939, he told his physician, Max Schur, "Now it's nothing but torture and makes no sense any more" (Schur, 1972, p. 529). The doctor had promised that he would not let Freud suffer needlessly. He administered three injections of morphine over the next 24 hours, each dose greater than necessary for sedation, and brought Freud's long years of pain to an end.

Instincts: The Propelling Forces of the Personality

instincts In Freud's system, mental representations of internal stimuli, such as hunger, that drive a person to take certain actions.

Instincts are the basic elements of the personality, the motivating forces that drive behavior and determine its direction. Freud's German term for this concept is *Trieb*, which is best translated as a driving force or impulse (Bettelheim, 1984). Instincts are a form of energy—transformed physiological energy—that connects the body's needs with the mind's wishes.

The stimuli (hunger or thirst, for example) for instincts are internal. When a need such as hunger is aroused in the body, it generates a condition of physiological excitation or energy. The mind transforms this bodily energy into a wish. It is this wish—the mental representation of the physiological need—that is the instinct or driving force that motivates the person to behave in a way that satisfies the need. A hungry person, for example, will act to satisfy his or her need by looking for food. The instinct is not the bodily state; rather, it is the bodily need transformed into a mental state, a wish.

When the body is in a state of need, the person experiences a feeling of tension or pressure. The aim of an instinct is to satisfy the need and thereby reduce the tension. Freud's theory can be called a homeostatic approach insofar as it suggests that we are motivated to restore and maintain a condition of physiological equilibrium, or balance, to keep the body free of tension.

Freud believed that we always experience a certain amount of instinctual tension and that we must continually act to reduce it. It is not possible to escape the pressure of our physiological needs as we might escape some annoying stimulus in our external environment. This means that instincts are always influencing our behavior, in a cycle of need leading to reduction of need.

People may take different paths to satisfy their needs. For example, the sex drive may be satisfied by heterosexual behavior, homosexual behavior, or autosexual behavior, or the sex drive may be channeled into some other form of activity. Freud thought that psychic energy could be displaced to substitute objects, and this displacement was of primary importance in determining an individual's personality. Although the instincts are the exclusive source of energy for human behavior, the resulting energy can be invested in a variety of activities. This helps explain the diversity we see in human behavior. All the interests, preferences, and attitudes we display as adults were believed by Freud to be displacements of energy from the original objects that satisfied the instinctual needs.

Types of Instincts

Freud grouped the instincts into two categories: life instincts and death instincts. The **life instincts** serve the purpose of survival of the individual and the species by seeking to satisfy the needs for food, water, air, and sex. The life instincts are oriented toward growth and development. The psychic energy manifested by the life instincts is the **libido**. The libido can be attached to or invested in objects, a concept Freud called **cathexis**. If you like your roommate, for example, Freud would say that your libido is cathected to him or her.

The life instinct Freud considered most important for the personality is sex, which he defined in broad terms. He did not refer solely to the erotic but included almost all pleasurable behaviors and thoughts. He described his view as enlarging or extending the accepted concept of sexuality.

> That extension is of a twofold kind. In the first place, sexuality is divorced from its too close connection with the genitals and is regarded as a more comprehensive bodily function, having pleasure as its goal and only secondarily coming to serve the ends of reproduction. In the second place, the sexual impulses are regarded as including all of those merely affectionate and friendly impulses to which usage applies the exceedingly ambiguous word "love." (Freud, 1925, p. 38)

Freud regarded sex as our primary motivation. Erotic wishes arise from the body's erogenous zones: the mouth, anus, and sex organs. He suggested that people are

life instincts The drive for ensuring survival of the individual and the species by satisfying the needs for food, water, air, and sex.

libido To Freud, the form of psychic energy, manifested by the life instincts, that drives a person toward pleasurable behaviors and thoughts.

cathexis An investment of psychic energy in an object or person.

 libido

predominantly pleasure-seeking beings, and much of his personality theory revolves around the necessity of inhibiting or suppressing our sexual longings.

death instincts The unconscious drive toward decay, destruction, and aggression.

aggressive drive The compulsion to destroy, conquer, and kill.

In opposition to the life instincts Freud postulated the destructive or **death instincts**. Drawing from biology, he stated the obvious fact that all living things decay and die, returning to their original inanimate state, and he proposed that people have an unconscious wish to die. One component of the death instincts is the **aggressive drive**, described as the wish to die turned against objects other than the self. The aggressive drive compels us to destroy, conquer, and kill. Freud came to consider aggression as compelling a part of human nature as sex.

Freud developed the notion of the death instincts late in life, as a reflection of his own experiences. He endured physiological and psychological debilitations of age, his cancer worsened, and he witnessed the carnage of World War I. One of his daughters died at the age of 26, leaving two young children. All these events affected him, and death and aggression became major themes in his theory. In his later years Freud dreaded his death, and exhibited hostility, hatred, and aggressiveness toward colleagues and disciples who disputed his views and left his psychoanalytic circle.

The concept of the death instincts achieved only limited acceptance, even among Freud's most dedicated followers. One psychoanalyst wrote that the idea should be "relegated to the dustbin of history" (Sulloway, 1979, p. 394). Another suggested that if Freud were a genius, then the suggestion of the death instincts was an instance of a genius having a bad day (Eissler, 1971).

The Levels of Personality

Freud's original conception divided personality into three levels: the conscious, the preconscious, and the unconscious. The conscious, as Freud defined the term, corresponds to its ordinary everyday meaning. It includes all the sensations and experiences of which we are aware at any given moment. As you read these words, for example, you may be conscious of the feel of your pen, the sight of the page, the idea you are trying to grasp, and a dog barking in the distance.

Freud considered the conscious a limited aspect of personality because only a small portion of our thoughts, sensations, and memories exists in conscious awareness at any time. He likened the mind to an iceberg. The conscious is the portion above the surface of the water—merely the tip of the iceberg.

More important, according to Freud, is the unconscious, that larger, invisible portion below the surface. This is the focus of psychoanalytic theory. Its vast, dark depths are the home of the instincts, those wishes and desires that direct our behavior. The unconscious contains the major driving power behind all behaviors and is the repository of forces we cannot see or control.

Between these two levels is the preconscious. This is the storehouse of memories, perceptions, and thoughts of which we are not consciously aware at the moment but that we can easily summon into consciousness. For example, if your mind strays from this page and you begin to think about a friend or about what you did last night, you would be summoning up material from your preconscious into your conscious. We often find our attention shifting back and forth from experiences of the moment to events and memories in the preconscious.

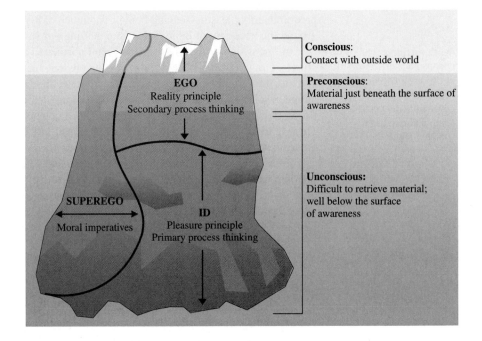

Conscious:
Contact with outside world

Preconscious:
Material just beneath the surface of awareness

Unconscious:
Difficult to retrieve material; well below the surface of awareness

FIGURE 2.1   *Freud's levels and structures of personality.* SOURCE: From *Psychology: Themes and Variations,* Second Edition, by W. Weiten, p. 428, Brooks/Cole Publishing Co., 1992.

The Structure of Personality: Id, Ego, and Superego

The Id

id To Freud, the aspect of personality allied with the instincts; the source of psychic energy, the id operates according to the pleasure principle.

Freud later revised this notion of three levels of personality and introduced three basic structures in the anatomy of the personality: the id, the ego, and the superego (see Figure 2.1). The **id** corresponds to Freud's earlier notion of the unconscious (although the ego and superego have unconscious aspects as well). The id is the reservoir for the instincts and libido (the psychic energy manifested by the instincts). The id is a powerful structure of the personality because it supplies all the energy for the other two components.

Because the id is the reservoir of the instincts, it is vitally and directly related to the satisfaction of bodily needs. As we noted earlier, tension is produced when the body is in a state of need, and the person acts to reduce this tension by satisfying the need. The id operates in accordance with what Freud called the **pleasure principle**; through its concern with tension reduction, the id functions to increase pleasure and avoid pain. The id strives for immediate satisfaction of its needs and does not tolerate delay or postponement of satisfaction for any reason. It knows only instant gratification; it drives us to want what we want when we want it, without regard for what anyone else wants. The id is a selfish, pleasure-seeking structure, primitive, amoral, insistent, and rash.

pleasure principle The principle by which the id functions to avoid pain and maximize pleasure.

The id has no awareness of reality. We might compare the id to a newborn baby who cries and waves its fists when its needs are not met but who has no knowledge of how to bring about satisfaction. The hungry infant cannot find food on his or her own. The only ways the id can attempt to satisfy its needs are through reflex action and wish-fulfilling hallucinatory or fantasy experience, which Freud labeled **primary-process thought**.

The Ego

Most children learn that they cannot take food from other people unless they are willing to face the consequences, that they must postpone the pleasure obtained from relieving anal tensions until they get to a bathroom, and that they cannot indiscriminately give vent to sexual and aggressive longings. The growing child is taught to deal intelligently and rationally with the outside world and to develop the powers of perception, recognition, judgment, and memory—the powers adults use to satisfy their needs. Freud called these abilities **secondary-process thought**.

We can sum up these characteristics as reason or rationality, and they are contained in Freud's second structure of personality, the **ego**, which is the rational master of the personality. Its purpose is not to thwart the impulses of the id but to help the id obtain the tension reduction it craves. Because it is aware of reality, the ego decides when and how the id instincts can best be satisfied. It determines appropriate and socially acceptable times, places, and objects that will satisfy the id impulses.

The ego does not prevent id satisfaction. Rather, it tries to postpone, delay, or redirect it in terms of the demands of reality. It perceives and manipulates the environment in a practical and realistic manner and so is said to operate in accordance with the **reality principle**. (The reality principle stands in opposition to the pleasure principle, by which the id operates.) The ego thus exerts control over the id impulses. Freud compared the relationship of the ego and the id to that of a rider on a horse. The raw, brute power of the horse must be guided, checked, and reined in by the rider; otherwise the horse could bolt and run, throwing the rider to the ground.

The ego serves two masters—the id and reality—and is constantly mediating and striking compromises between their conflicting demands. Also, the ego is never independent of the id. It is always responsive to the id's demands and derives its power and energy from the id.

It is the ego, the rational master, that keeps you working at a job you may dislike, if the alternative is the inability to provide food and shelter for your family. It is the ego that forces you to get along with people you dislike because reality demands such behavior from you as an appropriate way of satisfying id demands. The controlling and postponing function of the ego must be exercised constantly. If not, the id impulses might come to dominate and overthrow the rational ego. Freud argued that we must protect ourselves from being controlled by the id and proposed various unconscious mechanisms with which to defend the ego (see pages 56–59).

So far we have a picture of the personality in battle, trying to restrain the id while at the same time serving it, perceiving and manipulating reality to relieve the tensions of the id impulses. Driven by instinctual biological forces, which we

primary-process thought Childlike thinking by which the id attempts to satisfy the instinctual drives.

ego (psychology)

secondary-process thought Mature thought processes needed to deal rationally with the external world.

ego To Freud, the rational aspect of the personality, responsible for directing and controlling the instincts according to the reality principle.

reality principle The principle by which the ego functions to provide appropriate constraints on the expression of the id instincts.

continually try to guide, the personality walks a tightrope between the demands of the id and the demands of reality, both of which require constant vigilance.

The Superego

The id and the ego do not represent Freud's complete picture of human nature. There is a third set of forces—a powerful and largely unconscious set of dictates or beliefs—that we acquire in childhood: our ideas of right and wrong. In everyday language we call this internal morality a conscience. Freud called it the **superego**. The basis of this moral side of the personality is usually learned by the age of 5 or 6 and consists initially of the rules of conduct set down by our parents. Through praise, punishment, and example, children learn which behaviors their parents consider good or bad. Those behaviors for which children are punished form the **conscience**, one part of the superego. The second part of the superego is the **ego-ideal**, which consists of good, or correct, behaviors for which children have been praised.

In this way children learn a set of rules that earn acceptance or rejection from their parents. In time children internalize these teachings, and the rewards and punishments become self-administered. Parental control is replaced by self-control. We come to behave at least in partial conformity with these now largely unconscious moral guidelines. As a result of this internalization, we experience guilt or shame whenever we perform (or even think of performing) some action contrary to this moral code.

As the arbiter of morality, the superego is relentless, even cruel, in its quest for moral perfection. In terms of intensity, irrationality, and insistence on obedience, it is not unlike the id. Its purpose is not merely to postpone the pleasure-seeking demands of the id, as the ego does, but to inhibit them completely, particularly those demands concerned with sex and aggression. The superego strives neither for pleasure (as does the id) nor for attainment of realistic goals (as does the ego). It strives solely for moral perfection. The id presses for satisfaction, the ego tries to delay it, and the superego urges morality above all. Like the id, the superego admits no compromise with its demands.

The ego is caught in the middle, pressured by these insistent and opposing forces. Thus, the ego has a third master, the superego. To paraphrase Freud, the poor ego has a hard time of it, pressured on three sides, threatened by three dangers: the id, reality, and the superego. The inevitable result of this friction, when the ego is too severely strained, is the development of anxiety.

superego To Freud, the moral aspect of personality; the internalization of parental and societal values and standards.

conscience A component of the superego that contains behaviors for which the child has been punished.

ego-ideal A component of the superego that contains the moral or ideal behaviors for which a person should strive.

Anxiety: A Threat to the Ego

We already have a general idea of what the word *anxiety* means and how we feel when we are anxious. We know that anxiety is not unlike fear, although we may not know what we are frightened of. Freud described **anxiety** as an objectless fear; often, we cannot point to its source, to a specific object that induced it.

Freud made anxiety an important part of his personality theory, asserting that it is fundamental to the development of neurotic and psychotic behavior. He suggested that the prototype of all anxiety is the birth trauma, a notion elaborated on by a disciple, Otto Rank.

anxiety To Freud, a feeling of fear and dread without an obvious cause.

The fetus in its mother's womb is in the most stable and secure of worlds, where every need is satisfied without delay. But at birth the organism is thrust into a hostile environment. Suddenly it is required to begin adapting to reality because its instinctual demands may not always be immediately met. The newborn's nervous system, immature and ill prepared, is bombarded with diverse sensory stimuli. Consequently, the infant engages in massive motor movements, heightened breathing, and increased heart rate. This birth trauma, with its tension and fear that the id instincts won't be satisfied, is our first experience with anxiety. From it is created the pattern of reactions and feelings that will occur whenever we are exposed to some threat in the future.

When we cannot cope with anxiety, when we are in danger of being overwhelmed by it, the anxiety is said to be traumatic. What Freud meant by this is that the person, regardless of age, is reduced to a state of helplessness like that experienced in infancy. In adult life, infantile helplessness is reenacted to some degree whenever the ego is threatened.

Three Types of Anxiety

Freud proposed three types of anxiety: reality anxiety, neurotic anxiety, and moral anxiety. The first type of anxiety, the one from which the others are derived, is **reality** or **objective anxiety**. This involves a fear of tangible dangers in the real world. Most of us justifiably fear fires, hurricanes, earthquakes, and similar disasters. We run from wild animals, speeding cars, and burning buildings. Reality anxiety serves the positive purpose of guiding our behavior to escape or protect ourselves from actual dangers. Our fear subsides when the threat is no longer present. These reality-based fears can be carried to extremes, however. The person who cannot leave home for fear of being hit by a car or who cannot light a match for fear of fire is carrying reality-based fears beyond the point of normality.

The other kinds of anxiety, neurotic anxiety and moral anxiety, are more consistently troublesome to our mental health. **Neurotic anxiety** has its basis in childhood, in a conflict between instinctual gratification and reality. Children are often punished for overtly expressing sexual or aggressive impulses. Therefore, the wish to gratify certain id impulses generates anxiety. This neurotic anxiety is an unconscious fear of being punished for impulsively displaying id-dominated behavior. Note that the fear is not of the instincts, but of what may happen as a result of gratifying the instincts. The conflict becomes one between the id and the ego, and its origin has some basis in reality.

Moral anxiety results from a conflict between the id and the superego. In essence, it is a fear of one's conscience. When you are motivated to express an instinctual impulse that is contrary to your moral code, your superego retaliates by causing you to feel shame or guilt. In everyday terms, you might describe yourself as conscience-stricken.

Moral anxiety is a function of how well developed the superego is. A person with a strong inhibiting conscience will experience greater conflict than a person with a less stringent set of moral guidelines. Like neurotic anxiety, moral anxiety has some basis in reality. Children are punished for violating their parents' moral codes, and adults are punished for violating society's moral code. The shame and guilt feelings in moral anxiety arise from within; it is our conscience that causes the fear and the anxiety. Freud believed that the superego exacts a terrible retribution for violation of its tenets.

Anxiety serves as a warning signal to the person that all is not as it should be within the personality. Anxiety induces tension in the organism and thus becomes a drive (much like the hunger or thirst drives) that the individual is motivated to satisfy. The tension must be reduced.

Anxiety alerts the individual that the ego is being threatened and that unless action is taken, the ego might be overthrown. How can the ego protect or defend itself? There are a number of options: running away from the threatening situation, inhibiting the impulsive need that is the source of the danger, or obeying the dictates of the conscience. If none of these rational techniques works, the person may resort to defense mechanisms, which are nonrational strategies designed to defend the ego.

Defenses Against Anxiety

defense mechanism (psychology)

Anxiety is a signal that impending danger, a threat to the ego, must be counteracted or avoided. The ego must reduce the conflict between the demands of the id and the strictures of society or the superego. According to Freud, this conflict is ever present because the instincts are always pressing for satisfaction, and the taboos of society tend to limit such satisfaction. Freud believed that the defenses must, to some extent, always be in operation. Just as all behaviors are motivated by instincts, so all behavior is defensive in the sense of defending against anxiety. The intensity of the battle within the personality may fluctuate, but it never ceases.

defense mechanisms
Strategies the ego uses to defend itself against the anxiety provoked by conflicts of everyday life. Defense mechanisms involve denials or distortions of reality.

Freud postulated several **defense mechanisms** and noted that we rarely use just one; we typically defend ourselves against anxiety by using several at the same time (see Table 2.1). Also, some overlap exists among the mechanisms. Although defense mechanisms vary in their specifics, they share two characteristics: (1) they are denials or distortions of reality—necessary ones, but distortions

T A B L E   2 . 1   *Freudian defense mechanisms*

Repression	Involves unconscious denial of the existence of something that causes anxiety
Denial	Involves denying the existence of an external threat or traumatic event
Reaction Formation	Involves expressing an id impulse that is the opposite of the one truly driving the person
Projection	Involves attributing a disturbing impulse to someone else
Regression	Involves retreating to an earlier, less frustrating period of life and displaying the childish and dependent behaviors characteristic of that more secure time
Rationalization	Involves reinterpreting behavior to make it more acceptable and less threatening
Displacement	Involves shifting id impulses from a threatening or unavailable object to a substitute object that is available
Sublimation	Involves altering or displacing id impulses by diverting instinctual energy into socially acceptable behaviors

nonetheless, and, (2) they operate unconsciously. We are unaware of them, which means that on the conscious level we hold distorted or unreal images of our world and ourselves.

Repression

repression A defense mechanism that involves unconscious denial of the existence of something that causes anxiety.

Repression is an involuntary removal of something from conscious awareness. It is an unconscious type of forgetting of the existence of something that brings us discomfort or pain and is the most fundamental and frequently used defense mechanism. Repression can operate on memories of situations or people, on our perception of the present (so that we may fail to see some obviously disturbing event), and even on the body's physiological functioning. For example, a man can so strongly repress the sex drive that he becomes impotent.

Once repression is operating, it is difficult to eliminate. Because we use repression to protect ourselves from danger, in order to remove it, we would have to know that the idea or memory is no longer dangerous. But how can we find out that the danger no longer exists unless we release the repression? The concept of repression is basic to much of Freud's personality theory and is involved in all neurotic behavior.

Denial

denial A defense mechanism that involves denying the existence of an external threat or traumatic event.

The defense mechanism of **denial** is related to repression and involves denying the existence of some external threat or traumatic event that has occurred. For example, a person with a terminal illness may deny the imminence of death. Parents of a child who has died may continue to deny the loss by keeping the child's room unchanged.

Reaction Formation

reaction formation A defense mechanism that involves expressing an id impulse that is the opposite of the one that is truly driving the person.

One defense against a disturbing impulse is to actively express the opposite impulse. This is called **reaction formation**. A person who is strongly driven by threatening sexual impulses may repress those impulses and replace them with more socially acceptable behaviors. For example, a person threatened by sexual longings may reverse them and become a rabid crusader against pornography. Another person, disturbed by extreme aggressive impulses, may become overly solicitous and friendly. Thus, lust becomes virtue and hatred becomes love.

Projection

projection A defense mechanism that involves attributing a disturbing impulse to someone else.

Another way of defending against disturbing impulses is to attribute them to someone else. This defense mechanism is called **projection**. Lustful, aggressive, and other unacceptable impulses are seen as being possessed by other people, not by oneself. The person says, in effect, "I don't hate him. He hates me." Or a mother may ascribe her sex drive to her adolescent daughter. The impulse is still manifested, but in a way that is less threatening to the individual.

Regression

regression A defense
mechanism that involves
retreating to an earlier,
less frustrating period of
life and displaying the
usually childish behaviors
characteristic of that more
secure time.

In **regression**, the person retreats or regresses to an earlier period of life that was more pleasant and free of frustration and anxiety. Regression usually involves a return to one of the psychosexual stages of childhood development (see pages 59–65).

The individual returns to this more secure time of life by manifesting behaviors displayed at that time, such as childish and dependent behaviors.

Rationalization

rationalization A
defense mechanism that
involves reinterpreting our
behavior to make it more
acceptable and less
threatening to us.

Rationalization is a defense mechanism that involves reinterpreting our behavior to make it seem more rational and acceptable to us. We excuse or justify a threatening thought or action by persuading ourselves there is a rational explanation for it. The person who is fired from a job may rationalize by saying that the job wasn't a good one anyway. The loved one who turns you down now appears to have many faults. It is less threatening to blame someone or something else for our failures than to blame ourselves.

Displacement

displacement A defense
mechanism that involves
shifting id impulses from
a threatening object or
from one that is
unavailable to an object
that is available; for
example, replacing
hostility toward one's
boss with hostility toward
one's child.

If an object that satisfies an id impulse is not available, the person may shift the impulse to another object. This is known as **displacement**. For example, children who hate their parents or adults who hate their bosses, but are afraid to express their hostility for fear of being punished, may displace the aggression onto someone else. The child may hit a younger brother or sister, or the adult may shout at the dog. In these examples, the original object of the aggressive impulse has been replaced by an object that is not a threat. However, the substitute object will not reduce the tension as satisfactorily as the original object. If you are involved in a number of displacements, a reservoir of undischarged tension accumulates, and you will be driven to find new ways of reducing that tension.

Sublimation

sublimation A defense
mechanism that involves
altering or displacing id
impulses by diverting
instinctual energy into
socially acceptable
behaviors.

Whereas displacement involves finding a substitute object to satisfy id impulses, **sublimation** involves altering the id impulses. The instinctual energy is diverted into other channels of expression, ones that society considers acceptable and admirable. Sexual energy, for example, can be diverted or sublimated into artistically creative behaviors. Freud believed that a variety of human activities, particularly those of an artistic nature, are manifestations of id impulses that have been redirected into socially acceptable outlets. As with displacement (of which sublimation is a form), sublimation is a compromise. As such, it does not bring total satisfaction but leads to a buildup of undischarged tension.

As we noted, Freud suggested that defense mechanisms are unconscious denials or distortions of reality. We are, in a sense, lying to ourselves when we use these defenses, but we are not aware of doing so. If we knew we were lying to ourselves, the defenses would not be so effective. If the defenses are working well, they keep threatening or disturbing material out of our conscious awareness. As a result, we may not know the truth about ourselves. We may have a distorted picture of our needs, fears, and desires.

Our rational cognitive processes, such as problem solving, decision making, and logical thinking, may then be based on an inaccurate self-image. To Freud, we are driven and controlled by internal and external forces of which we are unaware and over which we can exercise little rational control.

There are situations in which the truth about ourselves emerges, when the defenses break down and fail to protect us. This occurs in times of unusual stress or when undergoing psychoanalysis. When the defenses fail, we are stricken with overwhelming anxiety. We feel dismal, worthless, and depressed. Unless the defenses are restored or new ones form to take their place we are likely to develop neurotic or psychotic symptoms. Thus, defenses are necessary to our mental health. We could not survive long without them.

Psychosexual Stages of Personality Development

psychosexual development

Freud believed that all behaviors are defensive but that not everyone uses the same defenses in the same way. All of us are driven by the same id impulses, but there is not the same universality in the nature of the ego and superego. Although these structures of the personality perform the same functions for everyone, their content varies from one person to another. They differ because they are formed through experience, and no two people have precisely the same experiences, not even siblings reared in the same house. Thus, part of our personality is formed on the basis of the unique relationships we have as children with various people and objects. We develop a personal set of character attributes, a consistent pattern of behavior that defines each of us as an individual.

A person's unique character type develops in childhood largely from parent-child interactions. The child tries to maximize pleasure by satisfying the id demands, while parents, as representatives of society, try to impose the demands of reality and morality. So important did Freud consider childhood experiences that he said the adult personality was firmly shaped and crystallized by the fifth year of life. What persuaded him that these early years are crucial were his own childhood memories and the memories revealed by his adult patients. Invariably, as his patients lay on his psychoanalytic couch, they reached far back into childhood. Increasingly, Freud perceived that the adult neurosis had been formed in the early years of life.

psychosexual stages of development To Freud, the oral, anal, phallic, and genital stages through which all children pass. In these stages, gratification of the id instincts depends on the stimulation of corresponding areas of the body.

Freud sensed strong sexual conflicts in the infant and young child, conflicts that seemed to revolve around specific regions of the body. He noted that each body region assumed a greater importance as the center of conflict at a different age. From these observations he derived the theory of the **psychosexual stages of development**; each stage is defined by an erogenous zone of the body (see Table 2.2). In each developmental stage a conflict exists that must be resolved before the infant or child can progress to the next stage.

TABLE 2.2   *Freud's psychosexual stages of development*

Stages	Ages	Characteristics
Oral	Birth–1	Mouth is the primary erogenous zone; pleasure derived from sucking: id is dominant.
Anal	1–3	Toilet training (external reality) interferes with gratification received from defecation.
Phallic	4–5	Incestuous fantasies; Oedipus complex; anxiety; superego development.
Latency	5–Puberty	Period of sublimation of sex instinct.
Genital	Adolescence–Adulthood	Development of sex-role identity and adult social relationships.

fixation A condition in which a portion of libido remains invested in one of the psychosexual stages because of excessive frustration or gratification.

Sometimes a person is reluctant or unable to move from one stage to the next because the conflict has not been resolved or because the needs have been so supremely satisfied by an indulgent parent that the child doesn't want to move on. In either case, the individual is said to be fixated at this stage of development. In **fixation**, a portion of libido or psychic energy remains invested in that developmental stage, leaving less energy for the following stages.

Central to the psychosexual theory is the infant's sex drive. Freud shocked his colleagues and the general public when he argued that babies are motivated by sexual impulses. Recall, however, that Freud did not define sex in a narrow way. He believed that the infant is driven to obtain a diffuse form of bodily pleasure deriving from the mouth, anus, and genitals, the erogenous zones that define the stages of development during the first five years of life.

The Oral Stage

oral stage

The oral stage, the first stage of psychosexual development, lasts from birth until some time during the second year of life. During this period the infant's principal source of pleasure is the mouth. The infant derives pleasure from sucking, biting, and swallowing. Of course the mouth is used for survival (for the ingestion of food and water) but Freud placed a greater emphasis on the erotic satisfactions derived from oral activities.

The infant is in a state of dependence on the mother or caregiver. She or he becomes the primary object of the child's libido. In more familiar terms, we might say the infant is learning, in a primitive way, to love the mother. How the mother responds to the infant's demands, which at this time are solely id demands, determines the nature of the baby's small world. The infant learns from the mother to perceive the world as good or bad, satisfying or frustrating, safe or perilous.

There are two ways of behaving during this stage: oral incorporative behavior (taking in) and oral aggressive or oral sadistic behavior (biting or spitting out). The oral incorporative mode occurs first and involves the pleasurable stimulation of the mouth by other people and by food. Adults fixated at the oral incorporative stage are excessively concerned with oral activities, such as eating, drinking, smoking, and kissing. If, as infants, they were excessively gratified, their adult oral personality

In the oral stage of psychosexual development, pleasure is derived from sucking, biting, and swallowing.

will be predisposed to unusual optimism and dependency. Because they were overindulged in infancy, they continue to depend on others to gratify their needs. As a consequence, they are overly gullible, swallow or believe anything they are told, and trust other people inordinately. Such people are labeled oral passive personality types.

The second oral behavior, oral aggressive or oral sadistic, occurs during the painful, frustrating eruption of teeth. As a result of this experience, infants come to view the mother with hatred as well as love. Persons fixated at this level are prone to excessive pessimism, hostility, and aggressiveness. They are likely to be argumentative and sarcastic, making so-called biting remarks and displaying cruelty toward others. They tend to be envious of other people and try to exploit and manipulate them in an effort to dominate.

The oral stage concludes at the time of weaning, although some libido remains if fixation has occurred. Then the infant's focus shifts to the other end.

The Anal Stage

Society, in the form of parents, tends to defer to the infant's needs during the first year of life, adjusting to its demands and expecting relatively little adjustment in return. This situation changes dramatically around the age of 18 months, when a new demand, toilet training, is made of the child. Freud believed that the experience of toilet training during the anal stage had a significant effect on personality development. Defecation produces erotic pleasure for the child, but with the onset of toilet training, the child must learn to postpone or delay this pleasure. For the first time, gratification of an instinctual impulse is interfered with as parents attempt to regulate the time and place for defecation.

As any parent can attest, this is a time of conflict for all concerned. The child learns that he or she has (or is) a weapon that can be used against the parents. The child has control over something and can choose to comply or not with the parents' demands. If the toilet training is not going well—for example, if the child has difficulty learning or the parents are excessively demanding—the child may react in one of two ways. One way is to defecate when and where the parents disapprove, thus defying their attempts at regulation. If the child finds this a satisfactory technique for reducing frustration and uses it frequently, he or she may develop an anal aggressive personality. To Freud, this was the basis for many forms of hostile and sadistic behavior in adult life, including cruelty, destructiveness, and temper tantrums. Such a person is likely to be disorderly and to view other people as objects to be possessed.

A second way the child may react to the frustration of toilet training is to hold back or retain the feces. This produces a feeling of erotic pleasure (derived from a full lower intestine) and can be another successful technique for manipulating the parents. They may become concerned if the child goes several days without a bowel movement. Thus, the child discovers a new method for securing parental attention and affection. This behavior is the basis for the development of an anal retentive personality. Stubborn and stingy, such a person hoards or retains things because feelings of security depend on what is saved and possessed and on the order in which possessions and other aspects of life are maintained. The person is likely to be rigid, compulsively neat, obstinate, and overly conscientious.

The Phallic Stage

phallic stage

A new set of problems arises around the fourth to fifth year, when the focus of pleasure shifts from the anus to the genitals. Again the child faces a battle between an id impulse and the demands of society, as reflected in parental expectations.

Children at the phallic stage display considerable interest in exploring and manipulating the genitals, their own and those of their playmates. Pleasure is derived from the genital region not only through behaviors such as masturbation, but also through fantasies. The child becomes curious about birth and about why boys have penises and girls do not. The child may talk about wanting to marry the parent of the opposite sex.

The phallic stage is the last of the pre-genital or childhood stages, and phallic conflicts are the most complex ones to resolve. They are difficult for many people to accept because they involve the notion of incest, a taboo in many cultures. Between incestuous desires and masturbation we can see the seeds of shock, anger, and suppression being sown in the parents of the typical 4-year-old. Reality and morality come to grips with the evil id once again.

Oedipus complex

Oedipus complex
During the phallic stage (ages 4 to 5), the unconscious desire of a boy for his mother, accompanied by a desire to replace or destroy his father.

The Oedipus complex in boys.   The basic conflict of the phallic stage centers on the unconscious desire of the child for the parent of the opposite sex. Accompanying this is the unconscious desire to replace or destroy the parent of the same sex. Out of Freud's identification of this conflict came one of his best-known concepts: the **Oedipus complex**. Its name comes from the Greek myth described in the play *Oedipus Rex*, written by Sophocles in the fifth century B.C. In this story, young Oedipus kills his father and marries his mother, not knowing who they are.

The boy comes to resolve the Oedipus complex by identifying with his father.

The Oedipus complex operates differently for boys and girls; Freud developed the male part of the complex more fully. In the Oedipus complex, the mother becomes a love object for the young boy. Through fantasy and overt behavior, he displays his sexual longings for her. However, the boy sees the father as an obstacle in his path and regards him as a rival and a threat. He perceives that the father has a special relationship with the mother in which he, the boy, is not allowed to participate. As a result, he becomes jealous of and hostile toward the father. Freud drew his formulation of the Oedipus complex from his childhood experiences. He wrote, "I have found love of the mother and jealousy of the father in my own case, too" (Freud, 1954, p. 223).

With the boy's desire to replace his father is the fear that the father will retaliate and harm him. He interprets his fear of his father in genital terms, becoming fearful that his father will cut off the offending organ (the boy's penis), which is the source of the boy's pleasure and sexual longings. And so **castration anxiety**, as Freud called it, comes to play a role, as it may have done in Freud's childhood. "There are a number of indications that [Freud's father] enjoined little Sigmund not to play with his genitals, and even threatened him with castration if he did" (Krüll, 1986, p. 110).

castration anxiety A boy's fear during the Oedipal period that his penis will be cut off.

Additional evidence to support this contention comes from Freud's later writings on masturbation, in which he saw such threats from fathers as common. Freud also reported that his adult dreams contained material relating to the fear of castration by his father.

Two other childhood events may have reinforced Freud's fear of castration. At around the age of 3, he and his nephew engaged in some rough sex play with his niece and discovered she did not have a penis. For a 3-year-old boy, this may have been sufficient evidence that penises can be cut off. In the opinion of one Freud biographer, "the threat of castration is particularly realistic to a Jewish boy, since it is easy to establish a connection between ritual circumcision and castration" (Krüll, 1986, p. 110). Freud confirmed this in his later writings.

So strong is the boy's fear of castration that he is forced to repress his sexual desire for his mother. To Freud, this was a way of resolving the Oedipal conflict. The boy replaces the sexual longing for the mother with a more acceptable affection and develops a strong identification with the father. In so doing, the boy experiences a degree of vicarious sexual satisfaction. To enhance the identification, he attempts to become more like his father by adopting his mannerisms, behaviors, attitudes, and superego standards.

The Oedipus complex in girls.   Freud was less clear about the female phallic conflict, which some of his followers termed the **Electra complex**. Like the boy's, the girl's first object of love is the mother, because she is the primary source of food, affection, and security in infancy. During the phallic stage, however, the father becomes the girl's new love object. Why does this shift from mother to father take place? Freud said it was the girl's reaction to her discovery that boys have a penis and girls do not.

Electra complex During the phallic stage (ages 4 to 5), the unconscious desire of a girl for her father, accompanied by a desire to replace or destroy her mother.

The girl blames her mother for her supposedly inferior condition and consequently comes to love her mother less. She may even hate the mother for what she imagines the mother did to her. She comes to envy her father and transfers her love to him because he possesses the highly valued sex organ. Freud wrote: "girls feel deeply their lack of a sexual organ that is equal in value to the male one; they regard themselves on that account as inferior and this envy for the penis is the origin of a whole number of characteristic feminine reactions" (Freud, 1925, p. 212). Thus, a girl develops **penis envy**, a counterpart to a boy's castration anxiety. She believes she has lost her penis; he fears he will lose his.

penis envy The envy the female feels toward the male because the male possesses a penis; this is accompanied by a sense of loss because the female does not have a penis.

This female Oedipus complex, Freud suggested, can never be totally resolved, a situation he believed led to poorly developed superegos in women. Freud wrote that an adult woman's love for a man is always tinged with penis envy, for which she can partially compensate by having a male child. The girl comes to identify with the mother and repress her love for her father, but Freud was not specific about how this occurs.

The phallic personality.   Phallic conflicts and their degree of resolution are of major importance in determining adult relations with and attitudes toward the opposite sex. Poorly resolved conflicts can cause lingering forms of castration anxiety and penis envy. The so-called phallic character or personality type evidences strong narcissism.

Although continually acting to attract the opposite sex, these persons have difficulty establishing mature heterosexual relationships. They need continual recognition and appreciation of their attractive and unique qualities. As long as they receive such support they function well, but when it is lacking they feel inadequate and inferior.

Freud described the male phallic personality as brash, vain, and self-assured. Men with this personality try to assert or express their masculinity through activities such as repeated sexual conquests. The female phallic personality, motivated by penis envy, exaggerates her femininity and uses her talents and charms to overwhelm and conquer men.

The tense drama of the phallic stage is repressed in all of us. Its effects motivate us as adults at the unconscious level, and we recall little, if anything, of the conflict.

The Latency Period

The storms and stresses of the oral, anal, and phallic stages of psychosexual development are the amalgam out of which most of the adult personality is shaped. The three major structures of the personality—the id, ego, and superego—have been formed by approximately the age of 5, and the relationships among them are being solidified.

Fortunately, because the child and parents certainly could use some rest, the next five or six years are quiet. The **latency period** is not a psychosexual stage of development. The sex instinct is dormant, temporarily sublimated in school activities, hobbies, and sports and in developing friendships with members of the same sex.

latency period To Freud, the period from approximately age 5 to puberty, during which the sex instinct is dormant, sublimated in school activities, sports, and hobbies, and in developing friendships with members of the same sex.

The Genital Stage

The genital stage, the final psychosexual stage of development, begins at puberty. The body is becoming physiologically mature, and if no major fixations have occurred at an earlier stage of development, the individual may be able to lead a normal life. Freud believed that the conflict during this period is less intense than in the other stages. The adolescent must conform to societal sanctions and taboos that exist concerning sexual expression, but conflict is minimized through sublimation. The sexual energy pressing for expression in the teenage years can be at least partially satisfied through the pursuit of socially acceptable substitutes and, later, through a committed adult relationship with a person of the opposite sex. The genital personality type is able to find satisfaction in love and work, the latter being an acceptable outlet for sublimation of the id impulses.

Freud emphasized the importance of the early childhood years in determining the adult personality. According to Freud, the first five years are the crucial ones. His personality theory pays less attention to later childhood and adolescence, and he was little concerned with personality development in adulthood. To Freud, what we are as adults—how we behave, think, and feel—is determined by the conflicts to which we are exposed and with which we must cope before many of us have even learned to read.

Questions About Human Nature

Freud's position is clear on the questions we posed about an image of human nature (see Figure 2.2). Freud did not present us with a flattering or optimistic picture. Quite the opposite. He suggested that each person is a dark cellar of conflict in which a battle continually rages. Human beings are depicted in pessimistic terms,

Free will — Determinism

Nature — Nurture

Past experiences — Present experiences

Uniqueness (ego and superego) — Universality (id)

Equilibrium — Growth

Optimism — Pessimism

FIGURE 2.2   *Freud's image of human nature*

condemned to a struggle with our inner forces, a struggle we are almost always destined to lose. Doomed to anxiety, to the thwarting of at least some of our driving impulses, we experience tension and conflict. We are endlessly defending ourselves against the forces of the id, which stand ever alert to topple us.

In Freud's system there is only one ultimate and necessary goal in life: to reduce tension. On the nature-nurture issue, Freud adopted a middle ground. The id, the most powerful part of the personality, is an inherited, physiologically based structure, as are the stages of psychosexual development. However, other parts of our personality are learned in early childhood, from parent-child interactions.

Although Freud recognized universality in human nature, in that we all pass through the stages of psychosexual development and are motivated by the same id forces, he asserted that part of the personality is unique to each person. The ego and superego perform the same functions for everyone, but their content varies from one person to another because they are formed through personal experience. Also, different character types can develop during the psychosexual stages.

On the issue of free will versus determinism, Freud held a deterministic view: Virtually everything we do, think, and dream is predetermined by the life and death instincts, the inaccessible and invisible forces within us. Our adult personality is determined by interactions that occurred before we were 5, at a time when we had limited control. These experiences forever hold us in their grip.

Freud also argued, however, that people who underwent psychoanalysis could achieve the ability to exercise increased free will and take responsibility for their choices. "The more the individual is able to make conscious what had been unconscious, the more he or she can take charge of his or her own life" (Solnit, 1992, p. 66). Thus, Freud suggested that psychoanalysis had the potential to liberate people from the constraints of determinism.

Freud's overall picture of human nature, painted in these bleak hues, reflects his personal view of humanity, which darkened with age and declining health. His judgment of people in general was harsh. "I have found little that is 'good' about human beings on the whole. In my experience, most of them are trash" (Freud, 1963, pp. 61–62). We can see this stern judgment in his personality theory.

Assessment in Freud's Theory

Freud considered the unconscious to be the major motivating force in life; our childhood conflicts are repressed out of conscious awareness. The goal of Freud's system of psychoanalysis was to bring these repressed memories, fears, and thoughts back to the level of consciousness. How can the psychoanalyst evaluate or assess this invisible portion of the mind, this dark arena that is otherwise inaccessible to us? Over the course of his work with patients, Freud developed two methods of assessment: free association and dream analysis.

Free Association

free association A technique in which the patient says whatever comes to mind. In other words, it is a kind of daydreaming out loud.

Freud's development of the technique of **free association** owes much to Josef Breuer, a Viennese physician who befriended Freud during Freud's early years in private practice. In treating a young woman who showed symptoms of hysteria, Breuer found that hypnotizing her enabled her to remember repressed events. Recalling the events—in a sense, reliving the experiences—brought relief of the disturbing symptoms.

catharsis The expression of emotions that is expected to lead to the reduction of disturbing symptoms.

Freud used the technique with some success and called the process **catharsis**, from the Greek word for purification. After a while, however, Freud abandoned hypnosis, partly because he had difficulty hypnotizing some of his patients. Also, some patients revealed disturbing events during hypnosis but were unable to recall those events when questioned later.

Seeking a technique other than hypnosis for helping a patient recall repressed material, Freud asked the person to lie on a couch while he sat behind it, out of sight. (Freud may have chosen this arrangement because he disliked being stared at.) He encouraged the patient to relax and to concentrate on events in the past. The patient was to engage in a kind of daydreaming out loud, saying whatever came to mind. He or she was instructed to express spontaneously every idea and image exactly as it occurred, no matter how trivial, embarrassing, or painful the thought or memory might seem. The memories were not to be omitted, rearranged, or restructured.

 resistance (psychoanalysis)

Freud believed that there was nothing random about the information uncovered during free association and that it was not subject to a patient's conscious choice.

The material revealed by patients in free association was predetermined, forced on them by the nature of their conflict.

He also found that sometimes the technique did not operate freely. Some experiences or memories were evidently too painful to talk about, and the patient would be reluctant to disclose them. Freud called these moments **resistances**. He believed they were significant because they indicate proximity to the source of the patient's problems. Resistance is a sign that the treatment is proceeding in the right direction and that the analyst should continue to probe in that area. Part of the psychoanalyst's task is to break down or overcome resistances so the patient can confront the repressed experience.

resistance In free association, a blockage or refusal to disclose painful memories.

dreams—analysis

Dream Analysis

Freud believed that dreams represent, in symbolic form, repressed desires, fears, and conflicts. So strongly have these feelings been repressed that they can surface only in disguised fashion during sleep.

In his technique of **dream analysis**, Freud distinguished two aspects of dreams: the manifest content, which refers to the actual events in the dream, and the latent content, which is the hidden symbolic meaning of the dream's events. Over the years, Freud found consistent symbols in his patients' dreams, events that signified the same thing for nearly everyone (see Table 2.3). For example, steps, ladders, and staircases in a dream represented sexual intercourse. Candles, snakes, and tree trunks indicated the penis, and boxes, balconies, and doors signified the female body. Freud warned that despite this apparent universality of symbols, many sym-

dream analysis A technique involving the interpretation of dreams to uncover unconscious conflicts. Dreams have a manifest content (the actual events in the dream) and a latent content (the symbolic meaning of the dream events).

T A B L E   2 . 3   *Dream symbols or events and their latent psychoanalytic meaning*

Symbol	Interpretation
Smooth-fronted house	Male body
House with ledges, balconies	Female body
King and queen	Parents
Small animals	Children
Children	Genital organs
Playing with children	Masturbation
Baldness, tooth extraction	Castration
Elongated objects (e.g., tree trunks, umbrellas, neckties, snakes, candles)	Male genitals
Enclosed spaces (e.g., boxes, ovens, closets, caves, pockets)	Female genitals
Climbing stairs or ladders; driving cars; riding horses; crossing bridges	Sexual intercourse
Bathing	Birth
Beginning a journey	Dying
Being naked in a crowd	Desiring to be noticed
Flying	Desiring to be admired
Falling	Desiring to return to a state (such as childhood) where one is satisfied and protected

bols are specific to the person undergoing analysis and could have a different meaning for someone else.

Dreams reveal conflicts in a condensed, intensified form. Dream events rarely result from a single cause; any event in a dream can have many sources. Dreams may also have mundane origins. Physical stimuli, such as the temperature of the bedroom or contact with one's partner, can induce a dream, and dreams can also be triggered by internal stimuli, such as a fever or an upset stomach.

It is interesting that of the more than 40 of his own dreams Freud described in his book *The Interpretation of Dreams*, only a few had a sexual content, despite his conviction that dreams typically involve some infantile sexual wish. The dominant theme in Freud's reported dreams was ambition, a characteristic he denied having.

Both of these Freudian assessment techniques—free association and dream analysis—reveal to the psychoanalyst a great deal of repressed material, but all of it is in disguised or symbolic form. The therapist then must interpret or translate the material for the patient. Freud compared this procedure with the task of an archeologist reconstructing a community that has been destroyed and buried under the accumulation of centuries. Just as the archeologist attempts to reconstruct a building from broken fragments, so a psychoanalyst reconstructs an experience from buried, fragmented memories. Thus, the evaluation or assessment of a patient's personality, the uncovering of his or her unconscious conflicts, depends on the skill, training, and experience of the analyst.

Research in Freud's Theory

case study A detailed history of an individual that contains data from a variety of sources.

Freud's major research method was the **case study.** We noted in Chapter 1 that the case study method has several limitations. It does not rely on objective observation, the data are not gathered in systematic fashion, and the situation (the psychoanalytic session) is not amenable to duplication and verification. We cannot systematically vary the conditions of childhood in which patients are reared, nor can we replicate in the laboratory a person's home environment. Thus, clinical observations cannot be repeated, as they can in controlled psychological experiments.

A fundamental criticism of Freud's case studies involves the nature of his data. He did not keep verbatim records of the therapy sessions and he warned analysts against taking notes during the sessions, believing it would distract their attention from their patients' words. Freud made notes several hours after seeing each patient. Describing his technique for recording his patients' comments, Freud said, "I write them down from memory in the evening after work is over" (quoted in Grubrich-Simitis, 1998, p. 20). Thus, it is possible that his data were incomplete, consisting only of what he later remembered.

It is also possible that his recollection was selective and that he recorded only the experiences that would support his theory, or that he interpreted those experiences in ways that would support his theory. Of course, Freud's notes may have been highly accurate, but we cannot be certain; we are unable to compare his case reports with what his patients said.

Even if Freud had kept a complete record of the therapy sessions, we cannot determine the validity of the patients' comments. Freud made few attempts to verify the accuracy of a patient's stories, which he might have done by questioning the patient's friends and relatives about the events described. Therefore, we must characterize the first step in Freud's research, the collection of data, as incomplete and inaccurate.

Some critics also suggest that Freud's patients did not actually reveal childhood sexual experiences because, in most cases, those experiences had never occurred. These writers argue that Freud inferred the stories of sexual seduction in childhood from his analysis of the patients' symptoms. For example, although Freud claimed that virtually all his women patients said they had been seduced by their fathers, his case notes do not show that any patient ever claimed that this had occurred (Kihlstrom, 1994).

Other critics agree that Freud was suggesting accounts of childhood seduction, without really hearing his patients say so, because he had already formed the hypothesis that such seductions were the true cause of adult neuroses. Still others charge that Freud may have used the power of suggestion to elicit or implant alleged memories of childhood seduction that had never taken place. "Where patients did not of their own accord provide material which could be construed in sexual terms, Freud did not hesitate to point them in the 'right' direction" (Webster, 1995, p. 197).

Another criticism of Freud's research is that it is based on a small and unrepresentative sample of people, restricted to himself and to those who sought psychoanalysis with him. Only a dozen or so cases have been detailed in Freud's writings, and most of these were of young, unmarried, upper-class women of good education. It is difficult to generalize from this limited sample to the population at large.

In addition, there may be discrepancies between Freud's notes on his therapy sessions and the case histories he published, which supposedly were based on these notes. Several investigators compared Freud's notes with the published case study of the Rat Man, one of his most famous patients. They found a lengthening of the period of analysis, an incorrect sequence of events disclosed by the patient, and unsubstantiated claims that the analysis resulted in a cure (Eagle, 1988; Mahoney, 1986). Thus, the published version of the case did not agree with the notes Freud made after his sessions with the patient. It is not possible to determine whether Freud deliberately made these changes to bolster his theory (or his ego) or whether they were the products of his unconscious. Nor do we know if such distortions characterize other Freudian case studies. It will remain a mystery because Freud destroyed most of his patient files not long after he compiled them.

Finally, it has been argued that none of Freud's handful of published case histories provides compelling supporting evidence for the theory. One of Freud's biographers concluded: "Some of the cases present such dubious evidence in favor of psychoanalytic theory that one may seriously wonder why Freud even bothered to publish them" (Sulloway, 1992, p. 160).

The criticisms leveled against Freud also apply to most of the later personality theorists who chose a neopsychoanalytic approach. They, too, used the case study as their primary research method and based their theories on their patients' reports. This does not mean that their work is devoid of merit; Freud and other analysts have offered a wealth of material about the human personality. If we accept their views as valid, however, we must do so on some basis other than experimental verification.

Although Freud was familiar with the experimental method, he had little confidence in it. An American psychologist once sent him information about experiments that had been conducted to validate Freudian concepts. Freud "threw the reprints across the table in a gesture of impatient rejection" and wrote to the psychologist that he did not "put much value on such confirmation" (Rosenzweig, 1985, pp. 171, 173). He believed there was no need for the kinds of experiments published in the psychology journals of the day because "they told him nothing more than he had already learned from his clinical encounters with patients" (Holzman, 1994, p. 190).

Freud insisted that his work was scientific and that he had amassed ample proof for his conclusions. Only psychoanalysts who used his techniques were qualified to judge the scientific worth of his work. Freud wrote that psychoanalysis was based on "an incalculable number of observations and experiences, and only someone who has repeated those observations on himself and on others is in a position to arrive at a judgment of his own upon it" (Freud, 1940, p. 144). Difficulty arises because Freud's observations cannot be repeated. We do not know exactly what he did in collecting his data and in translating his observations into hypotheses and generalizations.

Scientific Validation of Freudian Concepts

In the years since Freud's death in 1939, many of his ideas have been submitted to experimental testing. In an exhaustive analysis of some 2,500 studies in psychology, psychiatry, anthropology, and related disciplines, Seymour Fisher and Roger Greenberg evaluated the scientific credibility of some of Freud's ideas. In this evaluation, case histories were not considered. Every effort was made to restrict the investigation to data thought to have a high degree of objectivity (Fisher & Greenberg, 1977, 1996).

The researchers found that some Freudian concepts—notably the id, ego, superego, death wish, libido, and anxiety—could not be tested by the experimental method. Concepts that could be so tested, and which evidence appeared to support, included the oral and anal character types, the basic concept of the Oedipal triangle, castration anxiety, and the notion that females resolve the Oedipal dilemma by having a child as compensation for the lack of a penis.

Concepts not supported by research evidence include those of dreams as disguised expressions of repressed wishes, resolution of the male Oedipus complex by identification with the father and acceptance of the father's superego standards out of fear, and the idea that women have inadequately developed superegos. In addition, researchers found no evidence to support the psychosexual stages of development or a relationship between Oedipal variables and sexual difficulties later in life.

The unconscious.   The notion that unconscious forces can influence conscious thought and behavior is now well established. Psychologists also recognize that a great deal of the information processing involved in cognitive activities is unconscious. Some even propose that the causal mechanisms underlying *all* behavior and thought may be unconscious (Bargh & Chartrand, 1999; Wegner & Wheatley, 1999).

> It now appears that the unconscious is "smarter" than first thought, capable of processing complex verbal and visual information and even anticipating (and planning for) future events. . . . No longer simply a repository for drives and impulses, the unconscious appears to play a role in problem solving, hypothesis testing, and creativity. (Bornstein & Masling, 1998, p. xx)

subliminal perception
Perception below the threshold of conscious awareness.

Much research on the nature of the unconscious involves **subliminal perception** (also called subliminal psychodynamic activation), in which stimuli are presented to subjects below their level of conscious awareness. (The word *subliminal* derives from *sub*, meaning below, and *limen*, meaning threshold.) Despite their inability to perceive the stimuli, the subjects' conscious processes and behavior are activated by the stimuli. In other words, people can be influenced by stimuli of which they are not consciously aware.

When depressed subjects were exposed to subliminally presented verbal and pictorial stimuli representing aggressive behaviors, they became more depressed, as measured by self-ratings, than when they were exposed to neutral stimuli (Silverman, 1976, 1983). This supports Freud's contention that depression is caused by unconscious aggressive feelings toward others, which are then turned inward and directed against the self. The results of this research also indicate that the subjects were influenced by stimuli they could not consciously perceive.

In another representative study, subjects were shown a series of words and pictures for such a brief time that they could not consciously perceive them (Shevrin, 1977). Then they were asked to free-associate. What the subjects talked about reflected the stimuli they had been shown but had not actually been able to see. For example, when the stimulus was a picture of a bee, the associations included the words *sting* and *honey*. The subjects' thought processes were affected by the stimuli, even though they were unaware of having seen them. Many such studies using subliminal perception support the idea that cognitive activity is influenced by the unconscious. (For a review of additional relevant studies see Westen, 1998.)

Other imaginative research has demonstrated that the unconscious can influence emotional as well as cognitive processes. In one such study, the words *Mommy and I are one* were flashed for 4 milliseconds to subjects, along with a picture of a man and a woman joined together at their shoulders. Male schizophrenic patients exposed to this subliminally presented stimulus showed a greater improvement than did a control group not exposed to that message. Female schizophrenic patients showed no improvement when exposed to that message but did show improvement when presented with the subliminal message: *Daddy and I are one* (Silverman & Weinberger, 1985).

In other studies, the *Mommy and I are one* message was effective in helping a variety of subjects stop smoking and drinking, become more assertive, eat a more healthful diet, and reduce fears. Thus, a subliminally presented message of which the subjects have no conscious awareness has been shown to have therapeutic value (Weinberger & Silverman, 1990).

The ego. We noted that Freud viewed the ego's role as constantly mediating between reality and the insistent demands of the id. The ego is the rational part of the personality that must control and postpone the id's demands, balancing them with the circumstances of the real world. Psychoanalytic researchers have identified two components of the ego: ego control and ego resiliency.

Ego control, as you would expect from the name, is close to Freud's original conception. It refers to the amount of control we are able to exert over our impulses and feelings. The degree of ego control ranges from under-controlled (in which we are unable to restrain any impulses and feelings) to over-controlled (in which we tightly inhibit the expression of our impulses). Both extremes are considered maladaptive.

Ego resiliency refers to our flexibility in modulating, adjusting, or changing our typical level of ego control to meet the daily changes in our environment. Persons with little ego resiliency are referred to as "ego brittle," meaning they are unable to alter their level of ego control to meet challenges or difficult life situations. Those high in ego resiliency are flexible and adaptable, able to tighten or loosen their degree of ego control as the situation warrants.

Research has shown that children who score low on laboratory and observational measures of ego control are rated by their teachers as more aggressive and less compliant and orderly than children high on ego control. Children who score high on ego resiliency are rated by their teachers as better able to cope with stress, lower in anxiety, and less in need of reassurance than children low in ego resiliency.

High ego resiliency also correlated positively with general intelligence, good grades in school, and popularity with peers. Low ego control in boys and girls, and low ego resiliency in girls, was related positively to drug abuse in adolescence. Thus, important aspects of personality and behavior can be linked to ego control and ego resiliency (Block & Block, 1980; Shiner, 1988).

Another approach to defining ego control is in terms of three levels of development: pre-conformist, conformist, and post-conformist (Loevinger, 1976). The pre-conformist level is the most primitive, allowing the least control over impulse expression. The conformist level moderates impulse expression in terms of our awareness of the expectations of others and of the culture's rules of appropriate social conduct. At this stage of ego development we place a premium on being accepted by others. We are able to delay or redirect the manner, time, and place for expressing our impulses. The most mature stage of ego development is the post-conformist level. People at this level are highly conscientious and individualistic and rely more on personal goals and standards of appropriate conduct than on the standards of others.

A study of 248 identical and fraternal twins ages 16 to 70, separated at infancy and reared in different environments, used a self-report inventory to compare their levels of ego development. Although the subjects had been raised in different adoptive homes, the ego development of each pair of twins correlated significantly. The researchers concluded that their results indicated that ego development may be a heritable characteristic. Contrary to Freud's theory, the level of ego development among these subjects had been determined more by genetic factors than by child-parent interaction (Newman, Tellegen, & Bouchard, 1998).

Catharsis.   To Freud, catharsis involved the physical expression of an emotion by recalling a traumatic event, which often led to relief of the disturbing symptom. In popular culture, the term *catharsis* has come to refer to expressing one's emotion as a way of reducing hostility and aggression. Self-help books urge us to give vent to anger by taking it out on some inanimate object—beating a pillow, breaking a dish, or hitting a punching bag. Does this work? Does acting out aggressively reduce negative emotions? The answer is no.

In a 1999 study of catharsis, two groups of college students were exposed to messages that either supported or disputed the notion that cathartic behavior is a good way of relieving anger. Next, some of the students were experimentally provoked to anger; an essay they had written was severely criticized. They were told that their paper was one of the worst essays ever written!

Students who were thus provoked and who had read the pro-catharsis message were significantly more prone to act out their aggression by hitting a punching bag. In a second experiment, those who received the pro-catharsis message not only hit the punching bag but also behaved aggressively toward the person who had annoyed them by criticizing their writing. They even displayed heightened aggression toward innocent people who had played no role in promoting their anger. Apparently, striking the punching bag had not been cathartic. It had not dissipated their anger but might even have increased it (Bushman, Baumeister, & Stack, 1999).

Repression.   Experimental investigations of the Freudian defense mechanism of repression—the involuntary removal of some threatening idea or memory from conscious awareness—have provided supportive results, although some psychologists have questioned whether the work relates to repression precisely as Freud proposed it. In one study, subjects memorized two lists of words that were flashed on a screen (Glucksberg & King, 1967). Some words on the lists were conceptually similar; for example, *cats* and *dogs* are both animals. The subjects were given an electric shock with some words on the first list. No shocks were administered with the words on the second list. Then the subjects were tested on how well they remembered the words. The subjects forgot the words accompanied by the shock but recalled those not accompanied by the shock. They also repressed words on the second list that were conceptually similar to the words on the first list that had been accompanied by a shock. The researchers concluded that the threatening words had been pushed out of conscious awareness.

Research conducted in Australia identified subjects as "repressors" and "nonrepressors" based on personality test scores that showed repressors to be low in anxiety and high in defensiveness (Davis, 1987). Repressors were able to recall fewer emotional experiences from childhood, particularly those involving fear and self-consciousness, than were non-repressors. In related research, repressors and non-repressors were compared on several experimental tasks. When shown pictures of neutral, nonthreatening stimuli and pictures of embarrassing, threatening stimuli, repressors avoided looking at the latter. When repressors were asked to free-associate to phrases with sexual or aggressive content (presumably threatening material), physiological measurements showed them to be highly emotionally aroused, yet their verbal responses gave no hint of anger or sexual arousal because they had repressed their emotional reactions. Non-repressors did not inhibit their emotional reactions, and this was evident in their verbal responses (Davis, 1987).

Later research showed that repressors were significantly more likely than non-repressors to deny possessing personality traits they had identified as personally emotionally threatening (traits such as selfishness, laziness, rudeness, and dishonesty). Repressors also had fewer unpleasant or threatening emotional memories available for retrieval than did non-repressors because they had repressed them (Newman, Duff, & Baumeister, 1997; Schimmack & Hartmann, 1997).

In another study, repressors and non-repressors were shown a disturbing film about animal mutation and lingering death from the effects of nuclear testing. When then asked to recall a personal experience that made them happy, repressors could recall more pleasant events and thoughts than could non-repressors. The researchers concluded that the repressors coped with the negative stimuli in the film by accessing positive memories. Thus, repressors did not experience to the same frequency and degree as non-repressors the distressing emotional states engendered by the film. The repressors were not merely pretending to be unaffected; they had repressed the experience successfully (Boden & Baumeister, 1997).

In research using physiological measures to differentiate repressors and non-repressors, the galvanic skin response (GSR) was taken to indicate the presence of stress, anxiety, and fear. When college students identified earlier as repressors or non-repressors were given a stressful speech assignment, repressors showed a significantly greater increase in GSR activity than non-repressors. The researchers concluded that repressors react automatically to threatening situations with increased levels of physiological stress (Barger, Kircher, & Croyle, 1997).

Additional research dealt with subjects who denied or repressed psychological distress, reporting themselves to be free of such symptoms. However, their projective technique responses revealed evidence of psychological disturbance, which evidently they were repressing from conscious awareness. When the repressors were placed in situations (such as being asked to read aloud) believed to be stressful for highly defensive people, repressors scored higher on a measure of cardiac activity associated with heart disease than did non-repressors (Shedler, Mayman, & Manis, 1993).

Studies have also found links between the repressive coping style and (1) high cholesterol level and (2) high cortisol level (cortisol is a stress hormone) (Brown, Tomarken, Orth, Loosen, Kalin, & Davidson, 1996; Weinberger, 1995). Thus, repression may be effective in protecting us from anxiety, but its continued use may also be harmful to our physical health.

Other defense mechanisms. A different kind of research investigated the complexity of the Freudian defense mechanisms to determine whether they form a hierarchy (Brody, Rozek, & Muten, 1985; Cramer, 1987, 1990). Perhaps, it was postulated, the simplest mechanisms are used early in life, and the more complex ones emerge at a later age. Studies showed that denial (a simple, low-level defense mechanism) is used mostly by young children and less by adolescents. Identification, a more complex defense, is used considerably more by adolescents than by younger children.

In research on students from grades 2, 5, 8, 11, and first-year college classes, responses to the Thematic Apperception Test pictures showed clear age differences in defense mechanisms. The use of denial and projection decreased with age whereas identification increased with age (Porcerelli, Thomas, Hibbard, & Cogan, 1998).

Other research found that as children reach adolescence, they tend to reduce the use of defense mechanisms such as displacement and identification that involve directing aggressive impulses toward other people. At the same time, the adolescents in this study increased their use of repression, denial, and reaction formation (Levit, 1993).

Freud's contention that people with different forms of emotional disturbance tend to use different defenses has found moderate to strong research support. For example, people with obsessive-compulsive personalities are prone to use reaction formation as a defense, people with paranoid personalities are more likely to use projection, and people with passive-aggressive personalities are apt to rely on displacement (Busch et al., 1995; Sammallahti & Aalberg, 1995).

A longitudinal study of 90 subjects who were first tested in nursery school and later at age 23 found a link between pre-school personality and the use of denial as young adults. As we noted earlier, denial tends to be used as a defense mechanism mostly by children and its use typically declines with age. In this study, however, the male subjects who at age 23 were still using denial had a number of psychological problems that had been identified when they were in nursery school. Their childhood personalities were characterized as high in emotional immaturity and unworthiness and low in personal competence and ego resiliency. For female subjects, no such clear relationship was found between childhood personality and the continued use of denial at age 23. The authors of the study suggested that boys might be more vulnerable to stress than girls (Cramer & Block, 1998).

A study of 115 adult men found that those who tried to protect themselves from feelings of weakness by being more powerful and competitive and who avoided emotional expression tended to use more immature defense mechanisms. Those men who did not feel so great a need to be more powerful than others and who could express their emotions more freely used more mature defense mechanisms (Mahalik, Cournoyer, DeFrank, Cherry, & Napolitano, 1998).

Dreams.   Research on dreams has confirmed Freud's idea that dreams, in disguised or symbolic form, reflect emotional concerns. However, research does not appear to show that dreams represent a fulfillment of wishes or desires, as Freud proposed (Breger, Hunter, & Lane, 1971; Dement & Wolpert, 1958).

The Oedipus complex.   In an observational study to test the effects of the Oedipus complex, parents of boys and girls ages 3 to 6 years were asked to record affectionate behaviors and aggressive or hostile behaviors their children directed toward them. The results showed that acts of affection toward the parent of the opposite sex and displays of aggression toward the parent of the same sex occurred significantly more frequently than the reverse situation. These types of Oedipal behaviors were greatest around age 4 and began to decline by age 5 (Watson & Getz, 1990).

Dreams analyzed in research on the Oedipus complex supported Freud's theory in that significantly more men reported dreams reflecting castration anxiety, and significantly more women reported dreams reflecting castration wishes or penis envy (Hall & Van de Castle, 1965).

Freud proposed that penis envy in girls leads them to view the father as a love object, a desire later supplanted by the wish for a baby. In an experimental test of this proposal, college-age women subjects were exposed to subliminal messages containing pregnancy themes. Their later responses on an inkblot test were found to contain significantly more phallic imagery than the responses of women in the control group or of college-age men subjects exposed to the same stimuli. These results support Freud's belief that pregnancy has phallic significance for women (Jones, 1994).

Freud also suggested that the male Oedipus complex, with its hostile relationship with a threatening father, could be resolved by having boys identify with their fathers. However, one research study showed that 4- to 6-year-old boys formed a stronger identification with warm, nurturing fathers than with threatening, punitive fathers (Hetherington & Frankie, 1967).

Oral and anal personality types.   An investigation of the oral personality type showed a strong relationship between the oral orientation, as identified by the Rorschach, and obesity (Masling, Rabie, & Blondheim, 1967). This supports Freud's contention that oral types are preoccupied with eating and drinking. Another study found oral personality types to be more conforming to the suggestions of an authority figure than anal personality types (Tribich & Messer, 1974). According to Freud, oral personalities are dependent and submissive and should be more conforming than anal personalities; anal types tend to be hostile and can be expected to resist conformity. Freud also contended that women were more orally dependent than men were but later research found no such difference between the sexes (O'Neill & Bornstein, 1990). In general, then, research supports both the oral and anal personality types (Westen, 1998). There is little empirical evidence for the phallic personality type.

Aggression.   Another aspect of Freudian theory put to experimental test is the idea that aggression is instinctive and universal. Freud was not alone in taking this position. Scientists who observe animals in their natural surroundings also posit an aggressive instinct in humans and in lower animals, although data from anthropology and psychology have challenged this view. Anthropologists have observed that people in some so-called primitive cultures do not exhibit aggressive behavior. Psychologists who argue against an aggressive instinct suggest that aggressive behavior may be caused by frustration.

Considerable research has demonstrated that although frustration can trigger aggression, it does not always do so. Aggressive responses to frustration can be modified by training. This idea supports the role of learning in aggression. The psychologist Albert Bandura (Chapter 15) has shown that we learn aggressive behavior the same way we learn many social behaviors, primarily by observing aggression in other people and imitating what we have seen.

Age and personality development.   Freud proposed that personality was formed by about the age of 5 and was subject to little change thereafter. Studies of personality development over time indicate that the personality characteristics of preschool children changed dramatically, as shown by follow-up studies conducted over six to seven years (Kagan, Kearsley, & Zelazo, 1978). Other studies suggest that the middle childhood years (ages 7 to 12) may be more important in establishing adult personality patterns than the early childhood years.

Noted child development psychologist Jerome Kagan reviewed the literature and concluded that personality appears to depend more on temperament and experiences in later childhood than on early parent-child interactions (Kagan, 1999). Although there is no denying that our first five years of life affect our personality, it is now obvious that personality continues to develop well beyond that time.

The Freudian slip.   Finally, in our overview of research on Freudian concepts, we come to the well-known Freudian slip. According to Freud, what appears to be ordinary forgetting or a casual lapse in speech is actually a reflection of unconscious motives or anxieties (Freud, 1901).

In research to test this phenomenon, two groups of male subjects were shown the same pairs of words flashed on a computer screen (Motley, 1987). When a buzzer sounded, they were asked to say the words aloud. One group of subjects had electrodes attached and was told that during the experiment they would receive a painful electric shock. This situation was an experimental way of engendering anxiety. In the second group of subjects, the experimenter was an attractive, sexily dressed woman. This group was given a test of sexual anxiety.

Subjects anxious about the electric shock made verbal slips such as *damn shock* when the words on the screen were *sham dock*. Subjects in the sexual anxiety condition revealed that anxiety in verbal slips such as *nude breasts* for *brood nests*. Those who scored high on the sexual anxiety test made the highest number of sex-related Freudian slips. Men in a control group exposed to the same words but to neither anxiety-arousing condition did not make verbal slips. Not all lapses in speech are Freudian slips, of course, but research indicates that at least some may be what Freud said they were—hidden anxieties revealing themselves in embarrassing ways.

repressed memories

Repressed memories of childhood sexual abuse.   In the late 1980s, the issue of repressed memories resurfaced in sensational legal proceedings involving people who claimed they suddenly recalled incidents of abuse that had occurred years earlier. Women have brought criminal charges against fathers, uncles, and family friends; men have brought charges against priests, coaches, and teachers. These people allege sexual abuse that happened during their childhood, incidents they claim to have recalled only in adulthood. Some accused persons have been convicted and imprisoned on the basis of memories of incidents said to have taken place up to 20 years before.

How extensive is the repressed memory phenomenon in sexual abuse cases? How many adults who claim to have been abused as children seem to forget that abuse for years? The results of surveys vary. One study of 105 women (80 percent of whom were African Americans participating in court-ordered substance abuse treatment programs) found that 54 percent reported a history of childhood sexual abuse. Only 19 percent of these women said they had forgotten the abuse for some period of time and recalled it at a later date (Loftus, Polonsky, & Fullilove, 1994). A survey of 330 male and female psychologists found that 24 percent reported childhood abuse, and 40 percent of those had forgotten the abuse for some period. There were no significant sex differences in the reports of these temporarily repressed memories (Feldman-Summers & Pope, 1994).

These and similar studies rely on retrospective reports—recalling the abusive events up to 40 years after they allegedly occurred. But there is an obvious problem with retrospective research: How do we know the reported abuses really happened? One researcher interviewed adult women (86 percent were categorized as low-income Blacks) who were documented victims of childhood abuse. The evidence for the abuse consisted of hospital emergency room records and forensic evidence collected at the time of admission (Williams, 1994). Thus, in this study, we can be certain that the reported incidents had occurred. Interviews with the adult women revealed that 38 percent did not recall the abuse, a figure close to the incidence of repressed memory among the psychologist subjects but higher than the 19 percent reported by the women in the substance abuse treatment program. In the study of victims with documented childhood sexual abuse, the women most likely to have no memory of the event were those who were younger at the time of the abuse and who had been molested by someone they knew.

The debate continues about whether failure to recall childhood sexual abuse involves Freudian repression or simple forgetting (Brewin, Andrews, & Gotlib, 1993). Several researchers have suggested that people who forget an instance of abuse may not have fully understood the significance of the experience when it happened. If so, "then some of these children never 'knew' they were traumatized and thus had nothing to repress" (Loftus, Garry, & Feldman, 1994, p. 1178).

Although some repressed memories of sexual abuse are based on actual incidents, research has demonstrated how easily false memories can be implanted and recollections distorted, to the point where something that never occurred can be made conscious and appear genuine or threatening (Loftus & Ketcham, 1994; Ofshe & Watters, 1994).

In one study, 15 3- and 6-year-old children were interviewed 4 years after they had spent 5 minutes playing with a man while sitting across a table from him. The man never touched any of the children. During the follow-up interviews, the researchers created a climate of accusation by telling the children they would be questioned about an important event in their lives. "Are you afraid to tell?" they were asked. "You'll feel better once you've told" (Ceci & Bruck, 1993, p. 421). One-third of the children agreed with the interviewer's suggestion that, 4 years earlier, they had been hugged and kissed by the man. Two of the children agreed with the suggestion that they had been photographed in the bathroom; one agreed that the man had given her a bath.

A study involving 50 students at the University of Florence, Italy, showed that dream interpretation could be used to implant false memories. Half of the subjects were told by a persuasive psychologist who was a popular radio celebrity that their dreams were manifestations of repressed memories of traumatic childhood events. Examples of these incidents included being abandoned by their parents or being lost in an unfamiliar place. The other half of the subject population did not receive such interpretations of their dreams.

All subjects had been selected on the basis of questionnaire responses completed weeks earlier, when they had stated that no such traumatic events had occurred during their childhood. When questioned 10 to 15 days following the dream interpretations, the majority of the experimental subjects agreed that the traumatic experiences had really happened and that they had repressed the memories for years (Mazzoni, Lombardo, Malvagia, & Loftus, 1999).

Even innocuous, nontraumatic memories can be implanted. This was demonstrated in a study of 270 first-grade, third-grade, fourth-grade, and college-age students who watched a videotape about the everyday activities of two brothers at a summer camp. When the students were interviewed about the film, some of the questions dealt with actual scenes whereas other questions involved events that had not been depicted. Strongly worded questions about events not seen led to recall of these events as real when the subjects were re-interviewed a week later. These subjects were convinced that they had actually seen them in the film. Younger subjects exhibited a significantly greater tendency to accept false events than did college students, but even the college group was not immune to the implantation of false memories (Ackil & Zaragoza, 1998).

Surveys of clinical psychologists have shown that the reported incidence of repressed memories of childhood sexual abuse among women patients has declined. A possible explanation is the growing recognition that such memories may be false (Palm & Gibson, 1998; Polusny & Follette, 1996). However, it is important to keep in mind that childhood sexual abuse does occur. It is a haunting reality for many people and far more widespread than Sigmund Freud envisioned in the 19th century. The effects can be debilitating. Adults who were sexually abused as children exhibit strong tendencies toward anxiety, depression, self-destructiveness, low self-esteem, and suicide. Similarly severe effects have been noted in both male and female victims of abuse (Pilkington & Lenaghan, 1998; Westen, 1998).

Extensions of Freudian Theory

Several of the theorists we discuss in the chapters to follow developed positions in opposition to Freud's. Other theorists remained faithful to some of Freud's basic assumptions but attempted to expand, extend, or elaborate on his views. The goal of the latter group, which included Freud's daughter Anna, was to counteract what were seen as weaknesses or omissions in the Freudian psychoanalytic system.

Anna Freud

Anna Freud (1895–1982)

Although Anna Freud may have been an unplanned baby (she said she never would have been born had a safer contraceptive method been available to her parents), she became the only one of Sigmund Freud's six children to follow his path (Young-Bruehl, 1988). An unhappy child, Anna was jealous of the older sister favored by her mother and was ignored by her other siblings. She recalled "the experience of being . . . only a bore to them, and of feeling bored and left alone" (Appignanesi & Forrester, 1992, p. 273).

Anna was not ignored by her father. She became his favorite child and by the age of 14 was dutifully attending meetings of his psychoanalytic group, listening attentively to the case histories being presented and discussed. At 22, Anna began 4 years of psychoanalysis conducted by her father, who was later sharply criticized for analyzing his daughter. One historian called it "an impossible and incestuous treatment. . . . an Oedipal acting-in at both ends of the couch" (Mahony, 1992, p. 307). But another explained: "No one else would presume to undertake the task, for Anna's analysis would inevitably call into question Freud's role as her father" (Donaldson, 1996, p. 167). To analyze one's child was a serious violation of Freud's rules for the practice of psychoanalysis; the situation with Anna was kept secret for many years.

Anna Freud joined the Vienna Psychoanalytic Society, presenting a paper entitled *Beating Fantasies and Daydreams*. Although she claimed to be describing the experiences of a patient, she was actually relating her own fantasies. She spoke of an incestuous love relationship between father and daughter, a physical beating, and sexual gratification through masturbation.

She devoted her life to the care of her father and to his system of psychoanalysis. Whereas the elder Freud had worked only with adults, attempting to reconstruct their childhood by eliciting their recollections and analyzing their fantasies and dreams, Anna worked only with children. She established a clinic and a center to train analysts in the building next door to her father's London home. In 1927 she published *Four Lectures on Child Analysis*. Sigmund Freud approved of her work: "Anna's views on child analysis are independent of mine; I share her views, but she has developed them out of her own independent experience" (Freud quoted in Viner, 1996, p. 9).

Anna Freud substantially revised orthodox psychoanalysis by expanding the role of the ego, arguing that the ego operates independently of the id. This was a major extension of the Freudian system, one that involved a fundamental and radical change.

She proposed further refinements in *The Ego and the Mechanisms of Defense*, published in 1936, in which she clarified the operation of the defense mechanisms. The book received widespread praise and is considered a basic work on ego psychology. The standard defense mechanisms we discussed on pages 56–59 owe their full development and articulation to Anna Freud. This is among her most significant contributions to psychoanalytic theory.

Object Relations Theories

object relations (psychoanalysis)

We used the word *object* when we discussed Freud's concept of cathexis, which he defined as an investment of psychic energy in an object. By *object* he meant any person or activity that can satisfy an instinct. Thus, we may invest psychic energy in people, such as our mothers, who are able to satisfy our basic needs. Freud suggested that the first instinct-gratifying object in an infant's life is the mother's breast. Later, the mother as a whole person becomes an object. As the child matures, other people also become such objects, as long as they satisfy the child's instinctual needs.

object relations theories
Outgrowths of psychoanalytic theory that focus more on relationships with the objects (such as the mother) that satisfy instinctual needs, rather than on the needs themselves.

Object relations theories focus more on interpersonal relationships with such objects than they do on instinctual drives. Although drive satisfaction is important, it is secondary to the establishment of interrelationships. This primary emphasis on personal relations, over instinctual needs, tells us that unlike Freud, object relations theorists accept social and environmental factors as influences on personality.

They place particular emphasis on the mother-child relationship, suggesting that the core of personality is formed in infancy, at a younger age than Freud proposed. Although they differ on specifics, object relations theorists tend to agree that the crucial issue in personality development is the child's growing ability to become increasingly independent of its primary object: the mother. These theorists also see as critical the emergence in the early years of a strong sense of self and the maturing of relations with objects other than the mother.

Although there is no single viewpoint or system that commands the allegiance of all object relations theorists, several approaches can claim a following. We consider briefly the work of Heinz Kohut, Melanie Klein, and Margaret Mahler.

Heinz Kohut (1913–1981)

Kohut's emphasis is on the formation of the nuclear self, which he described as the foundation for becoming an independent person, capable of taking initiative and integrating ambitions and ideals. The nuclear self develops from the relationships that form between the infant and so-called *selfobjects* in the environment. These selfobjects are the people who play such a vital role in our lives that, as infants, we believe they are part of our selves.

Typically, the mother is the infant's primary selfobject. Kohut suggested that her role is to gratify not only the child's physical needs but also the psychological needs. To do this, the mother must act as a mirror to the child, reflecting back on the child a sense of uniqueness, importance, and greatness. By doing so, the mother confirms the child's sense of pride, which becomes part of the nuclear self. If the mother rejects her child, thus mirroring a sense of unimportance, then the child may develop shame or guilt. In this way, all aspects of the adult self (the positive and the negative) are formed by the child's initial relations with the primary selfobject.

Melanie Klein (1882–1960)

An unwanted child who felt rejected by her parents, Klein suffered periodic bouts of depression. She was estranged from her daughter, who later also became an analyst. The daughter accused Klein of interfering in her life and maintained that her brother, who died while mountain climbing, had actually committed suicide because of his poor relationship with their mother. Thus, Klein experienced difficulties both as a daughter and a mother. She went on to formulate a system of personality development that focused on the intense emotional relationship between infant and mother. She emphasized the first 5 to 6 months of a child's life, in contrast to Freud's stress on the first 5 years. She assumed babies are born with active fantasy lives that harbor mental representations (images) of Freudian id instincts, which the images temporarily satisfy. For example, a hungry baby can imagine sucking at the mother's breast and so, for a time, assuage the hunger.

These fantasies in infancy, which Klein called inner objects, are real and vivid, because infants lack the ability to distinguish between the real and the fantasy world. As a result, infants come to believe that every frustration, every thwarting of an instinct, is a personal attack inflicted by a hostile world.

Infants relate, initially, only to parts of objects, and the first such part-object for babies is the mother's breast. The breast either gratifies or fails to gratify an id instinct, and the infant comes to judge it as good or bad. The baby's world, as represented by this part-object, is thus seen as either satisfying or hostile. Gradually, as the world expands, infants relate to whole objects rather than part-objects, for example, to the mother as a person rather than solely a breast.

The infant derives pleasure from this whole person (the mother) and this increases self-confidence and the power to perceive and relate to other people. Thus, all other relationships develop out of the basic object relationship that began with the mother's breast. These experiences in infancy leave additional mental images that are stored and remain influential. The adult personality, then, is based on the relationship formed in the first few months of life.

Margaret Mahler (1897–1985)

Margaret Mahler, a pediatrician, observed the relationship that developed between infant and mother and became a psychoanalyst to learn more about it. She argued that newborns are incapable of distinguishing between themselves and everything else that is not themselves. She suggested, therefore, that initially, the infant perceives the mother as part of himself or herself.

The child's development of a separate sense of self, of a psychological identity, proceeds through three stages: normal autism, normal symbiosis, and separation-individuation. The first stage characterizes the first month of life. The infant is tended by the mother or caregiver during this time, assuming that she or he is attentive to the infant's needs. The infant does not have to exert any effort to satisfy his or her needs or be responsive to external stimuli. According to Mahler, this normal autism stage is one of complete narcissism or self-absorption.

In Mahler's second stage of development, normal symbiosis, which lasts until the age of 4 or 5 months, the infant becomes aware of objects that satisfy needs. The primary need-satisfying object is the mother. The infant must increasingly send signals or cues when feeling hunger or thirst, discomfort or pleasure, so that the mother can respond appropriately. The child recognizes the mother's face and begins to make distinctions between self and mother, and between self and other objects in his or her environment.

The third stage, separation-individuation, which lasts to approximately age 3, explains itself. This stage involves the development of a full-scale sense of self. The child begins to separate itself psychologically from the mother and to form a personal identity. This separate self becomes the basis for establishing healthy relationships with other people in adulthood.

There is a similarity between Mahler's developmental stages and Sigmund Freud's psychosexual stages in that the degree of success in advancing from one stage to the next will influence future personality development. The major difference is that Freud's stages involve sexual energy and goals whereas Mahler's stages involve investing psychic energy in interpersonal or object relationships.

It is important to remember that no matter how far the object relations theorists deviated from Freud's position by recognizing social and environmental influences, they remained Freudian in their basic approach. Their goal was to extend Freudian theory, not to replace it.

A Final Commentary

Freud's system of psychoanalysis has had a phenomenal impact on theory and practice in psychology and psychiatry, on our image of human nature, and on our understanding of personality. His influence has been felt in the general culture as well. As recently as 1998–1999, the Library of Congress in Washington, D.C., produced a popular touring exhibition entitled "Sigmund Freud: Conflict and Culture." Psychoanalysis contributed to the growing interest of American psychologists in the study of personality, beginning in the 1930s. In the 1940s and 1950s, the ideas of psychoanalysis influenced the emerging study of motivation in psychology. Contemporary psychology has absorbed many Freudian concepts, including the role of the unconscious, the importance of childhood experiences in shaping adult behavior, and the operation of the defense mechanisms. These and other ideas have generated a great deal of research.

We see further evidence of Freud's importance in the following chapters when we discuss the personality theorists who built on Freud's system or used it as a source of opposition for their ideas. Great ideas inspire not only by being considered valid, but also by being perceived as incorrect. Thus they stimulate the development of other viewpoints.

Freud's theory of personality remains more influential than his system of psychoanalytic therapy. Although research on Freud's ideas and experimental tests of his concepts continue to be plentiful, psychoanalysis as a therapeutic technique has declined in popularity. Growing numbers of people are seeking therapy for behavioral and emotional problems, but fewer are choosing the expensive, long-term approach Freud developed. Briefer courses of therapy, lasting from one to fifteen sessions, have become the norm, along with the increasing use of psychotherapeutic drugs.

The trend away from orthodox psychoanalysis in the United States has also been reinforced by the managed-care approach to total health care. It is less costly for insurance companies to approve a treatment regimen that involves prescribing a drug such as Prozac or Valium than a course of psychoanalysis lasting several years. In addition, managed care demands empirical evidence of the effectiveness of therapeutic treatment before providing insurance reimbursement and the evidence for the effectiveness of psychotherapy is weak.

We have already noted the flaws in the case study approach, Freud's primary method of research. In addition to those issues, raised mainly by experimental psychologists, there are questions asked by other personality theorists. Some argue that Freud placed too great an emphasis on instinctual biological forces as determinants of personality. Others challenge Freud's focus on sex and aggression as major motivating forces and believe we are shaped more by social experiences than by sexual ones. Some theorists disagree with Freud's deterministic picture of human nature, suggesting that we have more free will than Freud acknowledged, and that we can choose to act and grow spontaneously, in at least partial control of our fate.

Another criticism focuses on Freud's emphasis on past behavior to the exclusion of our goals and aspirations. These theorists argue that we are also influenced by the future, by our hopes and plans, as much as or more than by our experiences before age 5. Still other personality theorists think Freud paid too much attention to the emotionally disturbed, to the exclusion of the psychologically healthy and emotionally mature. If we wish to develop a theory of human personality, why not study the best and the healthiest, the positive human qualities as well as the negative ones? Theorists also take exception to Freud's views on women, specifically to the concepts of penis envy, women's poorly developed superegos, and women's inferiority feelings about their bodies.

Ambiguous definitions of certain Freudian concepts have been questioned. Critics point to confusion and contradiction in such terms as id, ego, and superego. Are they distinct physical structures in the brain? Are they fluid processes? In his later writings Freud addressed the difficulties of defining some of his concepts precisely, but the questions remain.

In addition, some of Freud's formulations may not be as appropriate today as when they were first proposed. "Many Freudian theses are no longer retained by psychoanalysts. . . . Revision—the discovery of new facts and the construction of new hypotheses—is a daily feature in the sciences; why should it be otherwise in psychoanalysis?" (Haynal, 1993, p. 129). As times change, psychologists seek new and better ways of describing the human personality.

This book is a history of modern insights into personality. In our personal and social growth we are never free of our past, nor should we want to be. The past offers the foundation on which to build, as later personality theorists have built on Freud's work. If psychoanalysis has served no other purpose than to inspire others and provide a framework within which to develop new insights, then Freud's importance to the world of ideas is secure. Every structure depends on the soundness and integrity of its foundation. Sigmund Freud gave personality theorists a solid, challenging base on which to build.

Chapter Summary

Instincts are mental representations of stimuli that originate within the body. Life instincts serve the purpose of survival and are manifested in a form of psychic energy called libido. Death instincts are an unconscious drive toward decay, destruction, and aggression.

The three structures of the personality are the id, ego, and superego. The id, the biological component of personality, is the storehouse of instincts and libido. It operates in accordance with the pleasure principle. The ego, the rational component of personality, operates in accordance with the reality principle. The superego, the moral side of personality, consists of the conscience (behaviors for which the child is punished) and the ego-ideal (behaviors for which the child is praised). The ego mediates among the demands of the id, the pressures of reality, and the dictates of the superego.

Anxiety develops when the ego is pressured too greatly. Reality anxiety is a fear of dangers in the real world. Neurotic anxiety is a conflict between instinctual gratification and reality. Moral anxiety is a conflict between the id and the superego. Defense mechanisms operate unconsciously. They are distortions of reality that protect the ego from the threat of anxiety. Defense mechanisms include repression, reaction formation, projection, regression, rationalization, displacement, and sublimation.

Children pass through psychosexual stages of development defined by erogenous zones of the body. The oral stage involves two modes of behavior: oral incorporative and oral aggressive. The anal stage involves the first interference with the gratification of an instinctual impulse. The phallic stage involves the Oedipus complex, the child's unconscious sexual longings for the parent of the opposite sex and feelings of rivalry and fear toward the parent of the same sex. Boys develop castration anxiety; girls develop penis envy. Boys resolve the Oedipus complex by identifying with their father, adopting their father's superego standards, and repressing their sexual longing for their mother. Girls are less successful in resolving the complex, which leaves them with poorly developed superegos. During the latency period, the sex instinct is sublimated in school activities, sports, and friendships with persons of the same sex. The genital stage, at puberty, marks the beginning of heterosexual relationships.

Freud's image of human nature is pessimistic. We are doomed to anxiety, to the thwarting of impulses, and to tension and conflict. The goal of life is to reduce tension. Much of human nature is inherited, but part is learned through parent-child interactions.

Two methods of personality assessment are free association and dream analysis. In free association, a patient spontaneously expresses ideas and images in random fashion. Sometimes resistances develop in which a patient resists talking about disturbing memories or experiences. Dreams have both a manifest content (the actual dream events) and a latent content (the symbolic meaning of those events).

Freud's research method was the case study, which does not rely on objective observation. It is not controlled and systematic, nor is it amenable to duplication and verification. Freud's data are not quantifiable, may be incomplete and inaccurate, and were based on a small and unrepresentative sample.

Some Freudian concepts have been supported by empirical research: the unconscious, repression, verbal slips, characteristics of oral and anal personality types, the Oedipal triangle, castration anxiety, and the resolution of the Oedipal dilemma in women by bearing a child. Major portions of Freud's theory (the id, superego, death wish, libido, catharsis, and anxiety) have not been scientifically validated. Two components of the ego have been identified: ego control and ego resiliency. With regard to repressed memories of childhood sexual abuse, some may be real, whereas others may be implanted and distorted.

Freud's theory has been modified by Anna Freud, who elaborated on the role of the ego, and by object relations theorists such as Kohut, Klein, and Mahler who focused on the mother-child relationship.

Personality theorists criticize Freud for placing too much emphasis on biological forces, sex, aggression, emotional disturbances, and childhood events. They also criticize his deterministic image of human nature, his negative views of women, and the ambiguous definitions of some of his concepts.

Review Questions

1. Give examples of how Freud's theory may reflect his childhood experiences and his personal conflicts about sex.

2. Describe the life instincts and the death instincts. How do they motivate behavior?

3. Describe the id, the ego, and the superego. How are they interrelated?

4. Describe three types of anxiety. What is the purpose of anxiety? How do we defend ourselves against anxiety?

5. Describe the oral and anal stages of psychosexual development. What activities characterize an adult fixated at the oral incorporative phase? At the anal retentive phase?

6. How do boys and girls resolve the conflicts of the phallic stage of psychosexual development? In your opinion, how would boys and girls reared by a single mother resolve these conflicts?

7. What are Freud's views on the relative influences of heredity and environment? What is Freud's position on the issue of free will versus determinism?

8. What kind of information can be revealed by free association? What are resistances?

9. Describe two aspects of dreams. Discuss research conducted to test Freud's ideas about dream contents. Which of the propositions in Freud's theory have received empirical support?

10. What criticisms can be made of the case study method?

11. Describe examples of research conducted on the concepts of the Freudian slip, the ego, and catharsis.

12. How does research on subliminal perception support Freud's views on the unconscious?

13. Describe behavioral and physiological reactions of subjects identified as repressors and non-repressors in coping with threatening memories.

14. At what ages are the defense mechanisms of denial, identification, and projection most likely to be used? Why?

15. Does the Freudian defense mechanism of repression explain all instances of re-pressed memories of childhood abuse? What other factors might account for such memories?

16. Describe some of the ways in which Anna Freud, Heinz Kohut, Melanie Klein, and Margaret Mahler extended and modified traditional Freudian theory.

17. What is the current status of psychoanalysis as a personality theory and as a method of psychotherapy?

Suggested Readings

Coles, R. (1993). *Anna Freud: The dream of psychoanaly-sis.* New York: Addison-Wesley. Describes Anna Freud's life, her work on defense mechanisms, and her hopes for the future of psychoanalysis.

Ellenberger, H. F. (1970). *The discovery of the uncon-scious: The history and evolution of dynamic psychi-atry.* New York: Basic Books. Traces the study of the unconscious from primitive times to Freudian psy-choanalysis and its derivatives.

Gay, P. (1988). *Freud: A life for our time.* New York: Nor-ton. An insightful work on Freud's life and career.

Hornstein, G. A. (1992). The return of the repressed: Psy-chology's problematic relations with psychoanalysis, 1909–1960. *American Psychologist, 47,* 254–263. Surveys the impact of Freudian psychoanalysis on American psychology from an initial skepticism, through experimental testing, to eventual absorption of some concepts into mainstream psychology.

Krüll, M. (1986). *Freud and his father.* New York: Norton. Examines the lives of Sigmund Freud and his father and analyzes the influences of Freud's experiences as a son on the development of psychoanalysis.

Lerman, H. (1986). *A mote in Freud's eye: From psycho-analysis to the psychology of women.* New York: Springer-Verlag. Describes how Freud's negative bias toward women developed from his personal experi-ences and permeated his theory of psychoanalysis.

Shows how Freud's stages of psychosexual develop-ment, as they apply to females, have been largely dis-proved, and offers criteria for a woman-based person-ality theory.

Roazen, P. (1975). *Freud and his followers.* New York: Knopf. A lively, well-written account of Freud's life and of the men and women who became his disci-ples, some of whom later broke away to form their own schools of thought.

Roth, M. S. (Ed.). (1998). *Freud: Conflict and culture.* New York: Knopf. Essays evaluating Freud's life, work, and contemporary influence, published in con-junction with a controversial exhibition of Freud arti-facts by the Library of Congress in Washington, DC.

Sulloway, F. J. (1979). *Freud, biologist of the mind: Be-yond the psychoanalytic legend.* New York: Basic Books. A biography that places Freud's work in the context of its times and disputes the legend that Freud was a lonely hero working in isolation.

Westen, D. (1998). The scientific legacy of Sigmund Freud: Toward a psychodynamically informed psy-chological science. *Psychological Bulletin, 124,* 333–371. Supports the relevance of Freudian psycho-dynamic theory for modern psychology in terms of its positions on unconscious processes, social forces in childhood, mental representations of the self, and aspects of the developmental stages.

The Neopsychoanalytic Approach

Several personality theorists, who initially were loyal to Freud and committed to his system of psychoanalysis, broke away because of their opposition to certain aspects of his approach. Carl Jung and Alfred Adler were associates of Freud's before they rebelled and offered their own views of personality. Karen Horney and Erich Fromm did not have a personal relationship with Freud but were orthodox Freudians before seeking different paths. Henry Murray, the first American theorist we discuss, developed a view of personality that provides a unique interpretation of formal psychoanalytic concepts. The work of Erik Erikson, presented in Chapter 8, is also derived from Freudian psychoanalysis.

These neopsychoanalytic theorists differ from one another on a number of points but are grouped here because of their shared opposition to two major points: Freud's emphasis on instincts as the primary motivators of human behavior and his deterministic view of personality. The neopsychoanalytic theorists present a more optimistic and flattering picture of human nature. Their work shows how quickly the field of personality diversified within a decade after it formally began.

> My life is a story of the self-realization of the unconscious. Everything in the unconscious seeks outward manifestation, and the personality too desires to evolve out of its unconscious conditions.
>
> —Carl Jung

T H R E E

Carl Jung

analytical psychology
Jung's theory of
personality.

    **analytical
        psychology**

        Carl Jung

Sigmund Freud once designated Carl Jung as his spiritual heir, but Jung went on to develop a theory of personality that differed dramatically from orthodox psychoanalysis. Jung fashioned a new and elaborate explanation of human nature quite unlike any other, which he called **analytical psychology**.

The first point on which Jung came to disagree with Freud was the role of sexuality. Jung broadened Freud's definition of libido by redefining it as a more generalized psychic energy that includes sex but is not restricted to it.

The second major area of disagreement concerns the direction of the forces that influence personality. Whereas Freud viewed human beings as prisoners or victims of past events, Jung argued that we are shaped by our future as well as our past. We are affected not only by what happened to us as children, but also by what we aspire to do in the future.

The third significant point of difference revolves around the unconscious. Rather than minimizing the role of the unconscious, as did other dissenters we discuss, Jung placed an even greater emphasis on it than Freud did. He probed more deeply into the unconscious and added a new dimension: the inherited experiences of human and prehuman species. Although Freud had recognized this phylogenetic aspect of personality (the influence of inherited primal experiences), Jung made it the core of his system of personality. He combined ideas from history, mythology, anthropology, and religion to form his image of human nature.

The Life of Jung (1875–1961)

An Unhappy Childhood

Black-frocked clergymen, deaths and funerals, neurotic parents in a failing marriage, religious doubts and conflicts, bizarre dreams and visions, and a wooden doll for a companion—all these marked Jung's difficult and unhappy childhood years. Born in Switzerland into a family that included nine clergymen (eight uncles and his father), Jung was introduced at an early age to religion and the classics. He was close to his father but considered him weak and powerless. Although kind and tolerant, Jung's father experienced periods of moodiness and irritability and failed to be the strong authority figure his son needed.

Jung's mother was the more powerful parent, but her emotional instability led her to behave erratically. She could change in an instant from cheerful and happy to mumbling incoherently and gazing vacantly into space. As a boy, Jung came to view his mother as being two different people inhabiting the same body. Not surprisingly, this belief disturbed him. One biographer suggested that "the whole maternal side of the family appeared to be tainted with insanity" (Ellenberger, 1978, p. 149).

As a result of his mother's odd behavior, Jung became wary of women, a suspicion that took many years to dispel. In his autobiography he described his mother as fat and unattractive, which may explain why he rejected Freud's notion that every boy has a sexual longing for his mother. Clearly, it did not reflect his own experience.

To avoid his parents and their continuing marital problems, Jung spent many hours alone in the attic of his home, carving a doll out of wood, a figure in whom he could confide. He had one sibling, a sister, who was born when he was 9 years old and who had little influence on his development; her arrival did nothing to ease his loneliness.

Dreams and Fantasies

Distrustful of his mother and disappointed in his father, Jung felt cut off from the external world, the world of conscious reality. As an escape he turned inward to his unconscious, to the world of dreams, visions, and fantasies, in which he felt more secure. This choice would guide Jung for the rest of his life. Whenever he was faced with a problem, he would seek a solution through his dreams and visions.

The essence of his personality theory was shaped in a similar way. When Jung was 3 years old, he dreamed he was in a cavern. In a later dream, he saw himself digging beneath the earth's surface, unearthing the bones of prehistoric animals. To Jung, such dreams represented the direction of his approach to the human personality. They prompted him to explore the unconscious mind, which lies beneath the surface of behavior. So strongly was he guided by these manifestations of his unconscious that he entitled his autobiography *Memories, Dreams, Reflections* (1961), and he believed his approach to personality resembled a subjective, personal confession. Thus, like Freud's work, Jung's personality theory was intensely autobiographical. In a lecture given at the age of 50, he acknowledged the influence of his life events on his theory.

As a child, Jung deliberately avoided other children. One of his few acquaintances from that time remembered Jung as an "asocial monster" (Wehr, 1987, p. 29). In describing his solitary childhood, Jung wrote, "The pattern of my relationship to the world was already prefigured; today as then I am a solitary" (Jung, 1961, pp. 41–42). Jung's loneliness is reflected in his theory, which focuses on the inner growth of the individual rather than on relationships with other people. In contrast, Freud's theory is concerned more with interpersonal relationships, perhaps because Freud, unlike Jung, did not have such an isolated and introverted childhood.

The Study of Medicine

Jung disliked school and resented the time he had to devote to formal studies rather than to ideas that interested him. He preferred to read on his own, particularly about religious and philosophical issues. To his delight, he was forced to miss 6 months of school because he had suffered a series of fainting spells. However, when Jung overheard his father say, "What will become of the boy if he cannot earn his living?" his illness suddenly disappeared, and he returned to school to work more diligently than before (Jung, 1961, p. 31). Jung later wrote that the experience taught him about neurotic behavior. He recognized that he had arranged the situation to suit himself, to keep him out of school, and that realization made him feel angry and ashamed.

Jung chose to study medicine at the University of Basel and decided, to the disappointment of his professors, to specialize in psychiatry, a field then held in low repute. He believed that psychiatry would give him the opportunity to pursue his interests in dreams, the supernatural, and the occult.

Beginning in 1900, Jung worked at a mental hospital in Zurich, under the direction of Eugen Bleuler, the psychiatrist who coined the term *schizophrenia*. In the years that followed, Jung lectured at the University of Zurich, developed an independent clinical practice, and conducted research using his word-association test to investigate the emotional reactions of his patients.

The Years with Freud

By the time he became associated with Sigmund Freud in 1907, Jung had already established a significant professional reputation. When Jung and Freud met for the first time, they were so congenial and had so much to share that they talked for 13 hours. Their friendship became a close one. "I formally adopted you as an eldest son," Freud wrote to Jung, "and anointed you as my successor and crown prince" (Freud & Jung, 1974, p. 218). Jung considered Freud a father figure. "Let me enjoy your friendship not as one between equals," he wrote to Freud, "but as that of father and son" (Freud & Jung, 1974, p. 122). Their relationship appeared to contain many of the elements of the Oedipus complex, with its inevitable wish of the son to destroy the father.

Also, their relationship may have been tainted, even doomed, by a sexual experience Jung had at the age of 18. A family friend, an older man who had been a father figure and confidant, made physical overtures to Jung, seeking a homosexual encounter. Repelled and disappointed, Jung broke off the relationship. Years later, when Freud, who was nearly 20 years older than Jung, attempted to designate Jung as son and heir, Jung may have felt Freud was, in a sense, forcing himself on Jung and changing the nature of their relationship. Because of Jung's earlier encounter with the older man, he may have been similarly disappointed in Freud and unable to sustain an emotionally close relationship with him.

For a time, however, the two men were close. Jung remained in Zurich, but he met with Freud periodically, continued a voluminous correspondence, and journeyed with Freud to the United States in 1909 to lecture at Clark University. Freud was grooming Jung to take over the presidency of the International Psychoanalytic Association. Concerned that psychoanalysis would be labeled a Jewish science (as it came to be called during the Nazi era) Freud wanted a non-Jew to assume titular leadership of the movement.

Contrary to Freud's hopes, Jung was not an uncritical disciple. Jung had his own ideas and unique view of the human personality, and when he began to express these notions, it became inevitable that they would part. They severed their relationship in 1913.

A Neurotic Episode

That same year, when Jung was 38 years old, he underwent a severe neurotic episode that lasted for 3 years. He believed he was in danger of losing contact with reality and was so distressed that he resigned his lectureship at the University of Zurich. At times he considered suicide; he "kept a revolver next to his bed in case he felt he had passed beyond the point of no return" (Noll, 1994, p. 207). Although he felt unable to continue with his scientific work, he persisted in treating his patients.

Freud had suffered a neurotic episode at approximately the same age and resolved it by analyzing his dreams, which formed a basis for his personality theory. Jung's situation offers a remarkable parallel. Jung overcame his disturbance by confronting his unconscious through the exploration of his dreams and fantasies. Although Jung's self-analysis was less systematic than Freud's, his approach was similar.

Out of Jung's confrontation with his unconscious he fashioned his approach to personality. He wrote, "The years when I was pursuing my inner images were the most important in my life—in them everything essential was decided" (Jung, 1961, p. 199). He concluded that the most crucial stage in personality development was not childhood, as Freud believed, but middle age, which was the time of Jung's own crisis.

Like Freud, Jung established his theory on an intuitive base, which derived from his personal experiences and dreams. It was refined along more rational and empirical lines by data provided by his patients. Nearly two-thirds of them were middle-aged and suffering from the same difficulties Jung faced.

The rest of Jung's long life was personally and professionally fruitful. He explored diverse cultures in the United States, Africa, and India to broaden his understanding of human nature. The University of Basel established a professorship for him, and a group of students organized a Jungian training institute in Zurich.

Jung remained productive in research and writing for most of his 86 years. His books became popular, and his analytical psychology attracted increasing numbers of followers. His ideas spread to the English-speaking world, and particularly to the United States, primarily through the generous financial support of the Rockefellers, the McCormicks, and the Mellons, all prominent American families. A number of family members sought analysis with Jung and in return arranged for the translation and publication of his books. Otherwise, Jung's works might have remained little known, inaccessible to all but the German-speaking community (Noll, 1997).

Psychic Energy

One of the first points on which Jung disputed Freud concerned the nature of libido. Jung did not agree that libido was primarily a sexual energy; he argued instead that libido was a broad, undifferentiated life energy. Interestingly, Jung, who minimized the importance of sex in his personality theory, maintained a vigorous, anxiety-free sex life and enjoyed a number of extramarital affairs. One of these relationships endured, with his wife's knowledge, for many years. He surrounded himself with adoring women patients and disciples who typically fell deeply in love with him. A biographer noted that this "happened with all of his female disciples sooner or later, as he often told them at the beginning of their treatment" (Noll, 1997, p. 253).

Contrast Jung's active sex life with Freud's troubled attitude toward sex and his cessation of sexual relations at the time he was fashioning a theory that focused on sex as the cause of neurotic behavior. "To Jung, who freely and frequently satisfied his sexual needs, sex played a minimal role in human motivation. To Freud, beset by frustrations and anxious about his thwarted desires, sex played the central role" (Schultz, 1990, p. 148).

libido To Jung, a broader and more generalized form of psychic energy.

psyche Jung's term for personality.

Jung used the term **libido** in two ways: first, as a diffuse and general life energy, and second, from a perspective similar to Freud's, as a narrower psychic energy that fuels the work of the personality, which he called the **psyche**. It is through psychic energy that psychological activities such as perceiving, thinking, feeling, and wishing are carried out.

When a person invests a great deal of psychic energy in a particular idea or feeling, that idea or feeling is said to have a high psychic value and can strongly influence the person's life. For example, if you are highly motivated to attain power, then you will devote most of your psychic energy to seeking power.

Opposites, Equivalence, and Entropy

Jung drew on ideas from physics to explain the functioning of psychic energy. He proposed three basic principles: opposites, equivalence, and entropy (Jung, 1928).

opposition principle Jung's idea that conflict between opposing processes or tendencies is necessary to generate psychic energy.

The **principle of opposites** can be seen throughout Jung's system. He noted the existence of opposites or polarities in physical energy, such as heat versus cold, height versus depth, creation versus decay. So it is with psychic energy: Every wish or feeling has its opposite. This opposition or antithesis—this conflict between polarities—is the primary motivator of behavior and generator of energy. Indeed, the sharper the conflict between polarities, the greater the energy produced.

equivalence principle The continuing redistribution of energy within a personality; if the energy expended on certain conditions or activities weakens or disappears, that energy is transferred elsewhere in the personality.

For his **principle of equivalence**, Jung applied to psychic events the physical principle of the conservation of energy. He stated that energy expended in bringing about some condition is not lost but rather is shifted to another part of the personality. Thus, if the psychic value in a particular area weakens or disappears, that energy is transferred elsewhere in the psyche. For example, if we lose interest in a person, a hobby, or a field of study, the psychic energy formerly invested in that area is shifted to a new one. The psychic energy used for conscious activities while we are awake is shifted to dreams when we are asleep.

The word *equivalence* implies that the new area to which energy has shifted must have an equal psychic value; that is, it should be equally desirable, compelling, or fascinating. Otherwise, the excess energy will flow into the unconscious. In whatever direction and manner energy flows, the principle of equivalence suggests that energy is continually redistributed within the personality.

entropy principle A tendency toward balance or equilibrium within the personality; the ideal is an equal distribution of psychic energy over all structures of the personality.

In physics, the **principle of entropy** refers to the equalization of energy differences. For example, if a hot object and a cold object are placed in direct contact, heat will flow from the hotter object to the colder object until they are in equilibrium at the same temperature. In effect, an exchange of energy occurs, resulting in a kind of homeostatic balance between the objects.

Jung applied this law to psychic energy and proposed that there is a tendency toward a balance or equilibrium in the personality. If two desires or beliefs differ greatly in intensity or psychic value, energy will flow from the more strongly held to the weaker. Ideally, the personality has an equal distribution of psychic energy over all its aspects, but this ideal state is never achieved. If perfect balance or equilibrium were attained, then the personality would have no psychic energy because, as we noted earlier, the opposition principle requires conflict for psychic energy to be produced.

The Systems of Personality

In Jung's view, the total personality, or psyche, is composed of several distinct systems or structures that can influence one another. The major systems are the ego, the personal unconscious, and the collective unconscious.

The Ego

ego To Jung, the conscious aspect of personality.

The **ego** is the center of consciousness, the part of the psyche concerned with perceiving, thinking, feeling, and remembering. It is our awareness of ourselves and is responsible for carrying out the normal activities of waking life. The ego acts in a selective way, admitting into conscious awareness only a portion of the stimuli to which we are exposed.

The Attitudes: Extraversion and Introversion

extraversion

introversion

extraversion An attitude of the psyche characterized by an orientation toward the external world and other people.

introversion An attitude of the psyche characterized by an orientation toward one's own thoughts and feelings.

Much of our conscious perception of and reaction to our environment is determined by the opposing mental attitudes of **extraversion** and **introversion**. Jung believed that psychic energy could be channeled externally, toward the outside world, or internally, toward the self. Extraverts are open, sociable, and socially assertive, oriented toward other people and the external world. Introverts are withdrawn and often shy, and they tend to focus on themselves, on their own thoughts and feelings.

According to Jung, everyone has the capacity for both attitudes, but only one becomes dominant in the personality. The dominant attitude then tends to direct the person's behavior and consciousness. The nondominant attitude remains influential, however, and becomes part of the personal unconscious, where it can affect behavior. For example, in certain situations an introverted person may display characteristics of extraversion, wish to be more outgoing, or be attracted to an extravert.

Psychological Functions

As Jung came to recognize that there were different kinds of extraverts and introverts, he proposed additional distinctions among people based on what he called the psychological functions. These functions refer to different and opposing ways of perceiving or apprehending both the external real world and our subjective inner world. Jung posited four functions of the psyche: sensing, intuiting, thinking, and feeling (Jung, 1927).

Sensing and intuiting are grouped together as nonrational functions; they do not use the processes of reason. These functions accept experiences and do not evaluate them. Sensing reproduces an experience through the senses the way a photograph copies an object. Intuiting does not arise directly from an external stimulus; for example, if we believe someone else is with us in a darkened room, our belief may be based on our intuition or a hunch rather than on actual sensory experience.

The second pair of opposing functions, thinking and feeling, are rational functions that involve making judgments and evaluations about our experiences. Although thinking and feeling are opposites, both are concerned with organizing and categorizing experiences. The thinking function involves a conscious judgment of whether an experience is true or false. The kind of evaluation made by the feeling function is expressed in terms of like or dislike, pleasantness or unpleasantness, stimulation or dullness.

Just as our psyche contains some of both the extraversion and introversion attitudes, so we have the capacity for all four psychological functions. And just as one attitude is dominant, so only one function is dominant. The others are submerged in the personal unconscious. Further, only one pair of functions is dominant—either the rational or the irrational—and within each pair only one function is dominant. A person cannot be ruled by both thinking and feeling or by both sensing and intuiting, because they are opposing functions.

Psychological Types

psychological types To Jung, eight personality types based on interactions of the attitudes (introversion and extraversion) and the functions (thinking, feeling, sensing, and intuiting).

Jung proposed eight **psychological types**, based on the interactions of the two attitudes and four functions. (See Table 3.1.)

The *extraverted thinking type* lives strictly in accordance with society's rules. These people tend to repress feelings and emotions, to be objective in all aspects of life, and to be dogmatic in thoughts and opinions. They may be perceived as rigid and cold. They tend to make good scientists because their focus is on learning about the external world and using logical rules to describe and understand it.

The *extraverted feeling type* tends to repress the thinking mode and to be highly emotional. These people conform to the traditional values and moral codes they have been taught. They are unusually sensitive to the opinions and expectations of others. They are emotionally responsive and make friends easily, and they tend to be sociable and effervescent. Jung believed this type was found more often among women than men.

TABLE 3.1   *Jung's psychological types*

Extraverted thinking	Logical, objective, dogmatic
Extraverted feeling	Emotional, sensitive, sociable; more typical of women than men
Extraverted sensing	Outgoing, pleasure-seeking, adaptable
Extraverted intuiting	Creative, able to motivate others and to seize opportunities
Introverted thinking	More interested in ideas than in people
Introverted feeling	Reserved, undemonstrative, yet capable of deep emotion
Introverted sensing	Outwardly detached, expressing themselves in aesthetic pursuits
Introverted intuiting	More concerned with the unconscious than with everyday reality

Extraverts channel the libido externally, toward the outside world.

The *extraverted sensing type* focuses on pleasure and happiness and on seeking new experiences. These people are strongly oriented toward the real world and are adaptable to different kinds of people and changing situations. Not given to introspection, they tend to be outgoing, with a high capacity for enjoying life.

The *extraverted intuiting type* finds success in business and politics because of a keen ability to exploit opportunities. These people are attracted by new ideas and tend to be creative. They are able to inspire others to accomplish and achieve. They also tend to be changeable, moving from one idea or venture to another, and to make decisions based more on hunches than on reflection. Their decisions, however, are likely to be correct.

The *introverted thinking type* does not get along well with others and has difficulty communicating ideas. These people focus on thought rather than on feelings and have poor practical judgment. Intensely concerned with privacy, they prefer to deal with abstractions and theories, and they focus on understanding themselves rather than other people. Others see them as stubborn, aloof, arrogant, and inconsiderate.

The *introverted feeling type* represses rational thought. These people are capable of deep emotion but avoid any outward expression of it. They seem mysterious and inaccessible and tend to be quiet, modest, and childish. They have little consideration for others' feelings and thoughts and appear withdrawn, cold, and self-assured.

The *introverted sensing type* appears passive, calm, and detached from the everyday world. These people look on most human activities with benevolence and amusement. They are aesthetically sensitive, expressing themselves in art or music, and tend to repress their intuition.

The *introverted intuiting type* focuses so intently on intuition that people of this type have little contact with reality. These people are visionaries and daydreamers—

aloof, unconcerned with practical matters, and poorly understood by others. Considered odd and eccentric, they have difficulty coping with everyday life and planning for the future.

The Personal Unconscious

personal unconscious
The reservoir of material that was once conscious but has been forgotten or suppressed.

The **personal unconscious** in Jung's system is similar to Freud's conception of the preconscious. It is a reservoir of material that was once conscious but has been forgotten or suppressed because it was trivial or disturbing. There is considerable two-way traffic between the ego and the personal unconscious. For example, our attention can wander readily from this printed page to a memory of something we did yesterday. All kinds of experiences are stored in the personal unconscious; it can be likened to a filing cabinet. Little mental effort is required to take something out, examine it for a while, and put it back, where it will remain until the next time we want it or are reminded of it.

Complexes

complex To Jung, a core or pattern of emotions, memories, perceptions, and wishes in the personal unconscious organized around a common theme, such as power or status.

As we file more and more experiences in our personal unconscious, we begin to group them into what Jung called **complexes**. A complex is a core or pattern of emotions, memories, perceptions, and wishes organized around a common theme. For example, we might say that a person has a complex about power or status, meaning that he or she is preoccupied with that theme to the point where it influences behavior. The person may try to become powerful by running for elective office, or to identify or affiliate with power by driving a motorcycle or a fast car. By directing thoughts and behavior in various ways, the complex determines how the person perceives the world.

Complexes may be conscious or unconscious. Those that are not under conscious control can intrude on and interfere with consciousness. The person with a complex is generally not aware of its influence, although other people may easily observe its effects.

Some complexes may be harmful, but others can be useful. For example, a perfection or achievement complex may lead a person to work hard at developing particular talents or skills. Jung believed that complexes originate not only from our childhood and adult experiences, but also from our ancestral experiences, the heritage of the species contained in the collective unconscious.

 collective unconscious

collective unconscious
The deepest level of the psyche containing the accumulation of inherited experiences of human and prehuman species.

The Collective Unconscious

The deepest and least accessible level of the psyche, the **collective unconscious** is the most unusual and controversial aspect of Jung's system; to critics, it is the most bizarre. Jung believed that just as each of us accumulates and files all of our personal experiences in the personal unconscious, so does humankind collectively, as a species, store the experiences of the human and prehuman species in the collective unconscious. This heritage is passed to each new generation.

Whatever experiences are universal—those that are repeated relatively unchanged by each generation—become part of our personality. Our primitive past becomes the basis of the human psyche, directing and influencing present behavior. To Jung, the collective unconscious was the powerful and controlling repository of ancestral experiences. Thus, Jung linked each person's personality with the past, not only with childhood but also with the history of the species. We do not inherit these collective experiences directly. For example, we do not inherit a fear of snakes. Rather, we inherit the potential to fear snakes. We are predisposed to behave and feel the same ways people have always behaved and felt. Whether the predisposition becomes reality depends on the specific experiences each of us encounters in life.

Jung believed that certain basic experiences have characterized every generation throughout human history. People have always had a mother figure, for example, and have experienced birth and death. They have faced unknown terrors in the dark, worshipped power or some sort of godlike figure, and feared an evil being. The universality of these experiences over countless evolving generations leaves an imprint on each of us at birth and determines how we perceive and react to our world. Jung wrote, "The form of the world into which [a person] is born is already inborn in him, as a virtual image" (Jung, 1953, p. 188).

A baby is born predisposed to perceive the mother in a certain way. Assuming the mother behaves the way mothers typically behave, in a nurturing and supportive manner, then the baby's predisposition will correspond with its reality.

Because the collective unconscious is such an unusual concept, it is important to note the reason Jung proposed it and the kind of evidence he gathered to support it. In his reading about ancient cultures, both mythical and real, Jung discovered common themes and symbols that appeared in diverse parts of the world. As far as he could determine, these ideas had not been transmitted or communicated orally or in writing from one culture to another.

In addition, Jung's patients, in their dreams and fantasies, recalled and described for him the same kinds of symbols he had discovered in ancient cultures. He could find no other explanation for these shared symbols and themes over such vast geographical and temporal distances than that they were transmitted by and carried in each person's unconscious mind.

archetypes

archetypes Images of universal experiences contained in the collective unconscious.

Archetypes

The ancient experiences contained in the collective unconscious are manifested by recurring themes or patterns Jung called **archetypes** (Jung, 1947). He also used the term *primordial images*. There are many such images of universal experiences, as many as there are common human experiences. By being repeated in the lives of succeeding generations, archetypes have become imprinted on our psyche and are expressed in our dreams and fantasies.

Among the archetypes Jung proposed are the hero, the mother, the child, God, death, power, and the wise old man. A few of these are developed more fully than others and influence the psyche more consistently. These major archetypes include the persona, the anima and animus, the shadow, and the self.

The word *persona* refers to a mask that an actor wears to display various roles or faces to the audience. Jung used the term with basically the same meaning. The **persona archetype** is a mask, a public face we wear to present ourselves as someone different from who we really are. The persona is necessary, Jung believed,

persona archetype The public face or role a person presents to others.

FIGURE 3.1   *The Yin-Yang symbol illustrates the complementary sides of our nature. The dark right side represents feminine aspects (the anima archetype) and the light left side represents masculine aspects (the animus archetype). The dot of the opposite color in each portion indicates the expression of the characteristics of the opposite archetype.*

because we are forced to play many roles in life in order to succeed in school and on the job and to get along with a variety of people.

Although the persona can be helpful, it can also be harmful. We may come to believe the persona reflects our true nature. Instead of merely playing a role, we may become that role. As a result, other aspects of our personality will not be allowed to develop. Jung described the process this way: The ego may come to identify with the persona rather than with the person's true nature, resulting in a condition known as inflation of the persona. Whether the person plays a role or comes to believe that role, he or she is resorting to deception. In the first instance, the person is deceiving others; in the second instance, the person is deceiving himself or herself.

The anima and animus archetypes refer to Jung's recognition that humans are essentially bisexual. On the biological level, each sex secretes the hormones of the other sex as well as those of its own sex. On the psychological level, each sex manifests characteristics, temperaments, and attitudes of the other sex by virtue of centuries of living together. The psyche of the woman contains masculine aspects (the **animus archetype**), and the psyche of the man contains feminine aspects (the **anima archetype**). (See Figure 3.1.)

anima archetype; animus archetype
Feminine aspects of the male psyche; masculine aspects of the female psyche.

These opposite sex characteristics aid in the adjustment and survival of the species because they enable a person of one sex to understand the nature of the other sex. The archetypes predispose us to like certain characteristics of the opposite sex; these characteristics guide our behavior with reference to the opposite sex.

Jung insisted that both the anima and the animus must be expressed. A man must exhibit his feminine as well as his masculine characteristics, and a woman must express her masculine characteristics along with her feminine ones. Otherwise, these vital aspects will remain dormant and undeveloped, leading to a one-sidedness of the personality.

shadow archetype The dark side of the personality; the archetype that contains primitive animal instincts.

The most powerful archetype Jung proposed has the sinister and mysterious name of the **shadow**, which contains the basic, primitive animal instincts and therefore has the deepest roots of all the archetypes. Behaviors that society considers evil and immoral reside in the shadow, and this dark side of human nature must be tamed

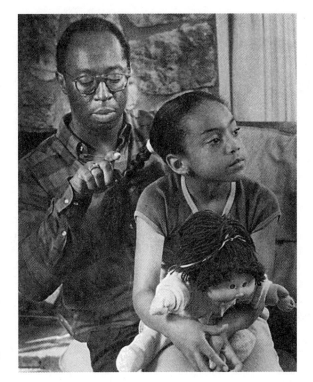

In the fully developed personality, a person will express behaviors considered characteristic of the opposite sex.

if people are to live in harmony. We must restrain, overcome, and defend against these primitive impulses. If we do not, society will likely punish us.

But we face a dilemma. Not only is the shadow the source of evil, it is also the source of vitality, spontaneity, creativity, and emotion. Therefore, if the shadow is totally suppressed, the psyche will be dull and lifeless. It is the ego's function to repress the animal instincts enough so that we are considered civilized while allowing sufficient expression of the instincts to provide creativity and vigor.

If the shadow is fully suppressed, not only does the personality become flat, but the person also faces the possibility that the shadow will revolt. The animal instincts do not disappear when they are suppressed. Rather, they lie dormant, awaiting a crisis or a weakness in the ego so they can gain control. When that happens, the person becomes dominated by the unconscious.

self archetype To Jung, the archetype that represents the unity, integration, and harmony of the total personality.

The **self archetype** represents the unity, integration, and harmony of the total personality. To Jung, the striving toward that wholeness is the ultimate goal of life. This archetype involves bringing together and balancing all parts of the personality. We have already noted Jung's principle of opposites and the importance of polarities to the psyche. In the self archetype, conscious and unconscious processes become assimilated so that the self, which is the center of the personality, shifts from the ego to a point of equilibrium midway between the opposing forces of the conscious and the unconscious. As a result, material from the unconscious comes to have a greater influence on the personality.

TABLE 3.2   *Jung's developmental stages*

Childhood	Ego development begins when the child distinguishes between self and others.
Puberty to young adulthood	Adolescents must adapt to the growing demands of reality. The focus is external, on education, career, and family. The conscious is dominant.
Middle age	A period of transition when the focus of the personality shifts from external to internal in an attempt to balance the unconscious with the conscious.

The full realization of the self lies in the future. It is a goal—something to strive for but rarely achieved. The self serves as a motivating force, pulling us from ahead rather than pushing us from behind (as with our past experiences).

The self cannot begin to emerge until the other systems of the psyche have developed. This occurs around middle age, a crucial period of transition in Jung's system, as it was in his own life. The actualization of the self involves goals and plans for the future and an accurate perception of one's abilities. Because development of the self is impossible without self-knowledge, it is the most difficult process we face in life and requires persistence, perceptiveness, and wisdom.

The Development of the Personality

Jung proposed that personality is determined by what we hope to be as well as by what we have been. He criticized Freud for emphasizing only past events as shapers of personality, to the exclusion of the future. Jung believed we develop and grow regardless of age and are always moving toward a more complete level of self-realization (see Table 3.2).

Jung took a longer view of personality than Freud, who concentrated on the early years of life and foresaw little development after the age of 5. Jung did not posit sequential stages of growth in as much detail as Freud but he wrote of specific periods in the overall developmental process (Jung, 1930).

Childhood to Young Adulthood

The ego begins to develop in early childhood, at first in a primitive way because the child has not yet formed a unique identity. What might be called the child's personality is, at this stage, little more than a reflection of the personalities of his or her parents. Obviously, then, parents exert a great influence on the formation of the child's personality. They can enhance or impede personality development by the way they behave toward the child.

Parents might try to force their personalities on the child, desiring him or her to be an extension of themselves. Or they might expect their child to develop a personality different from their own as a way of seeking vicarious compensation for their deficiencies. The ego begins to form substantively only when children become

Middle age is a time of transition, when one's focus and interests change.

able to distinguish between themselves and other people or objects in their world. In other words, consciousness forms when the child is able to say "I."

It is not until puberty that the psyche assumes a definite form and content. This period, which Jung called our psychic birth, is marked by difficulties and the need to adapt. Childhood fantasies must end as the adolescent confronts the demands of reality. From the teenage years through young adulthood, we are concerned with preparatory activities such as completing our education, beginning a career, getting married, and starting a family. Our focus during these years is external, our conscious is dominant, and, in general, our primary conscious attitude is that of extraversion. The aim of life is to achieve our goals and establish a secure, successful place for ourselves in the world. Thus, young adulthood should be an exciting and challenging time, filled with new horizons and accomplishments.

Middle Age

Major personality changes occur between the ages of 35 and 40. This period of middle age was a time of personal crisis for Jung and many of his patients. By then, the adaptational problems of young adulthood have been resolved. The typical 40-year-old is established in a career, a marriage, and a community. Jung asked why, when success has been achieved, are so many people gripped by feelings of despair and worthlessness? His patients all told him essentially the same thing: They felt empty. Adventure, excitement, and zest had disappeared. Life had lost its meaning.

The more Jung analyzed this period, the more strongly he believed that such drastic personality changes were inevitable and universal. Middle age is a natural time of transition in which the personality is supposed to undergo necessary and beneficial changes. Ironically, the changes occur because middle-aged persons have been so successful in meeting life's demands. These people had invested a great deal of energy in the preparatory activities of the first half of life, but by age 40 that preparation was finished and those challenges had been met. Although they still possess considerable energy, the energy now has nowhere to go; it has to be rechanneled into different activities and interests.

Jung noted that in the first half of life we must focus on the objective world of reality—education, career, and family. In contrast, the second half of life must be devoted to the inner, subjective world that heretofore had been neglected. The attitude of the personality must shift from extraversion to introversion. The focus on consciousness must be tempered by an awareness of the unconscious. Our interests must shift from the physical and material to the spiritual, philosophical, and intuitive. A balance among all facets of the personality must replace the previous one-sidedness of the personality (that is, the focus on consciousness).

Thus, at middle age we naturally begin the process of realizing or actualizing the self. If we are successful in integrating the unconscious with the conscious, we are in a position to attain a new level of positive psychological health, a condition Jung called individuation.

Individuation

individuation A condition of psychological health resulting from the integration of all conscious and unconscious facets of the personality.

Simply stated, **individuation** involves becoming an individual, fulfilling one's capacities, and developing one's self. The tendency toward individuation is innate and inevitable, but it will be helped or hindered by environmental forces, such as one's educational and economic opportunities and the nature of the parent-child relationship.

To strive for individuation, middle-aged persons must abandon the behaviors and values that guided the first half of life and confront their unconscious, bringing it into conscious awareness and accepting what it tells them to do. They must listen to their dreams and follow their fantasies, exercising creative imagination through writing, painting, or some other form of expression. They must let themselves be guided, not by the rational thinking that drove them before, but by the spontaneous flow of the unconscious. Only in that way can the true self be revealed.

Jung cautioned that admitting unconscious forces into conscious awareness does not mean being dominated by them. The unconscious forces must be assimilated and balanced with the conscious. At this time of life, no single aspect of personality should dominate. An emotionally healthy middle-aged person is no longer ruled by either consciousness or unconsciousness, by a specific attitude or function, or by any of the archetypes. All are brought into harmonious balance when individuation is achieved.

Of particular importance in the midlife process of individuation is the shift in the nature of the archetypes. The first change involves dethroning the persona.

Although we must continue to play various social roles if we are to function in the real world and get along with different kinds of people, we must recognize that our public personality may not represent our true nature. Further, we must come to accept the genuine self that the persona has been covering.

Next, we become aware of the destructive forces of the shadow and acknowledge the dark side of our nature with its primitive impulses, such as selfishness. We do not submit to them or allow them to dominate us but simply accept their existence. In the first half of life, we use the persona to shield this dark side from ourselves, wanting people to see only our good qualities. But in concealing the forces of the shadow from others, we conceal them from ourselves. This must change as part of the process of learning to know ourselves. A greater awareness of both the destructive and the constructive aspects of the shadow will give the personality a deeper and fuller dimension, because the shadow's tendencies bring zest, spontaneity, and vitality to life.

Once again we see this central theme in Jung's individuation process—that we must bring each aspect of the personality into harmony with all other aspects. Awareness of only the good side of our nature produces a one-sided development of the personality. As with other opposing components of personality, both sides of this dimension must be expressed before we can achieve individuation.

We must also come to terms with our psychological bisexuality. A man must be able to express his anima archetype or traditionally feminine traits such as tenderness, and a woman must come to express her animus or traditionally masculine traits such as assertiveness. Jung believed that this recognition of the characteristics of the other sex was the most difficult step in the individuation process because it represents the greatest change in our self-image. Accepting the emotional qualities of both sexes opens new sources of creativity and serves as the final release from parental influences.

Once the psyche's structures are individuated and acknowledged, the next developmental stage can occur. Jung referred to this as transcendence, an innate tendency toward unity or wholeness in the personality, uniting all the opposing aspects within the psyche. Environmental factors, such as an unsatisfactory marriage or frustrating work, can inhibit the process of transcendence and prevent the full achievement of the self.

Questions About Human Nature

Jung's image of human nature is quite different from Freud's. Jung did not hold such a deterministic view, but he did agree that personality may be partly determined by childhood experiences and by the archetypes. However, there is room in Jung's system for free will and spontaneity, the latter arising from the shadow archetype. (See Figure 3.2.)

On the nature-nurture issue, Jung took a mixed position. The drive toward individuation and transcendence is innate, but it can be aided or thwarted by learning and experience. The ultimate and necessary goal of life is the realization of the self. Although it is rarely achieved, we are continually motivated to strive for it.

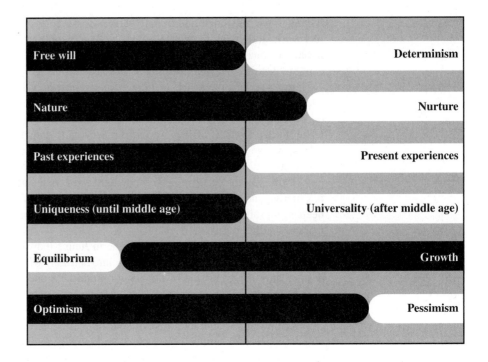

Jung's image of human nature

Jung disagreed with Freud on the importance of childhood experiences. Jung thought they were influential but did not completely shape our personality by age 5. We are affected more by our experiences in middle age and by our hopes and expectations for the future.

Each individual is unique, but only during the first half of life. When some progress toward individuation is made in middle age, we develop what Jung designated as a universal kind of personality in which no single aspect is dominant. Thus, uniqueness disappears, and we can no longer be described as one or another particular psychological type.

Jung presented a more positive, hopeful image of human nature than Freud did, and his optimism is apparent in his view of personality development. We are motivated to grow and develop, to improve and extend our selves. Progress does not stop in childhood, as Freud had assumed, but continues throughout life; we always have the hope of becoming better. Jung argued that the human species also continues to improve. Present generations represent a significant advance over our primitive ancestors.

Despite his basic optimism, Jung expressed concern about a danger he saw facing Western culture. He referred to this danger as a sickness of dissociation. By placing too great an emphasis on materialism, reason, and empirical science, we are in danger of failing to appreciate the forces of the unconscious. He argued that we must not abandon our trust in the archetypes that form our heritage. Thus, Jung's hopefulness about human nature was a watchful, warning kind.

Assessment in Jung's Theory

Jung's techniques for assessing the functioning of the psyche drew on science and the supernatural, resulting in both an objective and a mystical approach. He investigated a variety of cultures and eras and recorded their symbols, myths, religions, and rituals. He formed his personality theory on the basis of his patients' fantasies and dreams (as well as his own), and his explorations of ancient languages, alchemy, and astrology. Yet the work that first brought Jung to the attention of psychologists in the United States involved empirical and physiological assessments. His techniques were an unorthodox blend of opposites, which is not surprising for a theory based on a principle of opposition.

His sessions with patients were unusual, even chaotic. His patients did not lie on a couch. "I don't want to put the patient to bed," he remarked. Usually Jung and the patient sat in comfortable chairs facing each other, although sometimes Jung faced a window so he could look out at the lake near his house. Occasionally he took patients aboard his sailboat. And sometimes he could be rude. When one patient appeared at the appointed time, he said, "Oh no. I can't stand the sight of another one. Just go home and cure yourself today" (quoted in Brome, 1981, pp. 177, 185).

Jung believed that his patients' fantasies were real to them and he accepted them at face value. When Marie-Louise von Franz (1915–1998), who later became a lifelong disciple, first met Jung, he told her about a patient who lived on the moon. She replied that surely Jung meant the patient *acted* as though she lived on the moon. Jung said no, the woman truly did live on the moon. Von Franz decided that "either [Jung] was crazy or I was" (quoted in obituary for Marie-Louise von Franz, *New York Times,* March 23, 1998).

Three basic techniques Jung used to evaluate personality were the word association test, symptom analysis, and dream analysis. A widely used self-report personality test, the Myers-Briggs Type Indicator, was developed to assess Jung's psychological types.

Word Association

word-association test A projective technique in which a person responds to a stimulus word with whatever word comes to mind.

The **word-association test**, in which a subject responds to a stimulus word with whatever word comes immediately to mind, has become a standard laboratory and clinical tool in psychology. In the early 1900s, Jung used the technique with a list of 100 words he believed were capable of eliciting emotions (see Table 3.3). Jung measured the time it took for a patient to respond to each word. He also measured physiological reactions to determine the emotional effects of the stimulus words.

Jung used word association to uncover complexes in his patients. A variety of factors indicated the presence of a complex; these factors include physiological

TABLE 3.3   *Normal and neurotic responses to Jung's word-association test*

Stimulus word	Normal response	Neurotic response
Blue	Pretty	Color
Tree	Green	Nature
Bread	Good	To eat
Lamp	Bright	To burn
Rich	Beautiful	Money—I don't know
To sin	Much	This idea is totally alien to me; I do not acknowledge it
Needle	To prick	To sew
To swim	Healthy	Water

SOURCE: C. G. Jung. "The Association Method," 1909. In *The Collected Works of C.G. Jung,* Volume 2 (Princeton, NJ: Princeton University Press, 1973), pp. 442–444.

responses, delays in responding, making the same response to different words, slips of the tongue, stammering, responding with more than one word, making up words, or failing to respond.

Symptom Analysis

symptom analysis
Similar to catharsis, the symptom analysis technique focuses on the symptoms reported by the patient and attempts to interpret the patient's free associations to those symptoms.

Symptom analysis focuses on the symptoms reported by the patient and is based on the person's free associations to those symptoms. It is similar to Freud's cathartic method. Between the patient's associations to the symptoms and the analyst's interpretation of them, the symptoms will often be relieved or disappear.

Dream Analysis

dream analysis A technique involving the interpretation of dreams to uncover unconscious conflicts.

Jung agreed with Freud that dreams are the "royal road" into the unconscious. Jung's approach to **dream analysis** differed from Freud's in that Jung was concerned with more than the causes of dreams, and he believed that dreams were more than unconscious wishes. First, dreams are prospective; that is, they help us prepare for experiences and events we anticipate will occur. Second, dreams are compensatory; they help bring about a balance between opposites in the psyche by compensating for the overdevelopment of any one psychic structure.

Instead of interpreting each dream separately, as Freud did, Jung worked with a series of dreams reported by a patient over a period of time. In that way Jung believed he could discover recurring themes, issues, and problems that persisted in the patient's unconscious.

Jung also used amplification to analyze dreams. In Freudian free association, the patient begins with one element in a dream and develops a chain of associations from it by reporting related memories and events. Jung focused on the original dream element and asked the patient to make repeated associations and responses to it until he detected a theme. He did not try to distinguish between manifest and latent dream content.

TABLE 3.4   *Sample items from the Myers-Briggs Type Indicator*

Which answer comes closer to telling how you usually feel or act?

1. When you go somewhere for the day, would you rather
   (a) plan what you will do and when, or
   (b) just go?
2. Do you tend to have
   (a) deep friendships with a very few people, or
   (b) broad friendships with many different people?
3. When you have a special job to do, do you like to
   (a) organize it carefully before you start, or
   (b) find out what is necessary as you go along?
4. When something new starts to be the fashion, are you usually
   (a) one of the first to try it, or
   (b) not much interested?
5. When the truth would not be polite, are you more likely to tell
   (a) a polite lie, or
   (b) the impolite truth?

SOURCE: Consulting Psychologists Press. Copyright © 1976, 1977 by Isabel Briggs Myers. Copyright 1943, 1944, 1957 by Katharine C. Briggs and Isabel Briggs Myers.

The Myers-Briggs Type Indicator

Myers-Briggs Type Indicator (MBTI) An assessment test based on Jung's psychological types and the attitudes of introversion and extraversion.

An assessment instrument related to Jung's personality theory is the **Myers-Briggs Type Indicator (MBTI)**, developed in the 1920s by Katharine Cook Briggs and Isabel Briggs Myers (Briggs & Myers, 1943, 1976). Katharine Briggs was interested in the similarities and differences among personalities and pursued an independent study of the topic. In 1923 she read Jung's book *Psychological Types* and found that her view of personality was similar to Jung's. Without research grant support, university affiliation, or graduate students to assist her, she and her daughter Isabel developed a popular self-report inventory (see Table 3.4).

The MBTI is widely used for research and applied purposes, especially employee selection and counseling. The test has become the primary method for conducting research on Jung's eight psychological types and the attitudes of introversion and extraversion.

In 1975, Isabel Briggs Myers and Mary McCaulley established the Center for Applications of Psychological Type for MBTI training and research. In 1979, the Association for Psychological Type was founded. Two journals publish research reports on applications of the test. The MBTI is considered the most visible practical outgrowth of Jung's work on the human personality.

Research in Jung's Theory

life-history reconstruction Jung's type of case study that involves examining a person's past experiences to identify developmental patterns that may explain present neuroses.

Jung, like Freud, used the case study method, which Jung called **life-history reconstruction**. It involved an extensive recollection of a person's past experiences in which Jung sought to identify the developmental patterns he believed led to the present neurotic condition. The criticisms of Freud's data and research methods (see Chapter 2) also apply to Jung's work. Jung's data did not rely on objective observation and were not gathered in a controlled and systematic fashion. Further, the situations in which they were obtained—the clinical interviews—were not amenable to duplication, verification, or quantification.

Like Freud, Jung did not keep verbatim records of his patients' comments, nor did he attempt to verify the accuracy of their reports. Jung's case studies involved (as did Freud's) a small and unrepresentative sample of people, making it difficult to generalize to the population at large.

Jung's analysis of the data was subjective and unreliable. We do not know how he analyzed his data because he never explained his procedures. It is obvious that the data were subjected to some of the most unusual interpretations of any personality theory. We noted earlier that Jung studied a variety of cultures and disciplines. It was on this basis, and that of his own dreams and fantasies, that he interpreted the information gathered from his patients.

His work has been criticized for dealing with conclusions he may have slanted to fit his theory. It is also alleged that his visions, which he claimed to have experienced during his midlife confrontation with his unconscious, can be traced to published sources he had read (Noll, 1993, 1994).

As was the case with Freud's propositions, many of Jung's observations cannot be submitted to experimental test. Jung himself was indifferent to this criticism and commented that anyone who "wishes to know about the human mind will learn nothing, or almost nothing, from experimental psychology" (quoted in Ellenberger, 1970, p. 694).

Psychological Types

Despite Jung's negative view of experimental psychology, researchers have been able to submit aspects of Jungian theory to experimental test, with results that uphold some of Jung's propositions. Most of the supportive research uses the MBTI and focuses on the attitudes of introversion and extraversion. However, not all research supports the delineation of the psychological types (Cowan, 1989; DeVito, 1985; McCrae & Costa, 1989).

A study of college students found that their job interests were closely related to Jungian attitudes and psychological types (Stricker & Ross, 1962). Introverts showed strong interests in occupations that did not involve personal interaction, such as technical and scientific work. Extraverts were more interested in jobs that offered high levels of social interaction, such as sales and public relations.

Another study using the MBTI revealed that different psychological types are drawn to different professions (Hanewitz, 1978). The test was administered to a large sample of police officers, schoolteachers, and social work and dental school students. The teachers and social work students showed high levels of intuiting and feeling. Police officers and dental school students, who deal with people in a different way from teachers and social workers, scored high in extraversion and in sensing and thinking.

A study in which the MBTI was given to 130 female college students and 89 male college students found that those who scored high in intuiting were inclined toward more creative vocational interests. Those who scored high in sensing favored more conventional vocational interests (Apostal, 1991).

Jungian personality types appear to differ in cognitive or mental functioning. Researchers concluded that persons categorized as introverted thinking types have better memories for neutral or impersonal stimuli, such as numbers. Persons labeled extraverted feeling types have better memories for human stimuli with emotional overtones, such as facial expressions (Carlson & Levy, 1973).

Also, introverted thinking and extraverted feeling types differ in their ability to recall significant personal experiences (Carlson, 1980). When subjects were asked to recall their most vivid experiences involving such emotions as joy, anger, and shame, extraverted feeling types most often reported memories involving other people. Introverted thinking types more frequently recalled events that occurred when they were alone. In addition, extraverted feeling types recalled highly emotional details, whereas introverted thinking types remembered more emotionally neutral and actual experiences.

Persons classified as introverts or extraverts on the MBTI were compared on the quality of their classroom discussion in undergraduate psychology courses (Carskadon, 1978). Extraverts contributed little to the discussion, but introverts made frequent, thoughtful contributions. Students high in intuiting on the MBTI made the best classroom contributions, whereas those high in sensing made the poorest contributions.

Research on the origins of introversion and extraversion point to both genetic and environmental influences. Studies of twins provide evidence of an inherited component to the two attitudes (Wilson, 1977). Significant differences have been found among the parents of introverts and extraverts. Parents of introverts were described as rejecting and cold; parents of extraverts were more accepting and loving (Siegelman, 1988).

Dreams

In research on dreams to study the occurrence of the archetypes, subjects were asked to recall their most recent dream, their most vivid dream, and their earliest dream (Cann & Donderi, 1986). For approximately three weeks, they were asked to record the dreams of the previous night as soon as they awakened each morning. Subjects were also given the MBTI and another personality test.

The results showed that introverts were more likely than extraverts to recall everyday dreams, those that bore no relation to archetypes. Intuiting types recalled more archetypal dreams than did sensing types. Persons who scored high in neuroticism recalled fewer archetypal dreams than those who scored low in neuroticism. The researchers concluded that these findings agreed with predictions made on the basis of Jung's personality theory.

midlife crisis

The Midlife Crisis in Women

We noted that the onset of middle age, around age 40, was a time of crisis for Jung and many of his patients. Jung, and others who have studied this so-called midlife crisis, initially viewed it as a phenomenon more likely to affect men than women. More recently, however, the idea that women undergo a similar crisis has been recognized.

A survey of 88 women in their 50s, who had been studied periodically since their senior year in college, asked them to describe the most difficult period in their lives since graduation. A variety of ratings made of stability and adjustment (such as concern about impulses and potential and the search for an identity) revealed that the early 40s were the time of greatest conflict (Helson, 1992).

Other research demonstrated that many women in midlife undergo an intense period of self-evaluation, reviewing their lives and judging their relative success or failure. One study found that the midlife transition was less difficult for women who had actively pursued careers than for women who had focused solely on marriage and family. Many subjects in the latter group concluded that their marriage had been a partial or complete failure. Their regret over their choice led them to consider drastic changes. The career women felt significantly less need to make major changes at midlife (Levinson, 1996).

Research involving two samples of college-educated women confirmed these findings. Both subject groups graduated from college in the 1960s when the feminist movement was opening many new career paths. The women were studied initially as students and later when they were in their late 30s or early 40s. The majority of the women experienced a period of life reevaluation around age 40, as Jung had predicted. Approximately two-thirds made major life changes between the ages of 37 and 43 as a direct result of their self-evaluation. When asked at age 37 if they would opt again for the same life choices they had made when younger, 34 percent in the sample from an affluent private college and 61 percent in the sample from a large state university said they would not. If they could do it all over again, these women said they would pursue educational and career opportunities instead of family goals.

A sense of dissatisfaction at midlife motivated many women to change, but not all were able to return to school to enhance their skills or find a job that made full use of their abilities. Those women who were able to effect satisfactory life changes by age 43 reported significantly greater feelings of general well being than those women who were unable to make such changes. The changed group experienced an increased sense of personal identity and an enlarged view of their own capabilities. Thus, regret about their earlier choices led to positive changes in midlife (Stewart & Ostrove, 1998; Stewart & Vandewater, 1999).

Another longitudinal study followed women for 20 years after they graduated from college in the late 1950s. The results showed that the personalities of the women at midlife, based on ratings by independent judges, could be divided into three levels or prototypes: conflicted, traditional, and individuated. The lowest level, the conflicted prototype, was characterized by personal conflicts, psychological problems, poor relationships with others, anxiety, hostility, and rigidity. The women at this level were considered to be psychologically immature.

The second level, the traditional prototype, was characterized by devotion to others, feelings of guilt, an emphasis on fulfilling duties and obligations at the expense of their own self-development and self-expression, and a concern for societal standards and with receiving the approval of others. They were also described as competent adults and good citizens who focused on marriage rather than career but lacking a high degree of psychological maturity and self-understanding.

The third level, the individuated prototype, appears to correspond to Jung's concept of individuation, the ideal outcome of the midlife personality crisis. Women at this level were described as high in autonomy, creativity, responsiveness and closeness to others, self-actualization, individual achievement orientation, empathy, tolerance, ego resilience, and intellectual and cultural sophistication. In other words, they had reached the highest level of psychological maturity, a finding that supports Jung's view of individuation as the supreme state of psychological health and self-development (John, Pals, & Westenberg, 1998).

A Final Commentary

Jung's complex and unusual approach to the human personality has had considerable impact on a broad range of disciplines, notably psychiatry, cultural history, sociology, economics, political science, philosophy, and religion. Recognized by the intellectual community at large, Jung received honorary degrees from Harvard and Oxford universities and has been acknowledged as a powerful influence on the work of many scholars.

Jung made several important and lasting contributions to psychology. The word-association test is a standard projective technique and inspired the development of the Rorschach inkblot test and so-called lie-detection techniques. The concepts of psychological complexes and of introverted versus extraverted personalities are widely accepted in psychology today. The personality scales that measure introversion and extraversion are standard diagnostic and selection devices. Even today, important research is being done on the introversion-extraversion personality dimensions (see Chapter 10).

In the following chapters we see evidence of Jung's influence on the work of other theorists. Jung's notion of individuation, or self-actualization, anticipated the work of Abraham Maslow and other personality theorists. Jung was the first to emphasize the role of the future in determining behavior, an idea adopted by Alfred Adler. Portions of Henry Murray's theory can also be traced to Jung's ideas. Maslow, Erik Erikson, and Raymond Cattell embraced Jung's suggestion that middle age is a time of crucial personality change. The idea of a midlife crisis is now seen by many as a necessary stage of personality development and has been supported by considerable research.

Despite the significance of these formulations, the bulk of Jung's theory was not received enthusiastically by psychologists. One reason concerns the difficulty of understanding Jungian concepts. Sigmund Freud, Alfred Adler, Erich Fromm, and others wrote in a clear style that allows their books to be easily read and understood. Jung did not write for the general public. Reading his work can be frustrating, so beset are his books by inconsistencies and contradictions. Jung once said, "I can formulate my thoughts only as they break out of me. It is like a geyser. Those who come after me will have to put them in order" (quoted in Jaffé, 1971, p. 8). A contemporary Jungian scholar described one of Jung's major books as only partly intelligible.

"The connection between one thought and the next is not clear and . . . there are many internal contradictions" (Noll, 1994, p. 109). This criticism can be applied to many of Jung's writings. They are difficult to comprehend and lack internal consistency and systematization.

Jung's embrace of the occult and the supernatural is probably the source of most of the criticism directed at his theory. Evidence from mythology and religion is not in favor in an era when reason and science are considered the best approaches to knowledge and understanding. Critics charge that Jung accepted as scientific evidence the mythical and mystical occurrences his patients reported.

Paradoxically, the same mystical and religious content of Jung's theory may have been responsible for the burst of growth, vitality, and public acceptance enjoyed by Jungian psychology in the 1960s and 1970s. Several books about Jung and his analytical psychology were published during that time, and many people, particularly college students, found his ideas congenial with their interests in Eastern religions and existentialism and with a growing disaffection with materialism.

A surge of interest occurred in the late 1980s and 1990s. In an interview in the *APA Monitor*, a well-known Jungian analyst claimed Jung was "far better known today than he was 20 years ago" (Singer, quoted in DeAngelis, 1994, p. 41). One reason for this attention was the popular television series featuring the mythologist Joseph Campbell, who described the impact on modern life of the collective unconscious and the archetypes (see *The Power of Myth*, Campbell & Moyers, 1988). Another reason for Jung's contemporary relevance was a 1992 best-selling book, *Women Who Run with the Wolves*, by Clarissa P. Estes, a Jungian analyst. Estes identified the so-called wild-woman archetype, which she said derived from Jung's work.

Formal training in Jungian analysis is available in New York, San Francisco, Los Angeles, and several other American cities. There are also Jungian training institutes in a number of European countries. The Society of Analytical Psychology publishes the Jungian *Journal of Analytical Psychology*.

Chapter Summary

Jung broadened Freud's definition of libido, redefining it as a more generalized dynamic force. Jung argued that personality is shaped by the future as well as the past, and he placed greater emphasis on the unconscious. Jung used the term *libido* in two ways: a diffuse, generalized life energy and a narrower energy that fuels the psyche. The amount of energy invested in an idea or feeling is called a value. Psychic energy operates in accordance with the principles of opposites, equivalence, and entropy. The principle of opposites states that every aspect of the psyche has its opposite and that this opposition generates psychic energy. The principle of equivalence states that energy is never lost to the personality but is shifted from one part to another. The principle of entropy states that there is a tendency toward equilibrium in the personality.

The ego is the center of consciousness and is concerned with perceiving, thinking, feeling, and remembering. Part of our conscious perception is determined by the attitudes of introversion and extraversion, in which libido is channeled internally or externally. The psychological functions include thinking, feeling, sensing, and intuiting. Thinking and feeling are rational functions; sensing and intuiting are irrational. Only one attitude and function can be dominant. The psychological types are formed by combinations of the attitudes and functions.

The personal unconscious is a reservoir of material that was once conscious but has been forgotten or suppressed. Complexes, which may be conscious or unconscious, are patterns of emotions, memories, perceptions, and wishes centering on common themes. The collective unconscious is a storehouse of the experiences of humankind transmitted to each individual. Archetypes are recurring themes that express these experiences. The most powerful archetypes are the persona, anima, animus, shadow, and self.

Psychic birth occurs at puberty, when the psyche assumes a definite content. Preparatory activities mark the time from adolescence through young adulthood. In middle age, when success has been achieved, the personality changes. Psychic energy must be rechanneled into the inner world of the unconscious, and the attitude must shift from extraversion to introversion. Individuation (the realization of one's capabilities) can occur only in middle age, when people must confront the unconscious and abandon the behaviors and values that guided the first half of life. Transcendence involves the unification of the personality.

Jung's image of human nature was more optimistic and less deterministic than Freud's view. Jung believed that part of personality is innate, and part is learned. The ultimate life goal is individuation. Childhood experiences are important, but personality is more affected by midlife experiences and hopes for the future. Personality is unique in the first half of life but not in the second.

Jung's methods of assessment include the investigation of symbols, myths, and rituals in ancient cultures; the word-association test, used to uncover complexes; symptom analysis, in which patients free-associate to their symptoms; and dream analysis. The Myers-Briggs Type Indicator is an assessment instrument deriving from Jung's approach.

Jung's case study method, called life-history reconstruction, did not rely on objective observation, was not systematic and controlled, and was not amenable to duplication and verification.

Research has supported Jung's ideas on attitudes and functions, but broader aspects of his theory have resisted attempts at scientific validation. His work has had considerable influence in several fields. Widely accepted Jungian ideas include the word-association test, complexes, introversion-extraversion, self-actualization, and the midlife crisis.

Review Questions

1. Discuss three major points of difference between Jung's theory of analytical psychology and Freud's theory of psychoanalysis.
2. Describe the principles of opposites, equivalence, and entropy. How do they relate to the concept of psychic energy?

3. How does the principle of opposites apply to the attitudes and functions? Explain how the eight psychological types derive from the attitudes and functions.

4. What is the relationship between the ego and the personal unconscious? How does the personal unconscious differ from the collective unconscious?

5. What is a complex? How can a complex be helpful?

6. Distinguish between the persona archetype and the self archetype.

7. What are the similarities between Jung's concept of the shadow archetype and Freud's concept of the id?

8. Discuss Jung's ideas on the development of personality throughout the life span, especially the periods of adolescence and middle age.

9. What is individuation? How must our archetypes change if we are to achieve individuation?

10. How does Jung's image of human nature differ from Freud's?

11. What is the purpose of the word-association test? What are the purposes of dreams?

12. Describe research on the introverted and extraverted personality types. Describe research on the midlife crisis in women.

Suggested Readings

Clarke, J. J. (1992). *In search of Jung: Historical and philosophical enquiries.* London: Routledge. Assesses the impact of Jung's work on contemporary American culture.

Ellenberger, H. F. (1970). *The discovery of the unconscious: The history and evolution of dynamic psychiatry.* New York: Basic Books. Traces the study of the unconscious from primitive times to Freudian psychoanalysis and its derivatives. See Chapter 9, "Carl Gustav Jung and Analytical Psychology."

Freud/Jung letters. (1974). Princeton, NJ: Princeton University Press. Contains some 360 letters, dating from 1906 to 1913, that show the development and dissolution of the friendship between Sigmund Freud and Carl Jung. Edited by William McGuire.

Hannah, B. (1976). *Jung: His life and work.* New York: Putnam. A biographical memoir by a Jungian analyst who was a friend of Jung's for more than 30 years.

Iaccino, J. F. (1994). *Psychological reflections on cinematic terror: Jungian archetypes in horror films.* Westport, CT: Praeger. Uses Jungian archetypes to analyze recurrent themes in a wide range of significant horror movies, from classics to contemporary nightmare, alien, and vampire films.

Jung, C. G. (1961). *Memories, dreams, reflections.* New York: Vintage Books. Jung's recollections of his life, written at the age of 81.

Kerr, J. (1993). *A most dangerous method: The story of Jung, Freud, and Sabina Spielrein.* New York: Alfred A. Knopf. The story of a woman patient who became involved in a disastrous relationship with her analyst, Carl Jung.

Roazen, P. (1975). *Freud and his followers.* New York: Alfred A. Knopf. A lively, well-written account of Freud's life and of the men and women who became his disciples, some of whom later broke away to form their own schools of thought. See Part 6, "The 'Crown Prince': Carl Gustav Jung."

Schultz, D. (1990). *Intimate friends, dangerous rivals: The turbulent relationship between Freud and Jung.* Los Angeles: Jeremy Tarcher. Describes the personal and professional collaboration between Freud and Jung and the parallels and differences in their childhood, midlife crises, and relationships with women.

Stewart, A. J., & Ostrove, J. M. (1998). Women's personality in middle age: Gender, history, and midcourse corrections. *American Psychologist, 53,* 1185–1194. Focuses on the importance of the midlife period for women in terms of examining the past, defining an identity, and assessing one's confidence and power. Jung believed the middle years were a time of major personality change.

Tilander, A. (1991). Why did C. G. Jung write his autobiography? *Journal of Analytical Psychology, 36*(1), 111–124. Suggests that Jung chose to include in his autobiography the experiences that appeared to support his personality theory.

Whitmont, E. C., & Perera, S. B. (1989). *Dreams: A portal to the source.* London: Routledge & Kegan Paul. Provides a guide to the Jungian approach to understanding and interpreting dreams, which are seen as crucial to personality development.

> The goal of the human soul is conquest, perfection, security, superiority. Every child is faced with so many obstacles in life that no child ever grows up without striving for some form of significance.
>
> —Alfred Adler

F O U R

Alfred Adler

Alfred Adler

individual psychology
Adler's theory of
personality.

Alfred Adler fashioned an image of human nature that did not depict people as victimized by instincts and conflict and doomed by biological forces and childhood experiences. He called his approach **individual psychology** because it focused on the uniqueness of each person and denied the universality of biological motives and goals ascribed to us by Sigmund Freud.

In Adler's opinion, each individual is primarily a social being. Our personalities are shaped by our unique social environments and interactions, not by our efforts to satisfy biological needs. Although sex was of primary importance to Freud as a determining factor in personality, Adler minimized the role of sex in his system. To Adler, the conscious, not the unconscious, was at the core of personality. Rather than being driven by forces we cannot see and control, we are actively involved in creating our selves and directing our future.

With Adler and Freud we see two vastly different theories created by two men brought up in the same city in the same era and educated as physicians at the same university. There was only a 14-year difference in their ages. And as with Freud, aspects of Adler's childhood may have influenced his way of looking at human nature.

The Life of Adler (1870–1937)

Childhood and Adolescence

Adler's early childhood was marked by illness, an awareness of death, and jealousy of his older brother. He suffered from rickets (a vitamin D deficiency characterized by softening of the bones), which kept him from playing with other children. At the age of 3 his younger brother died in the bed next to his. At 4, Adler himself was close to death from pneumonia. When he heard the doctor tell his father, "Your boy is lost," he decided to become a doctor (Orgler, 1963, p. 16).

Pampered by his mother because of his sickness, the young Adler was dethroned at the age of 2 by the arrival of another baby. Biographers have suggested that Adler's mother may then have rejected him, but he was clearly his father's favorite. Therefore, his childhood relations with his parents were different from Freud's. (Freud was closer to his mother than to his father.) As an adult, Adler discarded the Freudian concept of the Oedipus complex because it was so foreign to his childhood experiences.

Adler was jealous of his older brother, who was vigorous and healthy and could engage in the physical activities and sports in which Alfred could not take part. "I remember sitting on a bench, bandaged up on account of rickets, with my healthy elder brother sitting opposite me. He could run, jump, and move about quite effortlessly, while for me, movement of any sort was a strain and an effort" (Adler quoted in Bottome, 1939, pp. 30–31).

Adler felt inferior to this brother and to other neighborhood children, who all seemed healthier and more athletic. As a result, he resolved to work hard to overcome his feelings of inferiority and to compensate for his physical limitations. Despite his small stature, clumsiness, and unattractiveness, the legacies of his illness, he forced himself to join in games and sports. Gradually he won his victory and achieved a sense of self-esteem and social acceptance. He developed a fondness for the company of other people and retained this sociability all his life. In his personality theory, Adler emphasized the importance of the peer group and suggested that childhood relationships with siblings and with children outside the family were much more significant than Freud believed.

In school (the same school Freud had attended) Adler was initially unhappy and was only a mediocre student. Believing the boy unfit for anything else, a teacher advised Adler's father to apprentice him to a shoemaker, a prospect Adler found frightening. He was particularly bad in mathematics, but he persisted and eventually rose from being a failing student to the top of his class.

In many ways, the story of Adler's childhood reads like a tragedy, but it is also a textbook example of his personality theory, of overcoming childhood weakness and inferiority to shape his destiny. The theorist who would give the world the notion of inferiority feelings spoke from the depths of his own childhood. "Those who are familiar with my life work will clearly see the accord existing between the facts of my childhood and the views I expressed" (quoted in Bottome, 1939, p. 9).

Adulthood

Fulfilling his childhood ambition, Adler studied medicine at the University of Vienna but graduated with no better than a mediocre academic record. He entered private practice as an ophthalmologist but soon shifted to general medicine. He was interested in incurable diseases but became so distressed at his helplessness to prevent death, particularly in younger patients, that he chose to specialize in neurology and psychiatry.

Adler's 9-year association with Freud began in 1902, when Freud invited Adler and three others to meet once a week at Freud's home to discuss psychoanalysis. Although their relationship never became close, Freud initially thought highly of Adler and praised his skill as a physician who was able to gain the trust of his patients. It is important to remember that Adler was never a student or disciple of Freud's and was not psychoanalyzed by him. One of Freud's colleagues charged that Adler did not have the ability to probe the unconscious mind and psychoanalyze people. It is interesting to speculate on whether this supposed lack led Adler to base his personality theory on the more easily accessible consciousness and to minimize the role of the unconscious.

By 1910, although Adler was president of the Vienna Psychoanalytical Society and co-editor of its journal, he was also an increasingly vocal critic of Freudian theory. He soon severed all connection with psychoanalysis and went on to develop his own approach to personality. Freud reacted angrily to Adler's defection. He belittled Adler's physical stature (Adler was five inches shorter than Freud) and called Adler loathsome, abnormal, driven mad by ambition, filled with venom and meanness, paranoid, intensely jealous, and sadistic. He described Adler's theory as worthless (Fiebert, 1997; Gay, 1988; Wittels, 1924).

Adler showed similar hostility toward Freud, calling him a swindler and denouncing psychoanalysis as filth (Roazen, 1975). Adler became irate whenever he was introduced or referred to as a student of Freud's. In his later years Adler appeared as embittered toward defectors from his own approach as Freud had toward those, like Adler, who deviated from psychoanalysis. Adler was known to "flare suddenly into heated anger when he felt his authority challenged" (Hoffman, 1994, p. 148).

In 1912, Adler founded the Society for Individual Psychology. He served in the Austrian army during World War I (1914–1918) and later organized government-sponsored child counseling clinics in Vienna. In his clinics, Adler introduced group training and guidance procedures, forerunners of modern group therapy techniques. In 1926, he made the first of several visits to the United States, where he taught and gave popular lecture tours.

He moved to the United States in 1929, settling in New York City, where he continued his work to develop and promote his individual psychology. A biographer noted that Adler's "personal traits of geniality, optimism, and warmth coupled with an intensely ambitious drive . . . soon catapulted him to American prominence as a psychological expert" (Hoffman, 1994, p. 160).

Adler's books and lectures brought him recognition on a national scale and he became America's first popular psychologist, a celebrity of the day. In 1937, while on an exhausting 56-lecture tour of Europe, Adler suffered a heart attack and died in Scotland.

Inferiority Feelings: The Source of Human Striving

inferiority feelings The normal condition of all people; the source of all human striving.

Adler believed that **inferiority feelings** are always present as a motivating force in behavior. "To be a human being means to feel oneself inferior," Adler wrote (1933/1939, p. 96). Because this condition is common to all of us, it is not a sign of weakness or abnormality.

compensation A motivation to overcome inferiority, to strive for higher levels of development.

Adler proposed that inferiority feelings are the source of all human striving. Individual growth results from **compensation**, from our attempts to overcome our real or imagined inferiorities. Throughout our lives, we are driven by the need to overcome this sense of inferiority and to strive for increasingly higher levels of development.

The process begins in infancy. Infants are small and helpless and are totally dependent on adults. Adler believed that the infant is aware of his or her parents' greater power and strength and of the hopelessness of trying to resist or challenge that power. As a result, the infant develops feelings of inferiority relative to the larger, stronger people around him or her.

Although this initial experience of inferiority applies to everyone in infancy, it is not genetically determined. Rather, it is a function of the environment, which is the same for all infants—an environment of helplessness and dependency on adults. Thus, inferiority feelings are inescapable, but more important, they are necessary because they provide the motivation to strive and grow.

The Inferiority Complex

Suppose a child does not grow and develop. What happens when the child is unable to compensate for his or her feelings of inferiority? An inability to overcome

Many people with physical disabilities strive to compensate for their weaknesses.

inferiority complex A condition that develops when a person is unable to compensate for normal inferiority feelings.

inferiority feelings intensifies them, leading to the development of an **inferiority complex**. People with an inferiority complex have a poor opinion of themselves and feel helpless and unable to cope with the demands of life. Adler found such a complex in the childhood of many adults who came to him for treatment.

An inferiority complex can arise from three sources in childhood: organic inferiority, spoiling, and neglect. The investigation of organic inferiority, Adler's first major research effort, was carried out while he was still associated with Freud, who approved of the notion. Adler concluded that defective parts or organs of the body shape personality through the person's efforts to compensate for the defect or weakness, just as Adler had compensated for rickets, the physical inferiority of his childhood years. For instance, a child who is physically weak might focus on that weakness and work to develop superior athletic ability.

History records many examples of such compensation: In ancient times the Greek statesman Demosthenes overcame a stutter to become a great orator. The sickly Theodore Roosevelt, 26th president of the United States, became a model of physical fitness as an adult. Efforts to overcome organic inferiority can result in striking artistic, athletic, and social accomplishments, but if these efforts fail, they can lead to an inferiority complex.

Adler's work is another example of a conception of personality developed along intuitive lines, drawn from the theorist's personal experience, and later confirmed by data from patients. Adler's office in Vienna was near an amusement park, and his patients included circus performers and gymnasts. They possessed extraordinary physical skills that, in many cases, were developed as a result of hard work to overcome childhood disabilities.

Spoiling or pampering a child can also bring about an inferiority complex. Spoiled children are the center of attention in the home. Their every need or whim is satisfied, and little is denied them. Under the circumstances, these children naturally develop the idea that they are the most important persons in any situation and that other people should always defer to them. The first experience at school, where these children are no longer the focus of attention, comes as a shock for which they are unprepared. Spoiled children have little social feeling and are impatient with others. They have never learned to wait for what they want, nor have they learned to overcome difficulties or adjust to others' needs. When confronted with obstacles to gratification, spoiled children come to believe that they must have some personal deficiency that is thwarting them; hence, an inferiority complex develops.

It is easy to understand how neglected, unwanted, and rejected children can develop an inferiority complex. Their infancy and childhood are characterized by a lack of love and security because their parents are indifferent or hostile. As a result, these children develop feelings of worthlessness, or even anger, and view others with distrust.

The Superiority Complex

superiority complex A condition that develops when a person overcompensates for normal inferiority feelings.

Whatever the source of the complex, a person may tend to overcompensate and so develop what Adler called a **superiority complex**. This involves an exaggerated opinion of one's abilities and accomplishments. Such a person may feel inwardly self-satisfied and superior and show no need to demonstrate his or her superiority with accomplishments. Or the person may feel such a need and work to become extremely successful. In both cases, persons with a superiority complex are given to boasting, vanity, self-centeredness, and a tendency to denigrate others.

Striving for Superiority or Perfection

Inferiority feelings are the source of motivation and striving, but to what end? Are we motivated simply to be rid of inferiority feelings? Adler believed that we work for something more; however, his view of our ultimate goal in life changed over the years.

First he identified inferiority with a general feeling of weakness or of femininity, in recognition of the inferior standing of women in the society of his day. He spoke of compensation for this feeling as the masculine protest. The goal of the compensation was a will or a drive toward power in which aggression, a supposedly masculine characteristic, played a large part. Later he rejected the idea of equating inferiority feelings with femininity and developed a broader viewpoint in which we strive for superiority or perfection.

striving for superiority The urge toward perfection or completion that motivates each of us.

Adler described his notion of **striving for superiority** as the fundamental fact of life (Adler, 1930). Superiority is the ultimate goal toward which we strive. He did not mean superiority in the usual sense of the word, nor did the concept relate to the superiority complex. Striving for superiority is not an attempt to be better than anyone else, nor is it an arrogant or domineering tendency or an inflated opinion of our abilities and accomplishments. What Adler meant was a drive for perfection. The word *perfection* is derived from a Latin word meaning to complete or to finish. Thus, Adler suggested that we strive for superiority in an effort to perfect ourselves, to make ourselves complete or whole.

This innate goal, the drive toward wholeness or completion, is oriented toward the future. Whereas Freud proposed that human behavior is determined by the past (that is, by the instincts and by our childhood experiences), Adler saw human motivation in terms of expectations for the future. He argued that instincts and primal impulses were insufficient as explanatory principles. Only the ultimate goal of superiority or perfection could explain personality and behavior.

Fictional Finalism

Adler applied the term *finalism* to the idea that we have an ultimate goal, a final state of being, and a need to move toward it. The goals for which we strive, however, are potentialities, not actualities. In other words, we strive for ideals that exist in us subjectively. Adler believed that our goals are fictional or imagined ideals that cannot be tested against reality. We live our lives around ideals such as the belief that all people are created equal or that all people are basically good. Adler's life goal was to conquer death; his way of striving for that goal was to become a physician (Hoffman, 1994).

These beliefs influence the ways we perceive and interact with other people. For example, if we believe that behaving a certain way will bring us rewards in a heaven or an afterlife, we will try to act according to that belief. Belief in the existence of an afterlife is not based on objective reality, but it is real to the person who holds that view.

fictional finalism The idea that there is an imagined or potential goal that guides our behavior.

Adler formalized this concept as **fictional finalism**, the notion that fictional ideas guide our behavior as we strive toward a complete or whole state of being. We direct the course of our lives by many such fictions, but the most pervasive one is the ideal of perfection. He suggested that the best formulation of this ideal developed by human beings so far is the concept of God.

There are two additional points about striving for superiority. First, it increases rather than reduces tension. Unlike Freud, Adler did not believe that our sole motivation was to reduce tension. Striving for perfection requires great expenditures of energy and effort, a condition quite different from equilibrium or a tension-free state. Second, the striving for superiority is manifested both by the individual and by society. Most of us are social beings. We strive for superiority or perfection not only as individuals but also as members of a group. We try to achieve the perfection of our culture. In Adler's view, individuals and society are interrelated and interdependent. People must function constructively with others for the good of all.

Thus, to Adler, human beings perpetually strive for the fictional, ideal goal of perfection. How in our daily lives do we try to attain this goal? Adler answered this question with his concept of the style of life.

Style of Life

style of life A unique character structure or pattern of personal behaviors and characteristics by which each of us strives for perfection. Basic styles of life include the dominant, getting, avoiding, and socially useful types.

The ultimate goal for each of us is superiority or perfection, but we try to attain that goal through many different behavior patterns. Each of us expresses the striving differently. We develop a unique pattern of characteristics, behaviors, and habits, which Adler called a distinctive character, or **style of life**.

To understand how the style of life develops, we return to the concepts of inferiority feelings and compensation. Infants are afflicted with inferiority feelings that motivate them to compensate for helplessness and dependency. In these attempts at compensation, children acquire a set of behaviors. For example, the sickly child may strive to increase physical prowess by running or lifting weights. These behaviors become part of the style of life, a pattern of behaviors designed to compensate for an inferiority.

Everything we do is shaped and defined by our unique style of life. It determines which aspects of our environment we attend to or ignore and what attitudes we hold. The style of life is learned from social interactions that occur in the early years of life. Adler suggested that the style of life is so firmly crystallized by the age of 4 or 5 that it is difficult to change thereafter.

The style of life becomes the guiding framework for all later behaviors. As we noted, its nature depends on social interactions, especially the person's order of birth within the family and the nature of the parent-child relationship. Recall that one condition that can lead to an inferiority complex is neglect. Neglected children may feel inferior in coping with the demands of life and therefore may become distrustful and hostile toward others. As a result, their style of life may involve seeking revenge, resenting others' success, and taking whatever they feel is their due.

The Creative Power of the Self

creative power of the self The ability to create an appropriate style of life.

You may have spotted an apparent inconsistency between Adler's notion of style of life and our observation that his theory is less deterministic than Freud's. Adler said we are in control of our fate, not victims of it. But now we find that the style of life is determined by social relationships in the early years and subject to little change after that. This seems almost as deterministic as the Freudian view, which emphasized the importance of early childhood in the formation of the adult personality. However, Adler's theory is not as deterministic as it may seem at first. He resolved the dilemma by proposing a concept he described as the **creative power of the self**.

Adler believed that the individual creates the style of life. We create our *selves*, our *personality*, our *character;* these are all terms Adler used interchangeably with *style of life*. We are not passively shaped by childhood experiences. Those experiences are not as important as our conscious attitude toward them. Adler argued that neither heredity nor environment provides a complete explanation for personality development. Instead, the way we interpret these influences forms the basis for the creative construction of our attitude toward life.

Adler argued for the existence of individual free will that allows each of us to create an appropriate style of life from the abilities and experiences given us by both our genetic endowment and our social environment. Although unclear on specifics,

Adler insisted that our style of life is not determined for us; we are free to choose and create it ourselves. Once created, however, the style of life remains constant throughout life.

Dominant, Getting, Avoiding, and Socially Useful Styles

Adler described several universal problems and grouped them in three categories:

1. problems involving our behavior toward others,
2. problems of occupation, and
3. problems of love.

He proposed four basic styles of life for dealing with these problems:

1. the dominant type,
2. the getting type,
3. the avoiding type, and
4. the socially useful type.

The first type displays a dominant or ruling attitude with little social awareness. Such a person behaves without regard for others. The more extreme of this type attack others and become sadists, delinquents, or sociopaths. The less virulent become alcoholics, drug addicts, or suicides; they believe they hurt others by attacking themselves.

The getting type (to Adler, the most common human type) expects to receive satisfaction from other people and so becomes dependent on them.

The avoiding type makes no attempt to face life's problems. By avoiding difficulties, the person avoids any possibility of failure.

These three types are not prepared to cope with the problems of everyday life. They are unable to cooperate with other people and the clash between their style of life and the real world results in abnormal behavior, which is manifested in neuroses and psychoses. They lack what Adler came to call *social interest*.

The socially useful type cooperates with others and acts in accordance with their needs. Such persons cope with problems within a well-developed framework of social interest.

Adler was generally opposed to rigidly classifying or typing people in this way, stating that he proposed these four styles of life solely for teaching purposes. He cautioned therapists to avoid the mistake of assigning people to mutually exclusive categories.

Social Interest

social interest Our innate potential to cooperate with other people to achieve personal and societal goals.

Adler believed that getting along with others is the first task we encounter in life. Our subsequent level of social adjustment, which is part of our style of life, influences our approach to all of life's problems. He proposed the concept of **social interest**, which he defined as the individual's innate potential to cooperate with other people to achieve personal and societal goals. Adler's term for this concept in the original German, *Gemeinschaftsgefuhl*, is best translated as "community feeling" (Stepansky, 1983, p. xiii). However, social interest has become the accepted term in English.

Although we are influenced more strongly by social than biological forces, in Adler's view, the potential for social interest is innate. In that limited sense, Adler's approach has a biological element. However, the extent to which our innate potential for social interest is realized depends on our early social experiences.

No one can avoid entirely other people or obligations toward them. From earliest times, people have congregated in families, tribes, and nations. Communities are indispensable to human beings for protection and survival. Thus, it has always been necessary for people to cooperate, to express their social interest. The individual must cooperate with and contribute to society to realize personal and communal goals.

The newborn is in a situation that requires cooperation, initially from the mother or primary caregiver, then from other family members and people at day care or school. Adler noted the importance of the mother as the first person with whom the baby comes in contact. Through her behavior toward the child, the mother can either foster social interest or thwart its development.

Adler believed the mother's role was vital in developing the child's social interest as well as other aspects of the personality. He wrote:

> This connection [between mother and child] is so intimate and far reaching that we are never able in later years to point to any characteristic as the effect of heredity. Every tendency which might be inherited has been adapted, trained, educated and made over again by the mother. Her skill or lack of skill will influence all the child's potentiality. (Adler quoted in Grey, 1998, p. 71)

The mother must teach the child cooperation, companionship, and courage. Only if children feel kinship with others can they act with courage in attempting to cope with life's demands. Children (and later, adults) who look upon others with suspicion and hostility will approach life with the same attitude. Those who have no feeling of social interest may become neurotics or even criminals. Adler noted that evils ranging from war to racial hatred to public drunkenness stemmed from a lack of community feeling.

It is interesting to note that early in his career, Adler suggested that people were driven by a lust for power and a need to dominate. He proposed this idea at the time he was struggling to establish his own point of view within the Freudian circle. After he broke with Freud and achieved recognition for his own work, he proposed that people are motivated more by social interest than by the needs for power and dominance.

When Adler was part of Freud's group, he was considered cantankerous and ambitious, quarreling over the priority of his ideas. But in later years he mellowed and his system also changed, from emphasizing power and dominance as motivating forces to stressing the more benign force of social or community interest.

Birth Order

birth order

One of Adler's most enduring contributions is the idea that order of birth is a major social influence in childhood, one from which we create our style of life. Even

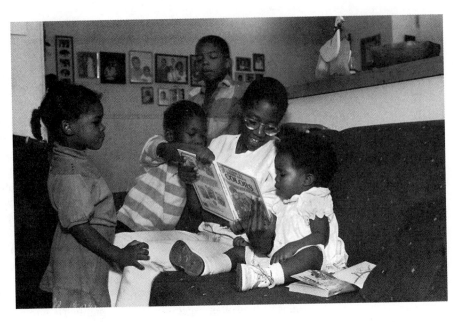

One's order of birth within the family—being older or younger than one's siblings—creates different conditions of childhood that can affect personality.

though siblings have the same parents and live in the same house, they do not have identical social environments. Being older or younger than one's siblings and being exposed to differing parental attitudes create different childhood conditions that help determine personality. Adler liked to amaze lecture audiences and dinner guests by guessing a person's order of birth on the basis of his or her behavior. He wrote about four situations: the first-born child, the second-born child, the youngest child, and the only child.

The First-Born Child

First-born children are, at least for a while, in a unique and enviable situation. Usually the parents are happy at the birth of the first child and devote considerable time and attention to the new baby. First-borns typically receive their parents' instant and undivided attention. As a result, first-borns have a happy, secure existence until the second-born child appears.

Then, no longer the focus of attention, no longer receiving constant love and care, first-borns are, in a sense, dethroned. The affection first-borns received during their reign must now be shared. They must often submit to the outrage of waiting until after the newborn's needs have been met, and they are admonished to be quiet so as not to disturb the new baby.

No one could expect first-borns to suffer this drastic displacement without putting up a fight. They will try to recapture their former position of power and privilege. The first-born's battle to regain supremacy in the family is lost from the beginning, however. Things will never be the same, no matter how hard the first-born tries.

For a time, first-borns may become stubborn, ill behaved, and destructive and may refuse to eat or go to bed. They are striking out in anger, but the parents will probably strike back, and their weapons are far more powerful. When first-borns are punished for their troublesome behavior, they may interpret the punishment as additional evidence of their fall and may come to hate the second child, who is, after all, the cause of the problem.

Adler believed all first-borns feel the shock of their changed status in the family, but those who have been excessively pampered feel a greater loss. Also, the extent of the loss depends on the first-born's age at the time the rival appears. In general, the older a first-born child is when the second child arrives, the less dethronement the first-born will experience. For example, an 8-year-old will be less upset by the birth of a sibling than will a 2-year-old.

Adler found that first-borns are often oriented toward the past, locked in nostalgia and pessimistic about the future. Having learned the advantages of power at one time, they remain concerned with it throughout life. They can exercise some power over younger siblings, but at the same time they are more subject to the power of their parents because more is expected of them.

First-borns take an unusual interest in maintaining order and authority. They become good organizers, conscientious and scrupulous about detail, authoritarian and conservative in attitude. Sigmund Freud was a first-born; Adler described him as a typical eldest son. First-borns may grow up to feel insecure and hostile toward others. Adler believed that neurotics, perverts, and criminals were often first-borns.

The Second-Born Child

Second-born children, the ones who caused such upheaval in the lives of first-borns, are also in a unique situation. They never experience the powerful position once occupied by the first-borns. Even if another child is brought into the family, second-borns do not suffer the sense of dethronement felt by the first-borns. Furthermore, by this time the parents have usually changed their child-rearing attitudes and practices. A second baby is not the novelty the first was; parents may be less concerned and anxious about their own behavior and may take a more relaxed approach to the second child.

From the beginning, second-borns have a pacesetter in the older sibling. The second child always has the example of the older child's behavior as a model, a threat, or a source of competition. Adler was a second-born child who had a lifelong competitive relationship with his older brother (whose name was Sigmund). Even when Adler became a famous analyst, he felt overshadowed by his brother.

> Alfred [Adler] always felt eclipsed by his "model brother" and resented his favored status in the family. . . . Even in middle age, he would feel moved to comment wearily that wealthy businessman Sigmund, "a good industrious fellow [who] was always ahead of me—is *still* ahead of me!" (Hoffman, 1994, p. 11)

Competition with the first-born serves to motivate the second-born, often stimulating a more rapid development than the first-born exhibited. Second-borns strive to catch up to and surpass the older sibling, a goal that spurs language and motor development. Second-borns usually begin to speak at an earlier age than first-borns. Not having experienced power, second-borns are not as concerned with it. They are more optimistic about the future and are likely to be competitive and ambitious, as Adler was.

Other outcomes may arise from the relationship between first-borns and second-borns. If, for example, the older sibling excels in sports or scholarship, the second-born may feel that he or she can never surpass the first-born and may give up trying. In this case, competitiveness would not become part of the second-born's style of life.

The Youngest Child

Youngest or last-born children never face the shock of dethronement by another child and often become the pet of the family, particularly if the siblings are more than a few years older. Driven by the need to surpass older siblings, youngest children often develop at a remarkably fast rate. Last-borns are often high achievers in whatever work they undertake as adults.

The opposite can occur if the youngest children are excessively pampered and come to believe they needn't learn to do anything for themselves. As they grow older, such children may retain the helplessness and dependency of childhood. Unaccustomed to striving and struggling, used to being cared for, these people find it difficult to adjust to adulthood.

The Only Child

Only children never lose the position of primacy and power they hold in the family; they remain the focus and center of attention. Spending more time in the company of adults than a child with siblings, only children often mature early and manifest adult behaviors and attitudes.

Only children are likely to experience difficulties when they find that in areas of life outside the home, such as school, they are not the center of attention. Only children have learned neither to share nor to compete. If their abilities do not bring them sufficient recognition and attention, they are likely to feel keenly disappointed.

With his ideas about order of birth, Adler was not proposing firm rules of childhood development. A child will not automatically acquire a particular kind of character based solely on his or her position in the family. What Adler was suggesting was the likelihood that certain styles of life will develop as a function of order of birth combined with one's early social interactions. The creative self in constructing the style of life uses both influences.

Questions About Human Nature

Adler's system provides a hopeful, flattering picture of human nature that is the antithesis of Freud's dreary view. (See Figure 4.1.) Certainly it is more satisfying to our sense of self-worth to consider ourselves capable of consciously shaping our development and destiny rather than being dominated by instinctual forces and childhood experiences over which we have no control.

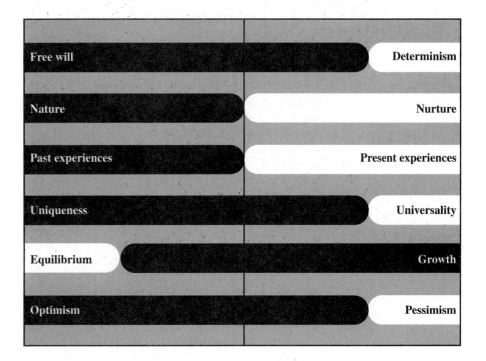

FIGURE 4.1   *Adler's image of human nature*

Adler's image is an optimistic one, simply that people are not driven by unconscious forces. We possess the free will to shape the social forces that influence us and to use them creatively to construct a unique style of life. This uniqueness is another aspect of Adler's flattering picture; Freud's system offered a depressing universality and sameness in human nature.

Although, in Adler's view, some aspects of human nature are innate—for example, the potential for social interest and striving for perfection—it is experience that determines how these inherited tendencies will be realized. Childhood influences are important, particularly order of birth and interactions with our parents, but we are not victims of childhood events. Instead, we use them to create our style of life.

Adler saw each person as striving to achieve perfection, and he viewed humanity in similar terms; he was optimistic about social progress. He was attracted to socialism and was involved in school guidance clinics and prison reform, expressing his belief in the creative power of the individual.

Assessment in Adler's Theory

Like Freud, Adler developed his theory by analyzing his patients; that is, by evaluating their verbalizations and behavior during therapy sessions. Adler's approach was more relaxed and informal than Freud's. Whereas Freud's patients lay on a couch while he sat behind them, Adler and his patients sat in comfortable chairs facing each other. The sessions were more like chats between friends than like the formal relationships maintained by Freud.

Adler also liked to use humor in his therapy, sometimes teasing his patients in a lighthearted, friendly way. He had a storehouse of jokes appropriate for various neuroses and believed that making a joke would sometimes lead a patient to "see how ridiculous his sickness is." When an adolescent patient told Adler he felt guilty when he masturbated, Adler replied: "You mean to say you masturbate and feel guilty? That is too much. One would be enough: either masturbate *or* feel guilty. But both is too much" (Hoffman, 1994, pp. 209, 273).

Adler assessed the personalities of his patients by observing everything about them: the way they walked and sat, their manner of shaking hands, even their choice of which chair to sit in. He suggested that the way we use our bodies indicates something of our style of life. Even the position in which we sleep is revealing. For example, according to Adler, restless sleepers and those who sleep flat on their back want to seem more important than they are. Sleeping on one's stomach shows a stubborn and negative personality. Curling in the fetal position shows that the person is fearful of interacting with others. Sleeping with the arms outstretched reveals a need to be nurtured and supported.

Adler's primary methods of assessment, which he referred to as the entrance gates to mental life, are order of birth (discussed above), early recollections, and dream analysis. In addition, contemporary psychologists have developed psychological assessment tests based on Adler's concept of social interest. Adler's purpose in assessing personality was to discover the patient's style of life and to determine whether it was the most appropriate one for that person.

Early Recollections

early recollections A personality assessment technique in which our earliest memories, whether of real events or fantasies, are assumed to reveal the primary interest of our life.

According to Adler, our personality is created during the first 4 or 5 years of life. Our **early recollections**, our memories from that period, indicate the style of life that continues to characterize us as adults. Adler found that it made little difference whether his clients' early recollections were of real events or were fantasies. In either case the primary interest of the person's life revolved around the remembered incidents.

Adler asked more than 100 physicians to describe their early memories. A majority of the recollections were concerned with illness or with a death in the family, which apparently led them to pursue a career in medicine, as was the case with Adler himself.

An early memory Adler recalled as an adult was that when he was 5 years old and had just started school, he was fearful because the path to school led through a cemetery (Adler, 1924/1963). He said he became terrified every time he walked to school, but he was also confused because other children seemed not to notice the cemetery. He was the only one who was afraid, and this experience heightened his sense of inferiority. One day Adler decided to put an end to his fears. He ran through the cemetery a dozen times, until he felt he had overcome his feelings.

Thereafter he was able to attend school without being frightened whenever he passed the cemetery.

Thirty years later Adler met a former schoolmate and, in the course of their conversation, asked if the old cemetery was still there. The man expressed surprise and told Adler there had never been a cemetery near the school. Adler was shocked; his recollection had been so vivid! He sought out other classmates and questioned them about the cemetery. They all told him the same thing: There had been no cemetery. Adler finally accepted that his memory of the incident was faulty. Nonetheless, it symbolized the fear and inferiority, and his efforts to overcome them, that characterized his style of life. That early recollection thus revealed an important and influential aspect of his personality.

Although Adler believed that each early memory should be interpreted within the context of the patient's style of life, he found commonalities among them. He suggested that memories involving danger or punishment indicated a tendency toward hostility. Those concerning the birth of a sibling showed a continued sense of dethronement. Memories that focused on one parent showed a preference for that parent. Recollections of improper behavior warned against any attempt to repeat the behavior.

dreams—analysis

Dream Analysis

Adler agreed with Freud about the value of dreams in understanding personality but disagreed on the way in which dreams should be interpreted. Adler did not believe that dreams fulfill wishes or reveal hidden conflicts. Rather, dreams involve our feelings about a current problem and what we intend to do about it.

One of Adler's own dreams illustrates this point. Before his first visit to the United States, Adler felt anxious and worried, concerned about how he and his theory about personality would be received. The night before he was scheduled to cross the Atlantic Ocean by ship, he dreamed that the ship, with him aboard, capsized and sank.

> All of Adler's worldly possessions were on it and were destroyed by the raging waves. Hurled into the ocean, Adler was forced to swim for his life. Alone he thrashed and struggled through the choppy waters. But through the force of will and determination, he finally reached land in safety. (Hoffman, 1994, p. 151)

This dream revealed Adler's fear about what he would face in the United States and his intention to land safely—in other words, to achieve success for himself and for his theory of individual psychology.

In the fantasies of our dreams (both night dreams and daydreams), we believe we can surmount the most difficult obstacle or simplify the most complex problem. Thus, dreams are oriented toward the present and future, not toward conflicts from the past.

Dreams should never be interpreted without knowledge of the person and his or her situation. The dream is a manifestation of a person's style of life and so is unique to the individual. Adler did find common interpretations for some dreams, however. Many people reported dreams involving falling or flying. Freud interpreted such dreams in sexual terms (see pages 68–69).

TABLE 4.1   *Dream events and their latent meanings*

Dream event	Adlerian interpretation
Being paralyzed	Facing insoluble problems
School exams	Being unprepared for situations
Wearing the wrong clothes	Being disturbed by one's faults
Sexual themes	Retreating from sex or inadequate information about sex
Rage	An angry or hostile life-style
Death	Unresolved issues about the dead person

SOURCE: Adapted from Grey, 1997, p. 93.

According to Adler, a dream of falling indicates that the person's emotional view involves a demotion or loss, such as the fear of losing self-esteem or prestige. A flying dream indicates a sense of striving upward, an ambitious style of life in which the person desires to be above or better than others. Dreams that combine flying and falling involve a fear of being too ambitious and thus failing. A dream of being chased suggests a feeling of weakness in relation to other people. Dreaming one is naked indicates a fear of giving oneself away. Additional Adlerian dream interpretations are shown in Table 4.1.

Measures of Social Interest

Adler had no desire to use psychological tests to assess personality. He argued that tests create artificial situations that provide ambiguous results. Instead of relying on tests, Adler thought therapists should develop their intuition. He did, however, support tests of memory and intelligence; it was tests of personality he criticized.

Psychologists have developed tests to measure Adler's concept of social interest. The Social Interest Scale (SIS) consists of pairs of adjectives (Crandall, 1981). Subjects choose the word in each pair that best describes an attribute they would like to possess. Words such as *helpful*, *sympathetic*, and *considerate* are thought to indicate one's degree of social interest. The Social Interest Index (SII) is a self-report inventory in which subjects judge the degree to which statements represent themselves or their personal characteristics (Greever, Tseng, & Friedland, 1973). The items, such as *I don't mind helping out friends,* were selected to reflect Adler's ideas and to indicate a person's ability to accept and cooperate with others. The Sulliman Scale of Social Interest has also been shown to be a promising measure of social interest (Mozdzierz, Greenblatt, & Murphy, 1988; Sulliman, 1973).

The Basic Adlerian Scales for Interpersonal Success—Version A (BASIS-A) is a 65-item self-report inventory that measures level of social interest and five lifestyle types: belonging, going along, wanting recognition, being cautious, and taking charge (Miranda, Frevert, & Kern, 1998).

Research in Adler's Theory

Adler's primary research method was the case study. Unfortunately, little of Adler's data survived. He did not publish case histories except for two fragments: one written by a patient, the other written by a patient's physician. Adler did not know the patients involved, but he analyzed their personalities by examining their writings.

Adler's data and research method are subject to the same criticisms we discussed for Freud and Jung. His observations cannot be repeated and duplicated, nor were they conducted in a controlled and systematic fashion. Adler did not attempt to verify the accuracy of his patients' reports or explain the procedures he used to analyze the data, and he had no interest in applying the experimental method.

Although most of Adler's propositions have resisted attempts at scientific validation, several topics have been the subject of research. These include dreams, early recollections, neglect in childhood, social interest, and order of birth.

Dreams.   Adler's belief that dreams help us solve current problems was investigated by exposing subjects to situations in which the failure to solve a puzzle was considered a threat to the personality. The subjects were then allowed to sleep. Some were permitted to dream; they were awakened only during non-rapid-eye-movement (NREM) sleep. Others were awakened during rapid-eye-movement (REM) sleep so that they could not dream. Subjects who dreamed recalled significantly more of the uncompleted puzzle than those who did not dream. The researchers concluded that dreaming enabled subjects to deal effectively with the current threatening situation—that is, the failure to solve the puzzle (Grieser, Greenberg, & Harrison, 1972).

In another study, the dreams of two groups of subjects were reported (Breger, Hunter, & Lane, 1971). One group consisted of college students who were anticipating a stressful psychotherapy session. The other group consisted of patients about to undergo major surgery. For both groups, the recalled dreams focused on their conscious worries, fears, and hopes. Both types of subjects dreamed about the current problems they were facing.

Early recollections.   Research has shown that the early memories of persons diagnosed as anxiety neurotics were concerned with fear; early memories of depressed persons centered on abandonment; and early memories of persons with psychosomatic complaints involved illness (Jackson & Sechrest, 1962). Early memories of alcoholics contained threatening events, as well as situations in which they were controlled by external circumstances rather than by their own decisions. The early memories of a control group of nonalcoholics showed neither of these themes (Hafner, Fakouri, & Labrentz, 1982).

Early recollections of adult criminals dealt with disturbing or aggressive interactions with other people. They contained more unpleasant events than the early recollections of a control group (Hankoff, 1987). The early memories of adolescent delinquents involved breaking rules, having difficulty forming social relationships, perceiving parents as untrustworthy and more likely to hurt than to help, and being unable to cope with life on their own. These themes were not present in the early memories of a control group (Davidow & Bruhn, 1990).

Recollections of psychiatric patients considered dangerous to themselves and to others showed more aggressive early memories than did recollections of nondangerous psychiatric patients. The recollections of the dangerous patients revealed that

Our earliest memories of childhood help reveal our style of life.

they felt vulnerable and powerless and saw others as hostile and abusive (Tobey & Bruhn, 1992).

Research using objective scoring systems for early recollections has shown that these memories tend to be subjective recreations rather than events that actually occurred, much like Adler's memory of the cemetery (Statton & Wilborn, 1991).

One study reported that when subjects were asked to make up early recollections that might have happened to someone else, the themes were similar to those revealed by their own recollections (Buchanan, Kern, & Bell-Dumas, 1991). This study also provided research support for Adler's contention that early recollections reveal one's current style of life and therefore can be used as a therapeutic device. (Table 4.2 summarizes possible themes of early recollections.)

During the 1980s and 1990s there has been a substantial increase in the amount of research on early recollections, most of it supportive of Adler's point of view (Watkins, 1992).

Neglect in childhood.   Adler suggested that children who were neglected or rejected by their parents developed feelings of worthlessness. A study of 714 adults hospitalized for depression found that the patients rated their parents as having been hostile, detached, and rejecting (Crook, Raskin, & Eliot, 1981). Interviews with siblings, relatives, and friends of the patients confirmed that the parents had indeed behaved in hostile and neglectful ways.

T A B L E   4 . 2   *Early recollections and style of life themes*

Recollection	Possible theme
First school memory	Attitudes toward achievement, mastery, and independence
First punishment memory	Attitude toward authority figures
First sibling memory	Evidence of sibling rivalry
First family memory	Functioning in social situations
Clearest memory of mother	Attitudes toward women
Clearest memory of father	Attitudes toward men
Memory of person you admire	Basis for role models
Happiest memory	Basis for how your strongest needs are best gratified

SOURCE: Adapted from A. R. Bruhn (1992). "The Early Memories Procedure." *Journal of Personality Assessment, 58*(1), 1–15.

In another study, parents of 8-year-old children completed a questionnaire to assess their child-rearing behaviors and their level of satisfaction with their children (Lefkowitz & Tesiny, 1984). Ten years later the children, then age 18, were given the depression scale of the Minnesota Multiphasic Personality Inventory (MMPI). Subjects whose test scores showed they were more depressed had been neglected in childhood by their parents. Those whose parents had not been indifferent or unloving scored lower on the depression scale.

Social interest.   Research using the SIS showed that persons higher in social interest reported less stress, depression, anxiety, and hostility than persons lower in social interest. High social interest scorers also scored higher on tests assessing cooperation with others, empathy, responsibility, and popularity than low social interest scorers (Crandall, 1980, 1981, 1984; Watkins, 1994; Watkins & St. John, 1994).

Studies with the SII showed that women who scored high in social interest were significantly higher in self-actualization, a characteristic of the healthy personality described by Abraham Maslow (see Chapter 11). Other research found that social interest was higher in women than in men and that it increased with age for both sexes (Greever, Tseng, & Friedland, 1973).

A study of 313 Latino men and women currently living in the United States found that subjects who were bicultural (well adjusted to living in both cultures) scored higher on social interest measures than subjects who were primarily acculturated to either the Latino lifestyle or the U.S. lifestyle alone (Miranda, Frevert, & Kern, 1998).

Order of birth.   Considerable research has been conducted on the effects of order of birth. Although not all of the studies have produced results supportive of Adler's ideas, he deserves credit for being the first personality theorist to suggest that order of birth influences behavior and personality. New directions for birth order research should include effects of blended families, stepchildren, adopted children, and children of gay parents.

According to Adler, first-borns are concerned with power and authority. One way for first-borns to gain power and authority as adults is through achievement in their work. If Adler was correct, then first-borns should score high on measures of achievement, an idea that has received much research support. In many areas, from college attendance to high-level management, first-borns have been found to be over-represented relative to their proportion of the population. More first-borns than later-borns become eminent, and they tend to attain greater intellectual achievement in academic settings and greater power and prestige in their careers (Breland, 1974; Schachter, 1963).

First-borns consistently scored higher than later-borns on a variety of achievement tests in English, mathematics, verbal skills, and verbal reasoning (Eysenck & Cookson, 1969; Kellaghan & MacNamara, 1972; Paulhus & Shaffer, 1981).

In general, evidence suggests that first-borns might be more intelligent than later-borns. The IQ scores of 400,000 European men were analyzed with respect to birth order (Belmont & Marolla, 1973). The results showed that first-borns had higher IQ scores than second-borns, second-borns had higher scores than third-borns, and so on. These findings were confirmed for men and women in several countries (Zajonc, Markus, & Markus, 1979). A possible explanation for the apparent higher intelligence of first-borns relates not to genetic differences but to the first-born's exclusive exposure to adults. Consequently, first-borns may have a more stimulating intellectual environment than later-borns.

Vocational preferences for first-borns were found to include teaching, medicine, science, and management (Bryant, 1987). First-borns' scores on an occupational interest inventory indicated a preference for socially oriented careers requiring good interpersonal skills (White, Campbell, Stewart, Davies, & Pilkington, 1997).

First-borns tend to be more dependent on other people and more suggestible. They are anxious in stressful situations and have a higher need for social relationships (Schachter, 1963, 1964). These findings could be predicted from Adler's theory. He noted that first-borns are made anxious when dethroned by a sibling, and they attempt to regain their position by eventually conforming to their parents' expectations. Accordingly, first-borns depend more than later-borns on the standards of others, including their parents, to guide their behavior and form the basis of their self-evaluations (Newman, Higgins, & Vookles, 1992).

Other research found that first-borns scored lower than later-borns on tests of depression and anxiety and higher on self-esteem (Gates, Lineberger, Crockett, & Hubbard, 1988). First-borns may also be more extraverted and conscientious than later-borns (Sulloway, 1995).

First-born girls were found to be more obedient and socially responsible than later-borns and tended to feel closer to their parents (Sutton-Smith & Rosenberg, 1970). Although first-borns are outgoing and enjoy socializing, research shows they are not especially popular. First-born boys were more likely than later-borns to exhibit behavior disorders and to be considered aggressive by their teachers (Lahey, Hammer, Crumrine, & Forehand, 1980).

Evidence also suggests that first-borns and only-borns exhibit some of the characteristics of the Type A personality, a pattern associated with heart disease (Ivancevich, Matteson, & Gamble, 1987).

Less research has been conducted on second-born children. There appears to be no support for Adler's contention that they are more competitive and ambitious than their siblings. One study found second-borns to be lower in self-esteem than first-borns or last-borns, particularly if the age difference between them and the other siblings was approximately 2 years (Kidwell, 1982).

Adler predicted that last-born children, if excessively pampered, would have adjustment problems as adults. One frequently suggested reason for alcoholism is that some people cannot cope with the demands of everyday life. If so, then according to Adler's theory, more last-borns than early-borns would be likely to become alcoholics. This prediction has been supported by many studies dealing with alcoholism and order of birth (Barry & Blane, 1977). Other research on last-borns shows that last-born children are more popular than first-borns or second-borns (Miller & Maruyama, 1976).

To Adler, only-born adults are overly concerned with being the center of attention, as they were in childhood. He also considered only-borns to be more selfish than children reared with siblings. Research has not consistently supported this contention. One study found that only-borns demonstrated more cooperative behaviors than first-borns or last-borns (Falbo, 1978). Another study found that only-borns were more self-centered and less popular than were children with siblings (Jiao, Ji, & Jing, 1986). An analysis of 115 studies of only-borns reported higher levels of achievement and intelligence than, and comparable social and emotional adjustment with, people who have siblings (Falbo & Polit, 1986). Later research (Mellor, 1990) confirmed those results and found that only children had higher levels of initiative, aspiration, industriousness, and self-esteem.

A Final Commentary

Adler's influence within psychology has been substantial. In later chapters we see examples of his ideas in the work of other personality theorists. These contributions make Adler's personality theory one of the most enduring. He was ahead of his time, and his cognitive and social emphases are more compatible with trends in psychology today than with the psychology of his own day. Abraham Maslow wrote: "Alfred Adler becomes more and more correct year by year. . . . As the facts come in, they give stronger and stronger support to his image of man" (Maslow, 1970a, p. 13).

Adler's emphasis on social forces in personality can be seen in the theories of Karen Horney and Erich Fromm. His focus on the whole person and the unity of personality is reflected in the work of Gordon Allport. The creative power of the individual in shaping his or her style of life, and the insistence that future goals are more important than past events, influenced the work of Abraham Maslow. A contemporary social-learning theorist, Julian Rotter, wrote that he "was and continues to be impressed by Adler's insights into human nature" (Rotter, 1982, pp. 1–2).

Adler's ideas also reached into Freudian psychoanalysis. It was Adler who proposed the aggressive drive more than 12 years before Freud included aggression with sex as primary motivating forces. The neo-Freudian ego psychologists, who focus more on conscious and rational processes and less on the unconscious, follow Adler's lead.

Adler disputed Freud's views on women, arguing that there was no biological basis, such as penis envy, for women's alleged sense of inferiority. Such a notion, Adler charged, was a myth invented by men to maintain their alleged sense of superiority. He acknowledged that women may feel inferior but believed that was attributable to social conditioning and sex-role stereotyping. He also believed in the idea of equality for the sexes and supported the women's emancipation movements of the day.

Specific Adlerian concepts of lasting importance to psychology include the early work on organic inferiority, which has influenced the study of psychosomatic disorders; the inferiority complex; compensation; and order of birth. Adler is also considered a forerunner of social psychology and group therapy.

Although his ideas have been widely accepted, Adler's public recognition declined after his death in 1937, and he has received relatively little subsequent praise or credit for his contributions. Many concepts have been borrowed from his theory without acknowledgment. A typical instance of this lack of recognition can be found in Sigmund Freud's obituary in the *Times* newspaper of London, which named Freud as the originator of the term *inferiority complex*. When Carl Jung died, the *New York Times* said *he* had coined the term. Neither newspaper mentioned Adler, the originator of the concept. However, Adler did receive one unique honor: a British composer named a string quartet for him.

As influential as Adler's work has been, it does have its critics. Freud charged that Adler's psychology was oversimplified and would therefore appeal to many people because it eliminated the complicated nature of the unconscious, had no difficult concepts, and ignored the problems of sex. Freud remarked that it could take two years or more to learn about his psychoanalysis, but "Adler's ideas and technique can be easily learned in two weeks, because with Adler there is so little to know" (quoted in Sterba, 1982, p. 156).

It is true that Adler's theory seems simpler than Freud's or Jung's, but that was Adler's intention. He wrote that it had taken him 40 years to make his psychology simple. One point that reinforces the charge of oversimplification is that his books are easy to read because he wrote for the general public and because some of them were compiled from his popular lectures. (See Figure 4.2.) A related charge is that Adler's concepts appear to rely heavily on commonsense observations from everyday life. A book reviewer in the *New York Times* noted: "Although [Adler] is one of the most eminent psychologists in the world, when he writes about psychology there is no other who can equal him in simplicity and non-technicality of language" (quoted in Hoffman, 1994, p. 276).

Critics allege that Adler was inconsistent and unsystematic in his thinking and that his theory contains gaps and unanswered questions. Are inferiority feelings the only problem we face in life? Do all people strive primarily for perfection? Can we become reconciled to a degree of inferiority and no longer attempt to compensate for it? These and other questions that have been posed cannot all be answered adequately by Adler's system; most theorists, however, leave us with unanswered questions.

FIGURE 4.2   *Adler's books achieved considerable popularity in the United States and spawned the genre of self-help books.* SOURCE: *Edward Hoffman,* The Drive for Self: Alfred Adler and the Founding of *Individual Psychology, Addison-Wesley, 1994.*

Some psychologists dispute Adler's position on the issue of determinism versus free will. Early in his career, Adler did not oppose the notion of determinism. It was broadly accepted in science at the time, and it characterized Freud's psychoanalytic theory. Later Adler felt the need to grant more autonomy to the self, and his final formulation rejected determinism. His doctrine of the creative self states that before age 5 we fashion a style of life from material provided by our heredity and environment. However, it is not clear how a child is able to make such momentous decisions. We know that Adler favored free will and opposed the idea that we are victims of innate forces and childhood events. That position is clear, but the specifics of forming the style of life are not.

Adler's followers claim that individual psychology remains popular among psychologists, psychiatrists, social workers, and educators. *Individual Psychology: The*

Journal of Adlerian Theory, Research and Practice is published quarterly by the North American Society of Adlerian Psychology. Other Adlerian journals are published in Germany, Italy, and France. Adlerian training institutes have been established in New York, Chicago, and other cities. Adlerian counseling techniques have been developed by Rudolph Dreikurs and others, and this work has influenced new generations of Adlerian clinicians in what Dreikurs calls family education centers. Dreikurs's work on child-rearing practices applies Adler's views to contemporary problems not only in child development, but also in the treatment of the family as a whole.

Chapter Summary

Alfred Adler's individual psychology differs from Freudian psychoanalysis in its focus on the uniqueness of the individual, on consciousness, and on social rather than biological forces. It minimizes the role of sex.

Inferiority feelings are the source of all human striving, which results from our attempts to compensate for these feelings. Inferiority feelings are universal and are determined by the infant's helplessness and dependency on adults. An inferiority complex (that is, an inability to solve life's problems) results from being unable to compensate for inferiority feelings. An inferiority complex can originate in childhood through organic inferiority, spoiling, or neglect. A superiority complex (an exaggerated opinion of one's abilities and accomplishments) results from overcompensation.

Our ultimate goal is superiority or perfection; that is, making the personality whole or complete. Fictional finalism refers to fictional ideas, such as perfection, that guide our behavior. Style of life refers to unique patterns of characteristics and behaviors by which we strive for perfection. The creative power of the self refers to our ability to create our selves from the materials provided by our heredity and environment. Four basic styles of life are the dominant or ruling type, the getting type, the avoiding type, and the socially useful type. Social interest is innate but the extent to which it is realized depends on early social experiences.

Order of birth is a major social influence in childhood from which one's style of life is created. First-borns are oriented toward the past, pessimistic about the future, and concerned with maintaining order and authority. Second-borns compete with first-borns and are apt to be ambitious. Last-borns, spurred by the need to surpass older siblings, may become high achievers. Only children may mature early but are apt to face a shock in school when they are no longer the center of attention.

Adler's image of human nature is more hopeful than is Freud's. In Adler's view, people are unique, and they possess free will and the ability to shape their own development. Although childhood experiences are important, we are not victims of them.

Adler's methods of assessment are order of birth, early recollections, and dream analysis. Research has provided support for Adler's views on the following: dreams, early memories, and childhood neglect; his belief that social interest is related to emotional well-being; the idea that first-borns are high achievers, dependent on others, suggestible, and anxious under stress; and the notion that last-borns are more likely to become alcoholics.

Adler's emphasis on social factors in personality, the unity of personality, the creative power of the self, the importance of goals, and cognitive factors has influenced many personality theorists.

Review Questions

1. In Alfred Adler's theory of individual psychology, what is the difference between inferiority feelings and the inferiority complex? How does each develop?

2. According to Adler, we are motivated by a tendency to strive for superiority or perfection. How does this idea compare with Freud's views on human motivation?

3. Distinguish between the concepts of striving for superiority and the superiority complex.

4. Describe the concept of fictional finalism. How does fictional finalism relate to the concept of striving for superiority?

5. How does the self develop? Do people play an active or a passive role in the development of the self?

6. Describe the four basic styles of life.

7. Discuss some parental behaviors that may foster a child's development of social interest. Which basic style of life is identified with social interest?

8. Describe the personality characteristics proposed by Adler that may develop in first-born, second-born, and youngest children as a result of their order of birth within the family.

9. Describe recent research on the personality of first-born and only-born children. Do the results support Adler's predictions?

10. How does Adler's image of human nature differ from Freud's?

11. What is the importance of early recollections in personality assessment? Give an example of how one of Adler's recollections revealed an aspect of his personality.

12. What is the purpose of dreams? Does contemporary research on sleep and dreaming support Adler's views?

Suggested Readings

Adler, A. (1930). Individual psychology. In C. Murchison (Ed.). *Psychologies of 1930* (pp. 395–405). Worcester, MA: Clark University Press. Offers a clear exposition of the basic principles of Adler's individual psychology.

Ansbacher, H. L. (1990). Alfred Adler's influence on the three leading cofounders of humanistic psychology.

Journal of Humanistic Psychology, 30(4), 45–53. Traces Adler's influence, in person and through his writings, on the development of the humanistic psychology movement in the United States, notably through his contact with Abraham Maslow (Chapter 11) and Carl Rogers (Chapter 12).

Ansbacher, R. R. (1997). Alfred Adler, the man, seen by a student and friend. *Individual Psychology, 53,* 270–274. Using Adler's technique of early recollections, the author describes and evaluates her memories of Adler's lectures and therapy sessions in New York and Vienna.

Ellenberger, H. F. (1970). *The discovery of the unconscious: The history and evolution of dynamic psychiatry.* New York: Basic Books. Traces the study of the unconscious from primitive times to Freudian psychoanalysis and its derivatives. See Chapter 8, "Alfred Adler and Individual Psychology."

Fiebert, M. S. (1997). In and out of Freud's shadow: A chronology of Adler's relationship with Freud. *Individual Psychology, 53,* 241–269. Reviews the 7-year correspondence between Adler and Freud showing the changes in their personal and professional relationships and their acrimonious breakup.

Grey, L. (1998). *Alfred Adler, the forgotten prophet: A vision for the 21st century.* Westport, CT: Praeger. A contemporary biography and assessment of the continuing influence of Adler's ideas.

Hoffman, E. (1994). *The drive for self: Alfred Adler and the founding of individual psychology.* Reading, MA: Addison-Wesley. Discusses Adler's contributions to personality theory, psychoanalysis, and popular psychology. Recounts events in Adler's life as the basis for familiar concepts such as inferiority complex, overcompensation, and lifestyle.

Orgler, H. (1963). *Alfred Adler, the man and his work: Triumph over the inferiority complex.* New York: New American Library. Provides an overview of Adler's life and an introduction to his ideas on personality. Discusses applications of individual psychology to child counseling and education.

Stepansky, P. E. (1983). *In Freud's shadow: Adler in context.* New York: Analytic Press. Discusses Adler's early status as a Freudian disciple and shows the relationship between his ideas on psychotherapy and his training in clinical medicine.

Sulloway, F. J. (1996). *Born to rebel: Birth order, family dynamics, and creative lives.* New York: Pantheon. Analyzes revolutions in social, scientific, and political thought, dating back to the 16th century, to demonstrate the crucial influence of birth order on personality development. Suggests that birth-order effects transcend gender, social class, race, national origin, and time.

> The basic evil is invariably a lack of genuine warmth and affection.
>
> —Karen Horney

F I V E

Karen Horney

Karen Danielsen Horney was another defector from the orthodox Freudian point of view. Although never a disciple or colleague of Freud's, Horney was trained in the official psychoanalytic doctrine. But she did not remain long in the Freudian camp.

Horney began her divergence from Freud's position by disputing his psychological portrayal of women. An early feminist, she argued that psychoanalysis focused more on men's development than on women's. To counter Freud's contention that women are driven by penis envy, Horney said that men are envious of women for their ability to give birth. "I know just as many men with womb envy as women with penis envy," she said (quoted in Cherry & Cherry, 1973, p. 75).

She began her career by insisting that her work was an extension of Freud's. In a letter she wrote, "I do not want to found a new school but build on the foundations Freud has laid" (quoted in Quinn, 1987, p. 318). By the time Horney completed her theory, her criticisms of Freud were so broad that she *had* founded a new school. Hers was a new approach to psychoanalysis that had little in common with Freud's views.

Horney's theory was influenced by her gender and her personal experiences, as well as by social and cultural forces that differed greatly from those that had influenced Freud. Horney formulated her theory in the United States, a radically different culture from Freud's Vienna. By the 1930s and 1940s, major changes had occurred in popular attitudes about sex and the roles of men and women. These changes were taking place in Europe, too, but they were considerably more pronounced in the United States.

Horney found that her American patients were so unlike her previous German patients, both in their neuroses and in their normal personalities, that she believed only the different social forces to which they had been exposed could account for the variation. Personality, she argued, cannot depend wholly on biological forces, as Freud proposed. If it did, we would not see such major differences from one culture to another.

Thus, Horney, like Alfred Adler, placed a greater emphasis than Freud did on social relationships as significant factors in personality formation. She argued that sex is not the governing factor in personality, as Freud had claimed, and she questioned his concepts of the Oedipus complex, the libido, and the three-part structure of personality. To Horney, people are motivated not by sexual or aggressive forces but by the needs for security and love. We shall see that this view reflected her personal experience.

The Life of Horney (1885–1952)

A Search for Love

Karen Horney

Karen Danielsen was born in a village near Hamburg, Germany. She was the second-born child, and from an early age she envied her older brother, Berndt. He was attractive and charming, the adored first-born, but she was smarter and more vivacious. She confided to her diary, "It was always my pride that in school I was better than Berndt, that there were more amusing stories about me than about him" (Horney,

1980, p. 252). She also envied him because he was a boy, and girls were considered inferior. "I know that as a child I wanted for a long time to be a boy, that I envied Berndt because he could stand near a tree and pee" (Horney, 1980, p. 252).

A stronger influence was her father. At the time she was born, he was a 50-year-old ship's captain of Norwegian background. Her mother was 33 and of a vastly different temperament. Whereas the father was religious, domineering, imperious, morose, and silent, the mother was attractive, spirited, and freethinking. Horney's father spent long periods away at sea, but when he was home, the opposing natures of the parents led to frequent arguments. Karen's mother made no secret of her wish to see her husband dead. She told Karen that she had married not out of love but out of fear of becoming a spinster.

We can see roots of Horney's personality theory in her childhood experiences. For most of her childhood and adolescence, she doubted that her parents wanted her. She believed they loved Berndt more than they loved her. At age 16, Horney wrote in her diary, "Why is everything beautiful on earth given to me, only not the highest thing, not love! I have a heart so needing love" (Horney, 1980, p. 30). Although Horney desperately wanted her father's love and attention, he intimidated her. She recalled his frightening eyes and stern, demanding manner, and she felt belittled and rejected because he made disparaging comments about her appearance and intelligence. "It must be grand to have a father one can love and esteem," she wrote (Horney, 1980, p. 21).

As a way of retaining her mother's affection, she acted the part of the adoring daughter, and until the age of 8 was a model child, clinging and compliant. Despite her efforts, she did not believe she was getting sufficient love and security. Her self-sacrifice and good behavior were not working, so she changed tactics and became ambitious and rebellious. Horney decided that if she could not have love and security, she would take revenge for her feelings of unattractiveness and inadequacy. "If I couldn't be beautiful, I decided I would be smart" (Horney quoted in Rubins, 1978, p. 14).

As an adult she came to realize how much hostility she had developed as a child. Her personality theory describes how a lack of love in childhood fosters anxiety and hostility, thus providing another example of a theory developed initially in personal and intuitive terms. A biographer concluded, "In all her psychoanalytic writings—Karen Horney was struggling to make sense of herself and to obtain relief from her own difficulties" (Paris, 1994, p. xxii).

At 14 she developed an adolescent crush on a male teacher and filled her diary with paragraphs about him. She continued to have such infatuations, searching desperately for love, confused and unhappy as many adolescents are. At 17 she awakened to the reality of sex, established a school newspaper for "super virgins," and roamed streets frequented by prostitutes. The following year she met a man she described as her first real love, but the relationship lasted only two days. Another man came into her life, prompting 76 pages of soul-searching in her diary. Horney decided that being in love eliminated, at least temporarily, her anxiety and insecurity; it offered an escape (Sayers, 1991).

Although Horney's quest for love and security was often thwarted, her search for a career was straightforward and successful. She decided at the age of 12, after being treated kindly by a physician, that she would become a doctor. Despite the medical establishment's discrimination against women and her father's strong opposition, she worked hard in high school to prepare herself for medical studies. In 1906 she entered the University of Freiburg medical school, only six years after the first woman had, reluctantly, been admitted.

Marriage and Career

During her time at medical school Horney met two men; she fell in love with one and married the other. Oskar Horney was studying for a Ph.D. in political science and after their marriage became a successful businessman. Karen Horney excelled in her medical studies and received her degree from the University of Berlin in 1913.

The early years of marriage were a time of personal distress. She gave birth to three daughters but felt overwhelming unhappiness and oppression. She complained of crying spells, stomach pains, chronic fatigue, compulsive behaviors, frigidity, and a longing for sleep, even death. In her diary she noted, "I considered the possibility of suicide yesterday. Absolute inability for self-control. Strong emotion against Oskar. Inability to work" (quoted in Paris, 1994, p. 58). The marriage ended in 1927, after 17 years.

During and after her marriage, Horney had a number of love affairs. Her husband also had affairs, and the two had agreed to conduct an open marriage, carrying out their extramarital relationships with discretion. Among the circle of upper-middle-class intellectuals of which they were a part, such arrangements were not unusual. When Karen Horney realized that these attachments were not helping to alleviate her depression and other emotional problems, she decided to undergo psychoanalysis.

Psychoanalysis and Compensation

The therapist Horney consulted, Karl Abraham (a loyal follower of Freud), attributed her problems to her attraction to forceful men, which he explained was a residue of her childhood Oedipal longings for her powerful father. "Her readiness to abandon herself to such patriarchal figures, said Abraham, was betrayed by her leaving her handbag [in Freud's view, a symbolic representation of the female genitals] in his office on her very first visit" (Sayers, 1991, p. 88). The analysis was not a success. "Won't I ever be getting well, completely well? I am beginning to despair of it" (Horney quoted in Paris, 1994, p. 3). She decided Freudian psychoanalysis was of only minimal help to her, and she turned instead to self-analysis, a practice she continued throughout her life.

During her self-analysis Horney was strongly influenced by Adler's notion of compensation for feelings of inferiority. She was particularly sensitive to Adler's remark that physical unattractiveness was a cause of inferiority feelings. She concluded that she "needed to feel superior because of her lack of beauty and sense of inferiority as a woman, which led her to masculine protest" by excelling in a male-dominated domain, such as medicine was at the time (Paris, 1994, p. 63). Apparently she believed that by studying medicine, and by promiscuous sexual behavior, she was acting more like a man.

Horney's search for love and security continued when she emigrated to the United States. During this period her most intense love affair was with the analyst Erich Fromm (see Chapter 6). When it ended after 20 years, she was deeply hurt. Although Fromm was 15 years younger, she may have seen him as a father figure. "To her great embarrassment, she once introduced Fromm to an American audience as 'Doctor Freud' [suggesting] Fromm's loyalty to Freud and the way this differentiated his work from her own" (Burston, 1991, p. 23).

One event that led to the breakdown of the relationship was that Horney persuaded Fromm to analyze her daughter Marriane. Fromm helped the woman understand her conflicts with her mother, giving Marriane the confidence to confront Horney for the first time in her life (McLaughlin, 1998).

From 1932 to 1952, Horney served on the faculty of psychoanalytic institutes in Chicago and New York. She was a founder of the Association for the Advancement of Psychoanalysis and the American Institute for Psychoanalysis. For many years she was a popular lecturer, writer, and therapist.

The Childhood Need for Safety

Horney agreed with Freud, in principle, about the importance of the early years of childhood in shaping the adult personality. However, they differed on the specifics of how personality is formed. Horney believed that social forces in childhood, not biological forces, influence personality development. There are neither universal developmental stages nor inevitable childhood conflicts. Instead, the social relationship between the child and his or her parents is the key factor.

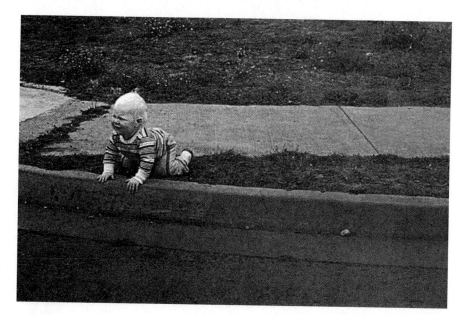

The state of helplessness in infancy can lead to neurotic behavior.

safety need A higher-level need for security and freedom from fear.

Horney thought childhood was dominated by the **safety need**, by which she meant the need for security and freedom from fear (Horney, 1937). Whether the infant experiences a feeling of security and an absence of fear is decisive in determining the normality of his or her personality development. A child's security depends entirely on how the parents treat the child. The major way parents weaken or prevent security is by displaying a lack of warmth and affection for the child. This was Horney's situation in childhood. (Her parents had provided little warmth and affection; it is interesting that as a parent, Horney behaved the same way toward her three daughters.) She believed children could withstand, without appreciable ill effect, much that is usually considered traumatic—such as abrupt weaning, occasional beatings, or even premature sexual experiences—as long as they feel wanted and loved and are, therefore, secure.

Parents can act in various ways to undermine their child's security and thereby induce hostility. These parental behaviors include obvious preference for a sibling, unfair punishment, erratic behavior, promises not kept, ridicule, humiliation, and isolation of the child from peers. Horney suggested that children know whether their parents' love is genuine. False demonstrations and insincere expressions of affection do not easily fool children. The child may feel the need to repress the hostility engendered by the parents' undermining behaviors for reasons of helplessness, fear of the parents, need for genuine love, or guilt feelings.

Horney placed great emphasis on the infant's helplessness. Unlike Adler, however, she did not believe all infants necessarily feel helpless, but when these feelings do arise, they can lead to neurotic behavior. Children's sense of helplessness depends on their parents' behavior. If children are excessively kept in a dependent state, then helplessness will be encouraged. The more helpless children feel, the less they dare to oppose or rebel against the parents. This means that the child will repress the resulting hostility, saying, in effect, "I have to repress my hostility because I need you."

Children can easily be made to feel fearful of their parents through punishment, physical abuse, or more subtle forms of intimidation. The more frightened children become, the more they will repress their hostility. In this instance the child is saying, "I must repress my hostility because I am afraid of you."

Paradoxically, love can be another reason for repressing hostility toward parents. In this case, parents tell their children how much they love them and how greatly they are sacrificing for them, but the warmth and affection the parents profess are not honest. Children recognize that these verbalizations and behaviors are poor substitutes for genuine love and security, but they are all that is available. The child must repress his or her hostility for fear of losing even these unsatisfactory expressions of love.

Guilt is yet another reason children repress hostility. They are often made to feel guilty about any hostility or rebelliousness. They may be made to feel unworthy, wicked, or sinful for expressing or even harboring resentments toward their parents. The more guilt the child feels, the more deeply repressed will be the hostility.

This repressed hostility, resulting from a variety of parental behaviors, undermines the childhood need for safety, and is manifested in the condition Horney called basic anxiety.

Basic Anxiety: The Foundation of Neurosis

anxiety

basic anxiety A
pervasive feeling of
loneliness and
helplessness; the
foundation of neurosis.

Horney defined **basic anxiety** as an "insidiously increasing, all-pervading feeling of being lonely and helpless in a hostile world" (Horney, 1937, p. 89). It is the foundation on which later neuroses develop, and it is inseparably tied to feelings of hostility.

Regardless of how we express basic anxiety, the feeling is similar for all of us. In Horney's words, we feel "small, insignificant, helpless, deserted, endangered, in a world that is out to abuse, cheat, attack, humiliate, betray" (1937, p. 92). In childhood we try to protect ourselves against basic anxiety in four ways: securing affection and love, being submissive, attaining power, or withdrawing.

By securing affection and love from other people, the person is saying, in effect, "If you love me, you will not hurt me." There are several ways by which we may gain affection, such as trying to do whatever the other person wants, trying to bribe others, or threatening others into providing the desired affection.

Being submissive as a means of self-protection involves complying with the wishes either of one particular person or of everyone in our social environment. Submissive persons avoid doing anything that might antagonize others. They dare not criticize or give offense. They must repress their personal desires and cannot defend against abuse for fear that such defensiveness will antagonize the abuser. Most people who act submissive believe they are unselfish and self-sacrificing. Such persons seem to be saying, "If I give in, I will not be hurt." This describes Horney's childhood behavior until the age of 8 or 9.

By attaining power over others, a person can compensate for helplessness and achieve security through success or through a sense of superiority. Such persons seem to believe that if they have power, no one will harm them. This could describe Horney's childhood once she decided to strive for academic success.

These three self-protective devices have something in common; by engaging in any of them the person is attempting to cope with basic anxiety by interacting with other people. The fourth way of protecting oneself against basic anxiety involves withdrawing from other people, not physically but psychologically. Such a person attempts to become independent of others, not relying on anyone else for the satisfaction of internal or external needs. For example, if someone amasses a house full of material possessions, then he or she can rely on them to satisfy external needs. Unfortunately, that person may be too burdened by basic anxiety to enjoy the possessions. He or she must guard the possessions carefully because they are the person's only protection against anxiety.

The withdrawn person achieves independence with regard to internal or psychological needs by becoming aloof from others, no longer seeking them out to satisfy emotional needs. The process involves a blunting, or minimizing, of emotional needs. By renouncing these needs, the withdrawn person guards against being hurt by other people.

The four self-protective mechanisms Horney proposed have a single goal: to defend against basic anxiety. They motivate the person to seek security and reassurance rather than happiness or pleasure. They are a defense against pain, not a pursuit of well-being.

Another characteristic of these self-protective mechanisms is their power and intensity. Horney believed they could be more compelling than sexual or other physiological needs. These mechanisms may reduce anxiety, but the cost to the individual is usually an impoverished personality.

Often, the neurotic will pursue the search for safety and security by using more than one of these mechanisms and the incompatibility among the four mechanisms can lay the groundwork for additional problems. For example, a person may be driven by the needs to attain power and gain affection. A person may want to submit to others while also desiring power over them. Such incompatibilities cannot be resolved and can lead to more severe conflicts.

Neurotic Needs

neurotic needs Ten irrational defenses against anxiety that become a permanent part of personality and that affect behavior.

Horney believed that any of these self-protective mechanisms could become so permanent a part of the personality that it assumes the characteristics of a drive or need in determining the individual's behavior. She listed 10 such needs, which she termed **neurotic needs** because they are irrational solutions to one's problems.

The 10 neurotic needs are as follows:

1. Affection and approval
2. A dominant partner
3. Power
4. Exploitation
5. Prestige
6. Admiration
7. Achievement or ambition
8. Self-sufficiency
9. Perfection
10. Narrow limits to life

These neurotic needs encompass the four ways of protecting ourselves against anxiety. Gaining affection is expressed in the neurotic need for affection and approval. Being submissive includes the neurotic need for a dominant partner. Attaining power relates to the needs for power, exploitation, prestige, admiration, and achievement or ambition. Withdrawing includes the needs for self-sufficiency, perfection, and narrow limits to life.

Horney noted that we all manifest these needs to some degree. For example, at one time or another, everyone seeks affection or pursues achievement. None of the needs is abnormal or neurotic in an everyday, transient sense. What makes them neurotic is the person's intensive and compulsive pursuit of their satisfaction as the only way to resolve basic anxiety. Satisfying these needs will not help us feel safe and secure but will aid only in our desire to escape the discomfort caused by our anxiety. Also, when we pursue gratification of these needs solely to cope with anxiety, we tend to focus on only one need and compulsively seek its satisfaction in all situations.

In her later writings, she reformulated the list of needs (Horney, 1945). From her work with patients, she concluded that the needs could be presented in three groups, each indicating a person's attitudes toward the self and others. She called these three categories of directional movement the neurotic trends (see Table 5.1).

TABLE 5.1   Horney's neurotic needs and neurotic trends

Needs	Trends
Affection and approval A dominant partner	Movement toward other people (the compliant personality)
Power Exploitation Prestige Admiration Achievement	Movement against other people (the aggressive personality)
Self-sufficiency Perfection Narrow limits to life	Movement away from other people (the detached personality)

Neurotic Trends

neuroticism

neurotic trends Three categories of behaviors and attitudes toward oneself and others that express a person's needs; Horney's revision of the concept of neurotic needs.

Because the **neurotic trends** evolve from and elaborate on the self-protective mechanisms, we can see similarities with our earlier descriptions. The neurotic trends involve compulsive attitudes and behaviors; that is, neurotic persons are compelled to behave in accordance with at least one of the neurotic trends. They are also displayed indiscriminately, in any and all situations.

The neurotic trends are:

1. movement toward other people (the compliant personality),
2. movement against other people (the aggressive personality), and
3. movement away from other people (the detached personality).

The Compliant Personality

compliant personality Behaviors and attitudes associated with the neurotic trend of moving toward people, such as a need for affection and approval.

The **compliant personality** displays attitudes and behaviors that reflect a desire to move toward other people: an intense and continuous need for affection and approval, an urge to be loved, wanted, and protected. Compliant personalities display these needs toward everyone, although they usually have a need for one dominant person, such as a friend or spouse, who will take charge of their lives and offer protection and guidance.

Compliant personalities manipulate other people, particularly their partners, to achieve their goals. They often behave in ways others find attractive or endearing. For example, they may seem unusually considerate, appreciative, responsive, understanding, and sensitive to the needs of others. Compliant people are concerned with living up to others' ideals and expectations, and they act in ways others perceive as unselfish and generous.

In dealing with other people, compliant personalities are conciliatory and subordinate their personal desires to those of other people. They are willing to assume blame and to defer to others, never being assertive, critical, or demanding. They do whatever the situation requires, as they interpret it, to gain affection, approval, and love. Their attitude toward themselves is consistently one of helplessness and weakness. Horney suggested that compliant people are saying, "Look at me. I am so weak and helpless that you must protect and love me."

Consequently, they regard other people as superior, and even in situations in which they are notably competent, they see themselves as inferior. Because the security of compliant personalities depends on the attitudes and behavior of other people toward them, they become excessively dependent, needing constant approval and reassurance. Any sign of rejection, whether actual or imagined, is terrifying to them, leading to increased efforts to regain the affection of the person they believe has rejected them.

The source of these behaviors is the person's repressed hostility. Horney found that compliant persons have repressed profound feelings of defiance and vindictiveness. They have a desire to control, exploit, and manipulate others—the opposite of what their behaviors and attitudes express. Because their hostile impulses must be repressed, compliant personalities become subservient, always trying to please and asking nothing for themselves.

The Aggressive Personality

aggressive personality
Behaviors and attitudes associated with the neurotic trend of moving against people, such as a domineering and controlling manner.

Aggressive personalities move against other people. In their world, everyone is hostile; only the fittest and most cunning survive. Life is a jungle in which supremacy, strength, and ferocity are the paramount virtues. Although their motivation is the same as that of the compliant type, to alleviate basic anxiety, aggressive personalities never display fear of rejection. They act tough and domineering and have no regard for others. To achieve the control and superiority so vital to their lives, they must consistently perform at a high level. By excelling and receiving recognition, they find satisfaction in having their superiority affirmed by others.

Because aggressive personalities are driven to surpass others, they judge everyone in terms of the benefit they will receive from the relationship. They make no effort to appease others but will argue, criticize, demand, and do whatever is necessary to achieve and retain superiority and power.

They drive themselves hard to become the best; therefore, they may actually be highly successful in their careers, although the work itself will not provide intrinsic satisfaction. Like everything else in life, work is a means to an end, not an end in itself.

Aggressive personalities may appear confident of their abilities and uninhibited in asserting and defending themselves. However, like compliant personalities, aggressive personalities are driven by insecurity, anxiety, and hostility.

The Detached Personality

detached personality
Behaviors and attitudes associated with the neurotic trend of moving away from people, such as an intense need for privacy.

People described as **detached personalities** are driven to move away from other people and to maintain an emotional distance. They must not love, hate, or cooperate with others or become involved in any way. To achieve this total detachment, they strive to become self-sufficient. If they are to function as detached personalities, they must rely on their own resources, which must be well developed.

Detached personalities have an almost desperate desire for privacy. They need to spend as much time as possible alone, and it disturbs them to share even such an experience as listening to music. Their need for independence makes them sensitive to any attempt to influence, coerce, or obligate them. Detached personalities must avoid all constraints, including timetables and schedules, long-term commitments such as marriages or mortgages, and sometimes even the pressure of a belt or necktie.

They need to feel superior, but not in the same way aggressive personalities do. Because detached people cannot actively compete with other people for superiority—that would mean becoming involved with others—they believe their greatness should be recognized automatically, without struggle or effort on their part. One manifestation of this sense of superiority is the feeling that one is unique, that one is different and apart from everyone else.

Detached personalities suppress or deny all feelings toward others, particularly love and hate. Intimacy would lead to conflict, and that must be avoided. Because of this constriction of their emotions, detached personalities place great stress on reason, logic, and intelligence.

You have probably noticed the similarity between the three personality types proposed by Horney and the styles of life in Adler's personality theory. Horney's compliant personality is similar to Adler's getting type, the aggressive personality is like the dominant or ruling type, and the detached personality is similar to the avoiding type. This is yet another example of how Adler's ideas influenced later explanations of personality.

Horney found that in the neurotic person, one of these three trends is dominant, and the other two are present to a lesser degree. For example, the person who is predominantly aggressive also has some need for compliance and detachment. The dominant neurotic trend is the one that determines the person's behaviors and attitudes toward others. This is the mode of acting and thinking that best serves to control basic anxiety and any deviation from it is threatening to the person. For this reason, the other two trends must actively be repressed, which can lead to additional problems. Any indication that a repressed trend is pushing for expression causes conflict within the individual.

conflict To Horney, the basic incompatibility of the neurotic trends.

In Horney's system, **conflict** is defined as the basic incompatibility of the three neurotic trends; this conflict is the core of neurosis. All of us, whether neurotic or normal, suffer some conflict among these basically irreconcilable modes. The difference between the normal person and the neurotic person lies in the intensity of the conflict; it is much more intense in the neurotic. Neurotic people must battle to keep the nondominant trends from being expressed. They are rigid and inflexible, meeting all situations with the behaviors and attitudes that characterize the dominant trend, regardless of their suitability.

In the person who is not neurotic, all three trends can be expressed as circumstances warrant. A person may sometimes be aggressive, sometimes compliant, and sometimes detached. The trends are not mutually exclusive and can be integrated harmoniously within the personality. The normal person is flexible in behaviors and attitudes and can adapt to changing situations.

The Idealized Self-Image

self-perception

Horney argued that all of us, normal or neurotic, construct a picture of ourselves that may or may not be based on reality. Horney's own search for self was difficult.

At age 21, she wrote, "There's still such chaos in me. Still so little firmly outlined. Just like my face: a formless mass that only takes on shape through the expression of the moment. The searching for our selves is the most agonizing" (Horney, 1980, p. 174).

In normal persons, the self-image is built on a realistic appraisal of our abilities, potentials, weaknesses, goals, and relations with other people. This image supplies a sense of unity and integration to the personality and a framework within which to approach others and ourselves. If we are to realize our full potential, a state of self-realization, our self-image must clearly reflect our true self.

Neurotic persons, who experience conflict between incompatible modes of behavior, have personalities characterized by disunity and disharmony. They construct an **idealized self-image** for the same purpose as normal persons do: to unify the personality. But their attempt is doomed to failure because their self-image is not based on a realistic appraisal of personal strengths and weaknesses. Instead, it is based on an illusion, an unattainable ideal of absolute perfection.

To attempt to realize this unattainable ideal, neurotic persons engage in what Horney called the **tyranny of the shoulds**. They tell themselves they should be the best or most perfect student, spouse, parent, lover, employee, friend, or child. Because they find their real self-image so undesirable, they believe they must act to live up to their illusory, idealized self-image, in which they see themselves in a highly positive light, for example, being virtuous, honest, generous, considerate, and courageous. In doing so, they deny their real selves and try to become what they think they should be or what they need to be to match their idealized self-image. However, their efforts are doomed to failure; they can never achieve their unrealistic self-image.

Although the neurotic or idealized self-image does not coincide with reality, it is real and accurate to the person who created it. Other people can easily see through this false picture, but the neurotic cannot. The neurotic person believes that the incomplete and misleading self-picture is real. The idealized self-image is a model of what the neurotic thinks he or she is, can be, or should be.

A realistic self-image, on the other hand, is flexible and dynamic, adapting as the individual develops and changes. It reflects strengths, growth, and self-awareness. The realistic image is a goal, something to strive for, and as such it reflects and leads the person. By contrast, the neurotic self-image is static, inflexible, and unyielding. It is not a goal but a fixed idea, not an inducement to growth but a hindrance demanding rigid adherence to its proscriptions.

The neurotic's self-image is an unsatisfactory substitute for a reality-based sense of self-worth. The neurotic has little self-confidence because of insecurity and anxiety, and the idealized self-image does not allow for correction of those deficiencies. It provides only an illusory sense of worth and alienates the neurotic from the true self. Developed to reconcile incompatible modes of behavior, the idealized self-image becomes just one more element in that conflict. Far from resolving the problem, it adds to a growing sense of futility. The slightest crack in the neurotic's idealized self-picture threatens the false sense of superiority and security the whole edifice was constructed to provide, and little is needed to destroy it. Horney suggested that the neurotic self-image may be like a house filled with dynamite.

idealized self-image For normal people, the self-image is an idealized picture of oneself built on a flexible, realistic assessment of one's abilities. For neurotics, the self-image is based on an inflexible, unrealistic self-appraisal.

tyranny of the shoulds An attempt to realize an unattainable idealized self-image by denying the true self and behaving in terms of what we think we should be doing.

externalization A way to defend against the conflict caused by the discrepancy between an idealized and a real self-image by projecting the conflict onto the outside world.

One way in which neurotics attempt to defend themselves against the inner conflicts caused by the discrepancy between idealized and real self-images is by **externalization**, projecting the conflicts onto the outside world. This process may temporarily alleviate the anxiety caused by the conflict but will do nothing to reduce the gap between the idealized self-image and reality.

Externalization involves the tendency to experience conflicts as though they were occurring outside of oneself. It also entails depicting external forces as the source of the conflicts. For example, neurotics who experience self-hatred because of the discrepancy between real and idealized selves may project that hatred onto other people or institutions and come to believe that the hatred is emanating from these external sources and not from themselves.

Feminine Psychology

feminine psychology To Horney, a revision of psychoanalysis to encompass the psychological conflicts inherent in the traditional ideal of womanhood and women's roles.

Early in her career, Horney expressed her disagreement with Freud's views on women. She began work on her version of **feminine psychology** in 1922, the year she became the first woman to present a paper on the topic at an international psychoanalytic congress. That meeting, held in Berlin, was chaired by Sigmund Freud.

Horney was especially critical of Freud's notion of penis envy, which she believed was derived from inadequate evidence (that is, from Freud's clinical interviews

Horney disputed Freud's views on the accepted sex stereotypes of men and women.

with neurotic women). Freud offered descriptions and interpretations of this alleged phenomenon from a male point of view in a place and time when women were considered second-class citizens. He suggested that women were victims of their anatomy, forever envious and resentful of men for possessing a penis. Freud also concluded that women had poorly developed superegos (a result of inadequately resolved Oedipal conflicts), and inferior body images, because women believed they were really castrated men.

Womb Envy

womb envy The envy a male feels toward a female because she can bear children and he cannot. Womb envy was Horney's response to Freud's concept of penis envy in females.

Horney countered these ideas by arguing that men envied women because of their capacity for motherhood. Her position on this issue was based on the pleasure she had experienced in childbirth. She uncovered in her male patients what she called **womb envy**. "When one begins, as I did, to analyze men only after a fairly long experience of analyzing women, one receives a most surprising impression of the intensity of this envy of pregnancy, childbirth, and motherhood" (Horney, 1967a, pp. 60–61).

Men have such a small part to play in the act of creating new life that they must sublimate their womb envy and overcompensate for it by seeking achievement in their work. Womb envy and the resentment that accompanies it are manifested unconsciously in behaviors designed to disparage and belittle women and to reinforce their inferior status. By denying women equal rights, minimizing their opportunities to contribute to society, and downgrading their efforts to achieve, men retain their so-called natural superiority. Underlying such typical male behavior is a sense of inferiority deriving from their womb envy.

Horney did not deny that many women believe themselves to be inferior to men. What she questioned was Freud's claim of a biological basis for these feelings. Although women may view themselves as inadequate compared to men, they do so for societal reasons, not because they were born female. If women feel unworthy, it is because they have been treated that way in male-dominated cultures. After generations of social, economic, and cultural discrimination, it is understandable that many women see themselves in this light.

The Flight from Womanhood

As a result of these feelings of inferiority, women may choose to deny their femininity and to wish, unconsciously, that they were men. Horney referred to this as the flight from womanhood, a condition that can lead to sexual inhibitions (Horney, 1926). Part of the sexual fear associated with this condition arises from childhood fantasies about the difference in size between the adult penis and the female child's vagina. The fantasies focus on vaginal injury and the pain of forcible penetration. This produces a conflict between the unconscious desire to have a child and the fear of intercourse. If the conflict is sufficiently strong, it can lead to emotional disturbances that manifest themselves in relations with men. These women distrust and resent men and reject their sexual advances.

The Oedipus Complex

Horney also disagreed with Freud about the nature of the Oedipus complex. She did not deny the existence of conflicts between children and parents, but she did not believe they had a sexual origin. By removing sex from the Oedipus complex, she reinterpreted the situation as a conflict between dependence on one's parents and hostility toward them.

Earlier in this chapter, we discussed parental behaviors that undermine the satisfaction of the childhood need for safety and security and lead to the development of hostility. At the same time, the child remains dependent on the parents so that expressing hostility is unacceptable; it could further damage the child's security. The child is saying, in effect, "I have to repress my hostility because I need you."

As we noted, the hostile impulses remain and create basic anxiety. To Horney, "The resulting picture may look exactly like what Freud describes as the Oedipus complex: passionate clinging to one parent and jealousy toward the other" (Horney, 1939, p. 83). Thus, her explanation for Oedipal feelings lies in neurotic conflicts that evolve from parent-child interactions. These feelings are not based on sex or other biological forces, nor are they universal. They develop only when parents act to undermine their child's security.

Freud did not respond to Horney's challenge to his views on women, nor did he alter his concept of the Oedipus complex. In a veiled allusion to Horney's work, he wrote, "We shall not be very greatly surprised if a woman analyst, who has not been sufficiently convinced of the intensity of her own wish for a penis, also fails to attach proper importance to that factor in her patients" (Freud, 1940). Of Horney herself, Freud remarked, "She is able but malicious" (quoted in Blanton, 1971, p. 65). Horney was bitter about Freud's failure to recognize the legitimacy of her views.

Motherhood or Career?

As an early feminist, Horney adopted several positions that have a contemporary ring. In 1934 she wrote an essay describing the psychological conflicts in defining women's roles, contrasting the traditional ideal of womanhood with a more modern view (Horney, 1967b). In the traditional scheme, promoted and endorsed by most men, the woman's role was to love, admire, and serve her man. Her identity was a reflection of her husband's. Horney suggested that women should seek their own identity by developing their abilities and pursuing careers.

These traditional and modern roles create conflicts that many women to this day have difficulty resolving. Drawing on Horney's work, a more contemporary feminist wrote that

> modern women are caught between wanting to make themselves desirable to men and pursuing their own goals. The competing purposes elicit conflicting behaviors: seductive versus aggressive, deferential versus ambitious. Modern women are torn between love and work and are consequently dissatisfied in both. (Westkott, 1986, p. 14)

dual-career families

It remains as troublesome for 21st-century women to combine marriage, motherhood, and career as it was for Karen Horney in the 1930s. Her decision to develop her abilities and focus on her work brought her enormous satisfaction, but she continued throughout her life to search for security and love.

Cultural Influences on Feminine Psychology

As we noted earlier, Horney recognized the impact of social and cultural forces on the development of personality. She also recognized that different cultures and social groups view women's roles in different ways. Thus there can be many different feminine psychologies. "The American woman is different from the German woman; both are different from certain Pueblo Indian women. The New York society woman is different from the farmer's wife in Idaho. . . . Specific cultural conditions engender specific qualities and faculties, in women as in men" (Horney, 1939, p. 119).

One example of the power of culture to shape women's lives and expectations can be found in traditional Chinese society. As far back as the first millennium B.C., women were considered subordinate to men. Society was governed by the belief that the universe contained two contrasting yet interacting elements, yin and yang. Yang represents the male element and contains all that is vital, positive, strong, and active. Yin represents the female element and contains all that is dark, weak, and passive. Over time, these elements came to form a hierarchy in which men were considered superior and women inferior.

This idea became part of the teaching of the Chinese philosopher Confucius (551–479 B.C.), whose work was the ruling ideology of China for centuries. Strict rules of conduct were established for women; they were expected to be submissive, obedient, respectful, chaste, and unselfish. The Chinese word for woman literally meant "inside person," denoting her status as restricted to the confines of the home.

> A respectable Chinese woman was not to be seen or heard. She was expected never to be freed from male domination, as her duty was to obey her father at home, her husband after marriage, and her eldest son when widowed. . . . Men were counseled against listening to women for fear that disaster would result. The exercise of willfulness and ambition, considered heroic in a man, was considered wicked and depraved in a woman. (Loo, 1998, p. 180)

If we contrast this attitude with the widely accepted views of a woman's place in 21st-century American society, we can easily accept Horney's position that the feminine psyche is influenced, even determined, by cultural forces.

Questions About Human Nature

Horney's image of human nature is considerably more optimistic than Freud's (see Figure 5.1). One reason for her optimism was her belief that biological forces do not condemn us to conflict, anxiety, neurosis, or a universality in personality. To Horney, each person is unique. Neurotic behavior, when it occurs, results from social forces in childhood. Parent-child relationships will either satisfy or frustrate the child's need for safety. If that need is frustrated, the outcome is neurotic behavior.

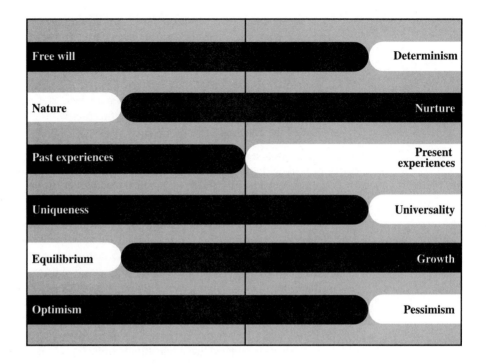

Free will | Determinism
Nature | Nurture
Past experiences | Present experiences
Uniqueness | Universality
Equilibrium | Growth
Optimism | Pessimism

FIGURE 5.1   *Horney's image of human nature*

Neuroses and conflicts can be avoided if children are raised with love, acceptance, and trust.

Each of us has the innate potential for self-realization, and this is our ultimate and necessary goal in life. Our intrinsic abilities and potential will blossom as inevitably and naturally as an acorn grows into an oak tree. The only thing that can obstruct our development is the thwarting in childhood of our need for safety and security.

Horney also believed that we have the capacity to consciously shape and change our personality. Because human nature is flexible, it is not formed into immutable shapes in childhood. Each of us possesses the capacity to grow. Therefore, adult experiences may be as important as those of childhood.

So confident was Horney of our capacity for self-growth that she emphasized self-analysis in her therapeutic work as well as in her own life. In her book entitled *Self-Analysis* (Horney, 1942), she argues in favor of our ability to help resolve our own problems. On the issue of free will versus determinism, then, Horney argued in favor of the former. We can all shape our lives and achieve self-realization.

Assessment in Horney's Theory

The methods Horney used to assess the functioning of the human personality were essentially those favored by Freud—free association and dream analysis—but with some modification. The most basic difference in technique between Horney and Freud was in the relationship between analyst and patient. Horney believed that Freud played too passive a role and was too distant and intellectual. She suggested that analysis should be an "exquisitely cooperative enterprise" between patient and therapist (Horney quoted in Cherry & Cherry, 1973, p. 84).

Although Horney kept a couch in her office, she did not use it with every patient. Adopting an attitude she called constructive friendliness, she approached the use of the couch as follows.

> This is something one needs to try through trial and error, asking if the patient operates better lying on the couch or sitting upright. It is particularly helpful to encourage a patient so he feels free to sit up, lie down, walk around, or whatever he wants. (Horney, 1987, p. 43)

With free association, Horney did not follow Freud's lead in trying to probe the unconscious mind. She believed that patients could easily distort or hide aspects of their inner lives or falsify feelings about events that they remembered. Instead, Horney focused on her patients' visible emotional reactions toward her, believing that these could explain her patients' attitudes toward other people. She pursued these attitudes through free association. She did not delve into presumed infantile sexual fantasies at the beginning of a course of analysis but inquired about the early years only after evaluating present attitudes, defenses, and conflicts.

Horney believed that each attitude or feeling resulted from a deeper, preexisting attitude, which in turn had resulted from a deeper one, and so on. Through free association, the analyst gradually uncovered the patient's early experiences and emotions, similar to peeling the layers of an onion.

dreams—analysis Horney also believed that dream analysis could reveal a person's true self, and that dreams represented attempts to solve problems, in either a constructive or a neurotic way. Dreams can show us a set of attitudes that may differ from those of our self-image. She did not offer a list of universal dream symbols but insisted that each dream be explained within the context of the patient's conflict. Focusing on a dream's emotional content, she concluded that the "safest clue to the understanding of a dream is in the feelings of the patient as he has them in the dream" (Horney, 1987, p. 61).

A 35-item self-report inventory, the CAD, was devised to measure Horney's three neurotic trends, the *C*ompliant, *A*ggressive, and *D*etached personality types (Cohen, 1967). Respondents are instructed to indicate whether each item is extremely desirable or extremely undesirable. Consider the following item: If I could live all alone in a cabin in the woods or mountains it would be [extremely desirable] or [extremely undesirable]. As you might have guessed, this item would be used to assess the detached personality.

Research in Horney's Theory

Horney used the case study method. Therefore, her approach, data, and interpretations are subject to the same criticisms made of the work of Freud, Jung, and Adler.

The weaknesses inherent in the case study method apply to her work no less than to theirs.

Horney was opposed to taking verbatim notes of her patients' recollections. "I don't see how anybody can employ a wholehearted receptivity and productivity of attention at the same time that he is anxiously scribbling everything down" (Horney, 1987, p. 30). As with Freud, Jung, and Adler, then, we do not have complete records of her analytic sessions and the data she collected during them. However, she tried to be rigorous and scientific in her clinical observations, formulating hypotheses, testing them in therapeutic situations, and maintaining that her data were tested the same way scientists in other fields test theirs.

Neurotic Trends

Researchers have studied Horney's three proposed neurotic trends, redefining them as follows: moving against people (ill-tempered), moving away from people (shy), and moving toward people (dependent) (Caspi, Elder, & Bem, 1987, 1988). The behavior of people belonging to each of these types in late childhood was compared with their behavior 30 years later to discover whatever continuities might exist.

Ill-tempered children, both boys and girls, tended to become ill-tempered adults, prone to divorce and downward occupational mobility. Gender differences were found in the shy and dependent types. Shy boys became aloof adults who experienced marital and job instability. On the other hand, shy girls manifested no such problems later in life. Dependent boys became agreeable, socially poised, warm, and giving adults with stable marriages and careers; the opposite was found for dependent girls (Caspi, Bem, & Elder, 1989).

A study dealing with the neurotic trends of moving against people (aggressive) and moving away from people (detached) compared measures from aggressive and detached children at ages 7 to 13 with their behavior five to seven years later (Moskowitz & Schwartzman, 1989). Those high in aggressiveness were found to be low in school achievement and to have psychiatric problems. Those who were detached or withdrawn were found to have inaccurate and negative self-images. The researchers concluded that Horney's proposed personality types had predictive value for later behavior.

Research using the CAD inventory found that college students preparing for careers in helping professions such as nursing and social work scored higher in compliance than did students considering careers in business or science. The business students, on a more competitive career path, scored higher on aggression. Science students scored highest on the detached scale. These results appear to be consistent with Horney's descriptions of the three neurotic trends (Cohen, 1967; Rendon, 1987).

Feminine Psychology

Some research applies indirectly to Horney's ideas on feminine psychology. In our discussion of research on the Oedipus complex (see Chapter 2), we mentioned a study on dreams that provided support for the Freudian concept of penis envy (Hall

& Van de Castle, 1965); this study fails to support Horney's questioning of the concept of penis envy. However, research that refutes Freud's notion that women have inadequately developed superegos and inferior body images can be taken to support Horney's views.

Neurotic Competitiveness

neurotic competitiveness
An indiscriminate need to win at all costs.

Horney spoke of **neurotic competitiveness** as a major aspect of contemporary culture. She defined it as an indiscriminate need to win at all costs. The feeling toward life of the person manifesting this need can be "compared to that of a jockey in a race, for whom only one thing matters—whether he is ahead of the others" (Horney, 1937, p. 189).

A self-report inventory, the Hypercompetitive Attitude Scale (HCA), was developed to test experimentally the concept of neurotic competitiveness (Ryckman, Thornton, & Butler, 1994). This 26-item scale contains such items as "Winning in competition makes me feel more powerful as a person." Subjects evaluate the items on a five-point continuum ranging from *never true of me* to *always true of me*.

Studies using the HCA and other measures of personality found that people who scored high on competitiveness were also high in narcissism, neuroticism, dogmatism, and mistrust, and low in self-esteem and psychological health. Hypercompetitive men were also found to be hypermasculine or macho, believing that women were sex objects who deserved neither respect nor consideration (Ryckman, Hammer, Kaczor, & Gold, 1990). These findings support Horney's description of the neurotic competitive personality.

A Final Commentary

Horney's contributions to psychology, although impressive, are not as well known or recognized as those of Freud, Jung, and Adler. Professionally, Horney suffered a disadvantage that limited the spread of her ideas: She never formed a group of disciples to disseminate and elaborate on her theory. Further, there is no professional journal dedicated to examining and propounding her ideas. On the other hand, her work drew a large public following, partly because of her personal qualities. A student recalled:

> There was about her an air of wholeness, of certainty, of total dedication and commitment, of a conviction that her ideas were valuable, that they were worth sharing with colleagues and students, because knowing them would make a difference to helping those in need. (Clemmens, 1987, p. 108)

These characteristics are evident in her books, which were written in a style readily understood by people who do not have professional analytical training. Her theory has a commonsense appeal and, to many people, seems applicable to their own personality or to that of a relative or friend.

Horney's ideas may be more relevant to problems inherent in American culture than the ideas of Freud, Jung, or Adler. Many personality researchers see Horney's conception of the neurotic trends as a valuable way to categorize deviant behavior. Others accept Horney's emphasis on self-esteem, the need for safety and security, the role of basic anxiety, and the importance of the idealized self-image. Her work had a significant impact on the personality theories developed by Erik Erikson and Abraham Maslow (see Chapters 8 and 11). Maslow used her concept of the real self and self-realization; her notion of basic anxiety is similar to Erikson's concept of basic mistrust.

Although Horney was trained in orthodox Freudian theory and paid tribute to Freud for providing the foundation and tools for her work, her theory deviated from psychoanalysis in several ways. Not surprisingly, she received a great deal of criticism from those who continued to adhere to Freud's position. To the Freudians, Horney's denial of the importance of biological instincts and her reduced emphasis on sexuality and the unconscious were obvious weaknesses.

Horney's personality theory is not as completely or consistently developed as Freud's. It has been suggested that because Freud's model was constructed so elegantly and precisely, it would have been better for Horney to reject it and start anew rather than attempt to refashion it along different lines. Another criticism is that although Horney's theory notes the impact of social and cultural forces on personality, it makes little use of research data from sociology and anthropology to detail precisely how social forces shape personality. A related charge is that her observations and interpretations were too greatly influenced by middle-class American culture. In her defense, it must be said that all personality theorists are affected by the class, culture, and time in which they work.

Primarily due to the women's movement that began in the 1960s, Horney's books have enjoyed renewed interest. Her writings on femininity and female sexuality may constitute the most influential of her contributions. "Had she written nothing else," a biographer stated, "these papers would have earned Horney a place of importance in the history of psychoanalysis" (Quinn, 1987, p. 211). Her adolescent diaries have been published, along with biographies in 1987 and 1994. The work of the Karen Horney Clinic and the Karen Horney Psychoanalytic Institute (a training center for analysts), both in New York City, attest to the lasting impact of her work.

Chapter Summary

Karen Horney differed from Freud in her views on feminine psychology and her emphasis on social rather than biological forces as shapers of personality.

The need for safety refers to security and freedom from fear. It depends on being loved and wanted as a child. When security is undermined, hostility is induced. The child may repress this hostility out of a sense of helplessness, fear of the parents, the need to receive parental affection, or guilt about expressing hostility. Repressing hostility leads to basic anxiety, defined as a feeling of being lonely and helpless in a hostile world.

Four ways to protect oneself against basic anxiety are by gaining affection, being submissive, attaining power, and withdrawing. Any of these protective devices may become a neurotic need or drive. Horney proposed 10 neurotic needs, which she later grouped as three neurotic trends: moving toward people (the compliant personality), moving against people (the aggressive personality), and moving away from people (the detached personality). Compliant types need affection and approval and will do what other people want. Aggressive types are hostile toward others and seek to achieve control and superiority. Detached types keep an emotional distance from others and have a deep need for privacy.

In the normal person, the idealized self-image is built on a realistic appraisal of one's abilities and goals. It helps the person achieve self-realization—the maximum development and use of one's potential. The idealized self-image in the neurotic person is based on an unrealistic, misleading appraisal of one's abilities.

Horney argued against Freud's contention that women have penis envy, poorly developed superegos, and inferior body images. She believed that men envy women because of their capacity for motherhood and, consequently, experience womb envy, which they sublimate through achievement. She rejected the sexual basis for the Oedipus complex, suggesting that it involved a conflict between dependence on parents and hostility toward them.

Horney's image of human nature is more optimistic than is Freud's. Each person is unique and is not doomed to conflict. Although childhood influences are important, later experiences also shape personality. The ultimate goal of life is self-realization, an innate urge to grow, which can be helped or hindered by social forces. According to Horney, we can consciously shape and change our personalities.

Horney's methods of assessment were free association and dream analysis, and her research method was the case study. Some psychologists see value in her concepts of neurotic trends, the need for safety, the role of anxiety, and the idealized self-image. The theory has been criticized for not being developed as fully as Freud's, for not using research data from sociology and anthropology, and for being heavily influenced by middle-class American culture.

Review Questions

1. Describe how Karen Horney's childhood experiences may be reflected in her personality theory.

2. Describe the childhood need for safety. What parental behaviors are necessary for a child's security?

3. What is the origin of basic anxiety? Describe four self-protective ways in which we may express basic anxiety.

4. Discuss the three neurotic trends and the behaviors associated with each.

5. How are the neurotic trends related to the self-protective defenses against anxiety?

6. Explain the difference between normal persons and neurotic persons in terms of the neurotic trends.

7. How does the idealized self-image of the normal, realistic person differ from the idealized self-image of the neurotic person?

8. Contrast the tyranny of the shoulds and the process of externalization.

9. Horney rejected Freud's contention of a biological basis for female inferiority. How did she account for women's feelings of inadequacy?

10. What was Horney's interpretation of the Oedipus complex?

11. Discuss the impact of cultural forces on women's roles. Give examples.

12. How does Horney's image of human nature differ from Freud's?

13. How did Horney's use of free association differ from Freud's?

14. Describe the results of research conducted on the neurotic trends and on neurotic competitiveness.

Suggested Readings

Berger, M. M. (Ed.). (1991, September). Special issue commemorating the 50th anniversary of the founding by Karen Horney, M.D. (1885–1952), of the Association for the Advancement of Psychoanalysis; the American Institute for Psychoanalysis; and *The American Journal of Psychoanalysis. American Journal of Psychoanalysis, 51(3).* Includes tributes to and personal recollections of Karen Horney, along with an overview and evaluations of her work.

Horney, K. (1937). *The neurotic personality of our time.* New York: Norton. Describes the development of conflict and anxiety within the personality and relates neuroses to past experiences and to the sociocultural climate.

Horney, K. (1980). *The adolescent diaries of Karen Horney.* New York: Basic Books. A publication of diary entries Horney wrote between the ages of 13 and 25; the entries are characterized by intense emotion and intellectual honesty.

Horney, K. (1987). *Final lectures.* New York: Norton. Contains lectures Horney delivered during the last year of her life. Presents refinements of her views on psychoanalytic techniques, such as free association and dream analysis.

Paris, B. J. (1994). *Karen Horney: A psychoanalyst's search for self-understanding.* New Haven, CT: Yale University Press. A study of Horney's life and work, exploring the relationship between her struggle for self-understanding and the evolution of her ideas. Assesses her later work as a contribution to psychology, psychoanalysis, and the study of gender and culture.

Quinn, S. (1987). *A mind of her own: The life of Karen Horney.* New York: Summit Books. Discusses Horney's life, her work on feminine psychology, and her conflicts with the orthodox Freudian establishment.

Sayers, J. (1991). *Mothers of psychoanalysis: Helene Deutsch, Karen Horney, Anna Freud, Melanie Klein.* New York: Norton. Describes the post-Freudian modification of psychoanalytic theory from patriarchal to matriarchal. Shows how the experiences of these influential women psychoanalysts changed the focus from sex, repression, and castration anxiety to identification, projection, and separation anxiety.

The most beautiful as well as the most ugly inclinations are not part of a fixed and biologically given human nature but result from the social processes which create [us].

—Erich Fromm

S   I   X

Erich Fromm

Erich Fromm, like Alfred Adler and Karen Horney, argued that we are not inflexibly shaped by instinctive biological forces, as Freud had proposed. Instead, Fromm suggested that personality is influenced by the social and cultural forces that affect the individual within a culture and by the universal forces that have influenced humanity throughout history.

Fromm's emphasis on the social determinants of personality is broader than that of Adler and Horney. We might say that Fromm takes a longer view of personality development than other theorists because of his concern with history. He suggested that we can find in historical events the roots of contemporary human loneliness, isolation, and insignificance. To find meaning in life, we need to escape these feelings of isolation and develop a sense of belonging. Paradoxically, the increasing freedom we have achieved over the centuries, both from nature and from rigid social systems, has intensified our loneliness and isolation. Too much freedom has become a trap, a negative condition from which we attempt to escape.

Fromm believed that the personal conflicts we suffer arise from the kinds of societies we construct. However, we are not doomed to suffering. Fromm was optimistic about our ability to create our own character and solve our problems—problems that we as a society have created. We do not passively accept the impact of social forces as determinants of personality or of society.

Fromm was a psychoanalyst, philosopher, historian, anthropologist, and sociologist. He assembled data from many sources beyond the psychoanalytic couch to offer a unique interpretation of the interaction between human nature and society.

The Life of Fromm (1900–1980)

A Troubled Childhood

Erich Fromm

Fromm was born in Frankfurt, Germany, in an Orthodox Jewish family. His father was a businessman, his grandfather a rabbi, and his mother's uncle a well-known scholar of the Talmud (writings on Jewish laws and traditions). As a child, Fromm was devoted to his religious studies; the moral fervor of the Old Testament affected him greatly. He was also influenced by the Jewish tradition of reason and intellect and by the emotional difficulties of being a member of a minority group. Fromm later severed all his connections with organized religion and referred to himself as an atheistic mystic.

His home life was not happy. Fromm characterized his family situation as tense. His father was moody, aloof, anxious, and morose, and his mother was frequently depressed. He described himself as an "unbearable, neurotic child" (quoted in Funk, 1982, p. 1). When Fromm was 12, he was shocked by the behavior of a friend of his parents, a 25-year-old artist who chose to abandon her painting and devote her life to her widowed father. Fromm may simply have been jealous, but he could not understand why the young woman preferred the company of this unattractive old man. Shortly after her father died, the woman killed herself. Her will stipulated that she be buried with her father in the same coffin. Troubled by the suicide, Fromm agonized over her decision and her attraction to her father.

I had never heard of an Oedipus complex or of incestuous fixations between daughter and father. But I was deeply touched. How is it possible that a beautiful young woman should be so in love with her father, that she prefers to be buried with him to being alive to the pleasures of life and of painting? (Fromm, 1962, p. 4)

It is not hard to see why Fromm later found meaning in Freud's work on the Oedipus complex, which seemed to explain this puzzling and tragic experience.

When Fromm was 14, another manifestation of irrationality unnerved him: the eruption of hysterical fanaticism in the German nation during World War I. He was astonished by the hatred that swept the country as people were whipped by government propaganda into a frenzy of maniacal thought and action. Fromm observed the changes in his relatives, friends, and teachers and wondered why so many otherwise normal people seemed to be going mad. After the war, Fromm wrote: "I was a deeply troubled young man who was obsessed with the question of how war was possible, by the wish to understand the irrationality of human mass behavior, by a passionate desire for peace and international understanding" (Fromm, 1962, p. 9).

Searching for Answers

It was primarily from these baffling personal experiences—his disturbing home life, the suicide, and the wartime behavior of an entire nation—that Fromm developed the need to seek an understanding of the causes of irrationality. He wrote, "My main interest was clearly mapped out. I wanted to understand the laws that govern the life of the individual man, and the laws of society" (Fromm, 1962, p. 9). He suspected that the human personality was profoundly affected by social, economic, political, and historical forces, and that a sick society produced sick people. Thus, his view of personality was shaped along intuitive lines, fashioned from his own experiences, and later refined along empirical lines.

Fromm began his search for the causes of irrational behavior at the University of Heidelberg, where he studied psychology, sociology, and philosophy. He read the works of such economic and political theorists as Karl Marx, Herbert Spencer, and Max Weber, and received his Ph.D. in sociology in 1922. Fromm underwent Freudian psychoanalytic training in Munich and at the Psychoanalytic Institute in Berlin. He married his first analyst, Frieda Reichmann, who was 10 years older than Fromm. A biographer of Horney suggested that Fromm, at this stage of his life,

had some kind of attachment to older women, mother-figures. . . . Erich's father is reported to have told Frieda Reichmann on her wedding day, "I'm glad you're going to be in charge of him now. Having been his mother's darling, Erich was very dependent, a prince who needed to be catered to." (Paris, 1994, p. 144)

By the 1930s, Fromm was writing critical articles disputing Freud's refusal to admit the impact of socioeconomic forces on personality. Like Horney, Fromm initially believed that his criticisms of Freudian psychoanalysis were intended merely to elaborate on Freud's position, not to replace it. He considered himself "like a pupil and translator of Freud who is attempting to bring out his most important discoveries in order to enrich them and to deepen them by liberating them from the somewhat narrow libido theory" (Evans, 1966, p. 59). However, Fromm moved so far beyond Freud's views in developing his approach to personality that he came to be "hated within the Freudian establishment with a special passion" (McLaughlin, 1998, p. 116).

In 1934, Fromm emigrated to the United States to escape the Nazi menace in Germany. He went to Chicago to work with Horney and then followed her to New York. He divorced his wife and began a long affair with Horney. During those years, Horney's ideas had a great impact on Fromm's work, a debt he rarely acknowledged.

Fromm presented his theory in several books written in a popular style, intended more for the general public than for colleagues. He taught at Columbia and Yale universities and established the department of psychoanalytic training at the medical school of the National University of Mexico. He became active in the peace movement of the 1960s and 1970s and helped to found SANE, the Organization for a Sane Nuclear Policy. He opposed the Cold War, the nuclear arms race, and the Vietnam War. He died at his home in Switzerland in 1980.

Freedom versus Security: The Basic Human Dilemma

The title of Fromm's first book, *Escape from Freedom* (1941), indicates his vision of the human condition: In the history of Western civilization, as people have achieved more freedom, they have come to feel more lonely, insignificant, and alienated. Conversely, the less freedom people had, the greater their feelings of belonging and security. Fromm contended that in the 20th century people had achieved greater freedom than in any other era yet felt more lonely, alienated, and insignificant than people did in centuries past.

Alienation from Nature

To understand this apparent paradox, we must consider the history of Western civilization, as Fromm interpreted it. He began by discussing human evolution, noting the distinction between animal nature and human nature. Humans are free of the instinctive biological mechanisms that guide animal behavior. Furthermore, humans are conscious beings, aware of themselves and their world. Through learning, we accumulate knowledge of the past. Through imagination, we can project ourselves far beyond the present. Because we possess a conscious awareness and the ability to master nature, we are no longer at one with nature, as are the lower animals. We have, in a sense, transcended nature. As a result, although we are subject to natural laws and cannot change them, we are left homeless, isolated, and alienated.

Fromm suggested that early peoples tried to cope with these feelings of alienation from nature by identifying with their tribes or clans. Sharing myths, religions, and tribal rites, they attained the security of belonging to a group. Membership in the group provided acceptance, affiliation, and a set of customs and rules. The religions that early peoples developed also helped reestablish the link with nature. Worship was focused on natural objects, such as the sun, the moon, fire, plants, and animals.

But this tenuous security could not last. Human beings are striving creatures who develop and grow, and post-primitive peoples revolted against subservience to the group. According to Fromm, each period of history has been characterized by increasing movement away from the group and toward individuality, as people have struggled to achieve independence, freedom, and the opportunity to express all their uniquely human abilities. This striving for individuality reached its peak between the Reformation in the 16th century and the present day, when, in Fromm's view, alienation has been matched by a high degree of freedom.

The Middle Ages: The Last Era of Stability

Fromm designated the Middle Ages (about AD 400–1400) as the last era of stability, security, and belonging. It was a time of virtually no individual freedom because the feudal system determined everyone's place in society. People remained in the role and class status to which they were born. There was no geographic or social mobility and little choice of occupation, social customs, or habits of dress. Although people were not free, they were also not alienated from others. The rigid social structure meant that a person's place in society was clear. There was no doubt or indecision about where, or to whom, one belonged.

The social upheavals of the Renaissance and the Protestant Reformation destroyed this stability and security by increasing personal freedom. People began to have more choice and more power over their lives. However, they achieved this freedom at the expense of the societal ties that had provided security and a sense of belonging. As a result, they were beset by feelings of insecurity, insignificance, and doubts about the meaning of life.

Psychic Escape Mechanisms

Fromm proposed three psychic mechanisms for escaping from the negative aspects of freedom and regaining our lost security: authoritarianism, destructiveness, and automaton conformity. **Authoritarianism** is manifested in either masochistic or sadistic strivings. People described as masochistic believe they are inferior and inadequate. They may complain of these feelings and declare they would like to be free of them, but they have a strong need for dependence on another person or group. They willingly submit to the control of other people or of social forces, and they behave in a weak and helpless manner. They achieve security by these actions because submissiveness assuages their feelings of loneliness.

Authoritarian persons described as sadistic strive for power over others. They may try to make others dependent on them and thus achieve control. They may exploit others by taking or using anything desirable the other person possesses, whether material goods or intellectual and emotional qualities. Or they may desire to see others suffer and to be the cause of that suffering. Although the suffering may involve physical pain, it most often is emotional suffering, such as embarrassment or humiliation.

The authoritarian escape mechanism involves some form of continuing interaction with an object or person. By contrast, **destructiveness** aims at eliminating that object or person. A destructive person says,

authoritarianism (personality trait)

authoritarianism A psychic mechanism for regaining security, displayed in either masochistic or sadistic feelings.

destructiveness A psychic mechanism for regaining security, displayed in a desire to eliminate threatening objects, persons, and institutions.

People can achieve a feeling of security by renouncing freedom and accepting a totalitarian system such as the Nazi regime.

> I can escape the feeling of my own powerlessness in comparison with the world outside of myself by destroying it. To be sure, if I succeed in removing it, I remain alone and isolated, but mine is a splendid isolation in which I cannot be crushed by the overwhelming power of the objects outside of myself. (Fromm, 1941, p. 179)

Fromm saw evidence of destructiveness in all societies. He believed that many human characteristics were used as a rationalization for destructiveness—including love, duty, conscience, and patriotism.

The escape mechanism Fromm described as having the greatest social significance is **automaton conformity**. Through this mechanism, we ease our loneliness and isolation by striving to become exactly like everyone else, by conforming to the societal rules that govern behavior. Fromm compared automaton conformity with the protective coloring of animals. Animals protect themselves by becoming indistinguishable from their surroundings. So it is with fully conforming human beings.

Although such people temporarily gain the security and sense of belonging they so desperately need, they do so at the price of the self. People who conform completely have sacrificed their personality; as Fromm said, there is no longer an "I," distinct from "them." The conforming person becomes part of "them," and a false self takes the place of the genuine self.

This loss of self leaves the person with insecurity and doubt. No longer possessing a separate identity or personality, the person functions reflexively and automatically, like an automaton or robot, in response to what others expect or demand. This new identity, the false one, can be maintained only through continued

automaton conformity
A psychic mechanism for regaining security, displayed in unconditional obedience to the prevailing rules that govern behavior.

conformity; there can be no relaxation. If the person were to do anything at variance with society's norms and values, then approval, recognition, and security would be lost.

Personality Development in Childhood

Fromm believed that the development of the individual in childhood parallels the development of the human species. In other words, the history of the species is repeated in the childhood of each human being. As children grow, they achieve increasing freedom and independence from their parents. Infants know little freedom but are secure in their dependent relationship. However, the less dependent children become, especially on the primary ties with the mother, the less secure they feel.

Because the normal maturation process involves some isolation and helplessness, children will attempt to regain the security of infancy and escape their growing freedom. They may use different behavior patterns similar to the psychic mechanisms described in the preceding section. The nature of the parent-child relationship determines the mechanism the child employs. Fromm proposed three forms of interpersonal relatedness between parent and child: symbiotic relatedness, withdrawal-destructiveness, and love.

symbiotic relatedness A childhood mechanism for regaining security in which children remain close to and dependent on their parents.

In **symbiotic relatedness**, children never achieve independence but escape their loneliness and insecurity by becoming part of someone else, either by "swallowing" or by being "swallowed" by that other person. Masochistic behavior arises from being swallowed; the child remains dependent on the parents and abnegates the self. Sadism arises from swallowing; the parents surrender authority to the child by submitting to the child's will. The child regains security by manipulating and exploiting the parents. In both cases, the relationship is one of closeness and intimacy; the child needs the parents for his or her security.

withdrawal-destructiveness A childhood mechanism for regaining security in which children distance themselves from their parents.

A distance and separation from others characterize the **withdrawal-destructiveness** interaction. Fromm stated that withdrawal and destructiveness are the passive and active forms of the same type of parent-child relationship. Which form the child's behavior takes depends on the parents' behavior. For example, parents who act destructively, attempting to subordinate or subjugate their child, will cause the child to withdraw.

love To Fromm, a form of parent-child interaction in which parents provide respect and a balance between security and responsibility.

Love is the most desirable form of parent-child interaction. In this instance, the parents provide the greatest opportunity for the child's positive personality development by offering respect and a balance between security and responsibility. As a result, the child feels little need to escape the growing freedom and is able to love the self as well as others.

Fromm agreed with Freud that the first five years of life are important, but Fromm did not believe that personality is fixed by the age of 5. Instead, he asserted that later events could also influence personality. He agreed with Freud that the family functioned as society's representative to the child; it is through family interactions that the child acquires character as well as appropriate ways of adjusting to society.

If the parent-child relationship is characterized by love, the child will feel little need to escape from freedom and will develop self-esteem and be able to love others.

TABLE 6.1   Fromm's psychological needs

Need	Characteristics
Relatedness	Need to form relationships with other people and be concerned with their well-being
Transcendence	Need to be involved in creative activities that use imagination and reason
Rootedness	Need to foster kinship with family, group, or community
Identity	Need to develop one's unique qualities and abilities
Frame of orientation	Need to develop a consistent viewpoint within which to organize our experiences, and to find a meaningful object or goal to which we commit ourselves
Excitation and stimulation	Need for a stimulating environment so that we can maintain peak alertness and energy to cope with the demands of everyday life

The Basic Psychological Needs

The drive to attain security and escape loneliness and the conflicting drive for freedom and the creation of the self are universal. The opposition of these drives determines all human cravings. This opposition is manifested in six basic human needs (see Table 6.1).

The need for **relatedness** arises from the disruption of our primary ties with nature. By virtue of our powers of reason and imagination, we are aware of our

relatedness need The need to maintain contact with other people, ideally through productive love.

separation from nature, our relative powerlessness, and the arbitrariness of birth and death. Because we have lost our instinctive relationship with nature, we must use reason to create a new relationship with other people. The ideal way to achieve this is through productive love, which involves caring, responsibility, respect, and knowledge. By loving, we become concerned with the growth and happiness of other people. We respond to their needs and respect and know them as they really are.

Productive love can be directed toward someone of the same sex (which Fromm described as brotherly or sisterly love), toward a person of the opposite sex (erotic love), or toward one's child (parental love). In all three forms, the person's ultimate concern is with the development and growth of the other person's self.

Failure to satisfy the need for relatedness results in narcissism. Narcissistic people cannot perceive the world in objective terms. Their only reality is the subjective world of their own thoughts, feelings, and needs. Because they focus solely on themselves, they cannot relate to others or cope with the outside world.

transcendence need The need to rise above our animal nature by becoming either creative or destructive.

Transcendence refers to the need to rise above a passive animal state, a state with which we cannot be satisfied because of our capacity for reason and imagination. We need to become creative and productive individuals. In the act of creation, whether of life (as in rearing children), or of material objects, art, or ideas, we surpass the animal state and enter a state of freedom and purposiveness. If a person's creative need is blocked, he or she will become destructive; that is the only alternative to creativity. Destructiveness and creativity are innate tendencies that satisfy the need for transcendence. Creativity, however, is the dominant tendency.

rootedness need The need to feel an attachment or sense of belonging to family, community, and society.

The need for **rootedness** also arises from the loss of our primary ties with nature. Because we stand detached and alone, we must establish new roots in our relationships with others to replace our earlier roots in nature. Feelings of kinship are the most satisfying kind of roots we can develop. The least satisfying way of achieving rootedness is to maintain childhood ties with the mother by clinging to the security of infancy. Such ties can generalize beyond the parent-child relationship to include the community and the nation. Indeed, Fromm referred to nationalism as a form of incest because it restricts our feelings of solidarity to a specific group, thus isolating us from humanity at large (Fromm, 1955).

identity need The need to achieve an awareness of our unique abilities and characteristics.

Fromm also suggested that people need a sense of **identity** as unique individuals. There are several ways of satisfying this need. A person could develop his or her unique talents and abilities or could identify with a group—for example, a religious sect, a union, or a nation—sometimes to the point of conformity. Fromm noted that conformity is an unhealthy way to satisfy the need for an identity because one's identity would then be defined only in reference to the qualities and characteristics of the group, rather than to the qualities of the self. Thus the self becomes a borrowed one, not a genuine one.

frame-of-orientation need The need for a consistent, coherent picture of our world within which to understand life events.

The need for a **frame of orientation** and **an object of devotion** stems from our powers of reason and imagination, which require a framework for making sense of the phenomena of the external world. We must develop a consistent and coherent view of our environment within which to perceive and understand what is going on around us. This frame of orientation can be based on rational or irrational considerations. A rational framework provides an objective perception of reality. An irrational one involves a subjective view, which eventually severs our connection with reality. In addition to a frame of orientation, we need an ultimate goal or an object to which we are devoted and through which we can find meaning and a sense of direction.

excitation need The need for a stimulating external environment so that the brain can function at a peak level of activity and alertness.

The need for **excitation and stimulation** refers to the drive for a stimulating external environment in which we can function at a peak of alertness and activity. The brain requires a certain level of stimulation to maintain optimal performance. Without such excitation, we would find it difficult to maintain our involvement with daily life.

The ways these psychological needs are satisfied depends on our cultural and social conditions and opportunities. Therefore, the way we cope with or adjust to society is to work out a compromise between our needs and our environment. As a result of our compromise, we develop the structure of the personality.

The Productive and Nonproductive Character Types

Fromm proposed a number of character or personality types that underlie human behavior and describe how we relate or orient ourselves to the real world. Pure forms of these types are rare; most personalities are a combination of types, although one is usually dominant.

Fromm distinguished between nonproductive and productive orientations. Nonproductive orientations are unhealthy ways of relating to the world. The nonproductive orientations in his original formulation are the receptive, exploitative, hoarding, and marketing character types. The productive type or orientation is the ideal state of human development.

He later proposed additional types:

- necrophilous (a nonproductive orientation)
- biophilous (a productive orientation)
- having (a nonproductive orientation)
- being (a productive orientation).

receptive orientation A character type that is highly dependent on others.

Individuals with **receptive** characters expect to get whatever they want—for example, love, knowledge, or pleasure—from some outside source, usually another person. People of this type are receivers in their relations with others, needing to be loved rather than loving, taking rather than creating. Such people are highly dependent on others and feel paralyzed when left on their own; they feel incapable of doing the smallest thing without outside help.

A similarity exists between the receptive character and Freud's oral incorporative personality type in that both find satisfaction in eating and drinking. This type of satisfaction is a major way of recognizing the receptive character type.

> The receptive type has great fondness for food and drink. These persons tend to overcome anxiety and depression by eating and drinking. The mouth is an especially prominent feature [of the receptive character type]; often the most expressive one; the lips tend to be open, as if in a state of continuous expectation of being fed. (Fromm, 1947, p. 63)

The receptive type is also similar to Horney's compliant personality type, the one described as moving toward people. The society that fosters the receptive character type is one in which the exploitation of one group by another is practiced.

exploitative orientation
A character type that
takes from others by force
or cunning.

In the **exploitative** character type, the person is also directed toward others for what he or she wants. However, instead of expecting to receive from others, people of this type take, either by force or by cunning. If something is given to them, they see it as worthless. They want only what belongs to and is valued by others, whether it be a spouse, an object, or an idea. To this type of person, what has to be stolen or appropriated has greater value than what is given freely.

The exploitative type is similar to Freud's oral aggressive type and is "symbolized by the biting mouth which is often a prominent feature in such people. It is not a play upon words to point out that they often make 'biting' remarks about others" (Fromm, 1947, p. 65). Examples of the exploitative orientation include corporate raiders and fascist leaders who clearly like to dominate others.

hoarding orientation A
character type that derives
security from amassing
and preserving material
possessions and personal
feelings.

In the **hoarding** type, the person derives security from what he or she can hoard and save. This miserly behavior applies not only to money and material possessions, but also to emotions and thoughts. Such people build walls around themselves and sit surrounded by all they have amassed, protecting it from outside intruders and letting out as little as possible. They are characterized by a compulsive orderliness about their possessions, thoughts, and feelings. They also give themselves away by their behavior.

> One can recognize these people too by facial expressions and gestures. Theirs is the tight-lipped mouth; their gestures are characteristic of their withdrawn attitude. While those of the receptive type are inviting and round, as it were, and the gestures of the exploitative type are aggressive and pointed, those of the hoarding type are angular, as if they want to emphasize the frontiers between themselves and the outside world. (Fromm, 1947, p. 66)

A parallel exists here with Freud's anal retentive personality and Horney's detached type (moving away from people). Fromm suggested that the hoarding orientation was particularly common in the 18th and 19th centuries in countries that had stable middle-class economies typified by the Protestant ethic of thrift, conservatism, and sober business practices.

marketing orientation A
character type that values
superficial qualities.

The **marketing** character type is a 20th-century phenomenon identified with capitalist societies, particularly that of the United States. In a commodity-based marketplace culture, success or failure depends on how well we sell ourselves. The set of values is the same for personalities as for goods; one's personality becomes simply a commodity to be sold. Thus, it is not our personal qualities, skills, knowledge, or integrity that count, but rather how nice a package we are. Superficial qualities such as smiling, being agreeable, and laughing at the boss's jokes become more important than inner characteristics and abilities.

Such an orientation cannot produce security because we are left without any genuine relatedness to other people. If the game is played long enough, we no longer have a relationship with or even an awareness of our selves. The packaged role we are forced to play obscures our true character from ourselves as well as from others. As a result, we become alienated, with no personal core and no meaningful relationships.

productive orientation
A character type that is
the ideal of self-
development.

The **productive** character type is the ideal and represents the ultimate goal of human development. This concept assumes our ability to use all our capacities to

For the marketing personality type found among American businessmen, superficial qualities are more important than knowledge or skills.

realize our potential and to develop the self. Productivity is not restricted to artistic creativity or to the acquisition of material things. Rather, the productive orientation is an attitude that each of us can attain. Although the productive character is the ideal both for people and for societies, it has not yet been achieved; the best we can accomplish within our present social structure is a combination of productive and nonproductive orientations.

The influence of the productive orientation may transform the nonproductive types. For example, the aggressiveness of the exploitative type can be transformed into initiative, and the miserliness of the hoarding type can become sound economy. Fromm believed that through social and cultural change, the productive orientation could become dominant.

In his 1964 book, *The Heart of Man*, Fromm introduced the necrophilous and biophilous orientations. The **necrophilous** character type (a nonproductive orientation) is attracted to death, corpses, decay, feces, and dirt. Such people seem happiest when talking about illness, death, and burials. They dwell on the past and tend to be cold and aloof. They are devoted to law and order, and to the use of force and power. Their dreams center on murder, blood, and skulls. Fromm suggested that Adolf Hitler was an example of the necrophilous type. Not all such people are savages, however. Some may appear harmless, although they leave a path of emotional destruction in their wake.

Fromm offered the example of a mother who is obsessively concerned with her child's failures and frequently makes gloomy predictions about the child's future.

necrophilous orientation
A character type attracted to inanimate objects and to things associated with death.

She will not respond to the child's joy; she will not notice anything new that is growing within him. . . . She does not harm the child in any obvious way, yet she may slowly strangle his joy in life, his faith in growth, and eventually she will infect him with her own necrophilous orientation. (Fromm, 1964, p. 39)

Necrophilous persons also have a passion for technology and tend to surround themselves with appliances such as sophisticated stereo or computer equipment, not for the joy of the music or the potential for data manipulation but for the love of the machine.

biophilous orientation A character type congruent with the productive orientation; this type is concerned with personal growth and development.

The opposite type, the **biophilous** character type, is a productive orientation. These people are in love with life and are attracted to growth, creation, and construction. They try to influence others, not by force or power, but by love, reason, and example. They are concerned with the development of the self and of others, and their view is toward the future.

Extreme forms of the necrophilous and biophilous character types are rare; most people are a blend of both types. The extreme necrophilous character would be psychotic or insane; the extreme biophilous character would be a saint. Neither would function well in the real world. Fromm viewed his formulation of the necrophilous and biophilous types as a return to Freudian ideas. A biographer noted:

Despite Fromm's resolutely anti-instinctivist posture, his thinking in his later years, polarized as it was between life- and death-promoting forces, came to resemble Freud's in many respects. (Burston, 1991, p. 73)

The having versus being character types were proposed in Fromm's later writings, *To Have or to Be?* (1976), and *The Art of Being* (1992).[1] Having is a nonproductive orientation; being is a productive orientation.

having orientation A character type in which the definition and meaning of one's life lies in possessions, in what one has rather than what one is.

In the **having** character type, the definition and meaning of a person's life lies in possessions, in the things he or she owns. This orientation involves not only material possessions such as cars, clothing, houses, or jewelry, but also people, and even intangibles such as ideas. "People of this type are saying to the world and to themselves, 'I am [equal to] what I have and what I consume.' . . . My property constitutes myself and my identity" (Fromm, 1976, pp. 27, 77). These people define their value in terms of how well their possessions compare with those of others. They are highly competitive and ceaseless in their struggle to surpass the worth of friends and acquaintances. In the process, they become alienated from others and antagonistic toward them.

Fromm suggested that the having character type was similar to Freud's proposed anal retentive personality. The Freudian type was described as stingy, stubborn, and orderly, focused on having, saving, and hoarding material possessions. Freud considered the anal retentive personality to be pathological and that a society of such personalities would inevitably be a sick society. Similarly, Fromm believed that any society in which the majority of the people were of the having type was a sick society.

being orientation A character type in which people define themselves in terms of what they are, not in terms of what they have; their self-worth comes from within, not from comparing themselves with others.

In the **being** character type, people define themselves in terms of what they are, not in terms of what they have. Being types are not so competitive; their definition

---

[1] *The Art of Being* comprises several chapters written for the 1976 book *To Have or to Be?* but not published until after Fromm's death.

of self-worth comes from within, not from comparing themselves with others. They cooperate, love, and live productively with other people. Sharing with others rather than striving to surpass them increases their enjoyment of life. You can see that the being character type has much in common with the biophilous type.

Fromm described people of the being character type as participating in life, experiencing, focusing on the present, and being at one with self and society. He argued that it was possible to develop a life of being through psychoanalysis and self-analysis. He described specific procedures for self-improvement, such as free association and autobiographical analysis, that would foster development of the productive being orientation.

Questions About Human Nature

Fromm presented an optimistic picture of human nature. In contrast to Freud, he did not consider people to be doomed to conflict and anxiety by immutable biological forces. According to Fromm, we are shaped by our society's social, political, and economic characteristics; however, these forces do not completely determine our character. We are not puppets reacting to the strings pulled by society. Instead, we have a set of psychological qualities or mechanisms by which we shape our own nature and our society (see Figure 6.1).

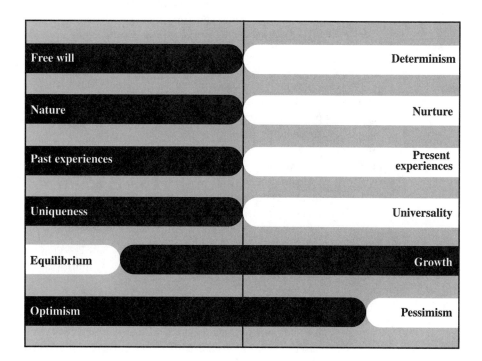

FIGURE 6.1   *Fromm's image of human nature*

Fromm believed we have an innate tendency to grow, develop, and realize our potential. This is our major task in life, our ultimate and necessary goal. Failure to attain a productive orientation, to become what we have the potential to become, results in unhappiness or even mental illness. Although Fromm proposed universality in personality, a common social character within a given culture, he also believed that each person is unique. To have an identity as a unique individual is a basic human need. He did not think we are inherently either good or evil, but rather that we can become evil if we fail to realize our potential.

humanistic communitarian socialism An ideal system of society typified by positive human relationships and the full expression of the productive orientation.

He believed that humanity would eventually reach a state of harmony and integration but was saddened by the lack of progress in his lifetime. He proposed an ideal society, which he called **humanistic communitarian socialism**, and described it as one in which love, brotherhood, and solidarity characterize all human relationships. The productive orientation will become dominant, and all feelings of loneliness, insignificance, and alienation will disappear.

Assessment in Fromm's Theory

The neopsychoanalytic theorists discussed in earlier chapters based their systems on the clinical data they obtained from patients and were clear about their methods of assessing or evaluating their patients' personalities. In contrast, Fromm wrote little about his assessment techniques. He occasionally referred to psychoanalytic observations but did not offer specific analytical findings or case studies. Colleagues of Fromm suggest that he focused primarily on those comments from his patients that supported his theories. He may have been "inattentive, impatient, or actually dismissive of those facets of their experience that did not coincide with his 'intuitive' sense of their problems and situations" (Burston, 1991, p. 82). Thus, the possibility exists that the data Fromm collected from his patients was highly selective.

Fromm used a form of free association and considered dream analysis an important therapeutic tool. However, his theory is largely based on generalizations and speculations derived from his interpretation of historical, social, and cultural events. He also drew on religious, economic, political, and anthropological sources.

Although Fromm did not use self-report techniques, he developed an interpretive questionnaire to assess the necrophilous character type (Fromm, 1973). The questionnaire included items such as "What is your opinion of women who use cosmetics?" Responses such as "Cosmetics are poisonous" or "Makeup makes women look like whores" were considered to indicate the necrophilous type.

Research in Fromm's Theory

We do not know how widely Fromm used the case study method, nor can we say how comprehensive were the case histories he developed on his patients. He did collect data of a psychoanalytic nature from his patients, however, and the criticisms of case studies discussed in earlier chapters also apply to Fromm. It is impossible to duplicate and verify Fromm's clinical observations or the conditions under which he made them.

Fromm remained convinced of the scientific worth and credibility of the case study as a research method. He admitted that the results could not be tested by experimental or correlational methods but insisted they could be tested by repeated analyses. A hypothesis generated from observations of one patient could be verified by observing additional patients. Nevertheless, no matter how carefully analysts make their observations, it remains impossible for anyone else to repeat them or to establish identical conditions.

Social Character in a Mexican Village

Late in his career, Fromm and his colleagues undertook a multidisciplinary study to test his idea of social character (Fromm & Maccoby, 1970). Over several years, psychologists, anthropologists, physicians, statisticians, and other specialists visited an isolated village in Mexico to analyze its history, its economic and social structure, and the health, attitudes, and dreams of its inhabitants. The investigators lived among the villagers and came to be accepted by them.

Through a combination of techniques including questionnaires, interviews, the Rorschach inkblot test, and the Thematic Apperception Test, the researchers found substantial support for the receptive, hoarding, and exploitative character types. No evidence was found for the marketing type. This is not surprising because Fromm described the marketing type as common to 20th-century capitalist societies, not to rural villages. Some evidence was found for the productive orientation. The personal characteristics of the villagers described as receptive, hoarding, exploitative, and productive were found to match the descriptions in Fromm's writings.

Social Character in American Business

Michael Maccoby, an anthropologist and psychiatrist who was coauthor of the Mexican village study, conducted research on Fromm's character types in American business. One study involved interviews with 250 male managers in 12 large U.S. corporations (Maccoby, 1976). Maccoby identified a personality type analogous to the marketing orientation and called it the "company man." Maccoby wrote, "When they describe themselves, they seem to be trying to give the right impression, to sell themselves to the interviewers. It is as though they are constantly working on themselves in order to have the right kind of personality to fit the job" (Maccoby, 1976, p. 92).

Like Fromm's marketing type, the company man focuses more on superficial personal qualities to attain success than on actual job skills, abilities, or knowledge. The personality or packaging of this type of person is all-important, and it can be changed to fit the perceived needs of superiors as readily as clothes are changed to fit different social situations.

A later study of corporate leaders suggested to Maccoby another character type, the self orientation (Maccoby, 1981). This type is a product of the turbulent American society of the 1960s, an era marked by the questioning of traditional authority, of the Protestant work ethic, and of the commitment to corporate success. Maccoby described the self orientation as cynical, rebellious, detached, undisciplined, self-indulgent, lacking in loyalty, and unconcerned with others' well-being.

Although Maccoby's research does not provide direct support for Fromm's proposed character types, it suggests types within the framework of Fromm's system that are products of historical, social, and cultural forces. Fromm believed that as these forces change so will the character types associated with them.

Using Fromm's interpretive questionnaire approach, Maccoby investigated a variety of subject samples and found evidence to support the necrophilous character type (Maccoby, 1972). Approximately 10 to 15 percent of those tested were judged to be necrophilous. Correlating the questionnaire responses with the subjects' political opinions revealed that persons labeled necrophilous supported military force against those they considered enemies and favored repressive measures against those who criticized the government. Necrophilous types also wanted to strengthen police forces and improve enforcement of anti-drug laws.

There is indirect evidence to support Fromm's receptive, exploitative, and hoarding character types. As we noted earlier, each of these types is similar to one of Sigmund Freud's oral or anal personality types. To the degree that empirical research support exists for Freud's types (see Chapter 2), by extension it exists for Fromm's similar orientations.

A Final Commentary

Fromm's books have been popular in many countries. He wrote for the general public because he wanted to reach the widest possible audience with his message about the type of society that will ensure the survival of human civilization. His books are highly readable, with a minimum of technical jargon. This does not mean that they are simple, but rather that he presented his ideas in an engaging and interesting manner. Fromm's importance to psychology lies in his focus on social, historical, and cultural forces and their role in shaping personality. We see similarities between Fromm's productive character type and Gordon Allport's concept of the mature personality (Chapter 9), as well as Abraham Maslow's description of the self-actualizing person (Chapter 11).

One criticism of Fromm's theory is that it lacks supporting empirical data. Fromm has also been faulted for not keeping current with developments in psychoanalysis. His major references were the works of Freud, Jung, and Horney; he did not recognize later ideas, such as those of the humanistic psychologists. In addition, some of Fromm's concepts are defined imprecisely and in terms that are often contradictory, thus making it difficult to test his propositions experimentally.

Scholars of the history and social conditions of the Middle Ages have challenged Fromm's suggestion that people during that period had attained security, identity, and belonging. They charge that Fromm painted an idealized picture of the Middle Ages and omitted calamities such as religious persecutions, witch hunts, plagues, wars, and other physical and psychological hardships. These scholars argue that the Middle Ages must have been a time not of security but of great instability and insecurity.

Nevertheless, Fromm presented us with a unique interpretation of the interaction between people and their society. He made us aware of the continuing and interrelated impact of social, economic, and psychological factors on human nature. He confirmed that personality is not the product of a single set of factors but the result of interplay of forces and events. He challenged us to think beyond the boundaries of any one discipline and goaded us to create a more humane society. Fromm's contributions extend beyond psychoanalysis and psychology to include the spectrum of social problems that concern us all.

Chapter Summary

Erich Fromm believed that as people throughout history gained increasing freedom, they came to feel more lonely and alienated. The less freedom people have, the greater their sense of belonging and security. The Middle Ages, a time of little individual freedom, was the last era of security and belonging, because everyone's place in society was fixed. Three psychic mechanisms of escape from too much freedom and from the loneliness and insignificance that accompany it are authoritarianism, destructiveness, and automaton conformity.

The development of an individual in childhood parallels the development of humankind throughout history. As children grow, they gain increasing independence and freedom at the expense of the security of the primary maternal ties. Children attempt to escape this freedom through symbiotic relatedness, withdrawal-destructiveness, or love. Six psychological needs that result from the polarity between the drive for security and the drive for freedom are relatedness, transcendence, rootedness, identity, a frame of orientation and an object of devotion, and excitation and stimulation.

Character types are grouped into nonproductive and productive orientations. Nonproductive orientations include the receptive, exploitative, hoarding, and marketing types. Receptive types depend on others for satisfaction of their needs. Exploitative types take what they need from others. Hoarding types derive security from what can be amassed and saved. Marketing types see themselves as commodities to be packaged and sold. Productive types represent the ultimate goal of human development: the achievement of self-realization.

Necrophilous (nonproductive) types are in love with death, power, and technology; biophilous (productive) types are in love with life, growth, and development; having (nonproductive) types define themselves by their possessions; and being (productive) types focus on cooperating, sharing, and living productively with others.

Fromm's image of human nature is optimistic. We have the ability to shape our personality and society. Life's ultimate, innate goal is the realization of our potentialities and capacities.

Fromm's research relied on psychoanalytic observations, which cannot be repeated or verified. Observational studies in a Mexican village and among American businessmen provide some support for his original character types. His theory has been criticized for ignoring post-Freudian developments in psychoanalysis, containing vague terminology, and presenting an idealized picture of the Middle Ages. His importance lies in his focus on broad social, historical, and cultural forces in the shaping of personality.

Review Questions

1. How does Fromm's approach to personality differ from those of the other personality theorists we have discussed?

2. What experiences in Fromm's early years influenced the direction of his work?

3. According to Fromm, why have people become less secure as they have achieved greater freedom?

4. Describe the three psychic mechanisms by which we can regain security and ease our feelings of loneliness.

5. Describe the parental behaviors that can foster symbiotic relatedness, withdrawal-destructiveness, and love.

6. Define the six psychological needs in Fromm's theory and describe how the satisfaction of each contributes to the creation of the self.

7. Describe the productive and nonproductive character orientations, and the having versus being orientations.

8. Distinguish between the biophilous and necrophilous character types.

9. What methods of assessment did Fromm use in developing his theory?

10. Which character orientation did Fromm consider typical of American society? Which orientations were supported by the Mexican village studies?

11. According to Fromm, what is the relationship between personality and society?

Suggested Readings

Burston, D. (1991). *The legacy of Erich Fromm.* Cambridge, MA: Harvard University Press. Portrays Fromm as a member of Freud's loyal opposition and places Fromm's work in the context of current intellectual thought.

Evans, R. I. (1966). *Dialogue with Erich Fromm.* New York: Harper & Row. Conversations with Fromm about his life and work.

Fromm, E. (1941). *Escape from freedom.* New York: Holt, Rinehart & Winston. Fromm's views on the human character and how it is affected by social and political forces.

Fromm, E. (1947). *Man for himself: An inquiry into the psychology of ethics.* New York: Holt, Rinehart & Winston. Describes the productive and nonproductive character orientations and relates them to ethical behavior for the individual and for society.

Fromm, E. (1968). *The revolution of hope: Toward a humanized technology.* New York: Harper & Row. Discusses the choice between a mechanistic and a humanistic world and argues for a psychospiritual renewal to deal with the problem.

Fromm, E. (1992). *The art of being.* New York: Continuum. Presents chapters originally written for an earlier book but not published until after Fromm's death. Describes practical steps people can take for self-improvement, to achieve a life of being, as opposed to having.

Fromm, E. (1998). *Love, sexuality, and matriarchy: About gender.* New York: Fromm International. Reprints essays written between 1933 and 1970 on topics such as sexual repression as an element of social control, the so-called "battle of the sexes," and the notion of monogamous marriage as the norm. Shows how ideas, once considered out of step with their times, can come to reflect a culture's dominant themes.

S E V E N

> For me, personality is [a] jungle without boundaries.
> —Henry Murray

Henry Murray

Henry Murray designed an approach to personality that includes conscious and unconscious forces; the influence of the past, present, and future; and the impact of physiological and sociological factors. The influence of Freudian psychoanalysis can be seen in Murray's recognition of the effect on adult behavior of childhood experiences and in his notions of the id, ego, and superego. Although Freud's imprint is clear, Murray gave unique interpretations to these phenomena. His deviations from orthodox psychoanalysis are so extensive that his system must be classified with the neo-Freudians rather than with the Freudian loyalists.

Two distinctive features of Murray's system are a sophisticated approach to human needs and the data source on which he based his theory. His proposed list of needs is still widely used in personality research and assessment and in clinical treatment. His data, unlike those of theorists discussed in earlier chapters, come from so-called normal individuals (undergraduate male students at Harvard University) rather than from patients undergoing psychotherapy. Also, some of the data were derived from more empirically based laboratory procedures rather than from case histories.

Because of his long affiliation with a major university instead of relative isolation in a clinic or private practice, and because of his personal charisma, Murray gathered and trained a large number of psychologists, many of whom have since achieved prominence and carried on his teachings.

The Life of Murray (1893–1988)

Childhood Depression and Compensation

depression, mental

Neither neurotic parents nor poverty marked Henry Murray's childhood. However, it contained elements of Adlerian compensation for a physical defect, a supernormal sensitivity to the sufferings of others, and a degree of maternal rejection to ensure that his childhood was not intolerably dull. Born into a wealthy family, Murray grew up in New York City, in a house on what is now the site of Rockefeller Center. His summers were spent on a Long Island beach. As a child, he accompanied his parents on four long trips to Europe. For the Adlerians among you, Murray reported that some of his earliest recollections focused on his privileged background (Triplet, 1992).

Another significant early memory is more intriguing. Murray called it "the marrow-of-my-being memory" (Murray, 1967, p. 299). At about age 4, he was looking at a picture of a sad woman sitting next to her equally sad son. This was the same kind of gloomy picture Murray later used in his Thematic Apperception Test. Murray's mother told him, "It is the prospect of death that has made them sad" (Murray, 1967, p. 299). Murray interpreted the memory as indicating the death of his emotional ties to his mother because she had abruptly weaned him when he was 2 months old, preferring, he believed, to lavish her affection on his siblings. He insisted that his mother's actions led to his lifelong depression, a condition that formed the core of his personality. Murray referred to his depression as a source of "misery and melancholy" and attempted to mask it in everyday behavior by an ebullient, cheerful, and outgoing manner (Murray, 1967). This lack of a childhood attachment to his mother later led Murray to question Freud's Oedipus complex because it did not coincide with his own experiences.

Another factor that made Murray sensitive to emotional problems and sufferings was his relationship with two emotionally disturbed aunts.

Murray was afflicted with crossed eyes, and at the age of 9 he underwent an operation that was performed in the dining room of his home. The condition was corrected, but a slip of the surgeon's blade left Murray with no stereoscopic vision. No matter how hard he tried, he was never able to succeed at games such as tennis or baseball because he could not focus both eyes on the ball. He remained unaware of his visual defect until he was in medical school, when a physician asked him if he had had trouble playing sports as a child.

Murray's physical ineptness and a speech impediment (a stutter) drove him to compensate for his limitations. When he tried to play football, he had to be quarterback, and when he was calling plays, he never stuttered. After being bested in a schoolyard fight, Murray took up boxing and won the local featherweight championship. He later agreed that "an Adlerian factor was at work" in these childhood efforts to compensate for his disabilities (Murray, 1967, p. 302).

Education

After attending Groton, a preparatory school, Murray enrolled at Harvard University. He studied history but earned mediocre grades because he preferred "the three Rs—Rum, Rowing, and Romanticism" (Robinson, 1992, p. 27). His career followed a devious route to the study of personality. He disliked the psychology course he took in college and dropped out after the second lecture. He did not attend another psychology course until years later, when he taught one himself.

In 1919 Murray graduated from Columbia University Medical School at the top of his class. He also earned an M.A. in biology from Columbia and taught physiology at Harvard. He served a two-year internship in surgery at a New York hospital where he helped care for a future U.S. president, Franklin D. Roosevelt, who was suffering from polio. Following the internship Murray spent two years at the Rockefeller Institute conducting biomedical research in embryology. He went abroad for further study and in 1927 received his Ph.D. in biochemistry from Cambridge University.

The Influence of Jung

Murray's sensitivity and empathy toward others were reinforced during his internship, when he became interested in the psychological factors in his patients' lives. In 1923 he read Carl Jung's book *Psychological Types* and found it fascinating. "I found this book at the medical school bookstore on the way home one night, and I read it all night long and all the next day" (Murray quoted in Anderson, 1988, p. 147).

A few weeks after finishing the book, Murray was faced with a serious personal problem. He had fallen in love with Christiana Morgan, a beautiful, wealthy, depressive married woman who was impressed by Jung's work. Murray did not want

to leave his wife of seven years—he claimed to abhor the idea of divorce—but neither did he want to give up his lover, whose spirited, artistic nature was the opposite
of his wife's. Murray insisted he needed both women.

He lived with the conflict for two years until, at Christiana Morgan's suggestion,
he went to Zurich to meet with Carl Jung. The two men spent a month together, and
Jung was able to resolve Murray's difficulty by instruction and example. Jung was
also having an affair with a younger woman, a relationship he maintained openly
while living with his wife. Jung counseled Murray to do the same, and Murray did
so for the next 40 years.

But first, the principal actors in this drama all found themselves in Zurich, with
Jung in the role of director. He decreed that Christiana Morgan's husband should be
analyzed by Toni Wolff, who was Jung's mistress. In addition, Jung spent many
hours with Christiana, analyzing her bizarre dreams and visions. Murray's wife,
Josephine, was reluctant to play her part. She spent 20 minutes listening to Jung
insist that Murray needed to live with both his wife and his mistress. Josephine
Murray quickly decided that Jung was a dirty old man (Robinson, 1992). In time,
however, both Murray's wife and Morgan's husband were persuaded to accept the
affair.

The experience with Jung and the resolution of Murray's marital dilemma
turned Murray toward a career in psychology. He had sought help for a personal
problem and psychology had provided an answer (Anderson, 1988). Thus, Jung did
more than resolve Murray's personal and career dilemmas; he made Murray aware
of the breadth and impact of unconscious forces. Murray wrote, "The great flood-
gates of the wonder-world swung open. I had experienced the unconscious" (1940,
p. 153).

Murray met with Jung several times but his attitude toward the man who helped
him through his early crises changed dramatically. His initial acceptance of Jung's
views turned to scathing dismissal. Murray said that Jung would "believe anything I
told him that was along the lines that he liked, but he would overlook what did not
fit his theories" (quoted in Anderson, 1988, p. 155).

The Harvard Psychological Clinic

Psychologist Morton Prince at the new Harvard Psychological Clinic, established
specifically to study personality, offered Murray an appointment. A former student
described the clinic as "wisteria on the outside, hysteria on the inside" (Smith, 1990,
p. 537). As part of his training, Murray underwent orthodox Freudian psychoanalysis and reported that his analyst became bored by the phlegmatic nature of his
childhood and his lack of complexes. Murray recalled that the analyst had little to
say. The analyst's stomach rumbled, and his office was "depressing, the color of
feces. . . .[a] miserable room . . . enough to send a patient into a morbid phase"
(quoted in Anderson, 1988, p. 159).

In the 1930s, Murray and Morgan developed the Thematic Apperception Test
(TAT), still one of the most widely used projective measures of personality (Morgan
& Murray, 1935). For many years it was thought that the TAT was primarily
Murray's work but in 1985, Murray revealed that Morgan had done most of the work

to develop the test. Further, the original idea for the test had come from one of his women students (Bronstein, 1988, p. 64).

The TAT became a best seller for Harvard University Press. Despite the magnitude of Morgan's contribution, her name was dropped from the publication, leaving Murray as sole author, an action taken with Murray's agreement (Douglas, 1993). This decision seems inexcusable, given her importance in the development of the test and in much of Murray's subsequent work. At age 94, long after Morgan's death, he acknowledged that she was "part of every paper he wrote and every lecture he gave, and that her very presence at the clinic raised the caliber of his thinking" (Douglas, 1993, p. 297).

In 1938 Murray published *Explorations in Personality: A Clinical and Experimental Study of Fifty Men of College Age*. This book assured his almost instant success as a leading personality theorist. Now considered a classic, it boosted the effort begun by Gordon Allport the year before (see Chapter 9) to make the study of personality an academically respectable part of American psychology.

During World War II, Murray joined the U.S. Army and became director of assessment for the Office of Strategic Services (the OSS; a forerunner of the CIA), screening candidates for dangerous assignments. He maintained an interest in literature, especially the work of Herman Melville, and in 1951 published an analysis of the psychological meaning of Melville's novel *Moby Dick*.

Murray remained at Harvard until his retirement in 1962, conducting research, refining his personality theory, and training new generations of psychologists. He received the American Psychological Foundation's Gold Medal Award and the American Psychological Association's Distinguished Scientific Contribution Award.

Although Murray lived to the age of 95, the debilitating effects of a stroke marred the last decade of his life. He came to view the sum of his career as a "series of failures and unfulfilled promises [and] could not escape the feeling that he had not quite made the grade" (Triplet, 1993, p. 386). At the end, as a biographer noted, Murray was

> certainly willing to be done with life, though never to the point of losing his sense of humor. "I am dead," he announced to his nurse. "No," she replied, pinching him gently on the cheek; "see, you're alive." "I'm the doctor," [he] snapped back, not without the hint of a smile—"I'm the doctor; you're the nurse; and I'm dead." Just days later, on Thursday, June 23, he had his way. (Robinson, 1992, p. 370)

The Principles of Personology

personology Murray's system of personality.

The first principle in Murray's **personology**, his term for the study of personality, is that personality is rooted in the brain. The individual's cerebral physiology guides and governs every aspect of the personality. A simple example of this is that certain drugs can alter the functioning of the brain, and so the personality. Everything on which personality depends exists in the brain, including feeling states, conscious and unconscious memories, beliefs, attitudes, fears, and values.

A second principle in Murray's system involves the idea of tension reduction. Murray agreed with Freud and other theorists that people act to reduce physiological and psychological tension, but this does not mean we strive for a tension-free state. It is the process of acting to reduce tension that is satisfying, according to Murray, rather than the attainment of a condition free of all tension.

Murray believed that a tension-free existence is itself a source of distress. We need excitement, activity, and movement, all of which involve increasing, not decreasing, tension. We generate tension in order to have the satisfaction of reducing it. Murray believed the ideal state of human nature involves always having a certain level of tension to reduce.

A third principle of Murray's personology is that an individual's personality continues to develop over time and is constructed of all the events that occur during the course of that person's life. Therefore, the study of a person's past is of great importance.

Murray's fourth principle involves the idea that personality changes and progresses; it is not fixed or static.

Fifth, Murray emphasized the uniqueness of each person while recognizing similarities among all people. As he saw it, an individual human being is like no other person, like some other people, and like every other person.

The Divisions of Personality

The Id

id To Murray, the id contains the primitive, amoral, and lustful impulses described by Freud, but it also contains desirable impulses, such as empathy and love.

Murray divided personality into three parts, using the Freudian terms id, superego, and ego, but his concepts are not what Freud envisioned.

Like Freud, Murray suggested that the **id** is the repository of all innate impulsive tendencies. As such, it provides energy and direction to behavior and is concerned with motivation. The id contains the primitive, amoral, and lustful impulses Freud described. However, in Murray's personological system the id also encompasses innate impulses that society considers acceptable and desirable.

Here we see the influence of Jung's shadow archetype, which has both good and bad aspects. The id contains the tendencies to empathy, imitation, and identification; forms of love other than lustful ones; and the tendency to master one's environment.

The strength or intensity of the id varies among individuals. For example, one person may possess more intense appetites and emotions than another. Therefore, the problem of controlling and directing the id forces is not the same for all people because some of us have greater id energy with which we must cope.

The Superego

superego To Murray, the superego is shaped not only by parents and authority figures, but also by the peer group and culture.

Murray defined the **superego** as the internalization of the culture's values and norms, by which rules we come to evaluate and judge our behavior and that of others. The substance of the superego is imposed on children at an early age by their parents and other authority figures.

Other factors may shape the superego, including one's peer group and the culture's literature and mythology. Thus, Murray deviated from Freud's ideas by allowing for influences beyond the parent-child interaction. According to Murray, the superego is not rigidly crystallized by age 5, as Freud believed, but continues to develop throughout life, reflecting the greater complexity and sophistication of our experiences as we grow older.

The superego is not in constant conflict with the id, as Freud proposed, because the id contains good forces as well as bad ones. Good forces do not have to be suppressed. The superego must try to thwart the socially unacceptable impulses, but it also functions to determine when, where, and how an acceptable need can be expressed and satisfied.

ego-ideal A component of the superego that contains the moral or ideal behaviors for which a person should strive.

While the superego is developing, so is the **ego-ideal**, which provides us with long-range goals for which to strive. The ego-ideal represents what we could become at our best and is the sum of our ambitions and aspirations.

The Ego

ego (psychology)

ego To Murray, the conscious organizer of behavior; this is a broader conception than Freud's.

The **ego** is the rational governor of the personality; it tries to modify or delay the id's unacceptable impulses. Murray extended Freud's formulation of the ego by proposing that the ego is the central organizer of behavior. It consciously reasons, decides, and wills the direction of behavior. Thus, the ego is more active in determining behavior than Freud believed. Not merely the servant of the id, the ego consciously plans courses of action. It functions not only to suppress id pleasure but also to foster pleasure by organizing and directing the expression of acceptable id impulses.

The ego is also the arbiter between the id and the superego and may favor one over the other. For example, if the ego favors the id, it may direct the personality toward a life of crime. The ego may also integrate these two aspects of the personality so that what we want to do (id) is in harmony with what society believes we should do (superego).

Opportunity exists in Murray's system for conflict to arise between the id and the superego. A strong ego can mediate effectively between the two, but a weak ego leaves the personality a battleground. Unlike Freud, however, Murray did not believe that this conflict was inevitable.

Needs: The Motivation of Behavior

Murray's most important contribution to theory and research in personality is his use of the concept of needs to explain the motivation and direction of behavior. He said that "motivation is the crux of the business and motivation always refers to something within the organism" (quoted in Robinson, 1992, p. 220).

need (psychology)

A need involves a physicochemical force in the brain that organizes and directs intellectual and perceptual abilities. Needs may arise either from internal processes such as hunger or thirst, or from events in the environment. Needs arouse a level of tension that the organism tries to reduce by acting to satisfy them. Needs energize and direct behavior. They activate behavior in the appropriate direction to satisfy the needs.

Murray's research led him to formulate a list of 20 needs (Murray, 1938, pp. 144–145). Not every person has all of these needs. Over the course of your lifetime

T A B L E   7 . 1   *Murray's list of needs*

Abasement	To submit passively to external force. To accept injury, blame, criticism, and punishment. To become resigned to fate. To admit inferiority, error, wrongdoing, or defeat. To blame, belittle, or mutilate the self. To seek and enjoy pain, punishment, illness, and misfortune.
Achievement	To accomplish something difficult. To master, manipulate, or organize physical objects, human beings, or ideas. To overcome obstacles and attain a high standard. To rival and surpass others.
Affiliation	To draw near and enjoyably cooperate or reciprocate with an allied other who resembles one or who likes one. To adhere and remain loyal to a friend.
Aggression	To overcome opposition forcefully. To fight, attack, injure, or kill another. To maliciously belittle, censure, or ridicule another.
Autonomy	To get free, shake off restraint, or break out of confinement. To resist coercion and restriction. To be independent and free to act according to impulse. To defy conventions.
Counteraction	To master or make up for a failure by restriving. To obliterate a humiliation by resumed action. To overcome weaknesses and to repress fear. To search for obstacles and difficulties to overcome. To maintain self-respect and pride on a high level.
Defendance	To defend the self against assault, criticism, and blame. To conceal or justify a misdeed, failure, or humiliation.
Deference	To admire and support a superior other. To yield eagerly to the influence of an allied other. To conform to custom.
Dominance	To control one's environment. To influence or direct the behavior of others by suggestion, seduction, persuasion, or command. To get others to cooperate. To convince another of the rightness of one's opinion.
Exhibition	To make an impression. To be seen and heard. To excite, amaze, fascinate, entertain, shock, intrigue, amuse, or entice others.
Harmavoidance	To avoid pain, physical injury, illness, and death. To escape from a dangerous situation. To take precautionary measures.
Infavoidance	To avoid humiliation. To quit embarrassing situations or to avoid conditions that may lead to the scorn, derision, or indifference of others. To refrain from action because of the fear of failure.
Nurturance	To give sympathy to and gratify the needs of a helpless other, an infant or one who is weak, disabled, tired, inexperienced, infirm, humiliated, lonely, dejected, or mentally confused.
Order	To put things in order. To achieve cleanliness, arrangement, organization, balance, neatness, and precision.
Play	To act for fun, without further purpose.
Rejection	To exclude, abandon, expel, or remain indifferent to an inferior other. To snub or jilt another.
Sentience	To seek and enjoy sensuous impressions.
Sex	To form and further an erotic relationship. To have sexual intercourse.
Succorance	To be nursed, supported, sustained, surrounded, protected, loved, advised, guided, indulged, forgiven, or consoled. To remain close to a devoted protector.
Understanding	To be inclined to analyze events and to generalize. To discuss and argue and to emphasize reason and logic. To state one's opinions precisely. To show interest in abstract formulations in science, mathematics, and philosophy.

you may experience all these needs, or there may be some needs you never experience. Some needs support other needs, and some oppose other needs (see Table 7.1).

Types of Needs

primary needs Survival and related needs arising from internal bodily processes.

secondary needs Emotional and psychological needs, such as achievement and affiliation.

Primary and secondary needs. **Primary needs** (viscerogenic needs) arise from internal bodily states and include those needs required for survival (such as food, water, air, and harmavoidance), as well as such needs as sex and sentience. **Secondary needs** (psychogenic needs) arise indirectly from primary needs, in a way Murray did not make clear, but they have no specifiable origin within the body. They are called secondary not because they are less important but because they develop after the primary needs. Secondary needs are concerned with emotional satisfaction and include most of the needs on Murray's original list.

reactive needs Needs that involve a response to a specific object.

proactive needs Needs that arise spontaneously.

Reactive and proactive needs. **Reactive needs** involve a response to something specific in the environment and are aroused only when that object appears. For example, the harmavoidance need appears only when a threat is present. **Proactive needs** do not depend on the presence of a particular object. They are spontaneous needs that elicit appropriate behavior whenever they are aroused, independent of the environment. For example, hungry people look for food to satisfy their need; they do not wait for a stimulus, such as a television ad for a hamburger, before acting to find food. Reactive needs involve a response to a specific object; proactive needs arise spontaneously.

The need for affection is expressed in cooperation, loyalty, and friendship.

Characteristics of Needs

Needs differ in terms of the urgency with which they impel behavior, a characteristic Murray called a need's prepotency. For example, if the needs for air and water are not satisfied, they come to dominate behavior, taking precedence over all other needs.

Some needs are complementary and can be satisfied by one behavior or a set of behaviors. Murray called this a fusion of needs. For instance, by working to acquire fame and wealth, we can satisfy the needs for achievement, dominance, and autonomy.

subsidiation To Murray, a situation in which one need is activated to aid in the satisfaction of another need.

The concept of **subsidiation** refers to a situation in which one need is activated to aid in satisfying another need. For example, to satisfy the affiliation need by being in the company of other people, it may be necessary to act deferentially toward them, thus invoking the deference need. In this case, the deference need is subsidiary to the affiliation need.

press The influence of the environment and past events on the current activation of a need.

Murray recognized that childhood events can affect the development of specific needs and, later in life, can activate those needs. He called this influence **press** because an environmental object or event presses or pressures the individual to act a certain way.

thema A combination of press (the environment) and need (the personality) that brings order to our behavior.

Because of the possibility of interaction between need and press, Murray introduced the concept of **thema** (or unity thema). The thema combines personal factors (needs) with the environmental factors that pressure or compel our behavior (presses). The thema is formed through early childhood experiences and becomes a powerful force in determining personality. Largely unconscious, the thema relates needs and presses in a pattern that gives coherence, unity, order, and uniqueness to our behavior.

Personality Development in Childhood

Complexes

Drawing on Freud's work, Murray divided childhood into five stages, each characterized by a pleasurable condition that is inevitably terminated by society's demands. Each stage leaves its mark on our personality in the form of an unconscious **complex** that directs our later development.

complex To Murray, a normal pattern of childhood development that influences the adult personality; childhood developmental stages include the claustral, oral, anal, urethral, and genital complexes.

According to Murray, everyone experiences these five complexes because everyone passes through the same developmental stages. There is nothing abnormal about them except when they are manifested in the extreme, a condition that leaves the person fixated at that stage. The personality is then unable to develop spontaneity and flexibility, a situation that interferes with the formation of the ego and superego. The stages of childhood and their corresponding complexes are shown in Table 7.2.

Stages of Development

The claustral stage. The fetus in the womb is secure, serene, and dependent, conditions we may all occasionally wish to reinstate. The *simple claustral complex* is experienced as a desire to be in small, warm, dark places that are safe and secluded.

TABLE 7.2   *The childhood stages and complexes in Murray's personology*

Stage	Complex
The secure existence within the womb	Claustral complexes
The sensuous enjoyment of sucking nourishment while being held	Oral complexes
The pleasure resulting from defecation	Anal complexes
The pleasure accompanying urination	Urethral complex
Genital pleasures	Genital or castration complex

For example, one might long to remain under the blankets instead of getting out of bed in the morning. People with this complex tend to be dependent on others, passive, and oriented toward safe, familiar behaviors that worked in the past. The *insupport* form of the claustral complex centers on feelings of insecurity and helplessness that cause the person to fear open spaces, falling, drowning, fires, earthquakes, or any situation of novelty and change. The *anticlaustral* or *egression* form of the claustral complex is based on a need to escape from restraining womb-like conditions. It includes a fear of suffocation and confinement and manifests itself in a preference for open spaces, fresh air, travel, movement, change, and novelty.

The oral stage.   The *oral succorance complex* features a combination of mouth activities, passive tendencies, and the need to be supported and protected. Behavioral manifestations include sucking, kissing, eating, drinking, and a hunger for affection, sympathy, protection, and love. The *oral aggression complex* combines oral and aggressive behaviors, including biting, spitting, shouting, and verbal aggression such as sarcasm. Behaviors characteristic of the *oral rejection complex* include vomiting, being picky about food, eating little, fearing oral contamination (such as from kissing), desiring seclusion, and avoiding dependence on others.

The anal stage.   In the *anal rejection complex*, there is a preoccupation with defecation, anal humor, and feces-like material such as dirt, mud, plaster, and clay. Aggression is often part of this complex and is shown in dropping and throwing things, firing guns, and setting off explosives. Persons with this complex may be dirty and disorganized. The *anal retention complex* is manifested in accumulating, saving, and collecting things, and in cleanliness, neatness, and orderliness.

The urethral stage.   Unique to Murray's system, the *urethral complex* is associated with excessive ambition, a distorted sense of self-esteem, exhibitionism, bed-wetting, sexual cravings, and self-love. It is sometimes called the Icarus complex, after the mythical Greek figure who flew so close to the sun that the wax holding his wings melted. Like Icarus, persons with this complex aim too high, and their dreams are shattered by failure.

The genital or castration stage.   Murray disagreed with Freud's contention that fear of castration is the core of anxiety in adult males. He interpreted the *castration complex* in narrower and more literal fashion as a boy's fantasy that his penis might be cut off. Murray believed such a fear grows out of childhood masturbation and the parental punishment that may have accompanied it.

Questions About Human Nature

Although Murray's personality theory is similar to Freud's in several ways, his image of human nature is quite different. Even the ultimate and necessary goal in life—which, like Freud's, is the reduction of tension—is considered from a different perspective. According to Murray, our goal is not a tension-free state but rather the satisfaction derived from acting to reduce the tension (see Figure 7.1).

On the free will versus determinism issue, Murray argued that personality is determined by our needs and by the environment. He accorded us some free will in our capacity to change and to grow. Each person is unique, but there are also similarities in the personalities of all of us.

Murray believed we are shaped by our inherited attributes and by our environment; each is of roughly equal influence. We cannot understand the human personality unless we accept the impact of the physiological forces and the stimuli in our physical, social, and cultural environments.

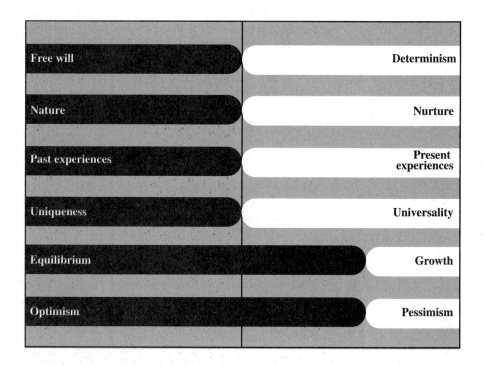

Free will	Determinism
Nature	Nurture
Past experiences	Present experiences
Uniqueness	Universality
Equilibrium	Growth
Optimism	Pessimism

FIGURE 7.1   *Murray's image of human nature*

Murray's view of human nature was optimistic. He criticized a psychology that projected a negative and demeaning image of human beings. He argued that, with our vast powers of creativity, imagination, and reason, we are capable of solving any problem we face. Also, our orientation is largely toward the future. Although Murray recognized the imprint of childhood experiences on current behavior, he did not envision people as captives of the past. The childhood complexes unconsciously affect our development, but personality is also determined by present events and by aspirations for the future.

We have the ability to grow and develop, and such growth is a natural part of being human. We can change through our rational and creative abilities and can reshape our society as well.

Assessment in Murray's Theory

Murray's techniques for assessing personality differ from those of Freud and the other neopsychoanalytic theorists. Because Murray was not working with emotionally disturbed persons, he did not use such standard psychoanalytic techniques as free association and dream analysis.

For his intensive evaluation of the normal personality, Murray used a variety of techniques to collect data from 51 male undergraduate students at Harvard University. The subjects were interviewed and given projective tests, objective tests, and questionnaires covering childhood memories, family relations, sexual development, sensory-motor learning, ethical standards, goals, social interactions, and mechanical and artistic abilities. This assessment program was so comprehensive that it took Murray's staff of 28 investigators six months to complete. We discuss these data in the section on research in Murray's theory.

The OSS Assessment Program

During the World War II years (1941–1945), Murray directed an assessment program for the Office of Strategic Services (OSS), a forerunner of the CIA. His goal was to select people to serve as spies and saboteurs, operating behind enemy lines in hazardous situations. Potential candidates for OSS positions were interviewed and given the Rorschach and the TAT projective tests and questionnaires covering a variety of topics. In addition, candidates participated in situational tests, which were stressful situations that simulated experiences they could expect to encounter on the job. Their behavior in these tests was closely observed (OSS Assessment Staff, 1948).

One such test required the candidate to build a bridge across a stream in a fixed period of time. No plans were provided, but the person was assigned a group of workers to assist him. In this way the candidate's ingenuity, ability to improvise, and leadership skills could be assessed in a realistic setting. To determine the candidate's reaction to frustration, the assistants included some stooges—people instructed to do everything possible to prevent the building of the bridge. Many candidates became enraged, and some were even reduced to tears, when faced with the lack of cooperation and the mounting frustration.

This pioneering attempt at employee selection through large-scale personality assessment has evolved into the successful assessment-center approach widely used in business today to select promising leaders and executives. The OSS program provides a striking example of the practical application of assessment techniques originally intended purely for research.

The Thematic Apperception Test

projective techniques

The assessment technique most often associated with Murray is the Thematic Apperception Test, which we described in Chapter 1. The TAT consists of a set of ambiguous pictures depicting simple scenes. The person taking the test is asked to compose a story that describes the people and objects in the picture, describing what might have led up to the situation and what the people are thinking and feeling.

Murray derived the TAT, which is a projective technique, from Freud's defense mechanism of projection. In projection, a person attributes or projects disturbing impulses onto someone else. In the TAT, the person projects those feelings onto the characters in the pictures and thereby reveals his or her troubling thoughts to the researcher or therapist (see Figure 7.2). Thus, the TAT is a device for assessing unconscious thoughts, feelings, and fears.

Interpreting the responses to the TAT pictures is a subjective process, as Murray admitted in an interview. He referred to the TAT as

> a kind of booby trap which may catch more embryo psychologists than patients. The patient reveals parts of himself when he composes a story to explain the picture. Then the psychologist may reveal parts of himself when he composes a formulation to explain the patient's story. (quoted in Hall, 1968b, p. 61)

In the hands of a trained clinician, the TAT can reveal considerable useful information. Because of its subjectivity, however, the information obtained should be used to supplement data from more objective methods rather than as the sole means of diagnosis.

Research in Murray's Theory

Murray's original research program involved the intensive study of the personalities of 51 male undergraduate students undertaken by a staff of psychiatrists, psychologists, and anthropologists. Thus, specialists with different training observed each subject using various techniques, in much the same way a complex medical diagnosis is prepared. Each observer presented his or her diagnosis to the Diagnostic Council, a committee of the five most experienced staff members. The council met with each subject for 45 minutes and rated the subject on several variables. As the data accumulated, the council reassessed its ratings, reviewed the information, and arrived at a final determination.

proceeding A basic segment of behavior; a time period in which an important behavior pattern occurs from beginning to end.

So much information was collected on each person's life that the data had to be divided into time segments; these were called proceedings and serials. The basic behavior segment, the **proceeding**, was defined as the period of time required for the

FIGURE 7.2   *The Thematic Apperception Test*

Picture contained in the Thematic Apperception Test (TAT). In describing a TAT picture, people may reveal their own feelings, needs, and values.

Typical Responses to TAT Card:

1. *This is the picture of a woman who all of her life has been a very suspicious, conniving person. She's looking in the mirror and she sees reflected behind her an image of what she will be as an old woman—still a suspicious, conniving sort of person. She can't stand the thought that that's what her life will eventually lead her to and she smashes the mirror and runs out of the house screaming and goes out of her mind and lives in an institution for the rest of her life.*

2. *This woman has always emphasized beauty in her life. As a little girl she was praised for being pretty and as a young woman was able to attract lots of men with her beauty. While secretly feeling anxious and unworthy much of the time, her outer beauty helped to disguise these feelings from the world and, sometimes, from herself. Now that she is getting on in years and her children are leaving home, she is worried about the future. She looks in the mirror and imagines herself as an old hag—the worst possible person she could become, ugly and nasty—and wonders what the future holds for her. It is a difficult and depressing time for her. (Pervin, 1984, p. 110)*

SOURCE: Reprinted by permission of the publishers from Henry A. Murray, *Thematic Apperception Test*, Cambridge, Mass.: Harvard University Press, Copyright © 1943 by the President and Fellows of Harvard College, © 1971 by Henry A. Murray.

occurrence and completion of a pattern of behavior—from beginning to end. A proceeding involves a real or fantasized interaction between the person and other people or objects in the environment. An imaginary interaction is called an internal proceeding; a real interaction is called an external proceeding.

Proceedings are linked in time and function. For example, on Monday a man may meet a woman (an external proceeding) and ask her for a Saturday night date. He may daydream about her throughout the week (internal proceedings) and may have his hair styled or wash his car (external proceedings) in preparation for the date. Each of these actions is a proceeding. Taken together, because they relate to the same function or purpose, they are called a **serial**.

Murray's approach to personality research was **idiographic** in that it involves the intensive study of a relatively small number of individuals using a variety of assessment techniques. This contrasts with the **nomothetic** approach, which deals with statistical differences among groups of subjects. Murray criticized followers of the nomothetic approach for not gathering enough data on the subjects they studied.

Considerable research has been conducted on several of the needs Murray proposed, notably the achievement and affiliation needs. We discuss the need for achievement in Chapter 17 as a limited-domain approach to personality.

The need for affiliation is strong in many people, particularly in stressful situations. In a classic experiment, subjects who knew they were going to receive an electric shock in an experiment were much more likely to prefer waiting in the company of others than were subjects who were not facing the stress of a potential electric shock (Schachter, 1959). Apparently, the presence of other people helped allay the anxiety associated with the stress of the anticipated shock. Another study found that people who had experienced severe effects of a thunderstorm, such as property damage, were much more likely to seek the company of others than were those who had experienced no such harmful effects of the storm (Strumpfer, 1970).

A group of college students kept a daily log of their stressful experiences and social interactions for two weeks. The results showed that the students were much more likely to want to affiliate with others after stressful events than after nonstressful periods (Cohen & Wills, 1985). Many people prefer the company of others even when not experiencing stress. Observations of college students showed that 60 percent of their activities involved at least one other person. Female students were much more likely than male students to associate with other people (Latané & Bidwell, 1977).

Additional research has found that people who score high in the affiliation need are unpopular, apt to avoid interpersonal conflicts, and likely to be unsuccessful as business managers. These tendencies may be due to their high level of anxiety about whether other people will like them. They may act in an overly assertive manner to avoid any possible rejection (McClelland, 1985; McClelland & Boyatzis, 1982).

The need for power is not on Murray's original list of needs, but several of his needs—including dominance, deference, aggression, and abasement—can be subsumed under what Murray referred to as the response to power. The power need, defined as the motivation to be in control, to give orders, and to command obedience, has been studied through responses to the TAT pictures and has been corre-

serial A succession of proceedings related to the same function or purpose.

idiographic research The intensive study of a relatively small number of subjects using a variety of assessment techniques.

nomothetic research The study of the statistical differences among large groups of subjects.

lated with other behaviors. Persons high in the need for power have tended to pursue careers as teachers, clergy, therapists, managers, and politicians. These fields afford the opportunity to exercise control and to dictate to others (McClelland, 1985; Winter, 1973).

Researchers also have related the need for power to excessive drinking (McClelland, David, Kalin, & Wanner, 1972), to the Type A personality (McClelland, 1979), and to the possession of high-status objects, such as expensive automobiles and stereo equipment (Winter, 1973). Male college students high in the need for power tend to be officers in campus organizations, to work in media activities, to follow fashion trends, and to marry dependent women (Winter, 1973).

A Final Commentary

Murray has exerted an impressive and lasting influence on the study of personality. Of particular importance is his list of needs, which is of continuing value for research, clinical diagnosis, and employee selection, and his techniques for assessing personality. Overall, these innovations, and the personal impact he made on at least two generations of personology researchers at Harvard, have had a more lasting effect than the details of his theory.

In 1978, the 40th anniversary of the publication of Murray's book *Explorations in Personality* was celebrated by a symposium at the annual convention of the American Psychological Association. An award was created in his name, and the Murray Research Center at Radcliffe College was dedicated. Several symposia have been held to discuss Murray's ideas (see, for example, Rabin, Zucker, Emmons, & Frank, 1990). The fact that psychologists today are carrying on work begun before many of them were born is an impressive tribute.

Murray's theory is not without its critics. One problem in evaluating his position is that only some portions of it have been published. His ingenuity and full range of thought were not widely revealed. Those who worked with him and had access to his broad speculations, which he offered in almost casual conversation, most keenly felt Murray's influence. Although students and colleagues have pursued some of these ideas, others have been lost to view.

Research has been conducted on some of Murray's ideas, such as the achievement and affiliation needs, the response to power, and the assessment techniques, but only limited portions of his theory have been put to experimental test. Of course, as we have seen in previous chapters, this criticism is not unique to Murray.

Murray's research method in the study of Harvard undergraduates has also been questioned. The Diagnostic Council may have been laudably democratic, but it was hardly scientific; to reach a scientific conclusion by majority rule is not the most objective procedure. In addition, some concepts, such as proceedings and serials, are defined too vaguely. What constitutes an important pattern of behavior? What happens to those judged insignificant? How long is a proceeding? These questions have not been answered satisfactorily.

Murray's classification of needs may be overly complex and a great deal of overlap exists among the needs. It is unclear how the needs relate to other aspects of personality and how the needs develop within an individual. However, the list of needs has had considerable impact on the construction of psychological tests. Further, the concept of need and the importance Murray placed on motivation in his system have influenced the modern study of personality.

Chapter Summary

The major principle of Murray's work is the dependence of psychological processes on physiological processes. Altering the level of need-induced tension is vital to the personality. We generate tension to have the satisfaction of reducing it.

Three basic divisions of personality are the id, superego, and ego. The id contains primitive, amoral impulses as well as tendencies to empathy, imitation, and identification. The superego is shaped by parents, peer groups, and cultural factors. The ego consciously decides and wills the direction of behavior.

Needs are physiologically based hypothetical constructs that arise from internal processes or environmental events. Needs arouse a tension level that must be reduced; thus, they energize and direct behavior. Needs may be primary (viscerogenic), arising from internal bodily processes, or secondary (psychogenic), concerned with mental and emotional satisfaction. Proactive needs are spontaneous and do not depend on environmental objects; reactive needs involve a response to a specific environmental object.

A need's prepotency is its urgency or insistence. The fusion of needs refers to needs that can be satisfied by one behavior or set of behaviors. Subsidiation involves a situation in which one need is activated to aid in the satisfaction of another need.

Press refers to the pressure, caused by environmental objects or childhood events, to behave in a certain way. Thema is an amalgamation of personal factors (needs) and environmental factors (presses).

Complexes are patterns formed in the five childhood stages of development that unconsciously direct adult development. The claustral complex involves the secure existence within the womb. The oral complex involves the sensuous enjoyment of sucking nourishment. The anal complex involves the pleasure resulting from defecation. The urethral complex involves the pleasure accompanying urination. The castration complex involves genital pleasure and the fantasy that the penis might be cut off.

According to Murray, the ultimate goal in life is to reduce tension. Although we have some free will, much of personality is determined by needs and by the environment. Each person is unique yet shares similarities, which are determined by inherited and environmental forces, with other people. Murray held an optimistic view of human nature, which is oriented toward the future and grants us the ability to grow and develop.

Murray and Christiana Morgan developed the TAT, based on the Freudian concept of projection. Considerable research has been conducted on Murray's proposed needs for achievement and affiliation and the response to power. His importance lies in his list of needs and his techniques for assessing personality.

Review Questions

1. Discuss the influence of Jung on Murray's personal life and theory of personality.

2. What is the relationship between physiological processes and psychological processes?

3. What is the role of tension in the development of personality? Is our ultimate goal a life free of tension? Why or why not?

4. How do Murray's views of the id, ego, and superego differ from Freud's conception of these structures of personality?

5. From what sources do needs arise? Describe ways of classifying needs, and give examples for each category.

6. Define the concepts of subsidiation, thema, and press.

7. Describe the five childhood stages of personality development and the complexes associated with each stage.

8. How does Murray's image of human nature differ from Freud's?

9. How is the Thematic Apperception Test used to assess personality? What criticisms can be made of projective techniques for personality assessment?

10. Distinguish between proceedings and serials, and between internal and external proceedings.

11. What type of data did Murray collect in his study of Harvard undergraduate students?

12. Is Murray's view of human nature optimistic or pessimistic? Why?

Suggested Readings

Anderson, J. W. (1988). Henry A. Murray's early career: A psychobiographical exploration. *Journal of Personality, 56(1),* 139–171. An analysis of Murray's life through his early thirties, examining his decision to become a psychologist, his involvement with psychoanalysis, and the impact of his personal and academic experiences on his work.

Douglas, C. (1993). *Translate this darkness: The life of Christiana Morgan.* New York: Simon & Schuster. A biography of the codeveloper of the Thematic Apperception Test, describing her career and her relationship with Henry Murray.

Murray, H. A. (1938). *Explorations in personality: A clinical and experimental study of fifty men of college age.* New York: Oxford University Press. Murray's classic work on personology. Includes the evaluation of a typical subject by the Diagnostic Council, the list of human needs, and the advantages of projective techniques for personality assessment.

Murray, H. A. (1967). Autobiography. In E. G. Boring & G. Lindzey (Eds.), *A history of psychology in autobiography* (Vol. 5, pp. 283–310). New York: Appleton-Century-Crofts. Murray's reflections on his life and work.

Murray, H. A. (1981). *Endeavors in psychology: Selections from the personology of Henry A. Murray.* New York: Harper & Row. A collection of Murray's writings on personality theory, human creativity, and the Thematic Apperception Test. Edited by Edwin S. Schneidman.

Robinson, F. G. (1992). *Love's story told: A life of Henry A. Murray.* Cambridge, MA: Harvard University Press. A biography of Murray that relates some of the more sensational aspects of his marriage and love affairs.

Smith, M. B. (1990). Henry A. Murray (1893–1988): Humanistic psychologist. *Journal of Humanistic Psychology, 30(1),* 6–13. A biographical sketch relating Murray's work to the humanistic psychology movement.

Triplet, R. G. (1992). Henry A. Murray: The making of a psychologist? *American Psychologist, 47,* 299–307. Assesses the impact of Murray's work at the Harvard Psychological Clinic on personality, abnormal psychology, and clinical psychology, and recounts the personal and academic disputes between the clinic and the psychology department.

The Life-Span Approach

Most personality theorists devote some attention to the way personality develops over time. Some describe stages in the development of specific aspects of personality; others posit general patterns of growth. Theorists also differ regarding the time period during which they believe personality continues to develop. For example, Sigmund Freud proposed that personality evolves through a sequence of steps until the age of 5; Henry Murray took a similar position. Carl Jung argued that middle age was the most important time of change for the personality.

The life-span approach, represented here by the work of Erik Erikson, focuses on the development of the personality over the entire course of life. Erikson's theory attempts to explain human behavior and growth through eight stages, from birth to death. Erikson believed that all aspects of personality could be explained in terms of turning points, or crises, we must meet and resolve at each developmental stage.

E   I   G   H   T

> The personality is engaged with the hazards of existence continuously, even as the body's metabolism copes with decay.
>
> —Erik Erikson

Erik Erikson

The work of Erik Erikson has had a profound influence on psychoanalysis and on our general culture. Erikson's books sold hundreds of thousands of copies, and his likeness appeared on the covers of *Newsweek* and the *New York Times Magazine*, an unusual sign of recognition for a personality theorist. His book on the origins of militant nonviolence, *Gandhi's Truth*, was awarded a Pulitzer Prize. And he achieved this prominence without ever earning a university degree.

Trained in the Freudian tradition by Sigmund Freud's daughter Anna, Erikson developed an approach to personality that broadened the scope of Freud's work while maintaining much of its core. Although Erikson offered significant innovations, his ties to the Freudian position were strong. "Psychoanalysis is always the starting point," he said (quoted in Keniston, 1983, p. 29). More recently, Erikson scholars confirmed that for all of his life, Erikson "publicly defined himself as a loyal Freudian, even as he departed substantially from orthodox psychoanalytic theory" (Anderson & Friedman, 1997, p. 1063).

Erikson extended Freud's theory in three ways. First, he elaborated on Freud's stages of development. Whereas Freud emphasized childhood and proposed that personality is shaped by approximately age 5, Erikson suggested that personality continues to develop in a succession of eight stages over the entire life span.

Erikson's second departure from Freudian theory was to place greater emphasis on the ego than on the id. In Erikson's view, the ego is an independent part of the personality; it is not dependent on or subservient to the id.

Third, Erikson recognized the impact on personality of cultural and historical forces. He argued that we are not governed entirely by innate biological factors at work in childhood. Although they are important, they do not provide the complete explanation for personality.

Because of his elaboration of these basic Freudian themes, Erikson could have been grouped with the neopsychoanalytic theorists in this book. But we have chosen instead to emphasize the life span, or developmental, aspect of his theory, which centers on the search for an ego identity.

The Life of Erikson (1902–1994)

Personal Identity Crises

Erik Erikson

It is not surprising that the theorist who gave us the concept of the identity crisis experienced several such crises of his own. Erikson was born in Frankfurt, Germany. His parents, who were not married, came from Denmark, and Erik's father left before the boy was born. His mother never told him his father's name. She moved to Karlsruhe, Germany, and married Dr. Theodore Homburger, Erik's pediatrician. Erik did not know for some years that Dr. Homburger was not his biological father, and he grew up unsure of his name and psychological identity. He retained the surname Homburger until age 37, when he became a United States citizen and adopted the name Erik Homburger Erikson.

Another crisis of identity occurred when Erikson started school. Despite his Danish parentage, he considered himself German, but his German classmates rejected him because his stepfather was Jewish. His Jewish peers rejected him because he was tall and blond and had Nordic features. His mother was Lutheran, and he later converted to Christianity. In school Erikson achieved mediocre grades. He showed some talent for art, however, and after graduating from high school he used that ability to try to establish his identity.

He dropped out of conventional society and traveled through Germany and Italy, reading, recording his thoughts in a notebook, and observing life around him. He described himself as morbidly sensitive and neurotic, even close to psychotic. He studied at two art schools and had his work exhibited at a gallery in Munich, but each time he left formal training to resume his wandering, his search for an identity. Later, discussing his proposed concept of the identity crisis, Erikson wrote, "No doubt, my best friends will insist that I needed to name this crisis and to see it in everybody else in order to really come to terms with it in myself" (Erikson, 1975, pp. 25–26).

As with many of the personality theorists described in this textbook, we can find a correspondence between Erikson's life experiences, particularly in childhood and adolescence, and the personality theory he developed as an adult. A biographer noted that what Erikson "saw and felt happening to himself (as with Freud's examination of his own dreams, memories, fantasies) became the 'research' that enabled a flow of ideas, articles, books" (Friedman, 1999, p. 16).

Child Development Studies

At the age of 25, Erikson received an offer to teach at a small school in Vienna established for the children of Sigmund Freud's patients and friends. Freud was attracting patients from all over the world. Being wealthy, they settled in Vienna with their families for the duration of their psychoanalysis. Erikson later confessed that he was drawn to Freud in part because of his search for a father. It was then that Erikson's professional career began and that he felt he had found an identity.

He trained in psychoanalysis and was analyzed by Anna Freud. The analytic sessions were held almost daily for three years; the fee was $7 per month. Anna Freud's interest was the psychoanalysis of children. Her influence, plus Erikson's own teaching experiences, made him aware of the importance of social influences on personality and led him to focus on child development. After he completed his program of study he became a member of the Vienna Psychoanalytic Institute.

In 1929, when attending a masked ball in Vienna, Erikson met Joan Serson, a Canadian-born artist and dancer who had been analyzed by one of Freud's disciples. They fell in love but when she became pregnant, Erikson refused to marry her. He explained that he was afraid to make a permanent commitment and he believed that his mother and stepfather would disapprove of a daughter-in-law who was not Jewish. Only the intercession of friends persuaded him that if he did not marry Joan, he would be repeating the behavior pattern of the man who had fathered him and condemning his child to the stigma of illegitimacy, which Erikson himself had felt so keenly.

When he did decide to marry Joan, he did so three times, in separate Jewish, Protestant, and civil ceremonies. Joan abandoned her career interests to become Erikson's life-long intellectual partner and editor. She provided a stable social and emotional foundation for his life and helped him develop his approach to personality. Erikson's half-sister commented that "He would have been nothing without Joan" (quoted in Friedman, 1999, p. 86). Erikson agreed.

In 1933, recognizing the growing Nazi menace, the Eriksons immigrated to Denmark and then to the United States, settling in Boston. Erikson established a private psychoanalytic practice specializing in the treatment of children. He became affiliated with Henry Murray's Harvard clinic, serving on the Diagnostic Council. He also joined a guidance center for emotionally disturbed delinquents and the staff of Massachusetts General Hospital.

Erikson began graduate work at Harvard, intending to obtain a Ph.D. in psychology, but he failed his first course and decided that a formal academic program was unsatisfying. In 1936 he was invited to the Institute of Human Relations at Yale University, where he taught in the medical school and continued his psychoanalytic work with children. Erikson and a Yale anthropologist collaborated on a study of the child-rearing practices of South Dakota's Sioux Indians. This research reinforced his belief in the influence of culture on childhood. Erikson continued to expand on his ideas at the Institute of Human Development of the University of California at Berkeley. Unlike many psychoanalysts, Erikson wanted his clinical experience to be as broad as possible, so he sought patients from diverse cultures and saw those he considered normal as well as those who were emotionally disturbed.

Identity Confusion

In his observations of American Indian peoples in South Dakota and in California, Erikson noted certain psychological symptoms that could not be explained by orthodox Freudian theory. The symptoms appeared to be related to a sense of alienation from cultural traditions and resulted in the lack of a clear self-image or self-identity. This phenomenon, which Erikson initially called *identity confusion*, was similar to the condition he had observed among emotionally disturbed veterans after World War II. Erikson suggested that those men were not suffering from repressed conflicts but rather from confusion brought about by traumatic war experiences and by being temporarily uprooted from their culture. He had described the veterans' situation as a confusion of identity about who and what they were.

In 1950 Erikson joined the Austen Riggs Center in Stockbridge, Massachusetts, a treatment facility for emotionally disturbed adolescents. Ten years later he returned to Harvard to teach a graduate seminar and a popular undergraduate course on the human life cycle, retiring in 1970. At the age of 84 Erikson published a book about old age. When he died in 1994, it was said that he was still distressed that he had never known who his father was.

Psychosocial Stages of Development and Basic Strengths

psychosocial stages of development To Erikson, eight successive stages encompassing the life span. At each stage, we must cope with a crisis in either an adaptive or a maladaptive way.

Erikson divided the growth of the personality into eight **psychosocial stages**. The first four are similar to Freud's oral, anal, phallic, and latency stages. The major difference between their theories is that Erikson emphasized psychosocial correlates, whereas Freud focused on biological factors.

Erikson suggested that the developmental process was governed by what he called the **epigenetic principle of maturation**. By this he meant that inherited forces are the determining characteristics of the developmental stages. The prefix *epi*

epigenetic principle of maturation The idea that human development is governed by a sequence of stages that depend on genetic or hereditary factors.

means "upon"; thus, development depends upon genetic factors. The social and environmental forces to which we are exposed influence the ways in which the genetically predetermined stages of development are realized. In this way, personality development is affected by both biological and social factors, or by both personal and situational variables.

In Erikson's theory, human development involves a series of personal conflicts. The potential for these conflicts exists at birth as innate predispositions; these will become prominent at different stages when our environment demands certain adaptations. Each confrontation with our environment is called a **crisis**. The crisis involves a shift in perspective, requiring us to refocus our instinctual energy in accordance with the needs of each stage of the life cycle.

crisis To Erikson, the turning point faced at each developmental stage.

Each developmental stage has its particular crisis or turning point that necessitates some change in our behavior and personality. We may respond to the crisis in one of two ways: a maladaptive (negative) way or an adaptive (positive) way. Only when we have resolved each conflict can the personality continue its normal developmental sequence and acquire the strength to confront the next stage's crisis. If the conflict at any stage remains unresolved, we are less likely to be able to adapt to later problems. A successful outcome is still possible, but it will be more difficult to achieve.

However, Erikson believed that the ego must incorporate maladaptive as well as adaptive ways of coping. For example, in infancy, the first stage of psychosocial development, we can respond to the crisis of helplessness and dependency by developing a sense of trust or a sense of mistrust. Trust, the more adaptive, desirable way of coping, is obviously the healthier psychological attitude. Yet each of us must also develop some degree of mistrust as a form of protection. If we are totally trusting and gullible, we will be vulnerable to other people's attempts to deceive, mislead, or manipulate us. Ideally, at every stage of development the ego will consist primarily of the positive or adaptive attitude but will be balanced by some portion of the negative attitude. Only then can the crisis be considered satisfactorily resolved.

basic strengths To Erikson, motivating characteristics and beliefs that derive from the satisfactory resolution of the crisis at each developmental stage.

Erikson also proposed that each of the eight psychosocial stages provides an opportunity to develop our **basic strengths**. These strengths, or virtues, emerge once the crisis has been resolved satisfactorily. He suggested that basic strengths are interdependent; one strength cannot develop until the strength associated with the previous stage has been confirmed (see Table 8.1).

TABLE 8.1   *Erikson's stages of psychosocial development and basic strengths*

Stage	Approximate ages	Adaptive vs. maladaptive ways of coping	Basic strength
Oral-sensory	Birth–1 year	Trust vs. mistrust	Hope
Muscular-anal	1–3 years	Autonomy vs. doubt, shame	Will
Locomotor-genital	3–5 years	Initiative vs. guilt	Purpose
Latency	6–11 years, to puberty	Industriousness vs. inferiority	Competence
Adolescence	12–18 years	Identity cohesion vs. role confusion	Fidelity
Young adulthood	18–35 years	Intimacy vs. isolation	Love
Adulthood	35–55 years	Generativity vs. stagnation	Care
Maturity and old age	55+ years	Ego integrity vs. despair	Wisdom

Trust Versus Mistrust

The oral-sensory stage of psychosocial development, paralleling Freud's oral stage of psychosexual development, occurs during our first year of life, the time of our greatest helplessness. The infant is totally dependent on the mother or primary caregiver for survival, security, and affection. During this stage the mouth is of vital importance. Erikson wrote that the infant "lives through, and loves with, [the] mouth" (1959, p. 57). However, the relationship between the infant and his or her world is not exclusively biological. It is also social. The baby's interaction with the mother determines whether an attitude of trust or mistrust for future dealings with the environment will be incorporated into his or her personality.

If the mother responds appropriately to the baby's physical needs and provides ample affection, love, and security, then the infant will develop a sense of trust, an attitude that will characterize the growing child's view of himself or herself and of others. In this way we learn to expect "consistency, continuity, and sameness" from other people and situations in our environment. Erikson said that this expectation provides the beginning of our ego identity (1950, p. 247), and he recalled that he had formed such a bond of trust with his mother.

On the other hand, if the mother is rejecting, inattentive, or inconsistent in her behavior, the infant develops an attitude of mistrust and will become suspicious, fearful, and anxious. According to Erikson, mistrust can also occur if the mother does not display an exclusive focus on the child. Writing in the 1950s and 1960s, Erikson expressed his belief that a new mother who resumes a job outside the home and leaves her infant in the care of relatives or in a day care center risks promoting mistrust in the child.

Although the pattern of trust or mistrust as a dimension of personality is set in infancy, the problem may reappear at a later developmental stage. For example, an ideal infant-mother relationship produces a high level of trust, but this secure sense of trust can be destroyed if the mother dies or leaves home. If that occurs, mistrust may overtake the personality. Childhood mistrust can be altered later in life through the companionship of a loving and patient teacher or friend.

The basic strength of *hope* is associated with the successful resolution of the crisis during the oral-sensory stage. Erikson described this strength as the belief that our desires will be satisfied. Hope involves a persistent feeling of confidence, a feeling we will maintain despite temporary setbacks or reverses.

Autonomy Versus Doubt and Shame

During the muscular-anal stage at the second and third years of life, corresponding to Freud's anal stage, children rapidly develop a variety of physical and mental abilities and are able to do many things for themselves. They learn to communicate more effectively and to walk, climb, push, pull, and hold on to an object or let it go. Children take pride in these skills and usually want to do as much as possible for themselves.

Of all these abilities, Erikson believed the most important involved holding on and letting go. He considers these to be prototypes for reacting to later conflicts in behaviors and attitudes. For example, holding on can be displayed in a loving way or in a hostile way. Letting go can become a venting of destructive rage or a relaxed passivity.

The important point is that during this stage, for the first time, children are able to exercise some degree of choice, to experience the power of their autonomous will. Although still dependent on their parents, they begin to see themselves as persons or forces in their own right and they want to exercise their newfound strengths. The key question becomes how much will society, in the form of parents, allow children to express themselves and do all they are capable of doing?

The major crisis between parent and child at this stage typically involves toilet training, seen as the first instance when society attempts to regulate an instinctual need. The child is taught to hold on and let go only at appropriate times and places. Parents may permit the child to proceed with toilet training at his or her own pace or may become annoyed. In that case, parents may deny the child's free will by forcing the training, showing impatience and anger when the child does not behave correctly. When parents thus thwart and frustrate their child's attempt to exercise his or her independence, the child develops feelings of self-doubt and a sense of shame in dealing with others. Although the anal region is the focus of this stage because of the toilet training crisis, you can see that the expression of the conflict is more psychosocial than biological.

The basic strength that develops from autonomy is *will*, which involves a determination to exercise freedom of choice and self-restraint in the face of society's demands.

Initiative Versus Guilt

The locomotor-genital stage, which occurs between ages 3 and 5, is similar to the phallic stage in Freud's system. Motor and mental abilities are continuing to develop, and children can accomplish more on their own. They express a strong desire to take the initiative in many activities. Initiative may also develop in the form of fantasies, manifested in the desire to possess the parent of the opposite sex and in rivalry with the parent of the same sex. How will the parents react to these self-initiated activities and fantasies? If they punish the child and otherwise inhibit these displays of initiative, the child will develop persistent guilt feelings that will affect self-directed activities throughout his or her life.

In the Oedipal relationship, the child inevitably fails, but if the parents guide this situation with love and understanding, then the child will acquire an awareness of what is permissible behavior and what is not. The child's initiative can be channeled toward realistic and socially sanctioned goals in preparation for the development of adult responsibility and morality. In Freudian terms, we would call this the *superego*.

The basic strength called *purpose* arises from initiative. Purpose involves the courage to envision and pursue goals.

Industriousness Versus Inferiority

Erikson's latency stage of psychosocial development, which occurs from ages 6 to 11, corresponds to Freud's latency period. The child begins school and is exposed to

Children take pride in developing new skills and abilities.

new social influences. Ideally, both at home and at school, the child learns good work and study habits (what Erikson referred to as industriousness) primarily as a means of attaining praise and obtaining the satisfaction derived from the successful completion of a task.

The child's growing powers of deductive reasoning and the ability to play by rules lead to the deliberate refinement of the skills displayed in building things. Here Erikson's ideas again reflect the sex stereotypes of the period in which he proposed his theory. In his view, boys will build tree houses and model airplanes; girls will cook and sew. However, whatever the activities associated with this age, the children are making serious attempts to complete a task by applying concentrated attention, diligence, and persistence. In Erikson's words, "The basic skills of technology are developed as the child becomes ready to handle the utensils, the tools, and the weapons used by the big people" (1959, p. 83).

Again, the attitudes and behaviors of parents and teachers largely determine how well children perceive themselves to be developing and using their skills. If children are scolded, ridiculed, or rejected, they are likely to develop feelings of inferiority and inadequacy. On the other hand, praise and reinforcement foster feelings of competence and encourage continued striving.

The basic strength that emerges from industriousness during the latency stage is *competence*. It involves the exertion of skill and intelligence in pursuing and completing tasks.

The outcome of the crisis at each of these four childhood stages depends on other people. The resolution is a function more of what is done to the child than of what the child can do for himself or herself. Although children experience increasing independence from birth to age 11, psychosocial development remains mostly under the influence of parents and teachers, typically the most significant people in our life at this time.

In the last four stages of psychosocial development, we have increasing control over our environment. We consciously and deliberately choose our friends, colleges, careers, spouses, and leisure activities. However, these deliberate choices are obviously affected by the personality characteristics that have developed during the stages from birth to adolescence. Whether our ego at that point shows primarily trust, autonomy, initiative, and industriousness, or mistrust, doubt, guilt, and inferiority, will determine the course of our life.

Identity Cohesion Versus Role Confusion: The Identity Crisis

ego identity The self-image formed during adolescence that integrates our ideas of what we are and what we want to be.

Adolescence, between ages 12 and 18, is the stage at which we must meet and resolve the crisis of our basic **ego identity**. This is when we form our self-image, the integration of our ideas about ourselves and about what others think of us. If this process is resolved satisfactorily, the result is a consistent and congruent picture.

Shaping an identity and accepting it are difficult tasks, often filled with anxiety. Adolescents experiment with different roles and ideologies, trying to determine the most compatible fit. Erikson suggested that adolescence was a hiatus between childhood and adulthood, a necessary psychological moratorium to give the person time and energy to play different roles and live with different self-images.

identity crisis

identity crisis The failure to achieve ego identity during adolescence.

People who emerge from this stage with a strong sense of self-identity are equipped to face adulthood with certainty and confidence. Those who fail to achieve a cohesive identity—who experience an **identity crisis**—will exhibit a confusion of

Adolescents who experience an identity crisis do not seem to know where they belong or what they want to become.

roles. They do not seem to know who or what they are, where they belong, or where they want to go. They may withdraw from the normal life sequence (education, job, marriage) as Erikson did for a time or seek a negative identity in crime or drugs. Even a negative identity, as society defines it, is preferable to no identity, although it is not as satisfactory as a positive identity.

Erikson noted the potentially strong impact of peer groups on the development of ego identity in adolescence. He noted that excessive association with fanatical groups and cults or obsessive identification with icons of popular culture could restrict the developing ego.

The basic strength that should develop during adolescence is *fidelity*, which emerges from a cohesive ego identity. Fidelity encompasses sincerity, genuineness, and a sense of duty in our relationships with other people.

Erikson's concept of ego identity apparently drew partly on earlier work of Erich Fromm (see Chapter 6). In Fromm's 1941 book, *Escape from Freedom*, he discussed the loss of identity and the efforts to seek an identity. Erikson was familiar with the book but never formally acknowledged the relevance of Fromm's ideas. Erikson's biographer later reported that this attitude upset Fromm greatly (Friedman, 1999).

Intimacy Versus Isolation

Erikson considered young adulthood to be a longer stage than the previous ones, extending from the end of adolescence to about age 35. During this period we establish our independence from parents and quasi-parental institutions, such as college, and begin to function as mature, responsible adults. We undertake some form of productive work and establish intimate relationships—close friendships and sexual unions. In Erikson's view, intimacy was not restricted to sexual relationships but also encompassed feelings of caring and commitment. These emotions could be displayed openly, without resorting to self-protective or defensive mechanisms and without fear of losing our sense of self-identity. We can merge our identity with someone else's without submerging or losing it in the process.

People who are unable to establish such intimacies in young adulthood will develop feelings of isolation. They avoid social contacts and reject other people, and may even become aggressive toward them. They prefer to be alone because they fear intimacy as a threat to their ego identity.

The basic strength that emerges from the intimacy of the young adult years is *love*, which Erikson considered to be the greatest human virtue. He described it as a mutual devotion in a shared identity, the fusing of oneself with another person.

Generativity Versus Stagnation

Adulthood—approximately ages 35 to 55—is a stage of maturity in which we need to be actively involved in teaching and guiding the next generation. This need extends beyond our immediate family. In Erikson's view, our concern will become broader and more long-range, involving future generations and the kind of society in which they will live. One need not be a parent to display generativity, nor does having children automatically satisfy this urge.

Erikson believed that all institutions—whether business, government, social service, or academic—provide opportunities for us to express generativity. Thus, in whatever organizations or activities we are involved, we can usually find a way to become a mentor, teacher, or guide to younger people for the betterment of society at large.

midlife crisis

When middle-aged people cannot or will not seek an outlet for generativity, they may become overwhelmed by "stagnation, boredom, and interpersonal impoverishment" (Erikson, 1968, p. 138). Erikson's depiction of these emotional difficulties in middle age is similar to Carl Jung's description of the midlife crisis (see Chapter 3). These people may regress to a stage of pseudo-intimacy, indulging themselves in childlike ways. And they may become physical or psychological invalids because of their absorption with their own needs and comforts.

Care is the basic strength that emerges from generativity in adulthood. Erikson defined care as a broad concern for others and believed it was manifested in the need to teach, not only to help others but also to fulfill one's identity.

Ego Integrity Versus Despair

During the final stage of psychosocial development, maturity and old age, we are confronted with a choice between ego integrity and despair. These attitudes govern the way we evaluate the whole of our life. At this time our major endeavors are at or nearing completion. We examine and reflect on our life, taking its final measure. If we look back with a sense of fulfillment and satisfaction, believing we have adequately coped with life's victories and failures, then we are said to possess ego integrity. Simply stated, ego integrity involves accepting one's place and one's past.

On the other hand, if we review our life with a sense of frustration, angry about missed opportunities and regretful of mistakes that cannot be rectified, then we will feel despair. We will become disgusted with ourselves, contemptuous of others, and bitter over what might have been.

At the age of 84, Erikson published a book reporting the results of a long-term study of 29 people in their 80s on whom life-history data had been collected since 1928. The title, *Vital Involvement in Old Age*, indicates Erikson's prescription for achieving ego integrity (Erikson, Erikson, & Kivnick, 1986). Older people must do more than reflect on the past. They must remain active, vital participants in life, seeking challenge and stimulation from their environment. They must involve themselves in such activities as grandparenting, returning to school, and developing new skills and interests.

The basic strength associated with this final developmental stage is *wisdom*. Deriving from ego integrity, wisdom is expressed in a detached concern with the whole of life. It is conveyed to succeeding generations in an integration of experience best described by the word *heritage*.

Basic Weaknesses

basic weaknesses
Motivating characteristics that derive from the unsatisfactory resolution of developmental crisis.

Similarly to the way basic strengths arise at each stage of psychosocial development, so may **basic weaknesses**. We noted earlier that the adaptive and maladaptive ways of coping with the crisis at each stage are incorporated in the ego identity in a kind

TABLE 8.2   *Erikson's maldevelopmental tendencies*

Stage	Way of coping	Maldevelopment
Oral-sensory	Trust	Sensory maladjustment
	Mistrust	Withdrawal
Muscular-anal	Autonomy	Shameless willfulness
	Doubt, shame	Compulsion
Locomotor-genital	Initiative	Ruthlessness
	Guilt	Inhibition
Latency	Industriousness	Narrow virtuosity
	Inferiority	Inertia
Adolescence	Identity cohesion	Fanaticism
	Role confusion	Repudiation
Young adulthood	Intimacy	Promiscuity
	Isolation	Exclusivity
Adulthood	Generativity	Overextension
	Stagnation	Rejectivity
Maturity and old age	Ego integrity	Presumption
	Despair	Disdain

SOURCE: Adapted from *Vital Involvement in Old Age,* by Erik H. Erikson, Joan M. Erikson, and Helen Q. Kivnick by permission of W. W. Norton & Company, Inc. Copyright © 1986 by Joan M. Erikson, Erik H. Erikson, and Helen Kivnick.

of creative balance. Although the ego should consist primarily of the adaptive attitude, it will also contain a share of the negative attitude.

In an unbalanced development, the ego consists solely of one attitude, either the adaptive or the maladaptive one. Erikson labeled this condition **maldevelopment**. When only the positive, adaptive, tendency is present in the ego, the condition is said to be "maladaptive." When only the negative tendency is present, the condition is called "malignant." Maladaptions can lead to neuroses; malignancies can lead to psychoses.

Erikson expected that both conditions could be corrected through psychotherapy. Maladaptions, which are the less severe disturbances, can also be relieved through a process of readaption, aided by environmental changes, supportive social relationships, or successful adaption at a later developmental stage. Table 8.2 lists the maldevelopmental characteristics for each of the eight stages.

maldevelopment A condition that occurs when the ego consists solely of a single way of coping with conflict.

Questions About Human Nature

A personality theorist who delineates basic human strengths would be thought to possess an optimistic view of human nature (see Figure 8.1). And so Erikson believed that although not everyone is successful in attaining hope, purpose, wisdom, and the other virtues, we all have the potential to do so. Nothing in our nature prevents it. Nor must we inevitably suffer conflict, anxiety, and neurosis because of instinctual biological forces.

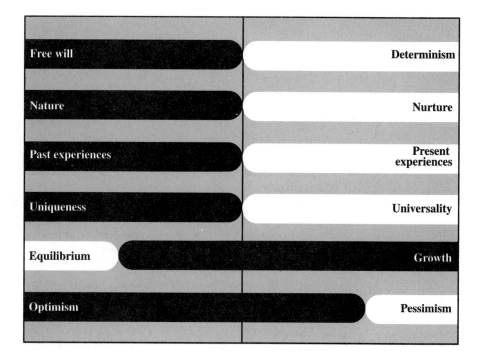

Free will	Determinism
Nature	Nurture
Past experiences	Present experiences
Uniqueness	Universality
Equilibrium	Growth
Optimism	Pessimism

FIGURE 8.1   *Erikson's image of human nature*

Erikson's theory allows for optimism because each stage of psychosocial growth, although centered around a crisis, offers the possibility of a positive outcome. We are capable of resolving each situation in a way that is adaptive and strengthening. Even if we fail at one stage and develop a maladaptive response or a basic weakness, there remains hope for change at a later stage.

We have the potential to direct consciously our growth throughout our lives. We are not exclusively products of childhood experiences. Although we have little control during the first four developmental stages, we gain increasing independence and the ability to choose ways of responding to crises and to society's demands. Childhood influences are important, but events at later stages can counteract unfortunate early experiences.

Erikson's theory is only partially deterministic. During the first four stages, the experiences to which we are exposed through parents, teachers, peer groups, and various opportunities, are largely beyond our control. We have more chance to exercise free will during the last four stages, although the attitudes and strengths we have formed during the earlier stages will affect our choices.

In general, Erikson believed that personality is affected more by learning and experience than by heredity. Psychosocial experiences, not instinctual biological forces, are the greater determinant. Our ultimate, overriding goal is to develop a positive ego identity that incorporates all the basic strengths.

Assessment in Erikson's Theory

Erikson agreed with certain of Freud's theoretical formulations but deviated from Freudian thinking in his methods of assessing personality. Erikson questioned the usefulness and even the safety of some Freudian techniques, beginning with the psychoanalytic couch. To Erikson, asking patients to lie on a couch could lead to sadistic exploitation. It could create an illusion of objectivity, foster an overemphasis on unconscious material, and engender excessive impersonality and aloofness on the part of the therapist. To promote a more personal relationship between therapist and patient and to ensure that they viewed each other as equals, Erikson preferred that patients and therapists face each other and be seated in comfortable chairs.

In dealing with his patients, Erikson relied less on formal assessment techniques than did Freud. Erikson occasionally used free association but rarely attempted to analyze dreams, a technique he called wasteful and harmful. He believed that assessment techniques should be selected and modified to fit the unique requirements of the individual patient.

In developing his personality theory, Erikson used data obtained primarily from play therapy, anthropological studies, and psychohistorical analysis. For work with emotionally disturbed children and in research on normal children and adolescents, Erikson chose play therapy. He provided a variety of toys and observed how the subjects interacted with them. The form and intensity of play revealed aspects of personality that might not be manifested verbally, because of a child's limited powers of verbal expression.

We mentioned earlier Erikson's anthropological studies of American Indian peoples. Living among these groups to observe them, Erikson recorded their behavior and interviewed the subjects at length, particularly with regard to child-rearing practices.

Psychohistorical Analysis

psychohistorical analysis
The application of Erikson's life-span theory, along with psychoanalytic principles, to the study of historical figures.

Erikson's most unusual assessment technique is **psychohistorical analysis**. These analyses are essentially biographical studies. Erikson used the framework of his life-span theory of personality to describe the crises and the ways of coping of significant political, religious, and literary figures, such as Gandhi, Martin Luther, and George Bernard Shaw. Erikson's psychohistories typically focus on a significant crisis, an episode that represents a major life theme uniting past, present, and future activities. Using what he called "disciplined subjectivity," Erikson adopted the subject's viewpoint as his own to assess life events through that person's eyes.

Psychological Tests

Although Erikson did not use psychological tests for personality assessment, several instruments have been based on his formulations. The Ego-Identity Scale is designed to measure the development of ego identity during adolescence (Dignan, 1965). The Ego Identity Process Questionnaire, also for adolescents, contains 32 items to mea-

TABLE 8.3   *Examples of items from a scale to measure generativity. Do these apply to any middle-aged people you know?*

1. I try to pass along to others the knowledge I have gained through my experiences.
2. I do not believe that other people need me.
3. I believe I have made a difference in the lives of other people.
4. Other people say I am a productive person.
5. I believe I have done nothing that will survive after I die.
6. People come to me for advice.
7. I believe that society cannot be responsible for providing sustenance and shelter for all homeless people.
8. I have important skills that I try to teach others.
9. I do not like to do volunteer work for charities.
10. Throughout my life I have made and kept many commitments to people, groups, and activities.

SOURCE: Adapted from D.P. McAdams & E. de St. Aubin (1992). A theory of generativity and its assessment through self-report, behavioral acts, and narrative themes in autobiography. *Journal of Personality and Social Psychology,* 62, 1003–1015.

sure the dimensions of exploration and commitment (Balistreri, Busch-Rossnagel, & Geisinger, 1995). The Loyola Generativity Scale (see Table 8.3) is a 20-item self-report inventory to measure the level of generativity or stagnation in adulthood (McAdams & de St. Aubin, 1992).

Research in Erikson's Theory

Erikson's primary research method was the case study. By now you are familiar with the weaknesses of this method—the difficulty of duplicating and verifying case material—but you also know that much useful information can be obtained through this technique. Erikson argued that case histories yield many insights into personality development and can help resolve a patient's problems.

Play Constructions

play constructions A personality assessment technique for children in which structures assembled from dolls, blocks, and other toys are analyzed.

Erikson used play therapy to conduct research on his theory, focusing on what he called **play constructions**. In one study, 300 boys and girls, ages 10 to 12, were asked to construct a scene from an imaginary movie using dolls, toy animals, automobiles, and wooden blocks. The girls tended to build static, peaceful scenes that contained low, enclosed structures. Intruders (animal figures or male figures, never female figures) tried to force their way into the interiors. By contrast, the boys focused on exteriors, action, and height. Their creations tended to be action-oriented, with tall towering structures and cars and people in motion (see Figure 8.2).

FIGURE 8.2   *Play constructions created by boys (top) and girls (bottom).* SOURCE: Redrawn from *Childhood and Society*, 2nd ed., by Erik H. Erikson, by permission of W. W. Norton & Company, Inc. Copyright 1950, © 1963 by W. W. Norton & Company, Inc. Copyright renewed 1978, 1991 by Erik H. Erikson.

sex differences

Trained as an orthodox Freudian, Erikson interpreted these play constructions along psychoanalytic lines. He wrote:

Sexual differences in the organization of a play space seem to parallel the morphology of genital differentiation itself: in the male, an external organ, erectable and intrusive in character . . . in the female, internal organs, with vestibular access, leading to a statically expectant ova. (Erikson, 1968, p. 271)

In other words, based on the determining effect of biological differences, girls would build low enclosures in which people are walled in, and boys would build towers.

Erikson has been criticized for this view, which suggests that women are victims of their anatomy and that their personalities are determined by the absence of a penis. Erikson admitted that differences in play constructions could also result from differences in society's sex-role training, in which girls are less oriented toward action, aggression, and achievement than boys are.

One replication of this study used younger subjects—boys and girls between the ages of 2 and 5 (Caplan, 1979). The results failed to support Erikson's findings. No significant sex differences were reported in the building of towers and enclosures. This raises the possibility that sex-role training was more complete in Erikson's 10- to 12-year-old subjects. Perhaps the younger children in this later study had not yet been sufficiently instructed in the behavior society expected of them.

Even today, more than 50 years after Erikson's research on play constructions, traditional gender stereotyping with regard to toys and play behaviors persists. Most children still prefer gender-based toys. Boys typically play with trucks, soldiers, and guns. Girls typically play with dolls, jewelry, and toy kitchen implements.

These patterns of toy preferences have been found to exist as early as age 2 and are taught and encouraged by the parents. It is the parents who purchase most of their children's toys (though often at the child's urging). Parents praise children for playing with the appropriate gender-typed toy and discourage them from playing with toys intended for the other sex. The message is learned quickly. One psychologist observed a boy who "had been playing with a race car and its driver when the driver's helmet fell off revealing long blond hair. The driver was a woman. The boy dropped the race car like it was a hot potato" (Martin, 1999, p. 49).

Studies show that fathers treat boys and girls in a more stereotypical way than mothers do. Thus, it is primarily the fathers who teach and reinforce gender-based play. They also instruct their sons and daughters in other gender-typed behaviors and attitudes. Fathers tend to reward passive, compliant behaviors in girls and assertive, aggressive behaviors in boys (Quiery, 1998).

Trust and Security

Erikson emphasized the importance of developing an early sense of trust if we are to achieve feelings of security and well-being later in life. This position has received strong research support (see, for example, Jacobson & Wille, 1986; Londerville & Main, 1981; Sroufe, Fox, & Pancake, 1983).

Studies of infants aged 12 to 18 months showed that those who had a strong emotional bond with their mother (therefore presumed to be high in trust) functioned, when observed three years later, at a higher social and emotional level than infants whose attachment to their mother was less secure. Children with a well-developed sense of trust were also more curious, sociable, and popular. They were more likely to be leaders at games and showed greater sensitivity to the needs and feelings of others. Those low in trust were more withdrawn socially and emotionally, reluctant to play with other children, less curious, and less forceful in pursuing goals.

The Psychosocial Stages

Other research has been concerned with the psychosocial developmental stages. Children aged 4, 8, and 11 were asked to make up stories based on several test pictures (Ciaccio, 1971). The stories were analyzed to determine which psychosocial stage they reflected. The results supported the themes proposed in Erikson's theory. For example, the stories of the 4-year-olds concerned autonomy (the stage just completed). Similarly, the stories of the older children reflected their developmental stages.

Psychohistorical analysis of the diaries, letters, and novels of Vera Brittain, a British feminist and writer, from age 21 into middle age, showed an initial concern with ego identity. This changed over time to a concern with intimacy and then generativity (Peterson & Stewart, 1990). These changes are in line with Erikson's developmental theory.

A study using the Inventory of Psychosocial Development, a test designed to assess adaptive and maladaptive development in Erikson's first six stages, found a significant relationship between happiness and adaptive development at each stage (Constantinople, 1969). Another study showed a high correlation between maladaptive development in the first six stages and a sense of alienation and uprootedness (Reimanis, 1974). These findings also offer support for Erikson's work.

Another study that supports Erikson's stages also used the Inventory of Psychosocial Development. Over a 22-year period the test was administered to a total of 474 college students. The results showed increasingly positive resolution of the crises of the psychosocial stages through the subjects' middle forties. As Erikson predicted, a favorable outcome at one stage was dependent on the successful resolution of the crisis at an earlier stage (Whitbourne, Elliot, Zuschlag, & Waterman, 1992).

Research conducted in South Africa on Black and White men and women aged 15 to 60 provides support for Erikson's theory as it applies to White subjects. Childhood aspects of personality were found to be strongly interrelated in White subjects, suggesting that the adaptive outcomes of each stage of childhood development had led to the formation of a cohesive personality. White females resolved their identity crisis at a younger age than other subjects did. The correlation between ego identity and emotional well-being was high for White male and female subjects. In general, Black males in the study did not form a positive ego identity until after the age of 40, considerably later than the adolescent stage of psychosocial development. Black females had difficulty resolving the crisis at every developmental stage (Ochse & Plug, 1986).

Using the Ego-Identity Scale, a researcher tested Erikson's contention that too weak or too strong an identification with the parent of the same sex can harm adolescent ego identity (Dignan, 1965). Scores on the Ego-Identity Scale and on a test of maternal identification were correlated for a group of female college freshmen and sophomores. The results confirmed Erikson's prediction. It was also found that female college students who had difficulty establishing an ego identity were more likely to have problems with alcohol abuse (Schnur & MacDonald, 1988). Other research showed that secure family relations in adolescence enhanced the development of ego identity. It was found that parental warmth and autonomy were predictors of a stable family environment, which, in turn, promoted identity development (Kamptner, 1988).

Psychologists tested Erikson's belief that positive outcomes in resolving the identity crisis are related to positive outcomes at prior developmental stages (Waterman, Buebel, & Waterman, 1970). Adolescents who developed trust, autonomy, initiative, and industriousness (adaptive ways of coping) in the first four stages of psychosocial development displayed a high level of identity cohesion rather than role confusion. Adolescents who had not resolved their identity crisis and who experienced role confusion had not developed adaptive ways of coping in the earlier stages.

Adolescent Development

An extensive research program on the adolescent stage of development identified five psychosocial types, or statuses, for that period (Marcia, 1966, 1980). These are identity achievement, moratorium, foreclosure, identity diffusion, and alienated achievement.

Identity achievement describes adolescents who are committed to occupational and ideological choices. A study of 74 college students found a positive correlation between achieved identity status and objective measures of commitment (Streitmatter, 1993). Such individuals have developed a strong ego identity. They were stable, concerned with realistic goals, and able to cope with changing environmental demands. They performed better on difficult tasks than adolescents experiencing role confusion. These stable adolescents majored in more difficult areas in college, attracted to courses in engineering and the physical sciences (Marcia & Friedman, 1970).

Moratorium, the second adolescent status, describes people who are still undergoing their identity crisis. Their occupational and ideological commitments are vague. They hold ambivalent views toward authority figures, alternately rebelling and needing guidance from them. Their behavior ranges from indecisive to active and creative (Blustein, Devenis, & Kidney, 1989; Podd, Marcia, & Rubin, 1968). They also tend to daydream, to believe in supernatural phenomena, and to enjoy behaving childishly (Bilsker & Marcia, 1991).

Foreclosure describes adolescents who have not experienced an identity crisis but who are firmly committed to an occupation and ideology. However, these commitments often have been determined by their parents and do not result from the adolescents' deliberate choice. These adolescents tend to be rigid and authoritarian and have difficulty coping with changing situations (Marcia, 1967). However, a study of 23 male and 37 female college students showed that those in the foreclosure status tend to be achievement-oriented and to focus their energy toward external rather than internal goals (Stephen, Fraser, & Marcia, 1992).

The *identity diffusion* status characterizes people who have no occupational or ideological commitments in adolescence and who may not have experienced an identity crisis. Their chosen lifestyle may actively reject commitments and in the extreme may result in aimless drifting. These adolescents have distant relationships with their parents, whom they see as indifferent and rejecting (Waterman, 1982).

The fifth status, *alienated achievement*, describes adolescents who have experienced an identity crisis, have no occupational goal, and cling to beliefs that are critical of the social and economic system. Their commitment to this rationale precludes any career that would entangle them in the very system they oppose. As students they tend to be cerebral, philosophical, and cynical (Marcia & Friedman, 1970; Orlofsky, Marcia, & Lesser, 1973).

Four of these statuses, in the following order—identity diffusion, foreclosure, moratorium, and identity achievement—represent increasingly successful resolutions of the identity problem. Erikson predicted that people who are close to achieving or who have achieved an integrated ego identity will have greater ego strength than those who are farther from resolving their identity dilemma. That prediction was supported by research on college men (Bourne, 1978a, 1978b). In cognitive and emotional terms, the identity-achievement and moratorium types functioned better than the foreclosure and identity-diffusion types. College men and women of the identity-achievement type were also found to be more confident (Berzonsky, Rice, & Neimeyer, 1990). In other research, sex differences were found in the resolution of the identity crisis. Men in one study showed a tendency toward separation and detachment from other people; women showed a tendency toward connection and attachment to others (Mellor, 1989).

Other studies support and extend that finding, showing that male identity focuses on individual competence and knowledge whereas female identity is more centered on relating to others. In other words, when women establish an identity, they depend heavily on social relationships. Men focus more on self and individual skills and abilities (Curry, 1998).

You may recall your own adolescence as a turbulent and stressful period. Three key elements for this developmental stage have been identified as follows.

1. Conflict with parents, characterized by a forceful resistance to adult authority,
2. Mood disruption, characterized by a volatile emotional life, mood swings, and episodes of depression, and
3. Risky behaviors, characterized by reckless, rule-breaking, and antisocial behavior that may harm themselves and others.

Studies have found that a stressful adolescence is far more likely to occur among White middle-class teenagers than among Mexican American or Asian American teenagers. However, the more acculturated minority-group members become, the more likely it is that their adolescents will experience the typical signs and symptoms of the majority population (Arnett, 1999).

Finally, it has been suggested that computer games and Internet sites may afford adolescents a unique, high-tech opportunity to do precisely what Erikson said was so necessary: to try different roles to see which offers the best fit. And when surfing the Web, one can do so anonymously. This was exemplified in the role-playing game called *Dungeons and Dragons*, once popular among young people. It allowed them to take on fictional personas to act out complex fantasies (Turkle, 1995).

The word *dungeon* is now used in specialized computer vocabulary to denote a virtual place. Virtual places shared by a number of computer users simultaneously are known as multi-user dungeons or MUDs. MUDs allow a player to interact with others and also to build a personal virtual world whose imaginary characters interact with others. Participants can play roles as like or unlike their real selves as they choose without revealing their real identity. "You can be whoever you want to be," one writer noted. "You can completely redefine yourself if you want" (Turkle, 1995, p. 184). That is precisely what Erikson urged us to do during adolescence, to experiment with different identities.

There is the danger that a person could become so absorbed in a virtual identity that it comes to replace the true developing self. But that can also happen in the real world by adopting a different persona. The point is that for some adolescents the Internet offers a secure way of trying to establish an identity.

Social Factors and Ego Identity

Erikson believed that social and historical factors affect the formation of ego identity, which in turn affects the nature of the personality. The women's movement of the 1960s and 1970s provided a real-world laboratory in which to test the effects of social forces. Specifically, psychologists asked whether women then at the adolescent stage of psychosocial development, the time of striving for an ego identity, were more influenced by the women's movement than women who were older at that time. It was assumed that the identity of the older women already had been formed.

Two studies answered yes. Both chose as subjects women who had graduated from one of three colleges during the 1940s to mid-1960s. Data were gathered from interviews, questionnaires, and self-report personality tests. Women attending college when the women's movement began were found to have greater aspirations. They valued their independence more than did the older women and eventually attained higher levels of education, job status, and income. They were more assertive and self-confident in middle age than were women who had passed through the adolescent stage before the advent of the women's movement (Duncan & Agronick, 1995; Helson, Stewart, & Ostrove, 1995).

One legacy of the women's movement is that most adolescent women today include a career orientation as part of their ego identity. This viewpoint has been found to affect dating behavior as well as age at the time of marriage (Matula, Huston, Grotevant, & Zamutt, 1992). Questionnaire studies of several hundred women college students revealed that those who are career oriented tend to marry later in life. They date less while in college and are more wary of committed relationships. The same study found the opposite situation for men. Questionnaire results for 56 college men revealed that the stronger their career identity, the more committed they were to a dating relationship. Indeed, they were unlikely to become involved in a dating relationship until they felt a definite commitment to an occupation.

Additional longitudinal research studied women who graduated from college in the 1960s and the men they married. It focused on changes in their emotional life over time, specifically,

- Changes in positive emotionality (PEM), defined as an active, happy involvement in one's work and social environments, and
- Negative emotionality (NEM), characterized by feelings of stress, anxiety, anger, and other negative emotions.

Measures of these two factors, taken at various ages from late 20s to middle 50s, showed that in young adulthood women tended to score higher on NEM than did their spouses and to score higher on PEM in late middle age. These findings were interpreted by the investigators to indicate that women showed greater feelings of social power, accomplishment, and breadth of interest, along with reduced stress and alienation, once the period of child rearing ended. Thus, social factors were seen to influence the affective dimension of ego identity (Helson & Klohnen, 1998).

Erikson defined identity consolidation as the process of dealing successfully with the social realities of adult life. This involves making adjustments to the changing demands of our social world. He believed that identity consolidation usually occurs during the 20s, as people assume adult responsibilities of marriage, family, and career. A study of women college graduates evaluated at ages 21 and 27 found that those who ranked high in ego resiliency and had found an identity in marriage were higher in identity consolidation than those who did not meet these criteria (Pals, 1999).

Psychologists in Israel tested another social factor believed to affect the formation of ego identity in adolescence, that is, minority-group or majority-group status in a culture in which these groups co-exist in a fundamentally hostile state. Using an ego-identity questionnaire developed specifically for this research, more than 2,000 Israeli-Jewish and Israeli-Arab teenagers were surveyed. The results were not in the anticipated direction. The researcher concluded that minority-group status in that culture did not have a negative effect on the formation of an ego identity in adolescence (Tzuriel, 1992).

The Identity Crisis

Some research has focused on the timing of the identity crisis. Erikson suggested that it began around age 12 and was resolved, one way or another, by approximately age 18. However, for some people the identity crisis may not occur until later. In one study, up to 30 percent of the subjects were still searching for an identity as late as age 24 (Archer, 1982). Also, college may delay the resolution of the identity crisis and prolong the period during which young adults experiment with different roles and ideologies (Cote & Levine, 1988). When college students were compared with people of the same age who held full-time jobs, it was found that employed persons had achieved ego identity at an earlier age than students had. The students remained longer in the moratorium status (Adams & Fitch, 1982).

Generativity

Research on the adulthood stage of psychosocial development has shown that generativity in middle-aged subjects is positively correlated with power and with intimacy motivation (McAdams, Ruetzel, & Foley, 1986). Thus, as Erikson's theory predicts, generativity evokes the needs to feel close to others and to feel strong in relation to them. Another study associated generativity with nurturance (Van de Water & McAdams, 1989). All these are necessary characteristics for teaching and mentoring the next generation.

Generativity in middle age appears to be significantly related to having experienced warm, affectionate parenting in childhood (Franz, McClelland, & Weinberger, 1991). Research supports the importance of both mother and father to a child's emotional well being. Middle-aged subjects who scored high in generativity tended to believe in the goodness and worth of human life and to feel happier and more satisfied with their own life than did people who scored low in generativity (McAdams & de St. Aubin, 1992; Van de Water & McAdams, 1989).

Other studies corroborated and extended these findings. People high in generativity also scored higher on extraversion, conscientiousness, and openness to new experiences than people low in generativity (Peterson, Smirles, & Wentworth, 1997). Those high in generativity were more likely to be involved in meaningful, satisfying social relationships, to feel strongly attached to their community, and to be more emotionally stable than those low in generativity (McAdams, Hart, & Maruna, 1998).

Two longitudinal studies of college-educated women tested and observed at intervals from ages 31 to 48 found that those who were high in generativity at midlife scored significantly higher in emotional well being than those low in generativity (Vandewater, Ostrove, & Stewart, 1997).

Further, as Erikson's theory predicted, subjects aged 37 to 42 scored higher on the Loyola Generativity Scale than did younger subjects (aged 22–27) or older subjects (67–72) (McAdams & de St. Aubin, 1992). It is also interesting to note a study of 158 men and women in their late 20s that used a questionnaire to obtain information about their personal life. The results showed that the subjects were already beginning to grapple with generativity issues much earlier than Erikson's proposed midlife period (Peterson & Stewart, 1993).

When a group of 70 men and women subjects were asked to describe the major themes of their life, persons who had previously scored high on the Loyola Generativity Scale revealed different issues from persons who had scored low. Common themes of the high scorers included some event of good fortune in their early life, sensitivity to the suffering of others, a stable personal belief system, and clear goals for themselves and for society. Low scorers did not record any of these themes (McAdams, Diamond, de St. Aubin, & Mansfield, 1997).

Maturity

Erikson believed that people in the maturity and old age stage of psychosocial development spend time recalling and examining their life, accepting or regretting past choices. A study using 49 psychologists as subjects found that most of their memories were of college and early adult years, the period involving the greatest number of critical decisions that affected the course of their life (Mackavey, Malley, & Stewart, 1991). Other research found that elderly subjects who scored high in ego integrity devoted time to reviewing their life to resolve troubling issues and come to a better understanding of their circumstances. In general, subjects scoring low in ego integrity reported that they did not engage in such self-examination (Taft & Nehrke, 1990).

Gender differences in aging may make it more difficult for women than for men to engage in a dispassionate process of reflection, or taking stock of life, such as Erikson described. A so-called double standard in our society considers aging as more negative for women and sees women as "old" at an earlier age than men. For example, a 50-year-old actor may be offered thoughtful, mature, powerful movie roles whereas a 50-year-old actress may be stereotyped as a widow or grandmother—if she is offered any movie roles at all.

In addition, women tend to live longer than men, so they are more likely to have to deal with issues of illness and incapacity, bereavement, loss of social support, and reduced income. This may contribute to the observation that women's retrospective reviews of their lives are often less positive than those of men and more likely to lead to the condition Erikson noted as despair in later years, rather than ego integrity (Rainey, 1998).

Ethnic Identity

ethnicity

One aspect of ego development not considered by Erikson is the impact of ethnic identity. Research on this topic consistently shows the importance of racial or ethnic identity to adolescents and young adults of minority groups. A large-scale study of 582 White and ethnic minority men and women, including adolescents and adults, found that Whites scored significantly lower on measures of racial and ethnic identity than did members of any of the minority groups studied (Gaines, et al., 1997).

Among Black women adolescents, ethnic identity was found to be the most significant factor in defining their sense of self (Aries & Moorehead, 1989). Other research showed that subjects of both sexes considered ethnic identity the most important factor in developing a strong ego identity (Helms, 1990). Low ethnic identity in Black college students was related to low self-esteem and to anxiety and inferiority feelings (Parham & Helms, 1985a, 1985b).

More recent research with 245 African American high school and college students failed to confirm any relationship between self-esteem and racial identity (Rowley, Sellers, Chavous, & Smith, 1998). However, a study of 126 Black and 292 White college students did find a significant positive relationship between self-esteem and level of ethnic identity; the higher the identity, the higher the self-esteem (Goodstein & Ponterotto, 1997). Thus, the issue of how self-esteem varies as a function of ethnic identity remains unclear.

Other research found that Black adolescents who scored high in ethnic identity expressed less positive attitudes toward drugs and more positive attitudes toward school, which were related to more positive behaviors at school. Those who scored high on a measure of anti-White attitudes were far more likely to use drugs, have negative attitudes toward school, and exhibit negative behaviors at school (Resnicow, Soler, Braithwaite, Selassie, & Smith, 1999).

A survey of 248 Black college students found that those who favored a strong Black nationalist identity, focusing on the uniqueness of the Black experience, had significantly lower grade-point averages than those who held a less extreme position. Black students who scored high on a questionnaire about assimilating into mainstream society earned lower grades than those who took a more moderate position (Sellers, Chavous, & Cooke, 1998). Research with 474 Black college students found that those high in ethnic identity were more likely to enroll in Black studies courses and to interact socially with other Black students. Those who emphasized the similarities between Blacks and other racial and ethnic groups rather than the uniqueness of the Black identity were more likely to interact socially with Whites. Students who attended Black colleges were far more likely to emphasize the uniqueness of the

Black experience than were Black students who attended primarily White colleges (Sellers, Rowley, Chavous, Shelton, & Smith, 1997).

Research has also found an absence of any relationship between ethnic identity in 701 Black college students and their perceived level of stress. In other words, ethnic identity was not shown to be a source of stress nor did it provide protection against stress (Chambers, Kambon, Birdsong, Brown, Dixon, & Robbins-Brinson, 1998).

A study of Black women and Hispanic women found that identity confusion (a conflict in identity between one's minority culture and the majority culture) may lead to eating disorders. Identification with a North American model of beauty that emphasizes extreme thinness created in some women a tendency to exhibit disorders such as anorexia. The researchers suggested that this condition resulted from an attempt to emulate the appearance standards of the ideal woman of the majority White culture (Harris & Koba, 1997).

Studies of Asian American and Hispanic American adolescents confirm that ethnicity is a central concern in forming an ego identity. A strong ethnic identity was associated with high self-esteem and with better peer and family relations (Phinney & Chavira, 1992). Asian American young people with a high ethnic identity showed a stronger resistance to drinking alcoholic beverages or smoking marijuana than did Asian American youth with a high degree of assimilation into the majority culture (Suinn, 1999).

One model of ethnic identity for Asian Americans in adolescence proposes five developmental stages (Atkinson, Morten, & Sue, 1989). The *conformity* stage involves a complete identification with and adoption of the cultural values of the Euro-American majority culture and a denigration and rejection of the Asian culture. At this stage, Asian Americans are saying, in effect, "Everything about the majority culture is desirable and worthwhile, while everything about my culture is worthless and undesirable. I want to act, be, look, and think like Euro-Americans."

In the *dissonance* stage, Asian Americans develop ambivalence toward the majority group, largely because of experiences with discrimination and rejection. They begin to question the beliefs and values they held during the conformity stage and sense a kinship with their own and with other minority groups.

The third stage, *resistance and immersion*, involves a reversal of the feelings and attitudes of the conformity stage. They reject the dominant group and embrace their Asian cultural values, wondering why they once felt ashamed of their ethnic identity. They develop an identification with and commitment to other Asian American groups and an interest in exploring Asian cultures and histories (Uba, 1994).

The *introspection* stage occurs when adolescents finally feel sufficiently secure about their ethnic identity to begin to question the dogmatic beliefs they held during the previous stage about the superiority of Asian culture. They come to recognize that the majority culture also has positive aspects that are worth incorporating in their ego identity.

By the final stage, *synergetic articulation and awareness*, Asian Americans acquire a genuine sense of self-worth as individuals and no longer define themselves solely in terms of their ethnic identity. They value their ethnic group but also are comfortable embracing beliefs and behaviors of other cultures.

The importance of this minority ego identity development model lies in the recognition of ethnic identity as a vital component of ego identity and in the suggestion that ethnic identity develops over a series of stages, similar to the concept of the psychosocial stages. As we noted, Erikson did not deal directly with the concept of ethnic identity, but this model adheres to the developmental pattern he proposed.

Gender Preference Identity

gender identity

Another aspect of ego identity currently generating research, though not considered directly by Erikson, is gender preference identity. As with ethnic identity, gender preference identity may have an impact on one's overall level of ego identity.

Researchers have proposed that homosexual or gay identity develops over a series of stages, similar to the way Erikson and others explained the development of ego or ethnic identity. One model lists four stages in the development of gender preference identity (Frable, 1997).

1. Sensitization. This stage, which occurs prior to adolescence, refers to one's initial perception of being different from peers of the same sex.
2. Identity confusion. This adolescent stage is marked by the confusing, perhaps frightening, realization that one's feelings and thoughts could be characterized as homosexual.
3. Identity assumption. During this stage the person comes to believe that he or she is homosexual and begins to accept the beginnings of a gay identity.
4. Commitment. In this stage the person fully accepts the gay identity as a way of life.

Studies have shown that people who score high on gay identity self-report inventories also score high on measures of mental and emotional well-being and express no desire to alter their identity or to conceal it from other people (Frable, 1997). A study of 825 homosexual and bisexual men found no differences in self-esteem, emotional well being, and general level of adjustment between those who believed they were stigmatized socially because of their gender preference and those who did not feel so stigmatized. However, men who kept their gender preference less visible in their social behaviors scored higher in self-esteem and well being than men who were more openly gay in their social behaviors (Frable, Wortman, & Joseph, 1997).

A Final Commentary

Erikson's substantial contributions to psychology include the recognition of personality development throughout the life span, the concept of the identity crisis in adolescence, and the incorporation in his theory of the impact of cultural, social, and historical forces. However, his system does not lack critics. Some point to ambiguous terms and concepts, conclusions drawn in the absence of supporting data, and an overall lack of precision (Rosenthal, Gurney, & Moore, 1981; Waterman, 1982).

Erikson agreed that these charges were valid and blamed them on his artistic temperament and lack of formal training in science. He wrote, "I came to psychology from art, which may explain, if not justify, the fact that at times the reader will find me painting contexts and backgrounds where he would rather have me point to facts and concepts" (Erikson, 1950, p. 13).

A more specific criticism relates to the incomplete description of the developmental stage of maturity, which Erikson attempted to correct in his 1986 book (Erikson, Erikson, & Kivnick, 1986). Also, some psychologists question whether personality development after age 55 is likely to be as positive as Erikson suggested with his concept of ego integrity. For many people, this stage of life is characterized by pain, loss, and depression, even for people who develop the basic strength of wisdom.

Erikson's position on sex differences, as revealed in his interpretation of the play-constructions research, has also come under attack. What he saw as biologically based differences in personality for boys and girls, emerging from the presence or absence of a penis, could as well be cultural differences or the result of sex-role training. Erikson later admitted these possibilities.

It has also been suggested that Erikson's developmental stages do not apply to women. When social psychologist Carol Tavris read Erikson's description of his so-called "stages of man," she wrote, "it was worrying. I wasn't having any of my crises in the right order. . . . My identity was shaky, although I was no longer a teenager, and I hadn't married when I was supposed to, which was putting my intimacy and generativity crises on hold" (Tavris, 1992, p. 37). She pointed out that other popular life-span theories, such as those of psychiatrists George Vaillant (*Adaptation to Life*, 1977) and Daniel Levinson (*The Seasons of a Man's Life*, 1978), also seemed to apply only to men.

Some critics charge that Erikson's personality theory does not apply to people in reduced economic circumstances who cannot afford a moratorium in adolescence to explore different roles and develop an ego identity. This stage may be a luxury available only to those with the means to attend college or take time out to travel (Slugoski & Ginsburg, 1989).

Erikson showed little interest in responding to his critics. He recognized that there are many ways of describing personality development and that no single view was adequate. His influence grew through his books and the work of succeeding generations of psychologists, psychiatrists, teachers, and counselors who found in his ideas useful ways to describe personality development from infancy through old age. His ideas have been recognized in both professional and popular circles. *Time* magazine called him the "most influential living psychoanalyst" (March 17, 1975), and *Psychology Today* described him as "an authentic intellectual hero" (Hall, 1983, p. 22). His concepts are useful in education, social work, vocational and marriage counseling, and clinical practice with children and adolescents. The Erikson Institute for Early Childhood Education was established at Chicago's Loyola University.

The field of life-span developmental psychology, which has seen a massive increase in research and theory in recent years, owes much of its spark to Erikson's approach, as does the current interest in developmental problems of middle and old age.

In addition, Erikson's method of play therapy has become a standard diagnostic and therapeutic tool for work with emotionally disturbed and abused children. Youngsters who cannot verbalize the details of a physical or sexual attack can express their feelings through play, using dolls to represent themselves and their abusers.

Chapter Summary

Erik Erikson built on Freud's theory by elaborating on the developmental stages, emphasizing the ego over the id, and recognizing the impact on personality of culture, society, and history. The growth of personality is divided into eight stages. A conflict at each stage confronts the person with adaptive and maladaptive ways of coping. Development is governed by the epigenetic principle; each stage depends on genetic forces but the environment helps determine whether they are realized.

The oral-sensory stage (birth to age 1) can result in trust or mistrust. The muscular-anal stage (ages 1 to 3) leads to an autonomous will or to self-doubt. The locomotor-genital stage (3 to 5) develops initiative or guilt. The latency stage (6 to 11) results in industriousness or inferiority. Adolescence (12 to 18) is the stage in which the ego identity is formed (the time of the identity crisis), leading to identity cohesion or role confusion. Young adulthood (18 to 35) results in intimacy or isolation. Adulthood (35 to 55) leads to generativity or stagnation. Maturity (over 55) is expressed in ego integrity or despair.

Each stage allows for the development of basic strengths that emerge from the adaptive ways of coping with the conflicts. The basic strengths are hope, will, purpose, competence, fidelity, love, care, and wisdom. Maldevelopment can occur if the ego consists solely of either the adaptive or the maladaptive tendency.

Erikson presented a flattering, optimistic image of human nature. We have the ability to achieve basic strengths, to resolve each conflict in a positive way, and to consciously direct our growth. We are not victims of biological forces or childhood experiences and are influenced more by learning and social interactions than by heredity.

Erikson's assessment methods were play therapy, anthropological studies, and psychohistorical analysis. His research relied on case studies. There is considerable research support for the first six stages of psychosocial development and for the concept of ego identity. However, the identity crisis may occur later than Erikson believed, and attending college may delay resolution of the crisis. Other research confirms the importance of developing a sense of trust early in life, and the benefits of generativity in middle age. Among minority group members, the formation of ethnic identity in adolescence may affect the development of ego identity and influence subsequent behavior. Gender preference identity may also affect characteristics of ego identity.

Criticisms of Erikson's theory focus on ambiguous terminology, incomplete descriptions of the psychosocial stages, and poorly supported claims of male-female personality differences based on biological factors.

Review Questions

1. In what ways does Erikson's theory extend psychoanalytic theory? How does Erikson's theory reflect his own experiences?

2. Discuss the identity crises of Erikson's early life.

3. Describe the role of conflict in the stages of psychosocial development.

4. Describe the four childhood stages of psychosocial development. Discuss the effects of various parental behaviors on the possible outcomes of each stage.

5. What is the major difference between the first four developmental stages and the last four developmental stages?

6. What factors affect the development of ego identity? Why do some people fail to achieve an identity at this stage?

7. What are the positive ways of resolving the conflicts of the adult stages of psychosocial development?

8. Describe the basic strengths at each stage of psychosocial development.

9. Distinguish between the two types of maldevelopment. How can these conditions be corrected?

10. How does Erikson's image of human nature differ from Freud's?

11. What methods of assessment did Erikson use in developing his theory?

12. Based on the results of his play-constructions research, what did Erikson conclude about sex differences in personality? On what grounds can we criticize these conclusions?

13. Describe research on the development of ego identity in adolescence.

14. Discuss how the ethnic identity of ethnic-minority adolescents can affect the formation of ego identity as well as subsequent attitudes and behavior.

15. Discuss the suggestion that some online Web sites can help adolescents establish an ego identity.

16. Describe the proposed stages for the development of gender preference identity.

Suggested Readings

Erikson, E. H. (1950). *Childhood and society.* New York: Norton. A collection of essays covering child-rearing practices, family life, and social and cultural structures, illustrating their relationship to personality development. The book was an instant success with scholars and the general public.

Erikson, E. H. (1968). *Identity: Youth and crisis.* New York: Norton. Erikson's classic work on the identity crisis and ways of coping with conflict at this stage of development.

Erikson, E. H. (1987). *A way of looking at things: Selected papers from 1930 to 1980.* New York: Norton.

A collection of Erikson's writings on children's play constructions, adult dreams, cross-cultural research, and development over the life cycle. Edited by Stephen Schlein.

Erikson, E. H., Erikson, J. M., & Kivnick, H. Q. (1986). *Vital involvement in old age.* New York: Norton. A sensitive psychosocial analysis of the need for stimulation and challenge in old age and a personal perspective on Erikson as he approached the age of 90.

Evans, R. I. (1967). *Dialogue with Erik Erikson.* New York: Harper & Row. Conversations with Erikson about his life and work.

Friedman, L. J. (1999). *Identity's architect: A biography of Erik H. Erikson.* New York: Simon & Schuster. A sympathetic treatment showing how Erikson's ideas of the identity crisis and the stages of the life cycle grew out of his own complicated life.

Hopkins, J. R. (1995). Erik Homburger Erikson (1902-1994). *American Psychologist, 50,* 796–797; Wallerstein, R. S. (1995). Erik Erikson (1902-1994). *International Journal of Psycho-Analysis, 76,* 173–175. Obituaries and tributes to Erik Erikson.

Josselson, R. (1996). *Revising herself: The story of women's identity from college to midlife.* New York: Oxford University Press. In an outgrowth of Erikson's theory, this longitudinal account compiled from interviews traces the cultural changes in women's roles and identities in the last third of the 20th century.

McAdams, D. P., & de St. Aubin, E. (Eds.). (1998). *Generativity and adult development: How and why we care for the next generation.* Washington, DC: American Psychological Association. Reports research and current thinking about the adulthood stage in Erikson's life cycle theory. Shows how generativity should involve growth beyond oneself, extending to mentoring younger generations and contributing to society at large.

Snarey, J. (1993). *How fathers care for the next generation: A four-decade study.* Cambridge, MA: Harvard University Press. Reports and analyzes a 30-year study of fatherhood and generativity conducted within the framework of Erikson's psychosocial theory of development.

5

The Trait Approach: The Genetics of Personality

A trait is a distinguishing personal characteristic or quality. In our daily lives we frequently use the trait approach to describe the personality of people we know. We tend to select outstanding characteristics or features to summarize what a person is like. We may say, "Allison is so self-assured," or "Ramon is great at math," or "Malik is really smart."

Grouping people by traits is easy and has a commonsense appeal, which may explain why the trait approach to personality has been popular for so long. Trait classifications date from the time of the Greek physician Hippocrates (460–377 B.C.), more than 2,000 years before the theories described in this book. Hippocrates distinguished four types of people: happy, unhappy, temperamental, and apathetic. The causes of these different types were internal bodily fluids, or "humors." He believed that these personality traits were constitutionally based, determined by biological functioning rather than by experience or learning.

In the 1940s, American physician William Sheldon (1899–1977) offered another constitution-ally based personality typology, based on body build (see Figure 9.1). He proposed three body types, each associated with a different temperament (Sheldon, 1942). Like the approach taken by Hippocrates, Sheldon's work considers personality traits or characteristics to be largely fixed, that is, constant and unvarying regardless of the situations in which we find ourselves.

Some personality psychologists criticized the notion that personality consists of distinct traits. Recall the person-situation debate of the 1960s and 1970s we noted in Chapter 1, about the relative impact on behavior of personal variables (traits) versus situational, or environmental, variables. The argument was advanced that if individual traits are sufficient to explain personality, then people will behave consistently in all situations. This idea is not supported by research. As we all know, human behavior tends to vary with the situation.

Participants in that debate sometimes overlooked the fact that later trait theorists, notably Gordon Allport and Raymond Cattell, never implied that

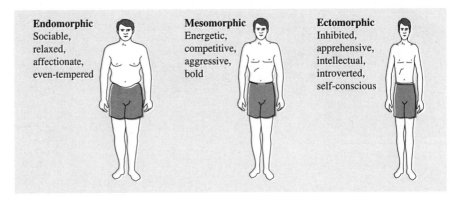

Endomorphic
Sociable,
relaxed,
affectionate,
even-tempered

Mesomorphic
Energetic,
competitive,
aggressive,
bold

Ectomorphic
Inhibited,
apprehensive,
intellectual,
introverted,
self-conscious

FIGURE 9.1   *The body types and personality characteristics proposed by Sheldon. The theory has not been supported by research.*

there was a cross-situational consistency in human behavior. Indeed, both theorists took into account the effect on behavior of specific events and of environmental and social influences. Theirs was an interactionist approach, a recognition that behavior is a function of the interaction between both personal and situational variables.

The trait approach to personality remains vital. The field begun by Allport and Cattell several decades ago is central to the study of personality today. These theorists differed from most of the others we have discussed in one important respect. Their insights are not based on the psychotherapeutic approach using case studies or interviews with emotionally disturbed patients on a couch or in a clinic. Instead, they studied personality by observing emotionally healthy persons in an academic laboratory

setting. Beyond that similarity, and the fact that their goal was to identify personality traits, Allport and Cattell each approached their study differently. (Allport may also be considered within the humanistic framework because he focused on the total human being and the innate potential for growth and self-realization.)

Allport and Cattell agreed on the importance of genetic factors in the formation of traits. A growing body of research evidence supports the notion that personality traits are influenced by inherited biological factors. In other words, there appears to be a significant genetic component to personality. After describing the theories of Allport and Cattell we discuss later approaches including the work of Hans Eysenck, the five-factor model, and the temperament theory.

As the individual matures, the bond with the past is broken.

—Gordon Allport

N I N E

Gordon Allport

Gordon Allport

During a career that spanned more than four decades, Gordon Allport became one of the most stimulating and provocative psychologists to study personality. Along with Henry Murray, Allport made personality an academically respectable topic. Psychoanalysis and the personality theories that derived from it were not considered part of mainstream scientific psychology. The systematic, formal study of personality was not recognized by the psychology establishment until the 1930s.

In 1937, Allport published *Personality: A Psychological Interpretation*. The book was an immediate success and remains a landmark in the study of personality. Thus, Allport served two purposes: he helped bring personality into the mainstream and he formulated a theory of personality development in which traits play a prominent role.

Allport disputed Sigmund Freud's psychoanalysis on several points. First, Allport did not accept the notion that unconscious forces dominate the personality of normal, mature adults. He suggested that emotionally healthy people function in rational and conscious terms, aware and in control of many of the forces that motivate them. According to Allport, the unconscious is important only in neurotic or disturbed behavior.

Second, with regard to historical determinism—the importance of the past in determining the present—Allport said that we are not prisoners of childhood conflicts and past experiences, as Freud believed. Rather, we are guided more by the present and by our view of the future. Allport wrote that people are "busy leading their lives into the future, whereas psychology, for the most part, is busy tracing them into the past" (Allport, 1955, p. 51).

Third, Allport opposed collecting data from pathological subjects. Whereas Freud saw a continuum between normal and abnormal personalities, Allport saw a clear distinction. To Allport, the abnormal personality functioned at an infantile level. The proper way to study personality was to collect data from emotionally healthy adults. Other populations—such as neurotics, children, and animals—should not be compared with normal adults. No functional similarity in personality existed between child and adult, abnormal and normal, or animal and human.

Another distinguishing feature of Allport's theory is his emphasis on the uniqueness of personality as defined by each person's traits. Allport opposed the traditional scientific emphasis on forming general constructs or laws to be applied universally. He argued that personality is not general or universal but is particular and specific to the individual.

The Life of Allport (1897–1967)

Isolation and Identity

Born in Montezuma, Indiana, Allport was the youngest of four sons. His mother was a teacher and his father was a salesman who decided to become a doctor. They were in such dire financial circumstances while the elder Allport attended medical school in Baltimore that he smuggled drugs from Canada into the United States and sold them to support the family. When the law came knocking on the front door, he skipped out the back and escaped over a fence (Rosenzweig & Fisher, 1997). He took the family to Indiana and opened a private practice. Allport believed that his own birth there was his father's first case.

Too young to be a playmate to his older brothers, Allport was isolated from children outside the family as well. He recalled, "I fashioned my own circle of activities. It was a select circle, for I never fitted the general boy assembly" (Allport, 1967, p. 4). He described himself as skillful with words but not at sports or games and as someone who worked hard to be the center of attention of the few friends he did have.

In Allport's personality theory, one of the major propositions is that psychologically healthy adults are unaffected by childhood events. Perhaps reflecting this belief, Allport revealed little information about his childhood years. What he did tell, however, demonstrates a parallel between his own early experiences and the theory he later developed.

Arising from his childhood conditions of isolation and rejection, Allport showed inferiority feelings for which he attempted to compensate by striving to excel. He wrote about the identity quest that resulted from his inferiority feelings with respect to his brothers and other children. As Allport grew older, he began to identify with his oldest brother, Floyd, perhaps envious of his brother's accomplishments. He followed in Floyd's footsteps by enrolling at Harvard and obtaining a Ph.D. in psychology, as Floyd had done. (Floyd Allport became a noted social psychologist.)

The attempt to emulate Floyd may have threatened Gordon's sense of identity. To assert his individuality, then, Gordon Allport may have been motivated to refute his identification with Floyd by declaring that his adult motives and interests were independent of his childhood feelings. He later formalized this idea as the concept of functional autonomy.

College Years

Although Allport ranked second in his high school graduating class of 100, he admitted to being uninspired about what to do next. At the end of the summer of 1915, he applied to Harvard and was accepted. He wrote, "Overnight my world was remade." Allport's college years were a great adventure for him as he discovered new frontiers of intellect and culture. But shocked by low grades on his first exams, he doubled his efforts and finished the year with straight As. Allport's interest in social ethics and social service, acquired from his parents, was reinforced at Harvard. He did volunteer work for a boy's club, a group of factory workers, and a contingent of foreign students. He also worked as a probation officer. He found these activities satisfying because he genuinely liked to help people. "It gave me a feeling of competence, to offset a generalized inferiority feeling." He believed this kind of service reflected his search for an identity (Allport, 1967, pp. 5–7).

He took undergraduate courses in psychology but at that time did not intend to pursue a career in the field. After graduation, he spent a year on the faculty of Robert College in Istanbul, Turkey, and later accepted the fellowship Harvard offered for graduate study in psychology.

The Meeting with Freud

On his return trip to the United States, Allport stopped in Vienna to see one of his brothers. While there, he sent a note to Sigmund Freud and received an invitation to visit the great man. When Allport entered Freud's office, he found Freud waiting patiently, expecting the young American to explain the purpose of his visit. The awkward period of silence lengthened until an uncomfortable Allport blurted out an account of an incident he had witnessed on the streetcar ride to Freud's office. He told of watching a small boy who had an obvious fear of dirt. Everything seemed dirty to the child. He even changed his seat, telling his mother not to let a dirty man sit beside him.

Freud studied the prim, proper, carefully groomed young man and asked, "Was that little boy you?" By asking this question, Freud was expressing his belief that Allport's behavior betrayed unconscious fears and conflicts. Allport appeared to Freud to be "neat, meticulous, orderly and punctual—possessing many of the characteristics [he] associated . . . with the compulsive personality" (Pervin, 1984, p. 267). Henry Murray later commented that "Freud just hit [Allport] right on the head, right on the nose" (quoted in J. W. Anderson, 1990, p. 326).

Allport was shaken by Freud's question. For the rest of his life Allport denied that he was the super-clean, proper little boy in the story but the incident clearly left a deep impression on him. Years later he wrote, "My single encounter with Freud was traumatic" (Allport, 1967, p. 22). He suspected that psychoanalysis probed the unconscious too deeply, as Freud tried to do with him. Psychology, Allport decided, should pay more attention to conscious or visible motivations. This was the path he chose for his study of personality.

The Study of Traits

Allport completed his Ph.D. at Harvard in 1922, after two years of graduate study. His dissertation, "An Experimental Study of the Traits of Personality," foreshadowed his lifelong work and was the first research conducted on personality traits in the United States. Awarded a traveling fellowship, Allport spent two years studying with noted psychologists in Germany and England. He returned to Harvard as an instructor, offering a course on the psychological and social aspects of personality, probably the first formal American college course on the subject. He spent nearly four decades at Harvard, conducting research on personality and social psychology and instructing several generations of students.

Considered an elder statesman in the field, Allport received many awards, including the American Psychological Foundation's Gold Medal, the American Psychological Association's Distinguished Scientific Contribution Award, and the presidencies of the American Psychological Association and the Society for the Psychological Study of Social Issues.

The Nature of Personality

In his book *Pattern and Growth in Personality*, Allport reviewed some 50 definitions of personality before offering his own. "Personality is the dynamic organization within the individual of those psychophysical systems that determine . . . characteristic behavior and thought" (Allport, 1961, p. 28).

Let us examine the key concepts in this definition. By *dynamic organization*, Allport means that although personality is constantly changing and growing, the growth is organized, not random. *Psychophysical* means that personality is composed of mind and body functioning together as a unit; personality is neither all mental nor all biological. By *determine*, Allport means that all facets of personality activate or direct specific behaviors and thoughts. The phrase *characteristic behavior and thought* means that everything we think and do is characteristic, or typical, of us. Thus, each person is unique.

Heredity and Environment

To support his emphasis on the uniqueness of the individual personality, Allport stated that we reflect both our heredity and our environment. Heredity provides the personality with raw materials (such as physique, intelligence, and temperament) that may be shaped, expanded, or limited by the conditions of our environment. In this way Allport invokes both personal and situational variables to denote the importance of both genetics and learning. However, our genetic background is responsible for the major portion of our uniqueness. An infinite number of possible genetic combinations exists, and, except for identical twins, the chance that someone else's genetic endowment will be duplicated in any one of us is too small to consider. Our genetic endowment interacts with our social environment, and no two people, not even siblings reared in the same house, have precisely the same environment. The inevitable result is a unique personality. Therefore, Allport concluded that to study personality, psychology must deal with the individual case and not with average findings among groups. (In Chapter 1 we described the research approach favored by Allport as *idiographic*, whereas the *nomothetic* approach deals with statistical differences among groups of subjects.)

Two Distinct Personalities

Allport considered personality to be discrete, or discontinuous. Not only is each person distinct from all others, but each adult is also divorced from his or her past. He found no continuum of personality between childhood and adulthood. Primitive biological urges and reflexes drive infant behavior, whereas adult functioning is more psychological in nature. In a sense there are two personalities: one for childhood and one for adulthood. The adult personality is not constrained by childhood experiences.

Thus we have Allport's unique view of the nature of personality. He emphasized the conscious rather than the unconscious, the present and future rather than the past. He recognized the uniqueness of personality rather than proposing generalities or similarities for large groups of people. And he chose to study the normal rather than the abnormal personality.

Personality Traits

traits To Allport, distinguishing characteristics that guide behavior. Traits are measured on a continuum and are subject to social, environmental, and cultural influences.

Allport considered personality **traits** to be predispositions to respond, in the same or a similar manner, to different kinds of stimuli. In other words, traits are consistent and enduring ways of reacting to our environment. He summarized the characteristics of traits as follows (Allport, 1937):

1. Personality traits are real and exist within each of us. They are not theoretical constructs or labels made up to account for behavior.
2. Traits determine or cause behavior. They do not arise only in response to certain stimuli. They motivate us to seek appropriate stimuli, and they interact with the environment to produce behavior.
3. Traits can be demonstrated empirically. By observing behavior over time, we can infer the existence of traits in the consistency of a person's responses to the same or similar stimuli.
4. Traits are interrelated; they may overlap, even though they represent different characteristics. For example, aggressiveness and hostility are distinct but related traits and are frequently observed to occur together in a person's behavior.
5. Traits vary with the situation. For example, a person may display the trait of neatness in one situation and the trait of disorderliness in another situation.

Initially, Allport proposed two types of traits: individual and common. *Individual traits* are unique to a person and define his or her character. *Common traits* are shared by a number of people, such as the members of a culture. It follows that people in different cultures will have different common traits. Common traits are also likely to change over time as social standards and values change. This demonstrates that common traits are subject to social, environmental, and cultural influences.

Personal Dispositions

personal dispositions These are traits that are peculiar to an individual, as opposed to traits shared by a number of people.

cardinal traits The most pervasive and powerful human traits.

central traits The handful of outstanding traits that describe a person's behavior.

secondary traits The least important traits, which a person may display inconspicuously and inconsistently.

Because Allport realized that some confusion could result from calling both of these phenomena *traits*, he later revised his terminology. He relabeled common traits as **traits** and individual traits as **personal dispositions**. Our personal dispositions do not all have the same intensity or significance. They may be cardinal traits, central traits, or secondary traits.

A **cardinal trait** is so pervasive and influential that it touches almost every aspect of a person's life. Allport described it as a "ruling passion," a powerful force that dominates behavior. He offered the examples of sadism and chauvinism. Not everyone has a ruling passion, and those who do may not display it in every situation.

Everyone has a few **central traits**, some five to ten themes that best describe our behavior. Allport's examples are aggressiveness, self-pity, and cynicism. These are the kinds of characteristics we would mention when discussing a friend's personality or writing a letter of recommendation.

The least influential individual traits are the **secondary traits**, which appear much less consistently than cardinal and central traits. Secondary traits may be so inconspicuous or weak that only a close friend would notice evidence of them. They may include, for example, a minor preference for a particular type of music or for a certain food.

Habits and Attitudes

As Allport developed his system, he then discussed traits and personal dispositions as being distinct from other characteristics, such as habits and attitudes. He agreed, however, that habits and attitudes are also capable of initiating and guiding behavior.

habits Specific, inflexible responses to specific stimuli; several habits may combine to form a trait.

You have only to consider your own **habits** to see how they influence the way you behave. Habits have a more limited impact than traits and personal dispositions because they are relatively inflexible and involve a specific response to a specific stimulus. Traits and personal dispositions are broader because they arise from the integration of several habits that share some adaptive function. In this way, habits may combine to form a single trait.

Children learning to brush their teeth or wash their hands before eating illustrate Allport's point. After a while these behaviors become automatic, or habitual. Taken together, these habits are directed toward the same purpose and form the trait we label *cleanliness*.

attitudes To Allport, attitudes are similar to traits. However, attitudes have specific objects of reference and involve either positive or negative evaluations.

It is more difficult to explain the difference between traits and **attitudes**. Consider patriotism: Is it a trait fostered by the traditions of a culture, or is it an attitude toward one's nation? Authoritarianism and extraversion, say, could be called traits or attitudes. Allport did not resolve the question except to note that both categories would be appropriate.

However, it is possible to distinguish between traits and attitudes in two general ways. First, attitudes have some specific object of reference. A person has an attitude toward something, for example, toward red-haired people, a musical group, or a brand of athletic shoe. A trait or personal disposition is not specifically directed toward a single object or category of objects. A person with the personal disposition of shyness will interact with most other people in the same way, regardless of their hair or shoes. Therefore, traits are broader in scope than attitudes.

Second, attitudes are positive or negative, for something or against it. They lead a person to like or hate, accept or reject, approach or avoid an object. Unlike a trait or personal disposition, an attitude involves a judgment or evaluation.

Personality and Motivation

personality and motivation

Allport believed that the central problem for any personality theory is how it treats the concept of motivation. Allport emphasized the influence of a person's present situation not only in his personality theory but also in his view of motivation. It is the individual's current state that is important, not what happened in the past during toilet training, schooling, or some other childhood crisis. Whatever happened in the past is exactly that: *past*. It is no longer active and does not explain adult behavior unless it exists as a current motivating force.

Cognitive processes—that is, our conscious plans and intentions—are also important. Allport criticized approaches such as Freud's that focused on unconscious, irrational forces at the expense of the conscious and rational. Deliberate intentions are an essential part of our personality. What we want and what we strive for are the keys to understanding our behavior. Thus, Allport attempted to explain the present in terms of the future rather than in terms of the past.

The Functional Autonomy of Motives

functional autonomy of motives The idea that motives in the normal, mature adult are independent of the childhood experiences in which they originally appeared.

Allport's concept of **functional autonomy** proposes that the motives of mature, emotionally healthy adults are not functionally connected to the prior experiences in which they initially appeared. Forces that motivated us early in life become autonomous, or independent, of their original circumstances. Similarly, when we mature, we become independent of our parents. Although we remain related to them, we are no longer functionally dependent on them and they should no longer control or guide our life. Allport offered the example of a tree. It is obvious that the tree's development can be traced to its seed. Yet when the tree is fully grown, the seed is no longer required as a source of nourishment. The tree is now self-determining, no longer functionally related to its seed.

Consider new college graduates embarking on a career in business and motivated to work hard to achieve financial success. Eventually their investment of time and energy pays off, and they amass enough money to be able to retire by age 50. Yet they continue to work just as hard as they did when first hired. Such behavior can no longer be for the same goal—the goal of financial security has been reached and surpassed. The motivation to work hard, once a means to a specific end (for money), has now become an end in itself. The motive has become independent of its original source.

We are all familiar with similar instances: the skilled craftsperson who insists on doing a meticulous job even when the extra effort brings in no additional monetary reward, or the miser who chooses a life of poverty while hoarding vast wealth. The behavior that once satisfied a specific motive now serves only itself. The original motive has been transformed into something autonomous. Therefore, adult motives cannot be understood by exploring a person's childhood. The only way to understand them is to investigate why people behave as they do today.

Perseverative Functional Autonomy

perseverative functional autonomy The level of functional autonomy that relates to low-level and routine behaviors.

Allport proposed two levels of functional autonomy: perseverative functional autonomy and propriate functional autonomy. **Perseverative functional autonomy**, the more elementary level, is concerned with such behaviors as addictions and repetitive physical actions such as habitual ways of performing some everyday task. The behaviors continue or persevere on their own without any external reward. The actions once served a purpose but no longer do so and are at too low a level to be considered an integral part of personality.

Allport cited both animal and human examples as evidence for perseverative functional autonomy. When a rat that has been trained to run a maze for food is given more than enough food it may still run the maze, but obviously for some purpose other than the food. At the human level, consider our preference for routine, familiar behaviors we maintain even in the absence of external reinforcement.

Propriate Functional Autonomy

propriate functional autonomy The level of functional autonomy that relates to our values, self-image, and lifestyle.

proprium Allport's term for the ego or self.

Propriate functional autonomy is more important than perseverative functional autonomy and is essential to the understanding of adult motivation. The word *propriate* derives from **proprium**, Allport's term for the ego or self. Propriate motives are unique to the individual. The ego determines which motives will be maintained and which will be discarded. We retain motives that enhance our self-esteem or self-image. Thus, a direct relationship exists between our interests and our abilities: We enjoy doing what we do well.

The original motivation for learning a skill such as playing the piano may have nothing to do with our interests. For example, in childhood we may be forced to take piano lessons and to practice. As we become proficient, we become more committed to playing the piano. The original motive (fear of parental displeasure) has disappeared, and the continued behavior of playing the piano becomes necessary to our self-image.

Our propriate functioning is an organizing process that maintains our sense of self. It determines how we perceive the world, what we remember from our experiences, and how our thoughts are directed. These perceptual and cognitive processes are selective. They choose from the mass of stimuli in our environment only those that are relevant to our interests and values. This organizing process is governed by three principles: (1) organizing the energy level, (2) mastery and competence, and (3) propriate patterning.

The first principle, *organizing the energy level*, explains how we acquire new motives. These motives arise from necessity, to help consume excess energy that we might otherwise express in destructive and harmful ways. For example, when people retire from their jobs, they have extra time and energy that, ideally, they should direct toward new interests and activities.

Mastery and competence, the second principle, refers to the level at which we choose to satisfy motives. It is not enough for us to achieve at an adequate level. Healthy, mature adults are motivated to perform better and more efficiently, to master new skills, and to increase their degree of competence.

The third principle, *propriate patterning*, describes a striving for consistency and integration of the personality. We organize our perceptual and cognitive processes around the self, keeping what enhances our self-image and rejecting the rest. Thus, our propriate motives are dependent on the structure or pattern of the self.

Allport noted that not all behaviors and motives could be explained by the principles of functional autonomy. Some behaviors—such as reflexes, fixations, neuroses, and behaviors arising from biological drives—are not under the control of functionally autonomous motives.

Personality Development in Childhood: The Unique Self

Allport chose the term *proprium* for the self or ego. He rejected the words *self* and *ego* because of the diversity of meanings ascribed to them by other theorists. We can best understand the word *proprium* by considering it in the sense of the adjective *appropriate*. The proprium includes those aspects of personality that are distinctive and thus *appropriate* to our emotional life. These aspects are unique to each of us and unite our attitudes, perceptions, and intentions.

TABLE 9.1   *The development of the proprium*

Stage	Development
1. Bodily self	Stages 1–3 emerge during the first three years. In this stage, infants become aware of their own existence and distinguish their own bodies from objects in the environment.
2. Self-identity	Children realize that their identity remains intact despite the many changes that are taking place.
3. Self-esteem	Children learn to take pride in their accomplishments.
4. Extension of self	Stages 4 and 5 emerge during the fourth through sixth year. In this stage, children come to recognize the objects and people that are part of their own world.
5. Self-image	Children develop actual and idealized images of themselves and their behavior and become aware of satisfying (or failing to satisfy) parental expectations.
6. Self as a rational coper	Stage 6 develops during ages 6–12. Children begin to apply reason and logic to the solution of everyday problems.
7. Propriate striving	Stage 7 develops during adolescence. Young people begin to formulate long-range goals and plans.
Adulthood	Normal, mature adults are functionally autonomous, independent of childhood motives. The function rationally in the present and consciously create their own lifestyles.

Stages of Development

Allport described the nature and development of the proprium over seven stages from infancy through adolescence (see Table 9.1).

Before the proprium begins to emerge, the infant experiences no self-consciousness, no awareness of self. There is not yet a separation of "me" from everything else. Infants receive sensory impressions from the external environment and react to them automatically and reflexively, with no ego to mediate between stimulus and response. Allport described infants as pleasure seeking, destructive, selfish, impatient, and dependent. He called them "unsocialized horrors." Our genetic inheritance, which is the basis of our eventual personality, does exist in infancy, but there is little of what could be called a "personality." The infant simply is driven by reflexes to reduce tension and maximize pleasure.

The first three stages in the development of the proprium span the years from birth to about age 4. The bodily self develops when infants begin to be aware of what Allport referred to as a "bodily me." For example, infants begin to distinguish between their own fingers and the object they are grasping. Next, the self-identity stage is marked by a sense of continuity of one's identity. Children realize that they remain the same people, despite changes in their bodies and their abilities. Self-identity is enhanced when children learn their name and see themselves as distinct from other people. Self-esteem develops when they discover that they can accomplish things on their own. They are motivated to build, explore, and manipulate objects, behaviors that sometimes can be destructive. If parents frustrate their child's need to explore at this stage, then the emerging sense of self-esteem can be thwarted, replaced by feelings of humiliation and anger.

Children develop actual and idealized self-images, reflecting how they actually see and would like to see themselves.

The extension-of-self stage involves the growing awareness of objects and people in the environment and the identification of them as belonging to the child. Children speak of "my house," "my parents," and "my school." A self-image develops next, incorporating how children see and would like to see themselves. These actual and ideal self-images develop from interaction with the parents, who make the child aware of their expectations and of the extent to which the child is satisfying or failing to satisfy those expectations. The self-extension and self-image stages typically occur between the ages of 4 and 6.

The self as a rational coper stage occurs between ages 6 and 12, when children realize that reason and logic can be applied to solving everyday problems. The propriate striving stage follows, when adolescents begin to formulate plans and goals for the future. Until they do so, their sense of self (their proprium) will remain incomplete.

Parent-Child Interactions

Our social interaction with our parents is vitally important throughout the stages of the development of the proprium, or self. Of particular significance is the infant-mother bond as a source of affection and security. If the mother or primary caregiver provides sufficient affection and security, the proprium will develop gradually and steadily, and the child will achieve positive psychological growth. Childhood motives will be free to be transformed into the autonomous propriate strivings of adulthood. A pattern of personal dispositions will form and the result will be a mature, emotionally healthy adult.

If childhood needs are frustrated, however, the proprium will not mature properly. The child becomes insecure, aggressive, demanding, jealous, and self-centered. Psychological growth is stunted. The result is a neurotic adult who functions at the level of childhood drives. Adult motives do not become functionally autonomous but remain tied to their original conditions. Traits and personal dispositions do not develop and the personality remains undifferentiated, as it was in infancy.

The Healthy Adult Personality

In Allport's view, the healthy personality changes from being a biologically dominated organism in infancy to a mature psychological organism in adulthood. Our motivations become separated from childhood and are oriented toward the future. As we noted, if our childhood needs for affection and security have been met, the proprium will develop satisfactorily. The adult personality grows out of childhood but is no longer dominated or determined by childhood drives. Allport did not explain whether the neurotic adult could counteract or overcome unfortunate childhood experiences; he was more interested in positive psychological growth. He described six criteria for the normal, mature, emotionally healthy, adult personality:

1. The mature adult extends his or her sense of self to people and to activities beyond the self.
2. The mature adult relates warmly to other people, exhibiting intimacy, compassion, and tolerance.

Normal, mature adults are functionally autonomous, independent of childhood motives. They function rationally in the present and consciously create their own lifestyles.

3. The mature adult's self-acceptance helps him or her achieve emotional security.
4. The mature adult holds a realistic perception of life, develops personal skills, and makes a commitment to some type of work.
5. The mature adult has a sense of humor and self-objectification (an understanding of or insight into the self).
6. The mature adult subscribes to a unifying philosophy of life, which is responsible for directing the personality toward future goals.

By meeting these six criteria, adults can be described as emotionally healthy and functionally autonomous, independent of childhood motives. As a result, they cope with the present and plan for the future without being victimized by the experiences of their early years.

Questions About Human Nature

Allport's conception of functional autonomy and personality development holds that emotionally healthy adults are not tied to or driven by childhood conflicts. Thus, his theory presents an optimistic view of adults in conscious control of their lives, rationally attending to current situations, planning for the future, and actively fashioning an identity. Always in the process of *becoming*, we creatively design and implement an appropriate style of life, influenced more by events of the present and plans for the future than by our past (see Figure 9.2).

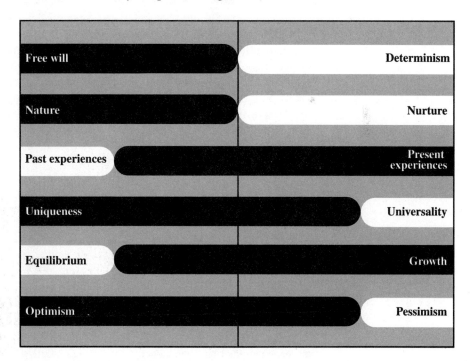

Free will	Determinism
Nature	Nurture
Past experiences	Present experiences
Uniqueness	Universality
Equilibrium	Growth
Optimism	Pessimism

FIGURE 9.2   *Allport's image of human nature*

Allport took a moderate stance on the question of free will versus determinism. He granted free choice in our deliberations about our future, but he also recognized that some behaviors are determined by traits and personal dispositions. Once these behaviors are formed, they are difficult to change. On the nature-nurture issue, he believed that both heredity and environment influence personality. Our genetic background explains a significant portion of personality, supplying our basic physique, temperament, and level of intelligence. These raw materials are shaped by learning and experience. Allport believed in each person's uniqueness. Although common traits show some universality in behavior, individual traits or personal dispositions describe our nature more precisely.

To Allport, the ultimate and necessary goal of life is not to reduce tension, as Freud proposed, but rather to increase tension, impelling us to seek new sensations and challenges. When we have met one challenge, we are motivated to seek another. The reward is the process of achieving rather than the specific achievement, striving for the goal rather than reaching it. We require goals to motivate us and to maintain an optimal level of tension in the personality.

Allport's optimistic image of human nature was reflected in his personal liberal stance and his interest in social reform. The humanistic attitude expressed in his work was mirrored in his own personality. His colleagues and students recall that he genuinely cared about people and that these feelings were reciprocated.

Assessment in Allport's Theory

Allport wrote more about personality assessment techniques than most other theorists did. In his popular book, *Pattern and Growth in Personality* (1961), he noted that, despite the existence of many approaches to assessment, there was no single best technique. Personality is so complex that to evaluate it we must employ many legitimate techniques. He listed 11 major methods (see Table 9.2) and relied heavily on the personal-document technique and the Study of Values. He also observed expressive behavior, which we discuss in the section on research in Allport's theory.

TABLE 9.2   *Allport's suggested methods for assessing personality*

Constitutional and physiological diagnosis
Cultural setting, membership, role
Personal documents and case studies
Self-appraisal
Conduct analysis
Ratings
Tests and scales
Projective techniques
Depth analysis
Expressive behavior
Synoptic procedures (combining information from several sources in a synopsis)

The Personal-Document Technique

personal-document technique A method of personality assessment that involves the study of a person's written or spoken records.

The **personal-document technique** involves examining diaries, autobiographies, letters, literary compositions, and other samples of a person's written or spoken records to determine the number and kinds of personality traits. Allport's most famous case is an analysis of a collection of more than 300 letters written over a 12-year period by a middle-aged woman identified as Jenny (Allport, 1965, 1966). It was later revealed that Jenny was the mother of Allport's college roommate and had written the letters to Allport and his wife (Winter, 1993a).

A similar analysis can be performed with third-person material, such as case histories and biographies. In Allport's technique, a group of judges would read the autobiographical or biographical material and record the traits they found in it. Given a reasonable degree of agreement among the judges, the assessments can be grouped into a relatively small number of categories. In the research with Jenny's letters, 36 judges listed nearly 200 traits. Because many terms were synonymous, Allport was able to reduce them to eight categories.

One of Allport's students performed a computer analysis on the letters to find categories of words that might indicate the existence of a particular trait (Paige, 1966). For example, words expressing anger, rage, hostility, and aggression were coded as constituting the trait of aggression. This approach is more sophisticated and quantitative than Allport's original analysis of the letters because it involves fewer subjective judgments. The computer analysis yielded eight prominent traits in Jenny's personality similar to the categories Allport identified. Because of that consistency, Allport concluded that his subjective approach to personality assessment provided information on traits that was valid and comparable to the more objective computer analysis.

The Study of Values

Allport and two colleagues developed an objective self-report assessment test called the Study of Values (Allport, Vernon, & Lindzey, 1960). They proposed that our personal values are the basis of our unifying philosophy of life, which is one of the six criteria for a mature, healthy personality. Our values are personality traits and represent strongly held interests and motivations. Allport believed that everyone possesses some degree of each type of value but one or two will be dominant in the personality. The categories of values are as follows.

1. *Theoretical values* are concerned with the discovery of truth and are characterized by an empirical, intellectual, and rational approach to life.
2. *Economic values* are concerned with the useful and practical.
3. *Aesthetic values* relate to artistic experiences and to form, harmony, and grace.
4. *Social values* reflect human relationships, altruism, and philanthropy.
5. *Political values* deal with personal power, influence, and prestige in all endeavors, not just in political activities.
6. *Religious values* are concerned with the mystical and with understanding the universe as a whole.

Research in Allport's Theory

Allport criticized psychologists who insisted that experimental and correlational methods were the only legitimate research approaches to the study of personality. He argued that not every aspect of personality could be tested in these ways. Therefore, psychologists should be more open and eclectic in their research methodology. He also opposed applying methods used with emotionally disturbed persons (such as case studies and projective techniques) to the study of emotionally healthy persons. Because case studies focus on the past, Allport considered them to be of no value for understanding normal adults because their personality is divorced from childhood influences.

Projective techniques, such as the Thematic Apperception Test and the Rorschach inkblot test, may present a distorted picture of the normal personality because they deal with unconscious forces that have little effect on the normal adult personality. Allport suggested that more reliable information could be obtained by simply asking people to describe themselves, a method that reveals their dominant traits.

Allport favored the idiographic approach—the study of the individual case—as indicated by his use of personal documents. However, he did use nomothetic methods when he believed them to be appropriate. Psychological tests such as the Study of Values employ the nomothetic approach.

Expressive Behavior

expressive behavior
Spontaneous and seemingly purposeless behavior, usually displayed without our conscious awareness.

coping behavior
Consciously planned behavior determined by the needs of a given situation and designed for a specific purpose, usually to bring about a change in one's environment.

Allport conducted considerable research on what he called **expressive behavior**, described as behavior that expresses our personality traits. He also identified **coping behavior**, which is oriented toward a specific purpose and is consciously planned and carried out. Coping behavior is determined by needs inspired by the situation and ordinarily is directed toward bringing about some change in our environment.

Expressive behavior is spontaneous and reflects basic aspects of the personality. In contrast to coping behavior, expressive behavior is difficult to change, has no specific purpose, and is usually displayed without our awareness. Allport offered the example of public speaking. The speaker communicates with the audience on two levels. The formal, planned level (coping behavior) includes the lecture's content. The informal, unplanned level (expressive behavior) consists of the speaker's movements, gestures, and vocal inflections. The speaker may be nervous, talk rapidly, pace, or fidget with an earring. These spontaneous behaviors express elements of his or her personality.

In his landmark study of expressive behavior, Allport gave subjects a variety of tasks to perform and then judged the consistency of their expressive movements over the different situations (Allport & Vernon, 1933). He found a high level of consistency in voice, handwriting, posture, and gestures. From these behaviors he deduced the existence of such traits as introversion and extraversion.

Additional research on expressive behavior has shown that personality can be assessed from audiotapes, films, and videotapes. Facial expressions, vocal inflections, and idiosyncratic gestures and mannerisms reveal personality traits to a trained observer. The expressive behaviors linked to specific traits have even been assessed from still photographs (Allport & Cantril, 1934; Berry, 1990, 1991; DePaulo, 1993; Riggio & Friedman, 1986; Riggio, Lippa, & Salinas, 1990).

Researchers have accumulated an impressive body of evidence to show that some people can form reliable impressions of a stranger's personality based solely on facial appearance and expression (Berry & Wero, 1993). For example, studies have shown that observers accurately assess personality factors such as anxiety from watching a film of the person as brief as 30 seconds (Ambody & Rosenthal, 1992). In another study, observers formed impressions of strangers by looking at their photographs. The assessments were found to be just as accurate as ratings made by classmates who had known the subjects for several weeks (Berry, 1990). These and similar studies provide strong support for Allport's proposition that expressive behavior reflects personality traits.

A long-term research program conducted by Paul Ekman identified facial expressions of seven emotions that can be objectively and consistently distinguished from one another. These emotions are anger, contempt, disgust, fear, sadness, surprise, and happiness (Ekman, Matsumoto, & Friesen, 1997). Other research has found that four of the Big Five factors of personality (see Chapter 10) can be characterized by facial expressions. For example, neuroticism reveals itself in looks of anger, contempt, and fear. Agreeableness shows in laughter and other expressions of friendly social interaction. Extraversion appears in smiles, laughter, and other expressions of enjoyment and amusement. Conscientiousness is marked by expressions of embarrassment including a tightly controlled smile, an averted gaze, and head movements down and away from the observer (Keltner, 1997).

Type A behavior   Type A behavior, the pattern associated with the potential for heart disease, has been distinguished from Type B behavior by expressions of disgust, glaring, grimacing, and scowling (Chesney, Ekman, Friensen, Black, & Hecker, 1997). A study of depressed patients in Switzerland found that facial expressions distinguished those who later attempted suicide from those who did not (Heller & Haynal, 1997). Obviously, we give away much of our inner self by the expression on our face.

Some facial expressions undergo changes too subtle to be observed directly but are measurable by techniques such as slow-motion analysis of filmed interviews (National Advisory Mental Health Council, 1995). For example, when subjects were asked merely to think about an emotion, such as recalling experiences that were happy or sad, increases in tension in certain facial muscles could be detected. Further, slow motion analysis showed that different muscle groups were involved with positive and with negative thoughts.

There is the question of the universality of facial expressions. Do the same expressions reveal the same personality factors from one culture to another? The evidence is not consistent. Studies of American and Chinese infants and adults found that some basic emotions were revealed by identical facial expressions in both cultures and in both age groups (Albright et al., 1997; Camras, Oster, Campos, Miyake, & Bradshaw, 1997). However, a study comparing facial expressions of American, Chinese, and Japanese infants reached a different conclusion. Chinese infants showed consistently less variety in facial expressive behavior than American and

Japanese infants. American infants differed significantly in facial expressions of emotions from Chinese infants but not so much from Japanese infants (Camras, 1998).

A Final Commentary

Although considerable research has been conducted on expressive behavior, Allport's theory as a whole has stimulated little research to test its propositions. His idiographic research approach ran counter to the main current of thought in contemporary psychology, which accepted nomothetic research instead (the study of large subject groups through sophisticated statistical analysis). Allport's focus on emotionally healthy adults was also at variance with the prevalent position in clinical psychology, which dealt with the neurotic and psychotic.

It is difficult to translate Allport's concepts into specific terms and operations suitable for study by the experimental method. For example, how do we observe functional autonomy or propriate striving in the laboratory? How can we manipulate them to test their effects or the impact of other variables on them?

Criticisms have been leveled against the concept of functional autonomy. Allport did not make clear how an original motive is transformed into an autonomous one. For example, once a person is financially secure, by what process is the motive to work hard for financial gain altered to become a motive to work hard for the sake of the task itself? If the mechanism of transformation is not explained, how can we predict which childhood motives will become autonomous in adulthood?

Allport's emphasis on the uniqueness of personality has been challenged because his position focuses so exclusively on the individual that it is impossible to generalize from one person to another. Many psychologists find it difficult to accept Allport's proposed discontinuity between child and adult, animal and human, normal and abnormal. They point out that research on the behavior of children, animals, and emotionally disturbed subjects has yielded considerable knowledge about the functioning of the normal, emotionally healthy adult.

Despite these criticisms, Allport's theory has been well received in the academic community. The approach to personality development, emphasis on uniqueness, and focus on the importance of goals are reflected in the work of the humanistic psychologists Carl Rogers and Abraham Maslow. Interest in Allport's work has been revived recently as part of the current focus on personality traits, which is providing empirical support for some of his ideas. His books are written in a readable style and his concepts have a commonsense appeal. The emphasis on conscious, rational determinants of behavior provides an alternative to the psychoanalytic position that sees people irrationally and unconsciously driven by uncontrollable forces. Allport's view that people are shaped more by future expectations than by past events is congenial with a hopeful and humanistic philosophy. His most enduring contributions to psychology are making the study of personality academically respectable and emphasizing the role of genetic factors within a trait approach to personality.

Chapter Summary

Gordon Allport focused on the conscious instead of the unconscious. He believed that personality is guided more by the present and future than by the past. He studied normal rather than emotionally disturbed persons. Personality is defined as the dynamic organization within the individual of those psychophysical systems that determine characteristic behavior and thought. It is a product of heredity and environment and divorced from childhood experiences.

Traits are consistent, enduring predispositions to respond in the same or a similar way to different stimuli. Individual traits (personal dispositions) are unique to the person; common traits are shared by many people. Habits are narrower than traits, are relatively inflexible, and involve a specific response to a specific stimulus. Attitudes have specific objects of reference and are for or against something. Cardinal traits are powerful and pervasive; central traits are less pervasive. Secondary traits are displayed less conspicuously and less consistently than other types of traits.

Functional autonomy means that a motive in the normal adult is not functionally related to the past experiences in which it originally appeared. Two levels of functional autonomy are perseverative (behaviors such as addictions and repeated physical movements) and propriate (interests, values, attitudes, intentions, lifestyle, and self-image related to the core of personality). Three principles of propriate functional autonomy are organizing the energy level, mastery and competence, and propriate patterning.

The proprium (self or ego) develops from infancy to adolescence in seven stages: bodily self, self-identity, self-esteem, extension of self, self-image, self as a rational coper, and propriate striving. An infant is controlled by drives and reflexes and has little personality. The mature, healthy adult personality is characterized by an extension of self to other people and activities, a warm relating to others, emotional security, a realistic perception, the development of skills, a commitment to work, self-objectification, and a unifying philosophy of life.

Allport presented an optimistic image of human nature and emphasized the uniqueness of the individual. We are not driven by childhood events. In conscious control of our lives, we creatively design a lifestyle and grow through an inherent need for autonomy, individuality, and selfhood. Our ultimate goal is for increases in tension that impel us to seek new sensations and challenges.

The personal-document approach to personality assessment involves the examination of diaries, letters, and other personal records to uncover personality traits. The Study of Values is a psychological test to assess six types of values. Allport's research on expressive behavior revealed a consistency in expressive movements and related them to a variety of emotions and personality patterns. Some research suggests a consistency of facial expressions from one culture to another.

Allport's theory has been criticized on the grounds that it is difficult to test empirically such concepts as functional autonomy. Allport's focus on the uniqueness of personality, on the stability and consistency of traits over all situations, and on the discontinuity between childhood and adult personalities has also been questioned.

Review Questions

1. Discuss the relative importance of personal variables versus situational variables as influences on personality. What was the outcome of this person-situation debate?

2. Explain Allport's definition of personality. How does his view differ from Freud's?

3. How was Allport's view of personality affected by his meeting with Freud and by his own childhood feelings of inferiority?

4. Describe four characteristics of traits. How do traits differ from attitudes?

5. According to Allport, what is the relationship between personality and motivation?

6. What is the role of cognitive processes in personality development?

7. What is the relationship between adult motives and childhood experiences? What was Allport's term for this situation?

8. Discuss the three principles of functional autonomy.

9. Define the concept of proprium and describe the seven stages in its development.

10. What parental behaviors are necessary for a child to achieve positive psychological growth?

11. How does Allport's theory account for emotional disturbances in adulthood?

12. What are the characteristics of the mature, healthy adult personality?

13. Describe the research findings on how expressive behavior can reveal aspects of our personality. Is there a universality of facial expressions over all cultures?

Suggested Readings

Allport, G. W. (1937). *Personality: A psychological interpretation*. New York: Holt. Allport's classic book that established the study of personality as an integral part of scientific academic psychology and defined the focus of personality psychology as the unique individual.

Allport, G. W. (1955). *Becoming: Basic considerations for a psychology of personality*. New Haven, CT: Yale University Press. Outlines Allport's approach to personality, emphasizing the human capacity for growth and development.

Allport, G. W. (1967). Autobiography. In E. G. Boring & G. Lindzey (Eds.), *A history of psychology in autobiography* (Vol. 5, pp. 1–25). New York: Appleton-Century-Crofts. Allport's account of his life and career.

Camras, L. A. (1998). Production of emotional facial expressions in European American, Japanese, and Chinese infants. *Developmental Psychology, 34,* 616–628. An outgrowth of Allport's work on expressive behavior, this cross-cultural study found significant differences in expressivity that may be related to early socialization experiences.

Elms, A. C. (1994). *Uncovering lives: The uneasy alliance of biography and psychology*. New York: Oxford University Press. Chapter 5, "Allport meets Freud and the clean little boy" (pp. 71–84), discusses Gordon Allport's 1920 encounter with Sigmund Freud.

Evans, R. I. (1971). *Gordon Allport: The man and his ideas*. New York: Dutton. Interviews with Allport about his life and work.

Kreitler, S., & Kreitler, H. (1990). *The cognitive founda-tions of personality traits.* New York: Plenum Press. Describes the study of personality traits as "alive and well" and asserts that no better building blocks of personality have thus far been proposed.

Rosenzweig, S., & Fisher, S. L. (1997). "Idiographic" vis–à–vis "idiodynamic" in the historical perspective of personality theory: Remembering Gordon Allport, 1897–1997. *Journal of the History of the Behavioral Sciences, 33,* 405–419. A reappraisal of Allport's focus on the uniqueness of the human personality. Considers the extent to which his personal spiritual-ity and religious views may have affected his image of human nature.

Personality is that which permits a prediction of what a person will do in a given situation.

—Raymond Cattell

T E N

Raymond Cattell, Hans Eysenck, and Other Trait Theorists

Cattell's goal in his study of personality was to predict what a person will do or how a person will behave in response to a given stimulus situation. Cattell made no reference to changing or modifying behavior from undesirable to desirable or from abnormal to normal, which had been the approach of some other personality theorists. These more clinically oriented theorists based their work on case studies of patients who sought a psychologist's services because they were unhappy or emotionally disturbed and wanted to change. In contrast, Cattell's subjects were so-called normal people. His aim was to study their personality, not to treat it. He believed it was impossible, or at least unwise, to attempt to change a personality before understanding fully what was to be modified.

Cattell's theory of personality, then, did not originate in a clinical setting. His approach is rigorously scientific, relying on observations of behavior and masses of data. In Cattell's research, it was not unusual for more than 50 kinds of measurements to be obtained from a single subject.

𝒢 **factor analysis**

factor analysis A statistical technique based on correlations between a number of measures, which may be explained in terms of underlying factors.

The hallmark of Cattell's approach was his treatment of the data. He submitted them to the statistical procedure called **factor analysis**, which involves assessing the relationship between each possible pair of measurements taken from a group of subjects to determine common factors. For example, scores on two different psychological tests or on two subscales of the same test would be analyzed to determine their correlation. If the two measures showed a high correlation, Cattell concluded that they measured similar or related aspects of personality. If the guilt-proneness and introversion subscales of a personality test, let us say, yielded a high correlation coefficient, we could infer that both subscales provided information on the same personality factor. Thus, two sets of data about a person are combined to form a single dimension, or factor, that describes the information provided by both sets of data.

Cattell referred to these factors as *traits*, which he defined as the mental elements of the personality. Only when we know someone's traits can we predict how that person will behave in a given situation. Thus, to understand someone fully, we must be able to describe in precise terms the entire pattern of traits that define that person as an individual.

The Life of Cattell (1905–1998)

Cattell was born in Staffordshire, England, where he had a happy childhood. His parents were exacting about the standards of performance they expected from their children but permissive about how the children spent their time. Cattell and his brothers and friends spent much time outdoors, sailing, swimming, exploring caves, and fighting mock battles. He recalled that they "occasionally drowned or fell over cliffs." When Cattell was 9, England entered World War I. A mansion near his home was converted to a hospital and he remembered seeing trainloads of wounded soldiers returning from the battlefields of France. He wrote that this experience made him unusually serious for a young boy and aware of the "brevity of life and the need to accomplish while one might." His intense dedication to work may have originated from these experiences. He also felt highly competitive with an older brother and wrote of the problems of maintaining his own freedom of development while confronted with this brother who could not be "overcome" (Cattell, 1974a, pp. 62–63).

At age 16 Cattell enrolled at the University of London to study physics and chemistry, graduating with honors in 3 years. His time in London intensified his interest in social problems but he realized that training in the physical sciences did not equip him to deal with social ills. He decided that the best solution was to master the study of the human mind. This was a courageous decision to make in 1924 because the field of psychology in England offered few professional opportunities and only six academic professorships. It was regarded as a discipline for eccentrics. Against the advice of friends, Cattell began graduate studies at the University of London, working with the eminent psychologist-statistician Charles E. Spearman, who had developed the technique of factor analysis.

Awarded his Ph.D. in 1929, Cattell found that his friends had been correct: There were few jobs for psychologists. He did some lecturing at Exeter University, wrote a book about the English countryside, and established a psychology clinic for the schools in the city of Leicester, all while pursuing his own research interests. Whereas Spearman had used factor analysis to measure mental abilities, Cattell resolved to apply the method to the structure of personality.

During this period Cattell developed chronic digestive disorders resulting from overwork, a deficient diet, and accommodations in a cold basement apartment. His wife left him due to his poor economic prospects and total absorption in his work. However, Cattell did claim some positive benefits to that time of hardship. The experience forced him to focus on practical problems rather than theoretical or experimental issues, which he might have done given more secure and comfortable circumstances. "Those years made me as canny and distrustful as a squirrel who has known a long winter. It bred asceticism, and impatience with irrelevance, to the point of ruthlessness" (Cattell, 1974b, p. 90).

Eight years after he earned his doctoral degree, Cattell finally received an opportunity to work full time in his chosen field. The prominent American psychologist Edward L. Thorndike invited Cattell to spend a year at Thorndike's laboratory at Columbia University in New York. The following year Cattell accepted a professorship at Clark University in Worcester, Massachusetts, and in 1941 moved to Harvard, where, he said, the "sap of creativity" rose (Cattell, 1974a, p. 71). His colleagues included Henry Murray, Gordon Allport, and William Sheldon, who was developing his theory of personality and body type. Cattell married a mathematician who shared his research interests, and at the age of 40 settled at the University of Illinois as a research professor. He published more than 450 articles and 40 books, a monumental accomplishment that reflects his dedication and perseverance.

> For the next twenty years, my life was that of a humming dynamo—smooth but powerful. I was generally the last out of the parking lot at midnight. There is a story that I arrived at the laboratory one day to find, to my amazement, not a soul there. I phoned and was told, "We are just sitting down to Thanksgiving dinner." All days were the same to me. (Cattell, 1993, p. 105)

In his seventies Cattell joined the graduate faculty of the University of Hawaii, where he permitted himself the luxury of swimming in the ocean every day. It was said that he worked "as hard as an assistant professor up for tenure and not sure that it will be granted" (Johnson, 1980, p. 300). He died in Honolulu at the age of 92.

In 1997 Cattell received the Gold Medal Award for Life Achievement in Psychological Science from the American Psychological Association. The citation noted,

> In a remarkable 70-year career, Raymond B. Cattell has made prodigious, landmark contributions to psychology, including factor analytic mappings of the domains of personality, motivation, and abilities. . . . Cattell stands without peer in his creation of a unified theory of individual differences in integrating intellectual, temperamental, and dynamic domains of personality. (Gold Medal Award, 1997, p. 797)

Cattell's Approach to Personality Traits

traits To Cattell, reaction tendencies, derived by the method of factor analysis, that are relatively permanent parts of the personality.

common traits Traits possessed in some degree by all persons.

Cattell defined **traits** as relatively permanent reaction tendencies that are the basic structural units of the personality. He classified traits in several ways (see Table 10.1).

Common Traits and Unique Traits

Cattell distinguished between common traits and unique traits. A **common trait** is one that is possessed by everyone to some degree. Intelligence, extraversion, and gregariousness are examples of common traits. Everyone has these traits, but some people have them to a greater extent than others. Cattell's reason for suggesting that

TABLE 10.1   *Ways of classifying traits*

Common traits	Everyone shares common traits, to some degree. For example, everyone has some measure of intelligence or of extraversion.
Unique traits	Each of us has unique traits that distinguish us as individuals; for example, a liking for politics or an interest in baseball.
Ability traits	Our skills and abilities determine how well we can work toward our goals.
Temperament traits	Our emotions and feelings (whether we are assertive, fretful, or easygoing, for example) help determine how we react to the people and situations in our environment.
Dynamic traits	These are the forces that underlie our motivations and drive our behavior.
Surface traits	These characteristics are composed of any number of source traits, or behavioral elements, and therefore may be unstable and impermanent, weakening or strengthening in response to different situations.
Source traits	Source traits are single, stable, permanent elements of our behavior.
Constitutional traits	These are source traits that have biological origins, such as the behaviors that result from drinking too much alcohol.
Environmental-mold traits	These are source traits that have environmental origins, such as the behaviors that result from the influence of our friends, our work environment, or the neighborhood we live in.

common traits are universal is that all people have a similar hereditary potential and are subject to similar social pressures, at least within the same culture.

People differ, as we said, in that they possess different amounts or degrees of these common traits. They also differ because of their **unique traits**, those aspects of personality shared by few other people. Unique traits are particularly apparent in our interests and attitudes. For example, one person may have a consuming interest in genealogy, whereas another may be passionately interested in Civil War battles or baseball or Chinese martial arts.

unique traits Traits possessed by one or a few persons.

Ability, Temperament, and Dynamic Traits

A second way to classify traits is to divide them into ability traits, temperament traits, and dynamic traits. **Ability traits** determine how efficiently we will be able to work toward a goal. Intelligence is an ability trait; our level of intelligence will affect the ways in which we strive for our goals. **Temperament traits** describe the general style and emotional tone of our behavior, for example, how assertive, easygoing, or irritable we are. These traits affect the ways we act and react to situations. **Dynamic traits** are the driving forces of behavior. They define our motivations, interests, and ambitions.

ability traits Traits that describe our skills and how efficiently we will be able to work toward our goals.

temperament traits Traits that describe our general behavioral style in responding to our environment.

dynamic traits Traits that describe our motivations and interests.

Surface Traits and Source Traits

A third class of traits is surface traits versus source traits according to their stability and permanence. **Surface traits** are personality characteristics that correlate with one another but do not constitute a factor because they are not determined by a single source. For example, several behavioral elements such as anxiety, indecision, and irrational fear combine to form the surface trait labeled *neuroticism*. Thus, neuroticism does not derive from a single source. Because surface traits are composed of several elements, they are less stable and permanent and therefore less important in describing personality.

Of greater importance are **source traits**, which are unitary personality factors that are much more stable and permanent. Each source trait gives rise to some aspect of behavior. Source traits are those individual factors derived from factor analysis that combine to account for surface traits.

surface traits Traits that show a correlation but do not constitute a factor because they are not determined by a single source.

source traits Stable, permanent traits that are the basic factors of personality, derived by the method of factor analysis.

Constitutional Traits and Environmental-Mold Traits

Source traits are classified by their origin as either constitutional traits or environmental-mold traits. **Constitutional traits** originate in biological conditions but are not necessarily innate. For example, alcohol intake can lead to behaviors such as carelessness, talkativeness, and slurred speech. Factor analysis would indicate that these characteristics are source traits.

Environmental-mold traits derive from influences in our social and physical environments. These traits are learned characteristics and behaviors that impose a pattern on the personality. The behavior of a person reared in an impoverished inner-city neighborhood is molded differently from the behavior of a person reared in upper-class luxury. A career military officer shows a different pattern of behavior

constitutional traits Source traits that depend on our physiological characteristics.

environmental-mold traits Source traits that are learned from social and environmental interactions.

T A B L E   1 0 . 2   *Cattell's source traits (factors) of personality*

Factor	Low scorers	High scorers
A	Reserved, aloof, detached	Outgoing, warmhearted, easygoing
B	Low in intelligence	High in intelligence
C	Low ego strength, easily upset, less emotionally stable	High ego strength, calm, emotionally stable
E	Submissive, obedient, docile, unsure, meek	Dominant, assertive, forceful
F	Serious, sober, depressed, worrying	Happy-go-lucky, enthusiastic, cheerful
G	Expedient, low in superego	Conscientious, high in superego
H	Timid, shy, aloof, restrained	Bold, adventurous
I	Tough-minded, self-reliant, demanding	Tender-minded, sensitive, dependent
L	Trusting, understanding, accepting	Suspicious, jealous, withdrawn
M	Practical, down-to-earth, concerned with detail	Imaginative, absentminded
N	Forthright, naive, unpretentious	Shrewd, worldly, insightful
O	Self-assured, secure, complacent	Apprehensive, insecure, self-reproaching
Q_1	Conservative, holds traditional values, dislikes change	Radical, liberal, experimenting, embraces change
Q_2	Group-dependent, prefers to join and follow others	Self-sufficient, resourceful, independent
Q_3	Uncontrolled, lax, impulsive	Controlled, compulsive, exacting
Q_4	Relaxed, tranquil, composed	Tense, driven, fretful

from a jazz musician. Thus, we see that Cattell recognized the interaction between personal and situational variables.

Source Traits: The Basic Factors of Personality

After more than two decades of intensive factor-analytic research, Cattell identified 16 source traits as the basic factors of personality (Cattell, 1965). These factors are best known in the form in which they are most often used, in an objective personality test called the Sixteen Personality Factor (16 PF) Questionnaire (see Table 10.2).

Cattell presented the traits in bipolar form, and, as you can see, the personality characteristics associated with these traits are expressed in words we are likely to use in everyday conversation when describing our friends and ourselves. No doubt you can tell at a glance whether you score high, low, or somewhere in between on these basic personality factors. Cattell later identified additional factors he designated *temperament traits* because they relate to the general style and emotional tone of behavior. He gave as examples excitability, zest, self-discipline, politeness, and self-assurance (Cattell, 1973; Cattell & Kline, 1977).

It is important to remember that in Cattell's system, source traits are the basic elements of personality just as atoms are the basic units of the physical world. He argued that psychologists cannot understand or generate laws about personality without describing precisely the nature of these elements.

Dynamic Traits: The Motivating Forces

We noted that Cattell described dynamic traits as the traits concerned with motivation, which is an important issue in many personality theories. Cattell believed that a personality theory that failed to consider the impact of dynamic, or motivating, forces is incomplete, like trying to describe an engine but failing to mention the type of fuel on which it runs.

Ergs and Sentiments

Cattell proposed two kinds of dynamic, motivating traits: ergs and sentiments. The word *erg* derives from the Greek word *ergon*, which means work or energy. Cattell used **erg** to denote the concept of instinct or drive. Ergs are the innate energy source or driving force for all behaviors, the basic units of motivation that direct us toward specific goals.

ergs Permanent constitutional source traits that provide energy for goal-directed behavior. Ergs are the basic innate units of motivation.

Cattell's factor-analytic research identified 11 ergs. These are:

anger
appeal
curiosity
disgust
gregariousness
hunger
protection
security
self-assertion
self-submission
sex

sentiments To Cattell, environmental-mold source traits that motivate behavior.

Whereas an erg is a constitutional source trait, a **sentiment** is an environmental-mold source trait because it derives from external social and physical influences. A sentiment is a pattern of learned attitudes that focuses on an important aspect of life, such as a person's community, spouse, occupation, religion, or hobby. Both ergs and sentiments motivate behavior, but there is a vital difference between them. Because an erg is a constitutional trait, it is a permanent structure of the personality. It may strengthen or weaken but it cannot disappear. A sentiment, because it results from learning, can be unlearned and can disappear so that it is no longer important to a person's life. (Cattell later called these learned traits SEMS, which stands for Socially Shaped Ergic Manifolds, which may be reason enough for us to continue to call them sentiments.)

Attitudes

attitudes To Cattell, attitudes are our interests in and emotions and behaviors toward some person, object, or event. This is a broader definition than typically used in psychology.

Cattell defined **attitudes** as our interests in and our emotions and behaviors toward some person, object, or event. As Cattell applied the term, it does not refer exclusively to an opinion for or against something, which is a commonplace usage of the word *attitude*. Cattell's definition is broader, encompassing all our emotions and actions toward an object or situation.

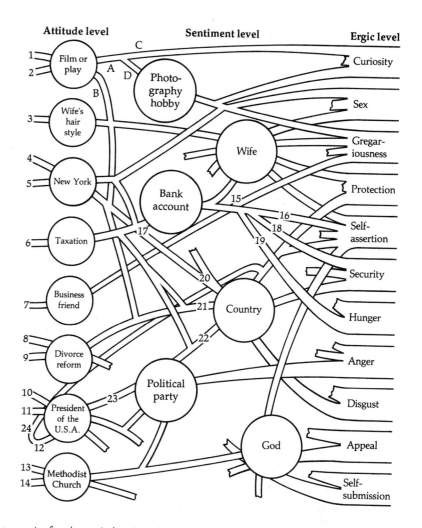

FIGURE 10.1   *Fragment of a dynamic lattice showing attitude subsidiation, sentiment structure, and ergic goals.* SOURCE: R. B. Cattell, *Personality: A Systematic Theoretical and Factual Study* (New York: McGraw-Hill, 1950), p. 158. Copyright 1950 by Raymond B. Cattell. Reprinted by permission.

Subsidiation

subsidiation To Cattell, the relationships among ergs, sentiments, and attitudes, in which some elements are subordinate to others.

dynamic lattice The representation in a chart or diagram of the relationships among ergs, sentiments, and attitudes.

Our dynamic traits—the ergs and sentiments—are related to our attitudes through the concept of **subsidiation**, which means simply that within the personality some elements *subsidiate*, or are subordinate to, other elements. Attitudes are subsidiary to sentiments; sentiments are subsidiary to ergs.

Cattell expressed these relationships in a diagram he called the **dynamic lattice** (see Figure 10.1). Our motivating forces, the ergs, are listed at the right. Sentiments are indicated in the circles at the center of the diagram. Note that each sentiment is subsidiary to one or more ergs. The attitudes, at the left, show the person's feelings and behaviors toward an object.

The Self-Sentiment

self-sentiment The self-concept, which is the organizer of our attitudes and motivations.

Each person's pattern of sentiments is organized by a master sentiment called the **self-sentiment**. This is our self-concept, reflected in virtually all of our attitudes and behaviors. The self-sentiment provides stability, coherence, and organization to the source traits and is linked to the expression of the ergs and sentiments. It is among the last of the sentiments to reach a full level of development. The self-sentiment contributes to the satisfaction of the dynamic traits and therefore controls all of the structures in the personality.

The Influences of Heredity and Environment

Cattell showed great interest in the relative influences of heredity and environment in shaping personality. He investigated the importance of hereditary and environmental factors by statistically comparing similarities found between twins reared in the same family, twins reared apart, nontwin siblings reared in the same family, and nontwin siblings reared apart. Thus, he was able to estimate the extent to which differences in traits could be attributed to genetic or to environmental influences.

The results of his analyses showed that for some traits, heredity plays a major role. For example, Cattell's data suggest that 80% of intelligence (Factor B) and 80% of timidity-versus-boldness (Factor H) can be accounted for by genetic factors. Cattell concluded that overall, one-third of our personality is genetically based, and two-thirds is determined by social and environmental influences.

Having demonstrated to his satisfaction that heredity is a significant influence on intelligence and other traits, Cattell suggested a policy of selective breeding to produce a more intelligent population. He called for the sterilization of low-IQ persons so that they would not have children, and he advocated incentives to encourage highly intelligent people to have a greater number of children.

Stages of Personality Development

Cattell proposed six stages in the development of personality covering the entire life span (see Table 10.3).

TABLE 10.3   Cattell's stages of personality development

Stage	Age	Development
Infancy	Birth–6	Weaning; toilet training; formation of ego, superego, and social attitudes
Childhood	6–14	Independence from parents and identification with peers
Adolescence	14–23	Conflicts about independence, self-assertion, and sex
Maturity	23–50	Satisfaction with career, marriage, and family
Late maturity	50–65	Personality changes in response to changes in physical and social circumstances
Old age	65+	Adjustment to loss of friends, career, and status

The period of infancy, from birth to age 6, is the major formative period for personality. The child is influenced by parents and siblings and by the experiences of weaning and toilet training. Social attitudes develop along with the ego and the superego, feelings of security or insecurity, attitudes toward authority, and a possible tendency to neuroticism. Cattell was not a follower of Freud's, but he incorporated in his theory several Freudian ideas, namely, that the early years of life are crucial in personality formation, and that oral and anal conflicts can affect personality.

Between ages 6 and 14, the childhood stage of personality formation, there are few psychological problems. This stage marks the beginning of a trend toward independence from parents and an increasing identification with peers. The childhood stage is followed by a more troublesome and stressful stage, adolescence, from 14 to 23. Emotional disorders and delinquency may be evident as young people experience conflicts centered on the drives for independence, self-assertion, and sex.

The fourth phase of development, maturity, lasts from approximately age 23 to age 50. It is generally a productive, satisfying time in terms of career, marriage, and family situations. The personality becomes less flexible, compared with earlier stages, and thus emotional stability increases. Cattell found little change in interests and attitudes during this period.

Late maturity, ages 50 to 65, involves personality developments in response to physical, social, and psychological changes. Health, vigor, and physical attractiveness may decline and the end of life may be in view. During this phase people reexamine their values and search for a new self. You will recognize here the similarity

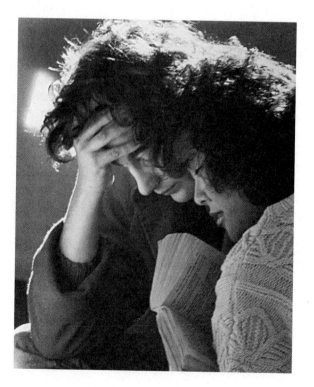

Adolescence can be a stressful stage of development.

In late maturity, after one's children have left home, there is often a reexamination of the values of one's life.

with Carl Jung's view of the midlife period. The final stage, old age, involves adjustments to different kinds of losses—the death of spouses, relatives, and friends; a career lost to retirement; loss of status in a culture that worships youth; and a pervasive sense of loneliness and insecurity.

Questions About Human Nature

Cattell's definition of personality gives us clues about his view of human nature. He wrote, "Personality is that which permits a prediction of what a person will do in a given situation" (Cattell, 1950, p. 2).

For behavior to be considered predictable, it must be lawful and orderly. Prediction would be difficult without regularity and consistency in the personality. For example, Cattell noted that one spouse can usually predict with considerable accuracy what the other spouse will do in a given situation because that person's past behavior has been consistent and orderly. Therefore, Cattell's view of human nature admits little spontaneity because that would make predictability more difficult. On the free will versus determinism issue, then, Cattell falls more on the side of determinism.

Cattell did not propose any ultimate or necessary goal that dominates behavior, no drive for self-actualization to pull us, no psychosexual conflicts to push us. Although Cattell noted the impact of early life events, we do not get the impression from his writings that he believed childhood forces determined the personality permanently. (See Figure 10.2.)

Cattell accepted the influence of both nature and nurture. For example, one's constitutional traits and ergs are innate, whereas environmental-mold traits are learned. On the uniqueness-universality issue, Cattell took a moderate position, noting the existence of common traits, which apply to everyone in a culture, and unique traits, which describe the individual.

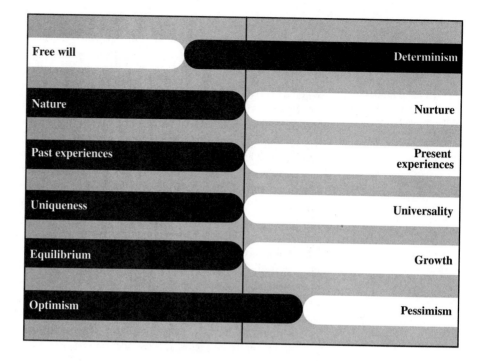

FIGURE 10.2   *Cattell's image of human nature*

Cattell's personal view of human nature is more clear. In his younger years he was optimistic about our ability to solve social problems. He predicted we would gain greater awareness of and control over our environment. He expected to see the level of intelligence rise, along with the development of "a more gracious community life of creatively occupied citizens" (Cattell, 1974b, p. 88). Reality did not live up to Cattell's expectations, and eventually he admitted that human nature and society had regressed.

Assessment in Cattell's Theory

Cattell's objective measurements of personality used three primary assessment techniques, which he called L-data (life records), Q-data (questionnaires), and T-data (tests).

L-data Life-record ratings of behaviors observed in real-life situations, such as in the classroom or office.

Life records (L-data).   The **L-data** technique involves observers' ratings of specific behaviors exhibited by subjects in real-life settings such as a classroom or office. For example, observers might record frequency of absence from work, grades at school, conscientiousness in performing job duties, emotional stability on the soccer field, or sociability in the office. The important point about L-data is that they involve overt behaviors that can be seen by an observer and occur in a naturalistic setting rather than in the artificial situation of a psychology laboratory.

Q-data Self-report questionnaire ratings of our characteristics, attitudes, and interests.

Questionnaires (Q-data). The **Q-data** technique relies on questionnaires. Whereas L-data calls for observers to rate the subjects, Q-data requires subjects to rate themselves. Various questionnaires have been used including standard self-report personality inventories, such as the MMPI, and scales to measure attitudes, interests, and opinions. Interviews have also been used. The subjects introspect and rate themselves on whatever aspect of behavior is being examined.

Cattell recognized the limitations of Q-data. First, some subjects may have only superficial self-awareness, so their answers will not reflect the true nature of their personality. Second, even if subjects do know themselves well, they may not want researchers to know them. Therefore, they may deliberately falsify their responses. This effect is aggravated by the fact that Q-data involves questionnaires; most subjects can easily figure out their purpose and judge what aspect of personality is being assessed. For example, if you were asked whether you preferred to be alone or in the company of other people, you would probably guess that the question relates to the trait of sociability. If you were sensitive about your shyness, you might say that you preferred to be with people just to conceal what you think is a disturbing personality trait. Because of this potential for bias, Cattell warned that Q-data must not automatically be assumed to be accurate.

T-data Data derived from personality tests that are resistant to faking.

Personality tests (T-data). The **T-data** technique involves the use of what Cattell called "objective" tests, in which a person responds without knowing what aspect of behavior is being evaluated. These tests circumvent the Q-data's shortcomings by making it difficult for a subject to know precisely what a test is measuring. If you cannot guess what the experimenter is trying to find out, then you cannot distort your responses to conceal your traits. For example, if you were shown an inkblot, you probably would not be able to predict whether the researcher's interpretation of your response revealed that you were conservative, relaxed, adventurous, or apprehensive.

Cattell considered such tests as the Rorschach, the Thematic Apperception Test, and the word-association test to be *objective* because they are resistant to faking. However, it is important to note that to most psychologists, this use of the word *objective* is misleading. As we stated in Chapter 1, such tests are usually called *subjective* because of the biases that affect scoring and interpretation.

The 16 PF (Personality Factor) Test

Cattell developed several tests to assess personality. The most notable is the 16 PF, which is based on the 16 major source traits. The test is intended for use with people 16 years of age and older and yields scores on each of the 16 scales. The responses are scored objectively; computerized scoring and interpretation are available. The 16 PF is widely used to assess personality for research, clinical diagnosis, and predicting occupational success.

Low Score Description	0	10	20	30	40	50	60	70	80	90	100	High Score Description

Percentile Rank

	High Score Description
Reserved	Outgoing
Less intelligent	More intelligent
Affected by feelings	Emotionally stable
Submissive	Dominant
Serious	Happy-go-lucky
Expedient	Conscientious
Timid	Adventurous
Tough-minded	Sensitive
Trusting	Suspicious
Practical	Imaginative
Forthright	Shrewd
Self-assured	Apprehensive
Conservative	Experimenting
Group-dependent	Self-sufficient
Uncontrolled	Controlled
Relaxed	Tense

FIGURE 10.3   *16 PF profile of a hypothetical airline pilot.* SOURCE: Based on Cattell, Eber, and Tatsuoka, 1970.

Consider the sample 16 PF Test profile for a hypothetical airline pilot (see Figure 10.3). By reading the high and low points of the plot of test scores, we can see that this person is emotionally stable, conscientious, adventurous, tough-minded, practical, self-assured, controlled, and relaxed. The pilot is not tense, apprehensive, or timid.

Cattell developed several variations of the 16 PF Test. For the assessment of emotional disturbances he compiled the Clinical Analysis Questionnaire. It measures 28 source traits, 16 from the 16 PF and 12 additional traits such as anxiety, guilt, and paranoia (Cattell & Kline, 1977). Tests are also available to assess personality factors in children and adolescents from ages 6 to 8, 8 to 12, and 12 to 18. Versions have been prepared to measure specific aspects of personality—such as anxiety, depression, and neuroticism—and for special purposes such as marriage counseling and performance evaluation of business executives.

Research in Cattell's Theory

Cattell's research approach is nomothetic. The method of factor analysis involves the study of large groups of people and the calculation of their average performance on various assessment instruments. However, he sometimes used the data to explain individual behavior. If you took the 16 PF Test, it would reveal the traits that are unique to you as an individual.

In discussing research methods, Cattell listed three ways to study personality: bivariate, clinical, and multivariate approaches. The *bivariate*, or two-variable, approach is the standard laboratory experimental method. The psychologist manipulates the independent variable to determine its effect on the subjects' behavior (the dependent variable). This approach has also been called univariate because only one variable is studied at a time. Cattell agreed that bivariate research is scientific, rigorous, and quantitative but argued that it dealt with only limited aspects of personality. In reality, personality is affected by many interacting variables. Also, in the typical artificial laboratory situation, significant emotional experiences cannot be manipulated and duplicated. Thus, for Cattell, the bivariate approach was too restrictive to reveal much about personality traits.

The *clinical* approach, which includes case studies, dream analysis, free association, and similar techniques, is highly subjective, as we noted in the chapters on the psychoanalytic theorists. These methods do not yield verifiable and quantifiable data. Cattell wrote, "The clinician has his heart in the right place, but perhaps we may say that he remains a little fuzzy in his head" (1959, p. 45).

Cattell chose to study personality through the *multivariate* approach, which yields highly specific data. It involves the sophisticated statistical procedure of factor analysis. Cattell favored two forms of factor analysis: the R technique and the P technique. The R technique involves collecting large amounts of data from a group of subjects. Correlations among all the scores are made to determine personality factors or traits. The P technique involves collecting a large amount of data from a single subject over a long period.

Let us consider only a few of the hundreds of factor-analytic studies Cattell and his associates conducted. We noted that he was interested in the relative effects on personality of heredity and environment. From a factor analysis of 16 PF data from 3,000 male subjects ages 12 to 18, Cattell concluded that three source traits were determined primarily by heredity (Cattell, 1982). These source traits are Factor F (serious versus happy-go-lucky), Factor I (tough-minded versus tender-minded or sensitive), and Factor Q_3 (uncontrolled versus controlled). Three other traits were found to be determined primarily by environmental influences: Factor E (submissive versus dominant), Factor G (expedient versus conscientious), and Factor Q_4 (relaxed versus tense).

Cattell also used the 16 PF Test to define the relationship between personality traits and marital stability (Cattell & Nesselroade, 1967). The subjects were married couples identified as having either a stable or an unstable marriage. The criterion for stability was whether a couple had taken steps toward dissolving the marriage. Factor analysis showed that marital stability could be predicted from the test scores. Partners in stable marriages had similar personality traits whereas partners in unstable marriages showed highly different personality traits.

Applying the P technique, Cattell studied a male college student for 40 days using various assessment measures (Cattell & Cross, 1952). The purpose was to compare the traits derived from factor analysis of the data on this single subject with traits derived from factor analysis of a large group of subjects. The results showed that traits unique to this individual were also similar to traits common to the large group.

Research on the Q_1 source trait (conservative versus radical and experimenting) asked subjects for their preferences for paintings that differed in complexity and ambiguity (Wilson, Ausman, & Mathews, 1973). Some paintings were clear representations of people and objects. Other paintings were abstract and nonrepresentational; it was not clear what these paintings were supposed to depict. As predicted, people scoring on the low, or conservative, end of Factor Q_1 preferred straightforward, representational works. People scoring on the high, or radical, end of Factor Q_1 preferred more abstract paintings.

A Commentary on Cattell

Despite Cattell's legitimate claim that factor analysis is an objective, precise technique, critics note that the opportunity exists for subjectivity to affect the outcome. At several stages in the research process, decisions are required that may be influenced by personal preferences. In the initial step of data collection the researcher must decide which tests to use and what aspects of behavior to measure. He or she then determines which factor-analytic technique to apply and what level of statistical significance will be accepted as appropriate. Once the factors, or traits, have been identified, the researcher labels them. If these names are ambiguous in any way, they may not accurately express the nature of the factors. This criticism does not suggest inherent weaknesses in Cattell's theory but that there is potential for subjective error in the factor-analytic approach. Perhaps it is this very subjectivity that accounts for the difficulty other researchers have had in replicating Cattell's findings and confirming his 16 basic source traits.

Cattell's theory demands consideration and respect. Few theories are so systematically constructed or firmly grounded in data. He organized a huge amount of research, accumulating monumental quantities of experimental data in an area frequently characterized by case histories, intuitions, and speculations. However, the sheer quantity of Cattell's work and the complexity of the factor-analytic method are among the reasons for a general lack of acceptance of his theory.

He understood his failure to persuade other psychologists of the wisdom of his views and defended his approach as the only one of value for studying personality. At the age of 85 he reiterated this point, criticizing contemporary psychologists for failing to master and apply factor analysis and lamenting that his work remained isolated from the mainstream of personality theorizing. He remained convinced that one day his work would allow for the prediction of human behavior with the same degree of accuracy with which astronomers predict the movements of planets (Cattell, 1974, 1990, 1993).

Cattell's publications may be described as widely respected but seldom read. Sales of his 1970 undergraduate textbook, *The Scientific Analysis of Personality*, were higher in England, Germany, Australia, and Japan than in the United States. European psychologists often rate his theory and research as being of greater relevance to the study of personality than American psychologists do.

Whatever the eventual outcome for Cattell's specific proposals, it is clear that the trait approach to personality and the investigation of genetic influences continue to fascinate contemporary researchers.

Behavioral Genetics

behavior genetics

behavioral genetics The study of the relationship between genetic or hereditary factors and personality traits.

In our introductory remarks to Chapters 9 and 10 on trait approaches to personality, we noted growing evidence supporting the idea that some traits are influenced by hereditary factors. The area of study on the connection between genetics and personality is called **behavioral genetics** and it has gained increasing acceptance and credibility. Regardless of the method used to evaluate or investigate personality, a significant genetic component must be considered. Allport and Cattell were among the first to suggest that inherited factors shape personality and rank in importance with environmental factors. In this section, we consider later researchers who have pursued this causal connection between our genetic inheritance and personality.

Hans Eysenck (1916–1997)

Hans Eysenck was born in Berlin, Germany, and emigrated to England in 1934, after Adolf Hitler came to power in Germany. Eysenck planned to study physics at the University of London but was told that he lacked the requisite academic background. Discouraged, he asked university officials if there was any other science in which he could major. Eysenck recalled, "I was told there was always psychology. 'What on earth is that?' I inquired in my ignorance. 'You'll like it,' they said. And so I enrolled in a subject whose scientific status was perhaps a little more questionable than my advisers realized" (Eysenck, 1980, p. 156). More than 40 years later the highly successful and productive Eysenck was asked if he had ever regretted his career choice. Often, he noted, but admitted that he was resigned to it.

Over the course of a long, productive career, Eysenck published approximately 75 books, including some for the general public, and more than 700 journal articles. He developed several personality assessment devices including the Eysenck Personality Inventory, the Maudsley Medical Questionnaire, and the Maudsley Personality Inventory. His work has been pivotal in supporting the role of inheritance in the description of personality.

The Dimensions of Personality

Eysenck spent most of his career at the University of London's Maudsley Hospital and Institute of Psychiatry, conducting research on the measurement of personality. He agreed with Cattell that personality is composed of traits, or factors, derived by the factor-analytic method. Nevertheless, Eysenck has been a critic of factor analysis and of Cattell's research because of the potential subjectivity in the technique and the difficulty in replicating Cattell's findings. Although Eysenck used factor analysis to uncover personality traits, he supplemented the method with personality tests and experimental studies that considered a wide range of variables.

Eysenck and his wife, Sybil (Ph.D., University of London), together developed many of the questionnaires used in their research. The Eysenck Personality Inventory (Eysenck & Eysenck, 1963) required 12 years of joint research and 20 factor analyses. Hans Eysenck wrote, "although published in our joint names, [it] is largely a monument to her skill, patience, and endurance" (Eysenck, 1980, p. 172). Few scientists in any discipline have been so straightforward in acknowledging the research contributions of their spouses.

The result of their efforts is a personality theory based on three dimensions, defined as combinations of traits or factors. We might think of the dimensions as "superfactors" (Eysenck, 1990a, 1990b; Eysenck & Eysenck, 1985). The three personality dimensions are as follows.

1. E—Extraversion versus introversion
2. N—Neuroticism versus emotional stability
3. P—Psychoticism versus impulse control (or superego functioning)

Eysenck noted that the dimensions of extraversion and neuroticism have been recognized as basic elements of personality since the time of the ancient Greek philosophers. He also suggested that formulations of the same dimensions could be found on nearly every personality assessment device ever developed (Eysenck, 1997).

Consider the list of personality traits associated with Eysenck's three personality dimensions (see Table 10.4). You can see clearly, for example, that people who score high on the traits of the E dimension would be classified as extraverts whereas people who score low would be classified as introverts.

Research has shown that the traits and dimensions Eysenck proposed remain stable throughout the life span from childhood through adulthood, despite the different social and environmental experiences each of us has. Our situations may change but the dimensions remain consistent. For instance, the introverted child tends to remain introverted as an adult.

TABLE 10.4   *Traits of Eysenck's personality dimensions*

Extraversion/introversion	Neuroticism/emotional stability	Psychoticism/impulse control
Sociable	Anxious	Aggressive
Lively	Depressed	Cold
Active	Guilt feelings	Egocentric
Assertive	Low self-esteem	Impersonal
Sensation seeking	Tense	Impulsive
Carefree	Irrational	Antisocial
Dominant	Shy	Creative
Venturesome	Moody	Tough-minded

Eysenck also conducted considerable research on intelligence. Although he did not list intelligence as a personality dimension, he considered it an important influence on personality. He noted that a person with an IQ of 120 is likely to have a more complex and multidimensional personality than is a person with an IQ of 80. He presented evidence to suggest that some 80 percent of our intelligence is inherited, leaving only 20 percent as the product of social and environmental forces (Eysenck & Eysenck, 1985).

extraversion

introversion

Extraversion

Based on your own experience, you can probably describe most extraverts and introverts with accuracy. Extraverts are oriented toward the outside world, prefer the company of other people, and tend to be sociable, impulsive, adventurous, assertive, and dominant. Introverts are quite the opposite. Eysenck was interested in how extraverts and introverts might differ biologically and genetically. He found that extraverts have a lower base level of cortical arousal than introverts do. Because the cortical arousal levels for extraverts are low, they need, and actively seek, excitement and stimulation. In contrast, introverts shy away from excitement and stimulation because their cortical arousal levels are already high (Eysenck, 1990b).

As a result, introverts react more strongly than extraverts to sensory stimulation. Studies have shown that introverts exhibit greater sensitivity to low-level stimuli and have lower pain thresholds than extraverts. Other research supports differential responses to sensory stimulation but reports less convincing evidence that such differences can be attributed to variations in cortical arousal levels (Bullock & Gilliland, 1993; Stelmack, 1990). Nevertheless, as Eysenck predicted, these differences are genetically based.

Neuroticism

Consider the traits associated with the neuroticism dimension. As you can see from Table 10.4, neurotics are characterized as anxious, depressed, tense, irrational, and moody. They may have low self-esteem and be prone to guilt feelings. Eysenck suggested that neuroticism is largely inherited, a product of genetics rather than learning or experience. It is manifested in biological as well as behavioral characteristics that differ from those of people at the emotional stability end of the neuroticism dimension.

People high in neuroticism show greater activity in those brain areas that control the sympathetic branch of the autonomic nervous system. This is the body's alarm system, which responds to stressful or dangerous events by increasing breathing rate, heart rate, blood flow to the muscles, and release of adrenaline. Eysenck argued that in neurotics, the sympathetic nervous system overreacts even to mild stressors, resulting in chronic hypersensitivity. This condition leads to heightened emotionality in response to almost any difficult situation. Indeed, neurotics react emotionally to events other people consider insignificant. According to Eysenck, these differences in biological reactivity on the neuroticism dimension are innate. People are genetically predisposed either toward neuroticism or toward emotional stability.

Psychoticism

People who score high in psychoticism are aggressive, antisocial, tough-minded, cold, and egocentric. Also, they have been found to be cruel, hostile, and insensitive to the needs and feelings of others. Paradoxically, they can also be highly creative. The research evidence tends to suggest a large genetic component. Men as a group generally score higher than women do on the psychoticism dimension. This finding led Eysenck to suggest that psychoticism may be related to male hormones. He also speculated that people who score high on all three dimensions may be apt to display criminal behavior but cited only modest empirical support for this idea (Eysenck & Gudjonsson, 1989).

In Eysenck's view, society needs the diversity provided by people characterized by all aspects of these three personality dimensions. An ideal society affords each person the opportunity to make the best use of his or her traits and abilities. However, some people will adapt to the social environment better than others will. The person high in psychoticism, for example, typified by hostile and aggressive behaviors, may become emotionally disturbed, or exhibit criminal tendencies, or channel the aggressive traits into a socially acceptable enterprise such as coaching college football.

How did Eysenck himself rate on his three dimensions of personality? In his autobiography he reported that his test scores were very stable. They showed, for neuroticism,

> a lack of apparent warmth, an inability to be artistically creative, [and] the absence of an elementary warning system modulated by incipient anxiety. On the [extraversion] dimension I am somewhat introverted, but not extremely so. And what about [psychoticism]? Pretty near the average; I don't think I show too much of the paranoid, cold aggressiveness so characteristic of the high P scores. (Eysenck, 1997, p. 298)

The Primary Role of Heredity

To Eysenck, then, traits and dimensions are determined primarily by heredity, although the research evidence shows a stronger genetic component for extraversion and neuroticism than for psychoticism. Eysenck did not rule out environmental and situational influences on personality, such as family interactions in childhood, but he believed their effects on personality were limited (Eysenck, 1990a).

His research design involved comparisons of identical (monozygotic) and fraternal (dizygotic) twins. The studies showed that identical twins are more alike in their personalities than are fraternal twins, even when the identical twins were reared by different parents in different environments during childhood. Studies of adopted children demonstrate that their personalities bear a greater similarity to the personalities of their biological parents than of their adoptive parents, even when the children had no contact with their biological parents. This is additional support for Eysenck's idea that personality owes more to our genetic inheritance than to our environment.

Cross-cultural research demonstrates that Eysenck's three personality dimensions have been found consistently in more than 35 nations including the United

States, England, Australia, Japan, China, Nigeria, and Sweden (see, for example, Bouchard, 1985; Eaves, Eysenck, & Martin, 1989; Floderus-Myrhed, Pedersen, & Rasmuson, 1980; Martin & Jardine, 1986; Tellegen et al., 1988). The confirmation of the same three personality dimensions in diverse cultures is further evidence for the primacy of inherited factors in the shaping of personality.

Robert McCrae and Paul Costa: The Five-Factor Model

five-factor model

Using the factor-analytic method, the personality traits Cattell and Eysenck derived varies in number. This does not suggest an inherent weakness in the method but instead reflects the way each theorist chose to measure personality. Some personality researchers have expressed dissatisfaction with both theories, suggesting that Eysenck has too few dimensions and Cattell has too many factors. More contemporary work has typically yielded no more than five broad personality factors (see, for example, Digman, 1990; Goldberg, 1990; Wiggins & Trapnell, 1997).

Working at the Gerontology Research Center of the National Institutes of Health in Baltimore, Maryland, Robert McCrae (1949–) and Paul Costa (1942–) embarked on an extensive research program that identified five so-called robust or Big Five factors (McCrae & Costa, 1985b, 1987). These factors are:

1. Neuroticism
2. Extraversion
3. Openness
4. Agreeableness
5. Conscientiousness

The factors were confirmed through a variety of assessment techniques including self-ratings, objective tests, and observers' reports. The researchers then developed a personality test, the NEO Personality Inventory, using an acronym derived from the initials of the first three factors. The consistent finding of the same factors from assessment procedures suggests that these factors can be relied on as distinguishing aspects of personality. The five factors and their characteristic traits are listed in Table 10.5.

Other researchers, following the lead provided by McCrae and Costa, developed adjective checklists that have proven to be quicker measures of the five factors. Subjects respond to the lists by selecting the words that best describe themselves. One such list uses 100 adjectives to measure the five factors; another uses only 40

TABLE 10.5   *McCrae and Costa's Big Five personality factors*

Factor	Description
Neuroticism	Worried, insecure, nervous, highly strung
Extraversion	Sociable, talkative, fun-loving, affectionate
Openness	Original, independent, creative, daring
Agreeableness	Good-natured, softhearted, trusting, courteous
Conscientiousness	Careful, reliable, hardworking, organized

(Goldberg, 1992; Saucier, 1994). Another successful approach to measuring the Big Five factors and their personality traits uses a structured interview consisting of 120 items to which subjects respond orally (Trull et al., 1998).

We can see a resemblance between the extraversion and neuroticism factors of McCrae and Costa and the extraversion and neuroticism dimensions of Eysenck's theory. Further, agreeableness and conscientiousness in the McCrae-Costa model may represent the low end of Eysenck's psychoticism dimension (impulse control). Openness shows a high positive correlation with intelligence. Similarly, agreeableness correlates with Alfred Adler's concept of social interest, which we discussed in Chapter 4 (McCrae & Costa, 1991; Zuckerman, 1991).

Studies of twins have found that four of the five factors show a stronger hereditary component: neuroticism, extraversion, openness, and conscientiousness. Agreeableness was found to have a stronger environmental component (Bergeman et al., 1993; Pedersen et al., 1988).

Cross-Cultural Consistency

The five factors have been consistently observed in Eastern as well as Western cultures, a finding that also supports a genetic component (Buss, 1991; Digman, 1989; Narayanan, Menon, & Levine, 1995; Paunonen et al., 1992). As McCrae and Costa noted, the Big Five factors and their traits appear to represent a "common human structure of personality" that transcends cultural differences (McCrae & Costa, 1997, p. 515). The diverse cultures in which these five factors and their traits have been found include the following: German, Portuguese, Hebrew, Chinese, Korean, Japanese, French, Filipino, and Canadian, as well as native-born and Spanish-speaking residents of the United States (Benet-Martinez, 1998; Jang & Livesley, 1998; McCrae & Costa, 1997; McCrae, Costa, Pilar, Rolland, & Parker, 1998; Trull & Geary, 1997).

Although the same factors are common to many cultures, major differences have been recognized in their relative importance and social desirability. For example, Australians consider extraversion and agreeableness to be more desirable to have than the other three factors. By contrast, Japanese consider conscientiousness to be more important than all other factors. In other words, in Japanese society it is more important for a person to be conscientious than to be extraverted, agreeable, open, or even emotionally stable.

In Hong Kong and in India agreeableness was found to be the most important factor. In Singapore, emotional stability was more important, whereas in Venezuela, the primary characteristic to praise is extraversion. No single factor was found to be more significant than others in Chile, Finland, Germany, the Netherlands, Norway, Turkey, and the United States (Williams, Satterwhite, & Saiz, 1998).

Stability of the Factors

The factors have been detected in children as well as adults. Longitudinal research studying the same subjects over a period of six years demonstrated a high level of stability for all five traits (Costa & McCrae, 1988). For example, persons high in agreeableness as children were likely to remain so as adults. A study in Finland of approximately 15,000 twins, ages 18 to 59, found a high degree of stability for both men and women on extraversion and neuroticism over that 40-year age span (Viken, Rose, Kaprio, & Koskenvuo, 1994). A study of 121 American men and women over 19 years, from late adolescence into adulthood, found modest but statistically significant stability for the extraversion and neuroticism factors (Carmichael & McGue, 1994).

More than 3,000 men and women college graduates were tested for extraversion when they were students and again 20 years later. The researchers found a significant positive correlation between the test scores at the two ages, suggesting that those who were extraverted in college remained so at midlife. The study also showed that those who scored high in extraversion were, as expected, more sociable and outgoing than were those who scored low. The high scorers were also more likely than the low scorers to seek social support when faced with stressful situations in midlife (Von Dras & Siegler, 1997).

In another study, preschool teachers were asked to predict what their students, then ages 3 to 6 years, would be like in 20 years' time. Their expectations, based on observations of the children's behavior, corresponded with the students' scores on the Big Five personality factors. These results suggest that the teachers assumed that preschool behavior would be closely related to adult behavior (Graziano, Jenson-Campbell, & Sullivan-Logan, 1998). This raises the question of whether such expectations will lead teachers and parents to reinforce certain behaviors to strengthen genetically based personality characteristics. In other words, would caregivers treat extraverted children differently from introverted children, thus strengthening each group's differential inherited behavioral tendencies?

Emotional and Behavioral Correlates

In several studies, extraversion was positively related to emotional well being, whereas neuroticism was negatively related to emotional well being. The researchers concluded that people high in extraversion and low in neuroticism were genetically predisposed to emotional stability (Costa & McCrae, 1984; Watson, Clark, McIntyre, & Hamaker, 1992). A study of 100 men and women college students found that those high in extraversion were able to cope with everyday life stress better than those scoring low in extraversion did. Extraverts were also more likely to seek social support to help them deal with stress (Amirkhan, Risinger, & Swickert, 1995). This agrees with the finding reported above that extraverts at midlife were more likely to seek social support in coping with stressful life events.

Research with college students found that over a 4-year period extraverts were likely to experience a greater number of positive events, such as a good grade, a pay raise, or marriage. Students scoring high in neuroticism were more predisposed to negative events such as illness, weight gain, traffic tickets, or rejection by graduate school (Magnus, Diener, Fujita, & Pavot, 1993). A study in Sweden of 320 pairs of identical and fraternal twins reared together and apart confirmed the relationship, for women subjects, between personality variables and desirable life events. Women who scored high on extraversion and openness to experience were significantly more likely to experience positive life events. Women who scored high on neuroticism were significantly more likely to experience negative life events (Saudino, Pedersen, Lichtenstein, McClearn, & Plomin, 1997).

In another study, persons high in agreeableness and conscientiousness showed greater emotional well being than persons low in these traits (McCrae & Costa, 1991). Other researchers found that people high in neuroticism were prone to depression, anxiety, and self-blame (Jorm, 1987; Parkes, 1986). More physical illness and psychological distress has been associated with high scores on the neuroticism factor (Larsen & Kasimatis, 1991; Ormel & Wohlfarth, 1991).

A group of 48 healthy adult males were asked to keep detailed diaries of their problems and moods over an 8-day period. The results showed that men who scored high in neuroticism reported having more frequent daily problems and finding them to be more distressing than did men who scored low in neuroticism (Suls, Green, & Hillis, 1998). Other research demonstrated that adults who scored low in neuroticism and high in extraversion and conscientiousness were also high in subjective vitality, which the investigators described in terms of energy, enthusiasm, and spirit (Ryan & Frederick, 1997).

People high in openness tend to have a wide range of intellectual interests and to seek challenges. They are more likely to change jobs, try different careers, and expect more varied life experiences than people scoring low in openness (McCrae & Costa, 1985a, 1985b).

Not surprisingly, people high in conscientiousness tend to be reliable, responsible, efficient, and dependable, and usually earn better grades in school than people low in conscientiousness (Goldberg, 1990). In research conducted in the workplace it was found that people who scored high in conscientiousness were more likely than low scorers to set high goals and strive to achieve them, to initiate desirable work behaviors, and to receive high performance ratings (Barrick & Mount, 1996; Barrick, Mount, & Strauss, 1993; Stewart, Carson, & Cardy, 1996). The conscientiousness factor was also shown to be a valid predictor of job performance for professional, police, managerial, sales, and skilled labor jobs (Salgado, 1997).

Research also indicates that high scorers on conscientiousness are likely to be healthier and to live longer. Longitudinal studies, some investigating the same subjects for nearly 70 years, showed that children who were high scorers turned out to be physically healthier and to live longer than children who were low scorers (Booth-Kewley & Vickers, 1994; Friedman et al., 1993, 1995; Marshall et al., 1994). A study of 196 college students in Australia found that high scores on conscientiousness were related to greater ego development for men subjects whereas high scores on the factor of openness were related to greater ego development among women (Einstein & Lanning, 1998). In other work, subjects high in the agreeableness factor were found to be cooperative, helpful, altruistic, honest, and selfless (Digman, 1990; John, 1990).

An 18-month study of 132 German university students from the beginning of their first year of college found significant effects of three of the Big Five personality factors on their social relationships. Students scoring high in extraversion made more friends during the 18-month period and were more likely to fall in love than students low in extraversion. Those high in agreeableness experienced less conflict with acquaintances of the opposite sex, and those high in conscientiousness were more likely to maintain contact with parents and siblings. The factor of openness showed no significant effect on social relationships (Asendorpf & Wilpers, 1998).

The evidence is clear from studies of a wide range of emotions and behaviors that the five-factor model of personality has a high predictive value. Most research uses the five factors as self-contained entities and not the individual traits of which they are composed (see Table 10.5). Research comparing the predictive value of the five factors and of the traits found that higher level factors and lower level traits have high predictive validities but that validities of the traits were higher than those of the factors (Paunonen, 1998).

Factor analyses of 14 studies of children, college students, and adults in the United States, Germany, and Hong Kong, including children in the United States of Asian ancestry, suggests the existence of two higher-order factors drawn from the five factor model. Factor α incorporates agreeableness, conscientiousness, and emotional stability and includes a constellation of traits that are considered socially desirable in many cultures. Factor β includes extraversion and an independent factor designated as "intellect." Extraversion in this case refers not only to sociability but also to an active, zestful, and venturesome attitude toward life. Intellect refers not to the standard conception of intelligence but rather to creative and divergent thinking and openness to new ideas (Digman, 1997).

Not all researchers accept McCrae and Costa's factors. Some critics argue that no list of a mere few factors can fully describe the complex human personality. Others agree that there may be five major factors but disagree on what they are. Nevertheless, McCrae and Costa's findings have been replicated and continue to inspire research. They provided an intriguing and well-supported approach to personality and to our understanding of the relative importance of heredity and environment.

Arnold Buss and Robert Plomin: The Temperament Theory

temperament

temperaments Inherited dispositions toward certain behaviors.

We noted that Cattell classified some personality factors as temperament traits, those traits that describe the general style and emotional level of our behavior. Beginning in the 1970s, Arnold Buss (1924–) of the University of Texas at Austin, and Robert Plomin (1948–) of Pennsylvania State University, identified three **temperaments** that they believe are the basic building blocks of personality. These are Emotionality, Activity, and Sociability. Buss and Plomin suggest that each person's personality is composed of different amounts of each temperament. The temperaments combine to form personality patterns or so-called supertraits, such as introversion or extraversion (Buss & Plomin, 1984, 1986). Their formulations have sparked a great deal of research interest (Bates, 1994).

Buss and Plomin developed two tests to assess personality: the Emotionality, Activity, Sociability Survey for Adults (EAS), and the Emotionality, Activity, Sociability Infant Temperament Survey (EASI) for children. For the latter test, the questionnaire is filled out by the parent or primary caregiver (Buss & Plomin, 1975, 1986). Based on extensive research with identical and fraternal twins, Buss and Plomin concluded that temperaments are primarily inherited, part of the genetic package with which we are equipped at birth. These findings have been replicated and supported by considerable independent research (see, for example, Saudino et al., 1995).

Because the three inherited temperaments are broad, they account for the range of individual differences in behavior that permits each of us to be unique. In addition, the temperaments persist throughout the life span, indicating the relatively minor impact of learning from environmental and social interactions (Plomin, Pedersen, McClearn, Nesselroade, & Bergeman, 1988).

However, Buss and Plomin do recognize some environmental effects. What we inherit is not a specific amount of a temperament but a range of response potential. One person will inherit more than another. What determines how much or how little of our potential for a given temperament we realize? Our social environment is the key. One researcher wrote, "We inherit dispositions, not destinies" (Rose, 1995, p. 648). Whether our genetic predispositions are realized depends on experience, particularly in childhood. Thus, Buss and Plomin do consider the impact of external stimulus or situational variables as well as of internal genetic variables. But they suggest limits on how greatly environment can modify temperament. If events force us to deviate from an innate temperamental tendency and to behave contrary to our nature for too long a period of time, the result will be conflict and stress.

Emotionality

The Emotionality temperament refers to our level of arousal or excitability. It consists of three components: distress, fearfulness, and anger. When we describe people as emotional, we mean they are easily upset and given to outbursts. At one extreme of the Emotionality continuum are people who appear unemotional in that nothing seems to disturb them. At the other extreme are people who are sensitive to the slightest provocation. Both extreme responses are maladaptive because they prevent a person from reacting to a given situation in an appropriate manner. An optimal degree of Emotionality arouses a person to respond quickly and alertly.

In Buss and Plomin's view, Emotionality refers to negative or unpleasant emotions such as distress, fearfulness, and anger, rather than to pleasant feelings such as happiness or love. This view agrees with our common usage of the word *emotional*. In general, we do not call people "emotional" when they appear well balanced and content. We usually reserve the term for those who are easily upset or agitated. The Emotionality components of distress, fearfulness, and anger have been observed in animal species as well as humans. Emotionality is relatively stable in childhood and continues into the adult years.

Activity

Buss and Plomin define the Activity temperament in terms of physical energy and vigor. We all know people who are more energetic and active than others and who display their energy in many different situations. They walk and talk fast and find it hard to sit still, fidgeting with their fingers or tapping their toes. Research with twins revealed an inherited component to Activity. It was found to be moderately stable through childhood and adulthood.

Sociability

The Sociability temperament refers to the degree of preference for contact and interaction with other people. Highly sociable persons prefer group activities and the company of others. Persons who are not sociable choose solitary activities and tend to avoid other people. Research suggests that Sociability is a persistent trait from infancy. Approximately 10 percent of the population has a high degree of Sociability at birth and 10 percent has a low degree of Sociability (Kagan, 1984).

Research on social inhibition shows that 15 to 20 percent of infants exhibit behaviors we may call "inhibited" when confronted with unfamiliar people (Kagan, Snidman, & Arcus, 1992). This social inhibition phenomenon may be related to a low level of the Sociability temperament. The temperament has been found to remain stable during childhood and to persist in adulthood.

Sociability is an adaptive characteristic. We must interact with other people to satisfy many of our needs and to obtain positive reinforcement. Many work and leisure activities are better accomplished socially than individually. The empirical evidence supporting the three temperaments is strongest for Sociability.

Twin Studies and Other Research

Much of the research on temperaments stems directly from the work of Buss and Plomin, whereas other studies focus more generally on the notion of inherited dispositions. We note the results of a few representative studies, most of which use the twin-comparison approach.

Identical twins, ages 42 to 57, were found to be more alike than fraternal twins on empathy, the ability to experience vicariously the feelings of others (Matthews,

The inherited nature of temperaments has been demonstrated by research comparing identical and fraternal twins.

Batson, Horn, & Rosenman, 1981). If empathy is inherited, then there may be a genetic basis for altruistic, or helping, behavior. Additional support for this proposition was found in a study of twins in England (Rushton, Fulker, Neale, Blizard, & Eysenck, 1984).

The results of twin studies on sociability support Buss and Plomin's position that this temperament is inherited. Identical twins during their first 12 months were found to be much more alike than fraternal twins on behaviors such as smiling at other people or displaying a fear of strangers (Freedman, 1974). When twins were compared on these behaviors at 18 and 24 months of age, researchers found the same differences in sociability between identical and fraternal twins (Matheny, 1983). Comparisons of twins between ages 6 and 10 showed that identical twins were much more similar than fraternal twins in their desire to affiliate with other people and on ratings of friendliness and shyness (Scarr, 1968).

A study involving two sets of parental ratings, taken 10 years apart, of adopted and nonadopted children measured extraversion, socialization, and stability. The results revealed that on average the children tended to change in the direction of the personalities of their biological parents (Loehlin, Horn, & Willerman, 1990). This evidence suggests that hereditary rather than environmental influences play the primary role in shaping personality.

In another study, children who at age 3 were described as restless were found at age 18 to be impulsive, aggressive, danger seeking, and alienated from others. Those who at age 3 were more inhibited scored significantly lower at age 18 on measures of impulsiveness (Caspi & Silva, 1994). These results support other findings suggesting that temperaments that define us as children are stable and persistent throughout life and thus are characteristic of us in adulthood.

In other work, 133 subjects were rated periodically from infancy to early adulthood in an attempt to establish a temperament labeled *difficult*. Infants thought to possess this temperament were described as hard to manage. Any new activity "became the occasion for noisy outbursts of crying. Sleeping and feeding schedules were irregular, and the children had many expressions of intense negative mood" (Thomas, 1986, p. 50). A high correlation was found between the Difficult temperament and the later development of behavior disorders (Thomas, Chess, & Korn, 1982).

Infants' temperaments can affect how their parents treat them. Mothers and fathers are typically considered to be environmental and social influences, yet there is obviously a genetic component to the relationship. One study compared irritable and nonirritable babies ranging in age from 1 to 6 months. Mothers of nonirritable babies treated their infants more positively than mothers of irritable babies did. The mothers in the first group were more responsive, stimulating, and soothing in their behavior and initiated significantly more frequent visual and physical contact (van den Boom & Hoeksma, 1994).

Twin studies on general personality attributes suggest that at least 50 percent of an individual's total personality is inherited. Supporting research was based on 850 pairs of twins in the United States (Loehlin & Nichols, 1976), 573 pairs of twins in England (Rushton et al., 1984), and data collected by researchers in Sweden on 13,000 pairs of twins (Floderus-Myrhed et al., 1980). It is important to remember that although these results support the influence of genetic factors on personality, the evidence for the heritability of Buss and Plomin's specific Emotionality, Activity, and Sociability temperaments is even stronger than for these general personality attributes.

These studies also indicate the role of the environment in shaping personality. Buss and Plomin, who do not dispute environmental or situational influences, recognize this point. In one study, researchers reported a significant relationship between shyness in adopted children and the sociability of their adoptive mothers (Daniels & Plomin, 1985). Because the adopted children and adoptive mothers share no genetic background, the researchers concluded that the subjects' similarity on Sociability was attributable to environmental influences.

Environmental factors affect the personality of siblings in different ways because experiences are different for each child. For example, parents treat sons differently from daughters and first-borns differently from later-borns. Brothers and sisters provide another set of social experiences. A dominant and assertive first-born may influence younger siblings in such a way that they develop passive, noncompetitive personalities (Rowe & Plomin, 1981).

Whatever the relative influence of heredity and environment on personality as a whole, strong evidence exists that temperaments remain stable from birth into adulthood and that the strength of that stability increases dramatically after age 3. Plomin also presented evidence to suggest that genetic factors influence our perception of stressful life events such as retirement or the death of a child or spouse (Plomin, Lichtenstein, Pedersen, McClearn, & Nesselroade, 1990). Thus, inherited temperaments exert pervasive, long-lasting influences on our behavior.

A Final Commentary

The theories presented in this chapter, together with their supporting research, indicate that inheritance may account for as much as 50 percent of personality (Brody, 1997; Buss, 1988, Stelmack, 1997). The evidence is greatest for the factors of extraversion, neuroticism, and psychoticism, but virtually every other dimension investigated by personality researchers displays a strong biological component. In many cases, a shared family environment has only a minor influence (Bouchard, 1994). Some researchers hold a more uncompromising view, arguing that twins, whether reared together or apart, will be alike in all facets of their personality regardless of family situation, suggesting that the genetic effect far outweighs the environmental effect (Rowe, 1994).

This area of research has practical and theoretical implications for personality psychologists, who in the past tended to concentrate on the family and social interactions in early childhood. Findings from behavioral genetics may require a restructuring of research efforts in the future if we are to account fully for the development of personality. However, caution is necessary. We must not conclude prematurely that family and other environmental factors can be discounted as shapers of personality. Plomin noted,

> It is good for the field of personality that it has moved away from simple-minded environmentalism. The danger now, however, is that the rush from environmentalism will

carom too far—to a view that personality is almost completely biologically determined. (Plomin, Chipuer, & Loehlin, 1990, pp. 225–226)

The various components of personality remain products of both our genetic makeup and the experiences of our life. The task for psychologists remains to determine the relative importance of each.

Chapter Summary

According to Cattell, factors, or traits, are the basic structural units of personality. We all possess the common traits to some degree; unique traits typify one or a few persons. Ability traits determine how efficiently we work toward a goal. Temperament traits define emotional style of behavior. Dynamic traits are concerned with motivation.

Surface traits are personality characteristics that correlate with one another but do not constitute a factor because they are not determined by a single source. The 16 source traits Cattell identified are single factors, and each is the sole source of some aspect of behavior. Source traits may be constitutional traits, which originate in internal bodily conditions, or environmental-mold traits, which derive from environmental influences.

Dynamic traits include ergs (the energy source for all behavior) and sentiments (learned patterns of attitudes). Ergs and sentiments are manifested in attitudes, which are a person's interests in some area, object, or other person. The self-sentiment is a person's self-concept and provides stability and organization to the source traits.

Cattell's research suggests that one-third of personality is genetically determined; the rest is determined by environmental influences. Thus, Cattell holds a deterministic view of personality. He does not suggest any ultimate life goals. Childhood influences are important in personality development, as are heredity and environment.

Cattell's three major assessment techniques are L-data (ratings made by observers), Q-data (self-ratings made through questionnaires, personality inventories, and attitude scales), and T-data (data from tests that are resistant to faking). Cattell developed the 16 PF and the Clinical Analysis Questionnaire. He used two forms of factor analysis: the R technique, which gathers large amounts of data from groups of subjects, and the P technique, which collects a large amount of data from a single subject over time. Cattell's work is highly technical, and the amount of supporting data is massive. Factor analysis has been criticized for its potential subjectivity.

Research on behavioral genetics shows a significant influence of genetic factors on personality. Eysenck demonstrated a genetic influence on the personality dimensions of extraversion, neuroticism, and psychoticism. McCrae and Costa proposed five biologically based factors: neuroticism, extraversion, openness, agreeableness, and conscientiousness. The factors are stable over the lifetime and appear in many cultures. The factors are valid predictors of emotions and behaviors. Buss and Plomin documented the innate potential for three temperaments: emotionality, activity, and sociability. Twin studies on personality attributes suggest that as much as 50 percent of personality is inherited.

Review Questions

1. How does Cattell's concept of personality traits differ from Allport's view of traits?

2. How does Cattell use factor analysis to identify traits?

3. Describe three ways to categorize traits.

4. Distinguish between ergs, sentiments, and attitudes. Distinguish between source traits and environmental-mold traits.

5. According to Cattell's research, which source traits are determined primarily by heredity?

6. What is the self-sentiment? What is its role in personality?

7. Identify the three types of data collected by Cattell. Give an example of each.

8. What is Cattell's position on free will versus determinism?

9. Describe the three personality types proposed by Eysenck. Does Eysenck suggest that personality traits are determined largely by genetic factors or by environmental factors?

10. Discuss Eysenck's research on identical and fraternal twins and on adopted children. How do the research results support his conclusion about the role of genetic factors in personality?

11. Describe McCrae and Costa's five factors of personality. What is the role of heredity and of environment in each of these factors?

12. In what ways do people who score high on extraversion and on conscientiousness differ from people who score low on these factors?

13. Describe the three temperaments proposed by Buss and Plomin. Discuss the importance of hereditary factors for each temperament and for personality in general.

Suggested Readings

Asendorpf, J. B., & Wilpers, S. (1998). Personality effects on social relationships. *Journal of Personality and Social Psychology, 74,* 1531–1544. Assessed the Big Five personality factors in a sample of college students over an 18-month period and noted how the relative strength of these traits predicted the number and quality of friendships and love relationships.

Buss, A. H. (1989). Personality as traits. *American Psychologist, 44,* 1378–1388. Discusses the trait approach to personality and notes that the goal of trait research is to understand people as combinations of traits.

Cattell, R. B. (1974). Autobiography. In G. Lindzey (Ed.), *A history of psychology in autobiography* (Vol. 6, pp. 59–100). Englewood Cliffs, NJ: Prentice-Hall; Travels in psychological hyperspace. In T. S.

Krawiec (Ed.), *The psychologists* (Vol. 2, pp. 85–133). New York: Oxford University Press. Two essays by Cattell about his life and work.

Cattell, R. B. (1993). Planning basic clinical research. In E. C. Walker (Ed.), *The history of clinical psychology in autobiography* (Vol. 2, pp. 101–111). Pacific Grove, CA: Brooks/Cole. Cattell's evaluation of his life's work, concluding that his approach to the measurement of personality structures and processes was the only correct one to pursue.

Eysenck, H. J. (1976). H. J. Eysenck. In R. I. Evans (Ed.), *The making of psychology: Discussions with creative contributors* (pp. 255–265). New York: Alfred A. Knopf. Interviews with Eysenck about his work, especially his criticisms of psychoanalysis and his controversial views on the genetic basis of intelligence.

Eysenck, H. J. (1990). Genetic and environmental contributions to individual differences: The three major dimensions of personality. *Journal of Personality, 58,* 245–261. Describes the relative impact of heredity and environment on Eysenck's proposed dimensions of personality (extraversion, neuroticism, and psychoticism) and emphasizes the importance to psychology of the study of behavioral genetics.

Eysenck, H. J. (1997). *Rebel with a cause: The autobiography of Hans Eysenck.* London: Transaction Publishers. Eysenck's reflections on his life and work. Notes how some of his ideas on personality dimensions have stood the test of time, and suggests the relative importance of heredity versus environment in his own personality.

Plomin, R. (1990). *Nature and nurture: An introduction to human behavioral genetics.* Pacific Grove, CA: Brooks/Cole. Reviews the research methods and empirical findings in the field of behavioral genetics. Discusses in a clear, readable style such issues as how heredity affects behavior and how these genetic influences can be detected.

Rowe, D. C. (1994). *The limits of family influence: Genes, experience, and behavior.* New York: Guilford Press. Documents the strong role of genetic factors in personality and intelligence, and the relatively weak effects of child-rearing practices and home environment.

Wright, L. (1997). *Twins and what they tell us about who we are.* New York: Wiley. Describes research and theories about twins and the relative effects on personality of genetic determinism versus environmental conditions. Suggests that theorists on both sides of the issue have used twin studies to bolster their position.

6

PART

The Humanistic Approach

Humanism is a system of thought in which human interests and values are of primary importance. The humanistic approach to personality is part of the humanistic movement in psychology that flourished in the 1960s and 1970s. The goal of the proponents of this movement was to alter psychology's methods and subject matter. Humanistic psychologists objected to psychoanalysis and to behaviorism, then the two major forces in American psychology, arguing that these systems presented too limited and demeaning an image of human nature.

Humanistic psychologists criticized Freud and others following the psychoanalytic tradition for studying only the emotionally disturbed side of human nature. They questioned how we could hope to learn about positive human characteristics and qualities if we focused on neuroses and psychoses. Instead, humanistic psychologists intended to study our strengths and virtues and to explore human behavior at its best, not worst.

The humanistic psychologists thought that the behavioral psychologists were narrow and sterile in their outlook because they disavowed conscious and unconscious forces to focus exclusively on the objective observation of overt behavior. But a psychology based on conditioned responses to stimuli depicts human beings as little more than mechanized robots, reacting to events in predetermined ways. The humanistic psychologists objected to this view, arguing that people are not big white rats or slow computers. Human behavior is too complex to be explained by the behaviorists' methods.

The term *humanistic psychology* was first used by Gordon Allport in 1930. Allport and Henry Murray are considered forerunners of the humanistic approach to personality, represented in this section by the works of Abraham Maslow and Carl Rogers. Their theories emphasize human strengths and aspirations, conscious free will, and the fulfillment of our potential. They present a flattering and optimistic image of human nature and describe people as active, creative beings concerned with growth and self-actualization.

> What humans can be, they must be. They must be true to their own nature.
>
> —Abraham Maslow

E L E V E N

Abraham Maslow

Abraham Maslow is considered the founder and spiritual leader of the humanistic psychology movement. He was strongly critical of behaviorism and of psychoanalysis, particularly Sigmund Freud's approach to personality. According to Maslow, when psychologists study only abnormal, emotionally disturbed examples of humanity, they ignore positive human qualities such as happiness, contentment, and peace of mind. A frequently quoted statement sums up Maslow's position: "The study of crippled, stunted, immature, and unhealthy specimens can yield only a cripple psychology" (Maslow, 1970b, p. 180).

We underestimate human nature, Maslow charged, when we fail to examine the best examples of humanity, society's most creative, healthy, and mature people. Thus, Maslow determined that his approach to personality would assess the best representatives of the human species. When you want to determine how fast humans can run, you study not the average runner but the fastest runner you can find. Only in this way is it possible to determine the full range of human potential.

Maslow's personality theory does not derive from case histories of clinical patients but from research on creative, independent, self-sufficient, fulfilled adults. Maslow concluded that each person is born with the same instinctive needs that enable us to grow, develop, and fulfill our potentials.

The Life of Maslow (1908–1970)

Inferiority Feelings and Compensation

The oldest of seven children, Abraham Maslow was born in 1908 in Brooklyn, New York. His parents were immigrants with little education and few prospects for rising above their marginal economic circumstances. At the age of 14, Maslow's father had walked and hitchhiked from Russia across Western Europe, so great was his ambition to reach the United States. The elder Maslow instilled in his son this intense drive to succeed.

Maslow's childhood was difficult. He told an interviewer, "with my childhood, it's a wonder I'm not psychotic" (quoted in Hall, 1968a, p. 37). In a statement recently uncovered in his unpublished papers Maslow wrote, "My family was a miserable family and my mother was a horrible creature" (quoted in Hoffman, 1996, p. 2). Isolated and unhappy, he grew up without close friends or loving parents. His father was aloof and periodically abandoned his unhappy marriage. Maslow said that his father "loved whiskey and women and fighting" (quoted in Wilson, 1972, p. 131). Eventually Maslow reconciled with his father but as a child and adolescent felt only hostility toward him.

Maslow's relationship with his mother was worse. A biographer reported that Maslow "grew to maturity with an unrelieved hatred toward [her] and he never achieved the slightest reconciliation" (Hoffman, 1988, p. 7). She was superstitious and would quickly punish Maslow for the slightest wrongdoing. She announced that God would retaliate for his misbehavior. Unaffectionate and rejecting of him, she openly favored the younger siblings. When Maslow brought home two stray kittens, his mother killed them, bashing their heads against a wall. Maslow never forgave her treatment of him, and when she died he refused to attend her funeral. The experience affected not only his emotional life but also his work in psychology. "The whole thrust of my life-philosophy, and all my research and theorizing . . . has its roots in a hatred for and revulsion against everything she stood for" (Maslow quoted in Hoffman, 1988, p. 9).

As a child, Maslow believed he was different from others. Embarrassed about his scrawny physique and large nose, he remembered his teenage years as marked by a huge inferiority complex. "I tried to compensate for what I felt was a great [physical] lack by forcing my development in the direction of athletic achievements" Maslow said (quoted in Hoffman, 1988, p. 13). Thus, the man who would later become interested in Alfred Adler's work was in many ways a living example of Adler's concept of compensation for inferiority feelings.

When Maslow's early attempts at compensation to achieve recognition and acceptance as an athlete did not succeed, he turned to books. The library became the playground of his childhood and adolescence, and reading and education marked the road out of the ghetto of poverty and loneliness. Maslow's early memories are significant because they indicate the style of life—the life of scholarship—he would fashion for himself. He recalled going to the neighborhood library early in the morning and waiting on the steps until the doors opened. He typically arrived at school an hour before classes began, and his teacher would let him sit in an empty classroom, reading the books she had loaned him. Although his grades remained mediocre, they were sufficient to gain him acceptance at City College of New York. He failed a course during his first semester and by the end of his freshman year was on academic probation, but with persistence his grades improved. He began the study of law, at his father's request, but decided after two weeks that he did not like it. What he really wanted to do was study *everything*.

From Monkeys to Self-Actualization

Maslow's desire for learning was matched by a passion for his cousin Bertha. He soon left home, first for Cornell University and then for the University of Wisconsin, where she joined him. He was 20 and she was 19 when they married. The union provided Maslow with a feeling of belonging and a sense of direction. He later said that life had little meaning until he married Bertha and began his studies at Wisconsin. Earlier, at Cornell, he had enrolled in a psychology course and pronounced that he found it "awful and bloodless." It had "nothing to do with people, so I shuddered and turned away from it" (quoted in Hoffman, 1988, p. 26). At Wisconsin, however, he found the behavioristic psychology of John B. Watson, leader of the revolution to make psychology a science of behavior. Like many people in the early 1930s, Maslow became enraptured, believing that behaviorism could solve all the world's problems. His training in experimental psychology included work on dominance and sexual behavior in primates. So obviously it was a giant step from this type of research in the behavioristic framework to the ideas of humanistic psychology—from monkeys to self-actualization.

Several influences brought about this profound shift in his thinking. He read the works of Freud, the Gestalt psychologists, and the philosophers Alfred North Whitehead and Henri Bergson. He was deeply affected by the onset of World War II and by the birth of his first child. About the baby he said, "I was stunned by the mystery and by the sense of not really being in control. I felt small and weak and feeble before all this. I'd say anyone who had a baby couldn't be a behaviorist" (quoted in Hall, 1968a, p. 56).

Maslow received his Ph.D. from the University of Wisconsin in 1934 and returned to New York, first for a postdoctoral fellowship under E. L. Thorndike at Columbia University, and later to teach at Brooklyn College, where he remained until 1951. Maslow took several intelligence and scholastic aptitude tests, scoring an IQ of 195, which Thorndike described as within the genius range. At first Maslow was surprised, but soon he accepted the revelation and thereafter considered it a triumph and frequently managed to work the information into social conversations.

Teaching in New York in the late 1930s and early 1940s Maslow had the opportunity to meet the wave of emigrant intellectuals fleeing Nazi Germany, including Erich Fromm, Karen Horney, and Alfred Adler. Maslow "talked about Adler all the time and was tremendously excited by his theories" recalled Bertha Maslow (quoted in Hoffman, 1988, p. 304). He also met the Gestalt psychologist Max Wertheimer and the American anthropologist Ruth Benedict. His admiration for Wertheimer and Benedict kindled his ideas about self-actualization.

In 1941 Maslow witnessed a parade shortly after Japan's surprise attack on the American naval base at Pearl Harbor in Hawaii, precipitating the onset of U.S. involvement in World War II. The experience changed his life. He resolved to devote himself to developing a psychology that would deal with the highest human ideals. He would work to improve the human personality and to demonstrate that people are capable of displaying better behaviors than prejudice, hatred, and aggression.

From 1951 to 1969, Maslow taught at Brandeis University in Massachusetts. A foundation grant enabled him to move to California to work on his philosophy of politics, economics, and ethics based on a humanistic psychology. He became an immensely popular figure in psychology and among the general public. He received many awards and honors and was elected president of the American Psychological Association in 1967.

Personality Development: The Hierarchy of Needs

need (psychology)

hierarchy of needs An arrangement of innate needs, from strongest to weakest, that activates and directs behavior.

instinctoid needs Maslow's term for the innate needs in his needs-hierarchy theory.

Maslow proposed a **hierarchy of five innate needs** that activate and direct human behavior (Maslow, 1968, 1970b). They are the physiological, safety, belongingness and love, esteem, and self-actualization needs (see Figure 11.1).

Maslow described these needs as **instinctoid**, by which he meant that they have a hereditary component. However, these needs can be affected or overridden by learning, social expectations, and fear of disapproval. Although we come equipped with these needs at birth, the behaviors we use to satisfy them are learned and therefore subject to variation from one person to another. The needs are arranged in order from strongest to weakest. Lower needs must be at least partially satisfied before higher needs become influential. For example, hungry people feel no urge to satisfy the higher need for esteem. They are preoccupied with satisfying the physiological need for food, not with obtaining approval and esteem from other people. It is only when people have adequate food and shelter, and when the rest of the lower needs are satisfied, that they are motivated by needs that rank higher in the hierarchy.

Need for self-
actualization

Esteem needs (from
self and others)

Belongingness
and love needs

Safety needs: security, order,
and stability

Physiological needs: food,
water, and sex

FIGURE 11.1   *Maslow's hierarchy of needs.*

Thus, we are not driven by all the needs at the same time. In general, only one need will dominate our personality. Which one it will be depends on which of the others have been satisfied. People who are successful in their careers are no longer driven by, or even aware of, their physiological and safety needs. These needs have been amply taken care of. Successful people are more likely to be motivated by the needs for esteem or self-actualization. However, Maslow suggested that the order of the needs can be changed. If an economic recession causes some people to lose their jobs, the safety and physiological needs may reassume priority. Being able to pay the mortgage becomes more prized than popularity with colleagues or an award from a civic organization.

Characteristics of Needs

Maslow described several characteristics of needs.

• The lower the need is in the hierarchy, the greater are its strength, potency, and priority. The higher needs are weaker needs.

• Higher needs appear later in life. Physiological and safety needs arise in infancy. Belongingness and esteem needs arise in adolescence. The need for self-actualization does not arise until midlife.

• Because higher needs are less necessary for actual survival, their gratification can be postponed. Failure to satisfy a higher need does not produce a crisis. Failure to satisfy a lower need does produce a crisis. For this reason, Maslow called lower needs **deficit** or **deficiency needs**; failure to satisfy them produces a deficit or lack in the individual.

• Although higher needs are less necessary for survival, they contribute to survival and growth. Satisfaction of higher needs leads to improved health and longevity. For this reason, Maslow called higher needs **growth** or **being needs**.

deficit (deficiency) needs The lower needs; failure to satisfy them produces a deficiency in the body.

growth (being) needs The higher needs; although growth needs are less necessary than deficit needs for survival, they involve the realization and fulfillment of human potential.

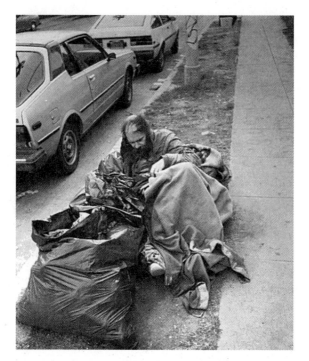

When the basic needs for food and shelter are unsatisfied, the higher needs, such as esteem and self-actualization, are of less importance.

• Satisfaction of higher needs is also beneficial psychologically. Satisfaction of higher needs leads to contentment, happiness, and fulfillment.

• Gratification of higher needs requires better external circumstances (social, economic, and political) than does gratification of lower needs. For example, pursuing self-actualization requires greater freedom of expression and opportunity than pursuing safety needs.

• A need does not have to be satisfied fully before the next need in the hierarchy becomes important. Maslow proposed a declining percentage of satisfaction for each need. Offering a hypothetical example, he described a person who satisfied, in turn, 85 percent of the physiological needs, 70 percent of the safety needs, 50 percent of the belongingness and love needs, 40 percent of the esteem needs, and 10 percent of the self-actualization need.

Physiological Needs

If you have ever been swimming and had to struggle for air while underwater, or if you have gone too long without eating, you may have realized how trivial the needs for love or esteem or anything else can be when your body is experiencing a physiological deficiency. As we noted, a starving person craves only food. But once that need is satisfied, the person is no longer driven by it. The need ceases to direct or control behavior.

This describes the situation for most people in an affluent, industrialized culture. It is rare for middle-class Americans to be concerned with satisfying their survival needs. Physiological needs have a greater personal impact as motivating forces in cultures where basic survival remains an everyday concern. Because a need that has been gratified no longer serves to motivate behavior, the physiological needs play a minimal role for most of us.

Safety Needs

Maslow believed that the needs for safety and security typically are important drives for infants and neurotic adults. Emotionally healthy adults have usually satisfied their safety needs, a condition that requires stability, security, and freedom from fear and anxiety. For infants and children, the safety needs can be seen clearly in their behavior because youngsters react visibly and immediately to any threat to their security. Adults have learned ways to inhibit their reactions to dangerous situations.

Another visible indication of children's safety needs is their preference for a structure or routine, for an orderly and predictable world. Too much freedom and permissiveness leads to an absence of structure and order. This situation is likely to produce anxiety and insecurity in children because it threatens their security. Some measure of freedom must be granted to children, but only within the limits of their capacity to cope. This freedom must be offered with guidance because children are not yet capable of directing their own behavior and realizing the consequences.

Neurotic and insecure adults also need structure and order because their safety needs still dominate their personality. Neurotics compulsively avoid new experiences. They arrange their world to make it predictable, budgeting their time and organizing their possessions. Pencils must be kept in a certain drawer, and shirts hung in the closet facing the same direction.

Maslow pointed out that although most normal adults have satisfied the safety needs, those needs may still have an impact on behavior. Many of us choose the predictable over the unknown; we prefer order to chaos. That is why we save for the future, buy insurance, and opt to remain in a secure job rather than risk a new venture. However, the safety needs are not as overwhelming a driving force for normal adults as they are for children or neurotics.

Belongingness and Love Needs

Once our physiological and safety needs have been reasonably well satisfied, we attend to the needs for belongingness and love. These needs can be expressed through a close relationship with a friend, lover, or mate, or through social relationships formed within a group.

The need to belong has grown more difficult to satisfy in our increasingly mobile society. Few of us live in the neighborhood where we grew up and keep friends from our early schooldays. We change schools, jobs, and communities too frequently to put down roots, to develop a secure sense of belonging. Many of us attempt to satisfy the need to belong in other ways, such as joining a church or a club, enrolling in a class, or volunteering for a service organization.

The need to give and receive love can be satisfied in an intimate relationship with another person. Maslow did not equate love with sex, which is a physiological need, but he recognized that sex is one way of expressing the love need. He suggested that the failure to satisfy the need for love is a fundamental cause of emotional maladjustment.

Belongingness and love needs can be satisfied through a relationship with a friend.

Esteem Needs

Once we feel loved and have a sense of belonging we may find ourselves driven by two forms of the need for esteem. We require esteem and respect from ourselves, in the form of feelings of self-worth, and from other people, in the form of status, recognition, or social success. Satisfaction of the need for self-esteem allows us to feel confident of our strength, worth, and adequacy, which will help us become more competent and productive in all aspects of our life. When we lack self-esteem, we feel inferior, helpless, and discouraged with little confidence in our ability to cope.

The Self-Actualization Need

self-actualization The fullest development of the self.

The highest need in Maslow's hierarchy, **self-actualization**, depends on the maximum realization and fulfillment of our potentials, talents, and abilities. Although a person may satisfy all the other needs in the hierarchy, if that person is not self-actualizing, he or she will be restless, frustrated, and discontent. Maslow wrote, "A musician must make music, an artist must paint, a poet must write . . . to be ultimately at peace" (1970b, p. 46).

The self-actualizing process may take many forms, but each person, regardless of occupation or interests, is capable of maximizing personal abilities and reaching the fullest personality development. Self-actualization is not limited to creative and intellectual superstars such as musicians, artists, and astrophysicists. What is important is to fulfill one's own potentials at the highest level possible, whatever one's chosen endeavor. Maslow put it this way, "A first-rate soup is more creative than a second-rate painting . . . cooking or parenthood or making a home could be creative, while poetry need not be" (1987, p. 159).

Several conditions are necessary in order for us to satisfy the self-actualization need.

1. We must be free of constraints imposed by society and by ourselves.
2. We must not be distracted by the lower-order needs.
3. We must be secure in our self-image and in our relationships with other people; we must be able to love and be loved in return.
4. We must have a realistic knowledge of our strengths and weaknesses, virtues and vices.

Although the hierarchy of needs Maslow proposed applies to most of us, there can be exceptions. Some people dedicate their lives to an ideal and willingly sacrifice everything for their cause. People have been known to fast until death in the service of their beliefs, thus denying their physiological and safety needs. Religious figures may abandon worldly goods to fulfill a vow of poverty, thus satisfying the self-actualization need while frustrating the lower-order needs. Artists throughout history have imperiled health and security for the sake of their work. A more common reversal in the hierarchy occurs when people place a greater importance on esteem than on love, believing that the belongingness and love needs can be satisfied only if they first feel self-confident.

Cognitive Needs

cognitive needs Innate needs to know and to understand.

Maslow proposed a second set of innate needs, the **cognitive needs**—to know and to understand, which exist outside the hierarchy we have described. The need to know is stronger than the need to understand. Thus, the need to know must be at least partially satisfied before the need to understand can emerge. Several points of evidence support the existence of cognitive needs (Maslow, 1970b).

• Laboratory studies show that animals explore and manipulate their environment for no apparent reason other than curiosity, that is, a desire to know and to understand.

• Historical evidence shows that people often have sought knowledge at the risk of their lives, thus placing the needs to know and to understand above the safety needs.

• Studies suggest that emotionally healthy adults are attracted to mysterious and unexplained events and are motivated to improve their knowledge about them.

• Emotionally healthy adults in Maslow's own clinical practice complained of boredom and a lack of zest and excitement in life. He described them as "intelligent people leading stupid lives in stupid jobs" and found that they improved when they took steps to fulfill the needs to know and to understand by becoming involved in more challenging activities.

The needs to know and to understand appear in late infancy and early childhood and are expressed by children as a natural curiosity. Because the needs are innate, they do not have to be taught, but the actions of parents and teachers can serve to inhibit a child's spontaneous curiosity. Failure to satisfy the cognitive needs is harmful and hampers the full development and functioning of the personality.

The hierarchy of these two needs overlaps the original five-need hierarchy. Knowing and understanding—essentially, finding meaning in our environment—are basic to interacting with that environment in an emotionally healthy, mature way to satisfy physiological, safety, love, esteem, and self-actualization needs. It is impossible to become self-actualizing if we fail to meet the needs to know and to understand.

Aesthetic Needs

aesthetic needs The needs for aesthetically pleasing experiences and beautiful surroundings.

Maslow suggested that some people need aesthetically pleasing experiences. When the **aesthetic needs** are not satisfied, the full development of the personality is hampered. People who have such highly developed aesthetic needs may become physically ill when confronted with ugliness.

Situational Variables

The needs Maslow proposed are innate, personal variables. Situational variables also play a role in Maslow's theory of personality development. We express our needs in our actions and behaviors as we relate to other people and to the various situations and events in our environment. In addition, we are responsible for creating much of the social and physical environment in which we function. The personal impact of these situations depends largely on how we perceive them. However, our perceptions may not accurately reflect a given situation. Thus, our response is a function of what we perceive the situation to be.

In sum, our behavior is determined by personal variables (the innate motivating needs), and by situational variables (the features of our world as we perceive them). Maslow proposed this interactionist viewpoint a decade before the eruption of the classic person-situation debate (see Chapter 1).

The Study of Self-Actualizers

self-actualization (psychology)

metamotivation The motivation of self-actualizers, which involves maximizing personal potential rather than striving for a particular goal object.

According to Maslow's theory, self-actualizing persons differ from others in terms of their basic motivation. Maslow proposed a distinct type of motivation for self-actualizers called **metamotivation** (sometimes called B-motivation or Being). The prefix *meta-* means after or beyond. Metamotivation, then, indicates that it goes beyond psychology's traditional idea of motivation.

Metamotivation

Metamotivation implies a condition in which motivation as we know it plays no role. Self-actualizing persons are not motivated to strive for a particular goal. Instead, they are said to be developing from within. Maslow described the motivation of people who are not self-actualizers as a condition of D-motivation or Deficiency. D-motivation involves striving for something specific to make up for something that is lacking within us. For example, failure to eat produces a deficiency in the body that we feel as discomfort. This feeling motivates us to take some action to reduce the resulting tension. Thus, a specific physiological need (hunger) that requires a specific goal object (food) produces a motivation to act to attain something we lack (we search for food). Maslow's writings about the development of B-motivation and D-motivation are incomplete, but apparently D-motivation applies not only to physiological needs, as in the example above, but also to the needs for safety, belongingness and love, and esteem (Maslow, 1971).

In contrast, self-actualizing persons are concerned with fulfilling their potential and with knowing and understanding their environment. In their state of metamotivation, they are not seeking to reduce tension, satisfy a deficiency, or strive for a specific object. Their goal is to enrich their lives by acting to increase tension to experience a variety of stimulating and challenging events. Because their lower-order deficiency needs have been met, self-actualizers function at a level beyond striving for specific goal object to satisfy a deficit. Thus, they are in a state of "being," spontaneously, naturally, and joyfully expressing their full humanity.

metaneeds States of growth or being toward which self-actualizers evolve.

Having explained that self-actualizers are thus, in a sense, unmotivated, Maslow proposed a list of **metaneeds** toward which self-actualizers evolve (see Table 11.1). Metaneeds are states of being—such as goodness, uniqueness, and

T A B L E 11.1   *Maslow's metaneeds and metapathologies*

Metaneeds	Metapathologies
Truth	Mistrust, cynicism, skepticism
Goodness	Hatred, repulsion, disgust, reliance only upon self and for self
Beauty	Vulgarity, restlessness, loss of taste, bleakness
Unity, wholeness	Disintegration
Dichotomy-transcendence	Black/white thinking, either/or thinking, simplistic view of life
Aliveness, process	Deadness, robotizing, feeling oneself to be totally determined, loss of emotion and zest in life, experiential emptiness
Uniqueness	Loss of feeling of self and individuality, feeling oneself to be interchangeable or anonymous
Perfection	Hopelessness, nothing to work for
Necessity	Chaos, unpredictability
Completion, finality	Incompleteness, hopelessness, cessation of striving and coping
Justice	Anger, cynicism, mistrust, lawlessness, total selfishness
Order	Insecurity, wariness, loss of safety and predictability, necessity for being on guard
Simplicity	Overcomplexity, confusion, bewilderment, loss of orientation
Richness, totality, comprehensiveness	Depression, uneasiness, loss of interest in the world
Effortlessness	Fatigue, strain, clumsiness, awkwardness, stiffness
Playfulness	Grimness, depression, paranoid humorlessness, loss of zest in life, cheerlessness
Self-sufficiency	Responsibility given to others
Meaningfulness	Meaninglessness, despair, senselessness of life

SOURCE: Adapted from *The Farther Reaches of Human Nature,* by A. H. Maslow. Copyright © 1971 by Bertha G. Maslow.

TABLE 11.2   *Characteristics of self-actualizing people*

Clear perception of reality
Acceptance of self, others, and nature
Spontaneity, simplicity, and naturalness
Dedication to a cause
Independence and need for privacy
Freshness of appreciation
Peak experiences
Social interest
Deep interpersonal relationships
Tolerance and acceptance of others
Creativeness and originality
Resistance to social pressures

metapathology A
thwarting of self-
development related to
failure to satisfy the
metaneeds.

perfection—rather than specific goal objects. Failure to satisfy metaneeds is harmful and produces a kind of **metapathology**, which thwarts the full development of the personality. Metapathology prevents self-actualizers from expressing, using, and fulfilling their potential. They may come to feel helpless and depressed, unable to pinpoint a source for these feelings or identify a goal that might alleviate the distress.

Characteristics of Self-Actualizers

Maslow's research on emotionally healthy people formed the basis of his personality theory (Maslow, 1970b, 1971). He did not find many examples of self-actualizers; he estimated that they constitute one percent or less of the population. However, he concluded that they share certain characteristics (see Table 11.2).

An efficient perception of reality.   Self-actualizers perceive their world, including other people, clearly and objectively, unbiased by prejudgments or preconceptions.

An acceptance of themselves, others, and nature.   Self-actualizers accept their strengths and weaknesses. They do not try to distort or falsify their self-image and they do not feel guilty about their failings. They also accept the weaknesses of other people and of society in general.

A spontaneity, simplicity, and naturalness.   The behavior of self-actualizers is open, direct, and natural. They rarely hide their feelings or emotions or play a role to satisfy society, although they may do so to avoid hurting other people. Self-actualizers are individualistic in their ideas and ideals but not necessarily unconventional in their behavior. They feel secure enough to be themselves without being overly assertive.

A focus on problems outside themselves.   Self-actualizers have a sense of mission, a commitment, to which they devote their energy. This dedication to a cause or vocation is a requirement for self-actualization. Self-actualizers find pleasure and ex-

Among the self-actualizers Maslow studied by analyzing biographies and other written records were the noted physicist Albert Einstein, and Harriet Tubman, a leader of the antislavery movement at the time of the American Civil War.

citement in their hard work. Through their intense dedication, self-actualizers are able to satisfy the metaneeds. A writer or scientist may search for truth, an artist for beauty, an attorney for justice. Self-actualizers do not undertake their tasks for money, fame, or power but rather to satisfy the metaneeds. Their commitment challenges and develops their abilities and helps define their sense of self.

A sense of detachment and the need for privacy.   Self-actualizers can experience isolation without harmful effects and seem to need solitude more than persons who are not self-actualizing. Self-actualizers depend on themselves, not on others, for their satisfactions. This independence may make them seem aloof or unfriendly, but that is not their intent. They are simply more autonomous than most people and do not crave social support.

A freshness of appreciation.   Self-actualizers have the ability to perceive and experience their environment with freshness, wonder, and awe. An experience may grow stale for someone who is not self-actualizing, but self-actualizers will enjoy each recurrence as though it was the first. Whether a sunset, a painting, or a symphony, a baseball game or a birthday gift—all can be seen with delight. Self-actualizers appreciate what they have and take little for granted.

Mystical or peak experiences. Self-actualizers know moments of intense ecstasy, not unlike deep religious experiences, that can occur with virtually any activity. Maslow called these events **peak experiences**, during which the self is transcended and the person feels supremely powerful, confident, and decisive. Maslow wrote that a peak experience involves

peak experience A moment of intense ecstasy, similar to a religious or mystical experience, during which the self is transcended.

> a feeling of great ecstasy and wonder and awe, the loss of placing in time and space with, finally, the conviction that something extremely important and valuable had happened, so that the subject is . . . transformed and strengthened. (Maslow, 1970b, p. 164)

Maslow noted differences among self-actualizers in the quantity and quality of their peak experiences. So-called *peakers* have more peak experiences than *nonpeakers* and the experiences of peakers tend to be more mystical and religious. Indeed, peakers may be described as more saintly and poetical than nonpeakers. Nonpeakers are more practical and more concerned with worldly affairs. Peakers have been identified among diverse occupational groups including artists, writers, scientists, business leaders, educators, and politicians. Maslow noted that it was possible for a person who is not self-actualizing occasionally to have a peak experience.

Social interest. Maslow adopted Alfred Adler's concept of social interest to indicate the sympathy and empathy self-actualizing persons have for all humanity. Although often irritated by the behavior of other people, self-actualizers feel a kinship with and an understanding of others as well as a desire to help them.

Profound interpersonal relations. Although their circle of friends is not large, self-actualizers have deep, lasting friendships. They tend to select as friends those with personal qualities similar to their own, just as we all choose as friends the people we find compatible. Self-actualizers often attract admirers or disciples. These relationships are usually one-sided; the admirer asks more of the self-actualizer than the self-actualizer is able or willing to give.

A democratic character structure. Self-actualizers are tolerant and accepting of the personality and behavior of others. They display no racial, religious, or social prejudice. They are willing to listen to and learn from anyone capable of teaching them and are rarely condescending.

Creativeness. Self-actualizing people are highly creative and exhibit inventiveness and originality in their work and other facets of life. They are flexible, spontaneous, and willing to make mistakes and learn from them. They are open and humble, in the way children are before society teaches them to be embarrassed or shy about possibly doing something foolish.

Resistance to enculturation. Self-actualizers are autonomous, independent, and self-sufficient. They feel free to resist social and cultural pressures to think or behave in a certain way. They do not openly rebel against cultural norms or social codes, but they are governed by their own nature rather than the strictures of society.

This is quite an amazing set of attributes. According to Maslow's research, self-actualizers seem almost perfect. But they do have human flaws and imperfections. On occasion they can be rude, even ruthless, and they experience doubts, conflicts, and tension. Nevertheless, such incidents are rare and less intense than for the person who is not self-actualizing.

Failure to Become Self-Actualizing

If the need for self-actualization is innate and therefore does not have to be taught and learned, then why isn't everyone self-actualizing? Why has less than one percent of the population reached this state of being? One reason is that the higher the need in Maslow's proposed hierarchy, the weaker it is. As the highest need, self-actualization is the least potent. Thus, it can easily be inhibited. For example, hostile or rejecting parents make it difficult for a person to satisfy love and esteem needs. In this case, the self-actualization need may not emerge. At a lower level, poor economic conditions can make it difficult to satisfy physiological and safety needs, so self-actualization assumes less importance.

Inadequate education and improper child-rearing practices can thwart the drive for self-actualization in adulthood. Maslow cited the typical sex-role training for boys, who are taught to inhibit such qualities as tenderness and sentimentality. Thus, this aspect of their nature is not encouraged to fully develop.

If children are overprotected and not permitted to try new behaviors, explore new ideas, or practice new skills, then they are likely to be inhibited as adults, unable to express themselves fully in activities vital to self-actualization. The opposite behavior—excessive parental permissiveness—can also be harmful. Too much freedom in childhood can lead to anxiety and insecurity, thus undermining the safety needs. To Maslow, the ideal situation in childhood is a balance of permissiveness and regulation.

Sufficient love in childhood is a prerequisite for self-actualization, as well as satisfaction of physiological and safety needs within the first two years of life. If children feel secure and confident in the early years, they will remain so as adults. This position is similar to Erik Erikson's emphasis on the development of trust in early childhood and to Karen Horney's ideas on the childhood need for security. Without adequate parental love, security, and esteem in childhood, it is difficult to strive for self-actualization in adulthood.

Jonah complex The fear that maximizing our potential will lead to a situation with which we will be unable to cope.

Another reason for the failure to self-actualize is what Maslow called the **Jonah complex**. This idea is based on the biblical tale of Jonah, described by Maslow as

> called by God to prophesy, but [Jonah] was afraid of the task. He tried to run away from it. But no matter where Jonah ran, he could find no hiding place. Finally, he understood that he had to accept his fate. (quoted in Hoffman, 1996, p. 50)

Thus, the Jonah complex refers to our doubts about our own abilities. We may fear that taking action to maximize our potential will lead to new situations with which we may be unable to cope. Simultaneously we are afraid of and thrilled by the possibilities but too often the fear takes precedence.

Self-actualization requires courage. Even when the lower needs have been satisfied, we cannot sit back and wait to be swept along some flower-strewn path to

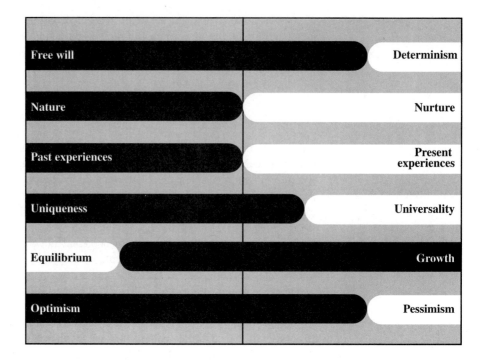

F I G U R E   1 1 . 2   *Maslow's image of human nature*

ecstasy and fulfillment. The self-actualizing process takes effort, discipline, and self-control. Thus, for many people, it may seem easier and safer to accept life as it is rather than seek new challenges. Self-actualizers will constantly test themselves by abandoning secure routines and familiar behaviors and attitudes.

Questions About Human Nature

Maslow's view of personality is humanistic and optimistic. He focused on psychological health rather than illness, growth rather than stagnation, virtues and potentials rather than weaknesses and limitations. He had a strong sense of confidence in our ability to shape our lives and our society (see Figure 11.2).

Maslow believed that we are capable of shaping our free will even in the face of negative biological and constitutional factors. He wrote,

> the reality of biological injustice and unfairness: that some babies are born healthy and others unhealthy, some smart and others stupid, and some beautiful and others ugly. . . . It is not something we can do anything about. It is determined. It is a limitation on free will. [Yet, everyone has] a great deal of leeway for free will, responsibility, and becoming an active agent rather than a pawn in life. There is a lot of leeway for helping myself rather than giving up and sinking, for doing the best that I can rather than whining. . . . What I *do* with my genetic endowment and my body is definitely more important than merely the given of my biological inheritance. (quoted in Hoffman, 1996, pp. 64–65)

We have the free will to choose how best to satisfy our needs and actualize our potential. We can either create an actualizing self or refrain from pursuing that supreme state of achievement. Thus, we are responsible for the level of personality development we reach.

Although the needs in Maslow's hierarchies are innate, the behaviors by which we satisfy them are learned. Therefore, personality is determined by the interaction of heredity and environment, of personal and situational variables. Although not explicit in his writings, Maslow seemed to favor the uniqueness of personality. Our motivations and needs are universal, but the ways in which the needs are satisfied will vary from person to person because these ways of behaving are learned. Even among self-actualizers, although they share certain qualities, their behaviors are not identical.

Maslow recognized the importance of early childhood experiences in fostering or inhibiting adult development, but he did not believe that we are victims of these experiences. We have more potential than we may realize to manage our life and our society and would be happier and more productive if we would learn to do so. Self-actualization as the ultimate and necessary goal reflects Maslow's belief that, given the proper conditions, we are capable of reaching the highest level of human functioning.

He argued that human nature is basically good, decent, and kind, but he did not deny the existence of evil. He believed some people were evil beyond reclamation and wrote in his journal that "nothing will work ultimately [with them] but shooting" (Maslow, 1979, p. 631). He suggested that wickedness was not an inherited trait but rather the result of an inappropriate environment. Maslow's compassion for humanity is clear in his writings, and his optimism is expressed in the belief that each of us is capable of fulfilling our vast human potential.

Assessment in Maslow's Theory

Maslow's work on self-actualization did not begin as a formal program of personality assessment and research. He started his investigation out of curiosity about two people who impressed him, the anthropologist Ruth Benedict and the Gestalt psychologist Max Wertheimer. Maslow admired them greatly and wanted to understand what made them so different from the other people he knew. After observing them carefully he concluded that they shared certain qualities that set them apart from the average individual.

Maslow then attempted to assess these characteristics in other people. His first subjects were college students, but he found only 1 out of 3,000 he could describe as self-actualizing. He decided that the characteristics for the self-actualizing personality, those qualities he had identified in Benedict and Wertheimer, were not developed in young people. His next step was to study middle-aged and older subjects. However, even among this group Maslow found less than one percent of the population capable of meeting his criteria for self-actualization.

The self-actualizers he finally identified included several dozen persons he designated as sure or probable cases, partial cases, or potential cases. Some were

TABLE 11.3   *Sample items from the Personal Orientation Inventory. Respondents select the item in each pair that is more descriptive of them.*

I do what others expect of me.
I feel free to not do what others expect of me.

I must justify my actions in the pursuit of my own interests.
I need not justify my actions in the pursuit of my own interests.

I live by the rules and standards of society.
I do not always need to live by the rules and standards of society.

Reasons are needed to justify my feelings.
Reasons are not needed to justify my feelings.

I only feel free to express warm feelings to my friends.
I feel free to express both warm and hostile feelings to my friends.

I will continue to grow only by setting my sights on a high-level, socially approved goal.
I will continue to grow best by being myself.

People should always control their anger.
People should express honestly felt anger.

SOURCE: From "An Inventory for the Measurement of Self-Actualization" by E. L. Shostrom, 1964, *Educational and Psychological Measurement, 24,* pp. 207–218.

Maslow's contemporaries. Others were historical figures such as Thomas Jefferson, Albert Einstein, George Washington Carver, Harriet Tubman, and Eleanor Roosevelt. Maslow used a variety of techniques to assess their personalities. For historical figures he worked with biographical material, analyzing written records for similarities in personal characteristics. For the living subjects he relied on interviews, free association, and projective tests. He found that many of these subjects were self-conscious when questioned, so often he was forced to study them indirectly, although he did not explain precisely how this was done.

The Personal Orientation Inventory

The Personal Orientation Inventory (POI), a self-report questionnaire, was developed by psychologist Everett Shostrom to measure self-actualization (Shostrom, 1964, 1974). The test consists of 150 pairs of statements. Subjects indicate which of each pair is more applicable to them (see Table 11.3).

The POI is scored for two major scales and ten subscales. The major scales are *time competence*, which measures the degree to which a person lives in the present, and *inner directedness*, which assesses how much a person depends on himself or herself rather than on others for judgments and values.

Research in Maslow's Theory

Maslow did not use case studies or the experimental or correlational methods in his research. Critics have charged that Maslow's methods for studying his self-actualizing subjects could not be described as rigorous or controlled. Maslow agreed; he knew his investigations failed to adhere to the requirements of scientific research. He wrote, "By ordinary standards of laboratory research, this simply was not research at all" (1971, p. 42). But he believed that because self-actualization could not be studied by accepted scientific procedures, the alternative was to wait until appropriate techniques were developed or not to study the issue at all.

Maslow was too impatient to postpone his research, too committed to the conviction that he could help humanity. He wrote that he did not have enough time to perform careful experiments. "They take too long in view of the years I have left and the extent of what I want to do" (1979, p. 694). He referred to his program as consisting of pilot studies only. Convinced that the results were valid, he expected other researchers to eventually confirm his theory. Maslow also suggested that to support and justify his conclusions, which he knew were correct, he somehow needed to collect less data than did other theorists.

Correlational Studies with the POI

The POI has been widely used for correlational research in which POI scores are correlated with other measures of behavior and personality. Scores indicating higher self-actualization have been positively related to several factors: emotional health, creativity, well being following therapy, academic achievement, autonomy, and racial tolerance. Other studies report negative correlations between high self-actualization scores and alcoholism, institutionalization for mental disturbances, neuroticism, depression, and hypochondriasis. These results are in the expected directions based on Maslow's description of self-actualizers. POI research on women, ages 19 to 55, confirmed Maslow's view that self-actualization occurs gradually over the life span.

It is important to remember that this research involves correlational studies and that there is no valid independent measure of self-actualization with which to correlate the POI scores. It does not necessarily follow that the POI is actually measuring self-actualization, even though it correlates well with variables believed to be associated with self-actualization.

The Hierarchy of Needs

In support of Maslow's theory, a study of men and women college students found that satisfaction of the needs for safety, belongingness, and esteem was negatively related to neuroticism and depression (Williams & Page, 1989). This research, using a test designed to measure the three needs, also showed that esteem needs were stronger than belongingness needs. The subjects exhibited less concern with safety needs, as expected among people of college age.

A study using the Need Satisfaction Inventory, a self-report questionnaire designed to measure how well a person satisfies Maslow's needs, correlated test scores of college students with their scores on the Eysenck Personality Inventory. Again, the results showed that subjects higher in need satisfaction were lower in neuroticism (Lester, 1990).

An elaborate test of the hierarchy using a sample representative of the general population supported the order of the five needs (Graham & Balloun, 1973). The study also demonstrated that the amount of concern people expressed about each need increased from the lowest to the highest need. Physiological needs, presumably well satisfied in these subjects, were of little concern to them. The self-actualization need was of the greatest interest, presumably because it was not so well satisfied.

Self-Esteem

self-esteem

Research supports Maslow's position that people high in self-esteem have greater self-worth and self-confidence. They also feel more competent and productive than do people low in self-esteem. People high in self-esteem function better in many situations. In a study of college students seeking jobs, those with high self-esteem received more job offers and were rated more favorably by recruiters than were students with low self-esteem (Ellis & Taylor, 1983). Another study found that people with high self-esteem coped more effectively with the difficulties of job loss than did those with low self-esteem (Shamir, 1986).

Research has also shown that people who measured low in self-esteem and who had been led to believe they had been deliberately excluded from a laboratory group by the other members, reported a significantly greater feeling of rejection than did people high in self-esteem (Nezlek, Kowalski, Leary, Blevins, & Holgate, 1997).

Even the accuracy of memory can be affected by self-esteem. In a study using college students, the subjects were given feedback about their personality, some of which was favorable and flattering, and some of which was unfavorable and unflattering. Those with high self-esteem recalled the favorable feedback far more accurately than did those with low self-esteem. Conversely, subjects low in self-esteem recalled the unfavorable feedback better than did those with high self-esteem (Story, 1998).

Research has suggested two dimensions or components of self-esteem: self-competence and self-liking. Self-competence refers to a person's sense of power, efficacy, or ability to perform a task well. Self-liking refers to one's sense of personal worth. When college student subjects were given feedback indicating that they were failing in a laboratory task, those low in self-liking were significantly less apt to persist at the task than those high in self-liking. There was no difference in persistence following failure feedback between those high in self-competence and those low in self-competence. Thus, the researchers concluded that people with a low sense of self-worth are less likely to persist at a task, such as school or learning a skill, if their initial attempt meets with failure (Tafarodi & Vu, 1997).

Finally, an analysis of 10 years of research studies on gender and self-esteem found that on average men possess greater self-esteem than women do. However, this difference varies with age and ethnicity. In the years prior to adolescence, no significant gender differences were found in self-esteem. Gender differences appear in early adolescence between ages 11 and 13, when boys exhibit higher self-esteem than do girls. These gender and age variables in self-esteem were shown to apply for White subjects but not for Black subjects (Major, Barr, Zubek, & Babey, 1999).

Self-Actualization and Peak Experiences

Industrial/organizational psychologists have conducted considerable research on self-actualization. Some of this work supported Maslow's view, prompting him to conclude that the application and testing of his ideas required a real-life setting, such as employees on the job, rather than the psychology laboratory. Some research showed that high-level business executives were more concerned with esteem and self-actualization needs than were low-level executives; presumably, the executives had satisfied their lower needs, allowing for the emergence of the higher needs. Longitudinal research failed to verify this conclusion. Other studies showed that higher needs did not emerge once lower needs were satisfied. However, the concept of self-actualization as a motivating force remains popular in the business community despite the lack of evidence to support it.

Research on peak experiences used a self-report test called the Peak Scale, which was developed to assess the tendency to have peak experiences, a characteristic of self-actualizers (Mathes, Zevon, Roter, & Joerger, 1982). Subjects who scored high on the Peak Scale also demonstrated on other measures having transcendental or mystical experiences and periods of intense happiness. High scorers reported guiding their lives by Maslow's Being values and ideas of beauty, truth, and justice. In other studies, people who reported peak experiences tended to show more self-awareness, greater tolerance for ambiguity, and greater social consciousness than those who did not have peak experiences (Thomas & Cooper, 1980; Wuthnow, 1978).

A study of college students found that 79 percent believed they had had peak experiences but only 20 percent had ever told anyone about them (Davis, Lockwood, & Wright, 1991). The most common reasons for not revealing the peak experiences were the following.

- subjects thought peak experiences were too personal to share
- subjects thought other people would make fun of them and fail to appreciate the value of the experiences
- subjects were unable to describe the experiences adequately

Another study compared the reported peak experiences of 123 college students with those of 29 artists who were older and had received more years of formal education. Although the groups differed on the kinds of events that triggered the peak experiences, the experiences themselves were remarkably alike and similar to those reported by Maslow's self-actualizing subjects (Yeagle, Privette, & Dunham, 1989). The results suggest that peak experiences may be independent of personal background variables.

A Final Commentary

Criticisms of Maslow's theory center on his research methods and lack of experimentally generated supporting data. The sample from which the data were derived, fewer than half of whom were interviewed, is too small for generalization to the population at large. The ways Maslow amassed information about his self-actualizing subjects are inconsistent and vague. He did not describe how he interpreted test results or analyzed biographical materials, nor did he indicate how free associations and interview responses led him to identify those particular subjects as self-actualizing. However, as we noted with other theorists, weakness in scientific methodology is not unique.

For his subjects Maslow selected people he admired, according to his criteria for self-actualization. These criteria were not specified at the time, and he later admitted that self-actualization was difficult to describe accurately. His list of characteristics of self-actualizers derives solely from his clinical interpretations of the data and may easily have been influenced by his personal philosophy and moral values. Thus, the descriptions may actually reflect Maslow's own ideal of the worthy and emotionally healthy individual.

Other criticisms have been directed at Maslow's definitions of various concepts such as metaneeds, metapathology, peak experiences, and self-actualization. His use of these terms could be inconsistent and ambiguous. Critics also have asked on what basis self-actualization is presumed to be innate. Why could it not be learned behavior, the result of some unique combination of childhood experiences? Maslow's defense was that although his theory was not widely supported by laboratory research, it was successful in social, clinical, and personal terms. He wrote, "It has fitted very well with the personal experience of most people, and has often given them a structured theory that has helped them to make better sense of their inner lives" (Maslow, 1970b, p. xii).

Partly because of Maslow's optimism and compassion, his theory, and the humanistic approach to psychology in general, became popular in the 1960s and 1970s. The trappings of a formal school of thought were then set in place. Journals and organizations relating to humanistic psychology were founded, and a division of humanistic psychology was created within the American Psychological Association. With the new millennium, the concerns of humanistic psychologists are experiencing a rebirth in the so-called "happy" personality (see Chapter 18).

As a pioneer of humanistic psychology, Maslow attracted admirers and disciples among students and professionals who had become disenchanted with behavioristic and psychoanalytic approaches to personality and to psychology. Few theories have had such a broad impact beyond the discipline. Teachers and counselors, business and government leaders, health care professionals, and many people trying to cope with everyday hassles have found Maslow's views compatible with their needs and useful in solving problems. Maslow issued a call to make psychology responsive to the problems of modern society. He argued forcefully that the survival of civilization depends on our ability to develop our full potential and to become self-actualizing.

Chapter Summary

Maslow argued that each person is born with instinctoid needs that lead to growth, development, and actualization. The hierarchy of needs includes physiological needs (for food, water, air, sleep, and sex) and the needs for safety, belongingness and love, esteem, and self-actualization. The lower needs must be satisfied before the higher needs emerge. The lower the need, the greater its strength. Lower needs are called deficit needs because failure to satisfy them produces a deficit in the body. Higher needs (growth or being needs) are less necessary for survival but enhance physical and emotional well being. Safety needs (for security, stability, order, and freedom from fear and anxiety) are most important in infants and neurotic adults. Belongingness and love needs can be satisfied through association with a group or affectionate relations with one person or with people in general. Esteem needs include self-esteem and esteem from others. Self-actualization involves the realization of one's potential and requires a realistic knowledge of one's strengths and weaknesses. The needs to know and to understand form a hierarchy of cognitive needs that emerges in late infancy and early childhood.

Motivation in self-actualizers (metamotivation) serves not to make up for deficits or reduce tension but to enrich life and increase tension. Metaneeds are states of growth toward which self-actualizers move. Frustration of metaneeds produces metapathology, a formless illness for which no specific cause can be identified. Self-actualizers constitute less than one percent of the population. They share the following characteristics: efficient perception of reality; acceptance of themselves and others; spontaneity and simplicity; focus on problems rather than self in which metaneeds are satisfied through commitment to work; privacy and independence; freshness of appreciation; peak experiences; social interest; intense interpersonal relationships; creativeness; democratic character structure; and resistance to enculturation. Not everyone becomes self-actualizing because self-actualization is the weakest need in the hierarchy and easily interfered with. Too much freedom or lack of security in childhood inhibits self-actualization. Also, some people fear realizing their highest potential, what Maslow termed the Jonah complex.

Maslow's image of human nature is optimistic, emphasizing free will, conscious choice, uniqueness, the ability to overcome childhood experiences, and innate goodness. Personality is influenced both by heredity and by environment. Our ultimate goal is self-actualization.

Maslow used interviews, free association, projective techniques, and biographical material to assess personality. The Personal Orientation Inventory is a self-report test to measure self-actualization. Some research supports the characteristics of self-actualizers, the relationship between self-esteem and self-competence and self-liking, the order of the needs in the hierarchy, and the greater concern with higher than lower needs. Maslow has been criticized for using too small a sample as the basis for his theory and for not making explicit his criteria for selecting self-actualizing subjects.

Review Questions

1. What criticisms did the humanistic psychologists make of behaviorism and psychoanalysis?

2. In what way can Maslow's childhood be considered an example of Adler's theory of personality?

3. Describe the hierarchy of needs Maslow proposed. How can each need be satisfied?

4. What are the differences between the higher needs and the lower needs?

5. At what age do we develop the needs to know and to understand? Which of these needs is the stronger?

6. What is the role of situational variables in determining the needs in the hierarchy?

7. Define metaneeds and metapathology.

8. Discuss the motivation and the characteristics of self-actualizing people.

9. What are peak experiences? Are they necessary for self-actualization?

10. List four factors that may explain why so few people satisfy the need for self-actualization.

11. How does Maslow's image of human nature differ from Freud's?

12. What does correlational research reveal about the relationship between self-actualization and certain personality characteristics?

13. How does self-esteem affect memory? How does it affect feelings of rejection? Describe gender and ethnic differences in self-esteem.

Suggested Readings

Hall, M. H. (1968, July). A conversation with Abraham H. Maslow. *Psychology Today,* pp. 35–37, 54–57. An interview with Maslow about the scope of his work.

Hoffman, E. (1988). *The right to be human: A biography of Abraham Maslow.* Los Angeles: Jeremy Tarcher. A biography based on published and unpublished material describing Maslow's difficult childhood and tracing his career from his early work with primates to his involvement with the human potential movement.

Maslow, A. H. (1968). *Toward a psychology of being (2nd ed.).* New York: Van Nostrand Reinhold. States Maslow's view that humans can be loving, noble, and creative and are capable of pursuing the highest values and aspirations. Also acknowledges the importance of Freud's concept of the unconscious.

Maslow, A. H. (1970). *Motivation and personality (2nd ed.).* New York: Harper & Row. Presents Maslow's theory of motivation and personality, emphasizing psychological health and self-actualization. A third edition (Harper & Row, 1987), revised and edited by Robert Frager and James Fadiman, includes material on Maslow's life, the historical significance of his work, and applications of self-actualization to management, medicine, and education.

Maslow, A. H. (1996). *The unpublished papers of Abraham Maslow.* Edited by E. Hoffman. Thousand Oaks, CA: Sage. Includes previously unpublished essays, articles, and papers with annotations and a biographical sketch written by the author of the Maslow biography cited above.

Mittelman, W. (1991). Maslow's study of self-actualization: A reinterpretation. *Journal of Humanistic Psychology, 31*(1), 114–135. Suggests that Maslow's self-actualizing subjects were distinguished not by some ability to actualize human potential but by their degree of openness. Defines openness as being highly receptive and responsive to information from one's self and from the environment, and not repressing or ignoring difficulties and problems.

Taylor, E. (1999). An intellectual renaissance of humanistic psychology? *Journal of Humanistic Psychology, 39*(2), 7–25. Reviews the historical background of humanistic psychology and its influence in the 1940s to 1960s. Reevaluates its status at the turn of the new century and recommends a more solid scientific basis for its premises.

Wertz, F. (Ed.). (1994). *The humanistic movement: Recovering the person in psychology.* Lake Worth, FL: Gardner Press. Describes the foundations and applied areas of humanistic psychology, including the contributions of Maslow, Rogers, and others.

The organism has one basic tendency and striving—to actualize, maintain, and enhance the experiencing organism.

—Carl Rogers

T W E L V E

Carl Rogers

Carl Rogers originated a popular approach to psychotherapy known initially as nondirective or client-centered therapy and later as person-centered therapy. This form of psychotherapy has generated an enormous amount of research and is widely applied in the treatment of emotional disturbances. Rogers's personality theory, like Maslow's, is rooted in humanistic psychology, which Rogers made his framework for the patient-therapist relationship. Rogers developed his theory not from experimental laboratory research but from his experiences working with clients. Thus, his formulations on the structure and dynamics of personality derive from his therapeutic approach.

Rogers's view of the therapeutic situation tells much about his view of human nature. Consider the phrase *person-centered therapy*. It suggests that the ability to change and improve personality is centered within the person. In other words, it is the person and not the therapist who directs such change. The therapist's role is to assist or facilitate the change.

Rogers believed that we are rational beings ruled by a conscious perception of our selves and our experiential world. Rogers did not ascribe much importance to unconscious forces or other Freudian explanations. He also rejected the notion that past events exert a controlling influence on present behavior. Although he recognized that childhood experiences affect the way we perceive our environment, and ourselves, Rogers insisted that current feelings and emotions have a greater impact on personality. Because of this emphasis on the conscious and the present, Rogers suggested that personality could only be understood from our own viewpoint, that is, based on our subjective experiences. Rogers dealt with reality as consciously perceived by each of us, and he noted that this perception did not always coincide with objective reality.

Rogers proposed a single, innate, overriding motivation: the inborn tendency to actualize, to develop our abilities and potentials, from the strictly biological to the most sophisticated psychological aspects of our being. This ultimate goal is to actualize the self, to become what Rogers called a *fully functioning person*. His approach to therapy and theory, and the optimistic and humanistic picture he painted, received enthusiastic acceptance in psychology, education, and family-life research.

The Life of Rogers (1902–1987)

A Reliance on His Own Experience

The fourth child in a family of six, Carl Rogers was born in 1902 in Oak Park, Illinois, a suburb of Chicago. His parents held strict religious views and emphasized moral behavior, the suppression of displays of emotion, and the virtue of hard work. Their fundamentalist teachings gripped Rogers like a vise, as he described it, throughout his childhood and adolescence. These beliefs forced him to live by someone else's view of the world rather than his own. He soon made them a target for revolt.

His parents promoted their influence in subtle and loving ways, as Rogers later did in his nondirective approach to counseling. It was understood by all the children that they did not "dance, play cards, attend movies, smoke, drink, or show any sexual interest" (Rogers, 1967, p. 344). Rogers had little social life outside his family.

Because he came to believe that his parents showed favoritism toward an older brother, there was considerable competitiveness between them. Rogers described himself as shy, solitary, dreamy, and often lost in fantasy. He read incessantly, any book he could find, even the dictionary and encyclopedia. His solitude led him to depend on his own resources and experiences, his personal view of the world. This characteristic remained with him throughout his life and became the foundation of his personality theory. In later years, he realized how strongly his loneliness had influenced his theory as well as his own personality.

> As I look back, I realize that my interest in interviewing and in therapy certainly grew out of my early loneliness. Here was a socially approved way of getting really close to individuals and thus filling some of the hunger I had undoubtedly felt. (Rogers, 1980, p. 34)

When Rogers was 12, the family moved to a farm 30 miles from Chicago. Rural life awakened his interest in science. First, he became fascinated by a species of moth he discovered in the woods. He observed, captured, and bred them over many months. Second, he became interested in farming, which his father pursued with modern, scientific methods. Rogers read about farming and agricultural experiments and came to appreciate the value of the scientific approach with its use of control groups, isolation of a variable for study, and the statistical analysis of data. It was an unusual undertaking for an adolescent. At the same time, his emotional life was in turmoil, the nature of which he never fully explained. He wrote, "My fantasies during this period were definitely bizarre, and probably would be classified as schizoid by a diagnostician, but fortunately, I never came in contact with a psychologist" (Rogers, 1980, p. 30).

He chose to study agriculture at the University of Wisconsin, the college his parents, two older brothers, and a sister had attended. But following his sophomore year, he abandoned the scientific study of agriculture to prepare for the ministry. In his junior year at Wisconsin, Rogers was selected to attend an international Christian student conference in Beijing, China. During his six months of travel he wrote to his parents that his philosophy of life was changing. His religious views had swung from fundamentalist to liberal. Freeing himself of his parents' ways grieved them, but the shift brought Rogers emotional and intellectual independence. This liberation, and the confidence and direction it gave him, reinforced Rogers's opinion that all human beings must learn to rely on their own experiences, ideas, and beliefs. But for Rogers, reaching this conclusion was a difficult process, and he paid a high emotional price. After being hospitalized for ulcers, which may have been stress induced, he remained at the family farm for a year to recuperate before returning to college.

A Unique Approach to Counseling

In 1924, Rogers graduated from the University of Wisconsin, married a childhood friend, and enrolled at Union Theological Seminary in New York. Still intending to become a clergyman, he nevertheless transferred after two years to Teachers College of Columbia University, across the street, to study clinical and educational psychology. He received his Ph.D. in 1931 and joined the staff of the Child

Study Department of the Society for the Prevention of Cruelty to Children in Rochester, New York. His job involved diagnosing and treating delinquent and underprivileged children.

In 1940 he moved from a clinical to an academic setting with an appointment as professor of psychology at Ohio State University. There, Rogers began to formulate his views on counseling for emotionally disturbed persons. He also worked to bring clinical psychology into the mainstream of contemporary psychological thought. He spent the years 1945 to 1957 at the University of Chicago, teaching and developing the Counseling Center. Once when he was unable to help a severely disturbed client, he became so upset that he fell ill himself, suffering what was then called a nervous breakdown. His self-confidence was shattered. He wrote that he felt "deeply certain of my complete inadequacy as a therapist, my worthlessness as a person, and my lack of any future in the field of psychology" (Rogers, 1967, p. 367). Rogers took three months off to undergo therapy to restore his sense of self-worth.

Rogers taught at the University of Wisconsin from 1957 to 1963. During these years he published many articles and books that brought his personality theory and person-centered therapy to a wide audience. His clinical experience while in academia was mostly with college students in the counseling centers. Thus, the kind of person he treated during that time—young, intelligent, highly verbal, and, in general, facing adjustment problems rather than severe emotional disorders—was vastly different from the kind of person treated by the Freudians or by clinical psychologists in private practice.

In 1964 Rogers became a resident fellow at the Western Behavioral Sciences Institute in California, working to apply his person-centered philosophy to international problems such as the reduction of tension between Protestants and Catholics in Northern Ireland, and Jews and Arabs in the Middle East. He served as president of the American Psychological Association in 1946 and received that organization's Distinguished Scientific Contribution Award and Distinguished Professional Contribution Award.

The Importance of the Self

During his trip to China, Rogers came to recognize the importance of an autonomous self as a factor in his own development. His early research reinforced the importance of the self in the formation of the personality. In the 1930s he developed a method for determining whether a child's behavior was healthy and constructive or unhealthy and destructive. He investigated the child's background and had the child rated on factors he believed would influence behavior. These factors included the family environment, health, intellectual development, economic circumstances, cultural influences, social interactions, and level of education. All of these factors are external, that is, part of the child's environment. Rogers also investigated a potential internal influence, the child's self-understanding or self-insight. Rogers described self-insight as an acceptance of self and reality, and a sense of responsibility for the self.

Approximately a decade later, William Kell, one of Rogers's students, adopted this evaluative approach in an attempt to predict the behavior of delinquent children.

Rogers suggested that the factors of family environment and social interactions would correlate most strongly with delinquent behavior, but he was wrong. The factor that most accurately predicted later behavior was self-insight.

Surprised to learn that family environment did not relate highly to later delinquent behavior, Rogers wrote, "I was simply not prepared to accept this finding, and the study was put on the shelf" (1987, p. 119). As we noted in Chapter 1, scientists sometimes reject data that do not agree with their views and expectations. Two years later, Helen McNeil replicated the study using a different group of subjects. She obtained similar results. One's level of self-insight was the single most important predictor of behavior.

This time, faced with an accumulation of data, Rogers accepted the findings and, on reflection, came to appreciate their significance. If one's attitude toward the self were more important in predicting behavior than the external factors widely thought to be so influential in childhood, then counselors and social workers were emphasizing the wrong things in trying to treat delinquent children and adolescents! Counselors traditionally focus on external factors such as a poor family environment and alter the circumstances by removing children from a threatening home situation and placing them in foster care. Instead, they should be trying to modify the children's self-insight. That realization was important to Rogers personally.

> This experience helped me decide to focus my career on the development of a psychotherapy that would bring about greater awareness of self-understanding, self-direction, and personal responsibility, rather than focusing on changes in the social environment. It led me to place greater emphasis on the study of the self and how it changes. (Rogers, 1987, p. 119)

Thus, the self became the core of Rogers's theory of personality, as it had become the core of his own life.

The Actualization Tendency

self-actualization (psychology)

actualization tendency
The basic human motivation to actualize, maintain, and enhance the self.

Rogers believed people are motivated by an innate tendency to actualize, maintain, and enhance the self. This drive toward self-actualization is part of a larger **actualization tendency**, which encompasses all physiological and psychological needs. By attending to basic requirements, such as the needs for food, water, and safety, the actualization tendency serves to maintain the organism, providing for sustenance and survival.

The actualization tendency begins in the womb, facilitating human growth by providing for the differentiation of the physical organs and the development of physiological functioning. It is responsible for maturation—the genetically determined development of the body's parts and processes—ranging from the growth of the fetus to the appearance of the secondary sex characteristics at puberty. These changes, programmed into our genetic makeup, are all brought to fruition by the actualization tendency.

Even though such changes are genetically determined, progress toward full human development is neither automatic nor effortless. To Rogers, the process involved struggle and pain. For example, when children take their first steps they may fall and hurt themselves. Although it would be less painful to remain in the crawling stage, most children persist. They may fall again and cry, but they persevere despite the pain because the tendency to actualize is stronger than the urge to regress simply because the growth process is difficult.

The governing process throughout the life span, as Rogers envisioned it, is the **organismic valuing process**. Through this process we evaluate all life experiences by how well they serve the actualization tendency. Experiences that we perceive as promoting actualization are evaluated as good and desirable; we assign them a positive value. Experiences perceived as hindering actualization are undesirable and thus earn a negative value. These perceptions influence behavior because we prefer to avoid undesirable experiences and repeat desirable experiences.

organismic valuing process The process by which we judge experiences in terms of their value for fostering or hindering our actualization and growth.

The Experiential World

In developing his theory Rogers weighed the impact of the experiential world, the environment or situation in which we operate daily. This provides a frame of reference or context that influences our growth. We are exposed to countless sources of stimulation, some trivial and some important, some threatening and others rewarding. He wanted to know how we perceive and react to this multifaceted world of experience.

He answered the question by saying that the reality of our environment depends on our perception of it, which may not always coincide with reality. We may react to an experience far differently from the way our best friend does. You may judge the behavior of your roommate in a dramatically different way than does someone decades older. Our perceptions change with time and circumstances. Your own opinion of acceptable collegiate behavior will be different by the time you are 70.

The notion that perception is subjective is an old one and not unique to Rogers. This idea, called *phenomenology*, argues that the only reality of which we can be sure is our own subjective world of experience, our inner perception of reality. The phenomenological approach within philosophy refers to an unbiased description of our conscious perception of the world, just as it occurs, without any attempt on our part at interpretation or analysis. In Rogers's view, the most important point about our world of experience is that it is private and thus can only be known completely to each of us.

As the actualization tendency in infancy leads us to grow and develop, our experiential world broadens. Infants are exposed to more and more sources of stimulation and respond to them as they are subjectively perceived. Our experiences become the only basis for our judgments and behaviors. Rogers wrote, "Experience is, for me, the highest authority. The touchstone of validity is my own experience" (1961, p. 23). Higher levels of development sharpen our experiential world and ultimately lead to the formation of the self.

The Development of the Self in Childhood

As infants gradually develop a more complex experiential field from widening social encounters, one part of their experience becomes differentiated from the rest.

This separate part, defined by the words *I*, *me*, and *myself*, is the self or self-concept. The formation of the self-concept involves distinguishing what is directly and immediately a part of the self from the people, objects, and events that are external to oneself. The self-concept is also our image of what we are, what we should be, and what we would like to be.

Ideally, the self is a consistent pattern, an organized whole. All aspects of the self strive for consistency. For example, people who are disturbed about having aggressive feelings and choose to deny them dare not express any obvious aggressive behaviors. To do so would mean taking responsibility for actions that are inconsistent with their self-concept, which they believe should lack aggressiveness.

Positive Regard

positive regard
Acceptance, love, and approval from others.

As the self emerges, infants develop a need for what Rogers called **positive regard**. This need is probably learned, although Rogers said the source was not important. The need for positive regard is universal and persistent. It includes acceptance, love, and approval from other people, most notably from the mother during infancy.

Infants find it satisfying to receive positive regard and frustrating not to receive it or to have it withdrawn. Because positive regard is crucial to personality development, infant behavior is guided by the amount of affection and love bestowed. If the mother does not offer positive regard, then the infant's innate tendency toward

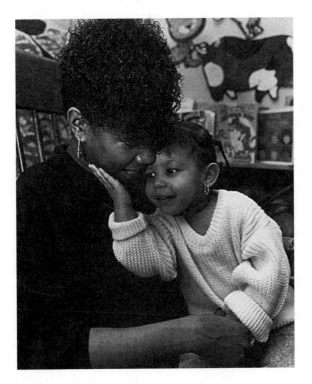

Ideally, a parent provides unconditional positive regard.

actualization and development of the self-concept will be hampered. Infants perceive parental disapproval of their behavior as disapproval of their newly developing self. If this occurs frequently, infants will cease to strive for actualization and development. Instead, they will act in ways that will bring positive regard from others, even if these actions are inconsistent with their self-concept.

Even though infants may receive sufficient acceptance, love, and approval, some specific behaviors may bring punishment. However, if positive regard for the infant persists despite the infant's undesirable behaviors, the condition is called **unconditional positive regard**. By this, Rogers meant that the mother's love for the child is granted freely and fully; it is not conditional or dependent on the child's behavior.

An important aspect of the need for positive regard is its reciprocal nature. When people perceive themselves to be satisfying someone else's need for positive regard, they in turn experience satisfaction of that need themselves. Therefore, it is rewarding to satisfy someone else's need for positive regard. Because of the importance of satisfying the need for positive regard, particularly in infancy, we become sensitive to the attitudes and behaviors of other people. By interpreting the feedback we receive from them (either approval or disapproval), we refine our self-concept. Thus, in forming the self-concept we internalize the attitudes of other people. In time, positive regard will come more from within ourselves than from other people, a condition Rogers called **positive self-regard**. Positive self-regard becomes as strong as our need for positive regard from others, and it may be satisfied in the same way. For example, children who are rewarded by their mothers with affection, approval, and love when they are happy come to generate positive self-regard whenever they behave in a happy way. Thus, in a sense, we learn to reward ourselves.

Positive self-regard, like positive regard, is reciprocal. When people receive positive regard and develop positive self-regard, in turn they may provide positive regard to others.

Conditions of Worth

Conditions of worth evolve from this developmental sequence of positive regard leading to positive self-regard. Positive self-regard is Rogers's version of the Freudian superego, and it derives from **conditional positive regard**. We noted that *unconditional* positive regard involves the parents' love and acceptance of the infant without conditions, independent of the child's behavior. *Conditional* positive regard is the opposite.

Parents may not react to everything their infant does with positive regard. Some behaviors annoy, frighten, or bore them and for those behaviors they may not provide affection or approval. Thus infants learn that parental affection has a price; it depends on behaving appropriately. They come to understand that sometimes they are prized, and sometimes they are not.

If a parent expresses annoyance every time the infant drops an object out of the crib, the child learns to disapprove of himself or herself for behaving that way. External standards of judgment become internal and personal. In a sense, then, children come to punish themselves as their parents did. Children develop self-regard only in situations that have brought parental approval, and in time the self-concept, thus

unconditional positive regard Approval granted regardless of a person's behavior. In Rogers's person-centered therapy, the therapist offers the client unconditional positive regard.

positive self-regard The condition under which we grant ourselves acceptance and approval.

conditions of worth To Rogers, a belief that we are worthy of approval only when we express desirable behaviors and attitudes and refrain from expressing those that bring disapproval from others; similar to the Freudian superego.

conditional positive regard Approval, love, or acceptance granted only when a person expresses desirable behaviors and attitudes.

formed, comes to function as a parental surrogate. These are conditions of worth. Children believe they are worthy only under certain conditions, the ones that brought parental positive regard and then personal positive self-regard. Having internalized their parents' norms and standards, they view themselves as worthy or unworthy, good or bad, according to the terms their parents defined.

Children thus learn to avoid behaviors that otherwise might be personally satisfying. Therefore they no longer function freely. Because they feel the need to evaluate their behaviors and attitudes so carefully, and refrain from taking certain actions, children are prevented from fully developing or actualizing the self. They inhibit their development by living within the confines of their conditions of worth.

Incongruence

Not only do children learn, ideally, to inhibit unacceptable behaviors, but they also may come to deny or distort unacceptable ways of perceiving their experiential world. By holding an inaccurate perception of certain experiences, they risk becoming estranged from their true self. We come to evaluate experiences, and accept or reject them, not in terms of how they contribute to the overall actualization tendency through the organismic valuing process, but in terms of whether they bring positive regard from others. This leads to **incongruence** between the self-concept and the experiential world, the environment as we perceive it.

incongruence A discrepancy between a person's self-concept and aspects of his or her experience.

Experiences that are incongruent or incompatible with our self-concept become threatening and are manifested as anxiety. For example, if our self-concept includes the belief that we love all humanity, once we meet someone toward whom we feel hatred, we are likely to develop anxiety. Hating is not congruent with our image of ourselves as loving persons. To maintain our self-concept, we must deny the hatred. We defend ourselves against the anxiety that accompanies the threat by distorting it, thus closing off a portion of our experiential field. The result is a rigidity of some of our perceptions.

Our level of psychological adjustment and emotional health is a function of the congruence or compatibility between our self-concept and our experiences. Psychologically healthy people are able to perceive themselves, other people, and events in their world much as they really are. Psychologically healthy people are open to new experiences because nothing threatens their self-concept. They have no need to deny or distort their perceptions because as children they received unconditional positive regard and did not have to internalize any conditions of worth. They feel worthy under all conditions and situations and are able to use all their experiences. They can develop and actualize all facets of the self, proceeding toward the goal of becoming a fully functioning person and leading what Rogers called "the good life."

Characteristics of Fully Functioning Persons

fully functioning person Rogers's term for self-actualization, for developing all facets of the self.

To Rogers, the fully functioning person is the desired result of psychological development and social evolution (Rogers, 1961). He described several characteristics of **fully functioning (self-actualizing) persons** (see Table 12.1).

TABLE 12.1   *Characteristics of fully functioning people*

Awareness of all experience; open to positive as well as negative feelings
Freshness of appreciation for all experiences
Trust in one's own behavior and feelings
Freedom of choice, without inhibitions
Creativity and spontaneity
Continual need to grow, to strive to maximize one's potential

Fully functioning persons exhibit an awareness of all experience.   No experience is distorted or denied; all of it filters through to the self. There is no defensiveness because there is nothing to defend against, nothing to threaten the self-concept. Fully functioning persons are open to positive feelings such as courage and tenderness, and to negative feelings such as fear and pain. They are more emotional in the sense that they accept a wider range of positive and negative emotions and feel them more intensely.

Fully functioning persons live fully and richly in each moment.   All experiences are potentially fresh and new. Experiences cannot be predicted or anticipated but are participated in fully rather than merely observed.

Fully functioning persons trust in their own organism.   By this phrase Rogers meant that fully functioning persons trust their own reactions rather than being guided by the opinions of others, by a social code, or by their intellectual judgments. Behaving in a way that feels right is a good guide to behaving in a way that is satisfying. Rogers did not suggest that fully functioning persons ignore information from their own intellect or from other people. Rather, he meant that all data are accepted as congruent with the fully functioning person's self-concept. Nothing is threatening; all information can be perceived, evaluated, and weighed accurately. Thus, the final decision about how to behave in a particular situation results from considering all experiential data. Fully functioning persons are unaware of making such considerations, however, because of the congruence between their self-concept and experience, so their decisions appear to be more intuitive and emotional than intellectual.

Fully functioning persons feel a sense of freedom to make choices without constraints or inhibitions.   This brings a sense of power because they know their future depends on their own actions and is not determined by present circumstances, past events, or other people. They do not feel compelled, either by themselves or by others, to behave in only one way.

Fully functioning persons are creative and live constructively and adaptively as environmental conditions change.   Allied with creativity is spontaneity. Fully functioning persons are flexible and seek new experiences and challenges. They do not require predictability, security, or freedom from tension.

Fully functioning persons may face difficulties.   The condition involves continually testing, growing, striving, and using all of one's potential, a way of life that

Fully functioning people feel a sense of freedom and have the ability to live richly and creatively in every moment.

brings complexity and challenge. Rogers did not describe fully functioning persons as happy, blissful, or contented, although at times they may be. More appropriately their personality may be described as enriching, exciting, and meaningful.

Rogers used the word *actualizing*, not *actualized*, to characterize the fully functioning person. The latter term implies a finished or static personality, which was not Rogers's intent. The development of the self is always in progress. Rogers wrote that being fully functioning is "a direction, not a destination" (Rogers, 1961, p. 186). If striving and growing cease, then the person loses spontaneity, flexibility, and openness. Rogers's emphasis on change and growth is neatly captured in the word *becoming* in the title of his book, *On Becoming a Person* (Rogers, 1961).

Questions About Human Nature

On the issue of free will versus determinism, Rogers's position is clear. Fully functioning persons have free choice in creating their selves. In other words, no aspect of personality is predetermined for them. On the nature-nurture issue, Rogers gave prominence to the role of the environment. Although the actualization tendency is innate, the actualizing process itself is influenced more by social than by biological forces. Childhood experiences have some impact on personality development, but experiences later in life have a greater influence. Our present feelings are more vital to our personality than the events of our childhood (see Figure 12.1).

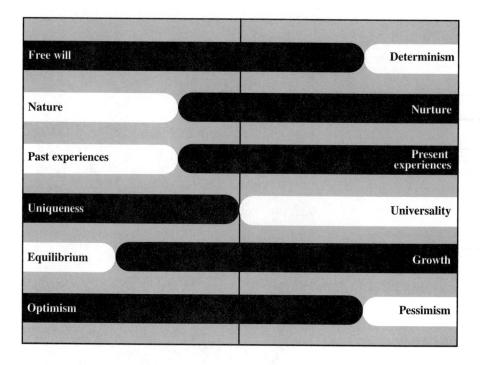

FIGURE 12.1   *Rogers's image of human nature.*

Rogers recognized a universality in personality when he noted that fully functioning persons share certain qualities. However, we may infer from his writings that there is opportunity for uniqueness in the ways these characteristics are expressed. The ultimate and necessary goal of life is to become a fully functioning person.

A personality theorist who credits people with the ability, motivation, and responsibility to understand and improve themselves obviously views people in an optimistic and positive light. Rogers believed we have a basically healthy nature and an innate tendency to grow and fulfill our potential. Rogers never lost this optimism. In an interview at the age of 85 he said, "in working with individuals and working with groups my positive view of human nature is continually reinforced" (Rogers, 1987, p. 118).

In Rogers's opinion, we are not doomed to conflict with our selves or with our society. We are not ruled by instinctive biological forces or controlled by events of the first five years of life. Our outlook is progressive rather than regressive, toward growth rather than stagnation. We experience our world openly, not defensively, and we seek challenge and stimulation instead of the security of the familiar. Emotional disturbances may occur, but these are uncommon. Through Rogers's person-centered therapy, people are able to overcome difficulties by using their inner resources, the innate drive for actualization.

I am quite aware that out of defensiveness and inner fear individuals can and do behave in ways which are incredibly cruel, horribly destructive, immature, regressive, antisocial, hurtful. Yet one of the most refreshing and invigorating parts of my experience is to work with such individuals and to discover the strongly positive directional tendencies which exist in them, as in all of us. (Rogers, 1961, p. 27)

The urge to become a fully functioning person benefits society as well. As more people in a given culture become self-actualizing, the improvement of society will naturally follow.

Assessment in Rogers's Theory

To Rogers, the only way to assess personality is in terms of the person's subjective experiences, the events in the person's life as he or she perceives them and accepts them as real. Rogers maintained that his clients had the ability to examine the roots of their problems and to redirect the personality growth that had been impeded by some incongruence between their self-concept and their experiences.

client-centered psychotherapy

person-centered therapy
Rogers's approach to therapy in which the client (not the "patient") is assumed to be responsible for changing his or her personality.

Person-Centered Therapy

In the technique of **person-centered therapy**, Rogers explored the client's feelings and attitudes toward the self and toward other people. He listened without preconceptions, trying to understand the client's experiential world. Although Rogers considered person-centered therapy the only worthwhile approach to personality assessment, he noted that it was not infallible. By focusing on subjective experiences, the therapist learns only about those events the client consciously expresses. Experiences that are not in conscious awareness remain hidden. The danger in trying to infer too much about these nonconscious experiences is that the inferences the therapist draws may represent the therapist's own projections more than the client's actual experiences. Also, what the therapist learns about a client depends on the client's ability to communicate. Because all forms of communication are imperfect, the therapist necessarily will see the client's world of experience imperfectly.

Within these limits, person-centered therapy provides a clearer view of a person's experiential world than other forms of assessment and therapy. One advantage Rogers claimed for his approach is that it does not rely on a predetermined theoretical structure (such as Freudian psychoanalysis) into which the therapist must fit the patient's problem. The only predetermined belief of the person-centered therapist is the client's inherent value and worth. Clients are accepted as they are. The therapist gives them unconditional positive regard and offers no judgments about their behavior or advice on how to behave. Everything centers on the client, including the responsibility for changing behavior and reevaluating relationships.

Rogers opposed assessment techniques such as free association, dream analysis, and case histories. He believed they made clients dependent on the therapist, who then assumed an aura of expertise and authority. These techniques removed personal responsibility from the clients by giving them the impression that the therapist knew all about them. Clients could conclude that the therapist would solve their problems and all they needed to do was sit back and follow the expert's instructions.

Encounter Groups

Rogers demonstrated that person-centered therapy could help individuals who were out of touch with their feelings and closed to life's experiences. Through the therapeutic process, people could develop or regain flexibility, spontaneity, and openness. With missionary zeal, Rogers wanted to bring this state of enhanced psychological health and functioning to greater numbers of people, so he developed a group technique in which people could learn more about themselves and how they related to, or encountered, one another. He called his approach the **encounter group** (Rogers, 1970). During the 1960s and 1970s, millions of people in the United States chose to take part in encounter-group experiences.

encounter groups A group therapy technique in which people learn about their feelings and about how they relate to (or encounter) one another.

Group size ranges from 8 to 15 people. They typically meet 20 to 60 hours over several sessions. They begin with no formal structure or agenda. The group facilitator is not a leader in the usual sense. He or she establishes an atmosphere in which group members can express themselves and focus on how others perceive them. The facilitator's job is to make it easier for members to achieve self-insight and become more fully functioning. Some people report feeling better and more aware of their true nature once they have participated in an encounter group. Rogers believed that most (though not all) participants would become more fully functioning.

Not all psychologists agree. A meta-analysis of 63 studies on encounter groups revealed that their efficacy was comparable to traditional psychotherapies (Faith, Wong, & Carpenter, 1995). The analysis also showed that larger groups that met more frequently produced more favorable outcomes than smaller groups that met less frequently. Encounter groups are no longer as popular as when Rogers himself was promoting them, but they are still conducted by his followers as a way of inducing people to enhance their potentials.

Psychological Tests

Rogers did not use psychological tests to assess personality, nor did he develop any tests. However, other psychologists have devised tests to measure aspects of the experiential world. The Experience Inventory (Coan, 1972), a self-report questionnaire, attempts to assess openness or receptivity to experience, a characteristic of the fully functioning person. The Experiencing Scale (Gendlin & Tomlinson, 1967) measures level of trust in ourselves. Persons being assessed by this test do not respond directly. They may talk about whatever they choose, and their tape-recorded comments are later rated for degree of self-trust; for example, how much they claim their feelings are an important source of information on which to base behavior, or how much they deny that personal feelings influence their decisions. The Experiencing Scale has been used with person-centered therapy. People who made the greatest improvement during therapy revealed an increase in self-trust from before therapy to after therapy. Those who showed little improvement during therapy showed a small or no increase in self-trust over the period. Those with less severe emotional disorders showed greater self-trust than those with more severe disorders (Klein, Malthieu, Gendlin, & Kiesler, 1969).

Although Rogers opposed testing to evaluate personality, he once agreed to take the Adjective Check List, the list of 300 adjectives to measure the self-concept (see Chapter 1). The results showed that Rogers possessed

> high creativity, intellectual quickness, and breadth of interests; low impulsiveness and a firm stance on ethical issues; emotional independence and effective goal-attainment; . . . gentleness and a valuing of inner feelings; tolerance of the fears and weaknesses of others, and a desire to bring people together. (Potkay & Allen, 1986, p. 254)

Research in Rogers's Theory

Rogers believed that person-centered interviews, which rely on clients' self-reports, were of greater value than experimental methods. In his view, the more orthodox scientific approaches yielded less information on the nature of personality than did his clinical approach. He said, "I never learned anything from research. Most of my research has been to confirm what I already felt to be true" (quoted in Bergin & Strupp, 1972, p. 314). Although Rogers did not use laboratory methods to collect data about personality, he did use them to attempt to verify and confirm his clinical observations. He was enthusiastic about research on the nature of the therapy sessions, an idea resisted by many clinicians who see it as a violation of privacy.

What Rogers did was to introduce what was then a radical procedure. He tape-recorded and filmed therapy sessions to enable researchers to study the client-therapist interaction. Before Rogers's innovation, the only data available from therapy sessions were the therapist's after-the-fact reconstructions. In addition to distortions of memory with the passage of time, a written record misses the client's emotional state and body language. Sometimes a facial expression or tone of voice reveals more than words. With recorded therapy sessions, everything became available for study. Rogers referred to it as a microscope with which to examine the "molecules of personality change" (Rogers, 1974, p. 120). He always obtained the client's permission to record the sessions and he found that the presence of the equipment did not impede the course of therapy.

Evaluating Person-Centered Therapy

Rogers and his associates also studied how the self-concept changes during a course of therapy. Using qualitative and quantitative techniques in the scientific tradition (despite Rogers's claim of not being a scientist), they analyzed the therapy sessions. By applying rating scales and content analyses of a client's verbalizations, they investigated changes in the self-concept. Much of the research used the **Q-sort technique,** a procedure developed by William Stephenson (Stephenson, 1953). In this technique, clients sort a large number of statements about the self-concept into categories that range from most descriptive to least descriptive. Thus the *Q* sort is a way of empirically defining the client's self-image.

Q-sort technique A self-report technique for assessing aspects of the self-concept.

TABLE 12.2   *Mrs. Oak's Q-sort statements of her perceived self before and after therapy*

Self before therapy	Self 12 months after therapy
I usually feel driven.	I express my emotions freely.
I am responsible for my troubles.	I feel emotionally mature.
I am really self-centered.	I am self-reliant.
I am disorganized.	I understand myself.
I feel insecure within myself.	I feel adequate.
I have to protect myself with excuses, with rationalizing.	I have a warm emotional relationship with others.

SOURCE: From "The Case of Mrs. Oak: A Research Analysis" by C. R. Rogers. In *Psychotherapy and Personality Change* by C. R. Rogers and R. F. Dymond, 1954, Chicago: University of Chicago Press.

Typical *Q*-sort statements include the following.

- I enjoy being alone.
- I feel helpless.
- I am emotionally mature.

self-perception

The *Q* sort can be used in several ways. For example, after sorting the statements in terms of the perceived self, clients can be asked to sort the same statements in terms of an ideal self, that is, the person they would most like to be.

Applying the correlational method, Rogers used *Q*-sort responses to determine how closely a client's self-image or perceived self corresponded to the ideal self. He also noted how greatly the self-concept changed from the period before therapy to the period following therapy. For one client, identified as "Mrs. Oak," the data yielded an initial correlation coefficient of $+.36$ between perceived self and ideal self. A year after therapy, the correlation coefficient had increased to $+.79$, indicating to Rogers that Mrs. Oak's perceived self had become much more congruent with her ideal or desired self (Rogers, 1954). He concluded that this dramatic change reflected an increase in emotional health.

Mrs. Oak chose different *Q*-sort phrases to describe herself before and after therapy. Prior to her sessions with Rogers, she saw her self-image as dependent and passive. She also felt rejected by other people. After the course of therapy, Mrs. Oak believed she was more like the self she really wanted to be. She felt more secure, less fearful, and better able to relate to other people (see Table 12.2).

A study by Rogers's associates measured the discrepancy between perceived self and ideal self in 25 clients (Butler & Haigh, 1954). The researchers found that the discrepancy decreased over time during and following therapy. Before therapy, the average correlation coefficient between perceived self and ideal self was $-.01$. After therapy it was $+.31$.

Incongruence and the Self-Concept

Research using the *Q* sort provides impressive evidence for the effectiveness of person-centered therapy but offers little information about the validity of Rogers's personality theory. Other studies have tested some of his concepts.

Rogers suggested that people defend themselves against experiences that are incongruent with their self-concept by denying or distorting these inconsistent aspects of reality. This idea was tested in college students who rated themselves on 100 socially desirable adjectives, indicating the degree to which each word described them (Suinn, Osborne, & Winfree, 1962). Five days later, the subjects were given a rating scale and told that it represented ratings made of them by two other students. These rating scales were fake. They contained some adjectives consistent with the subjects' self-ratings and some adjectives that were inconsistent. Two days after that, the subjects completed the 100-item adjective scale again, this time based on the ratings allegedly made of them, not on their own self-perceptions. In other words, they were asked to recall the phony ratings. The students' accuracy of recall was significantly higher for adjectives consistent with their own self-concept than it was for inconsistent adjectives. The researchers concluded that the subjects were defending themselves against incongruent material by being unable to recall it.

Openness to Experience

College students completed the *Q*-sort list to test Rogers's proposition that fully functioning persons are open to all experiences, whereas psychologically unhealthy persons erect defenses to protect themselves against experiences that threaten their self-image (Chodorkoff, 1954). A separate *Q*-sort description of each subject was prepared by clinicians who based their reports on a variety of data including responses to the Thematic Apperception Test and the Rorschach inkblot test. Based on these clinical measurements, the subjects were divided into good- and poor-adjustment groups.

Measures of perceptual defense against material perceived to be threatening were obtained from the subjects' reactions to neutral words such as *table* and to allegedly threatening words such as *penis*. The results showed that all subjects were slower to perceive threatening words than neutral words, but this response was more marked in the defensive subjects of the poorly adjusted group. Significantly less perceptual defense was shown by subjects in the good-adjustment group, presumed to be psychologically healthier. With regard to agreement between the subjects' self-descriptions and the clinicians' descriptions, researchers found that the closer the two sets of *Q*-sort statements, the better adjusted that person was found to be.

Acceptance of Self

A study of 56 mothers explored the relationship between their self-acceptance and the extent to which they accepted their children as they were, rather than as they desired them to be (Medinnus & Curtis, 1963). This research was based on Rogers's idea that people who accept their own nature realistically (whose perceived and ideal selves are congruent) are more likely to accept others as they really are. The results revealed significant differences between self-accepting mothers and those who were not self-accepting. Self-accepting mothers were more accepting of their children's nature. Also, the child's degree of self-acceptance depended to some extent on the mother's degree of self-acceptance.

Other studies support Rogers's belief that parental behavior affects a child's self-image. Parents who accept their children unconditionally and display democratic child-rearing practices were found to have children with higher self-esteem and greater emotional security than parents who failed to accept their children and who displayed authoritarian behavior (Baldwin, 1949). Parents of children with high self-esteem displayed their affection and used reward rather than punishment to guide their child's behavior. Parents of children with low self-esteem were more aloof, less loving, and more likely to use punishment (Coopersmith, 1967). Adolescents whose parents provided unconditional positive regard and allowed them to express themselves without restraint developed greater creative potential than did adolescents whose parents did not provide those conditions (Harrington, Block, & Block, 1987).

In another study, adolescents who received unconditional positive regard from their parents were found to be confident and hopeful about their ability to receive support from others in the future. They also engaged in more behaviors that were consistent with their perception of their interests and talents. Teens who received conditional positive regard from their parents lacked such confidence and hope. They took more actions that were inconsistent with their true selves in an effort to obtain support and approval from their parents (Harter, Marold, Whitesell, & Cobbs, 1996).

Emotional Adjustment

Several studies provide support for Rogers's suggestion that incongruence between perceived self and ideal self indicates poor emotional adjustment. Researchers have concluded that the greater the discrepancy, the higher the anxiety, insecurity, self-doubt, depression, social incompetence, and other psychological disorders. Also, high inconsistency between perceived and ideal self correlates with low levels of self-actualization and self-esteem (Achenbach & Zigler, 1963; Gough, Fioravanti, & Lazzari, 1983; Mahoney & Hartnett, 1973; Moretti & Higgins, 1990; Straumann, Vookles, Berenstein, Chaiken, & Higgins, 1991). Persons with a great discrepancy between perceived and ideal selves were rated by others as awkward, confused, and unfriendly (Gough, Lazzari, & Fioravanti, 1978).

Rogers believed that failure to realize our innate actualization tendency can lead to maladjustment. To test this idea, one researcher studied the inherited temperaments proposed by Buss and Plomin (Emotionality, Activity, and Sociability) in male and female college students (Ford, 1991). Using the EASI Temperament Survey to assess behavior, the college students' parents were asked to recall their children's temperaments when very young. These temperament profiles were compared with the college students' current self-perceptions on the three temperaments. The results supported Rogers's views. The greater the discrepancy in temperament between childhood potential and adult realization, the greater was the level of maladjustment.

A Final Commentary

Critics have faulted Rogers for failing to explain more precisely his proposed innate potential for actualization. Is it wholly physiological or does it have a psychological component? Are individual differences possible? Rogers did not provide answers to these and related questions. He described the actualization tendency as a kind of genetic blueprint for the organism's development but did not clarify how the mechanism operates.

Rogers insisted that the only way to explore personality is through person-centered therapy to examine a person's subjective experiences. Rogers did this by listening to a client's self-reports. Critics charge that he ignored those factors of which the client was not consciously aware but which could influence behavior. People may distort reports of their subjective experiences, repressing some events and elaborating on or inventing others, to conceal their true nature and present an idealized self-image.

Rogers's person-centered psychotherapy quickly became popular. Its rapid acceptance was fostered in part by social circumstances in the United States at the end of World War II (1945). Veterans returning from service overseas needed help readjusting to civilian life. The result was a demand for psychologists and for a counseling technique they could master and put into practice quickly. Training in traditional psychoanalysis required a medical degree and a lengthy period of specialization. Experimental psychology had no way to help. "Person-centered psychotherapy, however, was simple, informal, and brief, and it required little training" (deCarvalho, 1999, p. 142).

Rogers's therapy has found broad application not only as a treatment for emotional disturbances but also as a means of enhancing the self-image. In the business world it has been used as a training method for managers. In the helping professions it is used to train clinical psychologists, social workers, and counselors. In addition, psychotherapists of many different orientations have accepted some of Rogers's core concepts in their therapeutic work with clients.

His personality theory, although less influential than his psychotherapy, has also received wide recognition, particularly for its emphasis on the self-concept. However, Rogers did not believe he had influenced academic or scientific psychology. Nonetheless, his theory and therapy have stimulated research on the nature of psychotherapy, the client-therapist interaction, and the self-concept. His ideas have had a significant impact on psychology's theoretical and empirical definitions of the self.

Rogers's background was a unique combination of clinic, lecture hall, and laboratory. He drew on his considerable experience with emotionally disturbed clients and on the intellectual stimulation of colleagues and students. He attracted large numbers of followers who continue to test his ideas in the clinic and in the laboratory.

Chapter Summary

Rogers's person-centered theory proposes that we are conscious, rational beings not controlled by unconscious forces or past experiences. Personality can only be understood by a phenomenological approach, that is, from an individual's own viewpoint based on his or her subjective experiences (one's experiential field). Our goal is self-actualization, an innate tendency to growth and development. The organismic valuing process evaluates life experiences in terms of how well they serve the actualizing tendency. Experiences that promote actualization will be sought; experiences that hinder it will be avoided.

Positive regard is a need for acceptance, love, and approval from others, particularly from the mother, during infancy. In unconditional positive regard, the mother's love and approval are granted freely and are not conditional on the child's behavior. When love and approval are conditional, a state of conditional positive regard exists. Once we internalize the attitudes of others, positive regard comes from ourselves (positive self-regard). Conditions of worth (similar to the Freudian superego) involve seeing ourselves as worthy only under conditions acceptable to our parents. We avoid behaviors and perceptions that oppose our parents' conditions of worth. Incongruence develops between the self-concept and behaviors that threaten the self-image. We defend against anxiety by denying threatening aspects of the experiential field.

The fully functioning person represents the peak of psychological development. Characteristics of the fully functioning person are an awareness of all experiences, no conditions to defend against, the ability to live fully in each moment, trust in one's self, a sense of freedom and personal power, creativity, and spontaneity. Rogers's optimistic image of human nature encompassed a belief in free will, the prominence of environment over heredity, and some universality in personality. Individuals and societies can grow unhampered by past events.

Personality can be assessed in terms of subjective experiences as revealed in self-reports. In this person-centered approach, the therapist gives the client unconditional positive regard. Rogers opposed free association and dream analysis because they make the client dependent on the therapist. By recording therapy sessions, Rogers enabled researchers to investigate the nature of the client-therapist interaction.

The *Q*-sort technique, in which clients sort statements about their self-concept into categories ranging from most to least descriptive, is a way of quantifying the self-image. *Q*-sort research has revealed a greater correspondence between perceived self and ideal self after therapy. The better adjusted a person is, the greater the agreement between self-descriptions and descriptions made by others. Discrepancies between perceived self and ideal self indicate poor psychological adjustment. Rogers's work has been criticized for failing to define precisely the nature of self-actualization and for ignoring the impact of unconscious forces and the possible distortion of a client's subjective experiences in self-reports.

Review Questions

1. How did Carl Rogers's clinical experience differ from Sigmund Freud's?

2. Describe the research that influenced Rogers's view of the role of the self in personality.

3. How does the need to actualize promote biological and psychological growth?

4. What is the organismic valuing process?

5. What is the experiential field? How does our experiential field change with age?

6. What parental behaviors affect a child's development of positive self-regard?

7. Compare Rogers's concept of conditions of worth with Freud's concept of the superego.

8. Describe Rogers's concept of incongruence. How is incongruence related to anxiety?

9. Describe the characteristics of the fully functioning person.

10. How does the Rogerian clinical interview differ from the psychoanalytic clinical interview? What did Rogers call his approach? Why?

11. How does the Q-sort technique measure a person's self-image? What has Q-sort research shown about the self-concept before and after therapy?

12. What was Rogers's position on the importance of childhood experiences and adult experiences in personality development?

13. Discuss several criticisms of Rogers's theory.

Suggested Readings

DeCarvalho, R. J. (1999). Otto Rank, the Rankian circle in Philadelphia, and the origins of Carl Rogers' person-centered psychotherapy. *History of Psychology, 2,* 132–148. Traces the roots of Rogers's style of therapy to the psychiatric social work of the 1930s and the ideas of Otto Rank, a disciple of Sigmund Freud. Emphasizes the significance of the relationship between client and therapist.

Evans, R. I. (1975). *Carl Rogers: The man and his ideas.* New York: Dutton. Interviews with Rogers on the evolution of the self, techniques of person-centered therapy, and applications of his theory to education. Contrasts Rogers's humanistic views with B. F. Skinner's behaviorist views.

Kirschenbaum, H. (1979). *On becoming Carl Rogers.* New York: Delacorte Press. A biography of Rogers and his contributions to humanistic psychology.

Rogers, C. R. (1961). *On becoming a person: A therapist's view of psychotherapy.* Boston: Houghton Mifflin. Summarizes Rogers's views on psychotherapy, especially problems in communication and interpersonal relations. Discusses the effects of enhanced personal growth on personal and family life.

Rogers, C. R. (1967). Autobiography. In E. G. Boring & G. Lindzey (Eds.), *A history of psychology in autobiography* (Vol. 5, pp. 341–384). New York: Appleton-Century-Crofts. Rogers's assessment of his work and the influence of his early experiences.

Rogers, C. R. (1974). In retrospect: Forty-six years. *American Psychologist, 29,* 115–123. Rogers evaluates the impact of his work on the fields of counseling, psychotherapy, education, leadership, and international relations and on the empirical investigation of subjective phenomena.

Rogers, C. R. (1980). *A way of being.* Boston: Houghton Mifflin. Presents the work of Rogers's later years concerning individual and group psychotherapy, the helping professions, scientific progress, and personal growth.

Rogers, C. R. (1989). *The Carl Rogers reader.* Boston: Houghton Mifflin. A selection of Rogers's writings over 60 years, edited by Howard Kirschenbaum and Valerie Henderson. Includes personal recollections, case studies, and essays on personality change, psychotherapy, education, marriage, aging, international relations, and world peace.

The Cognitive Approach

If you look up the word *cognition* in a dictionary, you will find that it means the act or process of knowing. The cognitive approach to personality focuses on the ways in which people come to know their environment and themselves, how they perceive, evaluate, learn, think, make decisions, and solve problems. This is a truly *psychological* approach to personality because it focuses exclusively on conscious mental activities.

It may appear that this concentration on the mind or mental processes neglects ideas dealt with by other theorists. For example, in the cognitive approach we do not find needs, drives, or emotions as separate activities of the personality. Instead, they are aspects of personality under the control of the cognitive processes.

Contemporary psychoanalysts acknowledge the importance of cognitive processes. So, too, did Erik Erikson, who granted greater autonomy to the ego and to cognitive functioning. The humanistic psychologists Abraham Maslow and Carl Rogers dealt with perceptions, how we evaluate and mentally process our experiences. Henry Murray and Gordon Allport wrote about human reasoning, and Alfred Adler proposed a creative self, which results from our perception or interpretation of experience. Social-learning theorists (Chapters 15 and 16) also invoke cognitive processes. The difference between these approaches and George Kelly's cognitive theory of personality is that Kelly attempted to describe *all* aspects of personality, including its emotional components, in terms of cognitive processes.

> It occurred to me that what seemed true of myself
> was probably no less true of others. If I initiated my
> actions, so did they.
>
> —George Kelly

THIRTEEN

George Kelly

The Role of Cognitive Processes

personal construct theory Kelly's description of personality in terms of cognitive processes. We are capable of interpreting behaviors and events and using this understanding to guide our behavior and predict the behavior of other people.

Kelly's **personal construct theory** of personality differs greatly from other approaches discussed in this book. Kelly warned us we would not find in his system familiar concepts such as the unconscious, the ego, needs, drives, stimuli and responses, and reinforcement—not even motivation and emotion. The obvious question is how can we understand the human personality without considering these ideas, especially motivation and emotion?

Kelly's answer was that each person creates a set of cognitive constructs about the environment. By that he meant that we interpret and organize the events and social relationships of our lives in a system or pattern. On the basis of this pattern, we make predictions about ourselves and about other people and events, and we use these predictions to formulate our responses and guide our actions. Therefore, to understand personality, we must first understand our patterns, the ways we organize or construct our world. According to Kelly, our interpretation of events is more important than the events themselves.

The personality theory Kelly offered derived from his experience as a clinician. For several reasons, he interpreted his clinical experience differently from Freud and other theorists who treated patients. The model of human nature Kelly developed from his clinical work is unusual. He concluded that people function in the same way scientists do.

Scientists construct theories and hypotheses and test them against reality by performing experiments in the laboratory. If the results of their experiments support the theory, it is retained. If the data do not support the theory, it must be rejected or modified and retested.

As we have seen, this is how psychologists who study personality typically proceed. Yet Kelly noted that psychologists do not attribute to their subjects the same intellectual and rational abilities they ascribe to themselves. It is as if psychologists have two theories about human nature, one that applies to scientists and their way of looking at the world, and another that applies to everybody else. The logical assumption, then, is that psychologists view their subjects as incapable of rational functioning, as being motivated by all sorts of conflicting drives or as victims of rampant unconscious forces. Thus, human beings are believed to function largely on an emotional level, unlikely to use their cognitive processes to learn, think, evaluate experiences, or solve problems. Surely this is quite unlike the way psychologists function!

Are psychologists really superior beings? Kelly said they are no different from the people they study. What works for one works for the other; what explains one explains the other. Both are concerned with predicting and controlling the events in their lives, and both are capable of doing so rationally. Like scientists, all of us construct theories, which Kelly called *personal constructs*, by which we try to predict and control the events in our lives. He proposed that the way to understand someone's personality is to examine his or her personal constructs.

Kelly and the Cognitive Movement in Psychology

If you have studied the history of psychology, you might think at first glance that Kelly's cognitive theory is linked to the cognitive revolution in psychology that began around 1960 and now dominates mainstream American experimental psychology. However, the contemporary cognitive movement has not embraced Kelly's work, despite the similarity in terminology, because Kelly's theory is not consistent with its methods and subject matter.

Kelly's approach is that of the clinician dealing with the conscious constructs by which people arrange their lives. In contrast, cognitive psychologists are interested in both cognitive variables and overt behavior, which they study primarily in an experimental, not a clinical, setting. Also, cognitive psychologists do not limit their focus to personality. They study overt behavior and learning in social situations. They believe that cognitive processes such as learning influence a person's response to a given stimulus situation.

Although cognitive psychology took hold subsequent to Kelly's work, it had little influence on the movement. At best, Kelly's theory could be considered a precursor to contemporary cognitive psychology. The two approaches share the term *cognitive*, with its implied interest in conscious activities, but little else. Kelly's recognition of the importance of cognitive processes is noteworthy, but we must place it in perspective. It is not part of mainstream American psychology as defined by experimental psychologists, but that does not detract from its usefulness for studying personality.

The Life of Kelly (1905–1967)

George Kelly was born on a farm in Kansas. An only child, he received a great deal of attention and affection from his parents, who were fundamentalist in their religious beliefs and committed to helping the less fortunate. They opposed frivolous entertainment such as dancing and card playing. When Kelly was 4 years old, the family traveled by covered wagon to Colorado to try farming there but soon returned to Kansas. Kelly's early education was erratic and conducted as much by his parents as by schoolteachers. At 13 he went to high school in Wichita and seldom lived at home after that. In 1926 he earned a bachelor's degree in physics and mathematics from Park College in Parkville, Missouri. But his interests had shifted from science to social problems. Kelly's future was uncertain.

He worked briefly as an engineer, then took a teaching job at a labor college in Minneapolis. Next, he became an instructor in speech for the American Banking Association and also taught citizenship courses to immigrants. He then enrolled in graduate school and received a master's degree in educational sociology from the University of Kansas in Lawrence. Accepting a job offer from a junior college in Iowa, Kelly taught various subjects and coached the drama program. His career certainly showed no inclination toward psychology. In college, he had not been impressed by coursework in the field.

In the first course in psychology, I sat in the back row of a very large class, tilted my chair against the wall, made myself as comfortable as possible, and kept one ear cocked for anything interesting that might turn up. One day the professor, a very nice person who seemed to be trying hard to convince himself that psychology was something to be taken seriously, turned to the blackboard and wrote an "S," an arrow, and an "R." Thereupon I straightened up in my chair and listened, thinking to myself that now, after two or three weeks of preliminaries, we might be getting to the meat of the matter. (Kelly, 1969, p. 46)

Kelly paid attention for several more class meetings and then gave up. He did not comprehend what the arrow connecting the stimulus (S) and the response (R) stood for. He never did figure it out. The traditional behaviorist, experimental approach to psychology had failed to spark his interest. He also explored psychoanalysis. He wrote, "I don't remember which one of Freud's books I was trying to read, but I do remember the mounting feeling of incredulity that anyone could write such nonsense, much less publish it" (1969, p. 47).

Kelly's professional training took a different turn in 1929 when he was awarded a fellowship at the University of Edinburgh, Scotland. During his year there he earned a Bachelor of Education degree and developed an interest in psychology. He returned to the United States for doctoral studies at the State University of Iowa and received his Ph.D. in 1931.

An Intellectual Approach to Counseling

Kelly began his academic career at Fort Hays Kansas State College in the midst of the economic depression of the 1930s. There was little opportunity to conduct research in physiological psychology, the specialty in which he had trained, so he switched to clinical psychology for which there was a need. He developed a clinical psychology service for the local public school system and for the students at his college. He established traveling clinics, going from school to school, which gave him the opportunity to deal with a variety of problems and to try different approaches to treatment. Kelly was not committed to a particular therapeutic technique or to a specific theory about the nature of personality. He felt free to use traditional methods of assessment and treatment as well as those of his own design. His clinical experiences strongly influenced the nature of his personal construct theory. The people he treated were not severely disturbed psychotics in mental hospitals or neurotics with troublesome emotional problems. His patients were students who had been referred by their teachers for counseling.

Thus, unlike the emotionally maladjusted patients in a psychiatric ward or a psychoanalyst's office, Kelly's clients were much more capable of discussing their concerns rationally, of expressing their problems in intellectual terms, the level of functioning expected in an academic setting. In the classroom we are taught to analyze, to think and process information logically. This intellectual attitude carried over from the classroom to the counseling situation. Had circumstances placed Kelly during his formative professional years at work with schizophrenics in a mental institution, his theory might not have depended so heavily on cognitive information-processing abilities.

World War II interrupted Kelly's academic career. He joined the U.S. Navy and served as a psychologist in the Bureau of Medicine and Surgery in Washington, D.C. When the war ended in 1945, he taught for a year at the University of Maryland before joining the faculty of Ohio State University. There he spent 19 years teaching, refining his personality theory, and conducting research. Kelly also lectured at

universities throughout the world about how his personal construct theory of personality could be used to resolve international tensions. In 1965 he accepted an appointment to an endowed chair at Brandeis University but died shortly thereafter.

Kelly was a major force in the development of the clinical psychology profession during its rapid growth following World War II. He held several honored positions in the field, including the presidencies of the Clinical and Consulting divisions of the American Psychological Association and the American Board of Examiners in Professional Psychology.

Personal Construct Theory

Kelly suggested that people perceive and organize their world of experiences the same way scientists do, by formulating hypotheses about the environment and testing them against the reality of daily life. In other words, we observe the events of our life—the facts or data of our experience—and interpret them in our own way. This personal interpreting, explaining, or *construing* of experience represents our unique view of events, the pattern within which we place them. Kelly said that we look at the world through "transparent patterns that fit over the realities of which the world is composed" (Kelly, 1955, pp. 8–9).

We might compare these patterns to sunglasses that add a particular tint or coloring to everything we see. One person's glasses may have a bluish tint whereas another's may have a greenish tint. Several people can look at the same scene and perceive it differently, depending on the tint of the lenses that frame their point of view. So it is with the hypotheses or patterns we construct to make sense of our world. This special view, the unique pattern created by each individual, is what Kelly called our *construct system*.

construct An intellectual hypothesis that we devise and use to interpret or explain life events. Constructs are bipolar, or dichotomous, such as tall versus short or honest versus dishonest.

A **construct** is a person's unique way of looking at life, an intellectual hypothesis devised to explain or interpret events. We behave in accordance with the expectation that our constructs will predict and explain the reality of our world. Like scientists, we constantly test these hypotheses. We base our behavior on our constructs, and we evaluate the effects.

Consider a student who is in danger of failing an introductory psychology course and is trying to persuade the professor to give a passing grade. After observing the professor for most of the semester, the student concludes that the professor behaves in a superior and authoritarian manner in class and has an inflated sense of personal importance. From this observation, the student forms the hypothesis, or construct, that acting to reinforce the professor's exaggerated self-image will bring a favorable response.

The student tests this idea against reality. The student goes to the library, reads an article the professor has written, and praises it to the professor. If the professor feels flattered and gives the student a good grade, then the student's construct has been confirmed. It has been found to be useful and can be applied the next time the student takes a course with that professor or with any professor who behaves similarly. However, if the student receives a failing grade, then the construct was found to be inappropriate. A new one will be required for dealing with that professor.

Over the course of life we develop many constructs, one for almost every type of person or situation we encounter. We expand our inventory of constructs as we meet new people and face new situations. Further, we may alter or discard constructs periodically as situations change. Revising our constructs is a necessary and continuous process; we must always have an alternative construct to apply to a situation. If our constructs were inflexible and incapable of being revised (which is what would happen if personality was totally determined by childhood influences), then we would not be able to cope with new situations. Kelly called this adaptability **constructive alternativism** to express the view that we are not controlled by our constructs but are free to revise or replace them with other alternatives.

constructive alternativism The idea that we are free to revise or replace our constructs with alternatives as needed.

Anticipating Life Events

Kelly's personal construct theory is presented in a scientific format, organized into a fundamental postulate and 11 corollaries (see Table 13.1). The fundamental postulate states that our *psychological processes are directed by the ways in which we anticipate events.*

By using the word *processes*, Kelly was not suggesting some kind of internal mental energy. Rather, he believed that personality was a flowing, moving process. Our psychological processes are directed by our constructs, by the way each of us construes our world. Another key word in the fundamental postulate is *anticipate*. Kelly's notion of constructs is anticipatory. We use constructs to predict the future so that we have some idea of the consequences of our actions, of what is likely to occur if we behave in a certain way.

TABLE 13.1   *Corollaries of personal construct theory*

Construction	Because repeated events are similar, we can predict or anticipate how we will experience such an event in the future.
Individuality	People perceive events in different ways.
Organization	We arrange our constructs in patterns, according to our view of their similarities and differences.
Dichotomy	Constructs are bipolar; for example, if we have an opinion about honesty, that idea must also include the concept of dishonesty.
Choice	We choose the alternative for each construct that works best for us, the one that allows us to predict the outcome of anticipated events.
Range	Our constructs may apply to many situations or people, or they may be limited to a single person or situation.
Experience	We continually test our constructs against life's experiences to make sure they remain useful.
Modulation	We may modify our constructs as a function of new experiences.
Fragmentation	We may sometimes have contradictory or inconsistent subordinate constructs within our overall construct system.
Commonality	Although our individual constructs are unique to us, people in compatible groups or cultures may hold similar constructs.
Sociality	We try to understand how other people think and predict what they will do, and we modify our behavior accordingly.

The Construction Corollary

Similarities among repeated events.   Kelly believed no life event or experience could be reproduced exactly as it occurred the first time. An event can be repeated, but it will not be experienced in precisely the same way. For example, if you watch a movie today that you first saw last month, your experience of it will be different the second time. Your mood may not be the same, and during the elapsed month you were exposed to events that affected your attitudes and emotions. Maybe you read something unpleasant about an actor in the film. Or you may feel more content because your grades are improving.

However, although such repeated events are not experienced identically, recurrent features or themes will emerge. Some aspects of a situation will be similar to those experienced earlier. It is on the basis of these similarities that we predict or establish anticipations about how we will deal with that type of event in the future. Our predictions rest on the idea that future events, though they are not duplicates of past events, will nevertheless be similar. For example, some scenes in the movie probably affect you the same way every time. If you liked the car chase scenes the first time, you will probably like them again. You base your behavior on your anticipation of liking the chases, so that explains why you choose to watch the film again. Themes of the past reappear in the future, and we formulate our constructs on the basis of these recurring themes.

The Individuality Corollary

Individual differences in interpreting events.   With this corollary, Kelly introduced the notion of individual differences. He pointed out that people differ from one another in how they perceive or interpret an event. Because of construing events differently, people form different constructs. Our constructs do not so much reflect the objective reality of an event as they constitute the unique interpretation each of us places on it.

The Organization Corollary

Relationships among constructs.   We organize our individual constructs into a pattern according to our view of their interrelationships, that is, their similarities and differences. People who hold similar constructs may still differ from one another if they organize those constructs in different patterns.

Typically, we organize our constructs into a hierarchy, with some constructs subordinate to others. A construct can include one or more subordinate constructs. For example, the construct *good* may include among its subordinates the constructs *intelligent* and *moral*. Thus, if we meet someone who fits our idea of a good person, we anticipate that he or she will also have the attributes of intelligence and high moral standards.

The relationships among constructs are usually more enduring than the specific constructs themselves, but they, too, are open to change. A person who feels insulted by someone who appears more intelligent may switch the construct *intelligent* from a subordinate place under the construct *good* to a place under the construct *bad*. The only valid test for a construct system is its predictive efficiency. If the organization of our constructs no longer provides a useful way to predict events, we will modify it.

The Dichotomy Corollary

Two mutually exclusive alternatives.   All constructs are bipolar or dichotomous. This is necessary if we are to anticipate future events correctly. Just as we note similarities among people or events, we must also account for dissimilarities. For example, it is not enough to have a construct about a friend that describes the personal characteristic of *honesty*. We must also consider the opposite, *dishonesty*, to explain how the honest person differs from someone who is not honest. If we did not make this distinction—if we assumed that all people are honest—then forming a construct about honesty would not help us anticipate or predict anything about people we might meet in the future. A person can be expected to be honest only in contrast to someone who is expected to be dishonest. The appropriate personal construct in this example, then, is *honest versus dishonest*. Our constructs must always be framed in terms of a pair of mutually exclusive alternatives.

The Choice Corollary

Freedom of choice.   The notion that people have freedom of choice is found throughout Kelly's writings. According to the dichotomy corollary described above, each construct has two opposing poles. For every situation we must choose the al-

People differ from one another in the ways they perceive and interpret the same event.

ternative that works best for us, the one that allows us to anticipate or predict the outcome of future events.

Kelly suggested that we have some latitude in deciding between the alternatives, and he described it as a choice between security and adventure. Suppose you must decide which of two courses to take next semester. One is easy because it is not much different from a course you've already taken and is taught by a professor known to give high grades for little work. There is virtually no risk involved in choosing that course, but there may not be much reward either. You know the professor is dull, and you have already studied much of the course material. However, it is the secure choice, because you can make a highly accurate prediction about the consequences of deciding to take it.

The other course is more of a gamble. The professor is new and rumored to be tough, and you don't know much about the subject. It would expose you to a field of study you've been curious about. In this case, you cannot make an accurate prediction about the outcome of your choice. This more adventurous alternative means more risk but the potential reward and satisfaction are greater.

You must choose between the low-risk, minimal-reward secure option and the high-risk, high-reward adventurous option. The first has a high predictive efficiency, the second a lower predictive efficiency. Kelly believed we face such choices throughout life, choices between defining or extending our personal construct system. The secure choice, which is similar to past choices, further defines our construct system by repeating experiences and events. The more adventurous choice extends our construct system by encompassing new experiences and events.

The popular tendency to opt for the secure, low-risk alternative may explain why some people persist in behaving in an unrewarding way. For example, why does someone act aggressively toward other people even when continually rebuffed? Kelly's answer was that the person is making the low-risk choice because he or she has come to know what to expect from others in response to aggressive behavior. The hostile person does not know how people will react to friendliness because he or she has rarely tried it. The potential rewards may be greater for friendly behavior but so is the uncertainty for this person.

Remember that our choices are made in terms of how well they allow us to anticipate or predict events, not necessarily in terms of what is best for us. And it is Kelly's contention that each of us, in the best scientific tradition, desires to predict the future with the highest possible degree of certainty.

The Range Corollary

The range of convenience.   Few personal constructs are appropriate or relevant for all situations. Consider the construct *tall versus short*, which obviously has a limited **range of convenience** or applicability. It can be useful with respect to buildings, trees, or basketball players, but it is of no value in describing a pizza or the weather.

Some constructs can be applied to many situations or people, whereas others are more limited, perhaps appropriate for one person or situation. The range of convenience or relevance for a construct is a matter of personal choice. For example, we may believe that the construct *loyal versus disloyal* applies to everyone we meet or

range of convenience
The spectrum of events to which a construct can be applied. Some constructs are relevant to a limited number of people or situations; other constructs are broader.

to our family members or only to our pet dog. According to Kelly, if we are to understand personality fully, it is just as important to know what is excluded from a construct's range of convenience as it is to know what is included.

The Experience Corollary

Exposure to new experiences.   We have said that each construct is a hypothesis generated on the basis of past experience to predict or anticipate future events. Each construct is then tested against reality by determining how well it predicted a given event. Most of us are exposed to new experiences daily, so the process of testing the fit of a construct to see how well it predicted the event is ongoing. If a construct is not a valid predictor of the outcome of the situation, then it must be reformulated or replaced. Thus, we evaluate and reinterpret our constructs as our environment changes. Constructs that worked for us at age 16 may be useless, or even harmful, at age 40. In the intervening years, our experiences will have led us to revise our construct system.

If you never have any new experiences, then your construct system would never have to change. But for most of us, life involves meeting new people and coping with new challenges. Therefore, we must reconstrue our experiences and constructs accordingly.

The Modulation Corollary

permeability The idea that constructs can be revised and extended in light of new experiences.

Adapting to new experiences.   Constructs differ in their **permeability**. To permeate means to penetrate or pass through something. A permeable construct is one that allows new elements to penetrate or be admitted to the range of convenience. Such a construct is open to new events and experiences and is capable of being revised or extended by them.

How much our construct system can be modulated, or adjusted, as a function of new experience and learning depends on the permeability of the individual constructs. An impermeable or rigid construct is not capable of being changed, no matter what our experiences tell us.

For example, if a bigoted person applies the construct *high intelligence versus low intelligence* in a fixed or impermeable way to people of a certain ethnic minority group, believing that all members of this group have low intelligence, then new experiences will not penetrate or alter this belief. The prejudiced person will not modify that construct, no matter how many highly intelligent people of that ethnic group he or she meets. The construct is a barrier to learning and to new ideas.

The Fragmentation Corollary

Competition among constructs.   Kelly believed that within our construct system some individual constructs might be incompatible, even though they coexist within the overall pattern. Recall that our construct system may change as we evaluate new experiences. However, new constructs do not necessarily derive from old ones. A new construct may be compatible or consistent with an old one in a given situation, but if the situation changes, then these constructs can become inconsistent.

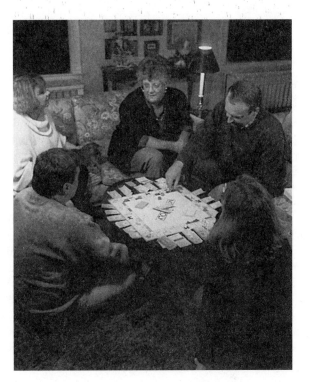

People may accept one another as friends in one situation, such as playing a board game, but may act as adversaries in another situation, such as a political debate.

Consider the following situation. A man meets a woman in a psychology class and decides that he is attracted to her. She is also a psych major, and her interests seem similar to his. She fits the *friend* alternative of the construct *friend versus enemy*. Thus, she is someone to be liked and respected. He sees her the next day at a political rally and is disappointed to find her loudly expressing conservative views that are the opposite of his own liberal opinions. Now she also fits the opposite alternative of the construct. She has become the *enemy*.

This inconsistency in the man's construct about this woman is at a subordinate level in his overall construct system. In one situation she is a friend, and in another situation she is an enemy. However, his broader construct, that liberals are friends and conservatives are enemies, remains undisturbed. According to Kelly, this is the process by which we tolerate subordinate inconsistencies without damaging our overall construct system.

The Commonality Corollary

Similarities among people in interpreting events.   Because people differ in the ways they construe events, each person develops unique constructs. However, people also show similarities in their ways of construing events. Kelly suggested that if several people construe an experience similarly, we can conclude that their cognitive processes are similar. Consider a group of people with the same cultural norms and ideals. Their anticipations and expectations of one another will have much in common and they will construe many of their experiences in the same way. People from the same culture may show a resemblance in their behaviors and characteristics even though they are exposed to different life events.

The Sociality Corollary

Interpersonal relationships.   We noted above that people in the same culture tend to construe events similarly. Although this accounts for some commonalities among people, it does not in itself bring about positive social relationships. It is not enough for one person to construe or interpret experiences in the same way as another person. The first person must also construe the other person's *constructs*. In other words, we must understand how another person thinks if we are to anticipate how that person will predict events.

Construing another person's constructs is something we do routinely. Think about driving a car. We stake our lives on being able to anticipate what the other drivers on the road will do. It is only when we can predict with some certainty what drivers, friends, bosses, or teachers will do that we can adjust our behaviors to theirs. And while we are adapting to them, they are doing the same to us.

Each person assumes a role with respect to others. We play one role with a partner, another with a child, another with our supervisor at work. Each role is a behavior pattern that evolves from understanding how the other person construes events. In a sense, then, we fit ourselves into the other person's constructs.

Questions About Human Nature

Kelly's personality theory presents an optimistic, even flattering, image of human nature (Kelly, 1969). Kelly treated people as rational beings capable of forming a framework of constructs through which to view the world. He believed we are the authors, not the victims, of our destiny. His view endows us with free will, the ability to choose the direction our life will take, and we are able to change when necessary by revising old constructs and forming new ones. We are not committed to a path laid down in childhood or adolescence. Our direction is clearly toward the future because we formulate constructs to predict or anticipate events (see Figure 13.1).

Thus, Kelly did not accept historical determinism. He did not consider past events to be the determinants of present behavior. We are not prisoners of toilet training, early sex experiences, or parental rejection, nor are we bound by biological instincts or unconscious forces. We need no push from internal drives or needs because we are motivated by the fact of being alive. Kelly saw no reason to invoke any other explanation.

Although Kelly did not discuss the role of heredity in personality, he noted that we are not totally determined by environmental influences. We live by constructs based on our interpretation of events. Therefore, it is the operation of our rational mental processes and not the specific events that influence the formation of personality. Kelly did not posit an ultimate and necessary life goal, but we may infer that our goal is to establish a construct system that enables us to predict events. On the question of uniqueness versus universality Kelly took a moderate position. The commonality corollary states that people in the same culture develop similar constructs,

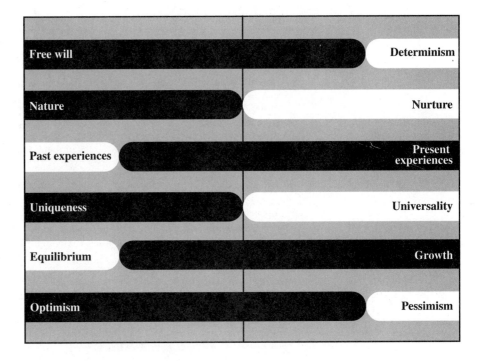

Free will	Determinism
Nature	Nurture
Past experiences	Present experiences
Uniqueness	Universality
Equilibrium	Growth
Optimism	Pessimism

FIGURE 13.1   *Kelly's image of human nature*

whereas the individuality corollary emphasizes the uniqueness of many of our constructs and therefore of the self.

Assessment in Kelly's Theory

The Interview

Kelly's primary assessment technique was the interview. He wrote, "If you don't know what is going on in a person's mind, ask him; he may tell you!" (1958, p. 330). Adopting what he called a "credulous attitude," Kelly accepted the client's words at face value, believing this was the best way to determine the person's constructs. He also recognized that a person might deliberately lie or distort the reported version of events. However, what the client said must be respected, even if not fully believed.

Self-Characterization Sketches

self-characterization sketch A technique to assess a person's construct system; that is, how a person perceives himself or herself in relation to other people.

Another technique used to assess a construct system is to have the person write a **self-characterization sketch**. Kelly's instructions to the client were as follows. "I want you to write a character sketch of [client's name] just as if he were the principal character in a play. Write it as it might be written by a friend who knew him very intimately and very sympathetically, perhaps better than anyone ever really could

TABLE 13.2　*Role title list from the Role Construct Repertory Test*

1. A teacher you liked.
2. A teacher you disliked.
3. Your wife/husband or present boyfriend/girlfriend.
4. An employer, supervisor, or officer under whom you worked or served and whom you found hard to get along with.
5. An employer, supervisor, or officer under whom you worked or served and whom you liked.
6. Your mother or the person who has played the part of a mother in your life.
7. Your father or the person who has played the part of a father in your life.
8. Your brother nearest your age or the person who has been most like a brother.
9. Your sister nearest your age or the person who has been most like a sister.
10. A person with whom you have worked who was easy to get along with.
11. A person with whom you have worked who was hard to understand.
12. A neighbor with whom you get along well.
13. A neighbor whom you find hard to understand.
14. A boy you got along well with when you were in high school.
15. A girl you got along well with when you were in high school.
16. A boy you did not like when you were in high school.
17. A girl you did not like when you were in high school.
18. A person of your own sex whom you would enjoy having as a companion on a trip.
19. A person of your own sex whom you would dislike having as a companion on a trip.
20. A person with whom you have been closely associated recently who appears to dislike you.
21. The person whom you would most like to be of help to or whom you feel most sorry for.
22. The most intelligent person whom you know personally.
23. The most successful person whom you know personally.
24. The most interesting person whom you know personally.

SOURCE: Reprinted from *The Psychology of Personal Constructs*, by George A. Kelly. Copyright © 1991 by Routledge, Chapman & Hall, Inc. Reprinted by permission.

know him" (1955, p. 323). Kelly found this technique useful for learning how clients perceive themselves in relation to other people.

The Role Construct Repertory Test

Kelly devised the Role Construct Repertory (REP) Test to uncover the constructs we apply to the important people in our lives. The client is asked to list by name the people who have played a significant role in his or her life such as mother, father, spouse, closest friend, and the most intelligent or interesting person he or she knows (see Table 13.2). The names are sorted, three at a time, and clients are asked to select from each group of three the two people who are most alike, noting how they differ from the third. For example, the client may be given the names of most threatening person, successful person, and attractive person and must describe how any two of them are similar in some aspect of behavior or character and how they differ from the other.

　　This information is presented in a diagram called a repertory grid (see Figure 13.2). For each row the client judges the three people indicated by the circles and

Constructs

Implicit Pole	Emergent Pole	Sort No.
Very religious	Don't believe in God	1
Complete different education	Same sort of education	2
Athletic	Not athletic	3
A boy	Both girls	4
Ideas different	Parents	5
Don't understand at all	Understand me better	6
Teach the wrong thing	Teach the right thing	7
Hasn't achieved a lot	Achieved a lot	8
No education	Higher education	9
Like other people	Don't like other people	10
Not religious	More religious	11
Not believing in too much education	Believe in higher education	12
Not sociable	More sociable	13
Not girls	Both girls	14
Not girls	Both girls	15
Low morals	Both have high morals	16
Think differently	Think alike	17
Different ages	Same age	18
Believe differently about me	Believe the same about me	19
Not friends	Both friends	20
Less understanding	More understanding	21
Don't understand music	Both appreciate music	22

Rows (roles):

Role	Sort No.
Ethical person	19
Happy person	18
Successful person	17
Boss	16
Rejected teacher	15
Accepted teacher	14
Attractive person	13
Threatening person	12
Pitied person	11
Rejecting person	10
Ex-pal	9
Pal	8
Ex-boyfriend/girlfriend	7
Spouse	6
Sister	5
Brother	4
Father	3
Mother	2
Self	1

FIGURE 13.2   A grid for the Role Construct Repertory Test. SOURCE: Reprinted from *The Psychology of Personal Constructs*, by George A. Kelly. Copyright © 1991 by Routledge, Chapman & Hall, Inc. Reprinted by permission.

formulates a construct about them, such as *happy versus sad*. The client writes a word or phrase that describes two of them in the column labeled *Emergent Pole* (in our example, the word *happy*). The client writes the opposite word (*sad*) to describe the third person in the group in the column labeled *Implicit Pole*. The client places a check mark in the squares of anyone else in the grid who shares the *Emergent Pole* characteristics, in this case, anyone significant in the client's life who could be described as happy.

The assumption underlying the REP Test is that people construe events in dichotomies, according to the dichotomy corollary, in terms of like versus unlike or similar versus dissimilar. By forcing clients to make repeated judgments about their social relationships, Kelly believed he could uncover their anticipations and expectations. The dichotomies or alternatives by which we guide our life will show the pattern of our personal constructs.

The REP Test has no objective scoring procedures. Its interpretation depends on the skill and training of the psychologist who administers it. Kelly did not intend the test to be a standardized, objective self-report inventory. He designed it as a way to assess constructs as a necessary stage in psychotherapy, to induce clients to reveal the constructs by which they organize their world. However, computer programs have since been developed to analyze individual repertory grids.

Fixed Role Therapy

fixed role therapy A psychotherapeutic technique in which the client acts out constructs appropriate for a fictitious person. This shows the client how the new constructs can be more effective than the old ones he or she has been using.

After assessing a client's system of personal constructs Kelly attempted to bring about a change in undesirable or ineffective constructs. He promoted a form of psychotherapy he called **fixed role therapy**. To help clients formulate new constructs and discard old ones, he asked them to write a self-characterization sketch describing themselves as the lead character in a play.

In fixed role therapy, the therapist prepares a fixed role sketch containing constructs that differ from the client's negative self-perceptions as revealed in the self-characterization sketch. The client is told that the fixed role sketch is about a fictitious character and is asked to act out that character in the therapist's office and later in everyday life. Through this role-playing the client is expected to project personal needs and values onto the fictitious character. The therapist expects the client to discover that the new constructs in the fixed role sketch work better in anticipating events than do the old constructs by which the client was living. Once the client realizes this, he or she can incorporate the new constructs into the overall construct system and function in a more satisfying and effective way.

Kelly developed fixed role therapy from observing a friend who began to live the role he was playing in a college dramatic production. The friend was so strongly influenced by the part that his behavior offstage gradually became more and more like the character. This example shows the intent of fixed role therapy: first to play a role and then to come to live it.

Consider the following example. Based on interviews with a male client, his written self-characterization sketch, and his REP Test results, the therapist concluded that the client was overly concerned with finding a female companion. His efforts were having a negative impact on his other social relationships. The client had difficulty being open and assertive because in his construct system assertiveness and extraversion were negative personality characteristics. Yet in dealing with other people he was convinced that his opinions were the correct ones and that everybody else was wrong. At work he felt isolated, believing he belonged to a higher social class than his colleagues.

The therapist's fixed role sketch for this client made no mention of the client's desire to have an intimate relationship with a woman. Instead, taking as a framework the client's skill at tennis, the therapist encouraged the client, through the fictitious character, to be more curious about and tolerant of different kinds of people and their views (Winter, 1992, pp. 270–271).

> Roy Taylor's philosophy of life very much reflects his approach to his favorite sport, tennis: it's not whether a player wins or loses that's important but whether they've played the game to the best of their ability. Whether at work or at play, he believes that if a job is worth doing it's worth doing well, and he brings to everything that he does a certain passion and conviction, which cannot fail to earn your respect. Although you might perhaps think that this would make him appear a little too serious and intense, once you get to know him you soon realize that his main concern is to live life to the full and that this includes having fun as well as working hard. Life doesn't always run smoothly for him, of course, but when he has a disappointment he always seems able to learn something from it, and to look to the future rather than brooding on his present or past misfortunes.
>
> One of his greatest strengths at tennis is his ability to anticipate the moves of the other players, be they his opponents or doubles partners. In other areas of his life, he also always tries to see the world through the eyes of the people with whom he comes into contact, perhaps because he has mixed with people from so many different walks of life. His lively curiosity in what makes other people tick is usually reciprocated and leads him, almost before he knows it, into some very rewarding relationships. He also, of course, has his fair share of disagreements with others, but when this happens he always makes an effort to understand the other person's point of view, even though he might not accept it. Because of this, he has a reputation both for commitment to those causes that are close to his heart and tolerance of the right of others to hold different opinions.

The therapist reviewed the fixed role sketch with the client and asked whether the character seemed like someone that the client might want to know. The client agreed to try behaving like the character in the sketch while in the therapist's office. He was asked to try acting, thinking, and talking like the character for the next two weeks. Behavioral changes instilled by fixed role therapy are reported to last far beyond the two-week role-playing period. However, positive case reports on treatment outcomes for individual clients must be balanced by the fact that there has been little controlled research on the technique's effectiveness.

Research in Kelly's Theory

Studies using the REP Test have shown that a person's constructs remain stable over time. One group of subjects took the test twice, using the names of different people as role figures each time. Although the role models changed, the constructs that were important to the subjects remained the same. However, research has shown that the validity of the REP test depends heavily on the skill of the psychologist interpreting the results.

One REP Test study investigated the complexity of a person's construct system. The results showed that the pattern becomes increasingly differentiated and integrated over the life span and can process more information as it is able to function in more abstract terms (Crockett, 1982). Another study suggested that forming friendships depends on a similarity of personal constructs. A group of students took the REP Test during their first week at college and again six months later. The data showed that the similarity in constructs or attitudes among friends did not develop during the six-month period but had existed before the relationships were formed. The researchers concluded that we seek as friends those people whose constructs are already similar to ours (Duck & Spencer, 1972). Also, for married subjects, spouses whose constructs were more alike reported greater happiness with their marriage than did couples whose constructs were more unlike (Neimeyer, 1984).

Other research showed a correspondence between one's personal characteristics and the ways of construing other people. Among a group of student nurses, those identified as highly anxious tended to use *anxious versus nonanxious* as a construct for evaluating others. Those who were judged by peers as friendly tended to view others in terms of a *friendly versus unfriendly* construct (Sechrest, 1968).

The REP Test has been used to study schizophrenics, neurotics, depressives, and persons with organic brain damage. Compared with normal subjects, schizophrenics were found to be unstable and inconsistent in construing other people. However, their construing of objects was stable and consistent, suggesting that their thought disorders applied only to social situations. Their thought processes were also characterized by paranoid delusions and irrational links between constructs (Bannister, Fransella, & Agnew, 1971; Bannister & Salmon, 1966; Winter, 1992).

A study using a modified version of the REP Test compared the personal construct systems of repeat patients in psychiatric hospitals with persons hospitalized for the first time. The repeat patients construed their social network as small, limited to a few people on whom they believed they could depend. First-time patients construed their social network as significantly larger (Smith, Stefan, Kovaleski, & Johnson, 1991). REP Test research with juvenile and adult offenders revealed that delinquents tended to identify with action-oriented television heroes rather than with real adults. Newly released prisoners showed poor self-esteem and lowered aspirations for the future. Rapists felt inadequate, immature, and preoccupied with personal failure (Needs, 1988).

Researchers have applied the REP Test in market research to assess the criteria consumers use to evaluate products. Industrial-organizational psychologists have used the REP Test for vocational counseling, employee selection, job performance evaluation, and evaluation of training programs.

Cognitive Complexity and Cognitive Simplicity

cognitive styles

An outgrowth of Kelly's work on personal constructs relates to cognitive styles, that is, differences in how we perceive or construe the persons, objects, and situations in

cognitive complexity A cognitive style or way of construing the environment characterized by the ability to perceive differences among people.

cognitive simplicity A cognitive style or way of construing the environment characterized by a relative inability to perceive differences among people.

our environment. Research on cognitive styles was derived from the REP Test and focuses on the concept of **cognitive complexity**.

A person's degree of cognitive complexity can be determined from the pattern of Xs on the repertory grid. A highly differentiated pattern of Xs indicates cognitive complexity, defined as the ability to discriminate in the process of applying personal constructs to other people. People high in cognitive complexity are able to see variety among people and can easily place a person in many categories.

The other extreme, **cognitive simplicity**, applies when the pattern of Xs on the repertory grid is the same or highly similar for each construct. This indicates that the person is less capable of perceiving differences when judging other people. Persons high in cognitive simplicity are likely to place others in only one or two categories, unable to see much variety.

Research has confirmed personality differences in terms of cognitive style. People high in cognitive complexity are better able to make predictions about other people's behavior. They more readily recognize differences between themselves and others, are more empathic, and deal better with inconsistent information in construing others than do people high in cognitive simplicity (Crockett, 1982). Studies of politicians in the United States and England found that conservatives were high in cognitive simplicity, whereas moderates and liberals displayed higher levels of cognitive complexity (Tetlock, 1983, 1984).

In Kelly's theory, cognitive complexity is the more desirable and useful cognitive style. Our goal in developing a construct system is to reduce uncertainty by being able to predict or anticipate what people will do. This gives us a guide for our own behavior. People with a more complex cognitive style will be more successful at this task than will people with a simpler cognitive style. Therefore, cognitive style is an important dimension of personality.

Studies show that cognitive complexity increases with age in that adults generally possess greater cognitive complexity than children do. However, age is not a complete explanation for cognitive complexity; many adults still possess cognitive simplicity. Much depends on the level of complexity of our childhood experiences. Adults high in cognitive complexity typically had more diverse experiences in childhood. Their parents were less authoritarian and more likely to grant autonomy than were parents of adults high in cognitive simplicity (Sechrest & Jackson, 1961).

A Final Commentary

Kelly developed a unique personality theory that did not derive from or build on other theories. It emerged from his interpretation, his own construct system, of data provided by his clinical practice. It is a personal view, and its originality parallels its message, that we are capable of developing the framework for our life.

Kelly's system has been criticized on several points. It focuses on intellectual and rational aspects of human functioning to the exclusion of emotional aspects. Kelly's image of a person rationally constructing the present and future, forming and testing hypotheses, and making predictions as the basis for behavior does not coincide with the everyday experiences of clinical psychologists who see more extreme examples of human behavior. Kelly's rational being seems to be an ideal that exists in the abstract but not in reality. Although Kelly did not deal explicitly with emotions, he recognized them as personal constructs, similar in their formation to other constructs.

We noted that Sigmund Freud's view of personality derived from his exposure to neurotic, middle-class Viennese patients, who presented him with a distorted, unrepresentative sample of human nature. Other theorists have been similarly criticized. Kelly's viewpoint was also unrepresentative, limited largely to Midwestern young adults in the process of defining a construct system that would help them cope with college life.

Kelly's theory, like many others, leaves unanswered questions. Each of us is able to construe events in a unique way, but why does one person construe an event in one way while another person construes the same event in a different way? What process or mechanism accounts for the difference? A person makes choices about defining or extending the construct system. What determines whether to opt for security or for adventure, for the safer or the riskier alternative?

Although personal construct theory has not gained wide acceptance in the United States, psychologists in Europe, Canada, and Australia are carrying on Kelly's work. In the mid-1980s, the Centre for Personal Construct Psychology was established in England to train clinicians in Kelly's psychotherapeutic techniques and to promote applications of the theory. The *International Journal of Personal Construct Psychology* began publication in the late 1980s, and in 1990 the first volume of the series *Advances in Personal Construct Psychology* appeared. Kelly's work is not as popular in the United States for several reasons. First, many psychologists see it as too different from prevailing ideas. Personality psychologists typically think in terms of the familiar concepts of motivation and emotion, unconscious forces, drives, and needs, which form no part of Kelly's system. Second, Kelly published few books, articles, or case studies, devoting most of his time to clinical work and to training graduate students. The writing style of his two major books is scholarly, not intended for the public or for the therapist seeking explanations of human passions and emotions, loves and hatreds, fears and dreams. Such was not the style of the man or his theory.

Kelly recognized the limitations of his program and made no pretense of setting forth a finished theory. Just as an individual's constructs change in light of new experiences, so Kelly expected the personal construct theory to change with further research and application. His contributions have been recognized with honors from the profession and from former students, and his theory is one of the most unusual to appear in a century of theorizing about the nature of the human personality.

Chapter Summary

Kelly viewed people as similar to scientists who construct hypotheses and test them against reality. A personal construct is a way of looking at events. Kelly's fundamental postulate states that psychological processes are directed by the ways we anticipate events and construe our world. The theory includes 11 corollaries. Kelly presented an optimistic image of human nature that depicts us as rational beings with free will, capable of directing our destiny. We are not bound by constructs developed at one stage of life or by past experiences, unconscious conflicts, and biological instincts. Our goal is to define a set of constructs that enables us to predict events.

Kelly assessed personality by accepting a person's words at face value, by having the person write a self-characterization sketch, and by the Role Construct Repertory (REP) Test. The REP Test uncovers dichotomies important in a person's life, revealing the pattern of personal constructs. Fixed role therapy involves having a client act out the constructs of an imaginary person to demonstrate how to implement new constructs that will be more effective than old ones. REP Test research has shown that constructs are stable over time. The validity of the test depends on the skill of the psychologist interpreting it. The test has been used for market research, performance appraisal, and vocational counseling.

People high in cognitive complexity are better able to predict the behavior of others. They more readily recognize differences between themselves and others, are more empathic, deal better with inconsistent information in construing others, and experienced greater complexity in childhood than did people high in cognitive simplicity.

Kelly's work has been criticized for omitting familiar concepts such as motivation and emotion, for focusing on the rational aspects of human functioning to the exclusion of emotional aspects, and for relying on an unrepresentative sample of subjects.

Review Questions

1. How does Kelly's approach to personality differ from the other approaches we have discussed?

2. What is the relationship between Kelly's cognitive theory and modern cognitive psychology?

3. How might Kelly's theory have been influenced by the kinds of clients he treated?

4. What is Kelly's definition of the term *construct?* Why must constructs be dichotomous?

5. What factors influence the ways we anticipate those events that are similar to past events?

6. How do we choose between the two alternatives offered by a construct?

7. What is a construct's range of convenience? In your construct system, what is the range of convenience for the construct *cheerful versus sad?*

8. What mechanism did Kelly propose to account for changes in a construct's range of convenience?

9. How is it possible to hold incompatible or inconsistent constructs?

10. What is Kelly's position on the issue of free will versus determinism?

11. What is the purpose of the Role Construct Repertory Test? What does research using the REP Test show about the cognitive styles of simplicity and complexity?

12. What is fixed role therapy?

Suggested Readings

Epting, F. R. (1984). *Personal construct counseling and psychotherapy*. New York: Wiley. The first major textbook on the principles of Kelly's personality theory and their clinical applications.

Fransella, F. (1995). *George Kelly*. London: Sage. Describes Kelly's life and the development and applications of personal construct theory. Reviews the concept of constructive alternativism using Kelly's personality as an example.

Jancowicz, A. D. (1987). Whatever became of George Kelly? Applications and implications. *American Psychologist, 42*, 481–487. Published on the 20th anniversary of Kelly's death, this article reviews and assesses the impact of Kelly's work.

Kelly, G. A. (1969). *Clinical psychology and personality: The selected papers of George Kelly*. New York: Wiley. Selections from Kelly's writings, edited by Brendan Maher. See Chapter 2, "The Autobiography of a Theory," for Kelly's description of the impact of his personal experiences on the development of his theory.

Thompson, G. G. (1968). George Alexander Kelly: 1905–1967. *Journal of General Psychology, 79*, 19–24. Reviews and assesses Kelly's life and work.

Winter, D. A. (1992). *Personal construct psychology in clinical practice: Theory, research and applications*. London: Routledge. Reviews 35 years of clinical work with personal construct theory and compares this approach to diagnosis and treatment with other major approaches.

The Behavioral Approach

In Chapter 1 we briefly considered the work of John B. Watson, the founder of behaviorism. His behaviorist psychology focused on overt behavior, on the experimental subjects' responses to external stimuli. This natural-science approach to psychology, based on careful experimental research and the precise quantification of stimulus and response variables, became immensely popular in the 1920s and remained a dominant force in psychology for more than 60 years.

Watson's behaviorism had no place for conscious or unconscious forces because they could not be seen, manipulated, or measured. Watson believed that whatever might be happening inside an organism— a person or an animal—between the presentation of the stimulus and the elicitation of the response had no value, meaning, or use for science. Why? Because scientists could not perform experiments on such internal conditions. In the behavioral approach, there-fore, we find no reference to anxiety, drives, motives, needs, or defense mechanisms, processes invoked by most other personality theorists. To behaviorists, personality is merely an accumulation of learned responses to stimuli, sets of overt behaviors, or habit systems. Personality refers only to what can be objectively observed and manipulated.

The behavioral approach to personality is represented here by the work of B. F. Skinner, whose ideas follow the Watsonian tradition. Skinner rejected as irrelevant any alleged internal forces or processes. His sole concern was with overt behavior and the external stimuli that shape it. Skinner attempted to understand what we call "personality" through laboratory research with rats and pigeons rather than clinical work with patients. His ideas have proved useful in the clinical setting, however, through the application of behavior-modification techniques.

It is the environment which must be changed.

—B. F. Skinner

F O U R T E E N

B. F. Skinner

Rats, Pigeons, and an Empty Organism

B. F. Skinner did not offer a personality theory that can easily be contrasted and compared with others discussed in this textbook. In fact, he did not offer a personality theory at all, nor does his research deal specifically with personality. His work attempted to account for all behavior, not just personality, in factual, descriptive terms. "You can't get results by sitting around and theorizing about the inner world. I want to say to those people: get down to the facts" (Skinner quoted in Hall, 1967, p. 70). Skinner argued that psychologists must restrict their investigations to facts, to what they can see, manipulate, and measure in the laboratory. That means an exclusive emphasis on the overt responses a subject makes and nothing more. Skinner's contention was that psychology is the science of behavior, of what an organism does.

We noted that this approach was popularized by John B. Watson. The spirit of Watson's behaviorist revolution in psychology, which influenced the young Skinner, lives on in Skinner's work, though in a more sophisticated and fully developed version. Skinner's study of behavior is the antithesis of the psychoanalytic, trait, lifespan, cognitive, and humanistic approaches, differing not only in subject matter but in methodology and aims.

In explaining personality, most other theorists look inside the person for clues. The causes, motives, and drives—the forces that direct our development and behavior—originate within each of us. In contrast, Skinner made no reference to internal, subjective states to account for behavior. Unconscious influences, defense mechanisms, traits, and other driving forces cannot be seen, and therefore have no place in a scientific psychology. They have no more value for science than the old theological concept of the soul. Skinner did not deny the existence of internal forces, only their usefulness for science. Skinner applied similar reasoning to physiological processes, which are not overtly observable and so have no relevance for science. He said, "The inside of the organism is irrelevant either as the site of physiological processes or as the locus of mentalistic activities" (quoted in Evans, 1968, p. 22).

And, indeed, he saw no need to look inside the organism for some form of inner activity. To Skinner, human beings are "empty organisms," by which he meant that there is nothing inside us that can be summoned to explain behavior in scientific terms. In the person-situation debate, then, Skinner was clearly and exclusively on the side of the environment or situation.

Another way Skinner differed from other theorists is in his choice of experimental subject. Some personality theorists focus on emotionally disturbed persons, others on normal or average individuals. At least one based his theory on the best and brightest people. Although Skinner's ideas about behavior have been applied to people, the research for his behavioral approach used rats and pigeons. What can we learn from pigeons about the human personality? Remember that Skinner's interest was in behavioral responses to stimuli, not in childhood experiences or adult feelings. Responding to stimuli is something animals do well, sometimes better than people do. Skinner admitted that human behavior is more complex than animal behavior but suggested that the differences are in degree, not in kind. He believed that the fundamental processes are similar. And because a science must proceed from simple to complex, the more elemental processes should be studied first. Thus, he chose animal behavior because it is simpler than human behavior.

Skinner's work has been of monumental importance in American psychology. The American Psychological Foundation awarded him its Gold Medal, and the American Psychological Association gave him the Distinguished Scientific Contribution Award (1958). The citation reads: "Few American psychologists have had so profound an impact on the development of psychology and on promising younger psychologists." Skinner's first book on behaviorism, *The Behavior of Organisms: An Experimental Analysis* (Skinner, 1938), was described as one of the few books to truly change the nature of the field (Thompson, 1988). Skinner also received the U.S. National Medal of Science and appeared on the cover of *Time,* headlined as the world's most famous American psychologist. His controversial 1971 book, *Beyond Freedom and Dignity,* became a best seller and made him a celebrity.

> Skinner was, for a short period, the hottest item on national and big-city talk shows. . . . Within a month, millions of Americans had read or heard about B. F. Skinner and *Beyond Freedom and Dignity.* He was "completely swamped" by mail, telephone calls, and visits. . . . Strangers often asked to shake his hand in restaurants. He had, as one writer noted, "acquired the celebrity of a movie or TV star." (Bjork, 1993, p. 192)

Skinner's work has had wide practical applications. He invented an automatic baby-tending device and was responsible for promoting the use of teaching machines. He published a successful novel that offers a program for behavioral control of human society. Therapeutic techniques derived from his research are being applied in clinical settings to treat a variety of disorders including psychoses, mental retardation, and autism. His behavior-modification techniques are used in schools, businesses, correctional institutions, and hospitals.

The Life of Skinner (1904–1990)

B.F. Skinner

B. F. Skinner was born in Susquehanna, Pennsylvania, the older of two sons; his brother died at the age of 16. His parents were hardworking people who instilled in their children clear rules of proper behavior. "I was taught to fear God, the police, and what people will think" (Skinner, 1967, p. 407). His mother never deviated from her strict standards. Her method of control was to say "tut tut." Skinner's grandmother made certain that he understood the punishments of Hell by pointing out the red-hot coals in the parlor stove. Skinner's father contributed to his son's moral education by teaching him the fate that befell criminals. He showed Skinner the county jail and took him to a lecture about life in a notorious New York state prison.

Skinner's autobiography contains many references to the impact of these childhood warnings on his adult behavior. He wrote of visiting a cathedral and taking care to avoid stepping on the gravestones set in the floor; as a child he had been instructed that such behavior wasn't proper. These and other instances made it clear to Skinner that his adult behaviors were determined by the rewards and punishments (the "reinforcements") he had received as a child. Thus, his system of psychology and his view of people as "complex system[s] behaving in lawful ways" reflected his own early life experiences (Skinner, 1971, p. 202).

Also prophetic of his view of people as machines that operate predictably were the many hours he spent constructing mechanical devices such as wagons, seesaws, carousels, slingshots, model airplanes, and a steam cannon that shot potato and carrot plugs over neighboring houses. Skinner also worked on a perpetual-motion machine, which perpetually failed. His interest in animal behavior also derived from childhood. He made pets of turtles, snakes, toads, lizards, and chipmunks. A flock of performing pigeons at a county fair fascinated him. The pigeons raced onstage, pulled a fire engine up to a burning building, and shoved a ladder against it. One trained pigeon wearing a firefighter's red hat climbed to an upper-story window to rescue a stranded pigeon. Skinner later would train pigeons to play Ping-Pong and to guide a missile to its target.

Finding an Identity

Skinner majored in English at Hamilton College and after graduation expected to become a novelist. Encouraged by favorable comment on his work from the eminent poet Robert Frost, Skinner built a study in the attic of his parents' home in Scranton, Pennsylvania, and sat down to write. The results were disastrous. He read, listened to the radio, played the piano, and built ship models while waiting for inspiration. He considered seeing a psychiatrist but his father argued that it would be a waste of money. Skinner was 22 years old and apparently a failure at the only thing he wanted to do.

He later referred to that time as his dark year, what Erik Erikson would call an identity crisis. Skinner's occupational identity as a writer, which he carefully constructed during his college years and which Robert Frost reinforced, had collapsed and took with it his sense of self-worth. He left Scranton for New York City's Greenwich Village but found he could not write there either. Worse, in his view, was that several women spurned his proclaimed love for them, leaving him so upset that he branded one woman's initial on his arm, where it remained for years (Skinner, 1983a).

Just when Skinner believed he had lost all hope, he discovered an identity that suited him, and to which he would cling for the rest of his life. He decided that since writing had failed him (rather than the other way around), he would study human behavior by the methods of science rather than the methods of fiction. He read books by Ivan Pavlov and John B. Watson, and chose to become a behaviorist. Thus, his self-image and identity became secure.

Skinner entered Harvard University in 1928 to study psychology. He had never taken a course in the field but earned his Ph.D. in three years. His choice of behaviorism led him to reject the feelings and emotions he had tried to draw on as a writer. One historian of psychology noted:

[There are] essential differences between a career devoted to writing poetry and fiction and one devoted to promoting the cause of behaviorism. The former requires commitment to such intrapsychic processes as inspiration, intuition, free association, the stream of consciousness, and the participation of the unconscious, as well as considering fantasies and feelings important parts of one's being. The latter denies it all—makes fantasies and feelings, indeed the entire intrapsychic domain, recede into a background of (to use Skinner's favorite term) "pre-scientific" notions, while attention is focused on observable behavior and the operations necessary to record, predict, and control it effectively. (Mindess, 1988, p. 105)

Psychic processes appear in Skinner's work only as objects of derision.

With postdoctoral fellowships, Skinner stayed at Harvard until 1936. He then taught at the University of Minnesota and Indiana University, returning to Harvard in 1947. In his 40s Skinner experienced a period of depression, which he resolved by returning to his failed identity as a writer. Skinner projected his emotional and intellectual discontent onto the protagonist of a novel, *Walden Two,* letting the character vent his personal and professional frustrations (Skinner, 1948). The book, which is still in print, has sold more than 2 million copies. It describes a society in which all aspects of life are controlled by positive reinforcement, which is the basic principle of Skinner's system of psychology.

Well into his 80s, Skinner continued to work with enthusiasm and dedication. He regulated his habits, recording his daily work output and the average time spent per published word (two minutes). Thus he became a living example of his definition of humans as complex systems behaving in lawful ways. He constructed in his house a personal Skinner box, a controlled environment that provided positive reinforcement. He slept in a yellow plastic tank large enough to contain a mattress, bookshelves, and a small television set. He went to bed each night at 10:00, slept for three hours, worked at his desk for an hour, slept three more hours, and rose at 5:00 a.m. for three more hours of work before walking a mile to his office at Harvard. He administered positive reinforcement each afternoon by listening to music. He once commented to a friend that he was cited in the psychology literature more frequently than Freud was. When asked if that had been his goal, Skinner said, "I thought I might make it" (quoted in Bjork, 1993, p. 214).

Reinforcement: The Basis of Behavior

Skinner's approach to behavior, simple in concept, is based on thousands of hours of well-controlled research. His fundamental idea is that behavior can be controlled by its consequences, that is, by what follows the behavior. Skinner believed that an animal or a human could be trained to perform virtually any act and that the type of reinforcement that followed the behavior would be responsible for determining it. Thus, whoever controls the reinforcers has the power to control human behavior, in the way an experimenter can control the behavior of a laboratory rat.

Respondent Behavior

respondent behavior
Responses made to or elicited by specific environmental stimuli.

Skinner distinguished between two kinds of behavior: respondent behavior and operant behavior. **Respondent behavior** involves a response made to or elicited by a specific stimulus. A reflexive behavior such as a knee jerk is an example of respondent behavior. A stimulus is applied (a tap on the knee) and the response occurs (the leg jerks). This behavior is unlearned. It occurs automatically and involuntarily. We do not have to be trained or conditioned to make the appropriate response.

Animals can be conditioned by reinforcing them with food when they exhibit desired behaviors.

classical conditioning

positive reinforcement

reinforcement The act of strengthening a response by adding a reward, thus increasing the likelihood that the response will be repeated.

extinction The process of eliminating a behavior by withholding reinforcement.

At a higher level is respondent behavior that is learned. This learning, called conditioning, involves the substitution of one stimulus for another. The concept originated in the work of the Russian physiologist Ivan Pavlov in the early 1900s. Later, Pavlov's ideas on conditioning were adopted by John B. Watson as the basic research method for behaviorism.

Working with dogs, Pavlov discovered that they would salivate to neutral stimuli such as the sound of their keeper's footsteps. Previously, the salivation response had been elicited by only one stimulus, the sight of food. Intrigued by this observation, Pavlov studied the phenomenon systematically. He sounded a bell shortly before feeding a dog. At first the dog salivated only in response to the food and not to the bell because the bell had no meaning. However, after a number of pairings of the bell followed by the food, the dog began to salivate at the sound of the bell. Thus, the dog had been conditioned, or trained, to respond to the bell. The dog's response shifted from the food to what previously had been a neutral stimulus.

This classic experiment by Pavlov demonstrated the importance of **reinforcement.** The dogs would not learn to respond to the bell unless they were rewarded for doing so. In this example the reward was food. Pavlov then formulated a fundamental law of learning: A conditioned response cannot be established in the absence of reinforcement. The act of reinforcing a response strengthens it and increases the likelihood that the response will be repeated.

However, an established conditioned response will not be maintained in the absence of reinforcement. Consider a dog conditioned to respond to the sound of a bell. Every time the bell rings, the dog salivates. Then the experimenter stops presenting food after sounding the bell. The dog hears the bell and nothing happens—no more food, no more reinforcement or reward. With successive ringings of the bell, the dog's salivary response decreases in frequency and intensity until no response occurs at all. This process is called **extinction.** The response has been wiped out or extinguished because reinforcers or rewards for it were no longer provided.

FIGURE 14.1   *A simple operant-conditioning apparatus*

Operant Behavior

operant behavior
Behavior emitted
spontaneously or
voluntarily that operates
on the environment to
change it.

Respondent behavior depends on reinforcement and is related directly to a physical stimulus. Every response is elicited by a specific stimulus. To Skinner, respondent behavior was less important than **operant behavior.** We are conditioned to respond directly to many stimuli in our environment, but not all behavior can be accounted for in this way. Much human behavior appears to be spontaneous and cannot be traced directly to a specific stimulus. Such behavior is emitted rather than elicited by a stimulus. It involves acting in a way that appears to be voluntary rather than reacting involuntarily to a stimulus to which we have been conditioned.

The nature and frequency of operant behavior will be determined or modified by the reinforcement that follows the behavior. Respondent behavior has no effect on the environment. In Pavlov's experiment, the dog's salivary response to the ringing bell did nothing to change the bell or the reinforcer (the food) that followed. In contrast, operant behavior operates on the environment and, as a result, changes it.

The Skinner Box and the Operant-Conditioning Process

 **operant
conditioning**

operant conditioning
The procedure by which a
change in the
consequences of a
response will affect the
rate at which the response
occurs.

To illustrate the **operant-conditioning** process, let us follow the progress of a rat in Skinner's operant-conditioning apparatus, also known as the Skinner box (see Figure 14.1). When a food-deprived rat is placed in the box, its behavior at first is spontaneous and random. The rat is active, sniffing, poking, and exploring its environment. These behaviors are emitted, not elicited; in other words, the rat is not responding to any specific stimulus in its environment.

At some time during this activity, the rat will depress a lever or bar located on one wall of the Skinner box, causing a food pellet to drop into a trough. The rat's behavior (pressing the lever) has operated on the environment and, as a result, has changed it. How? The environment now includes a food pellet. The food is a rein-forcer for the behavior of depressing the bar. The rat begins to press the bar more of-ten. What happens? It receives more food—more reinforcement—and so presses the bar even more frequently. The rat's behavior is now under the control of the rein-forcers. Its actions in the box are less random and spontaneous because it is spend-ing most of its time pressing the bar, and eating.

If we put the rat back in the box the next day, we can predict its behavior and we can control its bar-pressing actions by presenting or withholding the reinforcers or by presenting them at a different rate. Withholding the food extinguishes oper-ant behavior in the same way that it extinguishes respondent behavior. If the unre-inforced behavior no longer works, in that it no longer brings a reward, after a while it will stop. Thus, the person who controls the reinforcers controls the subjects' behavior.

Skinner believed that most human and animal behavior is learned through oper-ant conditioning. Consider how babies learn. An infant initially displays random, spontaneous behaviors, only some of which are reinforced (rewarded with food or hugs or toys, for example) by parents, siblings, or caregivers. As the infant grows, the positively reinforced behaviors, those of which the parents approve, will persist, whereas those of which the parents disapprove will be extinguished or discontinued. The concept is the same with the rat in the Skinner box. Behaviors that work (press-ing the bar to obtain food) are displayed frequently, and behaviors that do not work are not repeated. Thus, the organism's behavior operates on the environment. And in turn, the environment, in the form of reinforcement, operates on the organism's behavior.

You can see how powerful reinforcement can be in determining and controlling behavior. Skinner wrote, "Operant conditioning shapes behavior as a sculptor shapes a lump of clay" (1953, p. 91). If that lump of clay, that organism, needs the reinforcer badly enough, there is virtually no limit to how its behavior can be shaped—by an experimenter with a food pellet, a puppy owner with a dog biscuit, a mother with a smile, a boss with a pat on the back, or a government with a promise.

From infancy on we display many behaviors and those that are reinforced will strengthen and form patterns. This is how Skinner conceived of personality, as a pat-tern or collection of operant behaviors. What other psychologists called neurotic or abnormal behavior was nothing more mysterious to Skinner than the continued per-formance of undesirable behaviors that somehow have been reinforced.

Having demonstrated how behavior could be modified by continuous reinforce-ment—that is, by presenting a reinforcer after every response—Skinner decided to consider how behavior would change if he varied the rate at which it was reinforced. What led Skinner to this issue was a practical concern, a matter of expediency more than intellectual curiosity. It started with the food pellets used to reinforce the rats in his research. Today, packages of food pellets can be purchased from commercial pro-ducers, but in the 1930s, experimenters and their unlucky graduate students spent many tedious hours compounding food pellets by hand. Skinner's laboratory needed at least 800 pellets a day to keep the experiments going. One Saturday afternoon Skinner discovered that unless he spent the evening making pellets, the supply would be exhausted by Monday. Even for a dedicated researcher, a weekend spent with the pellet machine was not an attractive prospect. An alternative occurred to him: Why did he have to reinforce the rat on a continuous reinforcement schedule, that is, every time it made a response? What would happen if he rewarded the rat only once a minute, regardless of how often it pressed the lever for food? The startling result of this line of reasoning was that Skinner and his students spent less time making food pellets. He embarked on a research program that led to his most significant contribution: schedules of reinforcement.

Schedules of Reinforcement

Skinner pointed out that in everyday life outside the psychology laboratory, continuous reinforcement schedules are unlikely. Our behavior is rarely reinforced every time it occurs. A baby is not picked up and cuddled every time he or she cries. Baseball superstars do not hit a home run every time at bat. The bagger in the supermarket does not receive a tip for each bag packed. And your favorite singing group doesn't win a Grammy for every album it records. You can think of many more examples of behaviors that persist even though they are reinforced only occasionally.

reinforcement schedules
Patterns or rates of providing or withholding reinforcers.

After observing that his rats continued to press the bar at a fairly constant rate even when they were not being reinforced for each response, Skinner decided to investigate different **reinforcement schedules** to determine their effectiveness in controlling behavior. Among the rates of reinforcement he tested are the following.

- fixed interval
- fixed ratio
- variable interval
- variable ratio

A *fixed-interval schedule of reinforcement* means that the reinforcer is presented following the first response that occurs after a fixed time interval has elapsed. That interval might be 1 minute, 3 minutes, or any other fixed period of time. The timing of the reinforcement has nothing to do with the number of responses. Whether the rat responds 3 times or 20 times a minute during the fixed time interval, the reinforcer still arrives only after the passage of a given time period and the emission of the correct response.

Many situations operate in accordance with the fixed-interval reinforcement schedule. If your professor gives a midterm and a final examination, he or she is using a fixed-interval schedule. A job in which your salary is paid once a week or once a month operates on the fixed-interval schedule. You are not paid according to the number of items you produce or the number of sales you make (the number of responses) but by the number of hours, days, or weeks that elapse.

Skinner's research showed that the shorter the interval between presentations of the reinforcer, the greater the frequency of response. The response rate declined as the interval between reinforcements lengthened. How frequently reinforcers appeared also affected how quickly the response could be extinguished. The response stopped sooner if the rat had been reinforced continuously and the reinforcement was then stopped, than if the rat had been reinforced intermittently.

A parent's smile of
approval can reinforce
a child's behavior.

In the *fixed-ratio schedule of reinforcement*, reinforcers are given only after the organism has made a specified number of responses. For example, the experimenter could reinforce after every tenth or twentieth response. In this schedule, unlike the fixed-interval schedule, the presentation of reinforcers depends on how often the subject responds. The rat will not receive a food pellet until it emits the required number of responses. This reinforcement schedule brings about a faster rate of responding than does the fixed-interval schedule.

The higher response rate for the fixed-ratio reinforcement schedule also applies to humans. In a job in which your pay is determined on a piece-rate basis, how much you earn depends on how much you produce. The more items you produce, the higher your pay. Your reward is based directly on your response rate. The same is true for a salesperson working on commission. Income depends on the number of products sold; the more sold, the more earned. In contrast, a salesperson on a weekly salary earns the same amount each week regardless of the number of items sold.

But everyday life doesn't always permit a fixed-interval or fixed-ratio reinforcement schedule. Sometimes reinforcers are presented on a variable basis. In the *variable-interval schedule of reinforcement*, the reinforcer might appear after 2 hours in the first instance, after $1\frac{1}{2}$ hours the next time, and after 2 hours and 15 minutes the third time. A person who spends the day fishing might be rewarded, if at all, on a variable-interval basis. The reinforcement schedule is determined by the random appearance of fish nibbling at the bait.

A *variable-ratio schedule of reinforcement* is based on an average number of responses between reinforcers, but there is great variability around that average. Skinner found that the variable-ratio schedule is effective in bringing about high and stable response rates, as the people who operate gambling casinos can happily attest. Slot machines, roulette wheels, horse races, and the state lottery games pay on a variable-ratio reinforcement schedule, an extremely effective means of controlling behavior. Variable reinforcement schedules result in enduring response behaviors that tend to resist extinction. Most everyday learning occurs as a result of variable-interval or variable-ratio reinforcement schedules.

Skinner's research on reinforcement schedules provides an effective technique for controlling, modifying, and shaping behavior. If you are in charge of rats, salespeople, or assembly-line workers, or are trying to train your pet or your child, these operant-conditioning techniques can be useful in bringing about the behaviors you desire.

Successive Approximation: The Shaping of Behavior

In Skinner's original operant-conditioning experiment, the operant behavior (pressing the lever) is a simple behavior that a laboratory rat would be expected to display eventually in the course of exploring its environment. Thus, the chance is high that such a behavior will occur, assuming the experimenter has sufficient patience. It is obvious, however, that animals and humans demonstrate many more complex operant behaviors that have a much lower probability of occurrence in the normal course of events. How are these complex behaviors learned? How can an experimenter or a parent reinforce and condition a pigeon or a child to perform behaviors that are not likely to occur spontaneously?

successive approximation An explanation for the acquisition of complex behavior. Behavior such as learning to speak will be reinforced only as it comes to approximate or approach the final desired behavior.

Skinner answered these questions with the method of **successive approximation,** or shaping (Skinner, 1953). He trained a pigeon in a very short time to peck at a specific spot in its cage. The probability that the pigeon on its own would peck at that precise spot was low. At first, the pigeon was reinforced with food when it merely turned toward the designated spot. Then reinforcement was withheld until the pigeon made some movement, however slight, toward the spot. Next, reinforcement was given only for movements that brought the pigeon closer to the spot. After that, the pigeon was reinforced only when it thrust its head toward the spot. Finally, the pigeon was reinforced only when its beak touched the spot. Although this sounds like a time-consuming process, Skinner conditioned pigeons in fewer than three minutes.

The experimental procedure itself explains the term *successive approximation.* The organism is reinforced as its behavior comes in successive, or consecutive, stages to approximate the final behavior desired. Skinner suggested that this is how children learn the complex behavior of speaking. Infants spontaneously emit meaningless sounds, which parents reinforce by smiling, laughing, and talking. After a while, parents reinforce this babbling in different ways, providing stronger reinforcers for sounds that approximate words. As the process continues, parental reinforcement becomes more restricted, given only for appropriate usage and pronunciation. Thus, the

Parents teach their children acceptable behaviors by reinforcing those activities that approximate the final desired behaviors.

complex behavior of acquiring language skills is shaped by providing differential reinforcement in stages.

Skinner was once responsible for shaping the behavior of the psychoanalyst Erich Fromm, whose comments during a lecture annoyed him.

> Erich Fromm proved to have something to say about almost everything, but with little enlightenment. When he began to argue that people were not pigeons, I decided that something had to be done. On a scrap of paper I wrote [to a colleague] "Watch Fromm's left hand. I am going to shape a chopping motion" . . . [Fromm] gesticulated a great deal as he talked, and whenever his left hand came up, I looked straight at him. If he brought the hand down, I nodded and smiled. Within five minutes he was chopping the air so vigorously that his wristwatch kept slipping out over his hand. (Skinner, 1983a, pp. 150–151)

Superstitious Behavior

superstitious behavior

We know that life is not always as orderly or well controlled as events in the psychology laboratory. Sometimes we are reinforced accidentally after we have displayed some behavior. As a result, that behavior, which did not lead to or cause the reinforcement, may be repeated in a similar situation.

Consider an example from football. An offensive lineman for the Tampa Bay (FL) Buccaneers was having a terrible season early in his career. He asked his roommate to switch beds so that he could sleep closer to the bathroom. Immediately thereafter, his playing improved. For the rest of his career, he insisted on the bed nearest the bathroom door in every motel in which the team stayed. And the NFL kicker who hugged the goal posts before each game? He had done it once before making a successful kick, so because it had worked then, he continued the practice. He told a reporter that he wanted the goal posts to know he loved them and to implore them to stay still when he kicked.

superstitious behavior
Persistent behavior that has a coincidental and not a functional relationship to the reinforcement received.

Skinner called this phenomenon **superstitious behavior** and demonstrated it in the laboratory. A hungry pigeon was placed in the operant-conditioning apparatus and reinforced every 15 seconds on a fixed-interval schedule. It is likely that the pigeon would be doing something, displaying some behavior or activity, when the reinforcing food pellet was presented. It might be turning, raising its head, strutting, hopping, or standing still. Whatever behavior was being emitted at the moment of reward would be reinforced.

Skinner found that a single reinforcement was powerful enough to lead the pigeon to repeat the accidentally reinforced behavior more frequently for a while, which increased the probability that another food pellet would appear while the same behavior was being shown. And with short intervals between reinforcers, superstitious behaviors are learned quickly. Like the football players in the examples above, the superstitious behaviors offered by the pigeon have no functional relationship to the reinforcers. The connection is unintentional. In humans, such behaviors may persist throughout life and require only occasional reinforcement to sustain them.

The Self-Control of Behavior

Behavior is controlled and modified by variables that are external to the organism. There is nothing inside us—no process, drive, or other internal activity—that determines behavior. However, although these external stimuli and reinforcers are responsible for shaping and controlling behavior, we have the ability to use what Skinner called **self-control**, which he described as acting to alter the impact of external events. Skinner did not mean acting under the control of some mysterious "self." He suggested that to some extent we can control the external variables that determine our behavior.

self-control The ability to exert control over the variables that determine our behavior.

Skinner proposed several self-control techniques. In *stimulus avoidance*, for example, if the music from your roommate's stereo annoys you and interferes with your studying, you could leave the room and go to the library, removing yourself from an external variable that affects your behavior. By avoiding a person or situation that makes you angry, you reduce the control that person or situation has over your behavior. Similarly, alcoholics can act to avoid a stimulus that controls their behavior by not allowing liquor to be kept in their home.

Through the technique of *self-administered satiation*, we exert control to cure ourselves of bad habits by overdoing the behavior. Smokers who want to quit can chain-smoke for a period of time, inhaling until they become so disgusted, uncomfortable, or ill that they quit. This technique has been successful in formal therapeutic programs designed to eliminate smoking. The *aversive stimulation* technique of self-control involves unpleasant or repugnant consequences. Obese people who want to lose weight declare their intention to their friends. If they do not keep their resolution, they face the unpleasant consequences of personal failure, embarrassment, and criticism. In *self-reinforcement*, we reward ourselves for displaying good or desirable behaviors. A teenager who agrees to strive for a certain grade point average or to care for a younger brother or sister might reward himself or herself by buying concert tickets or new clothes.

To Skinner, then, the crucial point is that external variables shape and control behavior. But sometimes through our own actions we can modify the effects of these external forces.

Applications of Operant Conditioning

behavior modification A form of therapy that applies the principles of reinforcement to bring about desired behavioral changes.

Psychologists have applied Skinner's operant conditioning techniques to modify human behavior in clinical, business, and educational settings. **Behavior modification** has been successful with children and adults, with the mentally healthy and the mentally disturbed, and with individual as well as group behaviors.

Token Economy Programs

token economy A behavior-modification technique in which tokens, which can be exchanged for valued objects or privileges, are awarded for desirable behaviors.

The classic application is the **token economy**. In the pioneering study, a ward of more than 40 psychotic female patients in a state mental institution was treated as a giant Skinner box (Ayllon & Azrin, 1968). The patients could no longer be helped by conventional treatments. They had been institutionalized for a long time and were unable to care for themselves.

In this setting, the patients were offered opportunities to work at jobs, usually performed by paid hospital attendants, for which they would receive tokens. The tokens functioned like money, hence the term *token economy*. Like people outside the institution, the patients could buy goods and privileges to improve the quality of life. With a certain number of tokens they could purchase candy, cigarettes, lipstick, gloves, and newspapers. By paying with tokens, they could attend a movie on the ward, walk around the hospital grounds, or upgrade to a better room. The most expensive privileges, requiring 100 tokens, were an escorted trip into town and a private meeting with a social worker. A private meeting with a psychologist was worth only 20 tokens.

What kinds of behaviors did the patients have to emit to be reinforced and receive tokens? If they bathed at the time designated, brushed their teeth, made their bed, combed their hair, and dressed properly they earned a token for each activity. They would be paid up to 10 tokens for each work period in the hospital kitchen or laundry or for helping to clean the ward, run errands, or take other patients for walks. The tasks may seem simple to us, but before the token economy program began, these patients were considered helpless and aimless.

The conditioning worked dramatically. Not only did the patients groom themselves and clean their surroundings, but they also busied themselves at a variety of tasks. They interacted socially with one another and with the staff and assumed some responsibility for patient care. Their self-esteem improved markedly, and they became less dependent.

A note of caution about these impressive results: Token economies have been found to be effective only within the setting in which they are implemented. In general, the modified behaviors do not carry over to life outside the institution. Reinforcement must be continued if the desired behavior changes are to persist. When tokens are no longer provided, reinforced behaviors usually revert to their original state (Kazdin & Bootzin, 1972; Repucci & Saunders, 1974). However, if caregivers are trained to reward desirable behaviors with reinforcers such as smiles, praise, hugs, and other signs of affection, then behaviors conditioned in the institutional token-economy situation are more likely to be continued in the home setting (Kazdin, 1989).

behavior modification

Behavior Modification Programs

Operant-conditioning techniques have been applied to problems in business and industry. Behavior modification programs at major manufacturers, financial institutions, and government agencies have been shown to reduce absenteeism, lateness, and abuse of sick-leave privileges, and to lead to improvements in job performance and safety. The techniques can also be used to teach low-level job skills. Reinforcers used in business include pay, job security, recognition from supervisors, perks and status within the company, and the opportunity for personal growth. No attempt is made to deal with any alleged anxieties, repressed traumas, or unconscious motivating forces. The focus is on changing overt behavior, defining the nature of the appropriate reinforcers, and determining their optimal rate of presentation to modify behavior.

Punishment and Negative Reinforcement

punishment The application of an aversive stimulus following a response in an effort to decrease the likelihood that the response will recur.

Most operant-conditioning applications involve positive reinforcement rather than **punishment**. The token-economy patients were not punished for failing to behave appropriately. Instead, they were reinforced when their behavior changed in positive ways. Skinner said that punishment was ineffective in changing behavior from undesirable to desirable or from abnormal to normal. Positive reinforcement administered for desirable behaviors is much more effective than punishment.

> What's wrong with punishments is that they work immediately, but give no long-term results. The responses to punishment are either the urge to escape, to counterattack, or a stubborn apathy. These are the bad effects you get in prisons or schools, or wherever punishments are used. (quoted in Goleman, 1987)

negative reinforcement

negative reinforcement The strengthening of a response by the removal of an aversive stimulus.

Negative reinforcement is not the same as punishment. A negative reinforcer is an aversive or noxious stimulus, the removal of which is rewarding. In the laboratory or classroom, an operant-conditioning situation can be established in which the unpleasant stimulus (such as a loud noise or an electric shock) will continue until the subject emits the desired response. As with positive reinforcement, the environment

FIGURE 14.2   *Skinner's image of human nature*

changes as a consequence of the behavior; in this case, the noxious stimulus will disappear.

We can see examples of negative reinforcement in everyday situations. A person may stop smoking to avoid the aversive stimulus of a nagging spouse or colleague. The aversive stimulus (the nagging) should cease when the desirable behavior (not lighting a cigarette in the home or office) is displayed. Skinner opposed using noxious stimuli to modify behavior, noting that the consequences were not as predictable as with positive reinforcement. Also, negative reinforcement does not always work whereas positive reinforcement is more consistently effective.

Questions About Human Nature

Skinner's position is clear on the nature-nurture issue (see Figure 14.2). People are primarily products of learning, shaped more by external variables than genetic factors. We may infer that childhood experiences are more important in Skinner's view than are later experiences because our basic behaviors are formed in childhood. This does not mean that behavior cannot change in adulthood. What is learned in childhood can be modified, and new behavior patterns can be acquired at any age. The success of behavior modification programs verifies that assertion. Skinner's belief that behavior is shaped by learning also leads us to conclude that each person is unique. Because we are shaped by experience—and we all have different experiences, particularly in childhood—no two people will behave in precisely the same way.

Skinner did not address the issue of an ultimate and necessary goal. He made no reference to overcoming inferiority, reducing anxiety, or striving for self-actualization. Such motives assume internal, subjective states, which Skinner did not accept. Any indication of a life goal in Skinner's work seems to be societal, not individual. In his novel *Walden Two* and in other writings, he discussed his notion of the ideal human society. He stated that individual behavior must be directed toward the type of society that has the greatest chance of survival.

On the issue of free will versus determinism, people function like machines, in lawful, orderly, predetermined ways. Skinner rejected all suggestions of an inner being or autonomous self that determines a course of action or chooses to act freely and spontaneously.

From Skinner's scholarly writings to his popular novel about a utopian society based on operant conditioning his message is the same: Behavior is controlled by reinforcers. In a sense, this means that it is pointless to blame or punish people for their actions. A dictator who orders the mass killing of thousands of people, or a serial killer who murders a dozen, can no more be held responsible for their actions than can a driverless car that plunges down a hill. Both operate in lawful, predictable ways, controlled by external variables.

Are we left with a pessimistic conception of people as helpless and passive robots, unable to play an active role in determining their behavior? That is not Skinner's complete view. Despite his belief that behavior is controlled by external stimuli and reinforcers, we are certainly not victims. Although controlled by our environment, we are responsible for designing that environment. Our buildings, cities, consumer goods, factories, and government institutions are the result of human fabrication. So, too, are our social systems, languages, customs, and recreations. We constantly change our environment, often to our advantage. When we do so, we are acting as both controller and controlled. We design the controlling culture, and we are products of that culture.

> We may not be free agents, but we can do something about our lives, if we would only rearrange the controls that influence our behavior. . . . I am not trying to change people. All I want to do is change the world in which they live. (Skinner quoted in Bjork, 1993, pp. 16, 233)

The world may impose limits on our freedom to bring about change. In making changes, we will be guided and sometimes restricted by situations that provided positive reinforcement for us in the past. In acting to change our environment we will seek greater opportunities for positive reinforcement and in the process modify our own behavior. Skinner left us with a paradox, an image of person-as-machine capable of altering the environmental conditions that guide the machine's behavior.

Assessment in Skinner's Theory

Skinner did not use the typical assessment techniques favored by other theorists. There was no place in his work for free association, dream analysis, or projective techniques. Because he was not dealing directly with personality, he really had no interest in assessing it. He did, however, assess behavior. Note that in the application of his behavior modification techniques, it is necessary first to assess specific behaviors, both desirable and undesirable. Also to be assessed are the environmental factors that serve as reinforcers and that can be manipulated to alter behavior. No behavior can be modified appropriately without such prior assessment. Skinner's approach to assessing behavior is called **functional analysis** and it involves three aspects of behavior.

functional analysis An approach to the study of behavior that involves assessing the frequency of a behavior, the situation in which it occurs, and the reinforcers associated with it.

1. the frequency of the behavior
2. the situation in which the behavior occurs
3. the reinforcement associated with the behavior

Unless these factors have been evaluated, it is not possible to plan and implement a behavior modification program.

Consider a functional analysis for cigarette smokers who want to break the smoking habit. The smokers are asked to keep an accurate record of the number of cigarettes they smoke each day and the situations in which the cigarettes are smoked. Does smoking occur in a particular place or at a certain time? In the presence of others or alone? After meals or while driving? And what are the reinforcers? Most smokers smoke more frequently in the presence of certain stimuli. Identifying these stimuli is necessary because modifying them should lead to a change in the smoking behavior.

Direct Observation of Behavior

Three approaches to assessing behavior are direct observation, self-reports, and physiological measurements. Many behaviors can be assessed through direct observation. Usually, two or more people conduct the observation to assure accuracy and reliability. For example, in a classic report of a behavior modification situation, a woman sought treatment for her 4-year-old son whose behavior was considered unruly (Hawkins, Peterson, Schweid, & Bijou, 1966). Two psychologists observed the mother and child in their home to evaluate the nature and frequency of the child's undesirable behaviors, when and where they occurred, and the reinforcers the child received for the behaviors.

Nine undesirable behaviors were identified, including kicking, throwing things, biting, and pushing a sibling. The psychologists observed that the mother reinforced the child by giving him toys or food when he behaved badly. Her intention was to get him to stop misbehaving. Instead, she was rewarding him and thus reinforcing the misbehavior. The direct observation assessment lasted 16 hours, but without it the psychologists would not have known exactly which undesirable behaviors to try to eliminate or what reinforcers the child expected.

With a comprehensive direct-observation program, it is possible to plan a course of behavior modification. In this case the psychologists instructed the mother to use attention and approval as reinforcers when the child behaved in positive ways and never to reward him when he displayed one of the nine observed undesirable behaviors. The frequency of the undesirable behaviors, as determined in the direct observation assessment, provided a baseline against which to compare behavior during and after treatment.

Self-Reports of Behavior

Another approach to assessing behavior is the self-report technique carried out through interviews and questionnaires. The person observes his or her own behavior and reports on it to the examiner. Several self-report questionnaires have been published. For example, a questionnaire may assess the extent of a person's fear in situations such as driving a car, going to the dentist, or speaking in public.

Questionnaires for assessing behavior are similar in format to self-report inventories that assess personality. The difference lies in the way they are interpreted, as described by the **sign-versus-sample approach**. In the sign approach, which is used to assess *personality*, the psychologist infers the existence of character types, traits, or unconscious conflicts from the individual's responses. For example, if a person indicates that he or she is afraid of being in an elevator, this fear can be interpreted as a *sign*, or an indirect symptom, of some underlying motive or conflict.

In the sample approach, which is used to assess *behavior*, questionnaire responses are interpreted as directly indicative of a *sample* of behavior. No attempt is made to draw inferences or conclusions about the person's character or personality traits. The behavior itself and the stimulus associated with it are the important things. There is no concern with subjective motives, childhood experiences, or other mental processes.

Although Skinner did not use self-report personality inventories, he did agree, while in his 20s, to take several paper-and-pencil personality tests administered at a scientific meeting. He described the results as follows: He had better judgment than 95 percent of his colleagues who were tested, was more extraverted than 57 percent, and was more easily annoyed than 65 percent. Years later he took two projective tests, the Rorschach Inkblot Test and the Thematic Apperception Test. He gave his responses to the inkblots so fast that the examiner could not keep up with him, and he reported that he had nothing to say in response to the TAT pictures (Skinner, 1979).

sign-versus-sample approach In the sign approach to assessing *personality*, character types, traits, or unconscious conflicts are inferred from questionnaires and other self-report inventories. In the sample approach to assessing *behavior*, test responses are interpreted as directly indicative of present behavior, not of traits, motives, or childhood experiences.

Physiological Measurements of Behavior

Physiological assessments of behavior include heart rate, muscle tension, and brain waves. By recording such measurements, it is possible to evaluate the physiological effects of various stimuli. The measures can also be used to confirm the accuracy of information obtained by other assessment methods. For example, a person who is too embarrassed to reveal in an interview or on a questionnaire a fear of being in an elevator might exhibit a change in heart rate or muscle tension when asked in general about elevators.

Whatever assessment technique is chosen to assess behavior in different stimulus situations, the focus remains on what people do, not on what might have motivated them to do it. The ultimate goal is to modify behavior, not to change personality.

Research in Skinner's Theory

You can see that Skinner's assessment methods differ radically from those used by other theorists we have discussed. His research methods also diverged from mainstream experimental psychology. The usual procedure is to study large groups of animal or human subjects and to statistically compare their average responses. In contrast, Skinner preferred the intensive study of a single subject. He argued that data on the average performance of groups is of little value in dealing with a particular case. A science that deals with averages provides little information to help in understanding the unique individual.

Skinner believed that valid and replicable results could be obtained without statistical analysis, as long as sufficient data were collected from a single subject under well-controlled experimental conditions. The use of large groups of subjects forced the experimenter to deal with average behavior. The resulting data could not reflect individual response behavior and individual differences in behavior. Thus, Skinner favored the idiographic rather than the nomothetic approach.

reversal experimental design A research technique that involves establishing a baseline, applying an experimental treatment, and withdrawing the experimental treatment to determine whether the behavior returns to its baseline value or whether some other factor is responsible for the observed behavior change.

Skinner's single-subject experiments follow the **reversal experimental design**, which proceeds in four stages.

• The first stage involves establishing a *baseline*. The subject's behavior (the dependent variable) is observed to determine the normal rate of response before beginning the experimental treatment.

• The second stage is the *conditioning*, or experimental stage, when the independent variable is introduced. If this variable affects behavior, it will produce a notable change from the subject's baseline response rate.

• The third stage, called *reversal*, determines whether some factor other than the independent variable is responsible for the observed behavior change. During this stage, the independent variable is no longer applied. If the behavior returns to its baseline rate, then the researcher can conclude that the independent variable was responsible for the difference observed during the conditioning stage. If the behavior does not return to the baseline rate, then some factor other than the independent variable affected the behavior.

• The baseline, conditioning, and reversal stages are sufficient for most laboratory experiments. When the procedure is applied to behavior modification, a *reconditioning* stage is added. The independent variable is reintroduced, assuming it had been effective in changing behavior. Without the fourth stage, subjects in behavior modification programs would remain in reversal with behavior at their baseline level, unchanged by a treatment shown to be effective. It would be unethical not to restore the effective treatment.

Skinner and his followers conducted thousands of operant-conditioning experiments on topics such as reinforcement schedules, language acquisition, behavior shaping, superstitious behavior, and behavior modification. The results have been highly supportive of Skinner's ideas.

A Final Commentary

Skinner's approach has been criticized on several points. Those who oppose determinism find much to dislike in Skinner's views. The humanistic psychologists, who believe that people are more complex than machines or rats or pigeons object to Skinner's image of human nature. They argue that the exclusive emphasis on overt behavior ignores uniquely human qualities such as conscious free will. There has been criticism of the type of subject and the simplicity of the situations in Skinner's experiments. He made assertions and predictions about human behavior and society—about social, economic, religious, and cultural issues—with considerable confidence. But can we extrapolate from a pigeon pecking at a disc to a person functioning in the real world? The gap seems too vast to permit broad generalizations. Many aspects of human behavior cannot be reduced meaningfully to the level at which Skinner conducted his research.

Skinner's belief that all behaviors are learned was challenged by a former student. More than 6,000 animals of 38 species were conditioned to perform various behaviors for television commercials and tourist attractions. The animals included pigs, raccoons, chickens, hamsters, porpoises, whales, and cows. The animals displayed a tendency toward **instinctive drift** by substituting instinctive behaviors for the behaviors that had been reinforced, even when the instinctive behaviors interfered with receiving food.

instinctive drift The substitution of instinctive behaviors for behaviors that had been reinforced.

In one example, pigs and raccoons were conditioned to pick up a coin, carry it some distance, and deposit it in a toy bank (a *piggy* bank, of course). When the animals had deposited a certain number of coins, they were given food as a reinforcer. They learned the desired behaviors quickly,

> but after having performed the sequence nicely for some time, they began to engage in undesirable behaviors, at least from the viewpoint of the trainers. Pigs would stop on their way [to the bank], bury the coin in the sand, and take it out with their snout; raccoons would spend a lot of time handling the coin, with their well-known washing-like movements. This was at first amusing, but eventually it became time-consuming and would make the whole show appear very imperfect to the spectator. Commercially, it was a disaster. (Richelle, 1993, p. 68)

What had happened was that instinctive behavior—such as the pigs' rooting in the dirt and the raccoons' rubbing their paws as if washing their hands—came to take precedence over the learned behavior, even though it meant a delay in receiving the reinforcement (the food). The trainers published an article on the phenomenon and with Skinner's encouragement called it "The Misbehavior of Organisms" (Breland & Breland, 1961). This was a parody of the title of Skinner's groundbreaking book, *The Behavior of Organisms* (1938).

Skinner ignored most of the criticism his work received. He told an interviewer about one critic's book review, "I read a bit of it and saw that he missed the point. . . . There are better things to do with my time than clear up their misunderstandings" (quoted in Rice, 1968). When asked how he dealt with being misunderstood so frequently, he said, "I find that I need to be understood only three or four times a year" (quoted in Blackman, 1995, p. 126).

Skinner was a potent force in 20th-century American psychology. He shaped the field perhaps more than any other individual. In a survey dealing with the relative importance of more than 150 events in the history of psychology, Skinner's ideas and the behavior modification approach are ranked first and second (Gilgen, 1982). The *Journal of the Experimental Analysis of Behavior*, begun in 1958, publishes research on the behavior of individual subjects. In 1968, the *Journal of Applied Behavior Analysis* was established as an outlet for work on behavior modification techniques. Although Skinner's radical behaviorist position continues to be applied in laboratory, clinical, and organizational settings, it was challenged within the behaviorist framework by the cognitive-oriented positions of Albert Bandura and Julian Rotter (Chapters 15 and 16). In the 1960s, the study of consciousness returned to psychology, leading to a decline in the dominance of Skinnerian behaviorism.

Skinner conceded that his form of psychology lost ground to the cognitive approach (Goleman, 1987). Other psychologists agreed, noting that Skinnerian behaviorism had "fallen from favor among the majority of active workers in the field [and was] often referred to in the past tense" (Baars, 1986, pp. viii, 1). Despite the inroads of cognitive psychology, however, Skinner's position remains influential in many areas, from classrooms to assembly lines, from Skinner boxes to mental institutions. Skinner believed that with operant conditioning he offered a technique to improve human nature and the societies people design.

Chapter Summary

Skinner denied the existence of an entity called *personality* and did not seek causes of behavior within the organism. Mental and physiological processes are not overtly observable, so they have no relevance for science. The causes of behavior are external to the organism. Behavior can be controlled by its consequences, by the reinforcer that follows the behavior. Respondent behavior involves a response elicited by specific environmental stimuli. Conditioning (respondent behavior that is learned) involves substituting one stimulus for another. Pavlov demonstrated the importance of reinforcement. Conditioning will not occur without reinforcement. Operant behavior is emitted and is determined and modified by the reinforcer that follows it. Operant behavior cannot be traced to a specific stimulus; it operates on the environment and changes it. Personality is simply a pattern of operant behaviors.

Reinforcement schedules include fixed interval, fixed ratio, variable interval, and variable ratio. Shaping (successive approximation) involves reinforcing the organism only as its behavior comes to approximate the behavior desired. Superstitious behavior results when reinforcement is presented on a fixed- or variable-interval schedule. Whatever behavior is occurring at the moment of reinforcement will come to be displayed more frequently. Self-control of behavior refers to altering or avoiding certain external stimuli and reinforcers. Other self-control techniques are satiation, aversive stimulation, and self-reinforcement for displaying desirable behaviors.

Behavior modification applies operant-conditioning techniques to real-world problems. Desirable behaviors are positively reinforced; undesirable behaviors are ignored. The token-economy approach rewards desirable behaviors with tokens that can be used to acquire objects of value. Behavior modification deals only with overt behavior and uses positive reinforcement, not punishment. Negative reinforcement involves removing an aversive or noxious stimulus. It is less effective than positive reinforcement.

Skinner's image of human nature emphasizes determinism, uniqueness, the importance of the environment, and the design of a society that maximizes the opportunity for survival. Although people are controlled by the environment, they can exert control by designing that environment properly.

Skinner assessed behavior (not personality) using functional analyses to determine the frequency of the behavior, the situation in which the behavior occurred, and the reinforcers associated with the behavior. Three ways to assess behavior are direct observation, self-report, and physiological measures. Skinner's research was idiographic, focusing on the intensive study of a single subject. His reversal experimental design consists of baseline, conditioning, reversal, and reconditioning stages.

Skinner's system has considerable empirical support but has been criticized for its deterministic view, the simplicity of the experimental situations, the lack of interest in behavior other than response rate, and the failure to consider human qualities that set us apart from rats and pigeons.

Review Questions

1. How does Skinner's approach to personality differ from other approaches we have discussed?

2. Describe Pavlov's classical-conditioning experiment with dogs. How did Pavlov extinguish conditioned responses?

3. What is the difference between respondent behavior and operant behavior?

4. What is the role of reinforcement in modifying behavior? How does reinforcement relate to superstitious behavior?

5. Define positive reinforcement, negative reinforcement, and punishment. According to Skinner, how effective is each technique in modifying behavior?

6. Describe four reinforcement schedules. Which schedule applies to the person who sells computer software on commission? Which schedule applies to the child who is allowed to have an ice-cream cone only occasionally?

7. Explain how a complex behavior such as learning to speak is acquired through successive approximation.

8. Describe techniques for the self-control of behavior.

9. Describe the token-economy approach to behavior modification.

10. Why did Skinner prefer to study the individual case rather than groups of subjects? Describe the stages in a typical Skinnerian experiment with a human subject. Describe a typical Skinnerian experiment with a pigeon as the subject.

11. What was Skinner's position on the nature-nurture issue? On free will versus determinism?

12. What techniques do Skinnerians use to assess human behavior?

13. Discuss the impact of cognitive psychology on Skinnerian behaviorism.

Suggested Readings

Elms, A. C. (1981). Skinner's dark year and *Walden Two*. *American Psychologist, 36,* 470–479. Suggests that Skinner experienced an identity crisis in his youth when he failed as a writer and that writing his novel was a form of therapy when identity issues became important to him again in midlife.

Nye, R. D. (1992). *The legacy of B. F. Skinner: Concepts and perspectives, controversies and misunderstandings.* Pacific Grove, CA: Brooks/Cole. A primer on Skinner's basic concepts and their relevance for behavior in today's world. Examines controversies and misunderstandings surrounding Skinner's views and compares his system with those of Sigmund Freud and Carl Rogers.

Skinner, B. F. (1948). *Walden Two.* New York: Macmillan. Skinner's novel about human values and conduct in a utopian society based on behaviorist principles.

Skinner, B. F. (1976). *Particulars of my life; (1979). The shaping of a behaviorist; (1983). A matter of consequences.* New York: Alfred A. Knopf. Skinner's three-volume autobiography.

Skinner, B. F. (1987). *Upon further reflection.* Englewood Cliffs, NJ: Prentice-Hall. Essays on cognitive psychology, verbal behavior, education, and self-management in old age.

Skinner, B. F. (1987). Whatever happened to psychology as the science of behavior? *American Psychologist, 42,* 780–786. Charges that humanistic psychology, psychotherapy, and cognitive psychology are obstacles in the path of psychology's acceptance of his program for the experimental analysis of behavior.

PART 9

The Social-Learning Approach

The social-learning approach to personality, represented in this section by the works of Albert Bandura and Julian Rotter, is an outgrowth of Skinner's behaviorist approach. Like Skinner, Bandura and Rotter focus on overt behavior rather than on needs, traits, drives, or defense mechanisms. Unlike Skinner, Bandura and Rotter allow for internal cognitive variables that mediate between stimulus and response. Cognitive variables have no place in Skinner's system.

Bandura and Rotter have investigated cognitive variables with a high degree of experimental sophistication and rigor, drawing inferences from careful observations of behavior in the laboratory. They observe the behavior of human subjects in social set-

tings, whereas Skinner dealt with animal subjects in individual settings. Bandura and Rotter agree with Skinner that behavior is learned and that reinforcement is vital to learning, but they differ from Skinner in their interpretation of the nature of reinforcement.

Bandura, Rotter, and Skinner attempted to understand personality through laboratory rather than clinical work, but their principles have been applied in the clinical setting through behavior-modification techniques. Because Bandura and Rotter use cognitive variables, their work reflects and reinforces the cognitive movement in psychology. Their approach has also been called "cognitive behavioral" in recognition of this emphasis.

Virtually every phenomenon that occurs by direct experience can occur vicariously as well—by observing other people and the consequences for them.

—Albert Bandura

F I F T E E N

Albert Bandura

Bandura agrees with Skinner that behavior is learned, but with that point their similarity ends. Bandura criticized Skinner's emphasis on individual animal subjects rather than on human subjects interacting with one another. Bandura's approach is a *social* learning theory that investigates behavior as it is formed and modified in a social context. He argues that we cannot expect data from experiments that involve no social interaction to be relevant to the everyday world, because few people truly function in social isolation.

Although Bandura, like Skinner, recognizes that much learning takes place as a result of reinforcement, he also stresses that virtually all forms of behavior can be learned without directly experiencing any reinforcement. Bandura's approach is also called **observational learning**, indicating the importance in the learning process of observing other people's behavior. Rather than experiencing reinforcement ourselves for each of our actions, we learn through **vicarious reinforcement** by observing the behavior of other people and the consequences of that behavior. This focus on learning by observation or example, rather than always by direct reinforcement, is a distinctive feature of Bandura's theory.

Another feature of Bandura's observational-learning approach is its treatment of internal cognitive or thought processes. Unlike Skinner, Bandura believes that cognitive processes can influence observational learning. We do not automatically imitate the behaviors we see other people displaying. Rather, we make a deliberate, conscious decision to behave in the same way. To learn through example and vicarious reinforcement we must be capable of anticipating and appreciating the consequences of the behaviors we observe. We can regulate and guide our behavior by visualizing or imagining those consequences, even though we have not experienced them ourselves. No direct link exists between stimulus and response or between behavior and reinforcer, as Skinner proposed. Instead, our cognitive processes mediate between the two.

Bandura presents a less extreme form of behaviorism than Skinner. He emphasizes the observation of others as a means of learning, and he considers learning to be mediated by cognitive processes. His theory is based on rigorous laboratory research with normal human subjects in social interaction rather than a rat in a cage or a neurotic person on a couch.

 observational learning

observational learning
Learning new responses by observing the behavior of other people.

vicarious reinforcement
Learning or strengthening a behavior by observing the behavior of others, and the consequences of that behavior, rather than experiencing the reinforcement or consequences directly.

The Life of Bandura (1925–   )

Bandura was born in the province of Alberta, Canada. His high school had 20 students and 2 teachers. During the summer following his graduation, he took a construction job in the wilderness of the Yukon Territory, filling holes in the Alaska Highway. It was a fascinating experience for a bright, inquisitive young person.

> Finding himself in the midst of a curious collection of characters, most of whom had fled creditors, alimony, and probation officers, Bandura quickly developed a keen appreciation for the psychopathology of everyday life, which seemed to blossom in the austere tundra. (Distinguished Scientific Contribution Award, 1981, p. 28)

He attended the University of British Columbia in Vancouver as an undergraduate and earned his Ph.D. in 1952 from the University of Iowa. After a year at the

Wichita, Kansas, Guidance Center, he joined the faculty of Stanford University and has compiled an extensive record of publications. In 1973 he was elected president of the American Psychological Association and in 1980 received its Distinguished Scientific Contribution Award.

Bandura's sense of humor has often been directed at himself. When asked whether he walked to his office or drove his car, he said, "Both, sometimes in the same day." Having driven to work, he would be so absorbed in his ideas that he would absentmindedly walk home, leaving the car in the university parking lot. He once led a group of psychologists to New Orleans to investigate the city's facilities for an APA convention. Colleagues noted, "For a week, all we did was follow Al around and eat shrimp jambalaya" (Kiester & Cudhea, 1974, p. 27). Perhaps the accompanying psychologists received both direct and vicarious reinforcement for modeling their behavior after Bandura's.

Modeling: The Basis of Observational Learning

Bandura's basic idea is that learning can occur through observation or example rather than solely by direct reinforcement. Bandura does not deny the importance of direct reinforcement as a way to influence behavior, but he challenges the notion that behavior can be learned or changed *only* through direct reinforcement. He argues that operant conditioning, in which trial-and-error behavior continues until the person happens upon the correct response, is an inefficient and potentially dangerous way to learn skills such as swimming or driving. A person could drown or crash before finding the correct sequence of behaviors that brings positive reinforcement. To Bandura, most human behavior is learned through example, either intentionally or accidentally. We learn by observing other people and patterning our behavior after theirs.

Bobo Doll Studies

modeling A behavior modification technique that involves observing the behavior of others (the models) and participating with them in performing the desired behavior.

Through **modeling**, by observing the behavior of a model and repeating the behavior ourselves, it is possible to acquire responses that we have never performed or displayed previously and to strengthen or weaken existing responses. Bandura's now-classic demonstration of modeling involves the Bobo doll, an inflatable plastic figure 3 to 4 feet tall (Bandura, Ross, & Ross, 1963).

The subjects in the initial studies were preschool children who watched an adult hit and kick Bobo. While attacking the doll, the adult model shouted, "Sock him in the nose!" and "Throw him in the air!" When the children were left alone with the doll, they modeled their behavior after the example they had just witnessed. Their behavior was compared with that of a control group of children who had not seen the model attack the Bobo doll. The experimental group was found to be twice as aggressive as the control group.

The intensity of the aggressive behavior remained the same in the experimental subjects whether the model was seen live, on television, or as a cartoon character. The effect of the model in all three media was to elicit aggressive behavior, actions

In the Bobo doll studies, children exhibited aggressive behavior after observing an aggressive model.

that were not displayed with the same strength by children who had not observed the models.

Other Modeling Studies

In additional research on the impact of modeling on learning, Bandura compared the behavior of parents of two groups of children (Bandura & Walters, 1963). One group consisted of highly aggressive children, the other of more inhibited children. According to Bandura's theory, the children's behavior should reflect their parents' behavior. The research showed that the parents of the inhibited children were inhibited, and the parents of the aggressive children were aggressive.

Verbal modeling can induce certain behaviors, as long as the activities involved are fully and adequately explained. Verbal modeling is often used to provide instructions, a technique applicable to teaching such skills as driving a car. Verbal instructions are usually supplemented by behavioral demonstrations, such as when a driving instructor serves as a model performing the behaviors involved in driving.

Disinhibition

Research has shown that behaviors a person usually suppresses or inhibits may be performed more readily under the influence of a model (Bandura, 1973, 1986). This

disinhibition The weakening of inhibitions or constraints by observing the behavior of a model.

phenomenon, called **disinhibition**, refers to the weakening of an inhibition or restraint through exposure to a model. For example, people in a crowd may start a riot, breaking windows and shouting, exhibiting physical and verbal behaviors they would never perform when alone. They are more likely to discard their inhibitions against aggressive behavior if they see other people doing so.

The disinhibition phenomenon can influence sexual behavior. In an experiment that demonstrated how sexual responses could be disinhibited by models, a group of male undergraduate college students was shown a film that contained erotic pictures of nude males and females (Walters, Bowen, & Parke, 1963). The students were told that a spot of light would move over the film, indicating the eye movements of a previous subject, to show what parts of the pictures that subject looked at. These alleged eye movements of the previous subject represented the model. For half the subjects, the spot of light concentrated on breasts and genitals. For the other half, the light stayed in the background, as though the model had avoided looking at the naked bodies.

After watching the film, the subjects were shown stills from the movie while their eye movements were recorded. Those subjects whose model was considered uninhibited (who had looked directly at the erotic parts of the bodies) behaved similarly. Those subjects whose model had avoided looking at the nudes spent significantly more time examining the background of the pictures. The researchers concluded that modeling affected the subjects' perceptual responses to the stimuli. In other words, modeling determined not only what the subjects did but also what they looked at and perceived.

The Effects of Society's Models

On the basis of extensive research, Bandura concluded that much behavior—good and bad, normal and abnormal—is learned by imitating the behavior of other people. From infancy on, we develop responses to the models society offers us. Beginning with parents as models, we learn their language and become socialized by the culture's customs and acceptable behaviors. People who deviate from cultural norms have learned their behavior the same way as everyone else. The difference is that deviant persons have followed models the rest of society considers undesirable.

Bandura is an outspoken critic of the type of society that provides the wrong models for its children, particularly the examples of violent behavior that are standard fare on television and in movies and video games. His research clearly shows the effect of models on behavior. If what we see is what we become, then the distance between watching an aggressive animated character and committing a violent act ourselves is not very great.

Among the many behaviors children acquire through modeling are nonrational fears. A child who sees that his or her parents are fearful during thunderstorms or are nervous around strangers will easily adopt these anxieties and carry them into adulthood with little awareness of their origin. Of course, positive behaviors such as strength, courage, and optimism will also be learned from parents and other models. In Skinner's system, reinforcers control behavior; for Bandura, it is the models who control behavior.

Characteristics of the Modeling Situation

Bandura and his associates (Bandura, 1977, 1986) investigated three factors found to influence modeling:

1. the characteristics of the models
2. the characteristics of the observers
3. the reward consequences associated with the behaviors

Characteristics of the models.   The characteristics of the models affect our tendency to imitate them. In real life, we may be more influenced by someone who appears to be similar to us than by someone who differs from us in obvious and significant ways. In the laboratory, Bandura found that although children imitated the behavior of a child model in the same room, a child in a film, and a filmed cartoon character, the extent of the modeling decreased as the similarity between the model and the subject decreased. The children showed greater imitation of a live model than an animated character, but even in the latter instance the modeled behavior was significantly greater than that of the control group that observed no models.

Other characteristics of the model that affect imitation are age and sex. We are more likely to model our behavior after a person of the same sex than a person of the opposite sex. Also, we are more likely to be influenced by models our own age. Peers who appear to have successfully solved the problems we are facing are highly influential models.

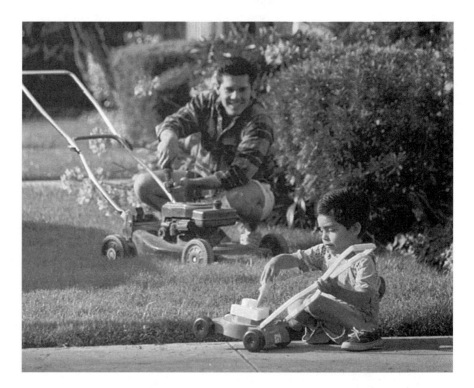

Children tend to imitate the behavior of an adult model of the same sex who is considered high in status.

Status and prestige are also important factors. It was found that pedestrians were much more likely to cross a street against a red light if they saw a well-dressed person crossing than if they saw a poorly dressed person crossing. Television commercials make effective use of high-status, high-prestige models with athletes, rock stars, or movie stars who claim to use a particular product. The expectation is that consumers will imitate their behavior and buy the advertised product.

The type of behavior the model performs affects the extent of imitation. Highly complex behaviors are not imitated as quickly and readily as simpler behaviors. Hostile and aggressive behaviors tend to be strongly imitated, especially by children.

Characteristics of the observers.   The attributes of the observers also determine the effectiveness of observational learning. People who are low in self-confidence and self-esteem are much more likely to imitate a model's behavior than are people high in self-confidence and self-esteem. A person who has been reinforced for imitating a behavior—for example, a child rewarded for behaving like an older sibling—is more susceptible to the influence of models.

The reward consequences associated with the behaviors.   The reward consequences linked to a particular behavior can affect the extent of the modeling and even override the impact of the models' and observers' characteristics. A high-status model may lead us to imitate a certain behavior, but if the rewards are not meaningful to us we will discontinue the behavior and be less likely to be influenced by that model in the future.

Seeing a model receiving reward or punishment for displaying a particular behavior affects imitation. In a Bobo doll study, some of the children watched as the model who hit the Bobo doll was given praise and a soda and candy. Another group of children saw the model receive verbal and physical punishment for the same aggressive behavior. The children who observed the punishment displayed significantly less aggression toward the Bobo doll than did the children who saw the model being reinforced (Bandura, 1965).

Observational Learning Processes

Bandura analyzed the nature of observational learning and found it to be governed by four related mechanisms: attentional processes, retention processes, production processes, and incentive and motivational processes (see Table 15.1).

Attentional Processes

cognitive learning

Observational learning or modeling will not occur unless the subject pays attention to the model. Merely exposing the subject to the model does not guarantee that the subject will be attentive to the relevant cues and stimulus events or even perceive the situation accurately. The subject must perceive the model accurately enough to acquire the information necessary to imitate the model's behavior.

TABLE 15.1   *Observational learning processes*

Attentional processes	Developing our cognitive processes and perceptual skills so that we can pay sufficient attention to a model, and perceiving the model accurately enough, to imitate displayed behavior. *Example:* Staying awake during driver's education class.
Retention processes	Retaining or remembering the model's behavior so that we can imitate or repeat it at a later time; for this, we use our cognitive processes to encode or form mental images and verbal descriptions of the model's behavior. *Example:* Taking notes on the lecture material or the video of a person driving a car.
Production processes	Translating the mental images or verbal symbolic representations of the model's behavior into our own overt behavior by physically producing the responses and receiving feedback on the accuracy of our continued practice. *Example:* Getting in a car with an instructor to practice shifting gears and dodging the traffic cones in the school parking lot.
Incentive and motivational processes	Perceiving that the model's behavior leads to a reward and thus expecting that our learning—and successful performance—of the same behavior will lead to similar consequences. *Example:* Expecting that when we have mastered driving skills, we will pass the state test and receive a driver's license.

Several variables influence attentional processes. In the real world, as in the laboratory, we are more attentive and responsive to some people and situations than to others. Thus, the more closely we pay attention to a model's behavior, the more likely we are to imitate it.

We have mentioned such characteristics as age, status, sex, and the degree of similarity between model and subject. These factors help determine how closely a subject attends to the model. It has also been found that celebrity models, experts, and those who appear confident and attractive command greater attention and imitation than models who lack these attributes. Some of the most effective models in American culture today appear on television. Viewers often focus on them even in the absence of reinforcement.

Attention to modeled behavior varies as a function of the observers' cognitive and perceptual skills and the value of the behavior being modeled. The more highly developed are our cognitive abilities and the more knowledge we have about the behavior being modeled, the more carefully we will attend to the model and perceive the behavior. When observers watch a model doing something they expect to do themselves, they pay greater attention than when the modeled behavior has no personal relevance. Observers also pay closer attention to modeled behavior that produces positive or negative consequences rather than neutral outcomes.

Retention Processes

Subjects must remember significant aspects of the model's behavior in order to repeat it later. To retain what has been attended to, we must encode it and represent it symbolically. These internal retention processes of symbolic representation and image formation are cognitive processes. Thus, Bandura recognizes the importance of cognitive processes in developing and modifying behavior. Recall, for comparison, that Skinner's focus was exclusively on overt behavior.

We retain information about a model's behavior in two ways: through an imaginal internal representational system or through a verbal system. In the imaginal system we form vivid, easily retrievable images while we are observing the model. This common phenomenon accounts for your being able to summon up a picture of the person you dated last week or the place you visited last summer. In observational learning we form a mental picture of the model's behavior and use it as a basis for imitation at some future time.

The verbal representational system operates similarly and involves a verbal coding of some behavior we have observed. For example, during observation we might describe to ourselves what the model is doing. These descriptions or codes can be rehearsed silently, without overtly displaying the behavior. For example, we might talk ourselves through the steps in a complicated skill, mentally rehearsing the sequence of behaviors we will perform later. When we wish to perform the action, the verbal code will provide hints, reminders, and cues. Together, these images and verbal symbols offer the means by which we store observed situations and rehearse them for later performance.

Production Processes

Translating imaginal and verbal symbolic representations into overt behavior requires the production processes, described more simply as *practice*. Although we may have attended to, retained, and rehearsed symbolic representations of a model's behavior, we still may not be able to perform the behavior correctly. This is most likely to occur with highly skilled actions that require the mastery of many component behaviors.

Consider learning to drive a car. We learn fundamental motions from a lecture and from watching a model drive. We may consider the symbolic representations of the model's behavior many times, but at first our translation of these symbols into actual driving behavior will be clumsy. We may shift into the wrong gear or overcorrect the steering. Our observations may not have been sufficient to ensure immediate and skilled performance of the actions. Practice of the proper physical movements, and feedback on their accuracy, is needed to produce the smooth performance of the behavior.

Incentive and Motivational Processes

No matter how well we attend to and retain behaviors we observe or how much ability we have to perform them, we will not do so without the incentive or motivation processes. When incentives are available, observation is more quickly translated into action. Incentives also influence the attentional and retention processes. We may not pay as much attention without an incentive to do so, and when less attention is paid, there is less to retain.

Our incentive to learn is influenced by our anticipation of the reinforcement or punishment for doing so. Seeing that a model's behavior produces a reward or avoids a punishment can be a strong incentive for us to pay attention to, remember, and perform a behavior correctly. The reinforcement is experienced vicariously during our observation of the model, after which we expect our performance of the same behavior to lead to the consequences we saw.

Bandura pointed out that although reinforcement can facilitate learning, reinforcement is not required for learning to occur. Many factors other than the reward consequences of the behavior determine what we attend to, retain, and rehearse. For example, loud sounds, bright lights, and exciting videos may capture our interest even though we may not have received any reinforcement for paying attention to them. Bandura's research showed that children watching a model on television imitate the model's behavior regardless of whether they have been promised a reward. Therefore, reinforcement can assist in modeling but is not vital to it. When reinforcement occurs, it can be given by another person, experienced vicariously, or administered by oneself.

The Self

In Bandura's approach to personality, the self is not some psychic agent that determines or causes behavior. Rather, the self is a set of cognitive processes and structures concerned with thought and perception. Two important aspects of the self are self-reinforcement and self-efficacy.

Self-Reinforcement

self-reinforcement
Administering rewards or punishments to oneself for meeting, exceeding, or falling short of one's own expectations or standards.

Self-reinforcement is as important as reinforcement administered by others, particularly for older children and adults. We set personal standards of behavior and achievement. We reward ourselves for meeting or exceeding these expectations and standards and we punish ourselves for our failures. Self-administered reinforcement can be tangible such as a new pair of gym shoes or a car, or it can be emotional such as pride or satisfaction from a job well done. Self-administered punishment can be expressed in shame, guilt, or depression about not behaving the way we wanted to. Self-reinforcement appears conceptually similar to what other theorists call *conscience* or *superego,* but Bandura denies that it is the same.

A continuing process of self-reinforcement regulates much of our behavior. It requires internal standards of performance, subjective criteria or reference points against which we evaluate our behavior. Our past behavior may become a reference point for evaluating present behavior and an incentive for better performance in the future. When we reach a certain level of achievement, it may no longer challenge, motivate, or satisfy us, so we raise the standard and require more of ourselves. Failure to achieve may result in lowering the standard to a more realistic level.

People who set unrealistic performance standards—who observed and learned behavioral expectations from unusually talented and successful models—may continue to try to meet those excessively high expectations despite repeated failures. Emotionally, they may punish themselves with feelings of worthlessness and depression. These self-produced feelings can lead to self-destructive behaviors such as alcohol and drug abuse or a retreat into a fantasy world.

We learn our initial set of internal standards from the behavior of models, typically our parents and teachers. Once we adopt a given style of behavior, we begin a lifelong process of comparing our behavior with theirs.

self-efficacy

self-efficacy Our feeling of adequacy, efficiency, and competence in coping with life.

Self-Efficacy

How well we meet our behavioral standards determines our **self-efficacy**. In Bandura's system, self-efficacy refers to feelings of adequacy, efficiency, and competence in coping with life. Meeting and maintaining our performance standards enhances self-efficacy; failure to meet and maintain them reduces it.

Another way Bandura described self-efficacy was in terms of our perception of the control we have over our life.

> People strive to exercise control over events that affect their lives. By exerting influence in spheres over which they can command some control, they are better able to realize desired futures and to forestall undesired ones. The striving for control over life circumstances permeates almost everything people do because it can secure them innumerable personal and social benefits. The ability to affect outcomes makes them predictable. Predictability fosters adaptive preparedness. Inability to exert influence over things that adversely affect one's life breeds apprehension, apathy, or despair. (Bandura, 1995, p. 1)

People low in self-efficacy feel helpless, unable to exercise control over life events. They believe any effort they make is futile. When they encounter obstacles, they quickly give up if their initial attempt to deal with a problem is ineffective. People who are extremely low in self-efficacy will not even attempt to cope because they are convinced that nothing they do will make a difference. Why, they ask, should they even try? Low self-efficacy can destroy motivation, lower aspirations, interfere with cognitive abilities, and adversely affect physical health.

People high in self-efficacy believe they can deal effectively with events and situations. Because they expect to succeed in overcoming obstacles, they persevere at tasks and often perform at a high level. These people have greater confidence in their abilities than do persons low in self-efficacy, and they express little self-doubt. They view difficulties as challenges instead of threats and actively seek novel situations. High self-efficacy reduces fear of failure, raises aspirations, and improves problem solving and analytical thinking abilities.

Sources of information about self-efficacy. Our judgment about our self-efficacy is based on four sources of information:

1. performance attainment
2. vicarious experiences
3. verbal persuasion
4. physiological and emotional arousal

The most influential source of efficacy judgments is *performance attainment*. Previous success experiences provide direct indications of our level of mastery and competence. Prior achievements demonstrate our capabilities and strengthen our feelings of self-efficacy. Prior failures, particularly repeated failures in childhood, lower self-efficacy.

Short-term failures in adulthood can lower self-efficacy. In one study, 60 college students were given a cognitive task. Ratings of item difficulty and feedback indicated that they performed either very well or very poorly. Self-report measures of their self-efficacy expectations for future tasks showed that persons who believed they had performed well on the cognitive task had a high self-efficacy expectancy for future performance. Those who thought they had performed poorly had a low expectation about their future performance (Sanna & Pusecker, 1994).

Vicarious experiences—seeing other people perform successfully—strengthen self-efficacy, particularly if the people we observe are similar in abilities. In effect, we are saying, "If they can do it, so can I." In contrast, seeing others fail can lower self-efficacy: "If they can't do it, neither can I." Therefore, effective models are vital in influencing our feelings of adequacy and competence. These models also show us appropriate strategies for dealing with difficult situations.

Verbal persuasion, which means reminding people that they possess the ability to achieve whatever they want to achieve, can enhance self-efficacy. This may be the most common of the four informational sources and one frequently offered by parents, teachers, spouses, coaches, friends, and therapists who say, in effect, "You can do it." To be effective, verbal persuasion must be realistic. It is probably not the best advice to encourage someone 5 feet tall to play professional basketball when other sports, such as martial arts, might be more appropriate.

A fourth source of information about self-efficacy is *physiological* and *emotional arousal*. How fearful or calm do we feel in a stressful situation? We often use this type of information as a basis for judging our ability to cope. We are more likely to believe we will master a problem successfully if we are not agitated, tense, or bothered by headaches. The more composed we feel, the greater our self-efficacy. Whereas the higher our level of physiological and emotional arousal, the lower our self-efficacy. The more fear, anxiety, or tension we experience in a given situation, the less we feel able to cope.

Bandura concluded that certain conditions increase self-efficacy:

1. Exposing people to success experiences by arranging reachable goals increases performance attainment.
2. Exposing people to appropriate models who perform successfully enhances vicarious success experiences.
3. Providing verbal persuasion encourages people to believe they have the ability to perform successfully.
4. Strengthening physiological arousal through proper diet, stress reduction, and exercise programs increases strength, stamina, and the ability to cope.

In his research Bandura applied these conditions to enhance self-efficacy in a variety of situations. He has helped subjects learn to play musical instruments, relate better to persons of the opposite sex, master computer skills, give up cigarette smoking, and conquer phobias and physical pain.

Developmental Stages of Modeling and Self-Efficacy

Childhood

In infancy, modeling is limited to immediate imitation. Infants have not yet developed the cognitive capacities (the imaginal and verbal representational systems) needed to imitate a model's behavior at some time after observing it. In infancy it is necessary for the modeled behavior to be repeated several times after the infant's initial attempt to duplicate it. Also, the modeled behavior must be within the infant's range of sensorimotor development. By about age 2, children have developed sufficient attentional, retention, and production processes to begin imitating behavior some time after the observation rather than immediately.

The behaviors we find reinforcing, and thus choose to imitate, will change with age. Younger children are reinforced primarily by physical stimuli such as food, affection, or punishment. Older children associate positive physical reinforcers with signs of approval from significant models and unpleasant reinforcers with signs of disapproval. Eventually these rewards or punishments become self-administered.

Self-efficacy also develops gradually. Infants begin to develop self-efficacy as they attempt to exercise greater influence over their physical and social environments. They learn about the consequences of their own abilities such as their physical prowess, social skills, and language competence. These abilities are in almost constant use acting on the environment, primarily through their effects on parents. Ideally, parents are responsive to their growing child's activities and attempts to communicate, and will provide stimulating surroundings that permit the child the freedom to grow and explore.

These early efficacy-building experiences are centered on the parents. Parental behaviors that lead to high self-efficacy in children differ for boys and girls. Studies have shown that high self-efficacy men had, when they were children, warm relationships with their fathers. Mothers were more demanding than fathers, expecting higher levels of performance and achievement. In contrast, high self-efficacy women experienced, as children, pressure from their fathers for high achievement (Schneewind, 1995).

The significance of parental influence diminishes as the child's world expands and admits additional models such as siblings, peers, and other adults. Like Adler, Bandura considered birth order within the family to be important. He argued that first-born children and only children have different bases for judging their own abilities than do later-born children. Also, siblings of the same sex are likely to be more competitive than are siblings of the opposite sex, a factor also related to the development of self-efficacy. Among playmates, children who are the most experienced and successful at tasks and games serve as high-efficacy models for other children. Peers provide comparative reference points for appraising one's own level of achievement.

Teachers influence self-efficacy judgments through their impact on the development of cognitive abilities and problem-solving skills, which are vital to efficient adult functioning. Children often rate their own competence in terms of their teachers' evaluations of them. In Bandura's view, schools that use ability groupings undermine self-efficacy and self-confidence in students assigned to the lower groups.

Competitive practices such as grading on a curve also doom poor achievers to average or low grades.

Adolescence

The transitional experiences of adolescence involve coping with new demands and pressures, from a growing awareness of sex to the choice of college and career. Adolescents must establish new competencies and appraisals of their abilities. Bandura noted that the success of this stage typically depends on the level of self-efficacy established during the childhood years.

Adulthood

Bandura divided adulthood into two periods, young adulthood and the middle years. Young adulthood involves adjustments such as marriage, parenthood, and career advancement. High self-efficacy is necessary for successful outcomes of these experiences. People who are low in self-efficacy will not be able to deal adequately with these situations and are likely to fail to adjust.

Studies show that adult women who feel high in self-efficacy about their parenting skills are likely to promote self-efficacy in their children. Women who believe they are good parents are less subject to despondency and emotional strain in their role as parent than are women low in self-efficacy (Olioff & Aboud, 1991; Teti & Gelfand, 1991). Other research showed that high self-efficacy mothers who work outside the home experience significantly less physical and emotional strain from work-family conflicts than do women low in self-efficacy (Bandura, 1995).

The middle years of adulthood are also stressful as people reevaluate their careers and their family and social lives. As we confront our limitations and redefine our goals, we must reassess our skills and find new opportunities for enhancing our self-efficacy.

Old Age

Self-efficacy reassessments in old age are difficult. Declining mental and physical abilities, retirement from active work, and withdrawal from social life force a new round of self-appraisal. A lowering of self-efficacy can further affect physical and mental functioning in a kind of self-fulfilling prophecy. For example, reduced self-confidence about sexual performance can lead to a reduction in sexual activity. Lower physical efficacy can lead to fatigue and a curtailing of physical activities. If we no longer believe we can do something we used to enjoy and do well, then we may not even try. To Bandura, self-efficacy is the crucial factor in determining success or failure throughout the entire life span.

Behavior Modification

behavior modification

Bandura's goal in developing his social-cognitive theory was to modify or change those learned behaviors that society considers undesirable or abnormal. Like Skinner's approach to therapy, Bandura's focuses on external aspects, those inappropriate or destructive behaviors, in the belief that they are learned, just as all behaviors are learned. Bandura does not attempt to deal with underlying unconscious conflicts. It is the behavior or symptom, rather than any presumed internal neurosis, that is the target of the social-learning approach.

Fears and Phobias

If modeling is the way we learn our behaviors originally, then it should also be an effective way to relearn or change behavior. Bandura applied modeling techniques to eliminate fears and other intense emotional reactions. In one early study, children who were afraid of dogs observed a child of the same age playing with a dog (Bandura, Grusec, & Menlove, 1967). While the subjects watched from a safe distance, the model made progressively bolder movements toward the dog. The model petted the dog through the bars of a playpen then went inside the pen and played with the dog. The observers' fear of dogs was considerably reduced as a result of this observational learning situation.

In a classic study of snake phobia, Bandura and his associates eliminated an intense fear of snakes in adult subjects (Bandura, Blanchard, & Ritter, 1969). The subjects watched a film in which children, adolescents, and adults made progressively closer contact with a snake. At first the filmed models handled plastic snakes, then touched live snakes, and finally let a large snake crawl over their body. The phobic subjects were allowed to stop the film whenever the scenes became too threatening. Gradually, their fear of snakes was overcome.

A technique called *guided participation* involves watching a live model and then participating with the model. For example, to treat a snake phobia, subjects watch through an observation window while a live model handles a snake. The subjects enter the room with the model and observe the handling of the snake at close range. Wearing gloves, subjects are coaxed into touching the middle of the snake while the model holds the head and tail. Subjects eventually come to touch the snake without gloves.

Modeling has been shown to be effective even in the absence of an observable model. In *covert modeling*, subjects are instructed to imagine a model coping with a feared or threatening situation; they do not actually see a model. Covert modeling has been used to treat snake phobias and social inhibitions.

You may not think that a fear of snakes is so terrible, but overcoming this fear brought about significant changes in the subjects' ability to cope with life, even for those who never encountered snakes. In addition to bolstering self-esteem and self-efficacy, eliminating a snake phobia changed personal and work habits. One subject was able to wear a necklace for the first time; previously she had not been able to do so because necklaces reminded her of snakes. A realtor treated successfully for snake phobia was able to increase his income because he no longer feared visiting properties in rural areas. Many other phobics treated by modeling therapy were freed from nightmares about snakes.

Phobias restrict our daily life. For example, many people who fear spiders react with rapid heartbeat, shortness of breath, and vomiting even from seeing a picture of a spider. Phobics doubt their self-efficacy in these fear-provoking situations and have little confidence in their ability to deal with the source of the phobia. To relieve people of these fears expands their environment and increases their self-efficacy.

Modeling therapy, particularly using film and video techniques, offers several practical advantages. Complex behaviors can be seen as a whole. Extraneous behaviors can be edited out so that the subject's time is spent viewing only relevant behaviors. Films can be repeated with many patients and used by several therapists simultaneously. Modeling techniques can also be used with groups, saving time and money in treating people with the same problem. The approach has been effective with phobias, obsessive-compulsive disorders, and sexual dysfunctions, and the positive effects have been reported to last for years.

Modeling techniques have been shown to affect our ability to tolerate pain. Male college students performing a pain-inducing isometric exercise were shown a videotape of models doing the same exercise. Some of the models appeared to tolerate the pain well, while others did not. Subjects who saw the pain-tolerant models continued to exercise for a significantly longer period of time and reported significantly less discomfort than did subjects whose models seemed more adversely affected by the pain. In addition, those subjects who viewed pain-intolerant models experienced the onset of pain sooner during the exercise period as well as an accelerated heart rate (Symbaluk, Heth, Cameron, & Pierce, 1997).

Considerable research has been conducted on self-efficacy during and after behavior modification therapy. The results have shown that as the subjects' self-efficacy improved during treatment, they were increasingly able to deal with the source of the fear. It was the therapeutic procedure itself that enhanced self-efficacy.

Anxiety

We noted that many behaviors can be modified through the modeling approach. We will consider two instances: fear of medical treatment and test anxiety.

Fear of medical treatment.   Some people have such an intense fear of medical situations that they are prevented from seeking treatment. One early study dealt with children who were scheduled for surgery and had never been in a hospital before. They were divided into two groups: an experimental group that watched a film about a boy's experience in the hospital, and a control group that saw a film about a boy taking a trip (Melamed & Siegel, 1975). The child in the hospital film was an exemplary model. Despite some initial anxiety, he coped well with the doctors and the medical procedures.

The children's anxiety was assessed by several techniques including direct observation of behavior, responses on self-report inventories, and physiological measures. These assessments were made the night before surgery and were repeated a few weeks later. The results showed that the modeling film had been effective in reducing anxiety. Subjects who had seen the hospital film had fewer behavior problems after hospitalization than did subjects in the control group.

Similar procedures have been used to reduce fear of hospitalization in adults as well as fear of dental treatment. One study involved a medical procedure considered so stressful that more than 80 percent of patients initially refused to undergo it or quit it prematurely (Allen, Danforth, & Drabman, 1989). Subjects who watched a video of a model having the procedure and describing how he coped with his distress were more likely to complete the treatment with less anxiety and a shorter hospital stay.

test anxiety

Test anxiety.   For some college students, test anxiety is so serious that their examination performance does not accurately reflect their knowledge of the material being tested. In the classic research, a sample of college students was divided into groups based on their personality test scores: those high in test anxiety and those low in test anxiety (Sarason, 1975b). Some of the students saw a filmed model talking about her anxiety when taking tests and her ways of dealing with it. Other students saw a film of the same model who talked about test anxiety but not about coping mechanisms. Under a third condition, students watched the filmed model talking about other college activities. The subjects were given a list of nonsense syllables to memorize and were tested on their ability to recall them. The results showed that subjects high in test anxiety were most strongly affected by the model who talked about coping mechanisms. They performed significantly better on the recall test than did high-anxiety subjects who had been exposed to the other two conditions.

Ethical Issues in Behavior Modification

Although the results of behavior modification are impressive, the techniques have drawn criticism from educators, politicians, and some psychologists. They have suggested that behavior modification exploits people, manipulating and controlling them against their will. Bandura believes these charges are misleading. Behavior modification does not occur without the client's awareness. Indeed, self-awareness and self-regulation are vital for any program of changing or relearning behaviors. Thus, modification techniques are not effective unless the person is able to understand what behaviors are being reinforced. Further, the clients themselves decide what they want to change. They are not being controlled by anyone else. People come to a therapist to eliminate specific fears and anxieties that inhibit their ability to function or cope with daily life. Bandura emphasized that the client-therapist relationship is a contract between two consenting individuals, not a relationship between a sinister master-controller and a spineless puppet.

Bandura also noted that far from manipulating or enslaving, modeling techniques actually increase personal freedom. People who are afraid to leave the house or who have a compulsion to wash their hands continually are not truly free. They are living within the constraints imposed by their phobic or compulsive behavior. Those constraints allow little choice. Removing them through behavior modification increases freedom and the opportunity for personal growth. Many behavior modification techniques have derived from Bandura's work. They have become increasingly popular alternatives to psychoanalysis and other therapeutic approaches.

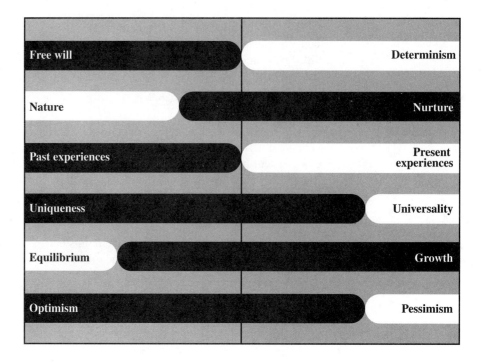

FIGURE 15.1   *Bandura's image of human nature*

Questions About Human Nature

reciprocal determinism
The idea that behavior is controlled or determined by the individual, through cognitive processes, and by the environment, through external social stimulus events.

triadic reciprocality The idea that behavior is determined through the interaction of behavioral, cognitive, and environmental or situational variables.

Bandura's position is clear on the issue of free will versus determinism (see Figure 15.1). Behavior is controlled by the person through the cognitive processes, and by the environment through external social situations. Bandura calls this view **reciprocal determinism.** He noted that people are neither "powerless objects controlled by environmental forces nor free agents who can become whatever they choose. Both people and their environments are reciprocal determinants of each other" (1977, p. vii). He later introduced the notion of **triadic reciprocality**, in which three factors—behavior, cognitive processes, and environmental variables—interact (Bandura, 1986).

Although our behavior is influenced by external social and environmental forces, we are not helpless with respect to them. Our reactions to stimuli are self-activated in accordance with our learned expectations. Following Bandura's rules for observational learning, we observe and interpret the potential effects of our actions and determine which behaviors are appropriate for a given situation. We encode and represent these external events symbolically and anticipate that a certain behavior will bring a certain response. Thus, we choose and shape our behavior to gain reinforcement and avoid punishment.

This viewpoint accepts self-awareness, self-reinforcement, and other internal forms of the regulation of behavior. Reinforcement does not automatically change behavior. When it does effect a change, it is usually because the individual is aware of what is being reinforced and expects the same reward for behaving that way again. Some degree of self-direction interacts with past and present events. Thus, we are influenced by external forces and in turn guide the extent and direction of such influences. The notion of self-direction of behavior represents an optimistic view of human nature. Bandura believes that individuals create their own environments. He suggests that abnormal behaviors, which he sees as little more than bad habits, can be changed by behavior modification techniques.

On the nature-nurture issue, Bandura proposes that most behaviors (except basic reflexes) are learned and that genetic factors play a minor role. However, he recognizes that hereditary factors such as body type, physical maturation, and appearance can influence the reinforcers people receive, particularly in childhood. For example, clumsy, unattractive children will receive different reinforcers than children who are graceful and attractive.

Childhood experiences are important in Bandura's theory. Childhood learning may be more influential than learning in adulthood. Our internal performance standards, which affect our self-efficacy, are established in childhood, along with a set of ideal behaviors. However, childhood experiences can be unlearned later in life, and new performance standards and behaviors may be substituted. We are not captives of the reinforcers we received in our early years. Because at least some behavior results from experience, it may be inferred that Bandura accepts the uniqueness of personality. Also, our ultimate and necessary goal in life is to set realistic performance standards to maintain an adequate level of self-efficacy.

Assessment in Bandura's Theory

Like Skinner, Bandura focuses on behavior rather than on internal motivating variables. He did not use assessment measures such as free association, dream analysis, or projective techniques. Unlike Skinner, Bandura accepted the operation of cognitive variables. It is these cognitive variables, as well as behavior, that can be assessed.

For example, in the modeling study we described involving children about to undergo surgery, assessment techniques included direct observation, self-report inventories, and physiological measurements. In studies of self-efficacy, behavioral and cognitive variables were assessed quantitatively. Self-efficacy with regard to phobias was assessed by the subjects' self-ratings of the number of tasks on a behavioral-avoidance test they expected to be able to complete. College students' test anxiety was assessed by personality inventories. Thus, the assessment of behavioral and cognitive variables is important in the social-learning approach to personality.

Research in Bandura's Theory

Bandura favors well-controlled laboratory investigations in the rigorous tradition of experimental psychology. We noted his use of experimental and control groups and the precise measurement of independent and dependent variables. He studies large subject groups and compares their average performance by statistical analysis. The subjects he has selected have shown diverse behavioral disorders, such as phobias, alcoholism, fetishism, and sexual dysfunctions. The ages of the subjects range from preschool through adult. Thus, his social-learning theory is based on a broad range of human subjects. This approach increases the generalizability and applicability of his research findings. To illustrate further the kind of research that has proceeded from Bandura's theory, we consider representative work on self-efficacy and on the effect of televised models on aggressive behavior.

Self-Efficacy

Age and gender differences.   Self-efficacy differs as a function of gender and age. Research with children and adults shows that on the average, men score higher than women in self-efficacy. These gender differences peak during the 20s and decline in later years. For both sexes, self-efficacy increases through childhood and early adulthood, peaks in middle age, and declines after age 60 (Gecas, 1989; Lachman, 1985).

Academic performance and career choice.   Research demonstrates a significant positive relationship between self-efficacy and academic performance. Teachers with a high degree of self-efficacy or confidence in their teaching abilities create more opportunities for their students to achieve at a high level. Self-efficacy in students is also positively related to motivation, level of effort, and persistence in classroom situations (Gibson & Dembo, 1984; Multon, Brown, & Lent, 1991; Zimmerman, 1995).

Bandura also found differences in the ways schools inculcate self-efficacy in their students. In high-achieving schools, principals were more concerned with education than with implementing policies and regulations, and teachers set high expectations and standards for their students. In low-achieving schools principals functioned more as administrators and disciplinarians than as educators, and teachers expected little in the way of academic performance from their students (Bandura, 1997).

Cultural differences have been shown to influence self-efficacy in children. A study was conducted with 800 elementary school students in grades two to six in East and West Germany, before those nations were reunified. Students in the East German communist-collectivist culture scored lower in self-efficacy than did children in the West German capitalist-individualist culture. The East German children had less confidence in their ability to perform well in school and considered themselves to be less intelligent than West German students (Oettingen & Maier, 1999).

Gender differences in self-efficacy can influence our choice of career. Research has shown that men perceive themselves to be high in self-efficacy for so-called traditional "male" as well as traditional "female" occupations. In contrast, women perceive themselves high in self-efficacy for so-called female occupations but low in self-efficacy for traditional male occupations. The men and women subjects in this research performed at comparable levels on standardized tests of verbal and quantitative skills. Thus, they possessed similar measurable abilities but perceived these abilities differently. Their feelings about their own competence for various careers differed as a function of gender (Hackett, 1995).

The higher the level of self-efficacy, the wider the range of career possibilities and the stronger the interest taken in them. Low self-efficacy may restrict the careers a person considers and contribute to indecisiveness about the options believed to be viable (Bores-Rangel, Church, Szendre, & Reeves, 1990). In one study, first-year women college students were found to be lower in self-efficacy than first-year men with regard to perceived ability to perform well in math courses (Lapan, Boggs, & Morrill, 1989). This affected the choice of college major and led women to avoid such programs as engineering and science, which in turn limited their career options.

Self-efficacy can affect the amount of time spent job-hunting as well as future job success. Employees high in self-efficacy set higher personal goals and were more committed to them than were employees low in self-efficacy. Those high in self-efficacy focused on analyzing and solving problems on the job, whereas those low in self-efficacy focused on personal deficiencies and the fear of failure, which undermined their productivity (Locke & Latham, 1990).

The significant positive relationship between self-efficacy and job performance was supported by a meta-analysis of 114 research studies involving more than 21,600 subjects. The higher our level of self-efficacy, the better is our performance on the job (Stajkovic & Luthans, 1998).

Physical health.   Self-efficacy also affects several aspects of physical well being. In one study, pregnant women who had been taught relaxation and breathing exercises to reduce pain during childbirth believed they had greater control over that pain than did women who had not been taught relaxation techniques. The higher the women's self-efficacy and feeling of control, the longer they were able to tolerate the discomfort experienced during delivery before requesting pain medication. In addition, the higher their perceived self-efficacy, the less pain medication they required (Manning & Wright, 1983).

Other research supports the positive relationship between self-efficacy and pain tolerance. Coping techniques that improve self-efficacy produce substantial increases in endorphins, which are the body's natural painkillers. In a study on chronic pain, 45 patients suffering low back pain were given a pain-rating scale and a self-efficacy rating scale. Their progress in a 3-week rehabilitation program was monitored. After six months it was found that patients higher in self-efficacy reported better physical functioning and less back pain than did patients lower in self-efficacy (Altmaier, Russell, Kao, Lehmann, & Weinstein, 1993).

Self-efficacy is also related to the maintenance of healthy behaviors.

> Life-style habits can enhance or impair health. This enables people to exert some behavioral control over their vitality and quality of health. Efficacy beliefs affect every phase of personal change—whether people even consider changing their health habits; whether they enlist the motivation and perseverance needed to succeed should they choose to do so; and how well they maintain the habit changes they have achieved. (Bandura, 1995, p. 28)

Consider cigarette smoking. Studies of adolescents show that the higher their self-efficacy, the more resistant they can be to peer pressure to take up smoking. Among college student smokers, high self-efficacy was found to be the best predictor of an expressed intention to reduce the number of cigarettes smoked or to quit (Schwarzer & Fuchs, 1995; Stacy, Sussman, Dent, Burton, & Floy, 1992). Other studies show that people high in self-efficacy are more likely to stop smoking because they are confident of success whereas people low in self-efficacy were unlikely even to try (Becona, Frojan, & Lista, 1988; DiClemente, Prochaska, & Gilbertini, 1985). For other subjects, self-efficacy measured before attempting to quit smoking was significantly related to smoking behavior a month after quitting. The higher the initial self-efficacy, the fewer cigarettes smoked during the month. Subjects who resisted smoking during that time period had greater self-efficacy than did those who resumed smoking (Garcia, Schmitz, & Doerfler, 1990). Further, high self-efficacy has been related to other health-enhancing behaviors such as exercise, weight control, and safe sex practices.

Self-efficacy affects recovery from physical illness. For example, one study found that people high in self-efficacy responded better to cognitive and behavioral treatment for pulmonary disease than did patients low in self-efficacy. Men who suffered heart attacks showed a higher rate of return to normal activities and less fear and depression when both they and their spouses believed in their cardiac fitness. The higher the patients' self-efficacy, the more likely they were to follow prescribed exercise programs and the more they improved (Kaplan, Atkins, & Reinsch, 1984; McLeod, 1986).

Mental health.   In Italy, a study of 282 boys and girls whose average age was 11.5 years found that children who rated themselves low in social and academic efficacy were significantly more likely to experience depression than were children who rated themselves high in efficacy. Low social efficacy has also been significantly related to depression in a sample of adolescents in the United States (Bandura, Pastorelli, Barbarelli, & Caprara, 1999).

A similar relationship was documented with adult subjects. Low social efficacy was found to contribute to feelings of depression, partly because a lack of coping skills inhibited the development of a social support network (Holahan & Holahan, 1987). These findings may indicate a circular relationship rather than simple cause-and-effect. Low self-efficacy can lead to depression, and depression can reduce self-efficacy. People who are depressed believe that they are far less capable than others of performing effectively in many areas of life and that they have little control over their situations (Bandura, 1997).

Coping with stress.   Enhanced self-efficacy and a sense of control over life events are positively related to the ability to cope with stress and to minimize its harmful effects on biological functioning. Bandura wrote, "It is not stressful life conditions *per se* but the perceived inability to manage them that produces the detrimental biological effects" (1995, p. 26). High self-efficacy has been associated with strengthening the body's immune system, lowering the release of stress-related hormones, and reducing susceptibility to respiratory infections.

Studies have shown that high self-efficacy can help women cope with the stress of abortion. A sample of 291 women completed questionnaires to rate perceived self-efficacy and to assess their mood immediately after the procedure and again 3 weeks later. Subjects higher in self-efficacy adjusted more satisfactorily with significantly less depression and higher mood states than did those lower in self-efficacy (Cozzarelli, 1993). Another study dealt with stress experienced following the birth of one's first child. Self-report inventories assessed self-efficacy, psychological distress, and background variables such as income, age, education, and marital satisfaction. Women higher in self-efficacy coped better with the demands than did those lower in self-efficacy (Ozer, 1995).

A study of refugees migrating from East to West Germany after the destruction of the Berlin Wall in 1990 showed that people higher in self-efficacy adapted significantly better to the change from an economically disadvantaged lifestyle under a communist system to an affluent lifestyle under a capitalist system.

> Perceived self-efficacy proved to be a powerful personal resource regarding the impact of migration stress on cognitive appraisals as well as on psychological and physical well-being. . . . Highly self-efficacious migrants perceived the demands in their new life more as challenges and less as threats. They experienced lower anxiety, better health, and fewer health complaints than low self-efficacious migrants. (Jerusalem & Mittag, 1995, p. 195)

television and aggression

Television and Aggressive Behavior

Bandura and many other researchers have demonstrated convincingly that in laboratory situations and in the real world, seeing violence begets violence whether on television, in movies, or in our homes, streets, and schools.

For example, a group of delinquent boys displayed significantly more violent behavior toward their peers after watching violent films than did a control group of boys who saw nonviolent films. The kinds of aggressive acts the boys committed frequently duplicated those depicted in the films (Leyens, Camino, Parke, & Berkowitz, 1975). In another study, 9-year-old children who watched numerous violent television programs were found to be more aggressive 10 years later. A follow-up 20 years later showed that the same subjects still expressed a high level of aggression. Other studies report similar relationships between viewing televised violence and behaving aggressively. These results have been confirmed in many countries including the United States, England, Belgium, Finland, Poland, and Australia (Eron, 1987; Huesmann, Eron, Dubow, & Seebauer, 1987).

In a different approach to the relationship between observed violence and aggressive behavior, researchers investigated the incidence of aggressive acts shortly after people viewed televised models committing violent acts. One analysis found a brief but sharp rise in violent actions peaking 3 to 4 days following highly publicized riots (Phillips, 1985). Murder rates in the United States were found to increase by more than 12 percent over the expected rate for the 3-day period following a televised championship boxing match, a phenomenon that was maintained over a 15-year period (Phillips, 1983). Self-directed violence also appears to increase following exposure to similar violence widely reported in the news media. The incidence of suicide tends to climb following the suicide of a movie star or other celebrity (Phillips, 1974).

A Final Commentary

Social learning theory focuses on overt behavior. Critics charge that this emphasis ignores distinctly human aspects of personality such as motivation and emotion. They draw an analogy with a physician whose patients have stomach pains. The physician who deals only with overt behavior may treat such patients by asking them to stop groaning and complaining and clutching their stomach. What may be required instead is medication or surgery. The physician must diagnose and treat the afflicted internal organ, the underlying cause of the pain. If just the symptom is treated and not the cause, critics say, substitute symptoms may appear.

However, the social-learning approach has several advantages. First, it is objective and amenable to laboratory methods of investigation, making it congruent with the current emphasis in experimental psychology. Most experimental psychologists reject theoretical work in personality that posits unconscious or other internal driving forces that cannot be manipulated or measured under laboratory conditions. Therefore, Bandura's approach boasts a great amount of empirical support.

Second, observational learning and behavior modification are compatible with the functional, pragmatic spirit of American psychology. More readily than other approaches, observational-learning techniques can be taken from the laboratory and applied to practical problems. The techniques also provide more immediate reinforcement for the practitioner than do other approaches. For example, in clinical situations, dramatic changes can be seen in client behavior within weeks or even days.

Many researchers and clinicians believe Bandura's social-learning theory is exciting and productive. The great number of books, articles, and research studies deriving from it attests to its popularity as a way to study behavior in the laboratory and to modify behavior in the real world. In 1980 the American Psychological Association formally recognized Bandura's contribution, his "masterful modeling as a researcher, teacher, and theoretician" (Distinguished Scientific Contribution Award, 1981, p. 27).

Chapter Summary

Behavior can be learned through vicarious reinforcement by observing the behavior of others and anticipating the rewards for behaving in the same way. Cognitive processes are the mediating mechanisms between stimulus and response, and bring about control of behavior through self-regulation and self-reinforcement. In the classic Bobo doll study, children patterned their behavior on the model's aggressive behavior whether the model was observed live, on television, or in a cartoon. Disinhibition involves weakening an inhibition through exposure to a model. Three factors that influence modeling are the model's characteristics, the observer's characteristics, and the behavior's reward consequences.

Observational learning is governed by attentional, retention, production, and incentive and motivational processes. The self is a set of cognitive processes concerned with thought and perception. Self-reinforcement requires internal performance standards against which to evaluate behavior. Self-efficacy refers to the ability to control life events. People low in self-efficacy feel helpless and give up quickly when faced with obstacles. People high in self-efficacy persevere at tasks and perform at a high level. Judgments of self-efficacy are based on performance attainment, vicarious experiences, verbal persuasion, and physiological arousal. Using these information sources, it is possible to increase self-efficacy. Infants and children are reinforced primarily by physical stimuli. Older children are reinforced more by others' approval or disapproval; this is internalized so that reinforcement becomes self-administered.

In behavior therapy, models are used to demonstrate ways of coping with threatening situations. Behavior can be modified through observation and guided participation. In covert modeling, subjects imagine how a model copes with a feared situation. Bandura's approach to behavior modification deals with overt behavior and cognitive variables, particularly self-efficacy. As self-efficacy improves during treatment, the client is increasingly able to deal with threatening situations. Behavior modification has been criticized for manipulating people against their will, but Bandura argues that with self-awareness and self-regulation, people undergoing behavior modification understand what is being reinforced.

Behavior is controlled by internal cognitive processes and external stimuli, a position Bandura calls reciprocal determinism. Triadic reciprocality refers to interaction among behavior, cognitive, and environmental variables. Most behavior is learned; genetic factors play a minor role. Learning in childhood may be more influential than learning in adulthood but adults are not victims of childhood experiences. Our ultimate goal is to set realistic performance standards to maintain an optimal level of self-efficacy. Self-efficacy varies with age and gender and can influence career choice, school performance, job performance, physical and mental health, and the ability to cope with stress.

Bandura assesses behavior and cognitive variables through direct observation, self-report inventories, and physiological measures. He favors controlled laboratory investigations using large groups of subjects and statistical analysis of data. Criticisms of Bandura's theory relate to his focus on overt behavior to the exclusion of emotions and conflicts, his treatment of symptoms rather than possible internal causes, and his failure to state precisely how cognitive variables affect behavior.

Review Questions

1. How does the observational-learning approach to personality differ from the other approaches we have discussed?

2. What is Bandura's position on the role of reinforcement?

3. Describe a typical modeling experiment. How does modeling vary as a function of the characteristics of the models, the characteristics of the observers, and the reward consequences of the behavior?

4. Describe how modeling can be used to change behavior. Give two specific examples.

5. What are the four processes of observational learning? How are they related?

6. How do the types of behaviors we acquire through modeling change with age?

7. What is the role of self-reinforcement?

8. How do people high in self-efficacy differ from people low in self-efficacy in terms of their ability to cope with life? On what sources of information do we base our judgment about our own level of efficacy?

9. Describe the developmental changes that occur in self-efficacy from infancy to old age. How can self-efficacy be increased?

10. Give an example of how modeling can be applied to the reduction of anxiety.

11. What is the relationship between self-efficacy and physical health? Between self-efficacy and mental health?

12. What is Bandura's position on the issue of free will versus determinism? On the relative influences of heredity and environment?

13. How does self-efficacy differ as a function of gender and age? In what ways can self-efficacy influence academic performance and career choice?

Suggested Readings

Bandura, A. (1976). Albert Bandura. In R. I. Evans (Ed.), *The making of psychology: Discussions with creative contributors* (pp. 242–254). New York: Alfred A. Knopf. Interviews with Bandura about his life and work.

Bandura, A. (1986). *Social foundations of thought and action: A social cognitive theory.* Englewood Cliffs, NJ: Prentice-Hall. Presents Bandura's theory of human nature emphasizing the self-regulation of behavior.

Bandura, A. (Ed.). (1995). *Self-efficacy in changing societies.* New York: Cambridge University Press. Discusses various ways in which self-efficacy beliefs shape lifestyles and goals. Considers these issues from life span and social-cultural perspectives.

Bandura, A. (1997). *Self-efficacy: The exercise of control.* New York: Freeman. Describes 20 years of research on the idea that we can accomplish what we truly want to accomplish; that we are capable of consciously directing our actions to achieve success. Extends the concept of efficacy to society at large—to political beliefs, social practices, and collective action.

Bandura, A., Pastorelli, C., Barbaranelli, C., & Caprara, G. V. (1999). Self-efficacy pathways to childhood depression. *Journal of Personality and Social Psychology, 76,* 258–269. Investigates the possible reciprocal influence of perceived social and academic self-efficacy and depression and problem behavior in boys and girls (average age 11).

Gecas, V. (1989). The social psychology of self-efficacy. *Annual Review of Sociology, 15,* 291–316. Evaluates the research literature on Bandura's concept of self-efficacy and discusses how social structure and group processes affect the development of self-efficacy over the life span.

Behavior does not occur in a vacuum. A person is continuously reacting to aspects of [the] external and internal environments.

—Julian Rotter

SIXTEEN

Julian Rotter

social learning theory

Like Bandura, Rotter looks both outside and inside the organism, to external reinforcement and internal cognitive processes, in his approach to explaining behavior. He refers to his work as a social-learning theory, expressing his belief that we learn behavior primarily through social experiences. Rotter is credited as the first person to use the term *social-learning theory*. He began writing about the approach in 1947 and published the book *Social Learning and Clinical Psychology* in 1954. Bandura did not use the term in print until several years later.

Rotter criticized Skinner's preference for studying single subjects isolated from social experiences, and he argued that Skinner's explanations did not reflect learning as it occurs in the real world where people must interact with others. Rotter also questioned Skinner's study of the responses of animal subjects to simple stimuli. He believes such research provides merely a starting point for understanding more complex human behavior.

In the research from which he developed his social-learning theory, Rotter and his followers studied normal human subjects, mostly children and college students. His theory is grounded in rigorous, well-controlled laboratory experiments, not clinical experiences. He deals with cognitive processes more extensively than Bandura did. Rotter suggests that we perceive ourselves as conscious beings, able to influence our experiences and make decisions that regulate our lives. External reinforcement is important, but the effectiveness of the reinforcement depends on our cognitive abilities. Rotter describes personality as the "interaction of the individual and his or her meaningful environment" (1982, p. 5).

Thus, behavior is influenced by several factors. We have a subjective expectation of the outcome or consequences of our behavior in terms of the reinforcement that will follow it. We estimate the likelihood that behaving a certain way will lead to a particular reinforcer or reward, and we guide our behavior accordingly. We place different values on different reinforcers and judge their relative worth in various situations. Because each of us functions in a unique psychological context or environment, a given reward may not have the same value or importance for everyone. Therefore, it is the task of our internal cognitive processes to determine the impact or significance of external social-psychological experiences.

External situations also direct behavior because we are motivated to strive for maximum positive reinforcement and the avoidance of punishment. Thus, Rotter's approach to personality attempts to integrate reinforcement theory and cognitive theory.

The Life of Rotter (1916–   )

Rotter was born in Brooklyn, New York, the youngest of three brothers. Rotter said they "fit quite well into Adler's descriptions of the oldest, the middle, and the 'fighting' youngest child" (1993, p. 273). The family lived comfortably until the beginning of the 1929 economic depression when Rotter's father lost his business. This dramatic change in circumstances was a pivotal event for the teenage boy. He wrote, "It began in me a lifelong concern with social injustice and provided me with a powerful lesson on how personality and behavior were affected by situational conditions" (1993, p. 274).

An insatiable reader, Rotter spent much time during his early years at the local public library. He discovered the writings of Freud and Adler and eagerly began interpreting his friends' dreams. He planned to study psychology and believed that Adler's insights about human nature influenced his understanding of himself and his family. Because of the depressed economic situation, however, he could give no serious thought to a career in psychology. Like so many people at that time, Rotter had to be pragmatic and choose a field in which he could earn a living. Because job prospects for psychologists were limited, Rotter chose to major in chemistry at Brooklyn College, but by the time he graduated, he had accumulated more credits in psychology than in science. He also attended the monthly discussion group at Adler's home about his system of individual psychology.

Two of Rotter's professors urged him to undertake graduate work in psychology at the State University of Iowa. Rotter arrived in Iowa City with only enough money to stay a few weeks but fortunately he obtained a research assistantship. After receiving his master's degree in 1938, he accepted an internship in clinical psychology at Worcester State Hospital in Massachusetts, a major training and research center in clinical psychology. The following year he went to Indiana University in Bloomington, receiving his Ph.D. in 1941.

Rotter hoped to find an academic job but the prejudices of the time were against him. He wrote, "At Brooklyn College and again in graduate school, I had been warned that Jews simply could not get academic jobs, regardless of their credentials. The warnings seemed justified" (1982, p. 346). He found work instead as a clinical psychologist at Norwich State Hospital in Connecticut. Following service as a psychologist with the U.S. Army during World War II, Rotter joined the faculty of Ohio State University, where George Kelly was director of the clinical psychology program.

It is interesting that two personality theorists whose work emphasizes cognition should have developed at the same institution. Kelly's ideas, however, were already well formulated by the time Rotter arrived. At Ohio State, Rotter advanced his social-learning approach to personality. His research program attracted many outstanding graduate students who went on to productive careers. One later referred to that time as the "glory days" at Ohio State, with "Rotter and Kelly right in the midst of refining their theoretical positions and writing their magnum opuses" (Sechrest, 1984, p. 228).

In 1963, Rotter left Ohio State for the University of Connecticut in Storrs. In 1988, he received the Distinguished Scientific Contribution Award from the American Psychological Association.

Social-Learning Theory

Two basic assumptions of Rotter's theory are the following:

1. Personality is learned.
2. Personality is motivated toward specific goals. Behaviors that move us closer to our anticipated goals will be reinforced more strongly than will other behaviors.

To explain how personality functions, Rotter proposed four primary concepts:

1. behavior potential,
2. expectancy,
3. reinforcement value, and
4. the psychological situation.

Rotter described the relationships among the concepts in this way. "The *potential* for a *behavior* to occur in any specific situation is a function of the *expectancy* that the behavior will lead to a particular *reinforcement* in that *situation* and the *value* of that reinforcement" (1975, p. 57).

Rotter completed his system by proposing two broader concepts, freedom of movement and the minimal goal level. We discuss the concepts and their interaction in the following sections.

Primary Concepts

Behavior Potential

behavior potential The likelihood that a particular behavior will occur in a given situation.

Behavior potential is the likelihood that of all the ways we could choose to act in a given situation, one specific behavior or response will be displayed. Our selection of one behavior over another is based on our subjective impression of the situation. Thus, the potential or the possibility that we will choose a particular way of behaving is affected by our circumstances and by our conscious preference for this behavior over all the behavioral alternatives available to us, according to our subjective perception of the situation.

cognitive learning

You can see how Rotter's view of behavior differs from Skinner's. Whereas Skinner dealt with objectively observable events, Rotter encompasses both overt actions and covert actions. The covert actions are our internal cognitive processes, which affect the ways we perceive and act in stimulus situations. These processes cannot be observed directly. They include rationalization, repression, consideration of alternatives, and planning. Skinnerian behaviorists do not consider these variables to be behavior at all.

Rotter insists that cognitive processes can be objectively observed and measured indirectly, such as inferring them from our overt behavior. For example, problem-solving behavior can be inferred or assumed by observing the behavior of subjects trying to complete an assigned task. If the subjects take more time to solve one problem than another, then this is evidence that they are considering alternative solutions.

It is difficult to investigate cognitive activities by objective means, but the principles that regulate the occurrence of these implicit behaviors are no different from those that regulate directly observable overt behaviors. Both are important in determining the potential that a particular behavior will occur.

expectancy Our belief that if we behave a certain way in a given situation, a predictable reinforcement will follow.

Expectancy

Expectancy refers to our belief that if we behave a certain way in a given situation, then we can predict the reward that will follow. We hold this belief, or expectation, in terms of a probability or likelihood ranging from zero to 100 percent that the re-

People have different expectations about the rewards they will receive for their behavior. Your expectation of a good test grade depends in part on the rewards you received in past test-taking situations.

inforcer will occur. This degree of expectancy is determined largely by past reinforcement and by generalization.

We consider the nature of past reinforcement for behaving that way in a similar situation. Did we receive the reward only once or many times? Did it occur yesterday or a year ago? Was the behavior reinforced occasionally or every time it was displayed? In this way, prior reinforcement will influence our expectancy about future reinforcement.

generalization The idea that responses made in one situation will also be made in similar situations.

Expectancy also depends on the extent of **generalization** from similar, but not identical, situations. We ask ourselves if past sequences of behavior followed by reinforcement are relevant to other situations in our lives. Generalized expectancies are particularly important when we face new situations because we cannot predict whether a given behavior will lead to a given reinforcer if we have never been in that situation before. Our expectation or belief about the outcome must be based on our past responses to similar events.

For example, a person running the 100-yard dash for the first time cannot, on the basis of past experience, determine his or her potential for winning the race. In this case, there has been no past experience. But expectancy can be based on a generalization from participation in other similar athletic events. When we have run the 100-yard dash several times, then the expectancy of winning can be based on past experience in that event. It will no longer be necessary to generalize our expectations from similar situations.

Reinforcement Value

reinforcement value The basis for preferring one reinforcer over another.

Reinforcement value refers to the extent of the preference you have for one reward over another. If you are in a situation in which it is equally likely that one of several reinforcers can occur, how much will you value one over the others?

People differ in terms of what they find reinforcing. For example, to occupy themselves on a quiet Sunday afternoon, some people choose to go to a movie, others to watch a football game on television. Some like to write letters or do a crossword puzzle, whereas others reserve the time for household chores. Different activities provide differing degrees of satisfaction and reinforcement. These preferences derive from associating past reinforcers with current ones, from which we develop expectancies for future reinforcement. Thus, Rotter relates the concepts of expectancy and reinforcement value: either can serve as a cue for the other.

Consider the person buying a $1 lottery ticket for which the prize is a lifetime income. Considering the low cost of the ticket, the reinforcement value is great. However, because of this unusually high reinforcement value, most people have a low expectation of winning. Few of us have had the experience of winning a multi-million-dollar prize. In contrast, many people have won much smaller prizes in a raffle or bingo game or the office football pool. Our expectancy of winning in these situations is greater, though the reinforcement value of the prize is lower. In this way, our expectation of success is partially determined by the reinforcement value of the anticipated reward.

The Psychological Situation

psychological situation
The combination of internal and external factors that influences our perception of and response to a stimulus.

We continuously react to our internal and external environments, and these environments themselves interact. Rotter calls this the **psychological situation** because we respond according to our psychological perception of the external stimulus situation.

To Rotter, behavior is predictable only when we know the psychological situation, not from knowledge of what some personality theorists call a "core" of personality. In the core approach, the prediction of behavior is based on the assumption of relatively constant personal elements such as motives and traits. A person

All situations contain cues that tell us what reinforcement—such as praise from the teacher or expulsion from the classroom—will follow if we behave in a particular way.

possessing a particular trait or characteristic is generally expected to behave in a certain way, regardless of the external situation. For example, the person a Freudian theorist labels an anal aggressive personality would be expected to behave aggressively under all circumstances.

Rotter suggests that our behavior varies with our perception of each situation. Thus, the anal aggressive person will probably not behave aggressively if the situational cues indicate that severe punishment will follow aggressive actions. You can see that this is an interactionist approach to the mutual influence of personal and situational variables. He criticized core theorists who focus solely on internal variables and also disputed the radical behaviorists who focus only on external variables. By ignoring the mediating effect of expectancies and other cognitive processes, Rotter noted, these behaviorists overlook the possibility that the same stimulus has different effects on behavior in different situations.

Imagine a gun collector examining a valuable weapon at a gun show or staring down the barrel of that weapon carried by a robber in a dark alley. The physical stimulus (the gun) is the same in both instances, but the psychological situation (the perception of the stimulus) differs sharply. As a result, the person's behavioral responses to the stimulus can be expected to differ.

Broader Concepts

Freedom of Movement

freedom of movement
The degree of expectancy that a certain behavior will bring a given reinforcement.

Freedom of movement is analogous to expectancy and involves a person's belief that certain behaviors will lead to the satisfaction of a need. Suppose you have a high need for recognition. There are several ways you could try to satisfy that need. You could study hard to earn high grades in college. You could practice diligently to achieve recognition as a tennis player. You might develop your social skills to enhance your popularity. Or take computer skills training to excel on the job.

If you succeed at any of these behaviors, then you will have a high expectancy that these and similar behaviors will lead to success in satisfying your need for recognition. This condition leads to high freedom of movement. If none of the behaviors results in satisfying the need for recognition, then your low level of expectancy leads to low freedom of movement. A person with high freedom of movement anticipates success in achieving goals, but a person with low freedom of movement anticipates failure or even punishment.

Low freedom of movement can be related to lack of knowledge about how to achieve a particular goal. For example, people with a low measured level of intelligence may have a low expectation of receiving high grades in school because they do not have the ability to learn the required behaviors. Or even though some people have sufficient intellectual ability, they may develop low freedom of movement because they have misinterpreted past situations. As children, they may have been punished for their behavior and generalize from those experiences to their present situation. As a result, they anticipate disapproval and failure in all life situations and have a low expectancy of success in attaining goals and satisfying needs.

When freedom of movement is low with regard to a goal or need that has a high value, we experience a state of conflict. We may develop avoidance behaviors and try to achieve the goal or meet the need only in a symbolic way, by retreating into a fantasy world in which there is no actual risk of punishment or failure. Rotter suggested that deviant or pathological behavior is usually designed to avoid the conflict between significant goals and low freedom of movement.

The Minimal Goal Level

minimal goal level The lowest level of potential reinforcement in a given situation that is perceived as satisfactory.

The **minimal goal level** is the lowest level of potential reward in a particular situation that we perceive as satisfactory. Reinforcers exist on a continuum, ranging from highly desirable to highly undesirable. The point at which desirable reinforcers become undesirable represents our minimal goal level. For example, when you apply for a job, the salary you are offered could range from unusually high to disappointingly low. Somewhere within that range is the lowest acceptable or satisfactory level. Working for a lower salary would not be reinforcing.

We set minimal goal levels in many situations, from college grades to the car, career, or spouse we expect to have. Different people can have different minimal goal levels in the same situation. You might be satisfied with nothing less than a grade of A in this course, whereas your roommate might happily settle for a C. And each of you would find the attainment of your goal to be reinforcing.

Suppose, however, that you receive a B. You may feel that you have failed. This feeling contributes to low freedom of movement, that is, a reduced expectation of success in future courses of this type. Your roommate would find your unhappiness hard to understand. He or she had expected only a C and would have been delighted to receive the B. For your roommate, receiving the grade of B would lead to higher freedom of movement and a higher expectancy of success in future courses.

The point at which we set our minimal goal levels affects our emotional health. The person with high minimal goal levels who does not achieve, who does not obtain reinforcement at or above these levels, develops low freedom of movement. Thus, setting unrealistic minimal goal levels can be harmful. In contrast, minimal goal levels that are too low for our ability and reinforcement history can leave us with high freedom of movement, but we would not be living up to our capacities. Students described as underachievers—who do not perform at levels consistent with their abilities—have set minimal goal levels that are too low.

We can raise or lower our minimal goal levels by changing our reinforcement values. We achieve this by pairing present values with higher or lower values. For example, a student may think that a B on an exam has a negative value, but if the grade is paired with the positive reinforcement of praise from the professor for classroom participation, then the grade of B can come to have a positive value as a reinforcer.

Psychological Needs

Our major motivation in life is to maximize positive reinforcement and minimize punishment. Here again Rotter focuses on the interaction between internal and external determinants of behavior. When he describes external conditions, he is dealing with *reinforcers*. When he speaks of internal cognitive conditions, he is referring to *needs*.

Our psychological needs are learned. In infancy and early childhood, these needs arise from experiences associated with satisfaction of physiological needs such as hunger, thirst, sensory stimulation, and freedom from pain. As children grow and develop language and cognitive skills, their psychological needs arise less from association with physiological needs and more from acquired or learned psychological needs. Cues from the social environment become more important than internal physiological states. Learned needs are considered social needs because they depend on other people. It is obvious that infants and children depend on other people, usually parents, for need satisfaction and reinforcers. Later, reinforcement becomes dependent on a broader range of people including teachers and friends. As adults we rely on other people for satisfaction of such needs as love, affection, and recognition.

Our behaviors, needs, and goals operate within functionally related systems. Rotter proposed the concept of **need potential** to indicate the possibility that within these systems, related behaviors leading to the same or similar reinforcers can occur at the same time. The types of behaviors he grouped into functionally related systems range from overt actions to covert cognitions. Also, the systems are arranged in hierarchies; needs higher on the scale can include needs lower on the scale. For example, the need potential for recognition is a broad category that includes lower need potentials such as the need potential for recognition in the classroom or in sports.

need potential The possibility that related behaviors leading to the same or similar reinforcers will occur at the same time

Categories of Needs

Rotter proposed six categories of needs (Rotter, Chance, Phares, 1972):

1. *Recognition/status needs.* The need to be considered competent in professional, social, occupational, or recreational activities. The need to gain social or vocational position, to be seen as more skilled or better than other people.
2. *Protection/dependency needs.* The need to have another person or group act on our behalf to prevent frustration or punishment or to provide for the satisfaction of our other needs.
3. *Dominance needs.* The need to direct and control the actions of other people including family members and friends. The need to have any action taken by others be the one that we suggest.
4. *Independence needs.* The need to make our own decisions and to rely on ourselves. The need to develop skills for obtaining satisfaction directly, without the mediation of other people.
5. *Love and affection needs.* The need for acceptance and liking by others.
6. *Physical comfort needs.* The need for physical satisfaction that becomes associated with achieving security.

Locus of Control

locus of control Our belief about the source of control of reinforcement.

Rotter proposed the concept of **locus of control**, which is a form of generalized expectancy, to explain personality differences in people's beliefs about the source of reinforcement. We noted earlier that people differ in their perception of whether a given event is satisfying or reinforcing. Rotter's research showed that some people believe reinforcers depend on their own behavior, whereas other people think reinforcers are controlled by outside forces.

We can suggest some similarity between locus of control and Bandura's concept of self-efficacy. Both deal with our perception or belief about the degree of control we have over the events in our life and our ability to cope with them. A major difference between the two concepts is that locus of control can be generalized over many situations whereas self-efficacy tends to be specific to a particular situation. However, Bandura insisted there was little overlap between the concepts of self-efficacy and locus of control. He wrote,

> Beliefs about whether one can produce certain actions *(perceived self-efficacy)* cannot, by any stretch of the imagination, be considered the same as beliefs about whether actions affect outcomes *(locus of control)*. (1997, p. 20)

internal locus of control
A belief that reinforcement is brought about by our own behavior.

external locus of control
A belief that reinforcement is under the control of other people, fate, or luck.

Persons who have been characterized as **internal locus of control** personalities believe that the reinforcement they receive is under the control of their own behaviors and attributes. Those with an **external locus of control** think that other people, fate, or luck controls the rewards they receive. In other words, they are convinced that they are powerless with respect to outside forces.

You can see that the source of our locus of control has considerable influence on our behavior. External locus-of-control people, who believe that their behaviors and abilities make no difference in the reinforcers they receive, may see little value in exerting any effort to improve their situation. Why should they try when they have little expectation of controlling present or future events? In contrast, internal locus-of-control people believe they have a firm grip on their situation and behave accordingly. They perform at a higher level on laboratory tasks than do external locus-of-control people. In addition, internals are less susceptible to attempts to influence them, place a higher value on their skills, and are more alert to environmental cues that they use to guide behavior. They report lower anxiety and higher self-esteem, are more responsible for their actions, and enjoy greater mental and physical health.

A Matter of Luck?

The locus-of-control concept, which Rotter called the "major discovery of his career," developed from an experiment on generalized expectancies and a chance comment by a colleague (Hunt, 1993, p. 334). The subjects in Rotter's experiment were told that they were being rated on their extrasensory perception (ESP) powers. They were shown a set of 10 cards and instructed to guess whether a square or a circle was on the reverse of each card. After completing one set, they were asked to estimate the number of cards they believed they would guess correctly on the next set. Some subjects expected to do worse on the second trial because they thought their successful guesses the first time had been a matter of luck. Others felt they would do better on the second trial because they believed their successful guesses the first time were due to high ESP skills.

At the time Rotter was conducting this research he was also supervising the clinical training of E. Jerry Phares, a psychotherapist. Phares told Rotter about one of his patients, a man in his 40s who complained about his poor social life. Phares urged the man to attend a college dance. Although several women danced with him, this apparent success had not altered the man's outlook about his social skills. He told Phares, "It was just lucky. It would never happen again." When Phares recounted the story to Rotter,

> [Rotter] realized there were always some subjects in our experiments whose expectancies, like this patient's, never went up even after successes. My graduate students and I had run various experiments in which we rigged the volunteers' success or failure. . . . Some volunteers, whether we told them they were right or wrong most of the time, didn't change their expectations that they'd get most of them wrong on the next set. Others, whatever we told them, thought they'd do better the next time.
>
> At that point I put together the two sides of my work—as practitioner and as scientist—and hypothesized that some people feel that what happens to them is governed by external forces of one kind or another, while others feel that what happens to them is governed largely by their own efforts and skills. (Rotter, quoted in Hunt, 1993, p. 334)

We are left to wonder whether some other psychologist would have developed the idea of locus of control, a useful and popular concept in contemporary personality theory, if Phares's patient had revised his outlook about his own sociability. Sometimes the formulation of new ideas in science is not straightforward, logical, or rational. Luck or chance can indeed play a role, regardless of one's locus of control.

Components of Perceived Control

A factor analysis of the scores of 3,033 Swiss male and female adolescents (ages 14 to 20) on a questionnaire assessing perception of control in nine everyday situations suggested two factors or components of the locus-of-control concept: expectancy and appraisal (Grob, Flammer, & Wearing, 1995). The expectancy component involves what we often think about when asked to describe the idea of control: "Can I do this? Can I accomplish that? Do I believe I can cope?" The appraisal component involves the question of how important the situation is and how necessary it is for us to have control in that situation: "Does it matter to me whether or not I am in control in this situation?" Obviously, if the situation is not important to us, then it is irrelevant whether we have control over it.

Thus, if perceived internal or external control does not apply to all situations, then locus of control may not be a generalized personality trait independent of the stimulus situation. We may need to believe in our ability to exert control only in situations that are important to us, situations with a high appraisal component.

Interpersonal Trust

interpersonal trust The degree of expectancy that a given person is trustworthy.

Rotter identified another form of generalized expectancy, **interpersonal trust**, which he defined as the expectation that the "word, promise, oral or written statement of another individual or group can be relied on" (1980, p. 1).

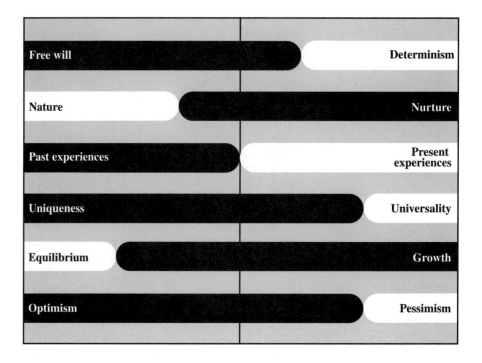

FIGURE 16.1   *Rotter's image of human nature.*

Rotter's research shows that people high in interpersonal trust are less likely to lie, cheat, or steal than are persons low in interpersonal trust. High scorers are more likely to respect the rights of others and to give them a second chance. However, highly trusting people are no more likely to be gullible or easily fooled. High interpersonal trust can have beneficial consequences. People high in interpersonal trust have been found to be more popular and less likely to be unhappy, maladjusted, or bothered by conflicts than people low in interpersonal trust.

Questions About Human Nature

On the free will versus determinism issue, Rotter appears to favor free choice, notably for people with an internal locus of control. It is clear from his emphasis on cognitive variables that Rotter believes we regulate our experiences and choose our behaviors. We may be influenced by external variables, but we shape the nature and extent of that influence. People with an external locus of control do not feel a strong sense of will. The possibility of free will is available to them, but they believe they are controlled by outside forces (see Figure 16.1).

To Rotter, most human behavior is learned and depends little on genetic factors. It is primarily nurture, not nature—experience, not inheritance—that shapes personality. Although what we learn in childhood is important, it does not determine behavior throughout the life span. Personality changes and grows; it is not fixed in the pattern established in our early years. Early experiences will affect our perception of later events but we are not victims, or captives, of our past. We react continuously to our internal and external environments, and as these change so does our perception of them.

Rotter's position on uniqueness versus universality in personality is reflected in his concept of the psychological situation. Each of us develops a personal view of the world, and we interpret and react to events according to our perceptions. It follows that each of us operates in a unique psychological situation. Rotter did not propose an ultimate and necessary life goal, such as self-actualization, but he stated that all behavior is directed toward some goal. Rather than being pulled toward some ideal state or pushed to escape anxieties, we act to achieve our personal goals. We are motivated to maximize positive reinforcement and minimize punishment, and we are capable of making conscious decisions about how best to achieve this state. Rotter's system offers an optimistic image of human nature. In summary, people are not passive victims of external events, inheritance, or childhood experiences but are free to shape the present and future.

Assessment in Rotter's Theory

Rotter used a variety of assessment techniques including interviews, projective tests, direct observation of behavior, and self-report inventories. He designed specific techniques to evaluate various concepts in his system. To measure reinforcement value Rotter used ranking and behavioral choice. In research using the *ranking method*, subjects are given verbal descriptions of reinforcers (such as praise from one's teacher) and are asked to rank the statements from most reinforcing to least reinforcing. In the *behavioral choice method*, subjects are asked to select behaviors they expect to be followed by a reinforcer of high value. Behavioral choice is also used to measure expectancy. When subjects choose one behavioral alternative over another, they are indicating a belief that the selected behavior has a higher expectancy of producing the desired reinforcement.

Another way to assess expectancy involves verbal techniques. For example, subjects are asked to predict the likelihood of receiving reinforcement in terms of alternatives on a scale of expectancy values. In another instance, subjects are graded on performance of a laboratory task. Before receiving the grade, however, they are asked about their expectation of success. The hypothesis is that the anticipated grades represent the level of expectancy the subjects are most confident of receiving.

Rotter developed self-report inventories to assess locus of control and interpersonal trust. The Internal-External (I-E) Scale (Rotter, 1966) consists of 23 forced-choice alternatives. From each pair of items, subjects select the one that best describes their beliefs (see Table 16.1). It is not difficult to determine which of each pair of alternatives represents an internal or an external locus of control. Another scale to assess locus of control is the Children's Nowicki-Strickland Internal-External Scale, a widely used 40-item test that has been translated into two dozen languages (Nowicki & Strickland, 1973; Strickland, 1989). An adult form of the scale is available, as well as a cartoon version for use with preschool children (Nowicki & Duke,

TABLE 16.1   *Sample items from the I-E Scale*

1. a. Many of the unhappy things in people's lives are partly due to bad luck.
   b. People's misfortunes result from the mistakes they make.
2. a. One of the major reasons why we have wars is because people don't take enough interest in politics.
   b. There will always be wars, no matter how hard people try to prevent them.
3. a. In the long run people get the respect they deserve in this world.
   b. Unfortunately, an individual's worth often passes unrecognized no matter how hard he or she tries.
4. a. The idea that teachers are unfair to students is nonsense.
   b. Most students don't realize the extent to which their grades are influenced by accidental happenings.
5. a. Without the right breaks one cannot be an effective leader.
   b. Capable people who fail to become leaders have not taken advantage of their opportunities.
6. a. No matter how hard you try some people just don't like you.
   b. People who can't get others to like them don't understand how to get along with others.

SOURCE: J. B. Rotter, "Generalized Expectancies for Internal versus External Control of Reinforcement," *Psychological Monographs, 80* (1966):11.

TABLE 16.2   *Sample items from the Interpersonal Trust Scale*

1. In dealing with strangers one is better off to be cautious until they have provided evidence that they are trustworthy.
2. Parents usually can be relied upon to keep their promises.
3. Parents and teachers are likely to say what they believe themselves and not just what they think is good for the child to hear.
4. Most elected public officials are really sincere in their campaign promises.

SOURCE: J. B. Rotter, "A New Scale for the Measurement of Interpersonal Trust," *Journal of Personality 35* (1967):654.

1983). Variants of the I-E Scale measure specific behaviors such as the relationship between locus of control and factors relating to successful dieting and weight loss.

The Interpersonal Trust Scale (Rotter, 1967) consists of 25 items to measure trust and 15 items to disguise the purpose of the test (see Table 16.2). Subjects indicate their extent of agreement or disagreement with each item.

Research in Rotter's Theory

Rotter used primarily the experimental and correlational research methods to formulate and test his theory. Much of his research relies on the I-E Scale and correlates those scores with measures of behavior and personality. We discuss here representative studies of the locus of control and interpersonal trust concepts.

Age and gender differences in locus of control.   We noted some of the characteristics of internal and external locus-of-control people. Additional research has been directed toward developmental aspects of this variable. Studies have shown that attempts to control our external environment begin in infancy, becoming more pronounced between ages 8 to 14. More college students have been found to show an internal rather than an external orientation. People apparently become more internally oriented as they grow older, reaching a peak in middle age (Heckhausen & Schulz, 1995; Milgram, 1971; Ryckman & Malikiosi, 1975).

In terms of overall scores on the I-E Scale, no significant differences between men and women were shown (DeBrabander & Boone, 1990). However, men and women respond differently to certain test items. In one study, men displayed greater internal locus of control than did women on questions relating to academic achievement (Strickland & Haley, 1980). External locus of control appears to increase in women after divorce, followed by a return to an internal locus of control (Doherty, 1983). Women who have been physically abused tend to show an external locus of control (Baron & Byrne, 1984).

Racial and socioeconomic differences in locus of control.   In early research with the I-E Scale, significant racial and socioeconomic differences were found. In general, the test performance of lower social classes and minority groups showed an external locus of control. This was confirmed in a study with children. Lower-class Black children were shown to be more externally oriented than were lower- and middle-class White children or middle-class Black children (Battle & Rotter, 1963; Coleman et al., 1966).

Studies conducted in Africa found that native Africans, like American-born Blacks in general, scored higher in external locus of control than did American-born Whites (Okeke, Draguns, Sheku, & Allen, 1999). In the African nation of Botswana, Black male and female adolescents scored higher in external locus of control than did White adolescents in the United States. In both countries, teens higher in socioeconomic status scored higher in internal control than did teens lower in socioeconomic status (Maqsud & Rouhani, 1991). A study of American high school students found that Hispanic American and Native American adolescents were more likely to be externally oriented than were White adolescents (Graves, 1961).

In general, Asians were shown to be more externally oriented than were Americans, a finding that may be explained in terms of cultural beliefs. Whereas American culture traditionally prizes self-reliance and individualism, Asian culture emphasizes community reliance and interdependence. Therefore, for Asians, success is viewed more as a product of external than internal factors. The more contact Asians have with Americans, the more internally oriented they seem to become. For example, Chinese residents of Hong Kong measured higher in external locus of control than did Americans of Chinese heritage, and Americans of Chinese heritage were more externally oriented than Americans of European heritage (Uba, 1994).

Behavioral differences in locus of control.   Internally oriented people are more likely than externally oriented people are to engage in significantly more daydreams about achievement and fewer daydreams about failure. They acquire and process more information in different situations, experience greater personal choice, and are more popular. In addition, internals are attracted to people they can manipulate, have higher self-esteem, and act in more socially skillful ways (Abdallah, 1989;

Brannigan, Hauk, & Guay, 1991; Lefcourt, Martin, Fick, & Saleh, 1985). People high in internal locus of control are less likely to have emotional problems or become alcoholics. They cope better with stress, experience less anxiety and depression, and are less likely to commit suicide (Benassi, Sweeney, & Dufour, 1988; Keltikangas-Jaruinen & Raikkonen, 1990; Lefcourt, 1982; Petrosky & Birkhimer, 1991).

For example, a study was conducted of 109 Israeli teenagers (69 males and 40 females) during the 1990 Persian Gulf War, when the explosion of 40 SCUD missiles caused widespread injury and destruction. The researcher found that adolescents who scored higher on perceived control experienced significantly less anxiety and fewer stress-related symptoms than did adolescents who scored lower in perceived control (Zeidner, 1993). Other research showed that people higher in internal locus of control earned higher grades in school and scored higher on standardized tests of academic achievement. They were more resistant to attempts at persuasion and coercion, more perceptive, and more inquisitive (Findley & Cooper, 1983; Lefcourt, 1982).

Physical health and locus of control.   Internally oriented people may be physically healthier than externally oriented people are. Research showed that internals tend to have lower blood pressure and fewer heart attacks. When they do develop cardiac problems, they cooperate better with the hospital staff and are released earlier than patients who are externally oriented. Internals tend to be more cautious about their health and are more likely to wear seat belts, to exercise, and to quit smoking (Phares, 1993; Seeman, Seeman, & Sayles, 1985; Segall & Wynd, 1990). Overall, the evidence seems clear that people who think they have control over their lives pay more attention to their health.

One study delineated four aspects of locus of control as it relates to physical health: self-mastery, illness prevention, illness management, and self-blame. The factor most closely associated with physical well being was self-mastery, defined as a belief in one's ability to overcome illness (Marshall, 1991).

Learning and locus of control.   Evidence suggests that locus of control is learned in childhood and is directly related to parental behavior. External control beliefs were likely to be expressed by children reared in homes without an adult male role model. Also, external control beliefs tended to increase with the number of siblings. This researcher concluded that children in large single-parent families headed by women are more likely to develop an external locus of control (Schneewind, 1995). Parents of children who possessed an internal locus of control were found to be highly supportive, to offer praise (positive reinforcement) for achievements, and to be consistent in their discipline. They were not authoritarian. As their children grew older, these parents continued to foster an internal orientation by encouraging independence (Wichern & Nowicki, 1976).

Interpersonal trust.   Rotter's early research on interpersonal trust showed that last-born children were less trusting than were other children. College students who express religious beliefs tended to be more trusting than those who express no such beliefs. The higher one's socioeconomic status, the higher the degree of interpersonal trust (Rotter, 1967). In laboratory experiments, subjects low in interpersonal trust were more likely to cheat when competing for a monetary prize. They worked less hard on an experimental task when they believed that they were not being monitored (Rotter, 1980). A study of high school girls showed that those low in interpersonal trust were more likely to shoplift than were those high in interpersonal trust. Those lower in trust were also more likely to believe that adults distrusted them (Wright & Kirmani, 1977). A study of 163 men and women college students found that those who scored low on interpersonal trust were significantly more envious, resentful, vindictive, and lacking in empathy for others than were those who scored high in interpersonal trust (Gurtman, 1992).

A Final Commentary

Rotter's focus on internal cognitive variables has been considered both a strength and a weakness. Some critics suggest that Rotter has gone too far, that his position deviates so greatly from orthodox behaviorism that it cannot be considered behavioral at all. Further, some of the assessment methods Rotter accepted, such as interviews and projective tests, are viewed as too subjective. However, his social-cognitive learning theory has attracted enthusiastic followers, primarily experimentally oriented researchers investigating the impact of cognitive variables. Rotter's emphasis on these variables is stronger than Bandura's, and his position represents a significant departure from Skinner's radical behaviorism.

Rotter offered concepts defined in precise, unambiguous terms that can be tested by experimental and correlational methods. He established a working relationship between cognitive variables and reinforcement and gave social-learning theory a strong motivational component. His research has been as rigorous and well controlled as the subject matter allows, and he used objective measures wherever possible. Studies have provided considerable empirical support. The I-E Scale has generated a wealth of research and has been applied in clinical and educational settings. Rotter noted that locus of control has become "one of the most studied variables in psychology" (1990, p. 489).

Chapter Summary

Rotter studied normal subjects and dealt more extensively with cognitive processes than Bandura did. Rotter's system integrates reinforcement and cognitive theories and is concerned with the interaction of the person and his or her unique environment.

Behavior potential refers to the likelihood that a specific behavior will occur relative to other behaviors that could be displayed in a given situation. Behavior includes directly observable acts as well as cognitive processes that can be inferred from overt behavior. Expectancy refers to the belief that if we behave in a certain way in a given situation a predictable reinforcer will follow. Reinforcement value refers to the degree of preference for one reinforcer over another. The psychological situation includes our internal and external environments, that is, both cognitive variables and external stimuli. Freedom of movement refers to a person's expectation that certain behavior will lead to success in satisfying a need. High expectancy leads to high freedom of movement; low expectancy leads to low freedom of movement. The minimal goal level refers to the lowest level of potential reinforcement in a given situation that we perceive as satisfactory. Setting unrealistic minimal goal levels may be harmful to our emotional health.

Behavior is directed toward maximizing positive reinforcement. Psychological needs are learned and are social in origin because they depend on other people. Six types of needs are recognition-status, protection-dependency, dominance, independence, love and affection, and physical comfort.

People who believe reinforcement depends on their own behavior have an internal locus of control. People who think reinforcement is controlled by outside forces have an external locus of control. People high in interpersonal trust are more popular and less likely to lie, cheat, and steal; more likely to respect the rights of others; and less likely to be unhappy and maladjusted. Rotter's image of human nature emphasizes free will, the importance of learning, the possibility that personality changes over the life span, uniqueness, and the goal of maximizing reinforcement and minimizing punishment.

To assess personality Rotter used interviews, projective tests, direct observation of behavior, and self-report inventories. He developed the Internal-External Scale and the Interpersonal Trust Scale. Research has shown that people become more internally oriented with age. People in lower social classes and in some minority groups tend to be externals. Internals feel a stronger sense of personal choice, experience fewer psychiatric symptoms and less anxiety, earn higher grades in school, and are physically healthier than externals. Parents of internally oriented children are supportive and consistent in their discipline, encouraging their children's independence.

For the interpersonal trust variable, last-born children have been found to be less trusting than their older siblings are. College students with deep religious beliefs are more trusting than those with no professed religious beliefs. The higher the social class, the greater the interpersonal trust.

When Rotter's theory was first proposed some psychologists criticized it for being too subjective because of the emphasis on cognitive variables. However, the theory has stimulated considerable research that has provided empirical support for its concepts.

Review Questions

1. How does Rotter's personality theory differ from Skinner's approach? What does Rotter's theory have in common with Bandura's approach?

2. According to Rotter, what is the role of cognitive factors in personality?

3. What factors influence our belief, or expectancy, that if we behave in a certain way in a given situation, a predictable reinforcement will follow?

4. What is the relationship between minimal goal levels and reinforcement values? How are we likely to respond to a minimal goal level too low for our abilities?

5. What is the difference between needs and goals? List the six categories of needs.

6. If external locus-of-control people heard that a tornado was approaching, would they be likely to think there was nothing they could do about it, or would they be likely to take immediate action to protect their family and property? Why?

7. What parental behaviors foster a child's internal locus of control?

8. Describe the differences in behavior between people high in interpersonal trust and people low in interpersonal trust.

9. What is Rotter's position on the issue of free will versus determinism? On the uniqueness of human behavior?

10. How does Rotter measure reinforcement value and expectancy?

11. Discuss racial and social class differences found in research on internal versus external locus of control.

Suggested Readings

Rotter, J. B. (1980). Interpersonal trust, trustworthiness, and gullibility. *American Psychologist, 35,* 1–7. Reviews the consequences for one's social life of being high or low in interpersonal trust.

Rotter, J. B. (1982). *The development and applications of social learning theory: Selected papers.* New York: Praeger. Covers the development of Rotter's theory and its applications to clinical, personality, and social psychology. Includes a biographical sketch.

Rotter, J. B. (1993). Expectancies. In C. E. Walker (Ed.), *The history of clinical psychology in autobiography* (Vol. 2, pp. 273–284). Pacific Grove, CA: Brooks/Cole. Covers Rotter's graduate training, academic experience, and the early work on locus of control. Also describes the growth of academic clinical psychology programs and related political controversies.

Strickland, B. R. (1989). Internal-external control expectancies: From contingency to creativity. *American Psychologist, 44,* 1–12. Reviews the research literature on internal versus external locus of control beliefs and relates the findings to measures of physical and psychological health.

The Limited-Domain Approach

Personality theorists have usually considered completeness to be their major theoretical goal, and we have seen that some theories come closer to achieving this than others do. However, an increasing number of personality psychologists have concluded that no theory can be a truly comprehensive explanation for all aspects of our personality and behavior. It is widely accepted today that such a goal may be unrealistic. This has given rise to a number of separate theories, smaller in scope and aim. Each has a narrower range of application, focusing on a restricted aspect of personality that can be experimentally tested more thoroughly than is possible with a global theory of the total personality.

It is easy to see why the global approach to personality theory characterized the field for so long. Early personality theorists—such as Freud, Jung, and Adler—treated individual patients in a clinical setting. They were attempting to modify or cure a patient's abnormal behaviors and emotional disturbances to help them function in the real world. Of necessity, then, these theorists focused on the whole person, not just one or two traits.

The focus shifted from the whole person when personality was brought out of the clinic and into the research laboratory. Experimental psychologists typically study one variable at a time, controlling or holding constant all others. In this way they concentrate on a limited domain or area of investigation. They collect large amounts of empirical data derived from their study of how the experimental variable relates to its antecedents and its behavioral consequences. Thus, limited-domain theories are characterized by a type of supporting data that is different from the data generated in the clinical approach.

Limited-domain theorists place less emphasis on the therapeutic value of their ideas. They typically are researchers, not clinicians, more interested in investigating personality than changing it. This does not mean that limited-domain theories have no treatment applications. Rather, it indicates that the theories were not developed *specifically* for use with patients, as was the case with many of the earlier personality theories.

Because personality study has become so much more experimentally oriented, we can expect the limited-domain approach to dominate the theoretical work of the 21st century. To date, more than a dozen well-formulated limited-domain theories have been proposed, and most are stimulating debate and research. Some of the areas proposed include the hardy personality, the authoritarian personality, the Type A/Type B personalities, altruism, cognitive dissonance, the power motive, self-disclosure, and optimal experience (also known as flow).

We have chosen to discuss three ideas: the need for achievement, sensation seeking, and learned helplessness. They represent three major orientations we have discussed in this text, respectively, the neopsychoanalytic, trait, and social-learning or social-cognitive. Thus, each limited-domain theory we describe encompasses not only a different aspect of personality but a different approach to the ultimate explanation of personality.

Achievement is one of the needs proposed by Henry Murray. It invokes the idea of tension reduc-tion and reflects the influence of Freud. The need or motivation to achieve is measured by the Thematic Apperception Test, a projective technique also based on Freudian concepts. *Sensation seeking* is one of the traits in Hans Eysenck's personality dimension E (extraversion versus introversion). It is primarily an inherited attribute and reflects the impact of behavioral genetics on personality. *Learned helplessness* is, by definition, a learned behavior. It has a strong cognitive component, reflecting the influence of the behaviorist, social learning, and cognitive movements in personality.

These theories are presented as examples of the limited-domain approach. They are not comprehensive systems of personality, nor are they the only examples of mini-theories in contemporary psychology. Our aim here is to give you the flavor of each theory and to acquaint you with the idea of studying personality in this limited-domain fashion.

David McClelland

Marvin Zuckerman

Martin E. P. Seligman

In recent years there has been a trend away from grand, comprehensive theories toward theories that are limited to conceptualizations about types of personality or about ways of personality functioning.

—Donald Fiske

SEVENTEEN

Limited-Domain Theories of Personality

David McClelland: The Need for Achievement

need for achievement
(nAch) The need to
achieve, overcome
obstacles, excel, and live
up to a high standard.

One of the needs posited by Henry Murray (Chapter 7) is the **need for achievement**, which he described as the need to overcome obstacles, to excel, and to live up to a high standard. David McClelland (1917–1998), affiliated with Harvard University, conducted a broad and intensive program to investigate this need. He refers to the need for achievement as *nAch* or *achievement motivation* and defines it as a drive that energizes and directs behavior in virtually all situations.

McClelland's work provides an excellent example of how much we can learn when the domain of research is restricted to a well-defined aspect of personality. It also shows the importance of the limited-domain approach in understanding the total personality. Although the focus of study is narrow, the ramifications are far reaching. McClelland and his associates developed a technique to measure a person's need for achievement and to show how behavior varies in different situations as a function of the level of the need. They also identified ways to promote achievement motivation in childhood. Applying his theory to broader social concerns, McClelland offered an empirical account of the economic growth and decline of ancient and contemporary cultures in terms of each society's level of achievement motivation. He demonstrated that it was possible to predict a nation's potential for economic growth or decline by measuring its achievement need.

The importance of McClelland's work was recognized in 1987 with the American Psychological Association's Distinguished Scientific Contribution Award. The association honored his pioneering studies and bold vision and the inspiration he provided for generations of followers.

Assessing the Need for Achievement

In his efforts to assess the need for achievement, McClelland was guided by the insights of Sigmund Freud and the requirements of the scientific method. From Freud he borrowed the approach of uncovering motives by analyzing patients' reported fantasies. Freud searched for fantasies in dreams and free associations. McClelland chose to use the Thematic Apperception Test (TAT), developed by Henry Murray and Christiana Morgan. McClelland analyzed fantasies by having his subjects interpret the TAT pictures and project their needs, fears, and values onto these ambiguous stimuli.

A colleague recalled the accidental manner in which McClelland chose the TAT for his work. McClelland and fellow researcher John Atkinson were sitting in McClelland's Harvard office, talking about how best to measure the achievement need. Another faculty member overheard the discussion as he passed through and said casually, "Why don't you try the TAT?" (Atkinson, quoted in Winter, 1998, p. 139). And so they did, though they decided not to use all of Murray's original TAT cards. Instead, they clipped pictures of everyday scenes from the pages of *The Saturday Evening Post* magazine.

In the initial research McClelland and his associates asked groups of male college students to write brief stories about the TAT pictures (McClelland, Atkinson, Clark, & Lowell, 1953). To vary the experimental conditions, the researchers gave different test-taking instructions to different groups, urging a high achievement need in one condition and a low achievement need in the other. The results showed that the stories written under the high-achievement condition contained significantly more references to attaining standards of excellence, desiring to achieve, and performing well. For example, one picture showed a young man sitting at a desk with an open book in front of him. Stories from high-need-achievement subjects involved working hard, striving for excellence, and doing one's best. Stories from low-need-achievement subjects dealt with sedentary activities such as daydreaming, thinking, and recalling past events.

McClelland concluded that TAT-induced stories could be used as a valid measure of the need to achieve, and thus the test became the basic tool for selecting subjects for his wide-ranging investigations. A later meta-analysis of nine studies of nearly 1,000 subjects confirmed the validity of this projective approach as a measure of need achievement, particularly as it relates to career success (Spangler, 1992).

Behavioral Studies

personality and academic achievement

McClelland's initial research explored behavioral differences between high- and low-need-achievement people. Although these early studies used only male subjects, later work included female subjects (McClelland, 1961). Subjects testing high in the need for achievement were found more often in middle and upper socioeconomic classes than in lower socioeconomic groups. They demonstrated a better memory for uncompleted tasks and were more likely to volunteer to serve as subjects for psychological research. They were more resistant to social pressures and less conforming than were subjects testing low in need achievement. Young people high in the need to achieve were more likely to attend college, earn higher grades, and be involved in college and community activities. High-need-achievement people were also more likely to cheat on examinations in certain situations. They got along better with other people and enjoyed greater physical health. Additional experiments revealed that high-need-achievement subjects believed certain tasks would be easier to perform than did low-need-achievement subjects. With cognitive tasks, experimentally induced anxiety facilitated the performance of the high-need achievers and impaired the performance of the low-need achievers (McClelland, 1985; Piedmont, 1988).

Do people high in achievement motivation perform better in every situation? To answer that question, McClelland and his colleagues tested various tasks. One experiment involved a repetitive chore, crossing out *E*s and *O*s in a long series of random letters. In this type of task there is little room for improvement, no way to learn to do the job better, only faster. The results showed that high- and low-need-achievement subjects performed at the same level. Other research confirmed that subjects high in need achievement do not perform better than subjects low in need achievement, unless the achievement motive is activated. Only when high-need-achievers are challenged to excel will they do so. From these findings McClelland predicted that people with a high need to achieve will seek life and career situations that allow them to satisfy this need. They will set personal achievement standards and work hard to meet them (McClelland, Koestner, & Weinberger, 1989).

In another study, competition increased intrinsic interest in a word game among the high-need-achievement subjects in a sample of 80 college students. Pitting their skills against other students also increased their enjoyment of the game. For low-need-achievement subjects, competitive conditions lowered their interest in the game (Epstein & Harackiewicz, 1992).

Behavior in the Workplace

People high in the need for achievement more frequently hold high-status jobs. They work harder, have a greater expectation of success, and report more job satisfaction than do people low in the need for achievement. High-need achievers choose jobs that provide personal responsibility, in which success depends primarily on their own efforts, and they are dissatisfied with jobs in which success depends on other people or on factors beyond their control (Reuman, Alwin, & Veroff, 1984).

Because high-need-achievement people prefer jobs with considerable responsibility, McClelland suggested that they prefer to be entrepreneurs, to operate their own business and be their own boss. This kind of work situation provides optimal challenge and authority. In a follow-up study of male college students 14 years after their achievement-motivation scores had first been measured it was found that 83 percent of those who had become successful entrepreneurs had scored high in the need to achieve. Only 21 percent of those who had become successful in nonentrepreneurial jobs had scored high in the need to achieve. Research in several countries supports the finding that high-need-achievement people are more attracted to entrepreneurial jobs (McClelland, 1965, 1987).

These early workplace studies were conducted with male subjects. To determine whether women entrepreneurs were also high in achievement motivation, psychologists studied 60 female business owners in Australia. Approximately 82 percent of these entrepreneurial women showed moderate to high levels of the need to achieve, a finding similar to McClelland's research with entrepreneurial men. The study of female subjects also found that those highest in need achievement were lowest in job satisfaction, suggesting to the researchers that the women were competing with impossible standards of excellence they had set for themselves (Langan-Fox & Roth, 1995).

These findings do not suggest that those of us who are not entrepreneurs—who work for organizations and have several levels of bosses—are low in the need to achieve. It has been found, for example, that successful corporate managers have higher need-achievement scores than do unsuccessful managers. In addition, McClelland showed a high positive correlation between need-achievement scores of executives and that company's economic success (McClelland, 1961). He noted, however, that in large corporations, a high level of the need to achieve might be beneficial only up to a certain managerial level.

> I shall not forget the moment when I learned that the president of one of the most successful achievement-oriented firms we had been studying scored exactly zero in the need for Achievement! Up to that point I had fallen into the easy assumption that an individual with a high need to Achieve does better work, gets promoted faster, and ultimately ends up as president of a company. How was it possible for a man to head an obviously

achieving company and yet score so low in the need for Achievement? (McClelland, 1993, p. 433)

McClelland then proposed that other characteristics, such as a need for power, become more important than the need to achieve once a person reaches higher levels of organizational leadership. At AT&T, a long-term study of managers, whose levels of need achievement were measured when they first joined the company, provided support for this idea. The research showed that the managers' need achievement levels were positively related to subsequent promotions but only up to a point. Need achievement was not related to success at higher levels of management (McClelland & Boyatzis, 1982).

Is the need to achieve relevant to a top leadership job such as the presidency of the United States? To answer this question, researchers evaluated inaugural speeches of 34 presidents from George Washington (1789) to Ronald Reagan (1981) seeking themes that might indicate a high need for achievement. A group of historians rated these presidents on their overall effectiveness and the ratings were compared with the need-achievement findings. The results showed that the higher the need for achievement as expressed in speeches, the lower their ratings on effective leadership (Spangler & House, 1991). We may conclude from these studies that a high level of need achievement is useful in facilitating the rise to a certain level, but beyond that level other attributes take precedence.

personality and culture

The Influence of Cultural Factors

McClelland investigated the link between the individual need for achievement and a nation's economic health (McClelland, 1961). Some of the theorists we have discussed noted ways in which cultural and societal forces influence individual personality development. Other theorists asserted that people are capable of acting deliberately to alter society. McClelland set out to discover whether a limited-domain personality variable—the need for achievement—would operate to affect or shape society.

The theoretical rationale for considering the possible connection between a culture's need for achievement and its economic growth grew out of the work of the German sociologist Max Weber. Weber wrote that the 16th-century Protestant Reformation had produced a new character type in Protestant countries, which gave impetus to the Industrial Revolution and the spirit of capitalism that followed. This orientation emphasized self-improvement and the needs to strive and to achieve (Weber, 1930). McClelland suggested that these cultural values of hard work and striving for excellence became the norm in Protestant cultures and were taught to each succeeding generation. The emphasis on individual achievement was then expressed in ways that advanced economic growth.

To test this relationship between individual need achievement and economic growth, McClelland compared average per capita consumption of electric power (a measure of economic development) for 12 Protestant and 13 Catholic countries. The data showed that the Protestant countries were the more economically advanced.

He also examined the relationship between achievement motivation and economic growth for three periods of ancient Greek civilization: times of growth, climax, and decline. His hypothesis was that if a causal relationship exists between a population's need to achieve and national economic prosperity, then achievement motivation should be higher during the growth period and lower during the period that precedes the decline.

To assess the need for achievement in an ancient culture, researchers could not ask people to write stories projecting achievement-related fantasies onto ambiguous stimulus pictures. Instead, the methodology involved analyzing stories written at the time for evidence of achievement themes on the assumption that the writers were reflecting their society's values. When McClelland compared these empirical measures of the need for achievement with measures of economic success during the three time periods, the results were as predicted. There was a high level of need achievement during the period of growth. During the climax period, the level of individual need achievement fell, which, McClelland suggested, contributed to the economic decline. Because the measures were indirect, he sought to confirm them in other cultures. Studies of Spain during the Middle Ages and of England from 1400 to the onset of the Industrial Revolution around 1830 showed high need achievement preceding economic growth and falling need achievement preceding economic decline. These studies of writings at the time support the idea that an individual personality characteristic, widely manifested in a given culture, affects the nature of that culture.

McClelland studied more than 20 countries to compare economic and achievement-need levels in 1925 and 1950. As a measure of the need for achievement, he analyzed stories in second- to fourth-grade schoolbooks. He chose children's stories because they reflect the motivations society wants its children to learn and the moral values it desires to teach the young generation. The results showed that the higher a nation's level of achievement motivation in 1925, the greater its economic growth rate between 1925 and 1950. It is important to note that the high achievement motivation came first; it was not the increased level of economic development that led to the higher need for achievement. Thus, by determining a country's 1925 achievement-need level, McClelland could predict that country's economic situation 25 years later.

Another historical study investigated the effects of war on achievement motivation. The period included more than 150 wars during the recorded history of Great Britain from 1603 to 1988. Historical documents—speeches of political leaders and sovereigns and communications among cabinet officers and other high government officials—were analyzed to determine achievement-related imagery. The findings consistently showed that the ending of a war was followed by a decline in achievement motivation (Winter, 1993b).

Cultural factors can also define the areas of success appropriate to satisfy a person's need for achievement. A cross-cultural study compared need achievement among 372 male and female high school and college students living in Hong Kong. Some of the students were from England (children of British parents working in Hong Kong); other students were native Chinese. The British students focused on individual achievement in competitive situations, that is, what they could accomplish for themselves. The Chinese students, with the stronger sense of collectivism fostered by their culture, focused more on affiliative achievement (family and group achievement) rather than acting to satisfy personal goals (Salili, 1994). An analysis of later research provides support for these cultural differences between European American and Asian subject samples. Studies show the first group to focus more on individualistic striving for personal goals and the second group more on group, community, and family goals (Church & Lonner, 1998).

Having provided impressive evidence for the impact of the need for achievement on society, McClelland's research program turned to the issue of how the need for achievement could be fostered. If enough people could become highly motivated to achieve, personal and societal consequences would be significant.

Developing the Need for Achievement in Adults

Drawing on principles of psychotherapy as well as research about human and animal learning and about ways to change attitudes, McClelland developed formal courses to teach achievement motivation to adult men (McClelland, 1965; McClelland & Winter, 1969). The initial training programs, offered in the United States, Mexico, and India, lasted 12 to 18 hours a day for up to 14 days. The first objective was to instill confidence in the participants that the program would be effective; this was an effort to increase the trainees' self-efficacy. Research has shown that training techniques are more likely to be effective if trainees believe they will develop the required skills and if they are made aware of how these skills relate to real-world problems.

Next, trainees were given information about achievement motivation and how to apply it, that is, how to translate theory into action. They examined personal and cultural values with respect to achievement motivation and learned how an enhanced need for achievement could be to their benefit and the benefit of society. Finally, they agreed to commit themselves to a specific course of action designed to achieve well-defined personal and career goals and to record their progress in attaining those goals.

The results showed significant increases in actions related to a high need for achievement for many of the trainees, behaviors that persisted up to two years later. Behaviors indicative of enhanced achievement motivation led to pay raises, promotion, increased corporate profits, and greater sales volume.

Developing the Need for Achievement in Children

Having demonstrated that adults could be taught to increase their need for achievement, McClelland focused on the family environment, on child-rearing practices that could account for the development of achievement motivation in childhood. One study detected differences in need-achievement levels in children as young as 5, differences traced to mothers' attitudes. Another study used as subjects 8- to 10-year-old boys divided into high- and low-need-achievement groups. Their mothers were interviewed about the demands they made on their children. It was found that mothers of high-need-achievement boys expected more *self-reliant mastery* than did mothers of boys with a low need for achievement. (Self-reliant mastery was defined as doing things on their own, taking responsibility, trying hard, and performing well.) Mothers of high-need-achievement boys also placed fewer restrictions on their

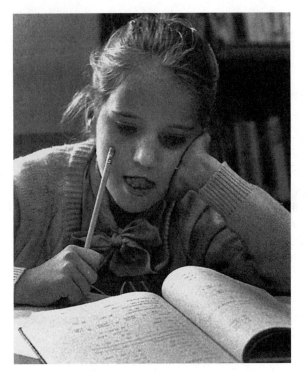

A child's desire to achieve can be enhanced by parents who set high but attainable standards and who express pleasure in the child's accomplishments.

sons but expected the restrictions they did impose to be followed at an earlier age. Boys found to be high in the need to achieve were encouraged to become independent at a younger age than were boys low in the need to achieve (Winterbottom, 1958).

In another set of experiments, parents of high- and low-need-achievement boys watched their sons performing such tasks as building towers out of blocks, playing ring-toss, and copying patterns with blocks. The parents were allowed to talk to their sons, and the parent-child interactions were observed. Parents of high-need-achievement boys set higher standards than did other parents, expecting their sons to build higher towers and to stand farther from the peg in the ring-toss game. McClelland concluded that to develop the need for achievement, one's parents should expect a high level of performance and set challenging standards.

Another difference between the two sets of parents was in the warmth of their comments to their children during the experimental tasks. While encouraging their sons to do well, parents of high-achievement-oriented boys were pleasant, calm, and offered good-natured bantering, more so than parents of low-achievement-oriented boys. Mothers of high-need-achievement boys tended to be more authoritarian than did mothers of low-need-achievement boys, whereas fathers of high-need-achievement sons were less authoritarian than were fathers of low-need-achievement sons. These findings, and similar results from other studies, led McClelland to suggest that a father's rigidity or authoritarian behavior could lower a son's need for achievement.

What emerges from this research is a sketch of parental behaviors likely to produce a high need for achievement in boys. These include setting realistic and challenging standards of performance at an age when such standards can be reached, not being overprotective or indulgent, not interfering with the child's efforts to achieve, and demonstrating genuine pleasure in the child's achievements.

In a longitudinal study, 89 men and women in their early 40s responded to stimulus pictures similar to those of the TAT. Their responses were coded for the presence or absence of TAT imagery. What makes this research unique is that the mothers of the subjects had been interviewed many years earlier when the subjects were 5 years old and questioned extensively about their child-rearing practices. Thus it was possible to compare differences in maternal behavior with the need-achievement levels of the children when they became adults. The results showed that parental pressure to achieve during the first two years of life led to higher levels of need achievement in adulthood, whereas pressure to achieve during later childhood years was not related to a high need achievement in adulthood. McClelland concluded from this research that parental behaviors during the first two years of life were crucial to the formation of a high level of need achievement in adulthood (McClelland & Franz, 1992).

Although need achievement apparently is established in childhood, the possibility exists that it could be enhanced or suppressed, strengthened or weakened, by expectations of caregivers in day-care centers or teachers in schools. If these adults do not expect a high level of performance and set challenging standards, the way parents of high need-achievement children were found to do, then they may be depriving children of an incentive to continue to achieve at a high level.

Some evidence suggests that this may operate with members of some minority groups. For example, when 392 White college students were asked to provide feedback on poorly written essays prepared, they were told, by Black or by White fellow students, the feedback was consistently less critical of Black writers than of White writers. Indeed, the comments were lenient and supportive of the work of the Black students whereas the comments offered to the White students were often harsh. Such inflated praise and gentle criticism in this example could deprive Black students of the high expectations and challenges provided to White students. That, in turn, could reduce the amount of effort and striving needed to maintain high achievement and result in lowered performance (Harber, 1998).

Age Differences

Evidence suggests that the need to achieve declines after middle age, when most people have passed the peak of their career. Older people tend to define success in different terms. No longer motivated to strive for the same goals they pursued in their 20s and 30s, they may still desire to strive for achievement, satisfaction, and challenge. If older persons have met work goals and gained status and financial security from their jobs, then these early career goals may be replaced by a quest for personal growth or for mentoring younger generations. Although these new goals may not require the same kind of competitive behavior, their attainment is nonetheless a kind of success.

Gender Differences

McClelland and his associates initially tested for gender differences in the need for achievement by comparing the performance of men and women subjects under experimental conditions designed to enhance achievement motivation (Veroff, Wilcox, & Atkinson, 1953). This research showed significant differences in the achievement need for men but not for women. This led McClelland to conclude that the TAT-based measure of need achievement was not valid for women subjects. Consequently, for many years, research on the need for achievement was conducted almost exclusively with male subjects. It is important to note, however, that the pioneering study of gender differences in achievement motivation was published in 1953. The accepted cultural norm was that women were not ambitious or desirous of achievement, or at least should not be. Obviously, people's views have changed over the last 50 years.

Research suggests that the need for achievement in women may be manifested in different ways, depending on their goals. Among college women oriented toward both career and family, those with high measured need achievement earned better grades, were more likely to complete college, and were more likely to marry and start a family at a relatively later age than were women with a lower need for achievement. Among women oriented more exclusively toward family rather than career goals, those with a high need to achieve expressed that need in activities related to dating, courtship, and marriage. They also placed greater emphasis on physical appearance than did career-oriented women with a high need to achieve (Elder & MacInnis, 1983). It is now accepted that some women make a conscious, deliberate, and careful choice of family over career or career over family, while other women try to balance both. Their need to achieve may be equally strong but the paths to satisfying that need are necessarily different.

Studies of children and adolescents suggest that some girls and young women do experience conflict at that age between the need to do their best and achieve at a high level versus the need to appear feminine, empathic, and caring. These subjects feared that achieving at too high a level would lead to unpopularity, especially with boys. A study of gifted third- to sixth-grade girls revealed several concerns they saw as barriers to achieving at a level appropriate to their abilities (Eccles, Barber, & Jozefowicz, 1999, p. 179):

- concern about hurting other people's feelings by winning
- concern about being seen as a show-off by expressing pride in one's achievements
- concern about reacting negatively to situations in which one is not successful
- concern about physical appearance and standards of beauty
- concern about being seen as too aggressive in classroom situations

Comment

McClelland's research program on the need for achievement demonstrates how a limited-domain approach to personality can have a wide domain of influence and application. The theory has a solid foundation of empirical support, and the data derive exclusively from experimental research. Whereas other theorists have speculated on the relationship between personality and social factors, McClelland has carefully described and investigated that relationship. His work has generated considerable research by a large network of followers. Interest in the theory continues today, some 50 years after the concept of need achievement was first introduced.

One new area of investigation deals with the distinction between the achievement need as an *approach* motive and that need as an *avoidance* motive. The question is whether behavior in achievement settings such as school or place of employment is directed primarily toward attaining success or toward avoiding failure. In other words, are we driven to win, or are we motivated instead to avoid losing? Perhaps it is some combination of the two and depends on the situation.

Studies of college students found that pursuing avoidance goals over the course of a semester led to a decline in self-esteem and in feelings of competence and control, as well as reduced vitality and overall life satisfaction. The researchers suggested that satisfying the achievement need by striving for success rather than acting to avoid failure is vital to subjective well being (Elliot & Church, 1997; Elliot & Sheldon, 1997).

Marvin Zuckerman: Sensation Seeking

sensation seeking The need for varied, novel, and complex sensations and experiences.

Since the early 1970s, psychologist Marvin Zuckerman (1928–), at the University of Delaware, has conducted research on a limited-domain aspect of personality that he calls **sensation seeking**. This trait has a large hereditary component initially noted by Eysenck (Chapter 10). Zuckerman describes sensation seeking as a desire for "varied, novel, complex, and intense sensations and experience, and the willingness to take physical, social, legal, and financial risks for the sake of such experience" (Zuckerman, 1994, p. 27).

Assessing Sensation Seeking

🎧 **sensation seeking**

To measure sensation seeking, Zuckerman constructed the Sensation Seeking Scale (SSS), a 40-item paper-and-pencil questionnaire. When developing this test, he administered it to many people whose behavior corresponded to his definition of sensation seeking. These included people who volunteered for psychological experiments that exposed them to novel experiences, people whose jobs involved physical danger (police officers and race-car drivers), and people who admitted to experimenting with drugs or varied sexual experiences. Their SSS scores were compared with the scores of people who chose to avoid novel or risky activities. Those people who deliberately sought unusual activities scored high on the SSS, and those who preferred less venturesome activities scored low. Sample items from the test are shown in Table 17.1.

Using the method of factor analysis, Zuckerman (1983) identified four components of sensation seeking.

1. *Thrill and adventure seeking*: a desire to engage in physical activities involving speed, danger, novelty, and defiance of gravity such as parachuting, scuba diving, or bungee jumping.

T A B L E   1 7 . 1   *Sample items from the Sensation Seeking Scale, Form V*

Choose the statement in each pair that you prefer.

_____ a. I like wild uninhibited parties.
_____ b. I prefer quiet parties with good conversation.

_____ a. I get bored seeing the same old faces.
_____ b. I like the comfortable familiarity of everyday friends.

_____ a. A sensible person avoids activities that are dangerous.
_____ b. I sometimes like to do things that are a little frightening.

_____ a. I would like to take off on a trip with no preplanned or definite routes or timetables.
_____ b. When I go on a trip I like to plan my route and timetable fairly carefully.

_____ a. I would like to try parachute jumping.
_____ b. I would never want to try jumping out of a plane with or without a parachute.

_____ a. There is altogether too much portrayal of sex in movies.
_____ b. I enjoy watching many of the sexy scenes in movies.

_____ a. I am not interested in experience for its own sake.
_____ b. I like to have new and exciting experiences and sensations even if they are a little frightening, unconventional, or illegal.

_____ a. People should dress according to some standard of taste, neatness, and style.
_____ b. People should dress in individual ways, even if the effects are sometimes strange.

SOURCE: From *Behavioral Expressions and Biosocial Bases of Sensation Seeking*, by M. Zuckerman, 1994, 389–392. Cambridge, England: Cambridge University Press.

2. *Experience seeking*: the search for novel experiences through travel, music, art, or a nonconformist lifestyle with similarly inclined persons.
3. *Disinhibition*: the need to seek release in uninhibited social activities.
4. *Boredom susceptibility*: an aversion to repetitive experiences, routine work, and predictable people, and a reaction of restless discontent when exposed to such situations.

Characteristics of Sensation Seekers

Zuckerman and his associates found that sensation seeking varies as a function of age. Younger people are more inclined to seek adventure, risk, and novel experiences than are older people. Test scores on subjects ranging from adolescents to 60-year-olds showed that sensation seeking begins to decrease in one's 20s. In a personal comment on how his own sensation-seeking behavior had changed with age, the 65-year-old Zuckerman noted that when he was younger, he enjoyed "late parties at [APA] conventions where one could 'talk psychology,' flirt, or just get drunk and disinhibited. These days I primarily go for the papers. Sensation seeking does decline with age" (1993, p. 49).

Significant gender differences were found in the four components of sensation seeking. Men scored higher on thrill and adventure seeking, disinhibition, and bore-

The need for sensation seeking manifests itself in the desire for varied, novel, and sometimes dangerous experiences.

dom susceptibility. Women scored higher on experience seeking. Similar results were obtained from subjects in the United States, England, Scotland, Japan, and Thailand. Researchers also found significant racial and cultural differences. Asians scored lower on the SSS than did people in Western countries. White subjects scored higher in sensation seeking than did non-Whites. No significant differences were reported as a function of educational level. College students did not score significantly higher or lower on the SSS than those who did not attend college.

Behavioral Differences

Although some people high in measured sensation seeking enjoy activities such as mountain climbing, hang gliding, auto racing, skiing, scuba diving, and parasailing, whereas those low in sensation seeking generally do not, the behavioral differences are not always so dramatic. Some high sensation seekers do prefer a variety of activities but not necessarily dangerous ones. These people may opt for encounter groups, meditation training, and novel "new age" experiences. Once the initial excitement has subsided, however, high sensation seekers usually discontinue the activities because they no longer provide the optimal level of stimulation.

Research showed that high sensation seekers were more likely than low sensation seekers to experiment with illicit drugs. Studies of more than 500 cocaine abusers and opiate addicts found that those who scored higher on the SSS exhibited more severe symptoms of drug abuse, including psychological impairment and the use of more than one drug, than did those who scored low on the SSS. High-scoring addicts started using drugs at an earlier age than low-scoring addicts did (Ball, Carroll, & Rounsaville, 1994; Kosten, Ball, & Rounsaville, 1994).

In addition, high sensation seekers were more likely to smoke cigarettes, drink alcohol, drive fast, have more car accidents and convictions for reckless or drunken driving, and engage in frequent sex. In Zuckerman's research, 16 percent of the high sensation seekers reported homosexual encounters, as compared with 7 percent of low sensation seekers. Among college men, high sensation-seeking scores correlated positively with risky sexual behavior the men knew could expose them to AIDS (Zuckerman, 1994). These findings were confirmed by research on older subjects. The correlation between sensation seeking scores and risky sexual behavior among gay men (both Blacks and Whites) was so strong that the researchers concluded that high-sensation-seeking males constitute a high-risk group for AIDS (Fisher & Misovich, 1990; Kalichman, Johnson, Adair, Rompa, Multhauf, & Kelly, 1994).

Physical risk-taking behavior has been related to sensation seeking. Skydivers, firefighters, riot-control police officers, and race-car drivers scored higher on the SSS than did groups not engaged in these activities. Research on male college under-graduate students in Israel found that high sensation seekers were more likely than low sensation seekers to participate in risky sports and to volunteer for army combat units (Hobfoll, Rom, & Segal, 1989).

Other findings describe different types of risk takers. Those identified as *anti-social* risk takers (drug addicts) or as adventurous risk takers (mountain climbers) showed significantly higher SSS scores than those identified as *prosocial* risk takers (police officers and firefighters). The researcher suggested that the motives of the prosocial group are related to factors other than thrill and adventure seeking (Levenson, 1990). High sensation seekers appear more willing than low sensation seekers to relocate from familiar to unfamiliar surroundings and to travel to exotic places, even when the journey involves physical hazards.

Personality Differences

Zuckerman and his colleagues correlated SSS scores with measures of other personality factors. One study showed that SSS scores, particularly on disinhibition, were related to Eysenck's factor of extraversion and to the asocial tendencies associated with psychoticism. Zuckerman suggested that high sensation seekers are ego-centrically extraverted, which means they are concerned with other people only as an audience or source of stimulation. They do not relate to other people in a dependent or nurturing way. High sensation-seeking scores also correlate positively with extraversion as described by Jung and measured by the Myers-Briggs Type Indicator (Morehouse, Farley, & Youngquist, 1990). However, investigations of sensation seeking and neuroticism as determined by psychological test scores showed no correlation. Zuckerman suggested that SSS scores did not point to abnormal or neurotic behavior but that neuroses such as phobias and obsessive-compulsive behaviors might be related to low sensation seeking.

High scores on the SSS correlate with a high degree of autonomy. High scorers openly express their emotions, are assertive in relating to others, are nonconforming, and are confirmed risk takers. They act independently of social conventions and of other people's needs and attitudes. Governed primarily by their own needs, they order their lives to maximize opportunities for self-fulfillment.

Cognitive Processes

Additional research related sensation seeking to cognitive processes of thought, perception, and intelligence. High sensation seekers were found to recognize symbols and figures more quickly than did low sensation seekers, which suggests that high sensation seekers process information more rapidly. High sensation seekers preferred greater complexity in visual stimulation, whereas low sensation seekers preferred stability, simplicity, and symmetry. High sensation seekers can focus their attention better than low sensation seekers. This was demonstrated in a study of 108 men and women college students who listened with headsets as different stimuli were presented to each ear simultaneously. When asked to repeat the words presented in one ear and to ignore the words presented in the other ear, high sensation seekers performed significantly better than did low sensation seekers on this task (Ball & Zuckerman, 1992).

Correlations between sensation seeking and intelligence test scores were positive but not high. High sensation seekers did not earn better grades in school. Zuckerman suggested that because high sensation seekers were more involved in recreational pursuits, they used less time for study. Tests of creativity and originality revealed that high sensation seekers have a greater capacity for original thinking but do not always express it in their schoolwork. High SSS scorers seem to be attracted to speculative, bizarre, pseudoscientific ideas. They tended to engage in what Sigmund Freud called primary-process thought. They may have images, dreams, and daydreams so vivid that the distinction blurs between these internal stimuli and the real world. Zuckerman suggested that because high sensation seekers continually search for novel experiences, if they cannot find them in external situations they look inward and create a fantasy world.

Occupational Preferences

Because high sensation seekers have a greater need for stimulating and varied experiences, they select different jobs than do low sensation seekers. On tests of vocational interests, such as the Kuder Preference Record, high and low sensation seekers showed significant differences. High SSS scores correlated positively with scientific interests and negatively with clerical interests. Men with high SSS scores also scored high on the Strong Vocational Interest Blank scales showing interest in the helping professions such as psychologist, physician, psychiatrist, social worker, and minister. Their scores correlated negatively with business sector jobs such as accountant, purchasing agent, and banker. Women with high SSS scores had high interest test scores for the profession of lawyer and low interest test scores for elementary school teacher, home economics teacher, and dietician. High sensation seekers of both sexes who were interested in the helping professions expressed a preference for risky, cutting-edge jobs such as crisis-intervention work or paramedic duty on emergency response teams.

Attitudes

High sensation seekers were shown to be more liberal in political and religious attitudes than were low sensation seekers. Those with high SSS scores are more likely to express atheistic views rather than belief in any conventional faith. High scorers on the SSS express more permissive attitudes toward sexual behavior, whether their own or that of other people. Low sensation seekers are more likely to be frequent churchgoers. They scored high on measures of authoritarianism, which is a personality style characterized by rigid opinions and prejudiced attitudes. Low sensation seekers also show a low tolerance for ambiguity. They believe ambiguous ideas and situations are threats rather than challenges (Zuckerman, 1994).

Physiological Differences

Zuckerman and his colleagues found that high and low sensation seekers showed different physiological responses to stimuli. High sensation seekers demonstrated stronger or more highly aroused physiological responses and higher tolerance thresholds for pain, loud noise, and other stressful stimuli (Zuckerman, 1990). Because high sensation seekers are better able to tolerate increases in arousal, Zuckerman suggested that they should cope better with stress than can low sensation seekers, who have a lower tolerance for arousal. This was confirmed in a study of 425 male and female high school varsity athletes. The students completed questionnaires assessing sensation seeking, emotional stability, coping skills, positive and negative life events, and positive and negative personal sports events such as injuries on the playing field. Low sensation seekers were found to have a significantly reduced ability to cope with stress (Smith, Ptacek, & Smoll, 1992).

In studies of high sensation seekers exposed to novel stimuli, researchers detected increases in the electrical activity of the brain and the level of sex hormones. The level of monoamine oxidase (an enzyme that controls the neurotransmitters, which produces rapid emotional swings) showed a decrease, which heightened feelings of excitement and euphoria (Zuckerman, Buchsbaum, & Murphy, 1980).

Heredity versus Environment

Research using the twin-comparison approach shows a strong hereditary basis for the sensation-seeking personality factor. A study by Eysenck suggested that 58 percent of this trait could be accounted for by genetic factors (Eysenck, 1983). A twin study conducted jointly by Zuckerman and Sybil Eysenck found an even greater genetic component (Zuckerman, 1993). Although sensation seeking is primarily inherited, Zuckerman also recognizes the influence of situational or environmental factors. One such factor is parental sensation seeking. Low-sensation-seeking parents may be overly fearful, protective, and inhibiting of their children, forbidding them to engage in adventurous behaviors. High-sensation-seeking parents may encourage

TABLE 17.2   *Self-descriptions of high and low sensation seekers*

High sensation seekers	Low sensation seekers
Enthusiastic	Frightened
Playful	Panicky
Adventurous	Tense
Elated	Nervous
Imaginative	Shaky
Daring	Fearful
Zany	Worried
Mischievous	Upset

SOURCE: From "Sensation Seeking" by M. Zuckerman. In *Dimensions of Personality* by H. London and J. E. Exner, Jr. (Eds.), 1978, New York: Wiley.

and reinforce their children for engaging in unusual activities, thus promoting additional sensation-seeking behaviors. Scores on the SSS also support the idea that first-borns and only-borns of both sexes are higher in sensation seeking than are later-borns. Because first-borns and only-borns receive more stimulation and attention from their parents at an early age, they are likely to be exposed to a greater optimal level of stimulation, which predisposes them to sensation seeking behavior as adults (Zuckerman, 1979).

Comment

Zuckerman's focus on the sensation-seeking personality trait has stimulated a great deal of research. Sensation seeking has been related to a wide range of behavioral, cognitive, personality, and physiological variables. Zuckerman's emphasis on the heritability of sensation seeking places his work in a different category from the behavioral and social-learning approaches to personality, which focus on the influences of situational factors and of learning.

Sensation-seeking theory has a commonsense appeal. It is easy to accept the idea that people differ in their need for excitement and risk, change and adventure. We can describe our own level of sensation seeking and make fairly accurate judgments about the levels of our friends and relatives by considering the activities they enjoy or avoid. Zuckerman asked high and low sensation seekers to choose from a list of adjectives those that best described themselves. Compare your own characteristics with the results shown in Table 17.2.

Martin E. P. Seligman: Learned Helplessness

learned helplessness A condition resulting from the perception that we have no control over our environment.

Since the mid-1960s, psychologist Martin Seligman (1943–) at the University of Pennsylvania has conducted research on a limited-domain aspect of personality he calls **learned helplessness**. He observed this phenomenon in a laboratory experiment on dogs on his first day as a graduate student. The dogs were subjects in a two-part conditioning experiment. In the first part, they were being conditioned to associate a high-pitched sound with an electric shock. This was a simple Pavlovian classical conditioning situation involving respondent behavior (the pairing of the tone with the shock).

In the second part of the experiment, the dogs were put individually in a large box that contained two compartments divided by a low wall. A shock was delivered through the floor of the compartment in which the dog was placed. To escape the shock, all the dog needed to do was emit the appropriate operant behavior—simply to jump over the low barrier into the other compartment where there was no electric shock. Once the dogs learned to jump the wall—something dogs can be expected to do quickly—they would be tested to see if the high-pitched tone without the electric shock would bring about the same response. The experiment's goal was to determine whether learning in the first situation (pairing the tone with the shock) carried over to the second situation (pairing the tone with the escape behavior).

The research did not work out the way it was planned. The dogs did not cross the barrier to escape the shock. Instead, when the shock was administered through the floor of their compartment, they lay down, whimpered, and made no effort to escape. The experimenters were baffled but Seligman thought he had a clue. He suggested that during the first part of the experiment, the dogs had learned that they were helpless. When the tone sounded, there was nothing they could do to avoid the paired shock. Why even try? This learned reaction apparently generalized to the second part of the experiment, even though a means of escape was available. Seligman wrote,

> I was stunned by the implications. If dogs could learn something as complex as the futility of their actions, here was an analogy to human helplessness, one that could be studied in the laboratory. Helplessness was all around us—from the urban poor to the newborn child to the despondent patient with his face to the wall. Was this a laboratory model of human helplessness, one that could be used to understand how it comes about, how to cure it, how to prevent it, what drugs worked on it, and who was particularly vulnerable to it? (1990, p. 20)

learned helplessness

Determined to find the answers to these questions, Seligman launched an intensive research program on learned helplessness, a condition he described as resulting from the perception that we have no control over our environment, that there is nothing we can do to change our circumstances.

Early Research

In Seligman's initial experiments, dogs were harnessed and exposed to painful, though not physically harmful, electric shock. There was no action the dogs could take to escape or avoid the shock. After a series of shocks, the dogs were placed in a two-compartment shuttle box. As in the first experiment Seligman had witnessed, a shock was administered through the floor of the compartment in which the dogs had been placed. The behavior of these dogs was then compared with that of a control group of dogs that had not been exposed to the first series of electric shocks.

When the dogs in the control group were placed in the box and given the shock through the floor, they raced about the compartment until they accidentally leaped the barrier into the safe compartment. On succeeding trials, they jumped the barrier more quickly each time, having learned that this was the way to escape. The dogs in the experimental group, who had received electric shocks *before* being placed in the shuttle box, behaved differently. After getting the shock through the compartment floor, they raced around for about 30 seconds and then gave up, dropping to the floor and whimpering. They never learned to escape, not even when experimenters tried to entice them over the barrier with food. These dogs had become passive and helpless and could make no attempt to alter their situation (Overmier & Seligman, 1967; Seligman & Maier, 1967).

The learned helplessness phenomenon was demonstrated for a variety of behaviors in animals including cats, goldfish, gerbils, guinea pigs, mice, and rats. It was also found that exposure to inescapable shock led to the production of endorphins, a natural morphine-like substance that alleviates pain. The researchers suggested that if the pain of the shock is thus reduced, this might help explain why the animals do not try to escape it (Peterson, Maier, & Seligman, 1993).

Learned helplessness was similarly demonstrated in humans. In one study, subjects in the experimental group were exposed to a loud, irritating noise and told they could turn it off if they pressed a series of buttons in the correct sequence. The conditions were arranged so that there was no correct sequence. No matter what action the subjects took, the noise continued. In the control group, the subjects could turn off the noise by pressing buttons in a sequence that was relatively easy to learn. In the next step, the experimental subjects were placed in a situation in which all they had to do to stop the noise was move their hand from one side of a box to the other in response to a light signal. Control-group subjects rapidly learned this series of behaviors but experimental subjects did not. They sat passively, making no effort to turn off the irritating noise (Hiroto, 1974).

Other studies with human subjects confirmed and extended these findings. Learned helplessness was found to occur after subjects observed helpless models, especially when the subjects recognized similarities between themselves and the models. The experimenters suggested that the subjects were saying, in effect, "If the models can't do anything about this, neither can I."

Learned helplessness was found to occur simply by suggestion, when subjects were told that they could do nothing to change their situation (Brown & Inouye, 1978; Maier & Seligman, 1976). In addition, research showed that subjects experiencing experimentally produced learned helplessness were slower to solve cognitive problems, were less competitive in games, showed a disrupted ability to learn, and manifested emotional difficulties such as frustration, anxiety, depression, and paranoid-like responses (Bodner & Mikulincer, 1998; Seligman, 1975).

A meta-analysis of 132 studies involving several thousand subjects found that the effects of inescapable shock were even stronger in human than in animal subjects. Learned helplessness effects have been found in many human subject groups including adult men and women, college students, adolescents, children, and patients in psychiatric hospitals (Villanova & Peterson, 1991).

Another study found that exposing college student subjects to a situation over which they had control (in which they were *not* helpless) produced a degree of protection or immunity against a later attempt to induce helplessness. A similar immunization effect was found in dogs and rats exposed to the same sequence of control versus no control situations (Ramirez, Maldonado, & Martos, 1992).

As we discuss additional research on this limited-domain personality theory, keep in mind that approximately one-third of the animal and human subjects studied did not succumb to the learned helplessness variable (Seligman, 1990).

Learned Helplessness in Elderly Persons

Applying the concept of learned helplessness to a real-world situation, psychologists investigated whether elderly residents of nursing homes, residing in a setting in which they had little control or choice, might learn to be helpless (Langer & Rodin, 1976). The researchers designed an experiment to determine whether offering nursing home residents greater control would affect their feelings of lethargy and their lack of motivation and activity. Perhaps the common listlessness stemmed from ceding control to the nursing home staff and from learning that their own behaviors and wishes had little effect on their living conditions.

Residents of one floor in the facility were given the opportunity to make decisions about their daily lives—for example, choosing what they wanted for breakfast, caring for the plants in their room, arranging their furniture. They were told that they would assume more responsibility for their care and make many decisions formerly controlled by the staff. Residents of the other floor of the nursing home remained under the authority of the staff. Their quarters, food, and recreational activities were identical to those on the experimental floor, but they had no personal influence or responsibility.

Behavioral differences became apparent within a few weeks. Residents who had been given a degree of personal control were happier and more physically active. They spent more time in social activities and less time alone in their room. The nursing staff reported that 93 percent of these residents showed enhanced social and emotional adjustment. Of the residents living under the old system, with no increase in personal control, only 21 percent showed positive changes. A follow-up visit 18 months later confirmed that the differences persisted. Also, of the residents given personal responsibility, 15 percent had died since the beginning of the study; in the more helpless group, 30 percent had died (Baltes & Bates, 1986).

Learned Helplessness and Emotional Health

The beneficial effects on psychological health of having control over one's life have been widely documented. In one example, researchers studied 71 men and women cancer patients, ages 29 to 80. They interviewed the patients and gave questionnaires to assess marital satisfaction, psychological adjustment, and perception of control. Patients with the highest perception of control were better adjusted than were patients who believed they had little control over their situation. This finding held even for patients severely debilitated by their physical condition. People who believed they could exert some influence over their illness and their emotions showed greater psychological adjustment than did people in better physical condition but with a low perception of control (Thompson, Sobolew-Shubin, Galbraith, Schwankovsky, & Cruzen, 1993).

Another study found that it was possible for people to learn to increase their feeling of control. A sample of 110 men and women (average age 55) scheduled for extensive dental work were assessed prior to treatment for their level of anxiety and their desire for control in a dental setting. Half the patients were shown a stress inoculation training video; the other half, the control group, was shown a video about the local sights. The results showed that patients with low control in a dental setting but with a strong desire for greater control benefited the most from seeing the stress training video. They believed they felt more control and less pain during the actual treatment than did similar patients in the control group who had received no stress training (Law, Logan, & Baron, 1994).

Animal Research on Learned Helplessness and Health

The results of the nursing home study raised the possibility that learned helplessness could affect physical health. To test this hypothesis, Seligman and his associates designed a study in which rats were injected with malignant tumor cells. The rats were exposed to one of three conditions: an electric shock from which they could escape, a shock from which they could not escape, and no shock (Visintainer, Volpicelli, & Seligman, 1982). Under normal circumstances, based on the number of cells injected, half the rats would be expected to reject the cells and survive. In the control group (no electric shock), 50 percent rejected the tumor as expected. Among the rats that received a shock but could escape, thus having some control over their situation, 70 percent rejected the tumor and survived. But in the learned helplessness group that could not escape the shock, only 27 percent of the rats rejected the malignant cells and survived.

These results were supported in a similar study of young rats. When the rats reached adulthood, they received injections of malignant cells and were exposed to the same three experimental conditions. The majority of the rats who had learned to be helpless when young failed as adults to reject the tumor. In contrast, the majority of the rats who had learned control when young rejected the tumor as adults (Seligman & Visintainer, 1985). Seligman concluded, "Childhood experiences proved to be crucial in tumor rejection by adults. Childhood mastery immunized, and early helplessness put adult rats at risk for cancer" (1990, p. 170).

Learned helplessness was also shown to weaken the rats' immune system (Maier, Laudenslager, & Ryan, 1985). The immune system forms a major part of the body's defense against illness. It contains several kinds of cells, including T-cells and NK (natural killer) cells, which resist viruses, bacteria, and tumor cells. In rats subjected to inescapable shock, T-cells no longer multiplied rapidly in response to specific invaders, and NK cells lost their ability to destroy other infections. These findings may provide a physiological explanation for the result that the helpless rats were unable to reject their tumor.

explanatory style

Explanatory Style: Optimism and Pessimism

Seligman expanded his theory as follows. He argued that it is not only the lack of control under conditions of learned helplessness that affects our health. Also important is how we explain this lack of control to ourselves. He proposed the

explanatory style A way of explaining to ourselves our relative lack of control over our environment. An optimistic explanatory style can prevent learned helplessness; a pessimistic explanatory style spreads helplessness to all facets of life.

optimism

pessimism

concept of **explanatory style** to account for this factor. An *optimistic* explanatory style prevents helplessness; a *pessimistic* explanatory style spreads helplessness to all facets of life.

People with an optimistic explanatory style tend to be healthier than are people with a pessimistic explanatory style. Pessimists tend to believe that their actions are of little consequence. For this reason, they are unlikely to try to prevent illness by changing their behavior with regard to smoking, diet and exercise, or timely medical attention. A study of 72 young adults found that optimistic people were less likely than pessimistic people were to get sick. However, when optimists did fall ill, they were far more likely to take responsibility for their care, such as resting, consulting a physician, or drinking appropriate fluids (Peterson, Maier, & Seligman, 1993).

In another investigation of explanatory style and physical health, researchers found that among college undergraduates, pessimists had twice as many infectious illnesses over a one-year period than did optimists. Among breast cancer patients experiencing a recurrence, the optimists lived longer over a 5-year period of study, independent of the severity of their illness. Optimists were also shown to develop stronger immune systems and to be more likely to recover from heart attacks (Peterson & Seligman, 1987; Peterson, Maier, & Seligman, 1993).

A study of 105 first-semester law school students found that those who scored high for an optimistic explanatory style had a significantly greater number of T-cells and NK cells, which protect against infections, than did those who scored low on optimism (Segerstrom & Taylor, 1998). Research on 100 adult men and women ages 30 to 45 found that those who scored high for a pessimistic explanatory style held more negative beliefs about their life and had higher blood pressure readings than did those who scored low on pessimism (Raikkonen, Matthews, Flory, Owens, & Gump, 1999).

The health of a group of 200 men was monitored from age 25 to their late 60s (Peterson, Seligman, & Vaillant, 1988). At the beginning of the study the subjects wrote essays that were analyzed for themes indicating an optimistic or a pessimistic explanatory style. The men were interviewed periodically and given questionnaires about life events. Every 5 years they were given a physical exam. No differences in health were reported up to age 45. By age 60, however, it was clear that the optimists were in far better health than the pessimists. Those subjects with an optimistic explanatory style evidenced fewer and less severe symptoms of the diseases of middle age than did the pessimists.

Optimism has been shown to be beneficial in coping with AIDS. In a study of 550 homosexual and bisexual men, some were diagnosed as HIV-negative and others as HIV-positive and thus likely to develop AIDS. The men were given questionnaires to assess their degree of optimism or pessimism as well as psychological adjustment, feeling of control, and concern about the disease. Those who scored high on optimism scored lower on psychological distress, had fewer worries about illness, believed they were at lower risk for developing AIDS, and believed they would have a higher degree of control over the disease than did those who scored low on optimism. Those who were already HIV-positive were found to be more optimistic about not developing AIDS than were those who were HIV-negative. The researchers explained,

They believe that they are safe from AIDS because they have probably developed an immunity. They believe that they can eliminate the virus from their system and that their immune systems are better able to accomplish this than those of other gay men. They believe that staying healthy and in good physical condition can prevent the development of AIDS. (Taylor, Kemeny, Aspinwall, Schneider, Rodriguez, & Herbert, 1992, p. 469)

Although such beliefs may be illusory, they also helped the subjects cope with a serious health threat and minimize the depression that accompanies a major illness. Further, the men highest in optimism were no more likely to engage in high-risk sexual behaviors than were those lowest in optimism. In general, those highest in optimism took better care of their health.

Optimism has been found to vary with the intensity of one's religious beliefs. Members of fundamentalist Jewish, Muslim, and Calvinist faiths scored higher on measures of optimism than did more moderate religious groups such as Conservative Jews, Lutherans, and Methodists. Similarly, the moderate group scored higher on optimism than did members of more liberal faiths such as Reform Jews and Unitarians. The researchers suggested that the greater optimism among fundamentalists was its association with "more hopefulness and less hopelessness. Fundamentalism is also associated with less personal blame for negative events" (Sethi & Seligman, 1994, p. 58).

Cultural differences in explanatory style have been investigated. Optimism-pessimism measures were taken from 257 college students in the United States, 312 college students in China, and 44 college students of Chinese American heritage. It was found that the American subjects were more optimistic than were the Chinese Americans, and that the Chinese Americans were more optimistic than were the mainland Chinese (Lee & Seligman, 1997).

Not surprisingly, research has shown that stressful life experiences can affect one's level of optimism. A group of adult subjects who were primary caregivers for relatives with Alzheimer's disease were compared on measures of optimism-pessimism with a group of adults who were not acting as caregivers. The caregivers grew increasingly pessimistic over a 4-year period and experienced greater anxiety, stress, and physical health complaints (Robinson-Whelen, Kim, MacCallum, & Kiecolt-Glaser, 1997).

Depression

depression, mental

Seligman's research program revealed an association between learned helplessness and depression. A major symptom of depression is the feeling of being unable to control the life events. Seligman referred to depression as the "ultimate pessimism." People who are severely depressed believe they are helpless. They see little point in trying to do anything because they do not expect that anything will work out well for them. Seligman observed several similarities between the symptoms of depression and the characteristics of learned helplessness (Seligman, 1990).

All of us experience occasional feelings of helplessness when we fail in some situation or when family or job pressures seem overwhelming. No matter how unhappy or angry we may feel at the moment, however, most people usually recover after a period of time. But some people do not recover quickly or easily. They may

People who are severely depressed believe they are helpless. They generalize their failure in one situation, such as a poor grade in one course, to all other aspects of life.

generalize their failure in one activity (say, earning a poor grade or failing to get a promotion) to other areas of life and to their personal sense of self-worth. Consequently, they can become helpless and depressed in all situations and lose their impetus to strive.

As you can see from Table 17.3, depression is associated with symptoms of poor health such as ulcers, stress, and norepinephrine deficiency. Depression also puts people at risk for physical illness by reducing the effectiveness of the immune system, suppressing NK cell activity and altering white blood cell count, findings confirmed by more than 40 studies over a 10-year period (Herbert & Cohen, 1993; Weisse, 1992).

According to Seligman, the important difference between people who recover from temporary depression and those who do not is their explanatory style.

> A pessimistic explanatory style changes learned helplessness from brief and local to long-lasting and general. Learned helplessness becomes full-blown depression when the person who fails is a pessimist. In optimists, a failure produces only brief demoralization. (1990, p. 76)

In addition, pessimists formulate explanations about negative situations in personal and pervasive terms, saying, for example, "It's all my fault," "It's always going to be this way," or "It's going to affect every aspect of my life."

Seligman's research with his undergraduate students as subjects supports the hypothesis that learned helplessness leads to depression in people with a pessimistic explanatory style. At the beginning of the semester, students were tested to determine their explanatory style and were asked to state the course grade they believed would represent personal failure. After the midterm exam, the students took a per-

TABLE 17.3 *Similarity of symptoms of learned helplessness and depression*

Learned helplessness	Depression
Passivity	Passivity
Difficulty learning that responses produce relief	Difficulty learning that responses produce outcomes
Lack of aggression	Introjected hostility
Weight loss and anorexia	Loss of libido
Norepinephrine depletion*	Norepinephrine depletion
Ulcers and stress	Ulcers and stress; feelings of helplessness

*Norepinephrine acts as a neurotransmitter; severe depression is associated with norepinephrine deficiency.

SOURCE: Adapted from *Learned Helplessness and Depression in Animals and Men*, by M. E. P. Seligman. Copyright © 1976 by General Learning Press, Morristown, NJ.

sonality test to measure their level of depression. The results showed that 30 percent of those with an optimistic explanatory style and who received grades they considered a personal failure showed symptoms of depression. Among those with a pessimistic explanatory style who received disappointing grades, 70 percent became depressed. Similar results were found in other research with college students and in studies of third-grade elementary school students. In both cases, explanatory style predicted the incidence of depression (Nolen-Hoeksema, Girgus, & Seligman, 1987; Zullow & Seligman, 1985).

The Attribution Model

The concept of explanatory style describes how people differ in the way they explain to themselves their feelings of learned helplessness or lack of control. Some people are devastated by learned helplessness. They appear to give up, become depressed, and experience health problems. Others facing similar situations recover after a period of time. Seligman proposed a cognitive explanation for these differences, a revised concept of learned helplessness called the **attribution model.** The key word is *attribution.* When we fail at something, we attribute that failure to some cause. This is how we explain to ourselves the source of our failure and our lack of control.

Seligman suggested that pessimists attribute personal failure to internal, stable, and global causes whereas optimists attribute failure to external, unstable, and specific causes. For example, if you fail a course and make an *internal* attribution, you are saying there is something wrong with you. Maybe you are not smart enough to pass. If you make an *external* attribution, you are saying that the cause lies elsewhere. Maybe the professor doesn't like you or your job doesn't leave you enough time to study.

If the cause of your failure cannot be changed, it is considered *stable*. If it can be modified, such as reducing your work hours so you have more time to study, it is considered *unstable*. If you make a *global* attribution, you are saying that whatever caused you to fail that course is likely to cause you to fail other courses. By making

attribution (social psychology)

attribution model The idea that we attribute our lack of control or failure to some cause.

a *specific* attribution you are limiting your failure to one course. That failure does not transfer to other courses of study or areas of life.

Seligman and his colleagues developed a test to measure explanatory or attributional style (Peterson, Semmel, Von Baeyer, Abramson, Metalsky, & Seligman, 1982). The Attributional Style Questionnaire (ASQ) presents 12 hypothetical situations. Six are positive events, such as becoming wealthy, and six are negative events, such as a disappointing social experience. Some events deal with achievement in school or on the job; other events involve getting along with people. When you take the test, you are asked to suggest a cause for each situation and to rate that cause on the three dimensions: internal versus external, stable versus unstable, and global versus specific.

In one study, the ASQ was given to first-year college students who had experienced negative events. Students who made internal, stable, and global attributions for their situations (the pessimistic style) received lower grades in their courses than those who made external, unstable, and specific attributions (the optimistic style) (Peterson & Barrett, 1987). Because both groups were of similar intelligence, that was not a factor in explaining the difference in grades. The researchers concluded that the pessimists responded to negative events and problems passively and made few attempts to alter their circumstances.

In another study, women who had recently undergone abortions and who made internal, stable, and global attributions were found to report more physical complaints and to expect more negative consequences than did women who made external, unstable, and specific attributions (Major, Mueller, & Hildebrandt, 1985).

Other research indicates that the global-versus-specific dimension has the greatest consequences for learned helplessness and depression. Subjects who failed in one situation and attributed that failure to a global cause also failed in other situations. Subjects who made global attributions also reported the intrusion of irrelevant thoughts that interfered with the performance of cognitive tasks. The experimenters suggested that people who think poorly of themselves will perform poorly, that is, in ways that continue to confirm their attributions. This in turn lowers their self-esteem and confidence about dealing with future situations (Mikulincer, 1986; Mikulincer & Nizan, 1988).

A study of 89 African American high school and college students found that those who made internal attributions for negative events also had low self-esteem. In other words, the students who blamed themselves for failures also felt bad about themselves (Belgrave, Johnson, & Carey, 1992).

The Development of Learned Helplessness in Childhood

Although learned helplessness can occur throughout life, Seligman believes we are particularly vulnerable to those feelings in infancy and early childhood. During these formative years the experience of learned helplessness can predispose us to the pessimistic explanatory style (Seligman, 1975). Infants begin life in a state of total helplessness, with no control over their environment. As they mature, they become increasingly able to exercise control. They can cry, which brings parents or caregivers to tend to their needs. They can crawl, walk, and speak, and the mastery of each skill brings greater possibilities for control—and for failure. Through these early interactions with the physical and social environments, a child's sense of helplessness, or of mastery and control, will be determined.

When infants make a response, that action may bring about some change such as food, a toy, or a hug, or it may have no effect whatever. At a primitive level, infants form associations between responses and outcomes. If there is no correlation between them—if the responses do not lead to successful outcomes—the condition of learned helplessness results. Infants learn that particular responses don't work, and they may generalize this idea to other responses, believing that none of them will work. This generalized learned helplessness accompanies a sense of having no control over life. In contrast, a high correlation between responses and outcomes provides positive feedback that leads to feelings of mastery and control. A consistent explanatory style develops by about age 8 and is strongly affected by the parents' explanatory style. Seligman remarked, "pessimistic parents also have pessimistic children" (Peterson, Maier, & Seligman, 1993, p. 293).

Learned helplessness can develop later in childhood in response to brutality from peers, a harsh school environment, or other negative experiences. Race and poverty are also factors in the development of learned helplessness. Students who are treated by teachers and peers as though they are less intelligent or skilled than other students may develop learned helplessness.

Comment

Learned helplessness is a popular and influential concept in the field of personality and has generated hundreds of research studies. Seligman and his associates have applied the concept to sports, politics, religion, child rearing, and job performance. However, critics note little difference between learned helplessness and Rotter's concept of external locus of control. Both express the idea that some people believe there is little they can do to influence their lives and therefore cease to try. Seligman admits the two concepts overlap but sees an important distinction.

> The difference is that locus of control is a belief about the nature of reinforcement—that is, about rewards and punishments in the world. Causal attributions are judgments about the causes of events. Although related, these are not the same. (Peterson, Maier, & Seligman, 1993, p. 145)

The learned helplessness limited-domain theory of personality leaves several questions unanswered. For example, does a person's explanatory style cause depression, or does depression cause a particular explanatory style? Is the effect of prolonged failure on self-esteem more important than its relationship to learned helplessness? Is the Attributional Style Questionnaire used to measure explanatory style truly valid?

Overall, a large, impressive body of data supports the learned helplessness concept. Seligman has lately turned his attention to a related idea called *learned optimism*. He is developing a program of exercises to teach optimism to adults and to children, thus applying his findings beyond the laboratory to the home and the workplace.

Chapter Summary

McClelland studied the need for achievement using the Thematic Apperception Test. Men high in the achievement need are typically middle-class, have a better memory for uncompleted tasks, are more active in college and community activities, and are more resistant to social pressures. People high in need achievement are more likely to attend college and do well, to take high-status jobs with a great deal of personal responsibility, and to expect to be successful. They often succeed as entrepreneurs or managers. McClelland found a high positive correlation between a nation's need-achievement level and its economic prosperity. When the need for achievement declined among the population, the economy declined. Parental behaviors likely to produce a high need for achievement in children include setting realistically high performance standards, not overprotecting or indulging, not interfering with the child's efforts to achieve, and showing pleasure in the child's achievements. Parental authoritarianism tends to lower a child's need for achievement. The need to achieve declines after middle age, perhaps as a result of the tendency to redefine success at this stage of life.

According to Zuckerman, sensation seeking is an inherited trait concerned with the need for novel and complex sensations and experiences. The Sensation Seeking Scale is designed to assess this aspect of personality. Four components of sensation seeking are thrill and adventure seeking, experience seeking, disinhibition, and boredom susceptibility. Research has shown higher levels of sensation seeking among White subjects, males, people from Western cultures, and young people from adolescence to their early 20s. High sensation seekers are more likely to use drugs, smoke cigarettes, drink alcohol, drive fast, engage in frequent sex, gamble, take physical risks, and travel to dangerous places. In terms of personality, high sensation seekers tend to be egocentrically extraverted, autonomous, assertive, nonconforming, and uninhibited in expressing emotions. In cognitive functioning, high sensation seekers recognize symbols and figures more quickly and prefer complexity in visual stimulation. Vocational interests of high-sensation-seeking males are oriented toward science and the helping professions. Low-sensation-seeking males are more oriented toward clerical and business concerns. High sensation seekers tend to hold more liberal religious and political attitudes. They are higher in tolerance for ambiguity, more permissive in sexual attitudes, and lower in authoritarianism. They display stronger physiological responses to novel stimuli. Sensation seeking is primarily inherited but can be influenced by environmental factors such as birth order and parental level of sensation seeking.

Learned helplessness, investigated by Seligman, results from our perception that we have no control over our environment. An optimistic explanatory style can prevent learned helplessness; a pessimistic style spreads helplessness to all facets of life and can lead to physical illness and depression. Pessimists make personal, permanent, and pervasive explanations to themselves about negative events. Thus, helplessness changes from brief and localized to long lasting and generalized. The attribution model of learned helplessness involves attributing a failure to some cause. Pessimists attribute their failures to internal, stable, and global causes. Optimists attribute their failures to external, unstable, and specific causes. The Attributional Style Questionnaire measures these causal dimensions. Although learned helplessness can occur at any age, infants and young children are particularly vulnerable. Infants learn that a correspondence exists between their responses and outcomes when responses bring changes in their environment; they learn helplessness when these responses do not bring about desired changes. Major causes of learned helplessness are maternal deprivation and an environment that provides a low level of stimulation and feedback.

Review Questions

1. How does McClelland's research on the need for achievement relate to the work of Freud and Murray?

2. Describe McClelland's technique for measuring achievement motivation.

3. Describe the differences between high and low achievers in terms of college and career performance.

4. What differences have been reported between men and women in the need for achievement?

5. What parental behaviors can influence the development of a child's need for achievement?

6. Define sensation seeking and describe its four components.

7. What does research show about differences in sensation seeking as a function of age, gender, culture, and race?

8. How do people high in sensation seeking differ from people low in sensation seeking in terms of personality and cognitive functioning?

9. Describe the occupational interests and political attitudes of high sensation seekers.

10. Discuss the relative importance of heredity and environment in determining sensation seeking.

11. Define learned helplessness and describe Seligman's early research.

12. In the study on elderly residents of nursing homes, how did having greater control over their lives affect the residents' behavior and attitudes?

13. How can learned helplessness affect physical health? How does it relate to depression?

14. Distinguish between optimistic and pessimistic explanatory styles. How can they affect health?

15. How does the attribution model of learned helplessness differ from Seligman's earlier version of learned helplessness?

Suggested Readings

The Need for Achievement

McClelland, D. C. (1961). *The achieving society.* New York: Free Press. Applies the methods of psychology to the evaluation of economic, historical, and social forces that explain the rise and fall of civilizations.

McClelland, D. C., & Winter, D. G. (1969). *Motivating economic achievement.* New York: Free Press. Describes psychological training programs to increase achievement motivation among business leaders to accelerate a nation's economic development.

Winter, D.G. (1998). "Toward a science of personality psychology": David McClelland's development of empirically derived TAT measures. *History of Psychology, 1,* 130–153. Discusses the implications of McClelland's scientific application of Henry Murray's humanistic-based TAT personality assessment instrument.

Sensation Seeking

Brannigan, G. G., & Merrens, M. R. (Eds.). (1993). *The undaunted psychologist: Adventures in research.* Philadelphia: Temple University Press. Essays by a diverse group of academic psychologists about the origins of their research interests. Includes chapters by McClelland and by Zuckerman about their personal and intellectual approaches to their research problems.

Zuckerman, M. (1990). The psychophysiology of sensation seeking. *Journal of Personality, 58,* 313–345. Summarizes research showing the differences in psychophysiological response of high and low sensation seekers to novel or intense stimuli.

Zuckerman, M. (1991). *Psychobiology of personality.* New York: Cambridge University Press. Outlines a behavioral genetics approach to personality and summarizes relevant research from neuropsychology, psychopharmacology, psychophysiology, and abnormal psychology.

Learned Helplessness

Robinson-Whelen, S., Kim, C., MacCallum, R. C., & Kiecolt-Glaser, J. K. (1997). Distinguishing optimism from pessimism in older adults. Is it more important to be optimistic or not to be pessimistic? *Journal of Personality and Social Psychology, 73,* 1345–1353. Describes longitudinal research on the persistence of optimism and pessimism among a sample of adults (mid-50s through 60s) facing significant life challenges and stresses, such as caring for a terminally ill relative.

Segerstrom, S. C., & Taylor, S. E. (1998). Optimism is associated with mood, coping, and immune change in response to stress. *Journal of Personality and Social Psychology, 74,* 1646–1655. Uses questionnaires and physiological measurements to study the effects of optimism on mood, expectations, coping behaviors, health behaviors, and changes in immune system among first-year law school students.

Seligman, M. E. P. (1975). *Helplessness: On depression, development, and death.* San Francisco: W. H. Freeman. Describes the early research on learned helplessness, its development in childhood, and its impact on depression and physical health.

Seligman, M. E. P. (1990). *Learned optimism.* New York: Alfred A. Knopf. Describes differences in explanatory style between optimists and pessimists and relates these styles to physical and mental health. Offers techniques for changing pessimism to optimism.

Personality in Perspective

In Chapter 1 we stated that our purpose was to explore the forces and factors that shape personality, to attempt to discover what makes us the way we are. We have discussed nearly two dozen theories, ranging from Sigmund Freud's work at the turn of the 20th century to contemporary developments at the beginning of the 21st century. Because we have covered so many diverse approaches, you may be tempted to conclude that the field of personality is marked more by chaos than certainty, more by differences than agreements.

Which theory is correct? Which solves the puzzle of personality? The most complete answer we can suggest is that all theories discuss factors that are influential, to some degree, in shaping our personality. Each theorist has contributed vital pieces to the puzzle. Now it is time to examine those pieces to try to see the whole picture. We will summarize these viewpoints in a brief and broad overview of the themes that emerge from the work of the various theorists. Let us consider the following issues.

- the genetic factor
- the environmental factor
- the learning factor
- the parental factor
- the developmental factor
- the consciousness factor
- the unconscious factor

The Genetic Factor

There is strong evidence that many personality traits or dimensions are inherited. These include the following:

- Eysenck's dimensions of psychoticism, neuroticism, and extraversion (the latter derived from the work of Jung)
- McCrae and Costa's five factors of neuroticism, extraversion, openness to experience, agreeableness, and conscientiousness
- Buss and Plomin's three temperaments of emotionality, activity, and sociability

In addition, Zuckerman's trait of sensation seeking is primarily influenced by genetic factors. Thus, the trait approach, with its emphasis on the impact of heredity, remains vital today and may be the fastest growing area of personality research. What remains to be determined is precisely how many inherited factors, traits, or temperaments there are. Cattell's 16, Eysenck's 3, McCrae and Costa's 5, Buss and Plomin's 3—or some as yet undiscovered number? Future research in behavior genetics may yield even more facets of personality shaped by inherited factors.

No matter what number of traits there may be, not even the most ardent proponent of the genetics approach argues that personality can be explained fully and totally by heredity. What we inherit are dispositions, not destinies; tendencies, not certainties. Whether our genetic predispositions are ever realized depends on social and environmental conditions, particularly those of childhood.

The Environmental Factor

Every personality theorist we have discussed acknowledged the importance of the social environment. Adler spoke of the impact of birth order, arguing that personality is influenced by our position in the family relative to our siblings. We are exposed to varying parental and social situations as a function of the extent of the age difference between siblings or whether we have siblings at all. In Adler's view, these different home environments can result in different personalities.

Horney believed that the culture and time period in which we are reared shows its effects, such as those she recorded in the neuroses exhibited by German and by American patients. She also pointed out the vastly different social environments to which boys and girls are exposed as children. She spoke of female inferiority developing from the way girls are treated in a male-dominated culture. She suggested that women raised in a matriarchal culture might have higher self-esteem and different personality characteristics.

Fromm subscribed to the influence of larger historical forces and events such as the type of society a people constructs. Each period in history—whether the Middle Ages, the Renaissance, the Protestant Reformation, or the Industrial Revolution, for example—helped shape different personality or character types appropriate to the needs of that era.

Even Allport and Cattell, who inaugurated the trait approach to the study of personality, agreed on the importance of the environment. Allport noted that although genetics supplies the basic raw material of personality, it is the social environment that shapes the material into the finished product. Cattell argued that heredity is more important for some personality factors than for others but that environmental factors ultimately influence every factor to some extent.

Erikson's eight stages of psychosocial development are innate but the environment determines the ways in which those genetically based stages are realized. He believed that social and historical forces influence the formation of ego identity. Maslow and Rogers contended that self-actualization was innate but recognized that environmental factors could inhibit or promote the self-actualization need.

Large-scale societal events such as wars and economic recessions can restrict life choices and influence the formation of self-identity. More ordinary life changes (becoming parents, getting divorced, and changing jobs) can also affect personality.

Finally, ethnic background and whether we are part of a minority or majority culture, helps determine personality. We saw examples of ethnic differences in such variables as sensation seeking, locus of control, and the need for achievement. We also learned that members of minority groups develop an ethnic identity as well as an ego identity and have to adapt to both cultures. The success of this adaptation affects personality and psychological health. For all these reasons, then, it is impossible to deny the impact of diverse environmental and social forces on personality. The most significant way in which that impact is exerted is through learning.

The Learning Factor

Evidence is overwhelming that learning plays a major role in influencing virtually every aspect of behavior. All of the social and environmental forces that shape personality do so by the techniques of learning. Even inherited facets of personality can be modified, disrupted, prevented, or allowed to flourish by the process of learning. Skinner (based on earlier work by Watson and Pavlov) taught us the value of positive reinforcement, successive approximation, superstitious behavior, and other learning variables in shaping what others call personality, although he described it simply as an accumulation of learned responses.

Bandura introduced the idea that we learn from watching models (observational learning) and through vicarious reinforcement. To Rotter, reinforcement is the key. He argued that our major motivation is to maximize positive reinforcement. Bandura and Rotter agreed with Skinner that most behaviors are learned and that genetics plays only a limited role.

We discussed many aspects of personality that have scientific evidence to show that they are learned, such as McClelland's need for achievement (originally proposed by Murray). In addition, considerable research has documented that learning will influence self-efficacy (Bandura), locus of control (Rotter), and learned helplessness (Seligman). These concepts appear to be related to a broader notion: level of control. People who believe they have control over their lives are high in self-efficacy, have an internal locus of control, and are not characterized by learned helplessness (which involves lack of control). In Seligman's terms, people who believe they are in control are optimistic rather than pessimistic.

Control is beneficial to many aspects of life and represents one of the most exciting developments in personality research in recent years. A high degree of control has been related to better coping mechanisms, fewer stress effects, greater mental and physical health, perseverance, higher aspirations and self-esteem, lower anxiety, higher grades, and greater social skills and popularity. By whatever name—self-efficacy, internal locus of control, or optimism—control is determined by social and environmental factors. It is learned in infancy and childhood, though it can change later in life. We saw that specific parental behaviors can foster a child's feeling of being in control. Thus, the notion of control is a learned dimension of personality for which parental behavior is paramount.

The Parental Factor

Although Freud was the first theorist to emphasize parental influences on the formation of personality, virtually every theorist echoed his views. Recall Adler's focus on the consequences for a child who feels unwanted or rejected by his or her parents. Such parental rejection can lead to insecurity, leaving the person angry and deficient in self-esteem. Horney wrote from her own experience about how lack of parental warmth and affection can undermine a child's security and result in feelings of helplessness. Fromm argued that the more independent a child is from the primary tie with the parents, the more insecure that child becomes.

Allport and Cattell, whose work was based on the importance of traits, also recognized the parental factor in personality formation. Allport considered the infant's relationship with the mother to be the primary source of affection and security, conditions crucial to later personality development. Cattell saw infancy as the major formative period, with the behavior of parents and siblings shaping the child's character. Erikson held that the child's relationship with the mother in the first year of life was vital in promoting a trusting attitude. Maslow commented on how necessary it was for parents to satisfy their child's physiological and safety needs in the first two years of life. This was a prerequisite for the emergence of higher-order needs. Rogers spoke of the parents' responsibility for supplying unconditional positive regard to their children.

We have also seen examples of how parental behaviors can determine specific aspects of personality, such as the need for achievement, self-efficacy, locus of control, and learned helplessness or optimism. Parental behaviors can influence primarily inherited traits such as sensation seeking. You can easily imagine how uncaring and punitive parents could stifle the emergence of inherited traits such as extraversion, sociability, agreeableness, and openness to experience.

A review of research on the relationship between early childhood experiences and adult psychopathology showed consistently that the childhood of depressed and anxious adults was related to inadequate parenting. The parents were found to be more rejecting and abusive, and less caring and affectionate, than parents of less troubled adults (Brewin, Andrews, & Gotlib, 1993). A study of more than 100 mothers rated them on the factors of emotionality and agreeableness. Mothers characterized by negative emotions and disagreeableness had children who scored higher in defiance, anger, disobedience, and other behavior problems than did mothers who did not exhibit negative emotional qualities (Kochanska, Clark, & Goldman, 1997).

What happens when parents are not the primary caregivers, that is, when parents share child-rearing responsibilities with day care workers, friends, or family members while they work outside the home? In a national longitudinal survey of more than 15,000 children ages 3 to 12, no significant problems with behavior or self-esteem were found when the mothers took a job outside the home. The researcher concluded that caregiving by someone other than the child's mother had no negative impact on the variables studied (Harvey, 1999).

A unique real-world laboratory in which to explore the issue of surrogate caregivers is the collective child-care arrangement in kibbutzim in Israel. In that situation, mothers attend to their infants' needs for the first few months of life. Then the primary responsibility for child care is assigned to professional caregivers. Children typically spend more time with these surrogate mothers and fathers than they do with their parents.

Overall, kibbutz children were found to function and adapt well, assuming they established a secure relationship with their parents during infancy. Indeed, the strength of that bond was the strongest predictor of children who became dominant, independent, and achievement oriented. However, the barracks-like sleeping arrangements (like summer camp or boarding school) in early childhood could lead to a more anxious, restrained, and emotionally flat personality. Adults reared on a kibbutz who failed to bond with their parents or caregivers showed introversion, diminished capacity for friendship, and reduced emotional intensity in interpersonal relations (Aviezer, Van Ijzendoorn, Sagi, & Schuegel, 1994).

A major controversy erupted in the late 1990s when it was suggested that parental attitudes and behaviors have no long-term effects on their child's personality outside the home (Harris, 1995, 1998). According to this idea, which seems questionable at first, peers influence a child's personality much more than do parents. Children adopt the behaviors, attitudes, values, and characteristics of their classmates and friends in an effort to win their acceptance and approval.

Proponents of this view do not completely deny the influence of parents on their child's personality. What they do dispute is the idea that parental influence is maintained outside the home environment. "Parents do influence their children's behavior. Of course they do. But the influence is in context, specific to the home. When children go out, they leave behind the behavior they acquired at home. They cast it off like the dorky sweater their mother made them wear" (Harris, quoted in Sleek, 1998, p. 9).

Modest support for this proposal was provided by a study of 839 pairs of twins in late adolescence. The results showed that twins who had more friends in common were more alike in personality than were twins who had fewer friends in common. This suggests that friends, rather than the home environment, had a greater impact on their personality (Loehlin, 1997).

Researchers who subscribe to the primacy of genetic factors in personality also tend to reject or minimize the parental effect, suggesting that the family environment contributes little to personality (Matthews & Deary, 1998). However this controversy is eventually resolved—whether personality is determined by parents, peers, genes, or some combination of factors—it leads us to another question. Is personality fixed in early life by these influences or can it be changed in later years? That question leads us to a consideration of the developmental factor.

The Developmental Factor

Freud believed that personality was shaped and fixed by the age of 5 and that it was difficult thereafter to alter any aspect of it. We accept that the childhood years are crucial to personality formation, but it is also clear that personality continues to develop well beyond childhood, perhaps throughout the entire life span. Theorists such as Cattell, Allport, Erikson, and Murray viewed childhood as important but agreed that personality could be modified in later years. Some theorists suggested that personality development is ongoing in adolescence. Jung, Maslow, Erikson, and Cattell noted middle age as a time of major personality change.

The question is, just how long does our personality continue to change and grow? Does your self at age 20 indicate what you will be like at 40? As with most questions concerning personality, this has become a highly complex issue. Perhaps it is not even the right question to ask.

It may not surprise you to learn that empirical evidence supports diverse viewpoints (see, for example, Matthews & Deary, 1998). Does personality change? Well, yes. Does personality also remain stable? Uh, probably, yes. But if we were to refine the question and ask whether *some* personality characteristics remain stable over a lifetime while other characteristics change, then we would be able to answer with an unqualified yes.

What has emerged from research is that our basic foundation of enduring personality dispositions (such as the traits described in McCrae and Costa's five-factor model) remains stable over many years. According to the evidence, these basic traits and capacities appear to be enduring from age 30 on. Research shows that the factors of neuroticism, extraversion, and openness decline from college age to middle age, whereas the factors of agreeableness and conscientiousness increase with age. Cross-cultural comparisons have demonstrated this consistency in such diverse countries as the United States, Germany, Italy, Portugal, Croatia, and South Korea (Costa & McCrae, 1997; McCrae et al., 1999).

What brings about personality change in adulthood? Theorists who favor the overriding influence of genetic factors suggest that any personality change is independent of environmental factors. Other theorists believe that the answer is rooted in social and environmental influences and in the adaptations we make to them. Changes in economic circumstances, leaving college, marriage and parenthood, divorce, job loss or advancement, midlife crises, aging parents all create problems to which adults must adjust. Two longitudinal studies of women examined the social factor of the women's liberation movement of the 1970s and its impact from the college years into middle age. Significant increases were found over time in the personality traits of dominance, self-acceptance, empathy, achievement, and self-focus. Decreases were noted in adherence to rules or norms (Agronick & Duncan, 1998; Roberts & Helson, 1997).

All such cultural and personal challenges leave their mark on personality. A contemporary theorist has suggested that personality can be described on three levels to explain its continuing development in adulthood. These levels are dispositional traits, personal concerns, and life narrative (McAdams, 1994).

Dispositional traits are inherited traits of the kind discussed by McCrae and Costa, those personality characteristics found to remain stable and relatively unchanging from about age 30 on. *Personal concerns* refer to conscious feelings, plans, and goals; for example, what we want, how we try to achieve it, and how we feel about the people in our life. These feelings, plans, and goals change often over the life span as a result of the diverse influences to which we are exposed, such as the examples noted above. All of these situations can mean changes in our feelings and intentions, yet the underlying dispositional traits (such as our basic level of neuroticism or extraversion), with which we confront these life situations, remain relatively unchanged.

The third level, *life narrative*, implies shaping the self, attaining an identity, and finding a unified purpose in life. We are constantly writing our life story, creating who we are and how we fit into the world. Like personal concerns, the life narrative changes in response to social and environmental demands. As adults, we add to and rewrite our narrative with each stage of life and its differing needs, challenges, and opportunities. In sum, then, this view holds that the underlying dispositional traits portion of personality remains constant, while our conscious judgments about who we are and who we would like to be are subject to change. That idea leads to another factor the theorists have considered, that of consciousness.

The Consciousness Factor

Almost every personality theory we have described deals explicitly or implicitly with conscious (cognitive) processes. Even Freud and Jung, who focused on the unconscious, wrote of an ego or conscious mind that perceives, thinks, feels, and remembers, enabling us to interact with the real world. Through the ego we are able to perceive stimuli and later recall an image of them. Jung wrote about rational functioning, making conscious judgments and evaluations of our experiences. Adler described humans as conscious, rational beings capable of planning and directing the course of our life. We formulate hopes, plans, and dreams and delay gratification. To use a term the social learning theorists adopted, we consciously *anticipate* future events.

Allport believed that people who are not neurotic will function in a conscious, rational way, aware and in control of the forces that motivate them. Rogers thought people were primarily rational beings, governed by a conscious perception of themselves and their world of experience. Maslow also recognized the role of consciousness; he proposed cognitive needs to know and to understand.

Kelly offered the most complete theory based on cognitive factors. He argued persuasively that we form constructs about our environment and about other people and that we make predictions (anticipations) about them based on these constructs. We formulate hypotheses about our social world and test them against the reality of our experience. Based on everyday evidence, it is difficult to deny that people construe, predict, and anticipate how others will behave and then modify or adapt their behavior accordingly.

Bandura credits people with the ability to learn through example and vicarious reinforcement. To do so, we must be able to anticipate and appreciate the consequences of the actions we observe in others. We visualize or imagine the results of or reinforcements for behaving the same way a model does, even though we may never have experienced those consequences personally. Rotter suggests that we perceive ourselves as conscious beings, capable of influencing events. We form conscious expectations about the reinforcer that is likely to follow a certain behavior, and to estimate the likelihood that behaving in a given way will lead to a particular reinforcer. Thus there is widespread agreement that consciousness exists and is an influence on personality. However, there is less agreement on the role or even the existence of another influence, that of the unconscious.

The Unconscious Factor

Sigmund Freud introduced us to the world of the unconscious, that murky repository of our darkest fears and conflicts, forces that affect our conscious thoughts and behaviors. Psychologists have found some evidence to support Freud's notion that thoughts and memories are repressed in the unconscious, and that repression (as well as other defense mechanisms) may operate at the unconscious level. Along with the cognitive movement in psychology have come not only an interest in conscious processes but also a renewed interest in the unconscious. Recent research confirms that the unconscious is a powerful force, perhaps even more pervasive in its influence than Freud suggested. However, the modern depiction of the unconscious is not the same as Freud's view. Contemporary researchers focus on unconscious cognitive processes and describe them as more rational than emotional.

The rational unconscious is often referred to as the *nonconscious*, to distinguish it from Freud's unconscious, his so-called dark cauldron of repressed wishes and desires. One method for studying the nonconscious involves subliminal activation, in which various stimuli are presented to subjects below their level of conscious awareness (see Chapter 2). Despite the subjects' inability to perceive the stimuli, their conscious processes and behaviors can be activated by those stimuli. The obvious conclusion to be drawn from such research is that people can be influenced by stimuli they can neither see nor hear. We also discussed in Chapter 2 the "Mommy and I are one" study about how subliminal presentation of certain stimuli influenced cognitive as well as emotional responses (Silverman & Weinberger, 1985). The subliminal stimuli had therapeutic value even though the subjects had no conscious awareness of the actual messages. Thus, the unconscious may have both a rational and an emotional component.

Although the unconscious is an ongoing research topic in psychology today, many of the personality theorists who followed Freud ignored it. We may suggest that the emotional unconscious as Freud envisioned it—the startling idea that signaled the formal beginning of the study of personality—remains the least understood factor and still very much what it was in Freud's time, mysterious and inaccessible.

The Happy Personality

Having reviewed several factors that contribute to the shaping of our personality, let us close the book on a positive note. The January 2000 issue of the *American Psychologist* journal focuses on "positive" psychology. This special issue on happiness, excellence, and optimal human functioning indicates the direction of contemporary personality theory and research for the new millennium.

You know from your own experience that some people you meet are more optimistic, open, and full of energy and vitality than are others. What causes them to be this way even when you know they are facing social or job or financial problems? Even if you are not one of these joyful people, we hope you have at least known temporary periods of happiness, when you have fallen in love, aced a tough exam, or gotten the job you really wanted, making you feel on top of the world.

Psychologists have variously labeled the happy personality in terms such as *subjective well being* or *life satisfaction* and define it as encompassing a cognitive evaluation of the quality of one's life experience and the possession of positive affect (McGregor & Little, 1998). (The word *affect* refers to moods and emotions.) Thus, happiness has both rational and emotional aspects.

Who are these happy personalities? As you might expect, research has covered demographic, social, cultural, racial, and personality factors.

Demographic and other factors.   Let us consider what may seem the most obvious determinant of happiness: money. That old adage is true; money does not buy happiness. However, the absence of money can lead to unhappiness. Research shows that an income adequate to fund basic needs is a necessary, though not sufficient, prerequisite for happiness. Surveys show that people who lack the money to provide for essentials are unhappy, but having money significantly beyond what is actually needed has little measurable effect on happiness. Even winning a huge amount in a lottery usually results in only a temporary increase in subjective well being (DeNeve & Cooper, 1998; Diener, Suh, Lucas, & Smith, 1999; King & Napa, 1998).

Is health related to happiness? Like money, the absence of good health can diminish happiness but being healthy in itself does not guarantee a happy personality. Thus, health appears to be a necessary but not sufficient condition for subjective well being (Myers & Diener, 1995). Age and gender likewise have little bearing on happiness. Studies show that life satisfaction does not decline with age and that men and women do not differ significantly in reported subjective well being (Diener, Suh, Lucas, & Smith, 1999; DeNeve & Cooper, 1998).

Marriage, however, does make a difference. The evidence is clear from studies conducted in several countries that married people report higher levels of happiness than do people who are divorced, separated, widowed, or who have never married. Married women have been found to be happier than unmarried women, and married men are happier than unmarried men (Mastekaasa, 1995).

Some evidence suggests that job satisfaction and level of education have a modest correlation with happiness but no relationship has yet been found between intelligence and happiness (Diener, Suh, Lucas, & Smith, 1999). Happiness does seem to vary across cultures, with a nation's relative wealth being of major importance. Countries marked by such poverty that satisfying basic needs is difficult have much lower reported levels of happiness among the population than do more economically advanced countries (Diener, Diener, & Diener, 1995). Evidence also suggests that subjective well being is markedly higher in individualistic societies such as the United States than in collectivist or group oriented cultures such as China (Diener, Suh, Smith, & Shao, 1995).

The impact of race was suggested by a study of 312 African American adults asked to rate their life satisfaction. Those who had experienced discrimination reported lower levels of life satisfaction than did those who had experienced no discrimination. Those who attended predominantly White schools had higher life satisfaction levels than those who went to predominantly Black or mixed race schools (Broman, 1997). Overall, then, we see that relatively little of the happy personality can be accounted for by demographic and social variables.

Personality factors.   It probably will be no surprise to learn that self-efficacy is significantly associated with happiness. We are happier and feel better when we have the ability to do things well and when we expect that situation to continue in the future. We feel more satisfied when we have goals to strive for and a sense of purpose. These give meaning to life, which is a consistently strong component of subjective well being (King & Napa, 1998; McGregor & Little, 1998). A study of more than 350 adults ages 44 to 65 linked three additional variables to life satisfaction: self-acceptance, environmental mastery, and autonomy. *Self-acceptance* includes making positive evaluations about oneself and one's life. *Environmental mastery* refers to the ability to deal effectively with challenges and problems. *Autonomy* implies a strong sense of self-determination (Schmutte & Ryff, 1997).

A meta-analysis of 148 studies involving more than 42,000 subjects described six other variables associated with the happy personality (DeNeve & Cooper, 1998).

1. *repressive-defensiveness*, an unconscious avoidance of threatening information that results in denying negative experiences and the negative emotions associated with those experiences; the lower a person's score on this factor, the higher is their subjective well being.
2. *trust*, the attribution a person makes about other people's motives; people who score high on trust tend to make optimistic attributions and to report greater life satisfaction.
3. *internal locus of control and desire for control*, the belief in and desire for control over one's life; the higher a person's score on these factors, the higher is their subjective well being.
4. *hardiness*, the tendency to minimize the effects of stressful events by adapting to and evaluating them in optimistic terms.
5. *emotional stability and positive affect*, being free of neuroses and of negative moods, feelings, and emotions; these conditions correlate positively with subjective well being.
6. *self-esteem*, people who feel good about themselves score high in subjective well being.

The personality correlates of the happy personality studied most extensively are the Big Five (Chapter 10). People who score low on the neuroticism factor and high on extraversion, agreeableness, and conscientiousness report high levels of subjective well being (DeNeve & Cooper, 1998). A comparison of more than 4,000 adults in the United States and in Germany confirmed that low neuroticism was the strongest predictor of well being (Staudinger, Fleeson, & Baltes, 1999). Many influences on the development of the happy personality remain for future investigation in the new millennium, but the idea is certainly a remarkably different explanation than that proposed by Sigmund Freud, who began the formal study of personality at the end of the 19th century.

Review Questions

1. Six questions about human nature were posed in Chapter 1 (p. 35). At the beginning of this course, we asked you to write down your own thoughts on these issues. Now that you have studied the diverse approaches to personality presented in this book, reconsider your answers to these questions to see how your views might have changed.

2. Think about the similarities and differences between your personality and the personality of your mother, father, or siblings. What factors do you see in common?

3.   Do you believe that you are a happy personality type? What factors do you think account for your answer. Why do you rate yourself high or low on subjective well being?

4.   Which of the approaches to personality discussed in this text do you find most helpful in understanding yourself? Which were of the least value to you?

GLOSSARY

ability traits Traits that describe our skills and how efficiently we will be able to work toward our goals.

actualization tendency The basic human motivation to actualize, maintain, and enhance the self.

aesthetic need The need for aesthetically pleasing experiences and beautiful surroundings.

aggressive drive The compulsion to destroy, conquer, and kill.

aggressive personality Behaviors and attitudes associated with the neurotic trend of moving against people, such as a domineering and controlling manner.

analytical psychology Jung's theory of personality.

anima archetype; animus archetype Feminine aspects of the male psyche; masculine aspects of the female psyche.

anxiety To Freud, a feeling of fear and dread without an obvious cause.

archetypes Images of universal experiences contained in the collective unconscious.

attitudes To Allport, attitudes are similar to traits. However, attitudes have specific objects of reference and involve either positive or negative evaluations. To Cattell, attitudes are our interests in and emotions and behaviors toward some person, object, or event. This is a broader definition than typically used in psychology.

attribution model The idea that we attribute our lack of control or failure to some cause.

authoritarianism   A psychic mechanism for regaining security, displayed in either masochistic or sadistic feelings.

automaton conformity   A psychic mechanism for regaining security, displayed in unconditional obedience to the prevailing rules that govern behavior.

basic anxiety   A pervasive feeling of loneliness and helplessness; the foundation of neurosis.

basic strengths   To Erikson, motivating characteristics and beliefs that derive from the satisfactory resolution of the crisis at each developmental stage.

basic weaknesses   To Erikson, motivating characteristics that derive from the unsatisfactory resolution of developmental crisis.

behavior modification   A form of therapy that applies the principles of reinforcement to bring about desired behavioral changes.

behavior potential   The likelihood that a particular behavior will occur in a given situation.

behavioral genetics   The study of the relationship between genetic or hereditary factors and personality traits.

behaviorism   The school of psychology, founded by John B. Watson, that focused on psychology as the study of overt behavior rather than of mental processes.

being orientation   A character type in which people define themselves in terms of what they are, not in terms of what they have; their self-worth comes from within, not from comparing themselves with others.

biophilous orientation   A character type congruent with the productive orientation; this type is concerned with personal growth and development.

cardinal traits   The most pervasive and powerful human traits.

case study   A detailed history of an individual that contains data from a variety of sources.

castration anxiety   A boy's fear during the Oedipal period that his penis will be cut off.

catharsis   The expression of emotions that is expected to lead to the reduction of disturbing symptoms.

cathexis   An investment of psychic energy in an object or person.

central traits   The handful of outstanding traits that describe a person's behavior.

cognitive complexity   A cognitive style or way of construing the environment characterized by the ability to perceive differences among people.

cognitive needs   Innate needs to know and to understand.

cognitive simplicity   A cognitive style or way of construing the environment characterized by a relative inability to perceive differences among people.

collective unconscious   The deepest level of the psyche containing the accumulation of inherited experiences of human and prehuman species.

common traits   Traits possessed in some degree by all persons.

compensation   A motivation to overcome inferiority, to strive for higher levels of development.

complex   To Jung, a core or pattern of emotions, memories, perceptions, and wishes in the personal unconscious organized around a common theme, such as power or status. To Murray, a normal pattern of childhood development that influences the adult personality; childhood developmental stages include the claustral, oral, anal, urethral, and genital complexes.

compliant personality   Behaviors and attitudes associated with the neurotic trend of moving toward people, such as a need for affection and approval.

conditional positive regard   Approval, love, or acceptance granted only when a person expresses desirable behaviors and attitudes.

conditions of worth   To Rogers, a belief that we are worthy of approval only when we express desirable behaviors and attitudes and refrain from expressing those that bring disapproval from others; similar to the Freudian superego.

conflict   To Horney, the basic incompatibility of the neurotic trends.

conscience   A component of the superego that contains behaviors for which the child has been punished.

constitutional traits   Source traits that depend on our physiological characteristics.

constructive alternativism   The idea that we are free to revise or replace our constructs with alternatives as needed.

construct   An intellectual hypothesis that we devise and use to interpret or explain life events. Constructs are bipolar, or dichotomous, such as tall versus short or honest versus dishonest.

control group   In an experiment, the group that does not receive the experimental treatment.

coping behavior   Consciously planned behavior determined by the needs of a given situation and designed for a specific purpose, usually to bring about a change in one's environment.

correlational method   A statistical technique that measures the degree of the relationship between two variables, expressed by the correlation coefficient.

creative power of the self   The ability to create an appropriate style of life.

crisis   To Erikson, the turning point faced at each developmental stage.

death instincts   The unconscious drive toward decay, destruction, and aggression.

defense mechanisms   Strategies the ego uses to defend itself against the anxiety provoked by conflicts of everyday life. Defense mechanisms involve denials or distortions of reality.

deficit (deficiency) needs   The lower needs; failure to satisfy them produces a deficiency in the body.

denial   A defense mechanism that involves denying the existence of an external threat or traumatic event.

dependent variable   In an experiment, the variable the experimenter desires to measure, typically the subjects' behavior or response to manipulation of the independent variable.

destructiveness   A psychic mechanism for regaining security, displayed in a desire to eliminate threatening objects, persons, and institutions.

detached personality   Behaviors and attitudes associated with the neurotic trend of moving away from people, such as an intense need for privacy.

disinhibition   The weakening of inhibitions or constraints by observing the behavior of a model.

displacement   A defense mechanism that involves shifting id impulses from a threatening object or from one that is unavailable to an object that is available; for example, replacing hostility toward one's boss with hostility toward one's child.

dream analysis   A technique involving the interpretation of dreams to uncover unconscious conflicts. Dreams have a manifest content (actual events in the dream) and a latent content (the symbolic meaning of the dream events).

dynamic lattice   The representation in a chart or diagram of the relationships among ergs, sentiments, and attitudes.

dynamic traits   Traits that describe our motivations and interests.

early recollections   A personality assessment technique in which our earliest memories, whether of real events or fantasies, are assumed to reveal the primary interest of our life.

ego   To Freud, the rational aspect of the personality, responsible for directing and controlling the instincts according to the reality principle. To Jung, the conscious aspect of personality. To Murray, the conscious organizer of all behavior; this is a broader conception than Freud's.

ego-ideal   A component of the superego that contains the moral or ideal behaviors for which a person should strive.

ego identity   The self-image formed during adolescence that integrates our ideas of what we are and what we want to be.

Electra complex   During the phallic stage (ages 4 to 5), the unconscious desire of a girl for her father, accompanied by a desire to replace or destroy her mother.

encounter groups   A group therapy technique in which people learn about their feelings and about how they relate to (or encounter) one another.

entropy principle   A tendency toward balance or equilibrium within the personality; the ideal is an equal distribution of psychic energy over all structures of the personality.

environmental-mold trait   Source traits that are learned from social and environmental interactions.

epigenetic principle of maturation   The idea that human development is governed by a sequence of stages that depend on genetic or hereditary factors.

equivalence principle   The continuing redistribution of energy within a personality; if the energy expended on certain conditions or activities weakens or disappears, that energy is transferred elsewhere in the personality.

ergs   Permanent constitutional source traits that provide energy for goal-directed behavior. Ergs are the basic innate units of motivation.

excitation need   The need for a stimulating external environment so that the brain can function at a peak level of activity and alertness.

expectancy   Our belief that if we behave a certain way in a given situation, a predictable reinforcement will follow.

experimental group   In an experiment, the group that is exposed to the experimental treatment.

explanatory style   A way of explaining to ourselves our relative lack of control over our environment. An optimistic explanatory style can prevent learned helplessness; a pessimistic explanatory style spreads helplessness to all facets of life.

exploitative orientation   A character type that takes from others by force or cunning.

expressive behavior   Spontaneous and seemingly purposeless behavior, usually displayed without our conscious awareness.

external locus of control   A belief that reinforcement is under the control of other people, fate, or luck.

externalization   A way to defend against the conflict caused by the discrepancy between an idealized and a real self-image by projecting the conflict onto the outside world.

extinction   The process of eliminating a behavior by withholding reinforcement.

extraversion   An attitude of the psyche characterized by an orientation toward the external world and other people.

factor analysis   A statistical technique based on correlations between a number of measures, which may be explained in terms of underlying factors.

feminine psychology   To Horney, a revision of psychoanalysis to encompass the psychological conflicts inherent in the traditional ideal of womanhood and women's roles.

fictional finalism   The idea that there is an imagined or potential goal that guides our behavior.

fixation   A condition in which a portion of libido remains invested in one of the psychosexual stages because of excessive frustration or gratification.

fixed role therapy   A psycotherapeutic technique in which the client acts out the constructs appropriate for a fictitious person. This shows the client how the new constructs can be more effective than the old ones he or she has been using.

frame-of-orientation need   The need for a consistent, coherent picture of our world within which to understand life events.

free association   A technique in which the patient says whatever comes to mind. In other words, it is a kind of daydreaming out loud.

freedom of movement   The degree of expectancy that a certain behavior will bring a given reinforcement.

fully functioning person   Rogers's term for self-actualization, for developing all facets of the self.

functional analysis   An approach to the study of behavior that involves assessing the frequency of a behavior, the situation in which is occurs, and the reinforcers associated with it.

functional autonomy of motives   The idea that motives in the normal, mature adult are independent of the childhood experiences in which they originally appeared.

generalization.   The idea that responses made in one situation will also be made in similar situations.

growth (being) needs   The higher needs; although growth needs are less necessary than deficit needs for survival, they involve the realization and fulfillment of human potential.

habits   Specific, inflexible responses to specific stimuli; several habits may combine to form a trait.

having orientation   A character type in which the definition and meaning of one's life lies in possessions, in what one has rather than what one is.

hierarchy of needs   An arrangement of innate needs, from strongest to weakest, that activates and directs behavior. The hierarchy includes physiological, safety, belongingness and love, esteem, and self-actualization needs.

historical determinism   The view that personality is basically fixed in the early years of life and subject to little change thereafter.

hoarding orientation   A character type that derives security from amassing and preserving material possessions and personal feelings.

humanistic communitarian socialism   An ideal system of society typified by positive human relationships and the full expression of the productive orientation.

id   To Freud, the aspect of personality allied with the instincts; the source of psychic energy, the id operates according to the pleasure principle. To Murray, the id contains the primitive, amoral, and lustful impulses described by Freud, but it also contains desirable impulses, such as empathy and love.

idealized self-image   For normal people, the self-image is an idealized picture of oneself built on a flexible, realistic assessment of one's abilities. For neurotics, the self-image is based on an inflexible, unrealistic self-appraisal.

identity crisis.   The failure to achieve ego identity during adolescence.

identity need   The need to achieve an awareness of our unique abilities and characteristics.

idiographic research   The intensive study of a relatively small number of subjects using a variety of assessment techniques.

incongruence   A discrepancy between a person's self-concept and aspects of his or her experience.

independent variable   In an experiment, the stimulus variable or condition the experimenter manipulates to learn its effect on the dependent variable.

individual psychology   Adler's theory of personality.

individuation   A condition of psychological health resulting from the integration of all conscious and unconscious facets of the personality.

inferiority complex   A condition that develops when a person is unable to compensate for normal inferiority feelings.

inferiority feelings   The normal condition of all people; the source of all human striving.

instinctive drift   The substitution of instinctive behaviors for behaviors that had been reinforced.

instinctoid needs   Maslow's term for the innate needs in his needs-hierarchy theory.

instincts   In Freud's system, mental representations of internal stimuli, such as hunger, that drive a person to take certain actions.

internal locus of control   A belief that reinforcement is brought about by our own behavior.

interpersonal trust   The degree of expectancy that a given person is trustworthy.

introversion   An attitude of the psyche characterized by an orientation toward one's own thoughts and feelings.

Jonah complex   The fear that maximizing our potential will lead to a situation with which we will be unable to cope.

L-data   Life-record ratings of behaviors observed in real-life situations, such as in the classroom or office.

latency period   To Freud, the period from approximately age 5 to puberty, during which the sex instinct is dormant, sublimated in school activities, sports, and hobbies, and in developing friendships with members of the same sex.

learned helplessness   A condition resulting from the perception that we have no control over our environment.

libido   To Freud, the form of psychic energy, manifested by the life instincts, that drives a person toward pleasurable behaviors and thoughts. To Jung, a broader and more generalized form of psychic energy.

life-history reconstruction   Jung's type of case study that involves examining a person's past experiences to identify developmental patterns that may explain present neuroses.

life instincts   The drive for ensuring survival of the individual and the species by satisfying the needs for food, water air, and sex.

locus of control   Our belief about the source of control of reinforcement.

love   To Fromm, a form of parent-child interaction in which parents provide respect and a balance between security and responsibility.

maldevelopment   A condition that occurs when the ego consists solely of a single way of coping with conflict.

marketing orientation   A character type that values superficial qualities.

metamotivation   The motivation of self-actualizing persons, which involves maximizing personal potential rather than striving for a particular goal object.

metaneeds   States of growth or being toward which self-actualizers evolve.

metapathology   A thwarting of self-development related to failure to satisfy the metaneeds.

minimal goal level   The lowest level of potential reinforcement in a given situation that is perceived as satisfactory.

modeling   A behavior-modification technique that involves observing the behavior of others (called "models") and participating with them in performing the desired behavior.

Myers-Briggs Type Indicator (MBTI)   An assessment test based on Jung's psychological types and the attitudes of introversion and extraversion.

necrophilous orientation   A character type attracted to inanimate objects and to things associated with death.

need for achievement (nAch)   The need to achieve, overcome obstacles, excel, and live up to a high standard.

need potential   The possibility that related behaviors leading to the same or similar reinforcers will occur at the same time.

negative reinforcement   The strengthening of a response by the removal of an aversive stimulus.

neurotic competitiveness   An indiscriminate need to win at all costs.

neurotic needs   Ten irrational defenses against anxiety that become a permanent part of personality and that affect behavior.

neurotic trends   Three categories of behaviors and attitudes toward oneself and others that express a person's needs; Horney's revision of the concept of neurotic needs.

nomothetic research   The study of the statistical differences among large groups of subjects.

object relations theories   Outgrowths of psychoanalytic theory that focus more on relationships with the objects (such as the mother) that satisfy instinctual needs, rather than on the needs themselves.

observational learning   Learning new responses by observing the behavior of other people.

Oedipus complex   During the phallic stage (ages 4 to 5), the unconscious desire of a boy for his mother, accompanied by a desire to replace or destroy his father.

operant behaviors   Behaviors, emitted spontaneously or voluntarily, that operate on the environment to change it.

operant conditioning   The procedure by which a change in the consequences of a response will affect the rate at which the response occurs.

opposition principle   Jung's idea that conflict between opposing processes or tendencies is necessary to generate psychic energy.

organismic valuing process   The process by which we judge experiences in terms of their value for fostering or hindering our actualization and growth.

peak experience   A moment of intense ecstasy, similar to a religious or mystical experience, during which the self is transcended.

penis envy   The envy the female feels toward the male because the male possesses a penis; this is accompanied by a sense of loss because the female does not have a penis.

permeability   The idea that constructs can be revised and extended in light of new experiences.

perseverative functional autonomy   The level of functional autonomy that relates to low-level and routine behaviors.

person-centered therapy   Rogers's approach to therapy in which the client (not "patient") is assumed to be responsible for changing his or her personality.

persona archetype   The public face or role a person presents to others.

personal construct theory   Kelly's description of personality in terms of cognitive processes. We are capable of interpreting behaviors and events and using this understanding to guide our behavior and to predict the behavior of other people.

personal dispositions   Traits that are peculiar to an individual, as opposed to traits shared by a number of people.

personal-document technique   A method of personality assessment that involves the study of a person's written or spoken records.

personal unconscious   The reservoir of material that was once conscious but has been forgotten or suppressed.

personality   The unique, relatively enduring internal and external aspects of a person's character that influence behavior in different situations.

personology   Murray's system of personality.

play constructions   A personality assessment technique for children in which structures assembled from dolls, blocks, and other toys are analyzed.

pleasure principle   The principle by which the id functions to avoid pain and maximize pleasure.

positive regard   Acceptance, love, and approval from others.

positive self-regard   The condition under which we grant ourselves acceptance and approval.

press   The influence of the environment and past events on the current activation of a need.

primary-process thought   Childlike thinking by which the id attempts to satisfy the instinctual drives.

primary needs   Survival and related needs arising from internal bodily processes.

proactive needs   Needs that arise spontaneously.

proceeding   A basic segment of behavior; a time period in which an important behavior pattern occurs from beginning to end.

productive orientation   A character type that is the ideal of self-development.

projection   A defense mechanism that involves attributing a disturbing impulse to someone else.

projective test   A personality assessment device in which subjects are presumed to project personal needs, fears, and values onto their interpretation or description of an ambiguous stimulus.

propriate functional autonomy   The level of functional autonomy that relates to our values, self-image, and lifestyle.

proprium   Allport's term for the ego or self.

psyche   Jung's term for personality.

psychoanalysis   Sigmund Freud's theory of personality and system of therapy for treating mental disorders.

psychohistorical analysis   The application of Erikson's life-span theory, along with psychoanalytic principles, to the study of historical figures.

psychological situation   The combination of internal and external factors that influences our perception of and response to a stimulus.

psychological types   To Jung, eight personality types on interactions of the attitudes (introversion and extraversion) and the functions (thinking, feeling, sensing, and intuiting).

psychosexual stages of development   To Freud, the oral, anal, phallic, and genital stages through which all children pass. In these stages, gratification of the id instincts depends on the stimulation of corresponding areas of the body.

psychosocial stages of development   To Erikson, eight successive stages encompassing the life span. At each stage, we must cope with a crisis in either an adaptive or a maladaptive way.

punishment   The application of an aversive stimulus following a response in an effort to decrease the likelihood that the response will recur.

Q-data   Self-report questionnaire ratings of our characteristics, attitudes, and interests.

Q-**sort technique**   A self-report technique for assessing aspects of the self-concept.

range of convenience   The spectrum of events to which a construct can be applied. Some constructs are relevant to a limited number of people or situations; other constructs are broader.

rationalization   A defense mechanism that involves reinterpreting our behavior to make it more acceptable and less threatening to us.

reaction formation   A defense mechanism that involves expressing an id impulse that is the opposite of the one that is truly driving the person.

reactive needs   Needs that involve a response to a specific object.

reality principle   The principle by which the ego functions to provide appropriate constraints on the expression of the id instincts.

receptive orientation   A character type that is highly dependent on others.

reciprocal determinism   The idea that behavior is controlled or determined by the individual, through cognitive processes, and by the environment, through external social stimulus events.

regression   A defense mechanism that involves retreating to an earlier, less frustrating period of life and displaying the usually childish behaviors characteristic of that more secure time.

reinforcement   The act of strengthening a response by adding a reward, thus increasing the likelihood that the response will be repeated.

reinforcement schedules   Patterns or rates of providing or withholding reinforcers.

reinforcement value   The basis for preferring one reinforcer over another.

relatedness need   The need to maintain contact with other people, ideally through productive love.

reliability   The consistency of response to a psychological assessment device. Reliability can be determined by the test-retest, equivalent-forms, and split-halves methods.

repression   A defense mechanism that involves unconscious denial of the existence of something that causes anxiety.

resistance   In free association, a blockage or refusal to disclose painful memories.

respondent behaviors   Responses made to or elicited by specific environmental stimuli.

reversal experimental design   A research technique that involves establishing a baseline, applying an experimental treatment, and then withdrawing the experimental treatment to determine whether the behavior under study returns to its baseline value or whether some other factor might be responsible for the observed change in behavior.

rootedness need   The need to feel an attachment or sense of belonging to family, community, and society.

safety need   A higher-level need for security and freedom from fear.

secondary-process thought   Mature thought processes needed to deal rationally with the external world.

secondary needs   Emotional and psychological needs, such as achievement and affiliation.

secondary traits   The least important traits, which a person displays inconspicuously and inconsistently.

self-actualization   The fullest development of the self.

self archetype   To Jung, the archetype that represents the unity, integration, and harmony of the total personality.

self-characterization sketch   A technique to assess a person's construct system; that is, how a person perceives himself or herself in relation to other people.

self-control   The ability to exert control over the variables that determine our behavior.

self-efficacy   Our feeling of adequacy, efficiency, and competence in coping with life.

self-reinforcement   Administering rewards or punishments to oneself for meeting, exceeding, or falling short of one's own expectations or standards.

self-report inventory   A personality assessment technique in which subjects answer questions about their behaviors and feelings.

self-sentiment   The self-concept, which is the organizer of our attitudes and motivations.

sensation seeking   The need for varied, novel, and complex sensations and experiences.

sentiments   To Cattell, environmental-mold source traits that motivate behavior.

serial   A succession of proceedings related to the same function or purpose.

shadow archetype   The dark side of the personality; the archetype that contains primitive animal instincts.

sign-versus-sample approach   In the sign approach to assessing *personality,* character types, traits, or unconscious conflicts are inferred from questionnaires and other self-report inventories. In the sample approach to assessing *behavior,* test responses are interpreted as directly indicative of present behavior, not of traits, motives, or childhood experiences.

social interest   Our innate potential to cooperate with other people to achieve personal and societal goals.

source traits   Stable, permanent traits that are the basic factors of personality, derived by the method of factor analysis.

standardization   The consistency or uniformity of conditions and procedures for administering an assessment device.

striving for superiority   The urge toward perfection or completion that motivates each of us.

style of life   A unique character structure or pattern of personal behaviors and characteristics by which each of us strives for perfection. Basic styles of life include the dominant, getting, avoiding, and socially useful types.

sublimation   A defense mechanism that involves altering or displacing id impulses by diverting instinctual energy into socially acceptable behaviors.

subliminal perception   Perception below the threshold of conscious awareness.

subsidiation   To Murray, a situation in which one need is activated to aid in the satisfaction of another need. To Cattell, the relationships among ergs, sentiments, and attitudes, in which some elements are subordinate to others.

successive approximation   An explanation for the acquisition of complex behaviors. Behaviors, such as learning to speak, are reinforced only as they come to approximate or approach the final desired behavior.

superego   To Freud, the moral aspect of personality; the internalization of parental and societal values and standards. To Murray, the superego is shaped not only by parents and authority figures, but also by the peer group and culture.

superiority complex   A condition that develops when a person overcompensates for normal inferiority feelings.

superstitious behaviors   Persistent behaviors that have a coincidental and not a functional relationship to the reinforcement received.

surface traits   Traits that show a correlation but do not constitute a factor because they are not determined by a single source.

symbiotic relatedness   A childhood mechanism for regaining security in which children remain close to and dependent on their parents.

symptom analysis   Similar to catharsis, the symptom analysis technique focuses on the symptoms reported by the patient and attempts to interpret the patient's free associations to those symptoms.

T-data   Data derived from personality tests that are resistant to faking.

temperament traits   Traits that describe our general behavioral style in responding to our environment.

temperaments   Inherited dispositions toward certain behaviors.

thema   A combination of press (the environment) and need (the personality) that brings order to our behavior.

token economy   A behavior-modification technique in which tokens, which can be exchanged for valued objects or privileges, are awarded for desirable behaviors.

traits   To Allport, distinguishing characteristics that guide behavior. Traits are measured on a continuum and are subject to social, environmental, and cultural influences. To Cattell, reaction tendencies, derived by the method of factor analysis, that are relatively permanent parts of the personality.

transcendence need   The need to rise above our animal nature by becoming either creative or destructive.

triadic reciprocality   The idea that behavior is determined through the interaction of behavioral, cognitive, and environmental or situational variables.

tyranny of the shoulds   An attempt to realize an unattainable idealized self-image by denying the true self and behaving in terms of what we think we *should* be doing.

unconditional positive regard   Approval granted regardless of a person's behavior. In Rogers's person-centered therapy, the therapist offers the client unconditional positive regard.

unique traits   Traits possessed by one or a few persons.

validity   The extent to which an assessment device measures what it is intended to measure. Types of validity include predictive, content, and construct.

vicarious reinforcement   Learning or strengthening a behavior by observing the behavior of others, and the consequences of that behavior, rather than experiencing the reinforcement or consequences directly.

withdrawal-destructiveness   A childhood mechanism for regaining security in which children distance themselves from their parents.

womb envy   The envy a male feels toward a female because she can bear children and he cannot. Womb envy was Horney's response to Freud's concept of penis envy in females.

word-association test   A projective technique in which a person responds to a stimulus word with whatever word comes to mind.

REFERENCES

Abdallah, T. M. (1989). Self-esteem and locus of control of college men in Saudi Arabia. *Psychological Reports, 65*(3, Pt. 2), 1323–1326.

Achenbach, T., & Zigler, E. (1963). Social competence and self-image disparity in psychiatric and nonpsychiatric patients. *Journal of Abnormal and Social Psychology, 67*, 197–205.

Ackil, J., & Zaragoza, M. (1998). Memorial consequences of forced confabulation: Age differences in susceptibility to false memories. *Developmental Psychology, 34*, 1358–1372.

Adams, D. (1954). *The anatomy of personality.* Garden City, NY: Doubleday.

Adams, G. R., & Fitch, S. A. (1982). Ego stage and identity status development: A cross-sequential analysis. *Journal of Personality and Social Psychology, 43*, 574–583.

Adams-Webber, J. R. (1970). An analysis of the discriminant validity of several repertory grid indices. *British Journal of Psychology, 60*, 83–90.

Adler, A. (1930). Individual psychology. In C. Murchison (Ed.), *Psychologies of 1930* (pp. 395–405). Worcester, MA: Clark University Press.

Adler, A. (1939). *Social interest: A challenge to mankind.* J. Linton & R. Vaughan (Trans.). New York: Putnam. (Original work published 1933)

Adler, A. (1963). *The practice and theory of individual psychology.* P. Radin (Trans.). Paterson, NJ: Littlefield, Adams. (Original work published 1924)

Agronick, G., & Duncan, L. E. (1998). Individual differences, life path, and importance attributed to the women's movement. *Journal of Personality and Social Psychology, 74*, 1545–1555.

Albright, L., Malloy, T. E., Dong, Q., Kenny, D. A., Fang, X., Winquist, L., & Yu, D. (1997). Cross-cultural consensus in personality judgments. *Journal of Personality and Social Psychology, 72*, 558–569.

Alderfer, C. P. (1972). *Existence, relatedness and growth: Human needs in organizational settings.* New York: Free Press.

Alderfer, C. P. (1989). Theories reflecting my personal experience and life development. *Journal of Applied Behavioral Science, 25*, 351–365.

Allen, K. D., Danforth, J. S., & Drabman, R. C. (1989). Videotaped modeling and film distraction for fear reduction in adults undergoing hyperbaric oxygen therapy. *Journal of Consulting and Clinical Psychology, 57*, 554–558.

Allport, G. W. (1937). *Personality: A psychological interpretation.* New York: Holt.

Allport, G. W. (1955). *Becoming: Basic considerations for a psychology of personality.* New Haven, CT: Yale University Press.

Allport, G. W. (1961). *Pattern and growth in personality.* New York: Holt.

Allport, G. W. (Ed.). (1965). *Letters from Jenny.* New York: Harcourt, Brace & World.

Allport, G. W. (1966). Traits revisited. *American Psychologist, 21,* 1–10.

Allport, G. W. (1967). Autobiography. In E. G. Boring & G. Lindzey (Eds.), *A history of psychology in autobiography* (Vol. 5, pp. 1–25). New York: Appleton-Century-Crofts.

Allport, G. W., & Cantril, H. (1934). Judging personality from voice. *Journal of Social Psychology, 5,* 37–55.

Allport, G. W., & Vernon, P. (1933). *Studies in expressive movement.* New York: Macmillan.

Allport, G. W., Vernon, P., & Lindzey, G. (1960). *A study of values* (3rd ed.). Boston: Houghton Mifflin.

Altmaier, E. M., Russell, D. W., Kao, C. F., Lehmann, T. R., & Weinstein, J. N. (1993). Role of self-efficacy in rehabilitation outcomes among chronic low back pain patients. *Journal of Counseling Psychology, 40,* 335–339.

Ambody, N., & Rosenthal, R. (1992). Thin slices of expressive behavior as predictors of interpersonal consequences: A meta-analysis. *Psychological Bulletin, 111,* 256–274.

Amirkhan, J. H., Risinger, R. T., & Swickert, R. J. (1995). Extraversion: A "hidden" personality factor in coping? *Journal of Personality, 63,* 189–212.

Anastasi, A. (1988). *Psychological testing* (6th ed.). New York: Macmillan.

Andersen, D. C., & Friedman, L. J. (1997). Erik Erikson on revolutionary leadership [Retrospective review of four books by Erikson]. *Contemporary Psychology, 42,* 1063–1067.

Anderson, J. W. (1988). Henry A. Murray's early career: A psychobiographical exploration. *Journal of Personality, 56*(1), 139–171.

Anderson, J. W. (1990). The life of Henry A. Murray: 1893–1988. In A. I. Rabin, R. A. Zucker, R. A. Emmons, & S. Frank (Eds.), *Studying persons and lives* (pp. 304–334). New York: Springer.

Apostal, R. A. (1991). College students' career interests and sensing-intuition personality. *Journal of College Student Development, 32,* 4–7.

Appignanesi, L., & Forrester, J. (1992). *Freud's women.* New York: Basic Books.

Archer, S. L. (1982). The lower age boundaries of identity development. *Child Development, 53,* 1551–1556.

Aries, E., & Moorehead, K. (1989). The importance of ethnicity in the development of identity of Black adolescents. *Psychological Reports, 65,* 75–82.

Arnett, J. J. (1999). Adolescent storm and stress, reconsidered. *American Psychologist, 54,* 317–326.

Asendorpf, J. B., & Wilpers, S. (1998). Personality effects on social relationships. *Journal of Personality and Social Psychology, 74,* 1531–1544.

Atkinson, D., Morten, G., & Sue, D. W. (1989). A minority development model. In D. Atkinson, G. Morten, & D. W. Sue (Eds.), *Counseling American minorities* (pp. 35–52). Dubuque, IA: William C. Brown.

Atkinson, J. W., Lens, W., & O'Malley, P. M. (1976). Motivation and ability: Interactive psychological determinants of intellectual performance, educational achievement, and each other. In W. H. Sewell, R. H. Hanser, & D. L. Featherman (Eds.), *Schooling and achievement in American society.* New York: Academic Press.

Atwood, G. E., & Tomkins, S. S. (1976). On the subjectivity of personality theory. *Journal of the History of the Behavioral Sciences, 12,* 166–177.

Aviezer, A., Van Ijzendoorn, M. H., Sagi, A., & Schuegel, C. (1994). "Children of the Dream" revisited: 70 years of collective early child care in Israeli kibbutzim. *Psychological Bulletin, 116,* 99–116.

Ayllon, T., & Azrin, N. (1968). *The token economy.* New York: Appleton-Century-Crofts.

Baars, B. J. (1986). *The cognitive revolution in psychology.* New York: Guilford Press.

Balay, J., & Shevrin, H. (1988). The subliminal psychodynamic activation method: A critical review. *American Psychologist, 43,* 161–174.

Baldwin, A. L. (1949). The effect of home environment on nursery school behavior. *Child Development, 20,* 49–61.

Balistreri, E., Busch-Rossnagel, N. A., & Geisinger, K. F. (1995). Development and preliminary validation of the Ego Identity Process Questionnaire. *Journal of Adolescence, 18,* 179–182.

Ball, S. A., Carroll, K. M., & Rounsaville, B. J. (1994). Sensation seeking, substance abuse, and psychopathology in treatment-seeking and community cocaine abusers. *Journal of Consulting and Clinical Psychology, 62,* 1053–1057.

Ball, S. A., & Zuckerman, M. (1992). Sensation seeking and selective attention: Focused and divided attention on a dichotic listening task. *Journal of Personality and Social Psychology, 63,* 825–831.

Baltes, M. M., & Bates, P. B. (1986). *Psychology of control and aging.* Hillsdale, NJ: Erlbaum.

Bandura, A. (1965). Influence of models' reinforcement contingencies on the acquisition of imitative responses. *Journal of Personality and Social Psychology, 1,* 589–595.

Bandura, A. (1973). *Aggression: A social learning analysis.* Englewood Cliffs, NJ: Prentice-Hall.

Bandura, A. (1977). *Social learning theory.* Englewood Cliffs, NJ: Prentice-Hall.

Bandura, A. (1978). The self system in reciprocal determinism. *American Psychologist, 33,* 334–358.

Bandura, A. (1986). *Social foundations of thought and action: A social cognitive theory.* Englewood Cliffs, NJ: Prentice-Hall.

Bandura, A. (1989). Human agency in social cognitive theory. *American Psychologist, 44,* 1175–1184.

Bandura, A. (1992). Self-efficacy mechanisms in psychobiologic functioning. In R. Schwarzer (Ed.), *Self-efficacy: Thought control of action* (pp. 355–394). Washington, DC: Hemisphere.

Bandura, A. (1995). Exercise of personal and collective efficacy in changing societies. In A. Bandura (Ed.), *Self-efficacy in changing societies* (pp. 1–45). Cambridge, England: Cambridge University Press.

Bandura, A. (1997). *Self-efficacy: The exercise of control.* New York: W. H. Freeman.

Bandura, A., Blanchard, E. B., & Ritter, B. (1969). The relative efficacy of desensitization and modeling approaches for inducing behavioral, affective, and attitudinal changes. *Journal of Personality and Social Psychology, 13,* 173–199.

Bandura, A., Grusec, J. E., & Menlove, F. L. (1967). Vicarious extinction of avoidance behavior through symbolic modeling. *Journal of Personality and Social Psychology, 5,* 16–22.

Bandura, A., Pastorelli, C., Barbaranelli, C., & Caprara, G. V. (1999). Self-efficacy pathways to childhood depression. *Journal of Personality and Social Psychology, 76,* 258–269.

Bandura, A., Ross, D., & Ross, S. A. (1963). Imitation of film-mediated aggressive models. *Journal of Abnormal and Social Psychology, 66,* 3–11.

Bandura, A., & Walters, R. (1963). *Social learning and personality development.* New York: Holt, Rinehart & Winston.

Bannister, D., Fransella, F., & Agnew, J. (1971). Characteristics and validity of the grid test on thought disorder. *British Journal of Social and Clinical Psychology, 10,* 144–151.

Bannister, D., & Salmon, P. (1966). Schizophrenic thought disorder: Specific or diffuse? *British Journal of Medical Psychology, 39,* 215–219.

Barger, S. D., Kircher, J. C., & Croyle, R. T. (1997). The effects of social context and defensiveness on the physiological responses of repressive copers. *Journal of Personality and Social Psychology, 73,* 1118–1128.

Bargh, J. A., & Chartrand, T. L. (1999). The unbearable automaticity of being. *American Psychologist, 54,* 462–479.

Baron, R., & Byrne, D. (1984). *Social psychology: Understanding human interaction* (4th ed.). Newton, MA: Allyn & Bacon.

Barrick, M. R., & Mount, M. K. (1996). Effects of impression management and self-deception on the predictive validity of personality constructs. *Journal of Applied Psychology, 81,* 261–272.

Barrick, M. R., Mount, M. K., & Strauss, J. P. (1993). Conscientiousness and performance of sales representatives. Test of the mediating effects of goal setting. *Journal of Applied Psychology, 78,* 715–722.

Barry, H., & Blane, H. T. (1977). Birth order of alcoholics. *Journal of Individual Psychology, 62,* 62–79.

Bates, J. E. (1994). Introduction. In J. E. Bates & T. D. Wachs (Eds.), *Temperament: Individual differences at the interface of biology and behavior* (pp. 1–14). Washington, DC: American Psychological Association.

Battle, E., & Rotter, J. B. (1963). Children's feelings of personal control as related to social class and ethnic group. *Journal of Personality, 31,* 482–490.

Becona, E., Frojan, M. J., & Lista, M. J. (1988). Comparison between two self-efficacy scales in maintenance of smoking cessation. *Psychological Reports, 62,* 359–362.

Belgrave, F. Z., Johnson, R. S., & Carey, C. (1992). Attributional style and its relationship to self-esteem and academic performance in Black students. In A. K. H. Burlew, W. C. Banks, H. P. McAdoo, & Azibo, D. A. Y. (Eds.), *African American psychology: Theory, research, and practice* (pp. 173–182). Newbury Park, CA: Sage.

Belmont, L., & Marolla, F. A. (1973). Birth order, family size and intelligence. *Science, 182,* 1096–1101.

Benassi, V. A., Sweeney, P. D., & Dufour, C. L. (1988). Is there a relationship between locus of control orientation and depression? *Journal of Abnormal Psychology, 97,* 357–367.

Benet-Martinez, V., & John, O. P. (1998). Los Cinco Grandes across cultures and ethnic groups: Multitrait multimethod analyses of the Big Five in Spanish and English. *Journal of Personality and Social Psychology, 75,* 729–750.

Ben-Porath, Y. S., & Butcher, J. N. (1989). Psychometric stability of rewritten MMPI items. *Journal of Personality Assessment, 53,* 645–653.

Ben-Porath, Y. S., & Butcher, J. N. (1991). The historical development of personality assessment. In C. E. Walker (Ed.), *Clinical psychology: Historical and research foundations* (pp. 121–156). New York: Plenum Press.

Bergeman, C. S., Chipeur, H. M., Plomin, R., Pedersen, N. L., McClearn, G. E., Nesselroade, J. R., Costa, P. T., Jr., & McCrae, R. R. (1993). Genetic and environmental effects on openness to experience, agreeableness, and conscientiousness: An adoption-twin study. *Journal of Personality, 61,* 159–179.

Bergin, A. E., & Strupp, H. H. (1972). *Changing frontiers in the science of psychotherapy.* New York: Aldine-Atherton.

Berry, D. S. (1990). Taking people at face value: Evidence for the kernel of truth hypothesis. *Social Cognition, 8,* 343–361.

Berry, D. S., & Wero, J. L. F. (1993). Accuracy in face perception: A view from ecological psychology. *Journal of Personality, 61,* 497–520.

Berzonsky, M. D., Rice, K. G., & Neimeyer, G. J. (1990). Identity status and self-construct systems: Process X structure interactions. *Journal of Adolescence, 13,* 251–263.

Bettelheim, B. (1984). *Freud and man's soul.* New York: Vintage Books.

Betz, N. E., & Hackett, G. (1981). The relationships of career-related self-efficacy expectations to perceived career options in college women and men. *Journal of Counseling Psychology, 28,* 399–410.

Bieri, J. (1955). Cognitive complexity-simplicity and predictive behavior. *Journal of Abnormal and Social Psychology, 51,* 263–268.

Bilsker, D., & Marcia, J. E. (1991). Adaptive regression and ego identity. *Journal of Adolescence, 14,* 75–84.

Bjork, D. W. (1993). *B. F. Skinner: A life.* New York: Basic Books.

Blackman, D. E. (1995). B. F. Skinner (1904–1990). In R. Fuller (Ed.), *Seven pioneers of psychology: Behaviour and mind* (pp. 107–129). London: Routledge.

Blanton, S. (1971). *Diary of my analysis with Sigmund Freud.* New York: Hawthorn Books.

Block, J. (1983). Differential premises arising from differential socialization of the sexes: Some conjectures. *Child Development, 54,* 1335–1354.

Block, J. H., & Block, J. (1980). The role of ego-control and ego-resiliency in the organization of behavior. In W. A. Collins (Ed.), *The Minnesota symposium on child psychology* (vol. 13, pp. 39–101). Hillsdale, NJ: Erlbaum.

Blustein, D. L., Devenis, L. E., & Kidney, B. A. (1989). Relationship between the identity formation process and career development. *Journal of Counseling Psychology, 36,* 196–202.

Boden, J., & Baumeister, R. (1997). Repressive coping: Distraction using pleasant thoughts and memories. *Journal of Personality and Social Psychology, 73,* 45–62.

Bodner, E., & Mikulincer, M. (1998). Learned helplessness and the occurrence of depressive-like and paranoid-like responses: The role of attentional focus. *Journal of Personality and Social Psychology, 74,* 1010–1023.

Booth-Kewley, S., & Vickers, R. R., Jr. (1994). Associations between major domains of personality and health behavior. *Journal of Personality, 62,* 281–298.

Bores-Rangel, E., Church, A. T., Szendre, D., & Reeves, C. (1990). Self-efficacy in relation to occupational consideration and academic performance in high school equivalency students. *Journal of Counseling Psychology, 37,* 407–418.

Bornstein, R. F., & Masling, J. M. (1998). Introduction: The psychoanalytic unconscious. In R. F. Bornstein & J. M. Masling (Eds.), *Empirical perspectives on the psychoanalytic unconscious* (pp. xiii–xxviii). Washington, DC: American Psychological Association.

Bottome, P. (1939). *Alfred Adler: A biography.* New York: Putnam.

Bouchard, T. J. (1985). Twins reared together and apart: What they tell us about human diversity. In S. W. Fox (Ed.), *Individuality and determinism: Chemical and biological bases* (pp. 147–184). New York: Plenum Press.

Bouchard, T. J. (1994). Genes, environment, and personality. *Science, 264,* 1700–1701.

Bourne, E. (1978a). The state of research on ego identity: A review and appraisal. Part I. *Journal of Youth and Adolescence, 7,* 223–257.

Bourne, E. (1978b). The state of research on ego identity: A review and appraisal. Part II. *Journal of Youth and Adolescence, 7,* 371–392.

Brannigan, G. G., Hauk, P. A., & Guay, J. A. (1991). Locus of control and daydreaming. *Journal of Genetic Psychology, 152,* 29–33.

Breger, L., Hunter, I., & Lane, R. W. (1971). *The effect of stress on dreams.* New York: International Universities Press.

Breland, H. M. (1974). Birth order, family configuration and verbal achievement. *Child Development, 45,* 1011–1019.

Breland, K., & Breland, M. (1961). The misbehavior of organisms. *American Psychologist, 16,* 681–684.

Brewin, C. R., Andrews, B., & Gotlib, I. H. (1993). Psychopathology and early experience: A reappraisal of retrospective reports. *Psychological Bulletin, 113,* 82–98.

Briggs, K. C., & Myers, I. B. (1943, 1976). *Myers-Briggs Type Indicator.* Palo Alto, CA: Consulting Psychologists Press.

Brody, L. R., Rozek, M. K., & Muten, E. O. (1985). Age, sex, and individual differences in children's defensive styles. *Journal of Clinical Child Psychology, 14,* 132–138.

Brody, N. (1997). Dispositional paradigms: Comment on Eysenck (1997) and the biosocial science of individual differences. *Journal of Personality and Social Psychology, 73,* 1242–1245.

Broman, C. L. (1997). Race-related factors and life satisfaction among African Americans. *Journal of Black Psychology, 23,* 36–49.

Brome, V. (1981). *Jung: Man and myth.* New York: Atheneum.

Bronstein, P. (1988). Personality from a sociocultural perspective. In P. Bronstein & K. Quina (Eds.), *Teaching a psychology of people: Resources for gender and sociocultural awareness* (pp. 60–68). Washington, DC: American Psychological Association.

Brown, J. B., Jr., & Inouye, D. K. (1978). Learned helplessness through modeling: The role of perceived similarity in competence. *Journal of Personality and Social Psychology, 36,* 900–908.

Brown, L. L., Tomarkin, A., Orth, D., Loosen, P., Kalin, N., & Davidson, R. (1996). Individual differences in repressive-defensiveness predict basal salivary cortisol levels. *Journal of Personality and Social Psychology, 70,* 362–371.

Brown, S. R., & Hendrick, C. (1971). Introversion, extraversion and social perception. *British Journal of Social and Clinical Psychology, 10,* 313–319.

Bruhn, A. R. (1990). Earliest childhood memories: Vol. 1. *Theory and application to clinical practice.* New York: Praeger.

Bruhn, A. R. (1992a). The early memories procedure: A projective test of autobiographical memory. Part 1. *Journal of Personality Assessment, 58*(1), 1–15.

Bryant, B. L. (1987). Birth order as a factor in the development of vocational preferences. *Individual Psychology, 43,* 36–41.

Buchanan, L. P., Kern, R., & Bell-Dumas, J. (1991). Comparison of content in created versus actual early recollections. *Individual Psychology, 47,* 348–355.

Buchanan, R. D. (1994). The development of the MMPI. *Journal of the History of the Behavioral Sciences, 30,* 148–161.

Bullock, W. A., & Gilliland, K. (1993). Eysenck's arousal theory of introversion-extraversion: A converging measures investigation. *Journal of Personality and Social Psychology, 64,* 113–123.

Burston, D. (1991). *The legacy of Erich Fromm.* Cambridge, MA: Harvard University Press.

Busch, F. N., Shear, M. K., Cooper, A. M., Shapiro, T., & Leon, A. (1995). An empirical study of defense mechanisms in panic disorder. *Journal of Nervous and Mental Disease, 183*(5), 299–303.

Bushman, B. J., Baumeister, R. F., & Stack, A. D. (1999). Catharsis, aggression, and persuasive influence: Self-fulfilling or self-defeating prophecies? *Journal of Personality and Social Psychology, 76,* 367–376.

Buss, A. H. (1988). *Personality: Evolutionary heritage and human distinctiveness.* Hillsdale, NJ: Erlbaum.

Buss, A. H., & Plomin, R. (1975). *A temperament theory of personality development.* New York: Wiley.

Buss, A. H., & Plomin, R. (1984). *Temperament: Early developing personality traits.* Hillsdale, NJ: Erlbaum.

Buss, A. H., & Plomin, R. (1986). The EAS approach to temperament. In R. Plomin & J. Dunn (Eds.), *The study of temperament: Changes, continuities and challenges* (pp. 67–79). Hillsdale, NJ: Erlbaum.

Buss, D. M. (1991). Evolutionary personality psychology. *Annual Review of Psychology, 42,* 459–491.

Butcher, J. N., Lim, J., & Nezami, E. (1998). Objective study of abnormal personality in cross-cultural settings: The Minnesota Multiphasic Personality Inventory (MMPI–2). *Journal of Cross-Cultural Psychology, 29,* 189–211.

Butcher, J. N., & Rouse, S. V. (1996). Personality: Individual differences and clinical assessment. *Annual Review of Psychology, 47,* 87–111.

Butcher, J. N., Williams, C. L., Graham, J. R., Archer, R. P., Tellegen, A., Ben-Porath, Y. S., & Kaemmer, B. (1992). *MMPI-A: Manual for administration, scoring, and interpretation.* Minneapolis: University of Minnesota Press.

Butler, J. M., & Haigh, G. V. (1954). Changes in the relationship between self-concepts and ideal concepts consequent upon client-centered counseling. In C. R. Rogers & R. F. Dymond (Eds.), *Psychotherapy and personality change.* Chicago: University of Chicago Press.

Campbell, J., & Moyers, B. (1988). *The power of myth.* Garden City, NY: Doubleday.

Camras, L. A. (1998). Production of emotional facial expressions in European American, Japanese, and Chinese infants. *Developmental Psychology, 34,* 616–628.

Camras, L. A., Oster, H., Campos, J. J., Miyake, K., & Bradshaw, D. (1997). Japanese and American infants' responses to arm restraint. In P. Ekman & E. L. Rosenberg (Eds.), *What the face reveals* (pp. 289–299). New York: Oxford University Press.

Cann, D. R., & Donderi, D. C. (1986). Jungian personality typology and the recall of everyday and archetypal dreams. *Journal of Personality and Social Psychology, 50,* 1021–1030.

Cantor, N., & Zirkel, S. (1990). Personality, cognition, and purposive behavior. In L. A. Pervin (Ed.), *Handbook of personality: Theory and research* (pp. 135–164). New York: Guilford Press.

Carlson, R. (1980). Studies of Jungian typology: II. Representations of the personal world. *Journal of Personality and Social Psychology, 38,* 801–810.

Carlson, R., & Levy, N. (1973). Studies of Jungian typology: I. Memory, social perception, and social action. *Journal of Personality, 41,* 559–576.

Carmichael, C. M., & McGue, M. (1994). A longitudinal family study of personality change and stability. *Journal of Personality, 62,* 1–20.

Carskadon, T. G. (1978). Use of the Myers-Briggs Type Indicator in psychology courses and discussion groups. *Teaching of Psychology, 5,* 140–142.

Carson, R. C. (1989). Personality. *Annual Review of Psychology, 40,* 227–248.

Caspi, A., Bem, D. J., & Elder, G. H. (1989). Continuities and consequences of interactional styles across the life course. *Journal of Personality, 57,* 375–406.

Caspi, A., Elder, G. H., & Bem, D. J. (1987). Moving against the world: Life course patterns of explosive children. *Developmental Psychology, 23,* 308–313.

Caspi, A., Elder, G. H., & Bem, D. J. (1988). Moving away from the world: Life course patterns of shy children. *Developmental Psychology, 24,* 824–831.

Caspi, A., & Silva, P. (1994). Temperamental qualities at age 3 predict personality traits in young adulthood: Longitudinal evidence from a birth cohort. Child Development, in press.

Cattell, R. B. (1950). *Personality: A systematic theoretical and factual study.* New York: McGraw-Hill.

Cattell, R. B. (1959). Foundations of personality measurement theory in multivariate expression. In B. M. Bass & I. A. Berg (Eds.), *Objective approaches to personality assessment* (pp. 42–65). Princeton, NJ: Van Nostrand.

Cattell, R. B. (1965). *The scientific analysis of personality.* Baltimore: Penguin Books.

Cattell, R. B. (1973). *Personality and mood by questionnaire.* San Francisco: Jossey-Bass.

Cattell, R. B. (1974a). Autobiography. In G. Lindzey (Ed.), *A history of psychology in autobiography* (Vol. 6, pp. 59–100). Englewood Cliffs, NJ: Prentice-Hall.

Cattell, R. B. (1974b). Travels in psychological hyperspace. In T. S. Krawiec (Ed.), *The psychologists* (Vol. 2, pp. 85–133). New York: Oxford University Press.

Cattell, R. B. (1982). *The inheritance of personality and ability: Research methods.* New York: Academic Press.

Cattell, R. B. (1990). Advances in Cattellian personality theory. In L. A. Pervin (Ed.), *Handbook of personality: Theory and research* (pp. 101–110). New York: Guilford Press.

Cattell, R. B. (1993). Planning basic clinical research. In C. E. Walker (Ed.), *The history of clinical psychology in autobiography* (Vol. 2, pp. 101–111). Pacific Grove, CA: Brooks/Cole.

Cattell, R. B., & Cross, K. P. (1952). Comparison of the ergic and self-sentiment structure found in dynamic traits by R- and P-techniques. *Journal of Personality, 21,* 250–271.

Cattell, R. B., Eber, H. W., & Tatsuoka, M. M. (1970). *Handbook for the Sixteen Personality Factor Questionnaire.* Champaign, IL: Institute for Personality and Ability Testing.

Cattell, R. B., & Kline, P. (1977). *The scientific analysis of personality and motivation.* New York: Academic Press.

Ceci, S. J., & Bruck, M. (1993). Suggestibility of the child witness: A historical review and synthesis. *Psychological Bulletin, 113,* 403–439.

Chambers, J. W., Jr., Kambon, K., Birdsong, B. D., Brown, J., Dixon, P., & Robbins-Brinson, L. (1998). Africentric cultural identity and the stress experience of African American college students. *Journal of Black Psychology, 24,* 368–396.

Chan, D. W. (1989). Dimensionality and adjustment correlates of locus of control among Hong Kong Chinese. *Journal of Personality Assessment, 53,* 145–160.

Chan, D. W., & Lee, H. B. (1995). Patterns of test usage in Hong Kong in 1993. *Professional Psychology: Research and Practice, 26,* 292–297.

Cherry, R., & Cherry, L. (1973, August 26). The Horney heresy. *The New York Times Magazine,* pp. 12ff.

Chesney, M. A., Ekman, P., Friesen, W. V., Black, G. W., & Hecker, M. H. L. (1997). Type A behavior pattern: Facial behavior and speech components. In P. Ekman & E. L. Rosenberg (Eds.), *What the face reveals* (pp. 456–466). New York: Oxford University Press.

Cheung, F. M., & Ho, R. M. (1997). Standardization of the Chinese MMPI-A in Hong Kong: A preliminary study. *Psychological Assessment, 9,* 499–502.

Cheung, F. M., & Leung, K. (1998). Indigenous personality measures: Chinese examples. *Journal of Cross-Cultural Psychology, 29,* 233–248

Chiu, C., Hong, Y., & Dweck, C. S. (1997). Lay dispositionism and implicit theories of personality. *Journal of Personality and Social Psychology, 73,* 19–30.

Chodorkoff, B. (1954). Self-perception, perceptual defense, and adjustment. *Journal of Abnormal and Social Psychology, 49,* 508–512.

Church, A. T., & Lonner, W. J. (1998). The cross-cultural perspective in the study of personality. *Journal of Cross-Cultural Psychology, 29,* 32–62.

Ciaccio, N. (1971). A test of Erikson's theory of ego epigenesis. *Developmental Psychology, 4,* 306–311.

Clemmens, E. R. (1987). Karen Horney, a reminiscence. In K. Horney, *Final lectures* (pp. 107–115). New York: Norton.

Coan, R. W. (1972). Measurable components of openness to experience. *Journal of Consulting and Clinical Psychology, 39,* 346.

Cohen, J. B. (1967). An interpersonal orientation to the study of consumer behavior. *Journal of Marketing Research, 4,* 270–278.

Cohen, S., & Wills, T. A. (1985). Stress, social support, and the buffering hypothesis. *Psychological Bulletin, 98,* 310–357.

Coleman, J. S., Campbell, E. Q., Hobson, C. J., McPartland, J., Mood, A. M., Weinfeld, F. D., & York, R. L. (1966). *Equality of educational opportunity.* Washington, DC: U.S. Office of Education.

Coles, R. (1998). Psychoanalysis: The American experience. In M. S. Roth (Ed.), *Conflict and culture* (pp. 140–151). New York: Knopf.

Constantinople, A. (1969). An Eriksonian measure of personality development in college students. *Developmental Psychology, 1,* 357–372.

Coopersmith, S. (1967). *The antecedents of self-esteem.* New York: W. H. Freeman.

Costa, P. T., Jr., & McCrae, R. R. (1984). Personality as a lifelong determinant of well-being. In C. Z. Malatesta & C. E. Izard (Eds.), *Emotion in adult development* (pp. 141–158). Beverly Hills, CA: Sage.

Costa, P. T., Jr., & McCrae, R. R. (1988). Personality in adulthood: A six-year longitudinal study of self-reports and spouse ratings on the NEO Personality Inventory. *Journal of Personality and Social Psychology, 54,* 853–863.

Costa, P. T., Jr., & McCrae, R. R. (1997). Longitudinal stability of adult personality. In R. Hogan, J. Johnson, & S. Briggs (Eds.), *Handbook of personality psychology* (pp. 269–290). San Diego: Academic Press.

Cote, J. E., & Levine, C. (1988). The relationship between ego identity status and Erikson's notions of institutionalized moratoria, value orientation stage, and ego dominance. *Journal of Youth and Adolescence, 17,* 81–99.

Cowan, D. A. (1989). An alternative to the dichotomous interpretation of Jung's psychological functions: Developing more sensitive measurement technology. *Journal of Personality Assessment, 53,* 459–471.

Cozzarelli, C. (1993). Personality and self-efficacy as predictors of coping with abortion. *Journal of Personality and Social Psychology, 65,* 1224–1236.

Cramer, P. (1987). The development of defense mechanisms. *Journal of Personality, 54,* 597–614.

Cramer, P. (1990). *The development of defense mechanisms: Theory, research and assessment.* New York: Springer-Verlag.

Cramer, P. (1996). *Storytelling, narrative, and the Thematic Apperception Test.* New York: Guilford.

Cramer, P., & Block, J. (1998). Preschool antecedents of defense mechanism use in young adults: A longitudinal study. *Journal of Personality and Social Psychology, 74,* 159–169.

Crandall, J. E. (1980). Adler's concept of social interest: Theory, measurement, and implications for adjustment. *Journal of Personality and Social Psychology, 39,* 481–495.

Crandall, J. E. (1981). *Theory and measurement of social interest: Empirical tests of Alfred Adler's concept.* New York: Columbia University Press.

Crandall, J. E. (1984). Social interest as a moderator of life stress. *Journal of Personality and Social Psychology, 47,* 164–174.

Crewsdon, J. (1988). *By silence betrayed: Sexual abuse of children in America.* Boston: Little, Brown.

Crockett, W. H. (1982). The organization of construct systems: The organization corollary. In J. C. Mancuso & J. R. Adams-Webber (Eds.), *The construing person.* New York: Praeger.

Crook, T., Raskin, A., & Eliot, J. (1981). Parent-child relationships and adult depression. *Child Development, 52,* 950–957.

Curry, C. (1998). Adolescence. In K. Trew & J. Kremer (Eds.), *Gender and psychology* (pp. 107–117). New York: Oxford University Press.

Daniels, D., & Plomin, R. (1985). Origins of individual differences in infant shyness. *Developmental Psychology, 21,* 118–121.

Davidow, S., & Bruhn, A. R. (1990). Earliest memories and the dynamics of delinquency: A replication study. *Journal of Personality Assessment, 54,* 601–616.

Davis, J., Lockwood, L., & Wright, C. (1991). Reasons for not reporting peak experiences. *Journal of Humanistic Psychology, 31,* 86–94.

Davis, P. J. (1987). Repression and the inaccessibility of affective memories. *Journal of Personality and Social Psychology, 53,* 585–593.

DeAngelis, T. (1994, July). Jung's theories keep pace and remain popular. APA Monitor, p. 41.

DeBrabander, B., & Boone, C. (1990). Sex differences in perceived locus of control. *Journal of Social Psychology, 130,* 271–272.

DeCarvalho, R. J. (1999). Otto Rank, the Rankian circle in Philadelphia, and the origin of Carl Rogers' person-centered psychotherapy. *History of Psychology, 2,* 132–148.

Dement, W. C., & Wolpert, E. A. (1958). The relationship of eye movements, body motility, and external stimuli to dream content. *Journal of Experimental Psychology, 55,* 543–553.

DeNeve, K., & Cooper, H. (1998). The happy personality: A meta-analysis of 137 personality traits and subjective well-being. *Psychological Bulletin, 124,* 197–229.

DePaulo, B. M. (1993). The ability to judge others from their expressive behaviors. In K. H. Craik, R. Hogan, & R. N. Wolfe (Eds.), *Fifty years of personality psychology* (pp. 197–206). New York: Plenum Press.

DeVito, A. J. (1985). Review of Myers-Briggs Type Indicator. In J. V. Mitchell, Jr. (Ed.), *Ninth mental measurements yearbook* (Vol. 2, pp. 1030–1032). Lincoln: University of Nebraska Press.

DiClemente, C. C., Prochaska, J. O., & Gilbertini, M. (1985). Self-efficacy and the stages of self-change of smoking. *Cognitive Therapy and Research.*

Diener, E., Diener, M., & Diener, C. (1995). Factors predicting the subjective well-being of nations. *Journal of Personality and Social Psychology, 69,* 851–864.

Diener, E., Suh, E. M., Lucas, R. E., & Smith, H. L. (1999). Subjective well-being: Three decades of progress. *Psychological Bulletin, 125,* 276–302.

Diener, E., Suh, E. M., Smith, H. L., & Shao, L. (1995). National differences in reported subjective well-being. *Social Indicators Research, 34,* 7–32.

Digman, J. M. (1989). Five robust trait dimensions: Development, stability, and utility. *Journal of Personality, 57,* 195–214.

Digman, J. M. (1990). Personality structure: Emergence of the five-factor model. *Annual Review of Psychology, 41,* 417–440.

Digman, J. M. (1997). Higher-order factors of the Big Five. *Journal of Personality and Social Psychology, 73,* 1246–1256.

Dignan, M. (1965). Ego identity and maternal identification. *Journal of Personality and Social Psychology, 1,* 476–483.

Distinguished Scientific Contribution Award. (1958). *American Psychologist, 13,* 729–738. [B. F. Skinner]

Distinguished Scientific Contribution Award. (1981). *American Psychologist, 36,* 27–42. [A. Bandura]

Doherty W. (1983). Impact of divorce on locus of control orientation in adult women: A longitudinal study. *Journal of Personality and Social Psychology, 44,* 834–840.

Donaldson, G. (1996). Between practice and theory: Melanie Klein, Anna Freud, and the development of child analysis. *Journal of the History of the Behavioral Sciences, 32,* 160–176.

Douglas, C. (1993). *Translate this darkness: The life of Christiana Morgan.* New York: Simon & Schuster.

Duck, S. W., & Spencer, C. (1972). Personal constructs and friendship formation. *Journal of Personality and Social Psychology, 23,* 40–45.

Duncan, L. E., & Agronick, G. W. (1995). The intersection of life stage and social events: Personality and life outcomes. *Journal of Personality and Social Psychology, 69,* 558–568.

Eagle, M. N. (1988). How accurate were Freud's case histories? [Review of Freud and the Rat Man]. *Contemporary Psychology, 33,* 205–206.

Eaves, L. J., Eysenck, H. J., & Martin, N. G. (1989). *Genes, culture, and personality: An empirical approach.* New York: Academic Press.

Eccles, J. S., Barber, B., & Jozefowicz, D. (1999). Linking gender to educational, occupational, and recreational choices. In W. B. Swann, Jr., J. H. Langlois, & L. A. Gilbert (Eds.), *Sexism and stereotypes in modern society* (pp. 153–192). Washington, DC: American Psychological Association.

Eccles, J. S., & Wigfield, A. (1995). In the mind of the actor: The structure of adolescents' achievement task values and expectancy-related beliefs. *Personality and Social Psychology Bulletin, 21,* 215–225.

Einstein, D., & Lanning, K., (1998). Shame, guilt, ego development, and the five-factor model of personality. *Journal of Personality, 66,* 555–582.

Eissler, K. R. (1971). *Talent and genius: The fictitious case of Tausk contra Freud.* New York: Quadrangle Books.

Ekman, P., Matsumoto, D., & Friesen, W. V. (1997). Facial expressions in affective disorders. In P. Ekman & E. L. Rosenberg (Eds.), *What the face reveals* (pp. 331–341). New York: Oxford University Press.

Elder, G. H., & MacInnis, D. J. (1983). Achievement imagery in women's lives from adolescence to adulthood. *Journal of Personality and Social Psychology, 45,* 394–404.

Ellenberger, H. F. (1970). *The discovery of the unconscious: The history and evolution of dynamic psychiatry.* New York: Basic Books.

Ellenberger, H. F. (1978). Carl Gustav Jung: His historical setting. In H. Reise (Ed.), *Historical explorations in medicine and psychiatry* (pp. 142–150). New York: Springer.

Ellenberger, H. F. (1993). The life and work of Hermann Rorschach (1884–1922). In M. S. Micale (Ed.), *Beyond the unconscious: Essays of Henri F. Ellenberger in the history of psychiatry* (pp. 192–236). Princeton, NJ: Princeton University Press.

Elliot, A. J., & Church, M. A. (1997). A hierarchical model of approach and avoidance achievement motivation. *Journal of Personality and Social Psychology, 72,* 218–232.

Elliot, A. J., & Sheldon, K. M. (1997). Avoidance achievement motivation: A personal goals analysis. *Journal of Personality and Social Psychology, 73,* 171–185.

Ellis, R. A., & Taylor, M. S. (1983). Role of self-esteem within the job search process. *Journal of Applied Psychology, 68,* 632–640.

Elms, A. C. (1994). *Uncovering lives: The uneasy alliance of biography and psychology.* New York: Oxford University Press.

Enns, C. Z. (1989). Toward teaching inclusive personality theories. *Teaching of Psychology, 16*(3), 111–117.

Epstein, J. A., & Harackiewicz, J. M. (1992). Winning is not enough: The effects of competition and achievement orientation on intrinsic interest. *Personality and Social Psychology Bulletin, 18,* 128–138.

Erikson, E. H. (1950). *Childhood and society.* New York: Norton.

Erikson, E. H. (1959). Identity and the life cycle: Selected papers. *Psychological Issues, 1* (Monograph 1).

Erikson, E. H. (1968). *Identity: Youth and crisis.* New York: Norton.

Erikson, E. H. (1975). *Life history and the historical moment.* New York: Norton.

Erikson, E. H., Erikson, J. M., & Kivnick, H. Q. (1986). *Vital involvement in old age.* New York: Norton.

Eron, L. (1987). The development of aggressive behavior from the perspective of a developing behaviorism. *American Psychologist, 42,* 435–442.

Eron, L., & Huesmann, L. (1984). The control of aggressive behavior by changes in attitudes, values, and the conditions of learning. In R. J. Blanchard & D. C. Blanchard (Eds.), *Advances in the study of aggression* (Vol. 1, pp. 130–171). New York: Academic Press.

Eron, L., Huesmann, L., Lefkowitz, M., & Walder, L. (1972). Does television violence cause aggression? *American Psychologist, 27,* 253–263.

Estes, C. P. (1992). *Women who run with the wolves.* New York: Ballantine.

Evans, R. I. (1966). *Dialogue with Erich Fromm.* New York: Harper & Row.

Evans, R. I. (1968). *B. F. Skinner: The man and his ideas.* New York: Dutton.

Exner, J. E., Jr. (1993). The Rorschach: A comprehensive system: Vol. 1. *Basic foundations* (3rd ed.). New York: Wiley.

Eysenck, H. J. (1947). *Dimensions of personality.* London: Routledge & Kegan Paul.

Eysenck, H. J. (1967). *The biological basis of personality.* Springfield, IL: Charles C Thomas.

Eysenck, H. J. (1980). Autobiography. In G. Lindzey (Ed.), *A history of psychology in autobiography* (Vol. 7, pp. 153–187). San Francisco: W. H. Freeman.

Eysenck, H. J. (1983). A biometrical-genetical analysis of impulsive and sensation seeking behavior. In M. Zuckerman (Ed.), *Biological bases of sensation seeking, impulsivity, and anxiety* (pp. 1–27). Hillsdale, NJ: Erlbaum.

Eysenck, H. J. (1990a). Genetic and environmental contributions to individual differences: The three major dimensions of personality. *Journal of Personality, 58,* 245–261.

Eysenck, H. J. (1990b). Biological dimensions of personality. In L. A. Pervin (Ed.), Handbook of personality: *Theory and research* (pp. 244–276). New York: Guilford Press.

Eysenck, H. J. (1997a). Personality and experimental psychology: The unification of psychology and the possibility of a paradigm. *Journal of Personality and Social Psychology, 73,* 1224–1237.

Eysenck, H. J. (1997b). *Rebel with a cause: The autobiography of Hans Eysenck.* New Brunswick, NJ: Transaction Publishers.

Eysenck, H. J., & Cookson, D. (1969). Personality in primary school children: 3. Family background. *British Journal of Educational Psychology, 40,* 117–131.

Eysenck, H. J., & Eysenck, M. W. (1985). *Personality and individual differences: A natural science approach.* New York: Plenum Press.

Eysenck, H. J., & Eysenck, S. (1963). *Eysenck Personality Inventory.* San Diego, CA: Educational and Industrial Testing Service.

Eysenck, H. J., & Gudjonsson, G. H. (1989). *The causes and cures of criminality.* New York: Plenum Press.

Faith, M. S., Wong, F. Y., & Carpenter, K. M. (1995). Group sensitivity training: Update, meta-analysis, and recommendations. *Journal of Counseling Psychology, 3,* 390–399.

Falbo, T. (1978). Only children and interpersonal behavior: An experimental and survey study. *Journal of Applied Social Psychology, 8,* 244–253.

Falbo, T., & Polit, D. F. (1986). Quantitative review of the only child literature: Research evidence and theory development. *Psychological Bulletin, 100,* 176–189.

Feldman-Summers, S., & Pope, K. S. (1994). The experience of ``forgetting" childhood abuse: A national survey of psychologists. *Journal of Consulting and Clinical Psychology, 62,* 636–639.

Fiebert, M. S. (1997). In and out of Freud's shadow: A chronology of Adler's relationship with Freud. *Individual Psychology, 53,* 241–269.

Findley, M. J., & Cooper, H. M. (1983). Locus of control and academic achievement: A literature review. *Journal of Personality and Social Psychology, 44,* 419–427.

Fisher, J. D., & Misovich, S. J. (1990). Social influence and AIDS-preventive behavior. In J. Edwards, R. S. Tindale, & E. J. Posavac (Eds.), *Social influence processes and prevention* (pp. 39–70). New York: Plenum Press.

Fisher, S. P., & Greenberg, R. P. (1977). *The scientific credibility of Freud's theories and therapy.* New York: Basic Books.

Fisher, S. P., & Greenberg, R. P. (1996). *Freud scientifically reappraised: Testing the theories and therapy.* New York: Wiley.

Fiske, D. W. (1949). Consistency of the factorial structures of personality ratings from different sources. *Journal of Abnormal and Social Psychology, 44,* 329–344.

Floderus-Myrhed, B., Pedersen, N., & Rasmuson, I. (1980). Assessment of heritability for personality, based on a short form of the Eysenck Personality Inventory: A study of 12,898 twin pairs. *Behavior Genetics, 10,* 153–162.

Ford, J. G. (1991). Inherent potentialities of actualization: An initial exploration. *Journal of Humanistic Psychology, 31*(3), 65–88.

Fowler, R. D. (1990). In memoriam: Burrhus Frederic Skinner, 1904–1990. *American Psychologist, 45,* 1203.

Frable, E. E. S. (1997). Gender, racial, ethnic, sexual, and class identities. *Annual Review of Psychology, 48,* 139–162.

Frable, D. E. S., Wortman, C., & Joseph, J. (1997). Predicting self-esteem, well-being, and distress in a cohort of gay men: The importance of cultural stigma, personal visibility, community networks, and positive identity. *Journal of Personality, 65,* 599–624.

Frank, G. (1992). The response of African Americans to the Rorschach: A review of the research. *Journal of Personality Assessment, 59,* 317–325.

Franz, C. E., McClelland, D. C., & Weinberger, J. (1991). Childhood antecedents of conventional social accomplishment in midlife adults: A 36–year prospective study. *Journal of Personality and Social Psychology, 60,* 586–595.

Freedman, D. G. (1974). *Human infancy: An evolutionary perspective.* Hillsdale, NJ: Erlbaum.

Freud, S. (1901). *The psychopathology of everyday life. In The standard edition of the complete psychological works of Sigmund Freud* (Vol. 6). J. Strachey (Ed. & Trans.). London: Hogarth Press.

Freud, S. (1914). On the history of the psychoanalytic movement. In *Standard edition* (Vol. 14, pp. 3–66). London: Hogarth Press.

Freud, S. (1925). An autobiographical study. In *Standard edition* (Vol. 20). London: Hogarth Press.

Freud, S. (1940). An outline of psychoanalysis. In *Standard edition* (Vol. 23, pp. 141–207). London: Hogarth Press.

Freud, S. (1954). *The origins of psychoanalysis: Letters to Wilhelm Fliess, drafts and notes: 1887–1902.* M. Bonaparte, A. Freud, & E. Kris (Eds.). New York: Basic Books.

Freud, S. (1963). *Psychoanalysis and faith: The letters of Sigmund Freud and Oskar Pfister.* H. Meng & E. Freud (Eds.). New York: Basic Books.

Freud, S. (1985). *The complete letters of Sigmund Freud to Wilhelm Fliess, 1887–1904.* J. M. Masson (Ed.). Cambridge, MA: Belknap Press of Harvard University.

Freud, S., & Jung, C. G. (1974). *The Freud/Jung letters.* W. McGuire (Ed.). Princeton, NJ: Princeton University Press.

Friedman, H. S., Schwartz, J. E., Tomlinson-Keasey, C., Tucker, J. S., Martin, L. R., Wingard, D. L., & Criqui, M. H. (1995). Childhood conscientiousness and longevity: Health behaviors and cause of death. *Journal of Personality and Social Psychology, 68,* 696–703.

Friedman, H. S., Tucker, J. S., Tomlinson-Keasey, C., Schwartz, J. E., Wingard, D. L., & Criqui, M. H. (1993). Does childhood personality predict longevity? *Journal of Personality and Social Psychology, 65,* 176–185.

Friedman, L. J. (1996). Psychological advice in the public realm in America, 1940–1970 [Review of the book The Romance of American Psychology]. *Contemporary Psychology, 41,* 219–222.

Friedman, L. J. (1999). *Identity's architect: A biography of Erik H. Erikson.* New York: Simon & Schuster.

Fromm, E. (1941). *Escape from freedom.* New York: Holt, Rinehart & Winston.

Fromm, E. (1947). *Man for himself: An inquiry into the psychology of ethics.* New York: Holt, Rinehart & Winston.

Fromm, E. (1955). *The sane society.* New York: Holt, Rinehart & Winston.

Fromm, E. (1962). *Beyond the chains of illusion: My encounter with Marx and Freud.* New York: Simon & Schuster.

Fromm, E. (1964). *The heart of man: Its genius for good or evil.* New York: Harper & Row.

Fromm, E. (1976). *To have or to be?* New York: Harper & Row.

Fromm, E. (1992). *The art of being.* New York: Continuum.

Fromm, E., & Maccoby, M. (1970). *Social character in a Mexican village.* Englewood Cliffs, NJ: Prentice-Hall.

Funk, R. (1982). Erich Fromm: *The courage to be human.* New York: Continuum.

Gaines, S. O., Jr., et al. (1997). Links between race/ethnicity and cultural values as mediated by racial/ethnic identity and moderated by gender. *Journal of Personality and Social Psychology, 72,* 1460–1476.

Garb, H. N., Florio, C. M., & Grove, W. M. (1998). The validity of the Rorschach and the Minnesota Multiphasic Personality Inventory: Results from meta-analyses. *Psychological Science, 9,* 402–404.

Garcia, M. E., Schmitz, J. M., & Doerfler, L. A. (1990). A fine-grained analysis of the role of self-efficacy in self-initiated attempts to quit smoking. *Journal of Consulting and Clinical Psychology, 58,* 317–322.

Gardner, H. (1993). *Creating minds.* New York: Basic Books.

Gates, L., Lineberger, M. R., Crockett, J., & Hubbard, J. (1988). Birth order and its relationship to depression, anxiety, and self-concept test scores in children. *Journal of Genetic Psychology, 149,* 29–34.

Gay, P. (1988). *Freud: A life for our time.* New York: Norton.

Gecas, V. (1989). The social psychology of self-efficacy. *Annual Review of Sociology, 15,* 291–316.

Geen, R. G. (1984). Preferred stimulation levels of introverts and extroverts: Effects on arousal and performance. *Journal of Personality and Social Psychology, 46,* 1303–1312.

Gelbort, K. R., & Winer, J. L. (1985). Fear of success and fear of failure: A multitrait multi-method validation study. *Journal of Personality and Social Psychology, 48,* 1009–1014.

Gendlin, E. T., & Tomlinson, T. M. (1967). The process conception and its measurement. In C. R. Rogers, E. T. Gendlin, D. J. Kiesler, & C. B. Truax (Eds.), *The therapeutic relationship and its impact: A study of psychotherapy with schizophrenics.* Madison: University of Wisconsin Press.

Gibson, S., & Dembo, M. H. (1984). Teacher efficacy: A construct validation. *Journal of Educational Psychology, 76,* 569–582.

Gilgen, A. R. (1982). *American psychology since World War II: A profile of the discipline.* Westport, CT: Greenwood.

Glucksberg, S., & King, L. J. (1967). Motivated forgetting mediated by implicit verbal chaining: A laboratory analog of repression. *Science, 158,* 517–519.

Gold Medal Award for Life Achievement in Psychological Science. (1997). *American Psychologist, 52,* 797–799. [Cattell]

Goldberg, L. R. (1990). An alternative "description of personality": The Big-Five factor structure. *Journal of Personality and Social Psychology, 59,* 1216–1229.

Goldberg, L. R. (1992). The development of markers for the Big-Five factor structure. *Psychological Assessment, 4,* 26–42.

Goleman, D. (1987, August 31). B. F. Skinner: On his best behavior. *The New York Times.*

Goodstein, R., & Ponterotto, J. G. (1997). Racial and ethnic identity: Their relationship and their contribution to self-esteem. *Journal of Black Psychology, 23,* 275–292.

Gough, H. G. (1987). *California Psychological Inventory: Administrator's guide.* Palo Alto, CA: Consulting Psychologists Press.

Gough, H. G., Fioravanti, M., & Lazzari, R. (1983). Some implications of self versus idealized self-congruence on the Revised Adjective Check List. *Journal of Personality and Social Psychology, 44,* 1214–1220.

Gough, H. G., & Heilbrun, A. B., Jr. (1983). *The Adjective Check List Manual* (rev. ed.). Palo Alto, CA: Consulting Psychologists Press.

Gough, H. G., Lazzari, R., & Fioravanti, M. (1978). Self versus ideal self: A comparison of five Adjective Check List indices. *Journal of Consulting and Clinical Psychology, 35,* 1085–1091.

Graham, W., & Balloun, J. (1973). An empirical test of Maslow's need hierarchy theory. *Journal of Humanistic Psychology, 13,* 97–108.

Graves, T. D. (1961). *Time perspective and the deferred gratification pattern in a tri-ethnic community.* Boulder: University of Colorado Institute of Behavioral Science.

Graziano, W. G., Jensen-Campbell, L. A., & Sullivan-Logan, G. M. (1998). Temperament, activity, and expectations for later personality development. *Journal of Personality and Social Psychology, 74,* 1266–1277.

Greever, K., Tseng, M., & Friedland, B. (1973). Development of the Social Interest Index. *Journal of Consulting and Clinical Psychology, 41,* 454–458.

Grey, L. (1998). *Alfred Adler, the forgotten prophet: A vision for the 21ˢᵗ century.* Westport, CT: Praeger.

Grieser, C., Greenberg, R., & Harrison, R. H. (1972). The adaptive function of sleep: The differential effects of sleep and dreaming on recall. *Journal of Abnormal Psychology, 80,* 280–286.

Grob, A., Flammer, A., & Wearing, A. J. (1995). Adolescents' perceived control: Domain specificity, expectations, and appraisal. *Journal of Adolescence, 18,* 403–425.

Grubrich-Simitis, I. (1998). "Nothing about the totem meal!" On Freud's notes. In M. S. Roth (Ed.), *Freud: Conflict and culture* (pp. 17–31). New York: Knopf.

Guanzon-La Pena, M. A., Church, A. T., & Carlota, A. J. (1998). Indigenous personality measures: Philippine examples. *Journal of Cross-Cultural Psychology, 29,* 249–270.

Gurtman, M. B. (1992). Trust, distrust, and interpersonal problems: A circumplex analysis. *Journal of Personality and Social Psychology, 62,* 989–1002.

Hackett, G. (1995). Self-efficacy in career choice and development. In A. Bandura (Ed.), *Self-efficacy in changing societies* (pp. 232–258). Cambridge, England: Cambridge University Press.

Hafner, J. L., Fakouri, M. E., & Labrentz, H. L. (1982). First memories of "normal" and alcoholic individuals. *Individual Psychology, 38,* 238–244.

Hall, C., & Van de Castle, R. (1965). An empirical investigation of the castration complex in dreams. *Journal of Personality, 33,* 20–29.

Hall, E. (1983, June). A conversation with Erik Erikson. *Psychology Today,* pp. 22–30.

Hall, M. H. (1967, September). An interview with "Mr. Behaviorist" B. F. Skinner. *Psychology Today,* pp. 21–23, 68–71.

Hall, M. H. (1968a, July). A conversation with Abraham H. Maslow. *Psychology Today,* pp. 35–37, 54–57.

Hamberger, L. K., & Hastings, J. E. (1992). Racial differences on the MCMI in an outpatient clinical sample. *Journal of Personality Assessment, 58,* 90–95.

Hanewitz, W. B. (1978). Police personality: A Jungian perspective. *Crime and Delinquency, 24,* 152–172.

Hankoff, L. D. (1987). The earliest memories of criminals. *International Journal of Offender Therapy and Comparative Criminology, 31,* 195–201.

Hanson, R. K. (1992). Thematic analysis of daily events as a method of personality assessment. *Journal of Personality Assessment, 58,* 606–620.

Harber, K. D. (1998). Feedback to minorities: Evidence of a positive bias. *Journal of Personality and Social Psychology, 73,* 622–628.

Harrington, D. M., Block, J. H., & Block, J. (1987). Testing aspects of Carl Rogers' theory of creative environments: Child-rearing antecedents of creative potential in young adolescents. *Journal of Personality and Social Psychology, 52,* 851–856.

Harris, D., & Kuba, I. (1997). Ethnocultural identity and eating disorders in women of color. *Professional Psychology, 28,* 341–347.

Harris, J. R. (1995). Where is the child's environment? A group socialization theory of development. *Psychological Review, 102,* 458–489.

Harris, J. R. (1998). *The nurture assumption: Why children turn out the way they do.* New York: Free Press.

Harter, S., Marold, D. B., Whitesell, N. R., & Cobbs, G. (1996). A model of the effects of perceived parent and peer support on adolescent false-self behavior. *Child Development, 67,* 360–374.

Harvey, E. (1999). Short-term and long-term effects of early parental employment on children of the National

Longitudinal Survey of Youth. *Developmental Psychology, 35,* 445–459.

Hawkins, R. P., Peterson, R. F., Schweid, E., & Bijou, S. W. (1966). Behavior therapy in the home: Amelioration of problem parent-child relations with the parent in a therapeutic role. *Journal of Experimental Child Psychology, 4,* 99–107.

Haynal, A. (1993). *Psychoanalysis and the sciences: Epistemology—history.* Berkeley: University of California Press.

Heath, A. C. (1991). The genetics of personality [Review of the book Nature's thumbprint: The new genetics of personality]. *Contemporary Psychology, 36,* 1063–1064.

Heath, A. C., Neale, M. C., Kessler, R. C., Eaves, L. J., & Kendler, K. S. (1992). Evidence for genetic influences on personality from self-reports and informant ratings. *Journal of Personality and Social Psychology, 63,* 85–96.

Heckhausen, J., & Schulz, R. (1995). A life-span theory of control. *Psychological Review, 102,* 284–304.

Heller, M., & Haynal, V. (1997). Depression and suicide faces. In P. Ekman & E. L. Rosenberg (Eds.), *What the face reveals* (pp. 398–407). New York: Oxford University Press.

Helms, J. (1990). *Black and white racial identity: Theory, research, and practice.* New York: Greenwood Press.

Helson, R. (1992). Women's difficult times and the rewriting of the life story. *Psychology of Women Quarterly, 16,* 331–347.

Helson, R., & Klohnen, E. C. (1998). Affective coloring of personality from young adulthood to midlife. *Personality and Social Psychology Bulletin, 24,* 241–252.

Helson, R., Stewart, A., & Ostrove, J. (1995). Identity in three cohorts of midlife women. *Journal of Personality and Social Psychology, 69,* 544–557.

Herbert, T. B., & Cohen, S. (1993). Depression and immunity: A meta-analytic review. *Psychological Bulletin, 113,* 472–486.

Hetherington, E. M., & Frankie, G. (1967). Effect of parental dominance, warmth, and conflict on imitation in children. *Journal of Personality and Social Psychology, 6,* 119–125.

Hilgard, E. (1987). *Psychology in America: A historical survey.* San Diego: Harcourt Brace Jovanovich.

Hiroto, D. S. (1974). Locus of control and learned helplessness. *Journal of Experimental Psychology, 102,* 187–193.

Hobfoll, S. E., Rom, T., & Segal, B. (1989). Sensation seeking, anxiety, and risk taking in the Israeli context. In S. Einstein (Ed.), *Drug and alcohol use: Issues and factors* (pp. 53–59). New York: Plenum Press.

Hoffman, E. (1988). *The right to be human: A biography of Abraham Maslow.* Los Angeles: Tarcher.

Hoffman, E. (1994). *The drive for self: Alfred Adler and the founding of individual psychology.* Reading, MA: Addison-Wesley.

Hoffman, E. (Ed.) (1996). *Future visions: The unpublished papers of Abraham Maslow.* Thousand Oaks, CA: Sage.

Holahan, C. K., & Holahan, C. J. (1987). Self-efficacy, social support, and depression in aging: A longitudinal analysis. *Journal of Gerontology, 42,* 65–68.

Holtzman, W. H. (1988). Beyond the Rorschach. *Journal of Personality Assessment, 52,* 578–609.

Holzman, P. S. (1994). Hilgard on psychoanalysis as a science. *Psychological Science, 5*(4), 190–191.

Horner, M. S. (1973). A psychological barrier to achievement in women: The motive to avoid success. In D. C. McClelland & R. S. Steele (Eds.), *Human motivation.* Morristown, NJ: General Learning Press.

Horney, K. (1937). *The neurotic personality of our time.* New York: Norton.

Horney, K. (1939). *New ways in psychoanalysis.* New York: Norton.

Horney, K. (1942). *Self-analysis.* New York: Norton.

Horney, K. (1945). *Our inner conflicts.* New York: Norton.

Horney, K. (1967a). The flight from womanhood: The masculinity-complex in women as viewed by men and by women. In H. Kelman (Ed.), *Feminine psychology.* New York: Norton.

Horney, K. (1980). *The adolescent diaries of Karen Horney.* New York: Basic Books. [Diaries written 1899–1911]

Horney, K. (1987). *Final lectures.* D. H. Ingram (Ed.). New York: Norton. [Lectures delivered 1952]

Huesmann, L., Eron, L., Dubow, E., & Seebauer, E. (1987). Television viewing habits in childhood and adult aggression. *Child Development, 58,* 357–367.

Hunt, M. (1993). *The story of psychology.* Garden City, NY: Doubleday.

Hurlburt, R. (1997). Randomly sampling thinking in the natural environment. *Journal of Consulting and Clinical Psychology, 65,* 941–949.

Ivancevich, J. M., Matteson, M. T., & Gamble, G. O. (1987). Birth order and the Type A coronary behavior pattern. *Individual Psychology, 43,* 42–49.

Jackson, M., & Sechrest, L. (1962). Early recollections in four neurotic diagnostic categories. *Journal of Individual Psychology, 18,* 52–56.

Jacobson, J. L., & Wille, D. E. (1986). The influence of attachment patterns on developmental changes in peer interaction from the toddler to the preschool period. *Child Development, 57,* 338–347.

Jacoby, L. L., & Kelley, C. M. (1987). Unconscious influences of memory for a prior event. *Personality and Social Psychology Bulletin, 13,* 314–336.

Jaffé, A. (1971). *The myth of meaning: Jung and the expansion of consciousness.* New York: Putnam.

Jang, K. L., & Livesley, W. J. (1998). Heritability of facet-level traits in a cross-cultural twin sample. *Journal of Personality and Social Psychology, 74,* 1556–1565.

Jerusalem, M., & Mittag, W. (1995). Self-efficacy in stressful life transitions. In A. Bandura (Ed.), *Self-efficacy in changing societies* (pp. 177–201). Cambridge, England: Cambridge University Press.

Jiao, S., Ji, G., & Jing, Q. (1986). Comparative study of behavioral qualities of only children and sibling children. *Child Development, 57,* 357–361.

John, O. P. (1990). The big five factor taxonomy: Dimensions of personality in the natural language and in questionnaires. In L. A. Pervin (Ed.), *Handbook of personality: Theory and research* (pp. 66–100). New York: Guilford Press.

John, O. P., Pals, J. L., & Westenberg, P. M. (1998). Personality prototypes and ego development: Conceptual similarities and relations in adult women. *Journal of Personality and Social Psychology, 74,* 1093–1108.

Johnson, R. C. (1980). Summing up [Review of the book Personality and learning theory, Vol. 1: The structure of personality in its environment]. *Contemporary Psychology, 25,* 299–300.

Jones, E. (1953, 1955, 1957). *The life and work of Sigmund Freud* (3 vols.). New York: Basic Books.

Jones, R. L. (1994). An empirical study of Freud's penis-baby equation. *Journal of Nervous and Mental Disease, 182*(3), 127–135.

Jorm, A. F. (1987). Sex differences in neuroticism: A quantitative synthesis of published research. *Australian and New Zealand Journal of Psychiatry, 21,* 501–506.

Josselson, R. L. (1982). Personality structure and identity status in women as viewed through early memories. *Journal of Youth and Adolescence, 11,* 293–299.

Jung, C. G. (1909). The association method. In *The collected works of C. G. Jung* (Vol. 2, pp. 442, 444). H. Read, M. Fordham, & G. Adler (Eds.). Princeton, NJ: Princeton University Press.

Jung, C. G. (1927). The structure of the psyche. In *Collected works* (Vol. 8, pp. 139–158). Princeton, NJ: Princeton University Press.

Jung, C. G. (1928). On psychic energy. In *Collected works* (Vol. 8, pp. 3–66). Princeton, NJ: Princeton University Press.

Jung, C. G. (1930). The stages of life. In *Collected works* (Vol. 8, pp. 387–403). Princeton, NJ: Princeton University Press.

Jung, C. G. (1953). *Two essays on analytical psychology.* New York: Pantheon.

Jung, C. G. (1961). *Memories, dreams, reflections.* New York: Vintage Books.

Kagan, J. (1984). *The nature of the child.* New York: Basic Books.

Kagan, J. (1989). Temperamental contributions to social behavior. *American Psychologist, 44,* 668–674.

Kagan, J. (1999). *Three seductive ideas.* Cambridge, MA: Harvard University Press.

Kagan, J., Arcus, D., & Snidman, N. (1993). The idea of temperament: Where do we go from here? In R. Plomin & G. E. McClearn (Eds.), *Nature, nurture, and psychology* (pp. 197–210). Washington, DC: American Psychological Association.

Kagan, J., Snidman, N., & Arcus, D. (1992). Initial reactions to unfamiliarity. *Current Directions in Psychological Science, 1,* 171–174.

Kalichman, S. C., Johnson, J. R., Adair, V., Rompa, D., Multhauf, K., & Kelly, J. A. (1994). Sexual sensation seeking: Scale development and predicting AIDS-risk behavior among homosexually active men. *Journal of Personality Assessment, 62,* 385–397.

Kamptner, N. L. (1988). Identity development in late adolescence: Causal modeling of social and familial influences. *Journal of Youth and Adolescence, 17,* 493–514.

Kaplan, R. M., Atkins, C. J., & Reinsch, S. (1984). Specific efficacy expectations mediate exercise compliance in patients with COPD. *Health Psychology, 3,* 223–242.

Karon, B., & Widener, A. (1997). Repressed memories and World War II. *Professional Psychology, 28,* 338–340.

Katcher, A. (1955). The discrimination of sex differences by young children. *Journal of Genetic Psychology, 87,* 131–143.

Kazdin, A. E. (1989). *Behavior modification in applied settings* (4th ed.). Pacific Grove, CA: Brooks/Cole.

Kazdin, A. E., & Bootzin, R. (1972). The token economy: An evaluative review. *Journal of Applied Behavioral Analysis, 5,* 343–372.

Kellaghan, T., & MacNamara, J. (1972). Family correlates of verbal reasoning ability. *Developmental Psychology, 7,* 49–53.

Kelly, G. A. (1955). *The psychology of personal constructs.* New York: Norton.

Kelly, G. A. (1969). *Clinical psychology and personality: The selected papers of George Kelly.* [B. Maher (Ed.).] New York: Wiley.

Keltikangas-Jaruinen, L., & Raikkonen, K. (1990). Healthy and maladjusted Type A behavior in adolescents. *Journal of Youth and Adolescence, 19,* 1–18.

Keltner, D. (1997). Facial expression, personality, and psychopathology. In P. Ekman & E. L. Rosenberg (Eds.), *What the face reveals* (pp. 450–452). New York: Oxford University Press.

Keniston, K. (1983, June). Remembering Erikson at Harvard. *Psychology Today,* p. 29.

Kidwell, J. (1982). The neglected birth order: Middleborns. *Journal of Marriage and the Family, 44,* 225–235.

Kiester, E., Jr., & Cudhea, D. (1974). Albert Bandura: A very modern model. *Human Behavior,* 27–31.

Kihlstrom, J. F., Barnhardt, M., & Tataryn, D. J. (1992). The psychological unconscious: Found, lost, and regained. *American Psychologist, 47,* 788–791.

King, L. A., & Napa, C. K. (1998). What makes a life good? *Journal of Personality and Social Psychology, 75,* 156–165.

Klein, M. H., Malthieu, P. L., Gendlin, E. T., & Kiesler, D. J. (1969). *The Experiencing Scale: A research and training manual.* Madison: Wisconsin Psychiatric Institute.

Kline, P. (1972). *Fact and fantasy in Freudian theory.* London: Methuen.

Kochanska, G., Clark, L. A., & Goldman, M. S. (1997). Implications of mothers' personality for their parenting and their young children's developmental outcomes. *Journal of Personality, 65,* 387–420.

Kosten, T. A., Ball, S. A., & Rounsaville, B. J. (1994). A sibling study of sensation seeking and opiate addiction. *Journal of Nervous and Mental Disease, 182,* 284–289.

Krüll, M. (1986). *Freud and his father.* New York: Norton.

Kurzweil, E. (1998). Freud's reception in the United States. In M. S. Roth (Ed.), *Freud: Conflict and culture* (pp. 127–139). New York: Knopf.

Lachman, M. E. (1985). Personal efficacy in middle and old age: Differential and normative patterns of change. In G. H. Elder, Jr. (Ed.), *Life course dynamics* (pp. 188–216). Ithaca, NY: Cornell University Press.

Lahey, B. B., Hammer, D., Crumrine, P. L., & Forehand, R. L. (1980). Birth order [and] sex interactions in child behavior problems. *Developmental Psychology, 16,* 608–615.

Langan-Fox, J., & Roth, S. (1995). Achievement motivation and female entrepreneurs. *Journal of Occupational and Organizational Psychology, 68,* 209–218.

Langer, E. J., & Rodin, J. (1976). The effects of choice and enhanced personal responsibility for the aged: A field experiment in an institutional setting. *Journal of Personality and Social Psychology, 34,* 191–198.

Lapan, R. T., Boggs, K. R., & Morrill, W. H. (1989). Self-efficacy as a mediator of investigative and realistic general occupational themes on the Strong-Campbell Interest Inventory. *Journal of Counseling Psychology, 36,* 176–182.

Larsen, R. J., & Kasimatis, M. (1991). Day-to-day symptoms: Individual differences in the occurrence, duration, and emotional concomitants of minor daily illness. *Journal of Personality, 59,* 387–423.

Latané, B., & Bidwell, L. D. (1977). Sex and affiliation in college cafeterias. *Personality and Social Psychology Bulletin, 3,* 571–574.

Laungani, P. (1999). Cultural influences on identity and behavior: India and Britain. In Y. T. Lee, C. R. McCauley, & J. G. Draguns (Eds.),, *Personality and person perception across cultures* (pp. 191–212). Mahwah, NJ: Erlbaum.

Law, A., Logan, H., & Baron, R. S. (1994). Desire for control, felt control, and stress inoculation training during dental treatment. *Journal of Personality and Social Psychology, 67,* 926–936.

Lee, Y. T., McCauley, C. R., & Draguns, J. G. (1999). Why study personality in culture? In Y. T. Lee, C. R. McCauley, & J. G. Draguns, (Eds.), *Personality and person perception across cultures* (pp. 3–22). Mahwah, NJ: Erlbaum.

Lee, Y. T., & Seligman, M. E. P. (1997). Are Americans more optimistic than the Chinese? *Personality and Social Psychology Bulletin, 23,* 32–40.

Lefcourt, H. M. (1982). *Locus of control: Current trends in theory and research* (2nd ed.). Hillsdale, NJ: Erlbaum.

Lefcourt, H. M., Martin, R. A., Fick, C. M., & Saleh, W. E. (1985). Locus of control for affiliation in social interactions. *Journal of Personality and Social Psychology, 48,* 755–759.

Lefkowitz, M. M., & Tesiny, E. P. (1984). Rejection and depression: Prospective and contemporaneous analysis. *Developmental Psychology, 20,* 776–785.

Lent, R. W., & Hackett, G. (1987). Career self-efficacy: Empirical status and future directions. *Journal of Vocational Behavior, 30,* 347–382.

Lerner, P. M. (1994). Current status of the Rorschach [Review of the book The Rorschach: A Comprehensive System: Vol. 1: Basic Foundations (3rd ed.)]. *Contemporary Psychology, 39,* 724–725.

Lester, D. (1990). Maslow's hierarchy of needs and personality. *Personality and Individual Differences, 11,* 1187–1188.

Levenson, M. R. (1990). Risk taking and personality. *Journal of Personality and Social Psychology, 58,* 1073–1080.

Levinson, D. J. (1978). *The seasons of a man's life.* New York: Knopf.

Levinson, D. J. (1996). *The seasons of a woman's life.* New York: Knopf.

Levit, D. B. (1993). The development of ego defenses in adolescence. *Journal of Youth and Adolescence, 22,* 493–512.

Leyens, J., Camino, L., Parke, R., & Berkowitz, L. (1975). Effects of movie violence on aggression in a field setting as a function of group dominance and cohesion. *Journal of Personality and Social Psychology, 32,* 346–360.

Liebert, R. M., Sprafkin, J. N., & Davidson, E. S. (1982). *The early window: Effects of television on children and youth* (2nd ed.). Elmsford, NY: Pergamon Press.

Locke, E. A., & Latham, G. P. (1990). *A theory of goal setting and task performance.* Englewood Cliffs, NJ: Prentice-Hall.

Loeb, R. C. (1975). Concomitants of boys' locus of control examined in parent-child interactions. *Developmental Psychology, 11,* 353–358.

Loehlin, J. C. (1997). A test of J. R. Harris's theory of peer influences on psychology. *Journal of Personality and Social Psychology, 72,* 1197–1201.

Loehlin, J. C., Horn, J. M., & Willerman, L. (1990). Heredity, environment, and personality change: Evidence from the Texas adoption project. *Journal of Personality, 58,* 221–243.

Loehlin, J. C., & Nichols, R. C. (1976). *Heredity, environment, and personality: A study of 850 sets of twins.* Austin: University of Texas Press.

Loftus, E., Garry, M., & Feldman, J. (1994). Forgetting sexual trauma: What does it mean when 38 percent forget? *Journal of Consulting and Clinical Psychology, 62,* 1177–1181.

Loftus, E., & Ketcham, K. (1994). *False memories and allegations of sexual abuse.* New York: St. Martin's Press.

Loftus, E., Polonsky, S., & Fullilove, M. T. (1994). Memories of childhood sexual abuse. *Psychology of Women Quarterly, 18,* 67–84.

Londerville, S., & Main, M. (1981). Security of attachment, compliance, and maternal training methods in the second year of life. *Developmental Psychology, 17,* 289–299.

Loo, C. M. (1998). *Chinese America: Mental health and quality of life in the inner city.* Thousand Oaks, CA: Sage.

Lowell, E. L. (1952). The effect of need for achievement on learning and speed of performance. *Journal of Psychology, 33,* 31–40.

Lubin, B., Larsen, R. M., Matarazzo, J. D., & Seever, M. (1985). Psychological test usage patterns in five professional settings. *American Psychologist, 40,* 857–861.

Maccoby, M. (1972, Winter). Emotional attitudes and political choices. *Politics and Society,* pp. 209–239.

Maccoby, M. (1976). *The gamesman.* New York: Simon & Schuster.

Maccoby, M. (1981). *The leader.* New York: Simon & Schuster.

Mackavey, W. R., Malley, J. E., & Stewart, A. J. (1991). Remembering autobiographically consequential experiences: Content analysis of psychologists' accounts of their lives. *Psychology and Aging, 6,* 50–59.

Magnus, K., Diener, E., Fujita, F., & Pavot, W. (1993). Extraversion and neuroticism as predictors of objective life events: A longitudinal analysis. *Journal of Personality and Social Psychology, 65,* 1046–1053.

Magnusson, D. (1990). Personality development from an interactional perspective. In L. A. Pervin (Ed.), *Handbook of personality* (pp. 193–222). New York: Guilford Press.

Mahalik, J. R., Cournoyer, R. J., DeFrank, W., Cherry, M., & Napolitano, J. M. (1998). Men's gender role conflict and use of psychological defenses. *Journal of Counseling Psychology, 45,* 247–255.

Mahoney, J., & Hartnett, J. (1973). Self-actualization and self-ideal discrepancy. *Journal of Psychology, 85,* 37–42.

Mahoney, P. J. (1986). *Freud and the Rat Man.* New Haven: Yale University Press.

Mahoney, P. (1992). Freud as a family therapist: Reflections. In T. Gelfand & J. Kerr (Eds.), *Freud and the history of psychoanalysis* (pp. 307–317). Hillsdale, NJ: Analytic Press.

Maier, S. F., Laudenslager, M., & Ryan, S. M. (1985). Stressor controllability, immune function, and endogenous opiates. In F. R. Brush and J. B. Overmier (Eds.), *Affect, conditioning, and cognition: Essays on the determinants of behavior* (pp. 203–210). Hillsdale, NJ: Erlbaum.

Maier, S. J., & Seligman, M. E. P. (1976). Learned helplessness: Theory and evidence. *Journal of Experimental Psychology, 105,* 3–46.

Major, G., Barr, L., Zubek, J., & Babey, S. H. (1999). Gender and self-esteem: A meta-analysis. In W. B. Swann, Jr., J. H. Langlois, & L. A. Gilbert (Eds.), *Sexism and stereotypes in modern society* (pp. 223–253). Washington, DC: American Psychological Association.

Major, B., Mueller, P., & Hildebrandt, K. (1985). Attributions, expectations, and coping with abortion. *Journal of Personality and Social Psychology, 48,* 585–599.

Malcolm, J. (1984). In the Freud archives. New York: Knopf.

Manning, M. M., & Wright, T. L. (1983). Self-efficacy expectancies, outcome expectancies, and the persistence of pain control in childbirth. *Journal of Personality and Social Psychology, 45,* 421–431.

Maqsud, M., & Rouhani, S. (1991). Relationships between socioeconomic status, locus of control, self-concept, and academic achievement of Botswana adolescents. *Journal of Youth and Adolescence, 20,* 107–114.

Marcia, J. E. (1966). Development and validation of ego-identity status. *Journal of Personality and Social Psychology, 3,* 551–558.

Marcia, J. E. (1967). Ego identity status: Relationship to change in self-esteem, general maladjustment and authoritarianism. *Journal of Personality, 35,* 118–133.

Marcia, J. E. (1980). Identity in adolescence. In J. Adelson (Ed.), *Handbook of adolescent psychology* (pp. 159–187). New York: Wiley.

Marcia, J. E., & Friedman, M. L. (1970). Ego identity status in college women. *Journal of Personality, 38,* 249–263.

Mariotto, M. J., & Paul, G. L. (1974). A multimethod validation of the Inpatient Multidimensional Psychiatric Scale with chronically institutionalized patients. *Journal of Consulting and Clinical Psychology, 42,* 497–509.

Markus, H. R., & Kitayama, S. (1991). Culture and the self: Implications for cognition, emotion, and motivation. *Psychological Review, 98,* 224–253.

Marshall, G. N. (1991). A multidimensional analysis of internal health locus of control beliefs: Separating the wheat from the chaff? *Journal of Personality and Social Psychology, 61,* 483–491.

Marshall, G. N., Wortman, C. B., Vickers, R. R., Jr., Kusulas, J. W., & Hervig, L. K. (1994). The five-factor model of personality as a framework for personality-health research. *Journal of Personality and Social Psychology, 67,* 278–286.

Martin, C. M. (1999). A developmental perspective on gender effects and gender concepts. In W. B. Swann, Jr., J. H. Langlois, & L. A. Gilbert (Eds.), *Sexism and stereotypes in modern society* (pp. 45–73). Washington, DC: American Psychological Association.

Martin, N., & Jardine, R. (1986). Eysenck's contributions to behaviour genetics. In S. Modgill & L. Modgill (Eds.), *Hans Eysenck: Consensus and controversy* (pp. 13–47). London: Falmer.

Masling, J. M., Rabie, L., & Blondheim, S. H. (1967). Obesity, level of aspiration, and Rorschach and TAT measures of oral dependence. *Journal of Consulting Psychology, 31,* 233–239.

Maslow, A. H. (1957). A philosophy of psychology: The need for a mature science of human nature. *Main Currents in Modern Thought, 13,* 27–32.

Maslow, A. H. (1968). *Toward a psychology of being* (2nd ed.). New York: Van Nostrand Reinhold.

Maslow, A. H. (1970a). Tribute to Alfred Adler. *Journal of Individual Psychology, 26,* 13.

Maslow, A. H. (1970b). *Motivation and personality* (2nd ed.). New York: Harper & Row.

Maslow, A. H. (1971). *The farther reaches of human nature.* New York: Viking Press.

Maslow, A. H. (1979). *The journals of A. H. Maslow.* [R. J. Lowry (Ed.).] Pacific Grove, CA: Brooks/Cole.

Maslow, A. H. (1987). *Motivation and personality* (3rd ed.). New York: Harper & Row.

Masson, J. M. (1984). *The assault on truth: Freud's suppression of the seduction theory.* New York: Farrar, Straus & Giroux.

Mastekaasa, A. (1995). Age variations in the suicide rates and self-reported subjective well-being of married and never married persons. *Journal of Community and Applied Social Psychology, 5,* 21–39.

Matheny, A. P. (1983). A longitudinal twin study of the stability of components from Bayley's Infant Behavior Record. *Child Development, 54,* 356–360.

Mathes, E. W., Zevon, M. A., Roter, P. M., & Joerger, S. M. (1982). Peak experience tendencies: Scale development and theory testing. *Journal of Humanistic Psychology, 22,* 92–108.

Matthews, G., & Deary, I. J. (1998). *Personality traits.* Cambridge, England: Cambridge University Press.

Matthews, K. A., Batson, C. D., Horn, J., & Rosenman, R. H. (1981). "Principles in his nature which interest

him in the fortune of others . . .": The heritability of empathic concern for others. *Journal of Personality, 49,* 237–247.

Matula, K. E., Huston, T. L., Grotevant, H. D., & Zamutt, A. (1992). Identity and dating commitment among women and men in college. *Journal of Youth and Adolescence, 21,* 339–356.

Mayer, J. D., & Carlsmith, K. M. (1997). Eminence rankings of personality psychologists as a reflection of the field. *Personality and Social Psychology Bulletin, 23,* 707–716.

Mazzoni, G. A. L., Lombardo, P., Malvagia, S., & Loftus, E. (1999). Dream interpretations and false beliefs. *Professional Psychology, 30,* 45–50.

McAdams, D. P. (1994). Can personality change? Levels of stability and growth in personality across the life span. In T. F. Heatherton & J. L. Weinberger (Eds.), *Can personality change?* (pp. 299–313). Washington, DC: American Psychological Association.

McAdams, D. P., & de St. Aubin, E. (1992). A theory of generativity and its assessment through self-report, behavioral acts, and narrative themes in autobiography. *Journal of Personality and Social Psychology, 62,* 1003–1015.

McAdams, D. P., Diamond, A., de St. Aubin, E., & Mansfield, E. (1997). Stories of commitment: The psychosocial construction of generative lives. *Journal of Personality and Social Psychology, 72,* 678–694.

McAdams, D. P., Hart, H. M., & Maruna, S. (1998). The anatomy of generativity. In D. P. McAdams & E. de St. Aubin (Eds.), *Generativity and adult development* (pp. 7–43). Washington, DC: American Psychological Association.

McAdams, D. P., Ruetzel, K., & Foley, J. M. (1986). Complexity and generativity at midlife: Relations among social motives, ego development, and adults' plans for the future. *Journal of Personality and Social Psychology, 50,* 800–807.

McClelland, D. C. (1961). *The achieving society.* New York: Free Press.

McClelland, D. C. (1965a). N achievement and entrepreneurship: A longitudinal study. *Journal of Personality and Social Psychology, 1,* 389–392.

McClelland, D. C. (1965b). Toward a theory of motive acquisition. *American Psychologist, 20,* 321–333.

McClelland, D. C. (1979). The need for power and sympathetic nervous system arousal. Paper presented at the meeting of the Society for Psychophysiological Research, Cincinnati, OH.

McClelland, D. C. (1985). *Human motivation.* Glenview, IL: Scott, Foresman.

McClelland, D. C. (1987). Characteristics of successful entrepreneurs. *Journal of Creative Behavior, 3,* 219–233.

McClelland, D. C. (1993). Motives and health. In G. G. Brannigan & M. R. Merrens (Eds.), *The undaunted psychologist: Adventures in research* (pp. 129–141). Philadelphia: Temple University Press.

McClelland, D. C., Atkinson, J. W., Clark, R. A., & Lowell, E. L. (1953). *The achievement motive.* New York: Appleton-Century-Crofts.

McClelland, D. C., & Boyatzis, R. E. (1982). The leadership motive pattern and long-term success in management. *Journal of Applied Psychology, 67,* 737–743.

McClelland, D. C., David, W. N., Kalin, R., & Wanner, E. (1972). *The drinking man.* New York: Free Press.

McClelland, D. C., & Franz, C. E. (1992). Motivational and other sources of work accomplishments in midlife: A longitudinal study. *Journal of Personality, 60,* 679–707.

McClelland, D. C., Koestner, R., & Weinberger, J. (1989). How do self-attributed and implicit motives differ? *Psychological Review, 96,* 690–702.

McClelland, D. C., & Winter, D. G. (1969). *Motivating economic achievement.* New York: Free Press.

McCrae, R. R., & Costa, P. T., Jr. (1985a). Openness to experience. In R. Hogan & W. H. Jones (Eds.), *Perspectives in personality* (Vol. 1, pp. 145–172).

McCrae, R. R., & Costa, P. T., Jr. (1985b). Updating Norman's "adequate taxonomy": Intelligence and personality dimensions in natural language and questionnaires. *Journal of Personality and Social Psychology, 49,* 710–721.

McCrae, R. R., & Costa, P. T., Jr. (1987). Validation of the five-factor model of personality across instruments and observers. *Journal of Personality and Social Psychology, 52,* 81–90.

McCrae, R. R., & Costa, P. T., Jr. (1989). Reinterpreting the Myers-Briggs Type Indicator from the perspective of the five-factor model of personality. *Journal of Personality, 57,* 17–40.

McCrae, R. R., & Costa, P. T., Jr. (1991). Adding Liebe und Arbeit: The full five-factor model and well-being. *Personality and Social Psychology Bulletin, 17,* 227–232.

McCrae, R. R., & Costa, P. T., Jr. (1997). Personality trait structure as a human universal. *American Psychologist, 52,* 509–516.

McCrae, R. R., Costa, P. T., Jr., Pilar, G. H. D., Rolland, J. P., & Parke, W. D. (1998). Cross-cultural assessment of the five-factor model: The revised NEO personality inventory. *Journal of Cross-Cultural Psychology, 29,* 171–188.

McCrae, R. R., Yi,, M. S. M., Trapnell, P. D., Bond, M. H., & Paulhus, D. L. (1998). Interpreting personality profiles across cultures: Bilingual, acculturation, and peer rating studies of Chinese undergraduates. *Journal of Personality and Social Psychology, 74,* 1041–1055.

McCrae, R. R., et al. (1999). Age differences in personality across the adult life span: Parallels in five cultures. *Developmental Psychology, 35,* 466–477.

McGregor, I., & Little, B. R. (1998). Personal projects, happiness, and meaning. *Journal of Personality and Social Psychology, 74,* 494–512.

McGuire, P. A. (1999, March). Multicultural summit cheers packed house. *APA Monitor,* p. 26.

McLaughlin, N. G. (1998). Why do schools of thought fail? Neo-Freudianism as a case study in the sociology of knowledge. *Journal of the History of the Behavioral Sciences, 34,* 113–134.

McLeod, B. (1986, October). Rx for health: A dose of self-confidence. *Psychology Today,* pp. 46–50.

McNulty, J. L., Graham, J. R., Ben-Porath, Y. S., & Stein, L. A. R. (1997). Comparadive validity of MMPI-2 scores of African American and Causasian mental health center clients. *Psychological Assessment, 9,* 464–470.

Medinnus, G., & Curtis, F. (1963). The relation between maternal self-acceptance and child acceptance. *Journal of Counseling Psychology, 27,* 542–544.

Meichenbaum, D., & Gilmore, J. B. (1984). The nature of unconscious processes: A cognitive-behavioral perspective. In K. Bowers & D. Meichenbaum (Eds.), *The unconscious reconsidered.* New York: Wiley.

Melamed, B. G., & Siegel, L. J. (1975). Reduction of anxiety in children facing hospitalization and surgery by use of filmed modeling. *Journal of Consulting and Clinical Psychology, 43,* 511–521.

Mellor, S. (1989). Gender differences in identity formation as a function of self-other relationships. *Journal of Youth and Adolescence, 18,* 361–375.

Mellor, S. (1990). How do only children differ from other children? *Journal of Genetic Psychology, 151,* 221–230.

Mikulincer, M. (1986). Attributional processes in the learned helplessness paradigm: Behavioral effects of global attributions. *Journal of Personality and Social Psychology, 51,* 1248–1256.

Mikulincer, M., & Nizan, B. (1988). Causal attribution, cognitive interference, and the generalization of learned helplessness. *Journal of Personality and Social Psychology, 55,* 470–478.

Milgram, N. A. (1971). Locus of control in Negro and white children at four age levels. *Psychological Reports, 29,* 459–465.

Miller, N., & Maruyama, G. (1976). Ordinal position and peer popularity. *Journal of Personality and Social Psychology, 33,* 123–131.

Mindess, H. (1988). *Makers of psychology: The personal factor.* New York: Human Sciences Press.

Miranda, A. O., Frevert, E. S., & Kern, R. M. (1998). Lifestyle differences between bicultural and low- and high-acculturation level Latino adults. *Individual Psychology, 54,* 119–134.

Mischel, W. (1968). *Personality and assessment.* New York: Wiley.

Mischel, W. (1973). Toward a cognitive social-learning reconceptualization of personality. *Psychological Review, 80*, 252–283.

Morehouse, R. E., Farley, F., & Youngquist, J. V. (1990). Type T personality and the Jungian classification system. *Journal of Personality Assessment, 54*, 231–235.

Moretti, M. M., & Higgins, E. T. (1990). Relating self-discrepancy to self-esteem: The contribution of discrepancy beyond actual-self ratings. *Journal of Experimental Social Psychology, 26*, 108–123.

Morgan, C. D., & Murray, H. A. (1935). A method for investigating fantasies. *Archives of Neurology and Psychiatry, 34*, 289–306.

Moskowitz, D. S., & Schwartzman, A. E. (1989). Life paths of aggressive and withdrawn children. In D. M. Buss & N. Cantor (Eds.), *Personality psychology: Recent trends and emerging directions* (pp. 99–114). New York: Springer-Verlag.

Motley, M. T. (1987, February). What I meant to say. *Psychology Today*, pp. 24–28.

Mozdzierz, G. J., Greenblatt, R. L., & Murphy, T. J. (1988). Further validation of the Sulliman Scale of Social Interest and the Social Interest Scale. *Individual Psychology, 44*, 30–34.

Mozdzierz, G. J., & Mozdzierz, A. B. (1997). A brief history of the journals of individual psychology. *Individual Psychology, 53*, 275–285.

Multon, K. D., Brown, S. D., & Lent, R. W. (1991). Relation of self-efficacy beliefs to academic outcomes: A meta-analytic investigation. *Journal of Counseling Psychology, 38*, 30–38.

Murray, H. A. (1938). *Explorations in personality: A clinical and experimental study of fifty men of college age.* New York: Oxford University Press.

Murray, H. A. (1940). What should psychologists do about psychoanalysis? *Journal of Abnormal and Social Psychology, 35*, 150–175.

Myers, D. G., & Diener, E. (1995). Who is happy? *Psychological Science, 6*, 10–19.

Narayanan, L., Menon, S., & Levine, E. L. (1995). Personality structure: A culture-specific examination of the five-factor model. *Journal of Personality Assessment, 64*, 51–62.

National Advisory Mental Health Council (1995). Basic behavioral science research for mental health. A national investment: Emotion and motivation. *American Psychologist, 50*, 838–845.

Needs, A. (1988). Psychological investigations of offending behaviour. In F. Fransella & L. Thomas (Eds.), *Experimenting with personal construct psychology* (pp. 493–506). London: Routledge & Kegan Paul.

Negy, C., & Woods, D. J. (1993). Mexican- and Anglo-American differences on the Psychological Screening Inventory. *Journal of Personality Assessment, 60*, 543–553.

Neimeyer, G. J. (1984). Cognitive complexity and marital satisfaction. *Journal of Social and Clinical Psychology, 2*, 258–263.

Neimeyer, G. J., & Rareshide, M. B. (1991). Personal memories and personal identity: The impact of ego identity development on autobiographical memory recall. *Journal of Personality and Social Psychology, 60*, 562–569.

Newman, D. L., Tellegen, A., & Bouchard, T. J. (1998). Individual differences in adult ego development: Sources of influence in twins reared apart. *Journal of Personality and Social Psychology, 74*, 985–995.

Newman, L. S., Duff, K. J., & Baumeister, R. F. (1997). A new look at defensive projection: Thought suppression, accessibility, and biased person perception. *Journal of Personality and Social Psychology, 72*, 980–1001.

Newman, L. S., Higgins, E. T., & Vookles, J. (1992). Self-guide strength and emotional vulnerability: Birth order as a moderator of self-affect relations. *Personality and Social Psychology Bulletin, 18*, 402–411.

Nezlek, J. B., Kowalski, R. M., Leary, M. R., Blevins, T., & Holgate, S. (1997). Personality moderators of reactions to interpersonal rejection: Depression and trait self-esteem. *Personality and Social Psychology Bulletin, 23*, 1235–1244.

Nolen-Hoeksema, S., Girgus, J., & Seligman, M. E. P. (1987). Learned helplessness in children: A longitudinal study of depression, achievement, and explanatory style. *Journal of Personality and Social Psychology, 51*, 435.

Noll, R. (1993). Personal communication.

Noll, R. (1994). *The Jung cult: Origins of a charismatic movement.* Princeton, NJ: Princeton University Press.

Noll, R. (1997). *The Aryan Christ: The secret life of Carl Jung.* New York: Random House.

Nowicki, S., & Duke, M. P. (1983). The Nowicki-Strickland life-span locus of control scales: Construct validation. In H. M. Lefcourt (Ed.), *Research with the locus of control construct* (Vol. 2, pp. 13–51). Orlando, FL: Academic Press.

Nowicki, S., & Strickland, B. R. (1973). A locus of control scale for children. *Journal of Consulting Psychology, 40*, 148–154.

Ochse, R., & Plug, C. (1986). Cross-cultural investigation of the validity of Erikson's theory of personality development. *Journal of Personality and Social Psychology, 50*, 1240–1252.

O'Connell, A. N. (1990). Karen Horney: 1885–1952. In A. N. O'Connell & N. F. Russo (Eds.), *Women in psychology: A bio-bibliographic sourcebook* (pp. 184–196). New York: Greenwood Press.

Oettingen, G., & Maier, H. (1999). Where political system meets culture: Effects on efficacy appraisal. In Y. T. Lee, C. R. McCauley, & J. G. Draguns (Eds.), *Person-*

ality and person perception across cultures (pp. 163–190). Mahwah, NJ: Erlbaum.

Ofshe, R., & Watters, E. (1994). *False memories, psychotherapy, and sexual hysteria.* New York: Scribner's.

Okeke, B. I., Draguns, J. G., Sheku, B., & Allen, W. (1999). Culture, self, and personality in Africa. In Y. T. Lee, C. R. McCauley, & J. G. Draguns (Eds.), *Personality and person perception across cultures* (pp. 139–162). Mahwah, NJ: Erlbaum.

Olioff, M., & Aboud, F. E. (1991). Predicting postpartum dysphoria in primiparous mothers: Roles of perceived parenting self-efficacy and self-esteem. *Journal of Cognitive Psychotherapy, 5,* 3–14.

O'Neill, R. M., & Bornstein, R. F. (1990). Oral-dependence and gender: Factors in help-seeking response set and self-reported pathology in psychiatric inpatients. *Journal of Personality Assessment, 55,* 28–40.

Orlofsky, J. L., Marcia, J. E., & Lesser, I. M. (1973). Ego identity status and the intimacy versus isolation crisis of young adulthood. *Journal of Personality and Social Psychology, 27,* 211–219.

Ormel, J., & Wohlfarth, T. (1991). How neuroticism, long-term difficulties, and life situation changes influence psychological distress: A longitudinal model. *Journal of Personality and Social Psychology, 60,* 744–755.

OSS Assessment Staff. (1948). *Assessment of men: Selection of personnel for the U.S Office of Strategic Services.* New York: Rinehart.

Overmier, J. B., & Seligman, M. E. P. (1967). Effects of inescapable shock upon subsequent escape and avoidance learning. *Journal of Comparative and Physiological Psychology, 63,* 28–33.

Ozer, E. M. (1995). The impact of childcare responsibility and self-efficacy on psychological health of professional working mothers. *Psychology of Women Quarterly, 19,* 315–335.

Palm, K., & Gibson, P. (1998). Recovered memories of childhood sexual abuse. *Professional Psychology, 29,* 257–261.

Pals, J. L. (1999). Identity consolidation in early adulthood: Relations with ego-resiliency, the context of marriage, and personality change. *Journal of Personality, 67,* 295–329.

Paris, B. J. (1994). *Karen Horney: A psychoanalyst's search for self-understanding.* New Haven, CT: Yale University Press.

Parkham, T., & Helms, J. (1985a). Attitudes of racial identity and self-esteem of black students: An exploratory investigation. *Journal of College Student Personnel, 26,* 143–147.

Parkham, T., & Helms, J. (1985b). Relation of racial identity and attitudes to self-actualization and affective states of black students. *Journal of Counseling Psychology, 32,* 431–440.

Paulhus, D., & Shaffer, D. R. (1981). Sex differences in the impact of number of younger and number of older siblings on scholastic aptitude. *Social Psychology Quarterly, 44,* 363–368.

Paunonen, S. V. (1998). Hierarchical organization of personality and prediction of behavior. *Journal of Personality and Social Psychology, 74,* 538–556.

Paunonen, S. V., & Ashton, M. C. (1998). The structured assessment of personality across cultures. *Journal of Cross-Cultural Psychology, 29,* 150–170.

Paunonen, S. V., Jackson, D. N., Trzebinski, J., & Forsterling, F. (1992). Personality structure across cultures: A multi-method evaluation. *Journal of Personality and Social Psychology, 62,* 447–456.

Pedersen, N. L., Plomin, R., McClearn, G. E., & Friberg, L. (1988). Neuroticism, extraversion, and related traits in adult twins reared apart and reared together. *Journal of Personality and Social Psychology, 55,* 950–957.

Pervin, L. A. (1984). *Current controversies and issues in personality* (2nd ed.). New York: Wiley.

Peterson, B. E., Smirles, K. A., & Wentworth, P. A. (1997). Generativity and authoritarianism: Implications for personality, political involvement, and parenting. *Journal of Personality and Social Psychology, 72,* 1202–1216.

Peterson, B. E., & Stewart, A. J. (1990). Using personal and fictional documents to assess psychosocial development: A case study of Vera Brittain's generativity. *Psychology and Aging, 5,* 400–411.

Peterson, B. E., & Stewart, A. J. (1993). Generativity and social motives in young adults. *Journal of Personality and Social Psychology, 63,* 186–198.

Peterson, C., & Barrett, L. C. (1987). Explanatory style and academic performance among college freshmen. *Journal of Personality and Social Psychology, 53,* 603–607.

Peterson, C., Maier, S. F., & Seligman, M. E. P. (1993). *Learned helplessness: A theory for the age of personal control.* New York: Oxford University Press.

Peterson, C., & Seligman, M. E. P. (1987). Explanatory style and illness. Special issue: Personality and physical health. *Journal of Personality, 55,* 237–265.

Peterson, C., Seligman, M. E. P., & Vaillant, G. (1988). Pessimistic explanatory style as a risk factor for physical illness: A 35-year longitudinal study. *Journal of Personality and Social Psychology, 55,* 23–27.

Peterson, C., Semmel, A., von Baeyer, C., Abramson, L. Y., Metalsky, G. I., & Seligman, M. E. P. (1982). The Attributional Style Questionnaire. *Cognitive Therapy and Research, 6,* 287–300.

Petrosky, M. J., & Birkhimer, J. C. (1991). The relationship among locus of control coping styles and psychological symptom reporting. *Journal of Clinical Psychology, 47,* 336–345.

Phares, E. J. (1993). From therapy to research: A patient's legacy. In G. G. Brannigan & M. R. Merrens (Eds.), *The undaunted psychologist: Adventures in research* (pp. 157–171). Philadelphia: Temple University Press.

Phillips, D. P. (1974). The influence of suggestion on suicide: Substantive and theoretical implications of the Werther effect. *American Sociological Review, 39,* 340–354.

Phillips, D. P. (1983). The impact of mass media violence on U.S homicides. *American Sociological Review, 48,* 560–568.

Phillips, D. P. (1985). The found experiment: A new technique for assessing impact of mass media violence on real-world aggressive behavior. In G. Comstock (Ed.), *Public communication and behavior* (Vol. 1). New York: Academic Press.

Phinney, J. S., & Chavira, V. (1992). Ethnic identity and self-esteem: An exploratory longitudinal study. *Journal of Adolescence, 15,* 271–281.

Piedmont, R. L. (1988). The relationship between achievement motivation, anxiety, and situational characteristics on performance on a cognitive task. *Journal of Research in Personality, 22,* 177–187.

Pilkington, B., & Lenaghan, M. (1998). Psychopathology. In K. Trew & J. Kremer (Eds.), *Gender and psychology* (pp. 179–191). New York: Oxford University Press.

Plomin, R., Chipuer, H. M., & Loehlin, J. C. (1990). Behavioral genetics and personality. In L. A. Pervin (Ed.), *Handbook of personality: Theory and research* (pp. 225–243). New York: Guilford Press.

Plomin, R., Lichtenstein, P., Pedersen, N. L., McClearn, G. E., & Nesselroade, J. R. (1990). Genetic influence on life events during the last half of the life span. *Psychology and Aging, 5,* 25–30.

Plomin, R., Pedersen, N. L., McClearn, G. E., Nesselroade, J. R., & Bergeman, C. S. (1988). EAS temperaments during the last half of the life span: Twins reared apart and twins reared together. *Psychology and Aging, 3,* 43–50.

Podd, M. H., Marcia, J. E., & Rubin, R. (1968). The effects of ego identity status and partner perception on a prisoner's dilemma game. *Journal of Social Psychology, 82,* 117–126.

Polusny, M. A., & Follette, V. M. (1996). Remembering childhood sexual abuse: A national survey of psychologists' clinical practices, beliefs, and personal experiences. *Professional Psychology, 27,* 41–52.

Popplestone, J. A., & McPherson, M. W. (1994). *An illustrated history of American psychology.* Madison, WI: Brown & Benchmark.

Porcerelli, J. H., Thomas, S., Hibbard, S., & Cogan, R. (1998). Defense mechanisms development in children, adolescents, and late adolescents. *Journal of Personality Assessment, 71,* 411–420.

Porter, L. A. (1961). A study of perceived need satisfactions in bottom and middle management jobs. *Journal of Applied Psychology, 45,* 1–10.

Potkay, C. R., & Allen, B. P. (1986). *Personality: Theory, research, and applications.* Pacific Grove, CA: Brooks/Cole.

Quiery, N. (1998). Parenting the family. In K. Trew & J. Kremer (Eds.), *Gender and psychology* (pp. 129–140). New York: Oxford University Press.

Quinn, S. (1987). *A mind of her own: The life of Karen Horney.* New York: Summit Books.

Rabin, A. I., Zucker, R. A., Emmons, R. A., & Frank, S. (Eds.). (1990). *Studying persons and lives.* New York: Springer.

Raeikkoenen, K., Matthews, K. A., Flory, J. D., Owens, J. F., & Gump, B. B. (1999). Effects of optimism, pessimism, and trait anxiety on ambulatory blood pressure and mood during everyday life. *Journal of Personality and Social Psychology, 76,* 104–113.

Rainey, N. (1998). Old age. In K. Trew & J. Kremer (Eds.), *Gender and psychology* (pp. 153–164). New York: Oxford University Press.

Ramirez, E., Maldonado, A., & Martos, R. (1992). Attributions modulate immunization against learned helplessness in humans. *Journal of Personality and Social Psychology, 62,* 139–146.

Raynor, J. O. (1970). Relationships between achievement-related motives, future orientation, and academic performance. *Journal of Personality and Social Psychology, 15,* 28–33.

Reimanis, G. (1974). Personality development, anomie, and mood. *Journal of Personality and Social Psychology, 29,* 355–357.

Rendon, D. (1987). Understanding social roles from a Horneyan perspective. *American Journal of Psychoanalysis, 47,* 131–142.

Repucci, N. D., & Saunders, J. T. (1974). Social psychology of behavior modification: Problems of implementation in natural settings. *American Psychologist, 29,* 649–660.

Resnicow, K., Soler, R. E., Braithwaite, R. L., Ben Selassie, M., & Smith, M. (1999). Development of a racial and ethnic identity scale for African American adolescents: The Survey of Black Life. *Journal of Black Psychology, 25,* 171–188.

Reuman, D. A., Alwin, D. F., & Veroff, J. (1984). Assessing the validity of the achievement motive in the presence of random measurement error. *Journal of Personality and Social Psychology, 47,* 1347–1362.

Reyes-Lagunes, E. L. G. M., Reyes-Lagunes, I., & Scott, R. L. (1994). MMPI-2 for Mexico: Translation and adaptation. *Journal of Personality Assessment, 63,* 105–116.

Richelle, M. N. (1993). *B. F. Skinner: A reappraisal.* Hillsdale, NJ: Erlbaum.

Riggio, R. E., & Friedman, H. S. (1986). Impression formation: The role of expressive behavior. *Journal of Personality and Social Psychology, 50,* 421–427.

Riggio, R. E., Lippa, R., & Salinas, C. (1990). The display of personality in expressive movement. *Journal of Research in Personality, 24,* 16–31.

Roazen, P. (1975). *Freud and his followers.* New York: Knopf.

Roazen, P. (1993). *Meeting Freud's family.* Amherst, MA: University of Massachusetts Press.

Robbins, P. R., Tanck, R. H., & Houshi, F. (1985). Anxiety and dream symbolism. *Journal of Personality, 53,* 17–22.

Roberts, B. W., & Helson, R. (1997). Changes in culture, changes in personality: The influence of individualism in a longitudinal study of women. *Journal of Personality and Social Psychology, 72,* 641–651.

Robinson, F. G. (1992). *Love's story told: A life of Henry A. Murray.* Cambridge, MA: Harvard University Press.

Robinson-Whelen, S., Kim, C., MacCallum, R. C., & Kiecolt-Glaser, J. K. (1997). Distinguishing optimism from pessimism in older adults. *Journal of Personality and Social Psychology, 73,* 1345–1353.

Rogers, C. R. (1954). The case of Mrs. Oak: A research analysis. In C. R. Rogers & R. F. Dymond (Eds.), *Psychotherapy and personality change.* Chicago: University of Chicago Press.

Rogers, C. R. (1961). *On becoming a person: A therapist's view of psychotherapy.* Boston: Houghton Mifflin.

Rogers, C. R. (1967). Autobiography. In E. G. Boring & G. Lindzey (Eds.), *A history of psychology in autobiography* (Vol. 5, pp. 341–384). New York: Appleton-Century-Crofts.

Rogers, C. R. (1970). *Carl Rogers on encounter groups.* New York: Harper & Row.

Rogers, C. R. (1974). In retrospect: Forty-six years. *American Psychologist, 29,* 115–123.

Rogers, C. R. (1980). *A way of being.* Boston: Houghton Mifflin.

Rogers, C. R. (1987). An interview with Carl Rogers. In A. O. Ross (Ed.), *Personality: The scientific study of complex human behavior* (pp. 118–119). New York: Holt, Rinehart & Winston.

Rose, R. J. (1995). Genes and human behavior. *Annual Review of Psychology, 46,* 625–654.

Rosenthal, D. R., Gurney, M. R., & Moore, S. M. (1981). From trust to intimacy: A new inventory for examining Erikson's stages of psychosocial development. *Journal of Youth and Adolescence, 10,* 525–536.

Rosenzweig, S. (1985). Freud and experimental psychology: The emergence of idiodynamics. In S. Koch & D. Leary (Eds.), *A century of psychology as science* (pp. 135–207). New York: McGraw-Hill.

Rossini, E. D., & Moretti, R. J. (1997). Thematic Apperception Test (TAT) interpretation. *Professional Psychology, 28,* 393–398.

Roth, M. S. (Ed.). (1998). *Freud: Conflict and culture.* New York: Knopf.

Rotter, J. B. (1966). Generalized expectancies for internal versus external control of reinforcement. *Psychological Monographs, 80* (Whole No. 609).

Rotter, J. B. (1967). A new scale for the measurement of interpersonal trust. *Journal of Personality, 35,* 651–665.

Rotter, J. B. (1975). Some problems and misconceptions related to the construct of internal versus external control of reinforcement. *Journal of Consulting and Clinical Psychology, 43,* 56–57.

Rotter, J. B. (1980). Interpersonal trust, trustworthiness, and gullibility. *American Psychologist, 35,* 1–7.

Rotter, J. B. (1982). *The development and applications of social learning theory: Selected papers.* New York: Praeger.

Rotter, J. B. (1990). Internal versus external control of reinforcement: A case history of a variable. *American Psychologist, 45,* 489–493.

Rotter, J. B. (1993). Expectancies. In C. E. Walker (Ed.), *History of clinical psychology in autobiography* (Vol. 2, pp. 273–284). Pacific Grove, CA: Brooks/Cole.

Rotter, J. B., Chance, J. E., & Phares, E. J. (1972). *Applications of a social learning theory of personality.* New York: Holt, Rinehart & Winston.

Rotter, J. B., & Hochreich, D. J. (1975). *Personality.* Glenview, IL: Scott, Foresman.

Rotter, J. B., & Rafferty, J. E. (1950). *Manual: The Rotter Incomplete Sentences Blank.* San Antonio, TX: Psychological Corporation.

Rowe, D. C. (1994). *The effects of nurture on individual natures.* New York: Guilford Press.

Rowe, D. C., & Plomin, R. (1981). The importance of nonshared (E1) environmental influences in behavioral development. *Developmental Psychology, 17,* 517–531.

Rowley, S. J., Sellers, R. M., Chavous, T. M., & Smith, M. A. (1998). The relationship between racial identity and self-esteem in African American college and high school students. *Journal of Personality and Social Psychology, 74,* 715–724.

Rubins, J. L. (1978). *Karen Horney: Gentle rebel of psychoanalysis.* New York: Dial Press.

Rushton, J. P., Fulker, D. W., Neale, M. C., Blizard, R. A., & Eysenck, H. J. (1984). Altruism and genetics. *Acta Geneticae et Gemellologiae, 33,* 265–271.

Ryan, R. M., & Frederick, C. (1997). On energy, personality, and health: Subjective vitality as a dynamic reflection of well-being. *Journal of Personality, 65,* 529–565.

Ryckman, R. M., Hammer, M., Kaczor, L. M., & Gold, J. A. (1990). Construction of a Hypercompetitive Attitude Scale. *Journal of Personality Assessment, 55,* 630–639.

Ryckman, R. M., & Malikiosi, M. X. (1975). Relationship between locus of control and chronological age. *Psychological Reports, 36,* 655–658.

Ryckman, R. M., Thornton, B., & Butler, J. C. (1994). Personality correlates of the Hypercompetitive Attitude Scale: Validity tests of Horney's theory of neurosis. *Journal of Personality Assessment, 62,* 84–94.

St. Clair, M. (1986). *Object relations and self psychology.* Monterey, CA: Brooks/Cole.

Salili, F. (1994). Age, sex, and cultural differences in the meaning and dimensions of need achievement. *Personality and Social Psychology Bulletin, 20,* 635–648.

Sammallahti, P., & Aalberg, V. (1995). Defense style in personality disorders. *Journal of Nervous and Mental Disease, 183,* 516–521.

Sanna, L. J., & Pusecker, P. A. (1994). Self-efficacy, valence of self-evaluation, and performance. *Personality and Social Psychology Bulletin, 20,* 82–92.

Sappington, H. A. (1990). Recent psychological approaches to the free will versus determinism issue. *Psychological Bulletin, 108,* 19–29.

Sarason, I. G. (1975b). Test anxiety and the self-disclosing coping model. *Journal of Consulting and Clinical Psychology, 43,* 148–153.

Sarris, A., Sawyer, M., & Quigley, R. (1993). Attitude of clinicians toward use of computers in hospital settings. *Professional Psychology: Research and Practice, 24,* 220–223.

Saucier, G. (1994). Mini-markers: A brief version of Goldberg's unipolar Big-Five markers. *Journal of Personality Assessment, 63,* 506–516.

Saudino, K. J., McGuire, S., Hetherington, E. M., Reiss, D., & Plomin, R. (1995). Parent ratings of EAS temperaments in twins, full siblings, half siblings, and step siblings. *Journal of Personality and Social Psychology, 68,* 723–733.

Saudino, K. J., Pedersen, N. L., Lichtenstein, P., McClearn, G. E., & Plomin, R. (1997). Can personality explain genetic influences on life events? *Journal of Personality and Social Psychology, 72,* 196–206.

Sayers, J. (1991). *Mothers of psychoanalysis: Helene Deutsch, Karen Horney, Anna Freud, Melanie Klein.* New York: Norton.

Scarr, S. (1968). Environmental bias in twin studies. *Eugenics Quarterly, 15,* 34–40.

Schachter, S. (1959). *The psychology of affiliation.* Stanford, CA: Stanford University Press.

Schachter, S. (1963). Birth order, eminence, and higher education. *American Sociological Review, 28,* 757–767.

Schachter, S. (1964). Birth order and sociometric choice. *Journal of Abnormal and Social Psychology, 68,* 453–456.

Schimmack, U., & Hartmann, K. (1997). Individual differences in the memory representation of emotional episodes. *Journal of Personality and Social Psychology, 73,* 1064–1079.

Schmutte, P. S., & Ryff, C. D. (1997). Personality and well-being. *Journal of Personality and Social Psychology, 73,* 549–559.

Schneewind, K. A. (1995). Impact of family processes on control beliefs. In A. Bandura (Ed.), *Self-efficacy in changing societies* (pp. 114–148). Cambridge, England: Cambridge University Press.

Schneiderman, N., McCabe, P. M., & Baum, A. (Eds.). (1992). *Stress and disease processes: Perspectives in behavioral medicine.* Hillsdale, NJ: Erlbaum.

Schnur, R. E., & MacDonald, M. L. (1988). Stages of identity development and problem drinking in college women. *Journal of Youth and Adolescence, 17,* 349–369.

Schultz, D. P. (1990). *Intimate friends, dangerous rivals: The turbulent relationship between Freud and Jung.* Los Angeles: Tarcher.

Schur, M. (1972). *Freud: Living and dying.* New York: International Universities Press.

Schwarz, N. (1999). Self-reports: How the questions shape the answers. *American Psychologist, 54,* 93–105.

Schwarzer, R., & Fuchs, R. (1995). Changing risk behaviors and adopting health behaviors: The role of self-efficacy beliefs. In A. Bandura (Ed.), *Self-efficacy in changing societies* (pp. 259–315). Cambridge, England: Cambridge University Press.

Sechrest, L. (1968). Personal constructs and personal characteristics. *Journal of Individual Psychology, 24,* 162–166.

Sechrest, L. (1984). Review of J. B. Rotter's The development and applications of social learning theory: Selected papers. *Journal of the History of the Behavioral Sciences, 20,* 228–230.

Sechrest, L., & Jackson, D. N. (1961). Social intelligence and accuracy of interpersonal predictions. *Journal of Personality, 29,* 169–182.

Seeman, M., Seeman, T., & Sayles, M. (1985). Social networks and health status: A longitudinal analysis. *Social Psychology Quarterly, 48,* 237–248.

Segall, M., & Wynd, C. A. (1990). Health conception, health locus of control, and power as predictors of smoking behavior change. *American Journal of Health Promotion, 4,* 338–344.

Segerstrom, S. C., & Taylor, S. E. (1998). Optimism is associated with mood, coping, and immune change in response to stress. *Journal of Personality and Social Psychology, 74,* 1646–1655.

Seligman, M. E. P. (1975). *Helplessness: On depression, development, and death.* San Francisco: W. H. Freeman.

Seligman, M. E. P. (1990). *Learned optimism.* New York: Knopf.

Seligman, M. E. P., & Maier, S. F. (1967). Failure to escape traumatic shock. *Journal of Experimental Psychology, 74,* 1–9.

Seligman, M. E. P., & Visintainer, M. (1985). Tumor rejection and early experience of uncontrollable shock in the rat. In F. R. Brush & J. B. Overmier (Eds.), *Affect, conditioning, and cognition: Essays on the determinants of behavior* (pp. 203–210). Hillsdale, NJ: Erlbaum.

Sellers, R. M., Chavous, T. M., & Cooke, D. Y. (1998). Racial ideology and racial centrality as predictors of African American college students' academic performance. *Journal of Black Psychology, 24,* 8–27.

Sellers, R. M., Rowley, S. A. J., Chavous, T. M., Shelton, J. N., & Smith, M. A. (1997). Multidimensional Inventory of Black Identity: A preliminary investigation of reliability and construct validity. *Journal of Personality and Social Psychology, 73,* 805–815.

Sethi, S., & Seligman, M. E. P. (1994). The hope of fundamentalists. *Psychological Science, 5,* 58.

Shamir, B. (1986). Self-esteem and the psychological impact of unemployment. *Social Psychology Quarterly, 49,* 61–72.

Shedler, J., Mayman, M., & Manis, M. (1993). The illusion of mental health. *American Psychologist, 48,* 1117–1131.

Sheldon, W. (1942). *The varieties of temperament: A psychology of constitutional differences.* New York: Harper & Row.

Shevrin, H. (1977). Some assumptions of psychoanalytic communication: Implications of subliminal research for psychoanalytic method and technique. In N. Freedman & S. Grand (Eds.), *Communicative structures and psychic structures.* New York: Plenum Press.

Shiner, R. L. (1998). How shall we speak of children's personalities in middle childhood? A preliminary taxonomy. *Psychological Bulletin, 124,* 308–332.

Shostrom, E. L. (1964). An inventory for the measurement of self-actualization. *Educational and Psychological Measurement, 24,* 207–218.

Shostrom, E. L. (1974). *Manual for the Personal Orientation Inventory.* San Diego: Educational and Industrial Testing Service.

Siegelman, M. (1988). "Origins" of extroversion-introversion. *Journal of Psychology, 69,* 85–91.

Silverman, L. H. (1976). Psychoanalytic theory: "The reports of my death are greatly exaggerated." *American Psychologist, 31,* 621–637.

Silverman, L. H. (1983). The subliminal psychodynamic activation method: Overview and comprehensive listing of studies. In J. Masling (Ed.), *Empirical studies in psychoanalysis* (Vol. 1). Hillsdale, NJ: Erlbaum.

Silverman, L. H., & Weinberger, I. (1985). Mommy and I are one: Implications for psychotherapy. *American Psychologist, 40,* 1296–1308.

Simon, L. (1998). *Genuine reality: A life of William James.* New York: Harcourt Brace.

Skinner, B. F. (1938). *The behavior of organisms: An experimental analysis.* New York: Appleton-Century.

Skinner, B. F. (1948). *Walden Two.* New York: Macmillan.

Skinner, B. F. (1953). *Science and human behavior.* New York: Free Press.

Skinner, B. F. (1967). Autobiography. In E. G. Boring & G. Lindzey (Eds.), *A history of psychology in autobiography* (Vol. 5, pp. 385–413). New York: Appleton-Century-Crofts.

Skinner, B. F. (1971). *Beyond freedom and dignity.* New York: Knopf.

Skinner, B. F. (1979). *The shaping of a behaviorist.* New York: Knopf.

Skinner, B. F. (1983a). *A matter of consequences.* New York: Knopf.

Sleek, S. (1998, October). Blame your peers, not your parents. *APA Monitor,* p. 9.

Slugoski, B. F., & Ginsburg, G. P. (1989). Ego identity and explanatory speech. In J. Shotter & K. F. Gergen (Eds.), *Texts of identity* (pp. 36–55). London: Sage.

Smith, D. (1986, March 31). What would Freud think? The uproar in the shrine of psychoanalysis. *New York,* pp. 38–45.

Smith, J. E., Stefan, C., Kovaleski, M., & Johnson, G. (1991). Recidivism and dependency in a psychiatric population: An investigation with Kelly's dependency grid. *International Journal of Personal Construct Psychology, 4,* 157–173.

Smith, M. (1980). An analysis of three managerial jobs using repertory grids. *Journal of Management Studies, 17,* 205–213.

Smith, M. B. (1990). Henry A. Murray (1893–1988): Humanistic psychologist. *Journal of Humanistic Psychology, 30*(1), 6–13.

Smith, R. E., Ptacek, J. T., & Smoll, F. L. (1992). Sensation seeking, stress, and adolescent injuries: A test of stress-buffering, risk-taking, and coping skills hypotheses. *Journal of Personality and Social Psychology, 62,* 1016–1024.

Solnit, A. J. (1992). Freud's view of mental health and fate. In E. E. Garcia (Ed.), *Understanding Freud: The man and his ideas* (pp. 64–77). New York: New York University Press.

Spangler, W. D. (1992). Validity of questionnaire and TAT measures of need for achievement: Two meta-analyses. *Psychological Bulletin, 112,* 140–154.

Spangler, W. D., & House, R. J. (1991). Presidential effectiveness and the leadership motive profile. *Journal of Personality and Social Psychology, 60,* 439–455.

Spence, J. T. (Ed.). (1983). *Achievement and achievement motives: Psychological and sociological approaches.* New York: W. H. Freeman.

Spranger, E. (1928). *Types of men.* [P. J. W. Pigors (Trans.).] Halle, Germany: Niemeyer.

Stacy, A. W., Sussman, S., Dent, C. W., Burton, D., & Floy, B. R. (1992). Moderators of peer social influence in adolescent smoking. *Personality and Social Psychology Bulletin, 18,* 163–172.

Stajkovic, A., & Luthans, F. (1998). Self-efficacy and work-related performance: A meta-analysis. *Psychological Bulletin, 124,* 240–261.

Statton, J. E., & Wilborn, B. (1991). Adlerian counseling and the early recollections of children. *Individual Psychology, 47,* 338–347.

Staudinger, U. M., Fleeson, W., & Baltes, P. B. (1999). Predictors of subjective physical health and global well-being: Similarities and differences between the United States and Germany. *Journal of Personality and Social Psychology, 76,* 305–319.

Steele, R. S. (1982). Freud and Jung: Conflicts of interpretation. London: Routledge & Kegan Paul.

Stelmack, R. M. (1997). Toward a paradigm in personality: Comment on Eysenck's (1997) view. *Journal of Personality and Social Psychology, 73,* 1238–1241.

Stepansky, P. E. (1983). *In Freud's shadow: Adler in context.* New York: Analytic Press.

Stephen, J., Fraser, E., & Marcia, J. E. (1992). Moratorium-achievement (MAMA) cycles in lifespan identity development: Value orientations and reasoning system correlates. *Journal of Adolescence, 15,* 283–300.

Stephenson, W. (1953). *The study of behavior: Q-technique and its methodology.* Chicago: University of Chicago Press.

Sterba, R. F. (1982). *Reminiscences of a Viennese psychoanalyst.* Detroit, MI: Wayne State University Press.

Stewart, A. J., & Ostrove, J. M. (1998). Women's personality in middle age: Gender, history, and midcourse corrections. *American Psychologist, 53,* 1185–1194.

Stewart, A. J., & Vandewater, E. A. (1999). "If I had it to do over again . . . ." Midlife review, midcourse corrections, and women's well-being in midlife. *Journal of Personality and Social Psychology, 76,* 270–283.

Stewart, G. L., Carson, K. P., & Cardy, R. L. (1996). The joint effects of conscientiousness and self-leadership training on employee self-directed behavior in a service setting. *Personnel Psychology, 49,* 143–164.

Stewart, R. A. C. (1968). Academic performance and components of self-actualization. *Perceptual and Motor Skills, 26,* 918.

Stewart, V., & Stewart, A. (1982). *Business applications of repertory grid.* New York: McGraw-Hill.

Story, A. L. (1998). Self-esteem and memory for favorable and unfavorable personality feedback. *Personality and Social Psychology Bulletin, 24,* 51–64.

Stotland, S., & Zuroff, D. C. (1990). A new measure of weight locus of control: The Dieting Beliefs Scale. *Journal of Personality Assessment, 54,* 191–203.

Straumann, T. J., Vookles, J., Berenstein, V., Chaiken, S., & Higgins, E. T. (1991). Self-discrepancies and vulnerability to body dissatisfaction and disordered eating.

Journal of Personality and Social Psychology, 61, 946–956.

Streitmatter, J. (1993). Identity status and identity style: A replication study. *Journal of Adolescence, 16,* 211–215.

Strelau, J. (1994). The concepts of arousal and arousability as used in temperament studies. In J. E. Bates & T. D. Wachs (Eds.), *Temperament: Individual differences at the interface of biology and behavior* (pp. 117–141). Washington, DC: American Psychological Association.

Stricker, L. J., & Ross, J. (1962). *A description and evaluation of the Myers-Briggs Type Indicator.* Princeton, NJ: Educational Testing Service.

Strickland, B. R. (1978). Internal-external expectancies and health-related behaviors. *Journal of Consulting and Clinical Psychology, 46,* 1192–1211.

Strickland, B. R. (1989). Internal-external control expectancies: From contingency to creativity. *American Psychologist, 44,* 1–12.

Strickland, B. R., & Haley, W. E. (1980). Sex differences on the Rotter I-E Scale. *Journal of Personality and Social Psychology, 39,* 930–939.

Strumpfer, D. (1970). Fear and affiliation during a disaster. *Journal of Social Psychology, 82,* 263–268.

Suinn, R. (1999, March). Scaling the summit: Valuing ethnicity. *APA Monitor,* p. 2.

Suinn, R., Osborne, D., & Winfree, P. (1962). The self-concept and accuracy of recall of inconsistent self-related information. *Journal of Clinical Psychology, 18,* 473–474.

Sulliman, J. R. (1973). The development of a scale for the measurement of social interest. *Dissertation Abstracts International, 34,* 567A (University Microfilms No. 73–31).

Sulloway, F. J. (1979). *Freud, biologist of the mind: Beyond the psychoanalytic legend.* New York: Basic Books.

Sulloway, F. J. (1992). Reassessing Freud's case histories: The social construction of psychoanalysis. In T. Gelfand & J. Kerr (Eds.), *Freud and the history of psychoanalysis* (pp. 153–192). Hillsdale, NJ: Analytic Press.

Sulloway, F. J. (1995). Birth order and evolutionary psychology: A meta-analytic overview. *Psychological Inquiry, 6*(1).

Suls, J., Green, P., & Hillis, S. (1998). Emotional reactivity to everyday problems, affective inertia, and neuroticism. *Personality and Social Psychology Bulletin, 24,* 127–136.

Sutton-Smith, B., & Rosenberg, B. C. (1970). *The sibling.* New York: Holt, Rinehart & Winston.

Symbaluk, D. G., Heth, C. D., Cameron, J., & Pierce, W. D. (1997). Social modeling, monetary incentives, and pain endurance: The role of self-efficacy in pain perception. *Personality and Social Psychology Bulletin, 23,* 258–269.

Tafarodi, R. W., & Vu, C. (1997). Two-dimensional self-esteem and reactions to success and failure. *Personality and Social Psychology Bulletin, 23,* 626–635.

Taft, L. B., & Nehrke, M. F. (1990). Reminiscences, life review, and ego integrity in nursing home residents. *International Journal of Aging and Human Development, 30,* 189–196.

Tavris, C. (1992). *The mismeasure of woman.* New York: Simon & Schuster.

Taylor, E. (1999). An intellectual renaissance of humanistic psychology? *Journal of Humanistic Psychology, 39* (2), 7–25.

Taylor, S. E., Kemeny, M. E., Aspinwall, L. G., Schneider, S. C., Rodriguez, R., & Herbert, M. (1992). Optimism, coping, psychological distress, and high-risk sexual behavior among men at risk for acquired immunodeficiency syndrome (AIDS). *Journal of Personality and Social Psychology, 63,* 460–473.

Tellegen, A., Lykken, D. T., Bouchard, T. J., Wilcox, K., Segal, N., & Rich, S. (1988). Personality similarity in twins reared apart and together. *Journal of Personality and Social Psychology, 54,* 1031–1039.

Teti, D. M., & Gelfand, D. M. (1991). Behavioral competence among mothers of infants in the first year: The mediational role of maternal self-efficacy. *Child Development, 62,* 918–929.

Tetlock, P. E. (1983). Cognitive style and political ideology. *Journal of Personality and Social Psychology, 45,* 118–126.

Tetlock, P. E. (1984). Cognitive style and political belief systems in the British House of Commons. *Journal of Personality and Social Psychology, 46,* 365–375.

Thomas, A. (1986). The New York Longitudinal Study: From infancy to early adult life. In R. Plomin & J. Dunn (Eds.), *The study of temperament* (pp. 39–52). Hillsdale, NJ: Erlbaum.

Thomas, A., Chess, S., & Korn, S. (1982). The reality of difficult temperament. *Merrill-Palmer Quarterly, 28,* 1–20.

Thomas, D. A. (1989). Measuring volunteers for exciting psychology experiments with the Sensation Seeking Scale. *Journal of Personality Assessment, 53,* 790–801.

Thomas, L., & Cooper, P. (1980). Incidence and psychological correlates of intense spiritual experiences. *Journal of Transpersonal Psychology, 12,* 75–85.

Thompson, S. C., Sobolew–Shubin, A., Galbraith, M. E., Schwankovsky, L., & Cruzen, D. (1993). Maintaining perception of control: Finding perceived control in low-control circumstances. *Journal of Personality and Social Psychology, 64,* 293–304.

Thompson, T. (1988). Benedictus behavior analysis: B. F. Skinner's magnum opus at fifty [Review of the book The behavior of organisms: An experimental analysis]. *Contemporary Psychology, 33,* 397–402.

Tobey, L. H., & Bruhn, A. R. (1992). Early memories and the criminally dangerous. *Journal of Personality Assessment, 59,* 137–152.

Tribich, D., & Messer, S. (1974). Psychoanalytic character type and states of authority as determiners of suggestibility. *Journal of Consulting and Clinical Psychology, 42,* 842–848.

Triplet, R. G. (1993). Book review of Love's story told: A life of Henry A. Murray. *Journal of the History of the Behavioral Sciences, 29,* 384–386.

Trull, T. J., & Geary, D. C. (1997). Comparison of the big-five factor structure across samples of Chinese and American adults. *Journal of Personality Assessment, 69,* 324–341.

Trull, T. J., Widiger, T. A., Useda, J. D., Holcomb, J., Doan, B., Axelrod, S. R., Stern, B. L., & Gershuny, B. S. (1998). A structured interview for the assessment of the five-factor model of personality. *Psychological Assessment, 10,* 229–240.

Turkle, S. (1995). *Life on the screen: Identity in the age of the Internet.* New York: Simon & Schuster.

Tzuriel, D. (1992). The development of ego identity at adolescence among Israeli Jews and Arabs. *Journal of Youth and Adolescence, 21,* 551–571.

Uba, L. (1994). *Asian Americans: Personality patterns, identity, and mental health.* New York: Guilford Press.

Vaillant, G. E. (1977). *Adaptation to life.* Boston: Little, Brown.

van den Boom, D. C., & Hoeksma, J. B. (1994). The effect of infant irritability on mother-infant interaction: A growth-curve analysis. *Developmental Psychology, 30,* 581–590.

Van de Water, D. A., & McAdams, D. P. (1989). Generativity and Erikson's "belief in the species." *Journal of Research in Personality, 23,* 435–449.

Vandewater, E. A., Ostrove, J. M., & Stewart, A. J. (1997). Predicting women's well-being in midlife: The importance of personality development and social role involvements. *Journal of Personality and Social Psychology, 72,* 1147–1160.

Vane, J. R., & Guarnaccia, V. J. (1989). Personality theory and personality assessment measures: How helpful to the clinician? *Journal of Clinical Psychology, 45,* 5–19.

Vernon, P. A., Jang, K. L., Harris, J. A., & McCarthy, J. M. (1997). Environmental predictors of personality differences: A twin and sibling study. *Journal of Personality and Social Psychology, 72,* 177–183.

Veroff, J. (1982). Assertive motivation: Achievement versus power. In A. J. Stewart (Ed.), *Motivation and society: A volume in honor of David C. McClelland* (pp. 99–132). San Francisco: Jossey-Bass.

Veroff, J., Wilcox, S., & Atkinson, J. W. (1953). The achievement motive in high school and college-age women. *Journal of Abnormal and Social Psychology, 48,* 108–119.

Viken, R. J., Rose, R. J., Kaprio, J., & Koskenvuo, M. (1994). A developmental genetic analysis of adult personality: Extraversion and neuroticism from 18 to 59 years of age. *Journal of Personality and Social Psychology, 66,* 722–730.

Villanova, P., & Peterson, C. (1991). Meta-analysis of human helplessness experiments. Unpublished data. Cited in Peterson, Maier, & Seligman, 1993.

Viner, R. (1996). Melanie Klein and Anna Freud: The discourse of the early dispute. *Journal of the History of the Behavioral Sciences, 32,* 4–15.

Visintainer, M., Volpicelli, J., & Seligman, M. E. P. (1982). Tumor rejection in rats after inescapable or escapable shock. *Science, 216,* 437–439.

Von Dras, D. D., & Siegler, I. C. (1997). Stability in extraversion and aspects of social support at midlife. *Journal of Personality and Social Psychology, 72,* 233–241.

Walters, R. H., Bowen, N. V., & Parke, R. D. (1963). *Experimentally induced disinhibition of sexual responses.* Cited in Bandura & Walters, 1963.

Waterman, A. S. (1982). Identity development from adolescence to adulthood: An extension of theory and a review of research. *Developmental Psychology, 18,* 341–358.

Waterman, C. K., Buebel, M. E., & Waterman, A. S. (1970). Relationship between resolution of the identity crisis and outcomes of previous psychosocial crises. *Proceedings of the 78th Annual Convention of the American Psychological Association, 5,* 467–468.

Watkins, C. E., Jr. (1992). Adlerian-oriented early memory research: What does it tell us? *Journal of Personality Assessment, 59,* 248–263.

Watkins, C. E., Jr. (1994). Measuring social interest. *Individual Psychology, 50,* 69–96.

Watkins, C. E., Jr., & St. John, C. (1994). Validity of the Sulliman scale of social interest. *Individual Psychology, 50,* 166–169.

Watson, D., Clark, L. A., McIntyre, C. W., & Hamaker, S. (1992). Affect, personality, and social activity. *Journal of Personality and Social Psychology, 63,* 1011–1025.

Watson, M. W., & Getz, K. (1990). The relationship between Oedipal behaviors and children's family role concepts. *Merrill-Palmer Quarterly, 36,* 487–505.

Weber, M. (1930). *The Protestant ethic and the spirit of capitalism.* New York: Scribner's.

Webster, R. (1995). *Why Freud was wrong.* New York: Basic Books.

Wegner, D. M., & Wheatley, T. (1999). Apparent mental causation: Sources of the experience of will. *American Psychologist, 54,* 480–492.

Weinberger, D. (1995). The content validity of the repressive coping style. In J. Singer (Ed.), *Repression and dissociation* (pp. 337–386). Chicago: University of Chicago Press.

Weinberger, I., & Silverman, L. H. (1990). Testability and empirical validation of psychoanalytic dynamic propositions through subliminal psychodynamic activation. *Psychoanalytic Psychology, 7,* 299–339.

Weisse, C. S. (1992). Depression and immunocompetence: A review of the literature. *Psychological Bulletin, 111,* 475–489.

Welsh, A. (1994). *Freud's wishful dream book.* Princeton, NJ: Princeton University Press.

West, S. G., Newsom, J. T., & Fenaughty, A. M. (1992). Publication trends in JPSP: Stability and change in topics, methods, and theories across two decades. *Personality and Social Psychology Bulletin, 18,* 473–484.

Westen, D. (1990). Psychoanalytic approaches to personality. In L. A. Pervin (Ed.), *Handbook of personality* (pp. 21–65). New York: Guilford Press.

Westen, D. (1998). The scientific legacy of Sigmund Freud. *Psychological Bulletin, 124,* 333–371.

Westkott, M. (1986). *The feminist legacy of Karen Horney.* New Haven, CT: Yale University Press.

Whitbourne, S. K., Elliot, L. B., Zuschlag, M. K., & Waterman, A. S. (1992). Psychosocial development in adulthood: A 22-year sequential study. *Journal of Personality and Social Psychology, 63,* 260–271.

White, J., Campbell, L., Stewart, A., Davies, M., & Pilkington, L. (1997). The relationship of psychological birth order to career interests. *Individual Psychology, 53,* 89–103.

Whitworth, R. H., & McBlaine, D. D. (1993). Comparisons of the MMPI and MMPI-2 administered to Anglo- and Hispanic-American university students. *Journal of Personality Assessment, 61,* 19–27.

Wichern, F., & Nowicki, S. (1976). Independence training practices and locus of control orientation in children and adolescents. *Developmental Psychology, 12,* 77.

Wiggins, J. S., & Trapnell, P. D. (1997). Personality structure: The return of the Big Five. In R. Hogan, J. Johnson, & S. Briggs (Eds.), *Handbook of personality psychology* (pp. 737–765). San Diego: Academic Press.

Williams, D. E., & Page, M. M. (1989). A multidimensional measure of Maslow's hierarchy of needs. *Journal of Research in Personality, 23,* 192–213.

Williams, J. E., Satterwhite, R. C., & Saiz, J. L. (1998). *The importance of psychological traits: A cross-cultural study.* New York: Plenum Press.

Williams, L. M. (1994). Recall of childhood trauma: A prospective study of women's memories of child sexual abuse. *Journal of Consulting and Clinical Psychology, 62,* 1167–1176.

Wilson, C. (1972). *New pathways in psychology.* New York: Taplinger.

Wilson, G. (1977). Introversion-extroversion. In T. Blass (Ed.), *Personality variables in social behavior.* Hillsdale, NJ: Erlbaum.

Wilson, G. D., Ausman, J., & Mathews, T. R. (1973). Conservatism and art preferences. *Journal of Personality and Social Psychology, 25,* 286–288.

Winter, D. A. (1992). *Personal construct psychology in clinical practice.* London: Routledge.

Winter, D. G. (1973). *The power motive.* New York: Free Press.

Winter, D. G. (1993a). Gordon Allport and Letters from Jenny. In K. H. Craik, R. Hogan, & R. N. Wolfe (Eds.), *Fifty years of personality psychology* (pp. 147–163). New York: Plenum Press.

Winter, D. G. (1993b). Power, affiliation, and war: Three tests of a motivational model. *Journal of Personality and Social Psychology, 65,* 532–545.

Winter, D. G. (1998). Toward a science of personality psychology: David McClelland's development of empirically derived TAT measures. *History of Psychology, 1,* 130–153.

Winterbottom, M. R. (1958). The relation of need for achievement to learning experiences in independence and mastery. In J. W. Atkinson (Ed.), *Motives in fantasy, action, and society.* Princeton, NJ: Van Nostrand.

Wittels, F. (1924). *Sigmund Freud: His personality, his teaching, and his school.* London: Allen & Unwin.

Wolfe, R. N. (1993). A commonsense approach to personality measurement. In K. H. Craik, R. Hogan, & R. N. Wolfe (Eds.), *Fifty years of personality psychology* (pp. 269–290). New York: Plenum Press.

Wolk, R. L., & Wolk, R. B. (1971). *Manual: Gerontological Apperception Test.* New York: Human Sciences Press.

Wolk, S., & DuCette, J. (1974). Intentional performance and incidental learning as a function of personality and task dimensions. *Journal of Personality and Social Psychology, 29,* 91–101.

Wood, R. E., & Bandura, A. (1989). Social cognitive theory of organizational management. *Academy of Management Review, 14,* 361–384.

Wright, T. L., & Kirmani, A. (1977). Interpersonal trust, trustworthiness, and shoplifting in high school. *Psychological Reports, 41,* 1165–1166.

Wuthnow, R. (1978). Peak experiences: Some empirical tests. *Journal of Humanistic Psychology, 18,* 59–75.

Yeagle, E. H., Privette, G., & Dunham, F. Y. (1989). Highest happiness: An analysis of artists' peak experiences. *Psychological Reports, 65,* 523–530.

Yik, M. S., Bond, M. H., & Paulhus, D. L. (1998). Do Chinese self-enhance or self-efface? *Personality and Social Psychology Bulletin, 24,* 399–406.

Young-Bruehl, E. (1988). *Anna Freud: A biography.* New York: Summit Books.

Zajonc, R. B., Markus, H., & Markus, G. B. (1979). The birth order puzzle. *Journal of Personality and Social Psychology, 37,* 1325–1341.

Zeidner, M. (1993). Coping with disaster: The case of Israeli adolescents under threat of missile attack. *Journal of Youth and Adolescence, 22,* 89–108.

Zimmerman, B. J. (1995). Self-efficacy and educational development. In A. Bandura (Ed.), *Self-efficacy in changing societies* (pp. 202–231). Cambridge, England: Cambridge University Press.

Zucker, R. A. (1990). Henry Murray's legacy: An epilogue. In A. I. Rabin, R. A. Zucker, R. A. Emmons, & S. Frank (Eds.), *Studying persons and lives* (pp. 335–340). New York: Springer.

Zuckerman, M. (1979). *Sensation seeking: Beyond the optimal level of arousal.* Hillsdale, NJ: Erlbaum.

Zuckerman, M. (1983). *Biological bases of sensation seeking, impulsivity, and anxiety.* Hillsdale, NJ: Erlbaum.

Zuckerman, M. (1990). The psychophysiology of sensation seeking. *Journal of Personality, 58,* 313–345.

Zuckerman, M. (1991). *Psychobiology of personality.* New York: Cambridge University Press.

Zuckerman, M. (1993). Out of sensory deprivation and into sensation seeking: A personal and scientific journey. In G. G. Brannigan & M. R. Merrens (Eds.), *The undaunted psychologist: Adventures in research* (pp. 45–57). Philadelphia: Temple University Press.

Zuckerman, M. (1994a). *Behavioral expressions and biosocial bases of sensation seeking.* Cambridge, England: Cambridge University Press.

Zuckerman, M. (1994b). Impulsive unsocialized sensation seeking: The biological foundations of a basic dimension of personality. In J. E. Bates & T. D. Wachs (Eds.), *Temperament: Individual differences at the interface of biology and behavior* (pp. 219–255). Washington, DC: American Psychological Association.

Zuckerman, M., Buchsbaum, M. S., & Murphy, D. L. (1980). Sensation seeking and its biological correlates. *Psychological Bulletin, 88,* 187–214.

Zuckerman, M., Eysenck, S., & Eysenck, H. J. (1978). Sensation seeking in England and America: Cross-cultural, age and sex comparisons. *Journal of Consulting and Clinical Psychology, 46,* 139–149.

Zullow, H., & Seligman, M. E. P. (1985). Pessimistic ruminations predict increase in depressive symptoms. Unpublished manuscript. [Cited in D. L. Rosenhan & M. E. P. Seligman, *Abnormal psychology* (2nd ed.). New York: Norton.]

Zuroff, D. C. (1980). Learned helplessness in humans: An analysis of learning processes and the roles of individual and situational differences. *Journal of Personality and Social Psychology, 39,* 130–146.

Author Index

Subject Index